40

T3-ALT-341

'A325
2009

OTHER A TO Z GUIDES FROM THE SCARECROW PRESS, INC.

1. *The A to Z of Buddhism* by Charles S. Prebish, 2001.
2. *The A to Z of Catholicism* by William J. Collinge, 2001.
3. *The A to Z of Hinduism* by Bruce M. Sullivan, 2001.
4. *The A to Z of Islam* by Ludwig W. Adamec, 2002. Out of Print. See No. 123.
5. *The A to Z of Slavery & Abolition* by Martin A. Klein, 2002.
6. *Terrorism: Assassins to Zealots* by Sean Kendall Anderson and Stephen Sloan, 2003.
7. *The A to Z of the Korean War* by Paul M. Edwards, 2005.
8. *The A to Z of the Cold War* by Joseph Smith and Simon Davis, 2005.
9. *The A to Z of the Vietnam War* by Edwin E. Moise, 2005.
10. *The A to Z of Science Fiction Literature* by Brian Stableford, 2005.
11. *The A to Z of the Holocaust* by Jack R. Fischel, 2005.
12. *The A to Z of Washington, D.C.* by Robert Benedetto, Jane Donovan, and Kathleen DuVall, 2005.
13. *The A to Z of Taoism* by Julian F. Pas, 2006.
14. *The A to Z of the Renaissance* by Charles G. Nauert, 2006.
15. *The A to Z of Shinto* by Stuart D. B. Picken, 2006.
16. *The A to Z of Byzantium* by John H. Rosser, 2006.
17. *The A to Z of the Civil War* by Terry L. Jones, 2006.
18. *The A to Z of the Friends (Quakers)* by Margery Post Abbott, Mary Ellen Chijioke, Pink Dandelion, and John William Oliver Jr., 2006
19. *The A to Z of Feminism* by Janet K. Boles and Diane Long Hoeveler, 2006.
20. *The A to Z of New Religious Movements* by George D. Chryssides, 2006.
21. *The A to Z of Multinational Peacekeeping* by Terry M. Mays, 2006.
22. *The A to Z of Lutheranism* by Günther Gassmann with Duane H. Larson and Mark W. Oldenburg, 2007.
23. *The A to Z of the French Revolution* by Paul R. Hanson, 2007.
24. *The A to Z of the Persian Gulf War 1990–1991* by Clayton R. Newell, 2007.
25. *The A to Z of Revolutionary America* by Terry M. Mays, 2007.
26. *The A to Z of the Olympic Movement* by Bill Mallon with Ian Buchanan, 2007.

27. *The A to Z of the Discovery and Exploration of Australia* by Alan Day, 2009.
28. *The A to Z of the United Nations* by Jacques Fomerand. 2009.
29. *The A to Z of the "Dirty Wars"* by David Kohut, Olga Vilella, and Beatrice Julian, 2009.
30. *The A to Z of the Vikings* by Katherine Holman, 2009.
31. *The A to Z from the Great War to the Great Depression* by Neil A. Wynn, 2009.
32. *The A to Z of the Crusades* by Corliss K. Slack, 2009.
33. *The A to Z of New Age Movements* by Michael York, 2009.
34. *The A to Z of Unitarian Universalism* by Mark W. Harris, 2009.
35. *The A to Z of the Kurds* by Michael M. Gunter, 2009.
36. *The A to Z of Utopianism* by James M. Morris and Andrea L. Kross, 2009.
37. *The A to Z of the Civil War and Reconstruction* by William L. Richter, 2009.
38. *The A to Z of Jainism* by Kristi L. Wiley, 2009.
39. *The A to Z of the Inuit* by Pamela K. Stern, 2009.
40. *The A to Z of Early North America* by Cameron B. Wesson, 2009.
41. *The A to Z of the Enlightenment* by Harvey Chisick, 2009.
42. *The A to Z of Methodism* edited by Charles Yrigoyen Jr. and Susan E. Warrick, 2009.
43. *The A to Z of the Seventh-day Adventists* by Gary Land, 2009.
44. *The A to Z of Sufism* by John Renard, 2009.
45. *The A to Z of Sikhism* by W. H. McLeod, 2009.
46. *The A to Z of Fantasy Literature* by Brian Stableford, 2009.
47. *The A to Z of the Discovery and Exploration of the Pacific Islands* by Max Quanchi and John Robson, 2009.
48. *The A to Z of Australian and New Zealand Cinema* by Albert Moran and Errol Vieth, 2009.
49. *The A to Z of African-American Television* by Kathleen Fearn-Banks, 2009.
50. *The A to Z of American Radio Soap Operas* by Jim Cox, 2009.
51. *The A to Z of the Old South* by William L. Richter, 2009.
52. *The A to Z of the Discovery and Exploration of the Northwest Passage* by Alan Day, 2009.
53. *The A to Z of the Druzes* by Samy S. Swayd, 2009.
54. *The A to Z of the Welfare State* by Bent Greve, 2009.

55. *The A to Z of the War of 1812* by Robert Malcomson, 2009.
56. *The A to Z of Feminist Philosophy* by Catherine Villanueva Gardner, 2009.
57. *The A to Z of the Early American Republic* by Richard Buel Jr., 2009.
58. *The A to Z of the Russo–Japanese War* by Rotem Kowner, 2009.
59. *The A to Z of Anglicanism* by Colin Buchanan, 2009.
60. *The A to Z of Scandinavian Literature and Theater* by Jan Sjåvik, 2009.
61. *The A to Z of the Peoples of the Southeast Asian Massif* by Jean Michaud, 2009.
62. *The A to Z of Judaism* by Norman Solomon, 2009.
63. *The A to Z of the Berbers (Imazighen)* by Hsain Ilahiane, 2009.
64. *The A to Z of British Radio* by Seán Street, 2009.
65. *The A to Z of The Salvation Army* by Major John G. Merritt, 2009.
66. *The A to Z of the Arab–Israeli Conflict* by P R Kumaraswamy, 2009.
67. *The A to Z of the Jacksonian Era and Manifest Destiny* by Terry Corps, 2009.
68. *The A to Z of Socialism* by Peter Lamb and James C. Docherty, 2009.
69. *The A to Z of Marxism* by David Walker and Daniel Gray, 2009.
70. *The A to Z of the Bahá'í Faith* by Hugh C. Adamson, 2009.
71. *The A to Z of Postmodernist Literature and Theater* by Fran Mason, 2009.
72. *The A to Z of Australian Radio and Television* by Albert Moran and Chris Keating, 2009.
73. *The A to Z of the Lesbian Liberation Movement: Still the Rage* by JoAnne Myers, 2009.
74. *The A to Z of the United States–Mexican War* by Edward H. Moseley and Paul C. Clark Jr., 2009.
75. *The A to Z of World War I* by Ian V. Hogg, 2009.
76. *The A to Z of World War II: The War Against Japan* by Anne Sharp Wells, 2009.
77. *The A to Z of Witchcraft* by Michael D. Bailey, 2009.
78. *The A to Z of British Intelligence* by Nigel West, 2009.
79. *The A to Z of United States Intelligence* by Michael A. Turner, 2009.

80. *The A to Z of the League of Nations* by Anique H. M. van Ginneken, 2009.
81. *The A to Z of Israeli Intelligence* by Ephraim Kahana, 2009.
82. *The A to Z of the European Union* by Joaquín Roy and Aimee Kanner, 2009.
83. *The A to Z of the Chinese Cultural Revolution* by Guo Jian, Yongyi Song, and Yuan Zhou, 2009.
84. *The A to Z of African American Cinema* by S. Torriano Berry and Venise T. Berry, 2009.
85. *The A to Z of Japanese Business* by Stuart D. B. Picken, 2009.
86. *The A to Z of the Reagan–Bush Era* by Richard S. Conley, 2009.
87. *The A to Z of Human Rights and Humanitarian Organizations* by Robert F. Gorman and Edward S. Mihalkanin, 2009.
88. *The A to Z of French Cinema* by Dayna Oscherwitz and MaryEllen Higgins, 2009.
89. *The A to Z of the Puritans* by Charles Pastoor and Galen K. Johnson, 2009.
90. *The A to Z of Nuclear, Biological, and Chemical Warfare* by Benjamin C. Garrett and John Hart, 2009.
91. *The A to Z of the Green Movement* by Miranda Schreurs and Elim Papadakis, 2009.
92. *The A to Z of the Kennedy–Johnson Era* by Richard Dean Burns and Joseph M. Siracusa, 2009.
93. *The A to Z of Renaissance Art* by Lilian H. Zirpolo, 2009.
94. *The A to Z of the Broadway Musical* by William A. Everett and Paul R. Laird, 2009.
95. *The A to Z of the Northern Ireland Conflict* by Gordon Gillespie, 2009.
96. *The A to Z of the Fashion Industry* by Francesca Sterlacci and Joanne Arbuckle, 2009.
97. *The A to Z of American Theater: Modernism* by James Fisher and Felicia Hardison Londré, 2009.
98. *The A to Z of Civil Wars in Africa* by Guy Arnold, 2009.
99. *The A to Z of the Nixon–Ford Era* by Mitchell K. Hall, 2009.
100. *The A to Z of Horror Cinema* by Peter Hutchings, 2009.
101. *The A to Z of Westerns in Cinema* by Paul Varner, 2009.
102. *The A to Z of Zionism* by Rafael Medoff and Chaim I. Waxman, 2009.

103. *The A to Z of the Roosevelt–Truman Era* by Neil A. Wynn, 2009.
104. *The A to Z of Jehovah's Witnesses* by George D. Chryssides, 2009.
105. *The A to Z of Native American Movements* by Todd Leahy and Raymond Wilson, 2009.
106. *The A to Z of the Shakers* by Stephen J. Paterwic, 2009.
107. *The A to Z of the Coptic Church* by Gawdat Gabra, 2009.
108. *The A to Z of Architecture* by Allison Lee Palmer, 2009.
109. *The A to Z of Italian Cinema* by Gino Moliterno, 2009.
110. *The A to Z of Mormonism* by Davis Bitton and Thomas G. Alexander, 2009.
111. *The A to Z of African American Theater* by Anthony D. Hill with Douglas Q. Barnett, 2009.
112. *The A to Z of NATO and Other International Security Organizations* by Marco Rimanelli, 2009.
113. *The A to Z of the Eisenhower Era* by Burton I. Kaufman and Diane Kaufman, 2009.
114. *The A to Z of Sexspionage* by Nigel West, 2009.
115. *The A to Z of Environmentalism* by Peter Dauvergne, 2009.
116. *The A to Z of the Petroleum Industry* by M. S. Vassiliou, 2009.
117. *The A to Z of Journalism* by Ross Eaman, 2009.
118. *The A to Z of the Gilded Age* by T. Adams Upchurch, 2009.
119. *The A to Z of the Progressive Era* by Catherine Cocks, Peter C. Holloran, and Alan Lessoff, 2009.
120. *The A to Z of Middle Eastern Intelligence* by Ephraim Kahana and Muhammad Suwaed, 2009.
121. *The A to Z of the Baptists* William H. Brackney, 2009.
122. *The A to Z of Homosexuality* by Brent L. Pickett, 2009.
123. *The A to Z of Islam, Second Edition* by Ludwig W. Adamec, 2009.

The A to Z of Islam

Second Edition

Ludwig W. Adamec

The A to Z Guide Series, No. 123

The Scarecrow Press, Inc.
Lanham • Toronto • Plymouth, UK
2009

Published by Scarecrow Press, Inc.
A wholly owned subsidiary of
The Rowman & Littlefield Publishing Group, Inc.
4501 Forbes Boulevard, Suite 200, Lanham, Maryland 20706
http://www.scarecrowpress.com

Estover Road, Plymouth PL6 7PY, United Kingdom

British Library Cataloguing in Publication Information Available

Library of Congress Cataloging-in-Publication Data

The hardback version of this book was cataloged by the Library of Congress as
follows:

Adamec, Ludwig W.
   Historical dictionary of islam / Ludwig W. Adamec. — 2nd ed.
     p. cm. — (Historical dictionaries of religions, philosophies, and movements ;
   no. 95)
   Includes bibliographical references.
   1. Islam—History—Dictionaries. I. Title.
BP50.A33 2009
297.03–dc22   2008052498

ISBN 978-0-8108-7160-1 (pbk. : alk. paper)
ISBN 978-0-8108-7020-8 (ebook)

⊗™ The paper used in this publication meets the minimum requirements of
American National Standard for Information Sciences—Permanence of Paper
for Printed Library Materials, ANSI/NISO Z39.48-1992.

Printed in the United States of America

To Rahella

Contents

Editor's Foreword   *Jon Woronoff*   xiii

Reader's Notes   xv

Map of the Islamic World   xvii

Acronyms and Abbreviations   xix

Chronology   xxi

Introduction   xxxvii

THE DICTIONARY   1

Appendix: Estimates of the Muslim Population of the World   345

Bibliography   349

About the Author   459

Editor's Foreword

All religions are hard to explain, but few seem to be as difficult as Islam. Indeed, the more it is explained—and it is explained a lot nowadays—the less it seems to be understood. There are various reasons for this, aside from any inherent complexities. One of the most pertinent is that Islam is undergoing considerable flux at present, swayed by various currents whose adherents hold different views, from the modernists and reformers, to the traditionalists and conservatives, to the fundamentalists and Islamists. And each differs in its interpretation of the traditions, precepts, and even sometimes facts, let alone just what one should believe and do as a practicing Muslim. Then there is the problem of vocabulary, most of it in Arabic, the meaning of which is difficult to convey to outsiders and not always entirely grasped even by Muslims.

No book could really overcome the many hurdles, but at least this revised edition of *The A to Z of Islam*, like its predecessor, seriously attempts to provide, in relatively simple language, the theory and practice, views and acts of the competing currents. In addition to surveying Islam today, it reviews Islam in its formative period and how it has evolved over many centuries. This is done first in the chronology and introduction, which also provide an overview of Islam as a world religion. Key aspects are further elucidated in the dictionary, which contains entries on crucial persons, including Muhammad and his Companions, imams and secular leaders, Koranic scholars and legal theorists, and even jihadists and terrorists. Other entries deal with significant stages in the expansion and development of Islam. And yet others present basic concepts and practices. As a guide, with no claim to completeness, a particularly useful section is the bibliography, including numerous sources for further study.

Unlike the authors of most "dictionaries" and similar reference works on Islam, Ludwig Adamec's views are more practical, his interests more pragmatic, and his presentation more accessible. This brings him closer to the concerns of ordinary laypersons and interested observers. Dr. Adamec has devoted over half a century to the study of the Middle East and the Islamic world, which he knows uncommonly well. Over this time he has taught at various universities, in particular the University of Arizona, and he has written extensively on Afghanistan, on which he is a leading authority, having written among other things successive editions of the *Historical Dictionary of Afghanistan*. This combination of study and teaching was indispensable in generating a handy guide, which should balance other existing guides to a religion that must absolutely become better understood. While maintaining most of the material from the very well-received first edition, this second edition fills in some of the gaps on earlier periods, and most important, brings the story up to date.

Jon Woronoff
Series Editor

Reader's Notes

The purpose of this work is to provide for the layperson as well as the serious student a concise dictionary of Islamic history, religion, philosophy, and political movements. Entries include biographies on and the thoughts of medieval thinkers as well as of modern members of the religious and political establishments. They describe the major sects, schools of theology, and jurisprudence, as well as aspects of Islamic culture, to present a brief introduction to the field of Islamic studies.

Muslims believe that the Koran is God's message in Arabic, revealed through the medium of the Prophet Muhammad for the guidance of the Arabs and subsequently for all humanity. Therefore, much of the Islamic terminology is Arabic, a fact that may pose some problems for the beginner.

Regarding names, in many parts of the Islamic world individuals have not adopted a family name. Some are known by their personal names (*ism*), such as 'Ali or Muhammad (as explained in the entry "Names and Name Giving"); others are identified under a group name (*nisba*) indicating a place of origin or residence, such as al-Baghdadi—the one from Baghdad, or al-Siqqilli—the Sicilian. They may be known by their patronymics (*nasab*), for example, Ibn Khaldun, the son of Khaldun (listed under "I") or Abu Muslim, the father of Muslim (listed under "A"). The Arabic article "al-" is ignored in the alphabetical order, and only the short name of an individual is given; for example, the full name of Taqi al-Din al-Maqrizi (listed under "M") is Abu 'l-'Abbas Ahmad ibn 'Ali ibn 'Abd al-Qadir al-Husayni Taqi al-Din al-Maqrizi (meaning the father of Abbas Ahmad, the son of Abd al-Qadir al-Husayni).

"Abd al-", meaning "the servant of," is also spelled Abdul; 'Abd Allah and 'Abdullah are variant spellings of the same name. The reader may ignore the diacritical mark "*ayn*" (ʿ), which stands for a certain sound in Arabic, as do the ligatures—dh, which non-Arabic speakers often pronounce like "z," and "kh," pronounced like "ch" in the German exclamation "ach." The article is transliterated "al" even in "sun letters," for example, al-Shafi'i (not ash-Shafi'i), al-Rashid (not ar-Rashid), al-Dajjal (not ad-Dajjal), al-Salam (not as-Salam), etc.

Where possible main entries are provided in English, with the equivalent term in Arabic; for example, the entry "Almsgiving" also provides the Arabic terms "zakat" and "sadaqa." The English word "judge" is followed by "qadhi" (also spelled "cadi" or "kadi" in Webster's dictionary). There are, however, a considerable number of proper names that cannot be cross referenced.

Terms in **boldface type** have their own entries. Some Islamic terms listed in Webster's Dictionary are given in the English spelling: Koran, rather than Qur'an; Medina, rather than Madina; and Mecca rather than Makka.

Citations from the Koran are from *The Holy Qur'an: English Translation of the Meanings and Commentary*, revised and edited by the Presidency of Islamic researches, IFTA, Call and Guidance, Kingdom of Saudi Arabia. Surahs and verses of the Koran are indicated listing the Surah first and the verse after a colon; for example, 22:36 indicates Surah 22 and verse 36.

Muslims reckon time from 622 CE, when Muhammad emigrated from Mecca to Medina; therefore, all dates in this volume are within our common era. It should be mentioned here that the dates of birth of individuals were usually not known and are often guesses and therefore less reliable than the dates of those persons' deaths. Also the records disagree on some dates, which may be reflected in this publication. The Islamic lunar year does not coincide with the Western solar year; some sources would list an event occurring in 911/912, but I have listed only the first date.

The chronology lists important dates and events, and the selected bibliography should enable the serious student to pursue more specialized research.

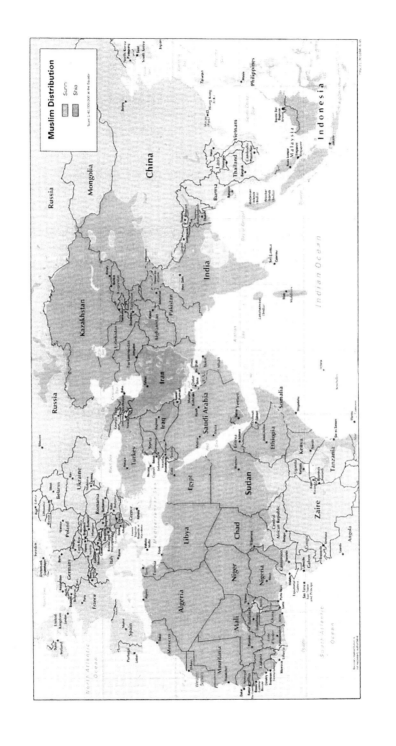

Acronyms and Abbreviations

CE	**Common Era**
d.	Died
EI2	*Encyclopaedia Islamica*
FIC	Front for Islamic Constitution
FIS	Front de Salut Islamique (Islamic Salvation Front)
ISNA	Islamic Society of North America
MCB	Muslim Council of Britain
MIK	Mujahidin-I Khalq
OIC	Organization of the Islamic Conference
NASIMCO	North American Shi'a Ithna-Asheri Muslim Communities Organization
NATO	North Atlantic Treaty Organization
PLO	Palestinian Liberation Organization
r.	ruled
UN	United Nations

Chronology

570 The traditional date of the birth of the Prophet Muhammad in the "Year of the Elephant." During this year (approximate date) Abraha, Christian king of Yemen, moves against Mecca with an elephant in his advance columns.

577 Muhammad's mother, Aminah b. Wahb, dies (his father had died soon after Muhammad's birth).

596 Muhammad marries Khadijah, a wealthy merchant woman.

602 Lakhmid dynasty at Hira ends.

ca. 610 "The Night of Destiny." Muhammad receives his first revelation from angel Gabriel. Khadija becomes his first convert.

613 First group of converts face persecution by the Quraysh, the major tribe of Mecca, which fears to lose its cultural and commercial dominance.

615 Exodus of some early converts to Ethiopia because of persecution by Meccans. Ascent of Muhammad to the seventh heaven.

617 Conversion of 'Umar ibn al-Khattab.

619 Death of Khadija and later Abu Talib, Muhammad's uncle and protector.

620 Prophet goes to Ta'if to win converts and find protection; docs not succeed. Night journey in which Muhammad is taken from Mecca to Jerusalem and from there to heaven.

621 First Aqabah covenant with 12 men from the Khazraj and Auz tribes, who convert to Islam.

622 **June:** Muslim converts in Yathrib (later Madinat al-Nabi, "City of the Prophet") promise loyalty and invite Muhammad to Yathrib. **July:** Muhammad flees to Yathrib. First of Muharram begins "Year One" of the Islamic lunar calendar.

623 Muhammad concludes marriage with 'A'ishah, daughter of Abu Bakr. Constitution of Madina establishes coexistence of Muslim and Jewish communities, *umma*. Fatima, daughter of Muhammad, marries 'Ali ibn Abi Talib, cousin of Muhammad.

624 **March:** Battle of Badr in which Muslims defeat a superior Meccan force. Jewish tribe, Banu Qaynuqa, accused of collaborating with Quraysh, expelled from Medina. The month of Ramadhan proclaimed as the period of fasting. Mecca, rather than Jerusalem, is designated as the *qiblah*, direction of prayer.

625 **March:** Battle of Uhud in which Muslim forces are defeated by Meccans, who do not follow up on their victory. Jewish tribe, Banu Nadir, accused of collaboration with enemy and expelled from Medina.

627 Battle of the Ditch. Meccans fail to conquer Medina, which is protected by a ditch (*kandaq*). Jewish tribe, Banu Qurayza, accused of collaborating with the enemy and destroyed.

628 Muhammad sets out on pilgrimage and is prevented from entering Mecca. Treaty of Hudaybiyyah establishes a 10-year truce with Meccans to permit Muslim pilgrims to enter Mecca.

629 Bedouin allies of the Quraysh break the Truce of Hudaybiyyah.

630 Muhammad, with about 10,000 men, enters Mecca without a fight. Muslims destroy the idols of the Ka'ba, declare the interior sacred, *harram*. "Farewell Pilgrimage" to Mecca by Muhammad.

630–631 "Year of Deputations." Tribal chiefs accept Islam. Abu Bakr leads pilgrimage to Mecca.

632 **March:** "Farewell Pilgrimage." **8 June:** Muhammad dies. Abu Bakr becomes successor (khalifa) of Muhammad (632–634). Beginning of the Rightly Guided Caliphate (632–657). Fatimah dies.

633 Wars of Apostasy (Ridda). Khalid b. al-Walid defeats Musaylamah; captures Hira. Ghassanids defeated at Marj Rahit.

634   Muslim forces defeat Byzantine army at Ajnadayn, occupy parts of Palestine. **August:** Abu Bakr dies, Umar b. Al-Khattab chosen as his successor (634–644).

635   Jews from Khaybar and Christians from Najran forced to settle in Syria. Arabian Peninsula unified under Islam. Khalid ibn Walid defeats Byzantines in Marj al-Suffar near Damascus.

636   Battle of Yarmuk expels Byzantines from Syria; Muslims are established in Damascus.

637   Sassanids defeated in the Battle of Qadisiyya.

638   Jerusalem captured.

639   First raid of 'Amr ibn. al-'As into Egypt.

640   Garrison towns (*amsar*) of Kufa and Basra founded.

641   'Amr ibn al-'As captures Babylon. Foundation of Fustat.

642   Sassanids defeated at Nihavand; Arabs rule Mesopotamia and parts of Persia. Muslims capture Alexandria for first time.

644   Caliph Umar assassinated. 'Uthman b. 'Affan elected as caliph (644–656).

646   Alexandria retaken by Muslims; under permanent control of Muslims.

649   Mu'awiyah, governor of Syria, takes Cyprus.

650   Koran edited in definitive version.

651   Eastern Persia occupied. Caliph 'Umar loses the ring of the Prophet; end of six good years of his rule.

653   Final version of Koran compiled.

655   Battle of the Masts. Arabs defeat Byzantine fleet.

656   'Uthman assassinated, accused of nepotism. Ali ibn Abi Talib proclaimed caliph (656–661). Talha, Zubayr, and 'A'ishah revolt, fight 'Ali in Battle of the Camel. 'A'ishah on camelback views the defeat.

657 Sixth Shi'ite imam, Jafar al-Sadiq, dies. Dispute over succession between Twelver and Sevener Shi'ahs.

657 Mu'awiyah challenges 'Ali, meets him in Battle of Siffin. Ali accepts arbitration and loses some of his followers, Kharijites, who reject arbitration. Kharijites develop into a puritanical sect that exists to this day.

658 Caliph Ali's forces defeat Kharijites at Nahrawan.

659 Adhruh Arbitration rejects claims of both 'Ali and Mu'awiyah.

660 Mu'awiyah proclaimed caliph in Syria, Egypt, and Hijaz. 'Ali recognized as caliph in Iraq and Iran.

661 'Ali assassinated in Kufa by a Kharijite. Mu'awiyah (661–680) proclaimed first Umayyad caliph (661–750). Husayn proclaimed caliph, cedes title to Mu'awiyah.

662 Ziyad ibn Abihi becomes governor of Basra, later also of Kufa (662–675).

670 Foundation of Qayrawan. 'Uqba ibn Nafi' conquers northwest Africa.

674–679 Muslim army besieges Constantinople.

680 Yazid, son of Mu'awiya, succeeds as caliph (680–683). **10 October:** (10th of Muharram) 'Ali's son Husayn is killed in the battle of Karbala near Kufa. Partisans of 'Ali, shiat 'Ali, eventually develop into a rival sect, counting the descendants of 'Ali as rightful successors of Muhammad. Shi'ites commemorate the 10th of Muharram (Islamic month) as the martyrdom of Husayn.

683 Reign of Caliph Mu'awiyah II (683–684). Medina sacked by Umayyads.

683–692 'Abd Allah ibn al-Zubayr proclaims himself caliph at Mecca.

684 Reign of Caliph Marwan (684–685). Battle of Marj Rahit and defeat of the Qays.

685 'Abd al-Malik elected caliph (685–705). Arabizes the administration and issues the first Islamic coins (693). Mukhtar leads 'Alid revolt at Kufa (685–687).

691 Dome of the Rock built in Jerusalem. Ibn al-Zubayr killed in battle.

692 Hajjaj occupies Mecca.

694 Hajjaj becomes governor of Iraq.

695–698 Consolidation of conquest of the Maghrib.

705 Walid I succeeds as caliph (705–715), founds the Umayyad Mosque in Damascus.

706–715 Qutayba b. Muslim conquers Transoxania.

711 Tariq b. Ziyad crosses Strait of Gibraltar (named after him Jabl al Tariq, Mountain of TarIq). Battle of Wadi Baakkah, conquest of Spain.

713 Zayd becomes imam of Fiver Shi'ites (Zaydis).

715 Sulaymand succeeds as caliph (715–717).

717 Umar II most respected of Umayyad caliphs (717–720). Siege of Constantinople (717–718).

720 Yazid II becomes caliph (720–724).

724 Reign of Hisham (724–743), noted for his administrative reforms.

728 Hasan al-Basri dies.

731–732 Charles Martel stops Arab advance in the Battle of Tours/ Poitiers.

743 Walid II (743–744) killed in a struggle between factions.

744 Yazid III succeeds to the caliphate. Ibrahim succeeds to the caliphate. Marwan II succeeds to the caliphate (744–750), last of the Umayyads.

746 Revolt of Abu Muslim, who raises the black banners of the Khorasanian army and assists in the establishment of the 'Abbasid Khalifate (749–1258).

749 Abu al-'Abbas al-Saffah proclaimed first 'Abbasid caliph (750–754).

750 Umayyad Caliph Marwan defeated at the Battle of the Greater Zab.

751 Battle on the Talas; Arabs defeat Chinese in Central Asia, capture paper makers; begin to manufacture paper.

754 Al-Mansur, brother of Abu al-'Abbas, becomes caliph (754–775).

756 Umayyad dynasty of Spain founded (756–1031) by 'Abd al-Rahman I (756–788).

762 Baghdad founded as capital of the 'Abbasid caliphate. 'Alid rebellions. Death of Isma'il; he becomes imam of the Isma'ili (or Sevener) shi'ites.

765 Jafar al-Siddiq, Sixth Shi'ite Imam, dies.

767 Death of Abu Hanifa, founder of Hanifite school.

775 Al-Mahdi becomes caliph (775–785).

778 Muqanna leads revolt in Khorasan.

780 Revolt of Muqanna, "The Veiled One," crushed.

785 Musa al-Hadi begins his short reign (785–786). Great mosque of Cordoba erected. Muqanna commits suicide.

786 Harun al-Rashid becomes caliph (786–809).

788 Idrisid dynasty founded.

793 Death of Malik ibn-Anas, founder of Malikite school.

796 Hakam I in Spain, revolts in Cordoba

800 Rise of the Aghlabid amirs.

803 End of Barmakid wazirate.

809 Al-Amin becomes caliph (809–813); his brother Ma'mun revolts.

813 Al-Amin assassinated and Ma'mun begins his caliphate (813–833), adopts Mu'tazilite school (827), and founds a university in Baghdad, the Bayt al-Hikma (house of wisdom) (830).

820 Death of Shafi'i, founder of Shafi'ite school.

821 Rise of the Tahirid amirs in Khurasan (822–873).

831 Palermo seized by the Arabs.

833 Al-Mu'tasim assumes caliphate (833–842). Mu'tazilite "rationalist" school gains ascendancy.

836 New 'Abbasid capital built in Samarra.

837 Sect of Babak destroyed.

842 Wathiq succeeds to caliphate (842–847).

847 Mutawakkil becomes caliph (847–861). Mu'tazilite school abandoned.

855 Death of Ahmad Ibn Hanbal, founder of Hanbalite school.

861 Mutawakkil assassinated. Caliphate of Muntasir begins.

862 Caliphate of Musta'in begins (862–866). Caliph moves from Samarra to Baghdad.

864 Zaydi shi'ism established in Daylam, Iran; continues until 1126.

866 Caliphate of Mu'tazz begins (866–869).

867 Rise of the Saffarid amirs in Eastern Iran.

868 Tulunid dynasty founded.

869 Zanj Rebellion of black slaves. Muhtadi becomes caliph (869–870). 'Ali ibn Muhammad founds kingdom of black slaves (869–883).

870 Mu'tamid becomes caliph (870–892). Conquest of Malta. Al-Bukhari dies.

871 Yaqub al-Saffar rules Persia (871–879).

873 Eleventh Shi'ite imam dies. Disappearance of the 12th Shia Imam and beginning of "Lesser Occultation" (873–940), followed by the "Greater Occultation" after 940, until the coming of the Mahdi.

874 Eleventh Shi'ite Imam dies.

875 Twelfth Imam goes into Occultation. End of direct rule of Shi'ite imams. Rise of the Samanid amirs in Transoxania.

877 Hamdan Qarmat revolts.

892 Caliphate of Mu'tadid begins (892–902).

894 Foundation of the Qarmatian state (894–977).

898 Foundation of a Zaydi state in Yemen; beginning of Rassi dynasty.

902 Al-Muktafi (902–908).

908 Al-Muqtadir becomes caliph (908–932); death of rival 'Abdallah ibn al-Mu'tazz.

909 'Ubaydullah al Mahdi becomes first Fatimid ruler (909–1171), assumes title of caliph in 911.

929 Rise of the Hamdanid amirs in Mesopotamia and Syria.

930 Qarmatians take Black Stone from Ka'ba. Abd al-Rahman II (912–961) assumes title of caliph in Spain.

932 Qahir becomes caliph (932–934). Buyid Mu'izz al-Dawlah becomes guardian of caliph, founds Buyid dynasty (932–1062).

934 Qahir blinded and deposed. Radhi becomes caliph (934–940).

935 Ikhshidid dynasty founded.

940 Beginning of "Grand Occultation" after fourth representative of the Hidden Imam. Muttaqi becomes caliph (940–944).

944 Muttaqi blinded and deposed. Mustakfi becomes caliph (944–946).

945 Buyids take Baghdad; rule Iraq and Iran (932–1062).

946 Muti' becomes caliph (946–974).

951 The Imam dies. Qarmatians return Black Stone to Mecca.

953 Mu'izz becomes Fatimid Caliph (953–975).

969 Fatimids conquer Egypt. Foundation of Cairo.

973 Fatimids found Al-Azhar mosque, the first Muslim university.

974 Ta'i' becomes caliph (974–991).

975 'Aziz becomes Fatimid caliph (975–996).

977 Beginning of Ghaznavid state (977–1186).

991 Qadir becomes caliph (991–1031). Recognizes independence of Mahmud of Ghazna and Ghaznawid dynasty (977–1186). Foundation in Baghdad of Shi'ite library, *Dar al'Ilm* (house of knowledge).

996 Al-Hakim becomes Fatimid ruler at Cairo (996–1021), revered by the Druzes as a deity. Fatimids destroy Church of the Holy Sepulcher in Jerusalem.

1027 Hisham III, Last Umayyad in Cordova (1027–1031).

1031 Qaim becomes caliph (1031–1075).

1036 Mustansir becomes Fatimid caliph (1036–1094).

1038 Almoravid (al-Morabitun) Berber Kingdom founded. Beginning of Seljuq sultanate (1038–1194).

1058 Al-Mawardi dies.

1062 Almoravid Yusuf ibn-Tashfin conquers Morocco.

1071 Battle of Manzikert. Rum Seljuks established in Anatolia.

1075 Al-Muqtadi becomes caliph (1075–1094).

1090 Hasan al-Sabbah captures Alamut fortress and begins rule of the Assassins.

1092 Nizam al-Mulk assassinated.

1094 Al-Mustazhir becomes caliph (1094–1118).

1099 Crusaders conquer Jerusalem.

1107 Muhammad Ibn-Tumart founds Almohad dynasty.

1111 Al-Ghazali dies.

1118 Al-Mustarshid becomes caliph (1118–1135).

1124 Death of Hasan al-Sabbah.

1130 Almohad (al-Muwahhidun) kingdom founded (1130–1269).

1135 Al-Rashid becomes caliph (1135–1136).

1136 Al-Muqtafi becomes caliph (1136–1160).

1160 Al-Mustanjid becomes caliph (1160–1170).

1170 Al-Mustadi' becomes caliph (1170–1180).

1171 Salah al-Din (Saladin) ends Fatimid regime in Egypt.

1174 Saladin captures Damascus and Syria. Ayyubid dynasty founded.

1180 Al-Nasir becomes caliph (1180–1225).

1187 Salah al-Din (Saladin) defeats crusaders at Battle of Hattin, captures Jerusalem.

1203 Denghlis Khan (Timuchin) founds Mongol empire.

1212 Almohades defeated at Battle of Las Navas de Tolosa.

1225 Al Zahir becomes caliph (1225–1226).

1226 Al Mustansir becomes caliph (1226–1242).

1230 End of Almohad rule in Spain.

1242 Al-Musta'sim becomes last 'Abbasid caliph (1242–1258).

1254 Mamluk rule in Egypt (1254–1517).

1256 Mongols captures Assassin fortress of Alamut.

1258 Mongols sack Baghdad; end of 'Abbasid caliphate at Baghdad.

1260 Mamluks defeat Mongols at 'Ayn Jalut.

1273 Jalal al-Din Rumi dies.

1324 Orkhan founds Ottoman empire (1324–1922).

1328 Ibn Taymiyyah dies.

1402 Timur-i Lang (Tamerlain) defeats Bayezid in Battle of Ankara.

1406 Ibn Khaldun dies.

1453 Ottomans capture Constantinople.

1492 Fall of Granada, the last Muslim kingdom in Spain.

1497 Babur captures Samarkand, becomes founder of Mughal dynasty (1526–1858).

1501 Shah Isma'il founds Safavid dynasty, imposes shi'ism in Iran.

1514 Selim defeats Shah Isma'il at Chalidran.

1517 Ottomans conquer Egypt.

1521 Ottomans capture Belgrade.

1529 Ottomans besiege Vienna.

1534 Ottomans capture Baghdad.

1538 Ottomans annex Hungary, capture Baghdad.

1556 Akbar begins rule of Moghul (Mughal) India

1683 Second siege of Vienna.

1722 Afghans defeat Safavid empire at Gulnabad.

1745 Emergence of the Wahhabi (Unitarian) movement.

1798 Napoleon invades Egypt (1798–1801).

1802 Wahhabis capture Mecca and Medina (1802–1804).

1805 Muhammad 'Ali founds Egyptian dynasty (1805–1952).

1812 Ibrahim, son of Muhammad 'Ali, takes Mecca and Medina.

1818 Ibrahim defeats Wahhabis.

1826 Massacre of the Janissaries under Mahmud II.

1828 Parts of Greece gain independence.

1830 French take Algeria.

1850 Execution of the Bab.

1869 Suez Canal opens.

1870 The "Mahdi" Muhammad Ibn 'Abdallah in Sudan.

1874 Aligarh school (later university) founded by Sir Sayyid Ahmad Khan.

1876 Abdul Hamid becomes sultan/caliph of the Ottoman empire.

1881 French occupy Tunisia. Agha Khan I dies.

1882   The Mahdi drives Egyptians out of Sudan. British invade Egypt, begin colonial rule (1882–1952).

1885   Khartum attacked and General Charles Gordon killed. Mahdi dies.

1898   Sir Sayyid Ahmad Khan dies.

1901   Wahhabi forces take Riyadh. The French invade Morocco.

1905–1911   Constitutional Revolt in Iran.

1907   Anglo–Russian Convention divides Iran, Afghanistan, and Tibet into spheres of influence.

1908   Young Turk revolt.

1914   Ottoman empire enters war against Triple Entente.

1916   **May:** Sykes–Picot Agreement. **June:** Arab Revolt.

1917   **November:** Balfour Declaration promises Jewish "Homeland" in Palestine.

1918   Armistice of Mudros between Ottomans and Allies.

1920   Ottoman government signs Treaty of Sèvres.

1921   Sons of Husayn, Sharif of Mecca, become kings. 'Abd Allah in Transjordan, Faysal in Iraq.

1922   Mustafa Kemal abolishes the sultanate.

1923   Turks defeat Greeks, sign Treaty of Lausanne, which repeals Treaty of Sèvres.

1924   Turks abolish the caliphate.

1928   Hasan al-Banna founds Muslim Brotherhood. Assassinated in 1949.

1938   Sir Muhammad Iqbal dies.

1941   Abu Ala Maududi founds Jama'at-i Islami.

1947   Pakistan founded as a state for Indian Muslims.

1948   State of Israel founded.

1970 Organization of Islamic Conference founded.

1974 Musa al-Sabr founds Movement of the Disinherited.

1975 Elijah Muhammad dies.

1977 **5 July:** General Zia ul-Haq deposes Zulfiqar Ali Bhutto.

1978 Imam Musa Sadr, leader of Twelver Shi'ites, disappears on a trip to Libya.

1979 **16 January:** Shah of Iran flees; Ruhullah Khomeyni establishes Islamic Republic of Iran.

1989 Islamic Salvation Front (FIS) founded. Khomeyni issues a fatwa against Salman Rushdie for writing the *Satanic Verses.*

1994 **5 November:** Emergence of the Taliban, students of religious schools, who capture Kandahar.

1995 **5 September:** Taliban capture Herat.

1996 **26 September:** Taliban take Kabul and two years later control most of Afghanistan.

1997 **6 October:** Taliban issue a decree prohibiting dolls for children and all photographic images of humans and animals.

1998 **22 April:** Court in Pakistan sentences a Christian, Ayyub Masih, to death for blaspheming Islam. The sentence is later suspended. **28 July:** The Taliban government decrees that Afghan parents must give their children "Islamic" names. **7 August:** Car bombs destroy U.S. embassies in Kenya and Tanzania. **20 August:** United States launches approximately 75 cruise missiles on a training camp of Osama bin Laden in Khost province of Afghanistan. **11 September:** Mullah Umar, head of the Taliban movement, issues a decree prohibiting forced marriages of women. **October:** Taliban require Hindus in Kandahar to wear yellow marks on their clothing. **4 November:** The United States offers a reward of $5 million for the capture of Osama bin Laden, who enjoys protection in Afghanistan.

1999 **12 October:** General Pervez Musharref stages coup, takes over government of Pakistan. **19 October:** Merve Kawakci is stripped of her citizenship and her seat in parliament after she appears in an Islamic head scarf. **4 November:** Roman Catholics and Orthodox Christians close their churches to protest Israeli decision to permit building a mosque next to the Church of the Annunciation in Nazareth. **14 November:** The United Nations imposes sanctions on Afghanistan for its refusal to surrender Osama bin Laden. **November 30:** A bill granting full political rights to women is rejected in Kuwait by a vote of 32 to 30. For approval, 33 votes would have been needed.

2000 **20 May:** Israeli troops withdraw from southern Lebanon as a result of casualties from Hizbullah campaigns. **1 August:** A group of six Iranian religious leaders issues a *fatwa* declaring that women could lead congregational prayers of their own gender. **6 October:** It is reported that the Bahrain government appointed to the consultative assembly four women, one Christian, and one Jew. **19 December:** The United Nations Security Council votes to impose sanctions on the Taliban government.

2001 **2 January:** Mulla Muhammad Umar of Afghanistan issues a decree making conversion from Islam to Christianity a capital crime. **26 February:** Mulla Muhammad Umar calls for the destruction of all statues because they are a threat to Islam. **6 March:** Destruction of the giant Buddha statues begins. **5 May:** Taliban government issues a ruling to prohibit foreigners from drinking alcohol, eating pork, listening to loud music, and being in contact with members of the opposite sex. **21 May:** A decree of Mulla Umar demands that Hindus wear a yellow mark on their clothing and homes and prohibits them from wearing a turban. **31 May:** The Taliban government prohibits foreign women from driving cars. **11 September:** Suicide bombers, believed to be members of Osama bin Laden's al-Qaeda organization, crash commercial airplanes into the World Trade Center and the Pentagon. **13 September:** The U.S. government mobilizes forces for action against the Taliban. **7 October:** American and British aircraft attack Taliban and al-Qaeda bases in Afghanistan. **22 December:** Afghan Interim Government begins its tenure.

2002 **11 January:** The first contingent of Taliban/al-Qaeda prisoners arrives at the American base at Guantanamo (Cuba). **13 August:** Iranian President Muhammad Khatami makes an official visit to Kabul. **4 September:** Gulbuddin Hekmatyar, an Afghan jihadist, proclaims jihad against American forces. **12 October:** Muslim radicals are blamed for a series of bombings, including at a night club in Bali in which 202 people are killed.

2003   **17 February:** Mulla Muhammad Umar calls for Afghans to join in holy war against Washington. **20 March:** United States launches war on Iraq.

2004   **4 January:** Afghan Great Council establishes Islamic State of Afghanistan. **11 March:** Terrorists bomb Madrid train, killing 190 people and injuring about 1,500.

2005   **7 July:** Terrorists bomb underground trains and a bus in London, killing 52 people and injuring 700. **21 July:** Terrorists attempt a repeat attack in London on underground trains and a bus, but none of the devices explodes.

2006   **8 June:** Abu Musab al-Zarqawi, head of al-Qaeda in Iraq, is killed in a U.S. air attack. **12 July:** Israel–Hizbullah war begins in Lebanon when Hizbullah forces cross into Israel and kill three soldiers and capture two others. A UN-brokered ceasefire ends war on 14 August.

2007   **December 27:** Benazir Bhutto, former prime minister and leader of the Pakistan People's Party, is assassinated at a campaign rally in Rawalpindi.

Introduction

The Arabian Peninsula, heartland of the Arab nation and birthplace of the Muslim Prophet Muhammad, is a vast expanse of deserts with oases on the periphery, covering an area of about 2,750,000 square kilometers. It is a plateau that slopes away from the west to the Persian/Arabian Gulf and Mesopotamia, the present Iraq. Its backbone is a range of mountains running parallel to the Red Sea coast, forming the **Hijaz** (barrier), which includes the holy cities of **Mecca** and **Medina**. The slope to the east is gradual and long, and the fall to the Red Sea is short and steep. Between the Nile and the Indus rivers is only one major river system: the Euphrates and Tigris and their tributaries. In the south-center lies the Rub' al-Khali, Empty Quarter, the largest expanse of sand in the world, comprising an area of about 640,000 square kilometers.

Sheltered by impenetrable barriers, nomad Bedouins eked out a precarious existence. Only they knew the location of the water holes that made survival possible. They grazed their livestock, moving within confined areas, some tending to limited agriculture in valleys and oases, others depending entirely on their flocks. Dates and the milk and meat from camels were the major items of nourishment. To possess the "two black ones"—that is, water and dates—is still the minimum requirement for survival. The camel was the nomad's nourisher, his means of transportation, and his medium of exchange. He still drinks its milk, feasts on its flesh, and makes his tent with its hair, which is fashioned into a felt. The **mahr** (dowry) of a bride, the price of blood, and the wealth of a chief were counted in terms of camels. The Bedouin has been called the parasite of the camel (Hitti, 1964, 21). Without the camel, the desert could not be crossed, and the Arabs could never have conquered an empire. Although the camel was the most useful, the horse was the most noble of all animals. In Arabia, the horse has been kept pure and free of admixtures; it provided the speed in raids (**ghazwah**), a necessity for survival.

Each tribe was an independent nation. It made war and peace with neighboring tribes, allied itself with other tribes, or became part of confederations on the basis of their common interests. There was no existence for the individual outside of the protection of his tribe. If a tribe was destroyed, its members had to attach themselves as clients to another tribe. To be expelled from one's tribe was tantamount to a sentence of death.

THE MESSAGE OF ISLAM

The period of some 150 years prior to the Prophet's message was called the jahiliyyah, the "age of **ignorance**." Arabia was then isolated from the rest of the Near East. Two superpowers ruled in the north: the Eastern Roman, or Byzantine, empire and the Sassanian Persian empire. They employed satellite kingdoms as buffer states to prevent the Arab nomads from raiding the northern territories. The Yemen in the south was contested by the empires of the north. In the "Year of the Elephant," in the 570s, an Abyssinian army under **Abrahah** moved against **Mecca** but was forced to return to Yemen.

Most of the Arabs were pagans, but some were Christian or Jewish. One of the most important cultural centers was the city-state of Mecca, ruled by an oligarchy of merchants from the tribe of **Quraysh**. The Quraysh were subdivided into a number of clans, one of which, the Banu Hashim (**Hashimites**), was the clan of the Prophet. The prosperity of Mecca depended on keeping the caravan routes free from attacks; therefore, they promoted two sacred periods during which raiding and blood feuds were temporarily stopped. Customary tribal law in Mecca was beginning to give way to hegemonic rule by the Quraysh. The Bedouin concept of honor was giving way to the idea of accumulating wealth.

Muhammad was born in the "Year of the Elephant." His mother, Amina, was of the clan of Zuhra, and his father, 'Abd Allah, was of the Hashimite clan of the Quraysh. His father died four months before his birth, and his mother died a few years later. As was the custom, he was raised by a Bedouin nurse, Halima, and then stayed with his grandfather, **'Abd al-Muttalib** and later with his uncle **Abu Talib**. At age 25, Muhammad married **Khadijah**, a wealthy woman of about 40 for whom he had conducted some business. Every year in the month of Rajab, Muhammad would go to Mount Hira and live there and fast. When he was 40, he came home one day, confessing to Khadijah that he heard voices. And one day in the month of **Ramadhan**, Muhammad had his first revelation. He heard a voice, commanding him to "Read!" Muhammad answered, "I cannot read!" The spirit gripped him again and said:

READ: IN THE NAME OF THY LORD WHO CREATED
CREATED MAN FROM A CLOT
READ: AND IT IS THY LORD THE MOST BOUNTIFUL
WHO TEACHETH BY THE PEN
TEACHETH EACH MAN THAT WHICH HE KNEW NOT.

Then the spirit disappeared and Muhammad went home to Khadijah. His wife covered him with a cloak, and Muhammad fell asleep. Suddenly the spirit returned and shouted:

O THOU THAT ARE CLOAKED, ARISE AND WARN!
THY LORD MAGNIFY! THY RAIMENT PURIFY!
AND FROM INIQUITY GET THEE AWAY.

Muhammad woke up and told Khadijah that the spirit had bid him to call men to God. He asked, "Whom shall I call? And who will believe me?" Khadijah was said to have answered, "Call me the first, for I believe in thee." Muhammad began to have additional revelations, and an angel—later identified as Gabriel—told Muhammad that he was chosen as the Messenger of God. He gained a small number of converts to his creed: After Khadijah, **'Ali**, his cousin and son-in-law, **Abu Bakr**, and the freed slave **Zayd ibn Harith** were among the first. The early converts came from three groups: young men of influential families who did not themselves wield any power; young men of weaker families and clans; and foreigners and men from outside the clan system who did not have any powerful protectors. The time was ripe for Muhammad's message; there was a social malaise as tribal traditional values and the existing social relationships were unable to cope with the problems faced by urban society. A new ideology was needed to replace the bonds of blood with the bonds of religion to provide a new concept of social justice and equality.

Muhammad was soon faced with opposition from the Quraysh, who feared that the new religion would threaten their social and commercial interests. Islam taught worship of one God and condemned the worship of idols. It propagated a philosophy of equality that threatened not only their pagan beliefs but also their wealth and political power. In 619, Muhammad lost his uncle and protector and soon afterward Khadija, his wife. **Abu Lahab**, an old enemy, now became head of the Hashimite clan. Some of Muhammad's followers, who did not enjoy the protection of a powerful tribe, were forced to migrate to Abyssinia, and Muhammad was forced to flee to **Yathrib**, subsequently called Madinat al-Nabi, "City of the Prophet," or simply Medina.

Members of the **Khazraj** and **Aws** tribes at Yathrib converted to Islam and invited Muhammad to come to their city, which was torn by disputes between two Arab and three Jewish tribes. The year 622, marking Muhammad's flight, became "Year One" of the Islamic era. In Medina, Muhammad was Prophet of the early Arab converts, and statesman and arbiter between them and the Jews. The "Charter of **Medina**" was the first constitution in Islam, regulating the coexistence of a heterogeneous community.

The growth of the Muslim community in Medina considerably alarmed the Quraysh, who feared that the caravan route to the north would be blocked. The first confrontation between the two city-states resulted in the Battle of **Badr** in 624, when a force of some 300 Muslims defeated a superior force of some 1,000 Meccans. This was a severe loss of prestige for Mecca, which lost a number of its most prominent leaders. For the Muslims it was confirmation that Allah was on their side. One of the Jewish tribes, the **Qaynuqah**, was accused of collaboration with the Meccans and expelled from Medina. Another engagement, the **Battle of Uhud** in 625, was a temporary setback, which Muhammad blamed on a lack of steadfastness among the Muslim forces. The second Jewish tribe, the Banu **Nadir**, was now expelled. In 627, the Meccans moved with an army of between 7,500 and 10,000 against Medina, but the Muslim community was saved by digging a trench that the Meccans were unable to cross. This came to be known as the Battle of the **Trench**. The last Jewish tribe, the **Qurayzah**, was accused of intriguing with the Meccans and was destroyed. Medina was now a Muslim Arab city, growing in power as converts joined the banners of the new faith.

Realizing the weakness of the Meccans, Muhammad decided to go on a pilgrimage to the **Ka'bah**, a cubelike building in Mecca that has been a shrine since pre-Islamic days. According to legend, the shrine was built by **Adam** and rebuilt by **Abraham** after the deluge. The angel **Gabriel** brought the **Black Stone** that is now in the Ka'bah and instructed the people about the pilgrimage. Muhammad set out in 628 for Mecca with some 1,400 Muslims, but he was not able to enter the city. He concluded with the Meccans the Treaty of **Hudaybiyah**, which was supposed to maintain peace for the subsequent ten years. Accusing the Meccans of violating the treaty, the Muslim forces took Mecca in 630, at the loss of two Muslim lives.

In the Year of **Deputations**, 630–631, delegations of tribes from all over the Arabian Peninsula came to Medina to offer their allegiance. They agreed to be instructed in the new faith and to pay a poor tax (**zakat**) for the institutional use of the Muslim community. The area of Mecca and Medina was declared **haram**, forbidden to non-Muslims, a prohibition that some believe was later extended to much of the Peninsula. By the time the Prophet Muhammad died in 632, virtually all the Arabs in the Peninsula had offered their allegiance (**bay'ah**), and the Arab nation and the Islamic state were one and the same.

The death of the Prophet caused considerable consternation. It was soon decided that a khalifah, successor or **caliph**, was to be elected to lead the Muslim community (**ummah**). Three factions in Medina seemed to vie for power: the emigrants, **muhajirun**, who came with Muhammad to Medina; the Helpers, **ansar**, Medinans who converted and supported the Prophet; and members of the Quraysh, Meccans who had now become Muslims and felt that their past leadership and blood relationship with the Prophet especially qualified them for assuming leadership of the state. An assembly of **Companions** of the Prophet seemed unable to agree about who would lead until **'Umar ibn al-Khattab** spontaneously offered bay'ah to Abu Bakr. Others followed suit, and he was elected the first caliph.

Abu Bakr did not have much time to institutionalize his functions as head of state. Many of the tribes who had nominally become Muslims considered themselves free of any obligation to Muhammad's successor. Therefore, most of the short reign of Abu Bakr was devoted to reuniting Arabia in the Wars of **Riddah**, defeating the apostates. He was ably assisted by **Khalid ibn al-Walid** and **'Amr ibn al-'As**, who eliminated the **Ghassanid** and **Lakhmid** buffer states and moved into Palestine.

Campaigns during the caliphate of 'Umar ibn al-Khattab (634–644) led the Islamic forces into North Africa and Mesopotamia. 'Umar adopted the title **Amir al-Mu'minin**, Commander of the Believers. The Byzantines were defeated in the Battle of al-**Yarmuk** (636), and the Persian Sassanids were defeated at the Battle of **Nihavand** (641). 'Umar was worried about overextending his forces, and he cautioned his reckless commander, 'Amr ibn al-As: "If my letter ordering thee to turn back from Egypt overtakes thee before entering any part of it then turn back; but if thou enter the land before the receipt of my letter, then proceed and solicit Allah's aid"(Hitti, 1964, 160). Surmising its contents, Amr did not open the letter until he had entered Egypt. At the siege of the fortress of Babylon, Cyrus, in charge of the fortress, tried to bribe the Muslim commander, but his negotiators found that it was impossible to corrupt the enemy. They reported:

> We have witnessed a people to each and every one of whom death is preferable to life, and humility to prominence, and to none of whom this world has the least attraction. They sit not except on the ground, and eat naught but on their knees. Their leader [amir] is like unto one of them: the low cannot be distinguished from the high, nor the master from the slave. And when the time of prayer comes none of them absents himself, all wash their extremities and humbly observe their prayer (Hitti, 1964, 163)

In 643, the Muslim armies reached the borders of India. When 'Umar was assassinated in 644, a council of five Companions elected **'Uthman ibn 'Affan** (644–656), an aristocratic member of the Quraysh, to lead the Islamic community. 'Uthman was a compromise candidate; he was old and weak and was soon dominated by members of his clan who wanted to take over leading positions in the state. The most important legacy of his rule is believed to be the final collection of the revelations in the **Koran** (Qur'an, the Holy Book of Muslims). Unrest continued in the empire; malcontents from Medina and disaffected groups in Egypt and Iraq turned against 'Uthman and murdered the 80-year-old caliph. **'Ali ibn Abi Talib** was the last of the Rashidun, the "**Rightly Guided Caliphs**" of Sunni Islam.

'Ali moved the capital of the Islamic state from Medina to Kufah. One reason may have been that Medina had been tainted by the murder of 'Uthman, another that he felt insecure in the old capital. He was immediately challenged by **Talhah**, **Zubayr**, and **'A'ishah**, Muhammad's widow. They blamed him for permitting 'Uthman's murderers to escape and finally met him in combat in the Battle of the **Camel** (656). Both Talhah and Zubayr were killed, and 'A'ishah was returned to Medina to resign herself to a life of seclusion. **Mu'awiyah**, the governor of Syria and a relative of 'Uthman, was next to challenge 'Ali's authority. He refused to swear allegiance to 'Ali and demanded that he first avenge the murder of 'Uthman. The two armies met in the Battle of **Siffin** (657). 'Ali's forces were about to gain the upper hand, when the Syrians appealed for arbitration and an end of the bloodshed. There was great reluctance among the soldiers to fight fellow Muslims. Each had relatives in the other camp, and 'Ali agreed to submit the dispute to arbitration. This marked the origins of the division of Islam into **Sunni**, or orthodox Muslims, and **Shi'ites**, the partisans of 'Ali, who felt that he was the rightful successor of the Prophet Muhammad. The **Kharijites**, or seceders, followers of 'Ali, turned against him because he had submitted to arbitration. A Kharijite assassinated 'Ali in 661. **Najaf**, 'Ali's burial place in present-day Iraq, is a holy city to Shi'ites.

Mu'awiyah had himself proclaimed caliph in 660 while 'Ali was still alive. He was a clever politician and presented himself as the model of an Arabian king. He was quoted as having said: "I apply not my sword where the lash suffices, nor my lash where my tongue is enough." He performed all the functions required of a caliph and said he would resign if all the Muslims could agree on a man more fit to lead them. He based his right to rule on the fact that he alone had sufficient power to maintain and defend the Islamic state. While he was still governor of Syria, Mu'awiyah built the first Islamic navy, and in the Battle of the **Masts** (655) he won a naval engagement with the Byzantine empire. New conquests in the east brought his forces into central Asia: Kabul in 664 and Bukhara in 674. One of his most important governors and military leaders was **Ziyad ibn Abihi** (Ziyad, the Son of His Father whose name was not known). Ziyad crushed the Kharijites again, as well as some of their Bedouin allies. Mu'awiyah assured the continuation of the **Umayyad Caliphate** (661–750) when he appointed his son, **Yazid** (680–683), as his successor. This continued the civil war into the second generation, when 'Abdullah, the son of 'Umar; 'Abdullah, the son of Zubayr; and **Husayn**, the son of 'Ali, refused to swear allegiance to Yazid. Husayn, expecting support from the Kufans, moved with a band of some 200 men into Iraq, but they were met by an Umayyad army of some 4,000 men, and he and his supporters were killed. His death at **Karbala** in 680 is still mourned by Shi'ites today. They observe the first ten days of the month of **Muharram** as days of lamentation. This event sealed the schism in Islam.

Yazid was able to defeat Abdullah Ibn al-Zubayr, who had proclaimed himself caliph, in Medina in 683. **'Abd al-Malik**, the "great Arabizer," succeeded in 685, marking the high point of Umayyad power. Assisted by his general, **al-Hajjaj**, 'Abd al-Malik captured Mecca in 692 and defeated a number of uprisings. He divided the empire into provinces, each of which was in charge of a governor; appointed **judges** (Qadhis) to the major towns; and established a large standing army. The first Muslim coins were struck, and the Arabic script was improved with the addition of vowel marks. The Umayyads expanded the territories of Islam from Bukhara and Samarkand to Spain; they reached southern France, but were stopped at the Battle of Poitiers (or Tours) in 731–732. Accused by the pious opposition of being Arab kings, rather than caliphs, resistance to the Umayyads began to grow. **'Umar ibn Abd al-Aziz** II (682–720), known as the "renovator" of Islam, was an exception.

With the capture of new lands, Arabs became a minority in the Islamic empire. Their secularism and lack of a clear ideology; ill treatment of the newly converted, who were taxed like non-Muslim subjects; and internecine warfare ended in a revolt that established the **'Abbasid Caliphate** (749–1258), with its capital in Baghdad.

The Umayyads were given bad press by 'Abbasid historians, in part to justify the 'Abbasid revolt, but also with some justification. Of the 14 caliphs, only Mu'awiyah, 'Abd al-Malik, and 'Umar were capable rulers, and with a weak man in charge, the empire was weakened. The Umayyads, like subsequent Muslim rulers, lacked a clear rule of succession; the Arabs did not follow the law of primogeniture. The practice of polygamy greatly increased the number of eligible successors, and several caliphs were the sons of slave women. If the oldest male relative was chosen to succeed, it was not necessarily a son; cousins, uncles, etc., had an equal claim. The result was a measure of internecine conflict that continued throughout the centuries in the Islamic world. The Umayyads failed to engender a sense of loyalty among their most deserving officials. They put to death some of their best generals and deposed their administrative officials to deprive them of their wealth. The Umayyads were Arab kings rather than theocratic rulers, enjoying the pleasures of life and more attuned to the culture of pre-Islamic times. Tribalism and conflicts between Arab tribes continued to divide the Arab-Islamic nation. Non-Arab converts, **mawlas**, were treated as second-class citizens, which encouraged them to join the Shi'ite opposition, attitudes to be expected in a period of transition from an Arab-Islamic nation to an Islamic empire.

The 'Abbasid assumption of power was not just a dynastic change; it was a revolution in the early history of Islam. The short rule of Abu al-'Abbas al-Saffah, "The Shedder of Blood" (749–754), was followed by al-**Mansur** (754–775), the real founder of a dynasty of 37 caliphs, which ended with the Mongol conquest of Baghdad in 1258. He established his capital at Baghdad. Ruthless to real or imagined rivals, he preserved the supremacy of Islamic law and was a good administrator. His thriftiness earned him the title "Father of the Penny" (the penny pincher). On his deathbed, he advised his successor, "Never allow a thing which has to be done today to remain over for tomorrow. Associate with people from whom you can get good advice. Keep the people and the army contented. Never make your treasury empty. Never go beyond the bounds of moderation," advice he himself did not often follow. Although the 'Abbasid state was hailed as a return to the theocratic state, it became increasingly patterned after an older, Persian model with the caliph the august, unapproachable, godlike autocrat. The 'Alids, who supported the revolution, were rudely disappointed when the 'Abbasids restored Sunni orthodoxy. Mansur has been called a treacherous man—he put to death his distinguished general, **Abu Muslim**, and cruelly killed his uncle Abdullah—but he preserved the supremacy of Islamic law and was a good administrator. The empire was organized after the Sassanian model, and ministries of the Army, the Seal, Finances, the Post, and Intelligence were set up. The only sphere in which Arabic continued to dominate was the religious sciences. The 'Abbasids gained valued help in their state building by drawing on the talents of the **Barmakids**, a Persian family of secretaries and viziers who were men of great ability and administrative skill and amassed considerable wealth.

The "Arabian Nights" period of the 'Abbassids began with **Harun al-Rashid** (786–809). He conducted a brilliant court, which attracted the talented and beautiful, including the **Barmakids**. But it was the end of an era. The Umayyad caliphate continued in Spain and, under Harun's successors, the empire began to lose control of the periphery. Harun hoped to prevent civil war after his death by arranging for an orderly succession; he appointed **Amin** as his successor at Baghdad and **Ma'mun** as governor of the eastern province of Khurasan and second in line of succession. It was not to be. Ma'mun prevailed in a struggle for power, and the unity of the Islamic world was ended with the establishment of independent sultanates in the periphery and the hegemony of the Turks, who came in as slaves and eventually became the masters of large parts of the Islamic world. Ma'mun tried to mend the Sunni–Shi'ite schism; he gave his daughter in marriage to the eighth Shi'ite imam, **'Ali al-Ridha**, and appointed him as his successor. This was not well received by the Sunni 'ulama', and only the premature death of al-Ridha brought an end to Ma'mun's efforts. Ma'mun began a short "age of rationalism," and the **Mu'tazilite** dogma became the accepted doctrine. He established the **Houses of Wisdom**, in which Arabic and foreign sciences were taught. Religion was freely debated among Christians, Jews, and Muslims of Baghdad; and Greek philosophers were translated and later retranslated from Arabic in the West.

Unlike the Umayyad caliphs, the 'Abbasids prided themselves on being the heads of a theocratic empire. They patronized the 'ulama' (doctors of Islamic sciences) and made a show of consulting them on matters of state and law. Culturally, first Persian and later Turkish influences dominated; with the loss of its tribal basis, the empire lost its democratic features, and the caliphate was transformed into monarchial despotism. The caliphs kept themselves aloof and surrounded themselves with an awe-inspiring court, and the vizier became the alter ego of the invisible caliph. The Muslim historian al-Fakhri said about the 'Abbasid caliphate:

It was a dynasty abounding in good qualities, richly endowed with generous attributes, wherein the wares of science found a ready sale, the merchandise of culture was in great demand, the observances of religion were respected, charitable bequests flowed freely, the world was prosperous, the Holy Shrines were well cared for, and the frontiers were bravely kept.

Under the Umayyads no true orthodoxy prevailed, and only with the beginning of 'Abbasid control do we have the creation of a systematic theology. Theological schools emerged in major cities, most importantly in Medina, Damascus, Basrah, and Kufah, which developed such disciplines as law, jurisprudence, grammar, and Koranic exegesis. In each of these towns, pious men gathered, usually in mosques, to discuss questions of theology. Certain men gained a reputation for their knowledge; others were famous for their asceticism. They argued such questions as free will and predestination, capital sin and the sinner's fate, and the divine unity and justice of Allah. The major philosophical trends were espoused by the rationalist Mu'tazilites; the uncommitted **Murji'ites**, who would leave judgment to God; the radical Kharijites, who declared a sinner a **kafir** to be killed; and the fundamentalist **Ash'arites**, whose doctrine became orthodox dogma. An important dogma in Islam is God's omnipotence, with the corollary that nothing happens without God's will. From that, it would follow that all is pre-ordained, and man can't help committing sins, but al-Ash'ari, with his doctrine of **kasb** (acquisition), stated that God produces the act, which is then "acquired" by the individual, giving him a choice, without infringing on God's omnipotence. Al-Ash'ari denied the existence of causality or a natural law, and he demanded the unquestioned acceptance of Divine Law and Revelation. He held that the Koran was the uncreated speech of God and espoused a literalism in which he used logic to expound an extreme fundamentalism.

The Mu'tazilite school, on the other hand, stood for free will and God's justice, giving man the certainty that choosing the good and avoiding evil will win salvation. They also held that the Koran was created. When Caliph Ma'mun supported the Mu'tazilite doctrine of the createdness of the Koran and forced its acceptance by the 'ulama', the 'Abbasid caliphs eventually lost their authority to interfere in matters of religion and law. Muslim historians call the period of the first 10 caliphs the golden age; Mansur (754) was the "Opener," Ma'mun (813) the "Middler," and Mu'tadid (892) the "Closer." The 21 caliphs after al-Mu'tadid were pawns and at times virtual captives of a new type of de facto political ruler, called **sultan**.

Sunni Muslims disagree about when the caliphate ended: some say it was after the four "Rightly Guided" caliphs (632–661) who were Companions of the Prophet; others that it ended with the Mongol conquest of Baghdad (1258). The Ottoman conquerors of western Asia and North Africa claimed to have been appointed by a member of the 'Abbasid clan when they captured Egypt in 1517. Thus the Ottoman sultanate/caliphate continued until its defeat in World War I. Shi'ites count the end of the imamat, respectively, with the fifth, seventh, or twelfth **imam**.

Political development in the Islamic world was a slow process: In pre-Islamic times and long afterward, the political unit was the biological and sociological unit: the family, the clan, and the tribe. Political unity meant the voluntary acceptance of arbitration, sharing resources, and providing for the common defense. An assembly (**majlis**) consisted of the male members of a tribe, who were to make decisions affecting the common interest. A chief (**shaykh**) presided, but he was essentially an arbitrator, a *primus inter pares*. The votes were weighed, not counted; the elders and more prosperous carried the day. There was no priestly class, only a shamanist type of soothsayer (**kahin**), who was the custodian of the idols, usually stones which were collected in the Ka'bah. The Kahin did not have any authority over the tribe. In urban areas, a kind of city council (*mala'*) existed, but it was not very effective.

Initially, Muhammad's community acted like a clan, but the bonds of Islam began to replace the bonds of blood. The early community consisted of two classes of **believers** (mu'minun): the Companions, who followed Muhammad to Medina (**muhajirun**), and the Helpers (**ansar**), Medinans of the Aws and Khazraj tribes who converted to Islam. But there were also three Jewish tribes in Medina, and together they formed the first Judeo–Muslim community (ummah). Muhammad became the ruler on the basis of a contract, called the Charter of **Medina**, which provided for the common defense and coexistence of the communities. Once Arabia was unified under Islam and new territories were conquered, the ummah included only Muslims, and non-Muslim subjects (dhimmis) continued to coexist in autonomous communities, subject to payment of a capitation tax (**jizyah**) and dispensations from military service.

Under the successors of Muhammad's rule, the caliphs served as heads of state, but since Islamic law consisted of God's commands—as collected in the Koran—sovereignty rested with God. The caliphs and subsequent rulers could not legislate; they had to enforce the God-given law. Only in matters not conflicting with divine law, the Koran, and Traditions (**shari'ah**), was legislation permitted. With 'Umar I (634–644) a new constitution came into force: No religion other than Islam was to be tolerated in the Arabian Peninsula. The Muslim Arabs were to be a warrior class, racially and political segregated from the conquered in garrison camps (**amsar**). They were not to hold any land outside the Arabian Peninsula, and the dhimmis were to have protection for their life, property, and religion. If they converted to Islam, they no longer had to pay that tax. A land tax, **kharaj**, was first levied only on non-Muslims in the newly conquered territories (as Arabs acquired land, they eventually also had to pay the land tax), and a cadastral survey was conducted for the assessment of taxes. **'Ushr** (a tenth) eventually became a tithe on property owned by Muslims, and a poor tax (zakat) came to be levied. A public register, the **Diwan**, was set up for the distribution of movable booty (**Ghanima** or **Khums**), of which at first one-fifth went to the ruler for his institutional use, while four-fifths was taken by the conquering soldiers. But soon the state took four-fifths and paid pensions to the soldiers, to Muhammad's wives, and to widows and families of martyrs. Pensions were paid on a scale depending on priority of conversion and nearness to the Prophet: wives, who got 10,000 dirhams; the Companions of the Prophet and those who had participated in the Battle of Badr (5,000 dirhams); etc. 'Umar divided the empire into provinces, each headed by a governor (**Wali**) who also acted as a judge and tax collector (**'Amil**), and judges were eventually appointed to the major towns.

Muslim political philosophers in the 10th and 11th centuries began to define the ideal character of an Islamic state. The caliph was the supreme head of state, ruling with the assistance of a consultative council (**shurah**). Sunnis believed in the principle of election, which was established with the election of the first four caliphs by a council of Companions of the Prophet. Nevertheless, dynastic succession was common, and the caliph was essentially an absolute monarch as long as he also held military power. Shi'ites held that the imam must be a descendant of Ali, nominated by his predecessor. The caliph had to be knowledgeable about Islamic law and the Traditions of the Prophet. He had to be of good character and piety, have good judgment in the functions of government and administration, and be of sound health and body. Eventually a doctrine of the caliphate was evolved. One Islamic jurist, al-**Mawardi** (974–1058), defined the functions of the caliph as follows: 1) protecting Islam from innovation, 2) providing justice, 3) protecting the borders of Islam, 4) executing the penalties of the shari'ah, 5) garrisoning the borders, 6) fighting unbelievers to convert or pay the poll tax, 7) levying taxes according to the Koran, 8) regulating the expenditures of the state, 9) appointing the right people to offices, and 10) supervising the administration.

However, when the sultans became de facto rulers, the institution of the sultanate was legitimized as long as sultans performed all the functions the caliph no longer could. For a time, the caliphs had the power to approve the legislation of a sultan, but eventually sultans, like the Shi'ite **Buyids**, ignored or defied the wishes of the caliph.

Already from the beginning of the 'Abbasid empire, the unity of the Islamic world was lost. In Spain, the Umayyad dynasty/caliphate continued from 756 to 1031 at the capitals of Seville and Cordova, ending the fiction of a united caliphate. The **Idrisids** (788–926) were the first Shi'ite dynasty in Islamic history, founded by Idris ibn 'Abdullah, and established in Morocco, but they fell prey to the **Fatimids** in the east and the Spanish Umayyads in the west. The **Tulunid dynasty** (868–905) was the first local principality of Egypt and Syria to gain autonomy from Baghdad. The **Ikhshidis** (935–969) established themselves in Egypt, but finally gave way to the Shi'ite Fatimids (909–1171). North Africa was subsequently ruled by the **Ayyubids** who, under Salah al-Din (Saladin, 1138–1193), defeated the crusaders at the battle of **Hittin** (1187) and captured Jerusalem. The **Mamluk** slave dynasties (1250–1517) gave way to the Ottoman empire (1342–1924), which reunited most of the Islamic world west of the Iranian border.

In the east, territory was lost to the short-lived **Tahirids** (820–873), who were replaced by the Saffarids (867–ca. 1495), who, in turn, were largely replaced by the **Samanids** (874–999). Turks were the founders of the **Ghaznavid dynasty** (977–1186), the **Saljuq dynasty** (1038–1194) (who replaced the Buyids), and the Ottoman empire. By the 16th century, the Islamic world was divided into the Ottoman empire, controlling the lands west of Iran; the **Safavid dynasty** (1501–1732), which founded modern Shi'ite Iran; and the Moghul (Mughal) Empire of India (1526–1858), which existed until defeated by Britain in 1858.

A body of **Islamic law** (shari'ah) also gradually evolved in the eight and ninth centuries based on the revelations of God's commands collected in the Koran. But it was soon felt that the Koran was not sufficient to cover all aspects of a complex society, and the jurists turned for guidance to the life of the Prophet. Acting on the premise that God would not have chosen Muhammad as prophet if he had not led an exemplary life, the Traditions (actions and sayings of the Prophet), collected in news items (**hadith**), were examined for guidance. A science of hadith criticism evolved in which news items, transmitted by an original witness through a chain of transmitters, were judged according to the reliability of the chain. Six major Sunni collections were compiled, with the one of Muhammad Ibn Isma'il al-**Bukhari** being the most authoritative, including some 7,000 Traditions with information on such topics as revelation, belief, prayer and ablutions, fasting, pilgrimage, marriage, and others. The Traditions thus became a second pillar of Islamic law.

Four **Schools of Law** developed in Sunni Islam, named after early legal scholars, the **Malikite**, named after **Malik ibn Anas** (d. 795), the Shafi'ite, named after ibn Idris al-**Shafi'i** (d. 819), the Hanbalite, named after Ahmad **ibn Hanbal** (d. 855), and the Hanafite, named after **Abu Hanifah** (d. 767). These schools recognize each other as orthodox but differ in the application and extent of two additional pillars of Islamic law. The Hanafite school has the largest number of adherents. It recognizes as a basis of jurisprudence, in addition to the Koran and the Sunnah, **ijma'** (consensus of the Muslim community) and **qiyas** (reasoning by analogy). Legal reasoning is called **ijtihad**, the struggle, or effort, in arriving at a legal decision. By the 10th century, Muslim jurists had decided by consensus that Islamic law was complete and that independent interpretation (ijtihad), was no longer permissible. Henceforth, Muslims were to follow, or imitate (**taqlid**), God's law and the body of decisions of the four schools. Islamic modernists as well as radical Islamists want to reopen the "Gate of Ijtihad" to permit a reinterpretation of Islamic law to meet new, modern requirements.

Judges (qadis) in shari'ah courts are to apply the law, subject to consultation with legal experts (**muftis**), who issue legal decisions (**fatwas**). A jurist (**faqih**) is trained in an Islamic college (**madrasah**) to serve as a lawyer, teacher, judge, or mufti. Punishments include the penalties for major offenses prescribed in the Koran (**hadd**, pl. hudud), discretionary and variable punishments (**ta'zir**), and **retaliation** (qisas).

Shi'ites find their sources of law in the Koran and the Traditions of the Prophet and the Infallible Imams. In the absence of the **Hidden Imam**, the Imami, or **Twelver Shi'ites**, are permitted to legislate on the basis of ijtihad of the qualified scholar (**mujtahid**). The shari'ah was unevenly enforced, and a dichotomy always existed between God's and the king's law (qanun or 'urf, customary law). The latter began to infringe on the former. The governor or his deputy presided over the police court or court of tort in cases that did not come under canon law. Muslims are enjoined to command virtue and prevent vice (*al-amr bi'l ma'ruf wa'n nahy 'an al-munkar*), and the governments institutionalized this in a Department of Promotion of Virtue and Suppression of Vice. It was to supervise public morals and command Muslims to attend the daily prayers. The **muhtasib**, overseer of public morals and market inspector, was appointed to maintain public order, resolve disputes between buyers and sellers, examine weights and measures, and check goods for quality and quantity. He had to be a jurist to be able to check the preaching of heretical doctrines. He could not act on suspicion, nor could he enter the closed doors of homes. His function was eventually taken over by the urban police in most countries.

With time, especially during the 19th and 20th centuries, the state increasingly restricted the application of Islamic law to personal law, matters of marriage, divorce, inheritance, etc. Under the influence of colonial rule and modernization, governments adopted, to varying degrees, Western legal systems.

In the postclassical age, a number of Islamic reform movements (**Salafiyyah**) emerged, often originating on the periphery of the Islamic world. Some were messianic, like the **Almohads** (1130–1269), **Almoravids** (1061–1147), **Wahhabis**, and the **Mahdi of the Sudan** (1880s–1899). Of these, only the Wahhabis, or Unitarians, as they call themselves, have had a lasting influence. An alliance between the revivalist Muhammad ibn **'Abd al-Wahhab** and the tribal chief Muhammad **ibn Sa'ud** in the late 18th century led to the establishment of the Kingdom of Saudi Arabia as an Islamic state, in which the shari'ah is enforced in all its provisions. Based on the Hanbali school of Sunni Islam, it is the most restrictive of the orthodox schools and, because of the country's relative isolation, it has scarcely been affected by the process of Westernization. The rest of the Islamic world has been affected to varying degrees by Western influences, as a result of colonization, integration into the world economy, the rise of nationalism, the Cold War, the emergence of Israel, and other factors.

Muslims differ in their interpretation of Islam. Secularists favor the separation of church and state. They tend to be cosmopolitan in outlook and favor the organization of the state along Western lines, and support mass education and scientific investigation. The secularist have achieved their objectives with the establishment of the Republic of Turkey and the victory of the secular policies of **Kemalism**. They can be found among the higher echelons of the military, the bureaucracy, and the urban intelligentsia.

Muslim modernists want to reinterpret Islam to adapt to the requirements of modern times. They feel that Islam and democracy are compatible and that selective borrowing from the West would benefit their societies and solve their socioeconomic problems. They are often the product of Western education, are urban, and belong to professional groups. Among its most important proponents have been **Sayyid Jamal a-Din Afghani** (d. 1897) and his disciple, **Muhammad 'Abduh** (d. 1905).

Numerically the largest segment of the Muslim population can be summarized under the label of traditionalists. They are devout, practicing Muslims, the products of **madrasahs** and Islamic elementary schools, as well as government schools, which accept the leadership of the 'ulama' and, although relatively tolerant, tend to reject alien ideas and practices. They tend to look to the classical and medieval periods of Islam as their model of the Islamic state. They feel that the Koran and the Traditions are sufficient for finding answers to the problems of today, and they are generally conservative. Most of the traditionalists come from the rural population, circles attached to the mosques and bazaars. They are farmers, craftsmen, and Muslim intellectuals who feel that the Islamic world is in danger. They favor the establishment of a Muslim, if not an Islamic, state, organized after the example of the classical and medieval models. A new, radical, **Islamist movement** has emerged in the 20th century, which wants to establish an Islamic state and draws its inspiration from the writings of the trinity of Sayyid Abu'l A'la al-**Maududi** (1903–1979), Hasan al-**Banna** (1906–1949), and Sayyid **Qutb** (1906–1966). To these should be added the Shi'ite Ayatollah **Khomeyni** (1900–1989), who was the first to achieve his objective of establishing a theocratic government in the **Islamic Republic of Iran** in 1979.

Islamism is a new term for a radical, fundamentalist movement that is gaining adherents among the youth of the Islamic world. They emerged on university campuses as the opponents of the leftists and developed a political ideology based on Islam that aims to restore power and influence to the Islamic world. The Islamists blame the backwardness and decline of the Islamic world on the rulers who did not enforce the injunctions of Islam and permitted the growth of Westernization. They share the basic beliefs of the 'ulama', but blame the traditional 'ulama' for having tolerated secular ideologies like nationalism and socialism. The Islamists proclaim holy war against the process of secularization. They maintain that sovereignty belongs to God; the amir is his representative, who rules with the advice of a council (shurah), which bases its decisions on the Koran and Traditions. The Islamists teach through political sermons and use violence to achieve their objectives, stating that no truly Islamic society existed after the first four Rightly Guided Caliphs (rashidun). The leaders are intellectuals who see themselves as avant guardistes and the only Islamic party, while their opponents characterize them as fascists. They are organized in centralized, disciplined groups, some in cells—like the communists and other clandestine parties. They are the product of government education, often members of the lower middle class. Some were attracted to Marxism and joined radical Islam after the fall of the communist empire. Many studied Marxism and Western thought, so as to be able to refute it. They want the consensus (ijma) of the community, not of the 'ulama'.

Their program consists of reeducating Muslims to accept their view of a purist Islam and starting a revolution to bring justice and happiness to the people. They accept the principle of private property and profit, but want to prevent social inequalities. They forbid lending money for interest and demand that taxes be on income and capital and that the poor be helped. The Islamists prohibit music, television, and games, and enforce attendance at prayers and wearing of traditional dress. Most will give women the right to education, but not coeducation. They build mosques in poor areas and provide social services that the governments failed to provide, such as soup kitchens and aid to families of their martyrs. The Islamists are missionaries who want to make "true" Muslims out of the believers and to eliminate all manifestations of Westernization.

A militant offshoot of the Islamists are the **Jihadis**, who have declared war on Muslim and Western governments and include some members of the **Taliban** and al-**Qaeda** and their supporters in the Islamic world and Europe. They have carried out **terrorist** attacks in Bali, Madrid, and London, as well as in **Afghanistan**, **Pakistan**, and Iraq. They have resorted to **suicide bombings**, which have taken a considerable toll on civilian lives.

There is both unity and variety in the Islamic world. Muslims are not a homogeneous, timeless people who can be explained solely by their normative texts, the Koran and the Sunnah. At the present time, the emergence of Islamic revivalism and its political impact is one example of the continuing process of redefinition. Although Muslims believe in the unity of the Islamic community (umma), there is no *homo islamicus* as sometimes represented in Orientalist literature.

THE DICTIONARY

– A –

ABADITES. *See* IBADITES.

'ABBAS IBN 'ABD AL-MUTTALIB (573–653). Paternal uncle of the Prophet and head of the Hashimite clan. He protected **Muhammad** from his Qurayshi enemies. Abbas fought in the Battle of **Badr** on the side of the Meccans and was taken prisoner by the Muslims. Ransomed, he converted to Islam in 630 and consolidated his link to Muhammad by giving him his sister-in-law, **Maymuna**, in **marriage**. In spite of his former opposition, he was accepted as one of the **Companions** of the Prophet, the "last of the refugees" (**muhajirun**). His great-grandson Abu al-Abbas al-Saffah was the eponymic founder of the **'Abbasid caliphate**.

'ABBASID CALIPHATE (749–1258). The dynasty that succeeded the **Umayyad caliphate** at the time when the Islamic community (**umma**) evolved from an Arab kingdom into an international Islamic empire. As the number of new converts increased, there was considerable discontent about discriminatory treatment by the Arabs, and a coalition of malcontents, partisans of **'Ali**, and the pious opposition in **Medina** supported the 'Abbasid revolt. To a certain extent an Iranian revivalism appeared under the guise of international Islam, led by the Khorasanian leader **Abu Muslim** (d. 755). He captured Marv in 747, defeated Marwan II in the battle of the Greater **Zab** in 750, and thus ended Umayyad rule. Abu 'l- 'Abbas al-Saffah (the Shedder of Blood) became the first 'Abbasid **caliph**. His title, al-Saffah, may have been adopted because of a tradition, according to which there would be three precursors to the **Mahdi** (Redeemer), one of them the

1

"Shedder of Blood." The empire enjoyed a period of greatness, which, however, did not last longer than about 100 years. Islamic unity was ended when **'Abd al-Rahman** continued the Umayyad dynasty in Spain (755–1031) and there existed two states with claims to the **caliphate**.

Al-**Mansur** was the real founder of the dynasty, supported by the army and bureaucracy; he established his capital at **Baghdad** (762), which became the intellectual center of the empire. Members of the **Barmakid** family held the position of first minister (**vizier**) of the state and were famous as builders and patrons of the arts. The empire reached its greatness during the reign of **Harun al-Rashid**, but decline began when two of his sons, al-**Amin** and al-**Ma'mun**, fought over succession, with the latter victorious. Under the influence of Greek philosophy, al-Ma'mun adopted the **Mu'tazilite** interpretation on such questions as the createdness of the **Koran**. This was followed by an inquisition (**mihna**) during which Islamic scholars were forced to accept the dogma that the Koran was created, an idea that was rejected some 25 years later. Ahmad **ibn Hanbal** (780–855), founder of the Hanbalite school of **Sunni** Islam, refused to recant.

Under al-Mu'tasim Turkic units, drafted to protect the ruler, became increasingly powerful and eventually became the real power behind the 'Abbasid throne. For his own protection and to appease the citizens of Baghdad, who resented the unruliness of the Turkic troops, al-Mu'tasim had to move the capital to **Samarra**, where it remained from 836 until 892. From the reign of al-Qahir to the time of al-Qaim, the 'Abbasids suffered the ignominy of being dominated by the **Shi'ite Buyids**. Trends toward Shi'ism were reversed when the Seljuq Turks established their empire at Baghdad, supporting **Sunni** orthodoxy and relegating the **caliphs** to an honored, but powerless, status. Finally, the **Mongol invasion** of the Middle East led to the destruction of Baghdad in 1258 and the massacre of members of the 'Abbasid clan. An uncle of al-Musta'sim continued the 'Abbasid line in **Cairo** until Egypt was captured by the **Ottomans** in 1517. The Ottomans later propagated the idea that the last of the 'Abbasids appointed Sultan Selim I as his successor.

The 'Abbasids included the following members:

749 Abu al-'Abbas al-Saffah
754 Al-Mansur
775 Al-Mahdi
785 Musa al-Hadi
786 Harun al-Rashid
809 Al-Amin
813 Al-Ma'mun
833 Al-Mu'tasim
842 Al-Wathiq
847 Al-Mutawakkil
861 Al-Muntasir
862 Al-Musta'in
866 Al-Mu'tazz
869 Al-Muhtadi
870 Al-Mu'tamid
892 Al-Mu'tadid
902 Al-Muktafi
908 Al-Muqtadir
923 Al-Qahir

934 Al-Radhi
940 Al-Muttaqi
944 Al-Mustakfi
946 Al-Muti'
974 Al-Ta'i
991 Al-Qadir
1031 Al-Qaim
1075 Al-Muqtadi
1094 Al-Mustazhir
1118 Al-Mustarshid
1135 Al-Rashid
1136 Al-Muqtafi
1160 Al-Mustanjid
1170 Al-Mustadi'
1180 Al-Nasir
1225 Al-Zahir
1226 Al-Mustansir
1242–58 Al- Musta'sim

The 'Abbasid assumption of power was a revolution in the early history of Islam. The **Rightly Guided caliphate** was an Islamic theocracy, the **Umayyad caliphate** was a kingdom of the Arabs, and the 'Abbasid caliphate was an Islamic empire. Culturally, first Persian and then Turkish influences prevailed. Only the **Arabic** language and **Sunni** orthodoxy remained. Politically, the 'Abbasid caliphate was a monarchical despotism; the caliphs held themselves aloof and surrounded themselves with an awe-inspiring court. Slaves gained influence in the administration and army. As the empire lost territory in the west, the center of power moved to the east. The golden age of the empire lasted until the death of the 10th caliph, Mutawakkil, in 861, and thereafter the decline began. Sectarian conflict prevailed, and a military feudalism spread. The **Mongol** invaders destroyed an empire that was already near disintegration.

'ABD. "Servant, slave." Used in a compound with one of the names of **Allah** ('Abd Allah), it designates a believer in the one God, Allah; it is also a common name. *See also* SLAVERY.

'ABD AL-'AZIZ IBN MUHAMMAD IBN SA'UD (1721–1803). *See* IBN SA'UD, 'ABD AL-'AZIZ IBN MUHAMMAD.

'ABD AL-AZIZ IBN SA'UD (1880–1953). *See* IBN SA'UD, ABD AL-AZIZ IBN 'ABD AL-RAHMAN AL-FAISAL AL-.

'ABD AL-HAMID II (r. 1876–1909). Ottoman sultan/caliph who fought a losing battle with domestic and foreign enemies. He promulgated the first Ottoman constitution in 1876 and assumed power as a constitutional monarch. But he prorogued parliament for 30 years when it was unable to agree on a budget and tried to limit his powers. The sultan continued his predecessor's reforms, including the construction of modern government buildings. He greatly expanded the educational system and founded the Dar al-Funun in 1900, which later became **Istanbul** University. Abd al-Hamid built a rail network, including the **Hijaz** railroad that connected Istanbul with **Medina** and was to facilitate **pilgrimages** as well as serve the strategic purpose of centralizing the powers of the state. To consolidate his power, he promoted **pan-Islamism**, Ottomanism, and Turkism to appeal to his varying constituencies, but foreign pressures increased. Great Britain occupied Cyprus (1878) and Egypt (1882), and France took Tunisia in 1881. Austria annexed Bosnia–Herzegovina in 1908. The rise of nationalism among the ethnic minorities and, finally, the Young Turk Revolution, led to the ouster of Abdul Hamid in 1909. He died in 1918.

ABD AL-JABBAR (d. 1025). Author, theologian, and jurist of the **Mu'tazila** school. He dictated the monumental Summa on the matter of Unity and Justice (al-Mughni fi abwab al-tawhid wa al-'adl). A native of Asadabad in western Iran, he studied at Qazvin, Hamadan, and Isfahan. Originally an **Ash'arite**, he gained a reputation as the most respected Mu'tazilite scholar in the Islamic world. He served as chief judge (qadhi al-qudhat) of Ray and was praised by some for his "goodness and high station in knowledge" but maligned by others for "corruption, greed, dim wits, and homosexuality." He was deposed by the **Buyid** ruler Mu'ayyid al-Dawla, according to some sources, when he refused to say the mercy prayer (*tarahhum*) for Ibn-Abbad, the man who had appointed him to the position of chief judge.

'ABD AL-KARIM AL-KHATABI (1882–1963). Hero in the fight against Spanish and French rule in North Africa and leader of the "Independent Republic of the Rif." He defeated a Spanish army of some 13,000 and conducted a successful guerilla war until a combined Spanish–French army of some 250,00 soldiers was able to defeat him in 1925. He surrendered to the French in 1926 was exiled to the island of Réunion. In 1947, he was freed and was given asylum by the Egyptian government, and for a number of years he presided over the Liberation Committee of the Arab West in Cairo

'ABD ALLAH IBN AL-ZUBAYR. *See* ZUBAYR, 'ABDALLAH IBN AL-.

'ABD AL-MALIK (646–705). Fifth **Umayyad caliph** (r. 685–705) and native of **Medina** who fought secessionist forces, defeating 'Abdallah ibn al-**Zubayr** in 692, who had proclaimed himself **caliph** in **Mecca**. He consolidated the state and centralized power, in which he was greatly assisted by his governor of Iraq, **Hajjaj ibn Yusuf**. More of an autocrat than **Mu'awiyah**, he was attuned to the pious opposition in the **Hijaz**. Described as dark, thickset, and with a long beard, he was an astute judge of character, appointing capable people to positions of power. He was known for his eloquence and miserliness, which earned him the nickname "Dew of the Stone."

'Abd al-Malik was the great Arabizer, substituting **Arabic** for Greek and Persian in the administration and issuing the first Islamic coins. During his reign, diacritical markings were added to the Arabic script, permitting greater accuracy in the rendition of Arabic speech. He established a regular postal service, which also served as a system for collecting intelligence. His policy of forcing newly converted Muslims to return to the land and to continue to pay their original taxes caused considerable resentment and contributed to hostility toward the Umayyad regime. Construction on **Dome of the Rock** began during his administration.

ABD AL-MUTTALIB IBN HASHIM. Grandfather of the Prophet and head of the **Banu Hashim**. He was the guardian and protector of **Muhammad** and died when Muhammad was eight years old. He is said to have rediscovered the **Zamzam** well and subsequently sold its water to pilgrims.

ABD AL-QADIR (1808–1883). Hero in the struggle against French colonial forces in Algeria and a noted scholar, poet, and man of religion. Variously described as of Berber ancestry or a **Sharif** (descendant of the Prophet), he headed an uprising against the French in 1832 and was proclaimed Emir of Oran in 1834. He remained a power in Algeria until 1847, when he surrendered to French forces and was imprisoned until 1852. He died in 1883 and is buried next to **Ibn Al-Arabi in Damascus**. After Algerian independence, his remains were transferred to Algeria.

'ABD AL-QADIR AL-JILANI. *See* JILANI, 'ABDUL QADIR AL-.

'ABD AL-RAHMAN (r. 756–787). Founder of the **Umayyad caliphate** of Spain (756–1031). He escaped the massacre of the Umayyad clan at **Baghdad** and made his way to Spain, where he was well received. He defeated the **'Abbasid** governor at Cordoba in 756 and made the city his capital. Cordoba became a famous center of **Arabic** culture and learning; it took its place as the most cultured city in Europe, and with Constantinople and **Baghdad** as one of the three cultural centers of the world.

> With its one hundred and thirteen thousand homes, twenty-one suburbs, seventy libraries and numerous bookshops, mosques and palaces, it acquired international fame and inspired awe and admiration in the hearts of travellers. (Hitti, 1964, 526)

Abd al-Rahman III (r. 912–961), the eighth in line of succession, proclaimed himself **caliph** in 929; his reign marked the height of Umayyad power in Spain.

'ABD AL-RAHMAN, 'UMAR (ABDUL RAHMAN, OMAR) (1938–). Egyptian Islamist leader, native of a village in Daqaliyah district in the Nile delta. He went blind in infancy, but he was able to study and obtain a doctorate from Al-**Azhar** University in 1977. Subsequently he taught at a branch of the university at Asyut. He went abroad and took a job as teacher of Islamic studies in Saudi Arabia.

Upon his return to Egypt, he was arrested for instigating the assassination of President Anwar Sadat but was freed in 1984 for lack of evidence. Abd al-Rahman is said to have inspired the **Islamist movements** Jama'at al-Islamiya and **Islamic Jihad** (al-Jihad al-Islami), which deny the legitimacy of any Muslim state that adopts Western governmental principles and demands the establishment of an Islamic state, governed on the basis of the **Koran** and Traditions (**Sunnah**). He fled to Sudan and went to the United States in 1990, where he continued his campaign against the Egyptian government. He was arrested and given a life sentence in 1994 for involvement in the bombing of the World Trade Center in New York on 26 February 1993.

'ABD AL-WAHHAB, MUHAMMAD IBN (1703–1792). 'Abd al-Wahhab studied theology with his father and then traveled widely in Arabia, Iran, and Iraq, before going to **Medina** to study **Islamic law** and theology. Influenced by the teachings of **Ibn Hanbal** (780–855) and **Ibn Taimiyyah** (1263–1328), he campaigned for a return to the practices of early Islam. He was shocked by what he considered sinful innovations in the great cities of Islam and allied himself with Muhammad **Ibn Sa'ud** of Dariya in Central Arabia to propagate his reformist ideas.

'Abd al-Wahhab presented his ideas in *The Book of Unity* (*Kitab al-tawhid*), in which he attacked as sinful innovations the doctrines of Sufism, saint cults, and intercession, and demanded the **Koran** and Traditions (**Sunnah**) be the sole bases of Islamic theology and jurisprudence. He was able to gain a considerable following among the Arab tribes and, although initially defeated, the alliance between the Islamist reformer and the clan of Al Sa'ud led to the conquest of Arabia and the establishment of **Wahhabism** in what came to be the Kingdom of Saudi Arabia.

ABD EL-KRIM. *See* 'ABD AL-KARIM AL-KHATABI.

'ABDUH, MUHAMMAD (1849–1905). Journalist, theologian, jurist, reformer, and one of the founders of Muslim modernism. Born in Egypt, he received the traditional education and earned the title of

hafiz when he had memorized the **Koran** at the age of 12. He graduated from Al-**Azhar** University in 1874 and immediately started to criticize the traditional **'ulama'** for its dogmatic and doctrinaire attitude in theology and jurisprudence. He called for a renaissance in the Islamic world and encouraged Muslims to study modern science and technology. He rejected imitation or emulation (**taqlid**) of the law as consolidated in the 10th century, and he advocated the adoption of independent reasoning and judgment (**ijtihad**) in revising **Islamic law**. As a teacher at Al-Azhar, he preached that **revelation** and reason were inherently harmonious. In his major publication, *The Message of Unity (Risalat al-tawhid*, 1887), he held that what was given in revelation should be rationally possessed.

As a result of the British invasion of Egypt in 1882, Abduh was suspended and joined his mentor, the **pan-Islamist** Sayyid Jamal al-Din al-**Afghani**, in Paris, where they published the journal *Al-'Urwa Al-Wuthqa* (*The Firmest Bond*). Exiled from France, he returned to Egypt in 1887, where his teachings and moderate views won him many followers. In 1889, Abdu was appointed grand mufti of Egypt and in 1894 was elected a member of the Supreme Council of Al-Azhar University. He issued liberal **fatwas** (legal decisions) proclaiming it legal to eat the meat of animals slaughtered by **Christians** and Jews; discouraging **polygamy**, as it would require equal treatment by a man of each wife, which was impossible; and fighting the misuse of **talaq**, **divorce** of **women** by men. Rashid **Ridha** (1865–1935) his biographer and the most important of his disciples, gradually abandoned his modernist views and moved toward a type of **fundamentalism** akin to contemporary **Islamism.**

'ABDUL. *See entries beginning with* 'ABD AL-.

ABLUTION. "Wudhu." Ritual washing prescribed before **prayers**. It is commanded on the authority of the **Koran**, which says: "O ye who believe! Approach not prayer. . . . Until after washing your whole body. If ye are ill, or on a journey, or one of you cometh from the privy, or ye have been in contact with **women**, and ye find no water, then take for yourselves clean sand (or earth), and rub therewith your faces and hands" (4:43). There are three types of ablutions: **ghusl** (greater ablution), which involves washing the entire body; **wudhu'**

(lesser ablution), washing the hands, mouth, nose, face, arms, head, and feet; and **tayammum**, in which, for lack of water, sand or earth is used instead. **Shi'ites** and **Kharijites** do not permit the use of tayammum. One Islamic scholar proclaimed:

> When a believer washes his face during ablution, every sin he contemplated with his eyes will come forth from his face along with the water; when he washes his hands, every sin they wrought will come forth from his hands with the water; when he washes his feet, every sin toward which his feet have walked will come out with the water, with the result that he will come forth pure from offenses. (Ghamari Tabrizi, 94)

ABODE OF WAR. *See* DAR AL-HARB.

ABORTION. "Isqat."Abortion is not mentioned in the **Koran**, but it is blameworthy in Islam except if the life of the pregnant mother is in danger (*Fatawi Alamgiri*). The practice of infanticide in pre-Islamic Arabia was outlawed in the Koran, which says: "Kill not your children for fear of want: We shall provide sustenance for them as well as for you. Verily the killing of them is a great sin" (S17:31). According to Tradition (**Sunnah**), 120 days after conception, the fetus receives its soul; therefore abortion is considered homicide. Female infanticide was rationalized by the Bedouins in pre-Islamic Arabia "because **women** have to be adorned in gold and silver only to be married off, thus resulting in a material loss." Women were seen as a liability in battle, as they could not serve as fighters, and they were carried off as part of the booty.

ABRAHAH (ca. 540–570). Christian viceroy of the Negus in Yemen who invaded the **Hijaz** in about 570 but was not able to capture **Mecca**. He brought war elephants with his army, animals not known by the desert Arabs; therefore, they named the year of the campaign the "**Year of the Elephant**." This is traditionally claimed to be the year of the birth of the Prophet **Muhammad**. Abraha's troops were decimated by smallpox and forced to retreat. The **Koran** says:

> Seest thou not how thy Lord dealt
> With the companions of the Elephant
> Did he not make their treacherous plan go astray?
> And he sent against them flights of birds,

Striking them with stones of baked clay.
Then did he make them like an empty field. (105:1–5)

ABRAHAM (IBRAHIM). The biblical ancestor of the Arabs and Jews. He rebuilt the **Ka'bah**, established the **pilgrimage** to **Mecca**, and destroyed the idols in the temple (2:125–127, 3:96, 22:26). According to the **Koran**, Abraham was neither **Christian** nor Jew, but a **hanif**, monotheist. He is reckoned to be one of six prophets to whom God delivered special laws. Legend has it that Abraham was buried under a **mosque** in Hebron.

ABROGATION. "Naskh." The repeal of a **revelation** by another. The **Koran** says: "**Allah** doth blot out or confirm what He pleaseth; with Him is the Mother of the Book"(13:39) and "When We substitute one revelation for another—and Allah knows best what He reveals (in stages)—They say, 'Thou art but a forger' but most of them know not"(16:01). This refers to changes in legal and practical matters, such as the prayer direction (**qiblah**), matters of **inheritance**, and penalties for **adultery**.

ABU. "Father, or owner of"; indicates possession, state, property, or father of the person named; for example, Abu Musa means the father of Musa.

ABU AL-'ABBAS AL-SAFFAH (r. 750–754). *See* 'ABBASID CALIPHATE.

ABU BAKR (573–634). First of the **Rightly Guided Caliphs** and father of **'A'ishah**, the favorite wife of **Muhammad**. He was one of the first three male converts to Islam and the first in a socially prominent position. He was called al-Siddiq (the Sincere) and described as a man of fair complexion, thin frame, with a stoop. He spent much of his fortune buying and manumitting slaves, which was reckoned to be a good deed, to be rewarded on the **Day of Judgment**. He was elected as khalifa, successor to the Prophet, in 632 by a council in which members of the Helpers (**ansar**) contested the choice of the Immigrants (**muhajirun**). Abu Bakr suggested the selection of

'**Umar ibn al-Khattab**, but he in turn offered allegiance (**bay'ah**) to Abu Bakr, and the council accepted the choice.

Many of the tribes that had allied themselves with Muhammad considered themselves free of any obligation to his successor. Rival prophets appeared, most importantly **Musaylimah** (Maslama). Therefore, Abu Bakr's short reign (632–634) was devoted to forcing the tribes to renew their allegiance in what came to be known as the War of **Riddah** (**apostasy**). Abu Bakr's election established the elective principle of leadership in **Sunni** Islam (although, in fact, it was largely dynastic) and the principle of the oath of loyalty by members of the community. The seeds of schism were sown when the partisans of '**Ali**, son of **Abu Talib** and cousin of Muhammad, disputed the election. The partisans of 'Ali (*shi'at 'ali*) later evolved into the **Shi'ite sect**. Abu Bakr's major achievements included the consolidation of the young Muslim state. He made the first attempt to collect the scattered **revelations**, which were subsequently collected in the **Koran** (Qur'an), and he established government by consultation (**shurah**). Abu Bakr nominated 'Umar as his successor before he died in 634 in **Medina**.

ABU DAWUD. *See* SIJISTANI, SULAYMAN ABU DAWUD AL-.

ABU AL-FARAJ. *See* ISFAHANI, ABU AL-FARAJ AL-.

ABU HAMZA. *See* MASRI.

ABU HANIFAH, AL-NU'MAN IBN THABIT (ca. 700–767). Great **Sunni** jurist and eponymic founder of the Hanafi **school of law**, the largest of the four orthodox schools (**madhhab**) and the dominant school in the **Ottoman empire**. He was born in **Kufah** and died in prison in **Baghdad** because he refused to serve as a judge (**qadhi**), or more likely, because he was a supporter of the Zaidi revolt. He derived his income from trading in silks and did not need government patronage. **Ibn Khallikan** described him as tall, of medium weight, with a somber disposition, "a learned man and a practiser (of good works), remarkable for self-denial, piety, devotion and the fear of **God**; humble in spirit and constant in his acts of submission to the

Almighty." He embarked on the study of law with **Ja'far al-Sadiq** in **Medina** as well as with other famed **mujtahids**.

With Abu Hanifa, the science of Muslim jurisprudence (**fiqh**) really began. Before him, doctrines were formulated in response to actual problems, whereas he attempted to solve future problems. He did not declare a sinner to have become an infidel, accepted reasoning by analogy (**qiyas**), and permitted the use of personal opinion (**ra'y**) in the interpretation of law. Because of this, he and his followers were also called *ahl al-ra'y*, the "people of opinion." Abu Hanifa dictated his teachings to his disciples, Abu Yusuf (d.799), Muhammad ibn al-Hasan, and others, who subsequently compiled them.

ABU HURAYRAH (d. 681). "Father of the kitten," so named because of his liking for kittens. Before his conversion, his name was Abd al-Rahman al-Dawsi. He was a **Companion** of the Prophet, whom he joined in **Medina** in 629, and was appointed governor of Bahrain by Caliph **'Umar** I. Described as having a reputation for piety and a fondness for jesting, he was one of the most prolific transmitters of **hadiths**. There is, however, some doubt that many attributed to him are genuine. He died in Medina at the age of 78.

ABU JAHL (d. 624). His real name was Amr ibn Hisham, but he was named by the Prophet "Father of Ignorance." A mortal enemy of the Prophet, he suggested that **Muhammad** be killed by a group of Qurayshis who would strike together, so that the **Hashimites** could not fight them all and would have to accept blood money. Aware of the plot, Muhammad hid in a cave and after four days traveled with Abu Bakr to **Medina**, where he started the first Muslim community. Abu Jahl was killed in the Battle of **Badr**.

ABU LAHAB. "Father of the flame"(hellfire), a name given by **Muhammad** to his uncle, whose name was 'Abd al 'Uzza. He was a mortal enemy of the early Islamic community. After the death of **Abu Talib**, head of Muhammad's clan, the Banu **Hashim**, Abu Lahab withdrew the clan's protection from Muhammad, forcing him to flee to **Medina** (**hijrah**). The **Koran** says: "Perish the hands of the Father of Flame! Perish he! No profit to him from all his wealth, and all his gains! Burnt soon he will be in a fire of blazing flame! His wife shall carry the (crackling) wood as fuel! A twisted rope of palm-leaf fibre round her (own) neck!" (111:1–5). Abu Lahab died shortly after the Battle of **Badr** in 624.

ABU MUSA AL-ASH'ARI (614–663). A native of Yemen and **Companion** of the Prophet, who converted to Islam after 628. He was a military commander in Yemen, Persia, and Mesopotamia and a transmitter of a number of **hadith**. Governor of **Basra** and **Kufah** under caliphs **'Umar** and **'Uthman**, he was appointed by **'Ali ibn Abi Talib** to represent him at the **Adhruh Arbitration** in 659, which demanded that Ali and **Mu'awiyah** resign their claim to the **caliphate**.

ABU MUSLIM (d. 755). Son of a Persian slave woman, he was born at Marw (or near Isfahan) and raised in **Kufah**. He conducted pro-**'Abbasid** propaganda and headed the Khorasanian forces, which brought the 'Abbasids to power. The rebels, consisting of Persian converts (mawalis), **Shi'ites**, and Himyarite Arabs, raised the black banners of **Muhammad** and invaded Iraq. He defeated **Umayyad Caliph** Marwan II in 750, and Abdullah, uncle of the 'Abbasid caliph al-**Mansur**, at Nasibin in 754. He thus secured the **caliphate** for al-Mansur. He was appointed governor of Khorasan, where his tenure contributed to a revival of Persian culture. He apparently became too powerful for the caliph, who invited Abu Muslim to the court and had him treacherously assassinated. He was described as "low in stature, of a tawny complexion, with handsome features and engaging manners, his skin was clear, his eyes large, his forehead lofty, and his beard ample and bushy . . . his legs and thighs short, and his voice soft. . . . He abstained from intercourse with females, except once in each year. 'Such an act,' said he, 'is a sort of folly, and it is quite enough for a man to be made once a year.'" (Khallikan, trans. Slane, II, 103)

ABU NUWAS (753–813/815). "Father of the lock of hair," whose real name was Hasan ibn Hani. A native of Khuzistan, Iran, he was educated in **Basra** and **Kufah** in Islamic studies and lived with Bedouins to acquire a command of "pure" **Arabic**. He was a famed poet and boon companion of Caliphs **Harun al-Rashid** and his son al-**Amin**. He glorified Bedouin life and also wrote hunting and drinking songs (*Khamriyyah*), elegies, panegyrics, satires, and religious poems. His drinking and debauchery got him repeatedly imprisoned, but the elegance of his style and command of Arabic and his accomplishments as a poet, as well as his supposed remorse in old age, saved him from a violent death. From prison, he wrote to Fadhl, the **Barmakid vizier**:

> Fadhl, who hast taught and trained me up to goodness
> (And goodness is but habit), thee I praise.
> Now hath vice fled and virtue me revisits,
> And I have turned to chaste and pious ways. (Nicholson, 1962, 293)

Ibn Khallikan quotes one contemporary saying:

> I never saw a man of more extensive learning than Abu Nuwas, nor one who, with a memory so richly furnished, possessed so few books; after his decease we searched his house, and could only find one book-cover, containing a quire of paper, in which was a collection of rare expressions and grammatical observations. (I, 392)

ABU AL-QASIM (939–1013). Famous surgeon, known as Albucasis in the West, who greatly influenced European surgical practices until the 16th century. He was court physician of **Umayyad Caliph Abd al-Rahman** III (d. 961) at Cordoba, Spain, and there he published his famous treatise *The Method* (*al-Tashrif liman 'jaz'an al-ta'lif*). It was translated into Latin in the 12th century and served as the leading text on surgery.

ABU SUFYAN (d. 651). Head of the **Umayyad** clan and leader of a Meccan force that fought **Muhammad** in the Battle of **Badr** (624) and the Battle of the **Trench** (627). He submitted to Islam when Muhammad took **Mecca** in 630. His ties to the Prophet were strengthened when he gave him his daughter, **Umm Habibah**, in **marriage**. His son, **Mu'awiyah**, became the founder of the **Umayyad caliphate**.

ABU TALIB (d. 619). Uncle and guardian of the Prophet and father of **'Ali**, fourth of the **Rightly Guided Caliphs**. He was head of the Banu **Hashim**, and he protected **Muhammad** from persecution by the Meccans, but he never became a Muslim. When he died, **Abu Lahab** succeeded to leadership of the Banu Hashim and Muhammad was forced to flee to **Medina**.

ABU 'UBAYDAH. *See* 'UBAYDAH, IBN AL-JARRAH.

'ABU AL-WAFA (BUZJANI, 940–997). *See* WAFA', ABU AL-.

ADAB. Polite behavior, good morals, also belles lettres. The *Book of Adab* of al-**Bukhari** specifies, for example, how Muslims should greet others: A small group of people should first greet a large one, a riding person should greet the walking person, and the standing person should first greet the sitting one. *See also* EDUCATION.

'ADAH (ADAT). "Custom." In Islamic jurisprudence, *'adah* is customary law, synonymous with **'urf** or **qanun**. It complements divine law, **shari'ah**, but must not be contrary to it.

ADAM. The first man and prophet; he had the title "God's Chosen One." God made him of dried clay, and the **angels** were ordered to prostrate before him; only one, **Iblis** (satan), refused, claiming superiority because he was made of fire (15:26–32). Adam was separated from Eve after they were driven from paradise, but he was reunited with her in the valley of '**Arafat** near **Mecca**. According to tradition, he built the **Ka'bah** and died in Mecca.

'ADAWIYYAH, RABI'AH AL-. *See* RABI'AH AL-'ADAWIYYAH.

ADHAN (AZAN). *See* CALL TO PRAYER.

ADHRUH ARBITRATION (659). As a result of the Battle of **Siffin** (657), in which **Mu'awiyah** challenged Caliph **'Ali**, demanding vengeance for the murder of Caliph **'Uthman**, 'Ali agreed to arbitration at a time when his forces seemed to have the upper hand. Following a suggestion by **'Amr ibn al-'As**, the Syrians had fastened copies of the **Koran** on their lances and called for an appeal to the "Law of the Lord." This appeal resulted in the appointment of two intermediaries, 'Amr for Mu'awiyah and **Abu Musa al-Ash'ari** for 'Ali, who were to consult the Holy Book as a basis for arbitration. Instead, it became an arbitration by men. Now a large number of 'Ali's forces seceded and the Seceders (**Kharijites**) turned against their **caliph**.

The arbiters met at Adhruh in February 658, and 'Amr convinced Abu Musa that both candidates should resign, to which the latter agreed. According to the traditional account, Abu Musa was tricked into announcing the demotion of 'Ali, after which 'Amr proclaimed Mu'awiyah caliph. According to the Orientalist Wellhausen, there was no treachery, and it was 'Ali who refused to step down. 'Ali was subsequently assassinated by a Kharijite, and Mu'awiyah became the first of the Umayyad caliphs

ADL, AL-. "Justice," due to every Muslim. In jurisprudence, a person whose testimony is valid. Al-Adl is one of the 99 names of **Allah**, meaning the Just.

'ADN. The Garden of Eden. *See also* HEAVEN.

ADULTERY. "Zinah." Adultery is forbidden and punished by stoning, but the penalty requires that there be either four witnesses to the act or else the confessions of the culprits. Because four witnesses are not easily found, this penalty has rarely been exacted. If a husband catches his wife in flagrante delicto, he is authorized to kill her and her partner. The culprits must be free Muslims of maturity and married; the punishment for fornication is 100 lashes, and only half that number for slaves. False accusation of adultery is punished with 80 lashes. Muslim modernists claim that since witnesses cannot usually be found, this drastic penalty should not be inflicted (24:2-4). In most parts of the Islamic world, zinah is not a capital crime. Islamist radicals, such as the **Taliban** of Afghanistan, wanted to reintroduce these as well as other Islamic (**hadd**) punishments. Zinah also includes **fornication**. *See also* LI'AN.

AFGHANI, SAYYID JAMAL AL-DIN (1838–1897). Father of the **pan-Islamist** movement, Muslim modernist, and political propagandist who called for the unity of the Islamic world and selective borrowing from the West for the purpose of stemming the tide of Western imperialism. Afghani was the adviser of Muslim rulers in many parts of the Middle East and a political activist in Iran, Afghanistan, India, Egypt, and the **Ottoman empire**. Frequently opposed by the **'ulama'** and suspected as an intriguer by the temporal powers, he was often on the run. When one of his followers assassinated the Persian ruler Nasr al-Din Shah (r. 1848–1896), Afghani was placed under house arrest by the Ottoman **Sultan Abdul Hamid** (r. 1876–1907). Afghani died in **Istanbul** in 1897.

He was not a prolific writer and varied his message to suit a particular audience. He wrote a *Refutation of the Materialists* (*al-Radd 'ala al-dahriyin*) and published the periodical *The Firmest Bond* (*al-'Urwa al-Wuthqa*) with his disciple Muhammad **Abduh**. Afghani was the precursor of the **Islamist** movement. Afghans revere his memory and believe him to be a descendant of a family of Sayyids from Asadabad in Kunar province of Afghanistan. Western and Iranian scholars agree that his origin was Iranian.

AFGHANIS. Radical **Islamists**, mostly of Arab nationality but also from other Muslim countries, who participated in the war against the communist regime in Afghanistan. Many returned to their countries and continued the **jihad** against their governments with the intention of establishing an "Islamic state." They are said to include some 5,000 Saudis, 3,000 Yemenis, 2,000 Egyptians, 2,800 Algerians, 400 Tunisians, 370 Iraqis, 200 Libyans, some Jordanians, and citizens of other Muslim countries. They are a serious threat to the military regime in Algeria, have started terrorist activities in Egypt, and are fighting in regional wars from Bosnia to Kashmir. **Osama bin Laden** is an "Afghani," accused of instigating the bombings of American embassies in Nairobi and Dar es Salam. He is a wealthy Saudi citizen who had taken refuge with the **Taliban** regime in Afghanistan, as have several thousand others, including Islamboli, a brother of the assassin of the Egyptian President Anwar al-Sadat.

AFGHANISTAN. The "Land of the Afghans" was founded as a political entity in 1747 when Ahmad Shah (r. 1747–1773) was crowned king of a tribal confederation that was welded into a state by Amir Abd al-Rahman (r. 1880–1901). For some time Afghanistan became a buffer between the Russian and British-Indian empires, after unsuccessful British attempts to exert direct control over the country. Afghanistan fought three wars with British-India. The First Anglo–Afghan War (1839–1842) resulted in the virtual destruction of the British army; in the Second Anglo–Afghan War (1878–1881) the

British army evacuated Afghanistan to avoid increasing harassment by Afghan forces; and the Third Anglo–Afghan War (1919) resulted in Afghan independence from British suzerainty. King Amanullah (r. 1919–1929) was the first Afghan ruler to introduce modern reforms, including constitutional government and participation of **women** in the social and economic life of the country. He was ousted by tribal forces who opposed his reforms and, after a period of anarchy, Nadir Shah (r. 1929–1933) and his son Zahir Shah (r. 1933–1975) resumed the process of modernization, resulting in the Constitution of 1963 and permission for women to discard the veil and become active in the professions and economic life. A coup by Muhammad Daud in 1975 established a republican government, which was followed by a Marxist coup in 1978 and Soviet intervention during the subsequent 10 years. American and international support brought thousands of Muslim volunteers to Afghanistan to fight the communist government, forcing the withdrawal of Soviet forces in 1989 and the fall of the Marxist government in 1992. A period of civil war lasted until the **Taliban** emerged as a political force in 1994 and within two years controlled most of the country. **Mulla Muhammad Umar** was proclaimed "Commander of the Faithful" (**amir al-mu'minin**), and the "Islamic Emirate of Afghanistan" was declared the new center of an Islamic state, with the **shari'ah** (Islamic law) as sole law of the country. Women were restricted to their homes, girls' schools were closed, men had to grow **beards**, and the religious police enforced the new edicts. The Taliban government gave shelter to **al-Qaeda**, the party of **Osama bin Laden**, which had declared war on the United States.

A veritable "foreign legion" of volunteers came to Afghanistan to be trained for military action in Central Asia, Kashmir, and elsewhere. The attacks by suicide bombers on the World Trade Center and the Pentagon on 11 September 2001, finally led to American and British intervention and the ouster of the Taliban regime. A new government was established in December 2004 in Kabul, headed by Hamed Karzai, and the United States and its allies started the process of consolidating the country. As of this writing, both Mulla Muhammad Umar and Osama bin Laden have not been captured after seven years of fighting, and the remnants of the Islamic government have still not been eliminated.

AFSHARID DYNASTY (r. 1736–1795). Founded by Nadir Shah Af-shar, who was born in 1688 as Nadir Quli in northern **Khorasan**, the son of Imam Quli, a member of a clan affiliated with the Afshar tribe. He started life as a raider for booty and became one of the last great nomadic conquerors of Asia. He ended the Ghilzai dream of ruling an empire after Mahmud, son of Mir Wais, captured Isfahan in 1722. Nadir defeated the Afghans and drove them out of Iran. He attacked Herat and invaded India, where he defeated the Mughal army at Kar-nal, near Delhi, in 1739. Ruling over a heterogeneous population, he wanted to unite his subjects by proclaiming **Shi'ism** the fifth (Ja-farite) orthodox school of **Sunni** Islam. The **Shi'a** clergy objected to this. Nadir became increasingly tyrannical and was eventually killed by his own tribesmen.

AFTERLIFE. *See* HEREAFTER, THE.

AGA KHAN. **Imam** of the Nizari branch of the **Isma'ilis.** The Qajar rulers of Iran at times bestowed this title on notables. In 1818, Fath 'Ali Shah gave the title Agha Khan I to Abu al-Hasan 'Ali Shah Ma-hallati (1800–1881), governor of Kerman province. He fled Iran af-ter an unsuccessful revolt in 1841 and settled in Bombay. He was able to organize Isma'ili communities in India, supported by a court order that gave him control of the **sect**'s property. He was succeeded by 'Ali Shah (1881–1885), who became the official representative of Iran to the government of India. The third Agha Khan (1877–1957), Sultan Sir Muhammad Shah, was very active. Born in Karachi, he be-came the head of the Isma'ili community at the age of eight. Al-though he moved to Europe in 1898, he continued to take charge of the interests of the sect from there. Agha Khan III gave his support to the Allies in the First and Second World Wars. He was president of the All-India Muslim League and involved in raising **Aligarh** Col-lege to the status of a university in 1920. In 1937, he was elected president of the League of Nations.

The present Agha Khan is Karim IV (b. 1937), who counts himself the 49th successor of the Nisari Isma'ili Imam. He attends to the wel-fare of the Isma'ili community in Africa, Syria, Iran, Tajikistan, In-dia, United States, Pakistan, and Afghanistan. He founded a charita-ble organization, the **Aga Khan Foundation**, in 1967 with headquarters in Geneva, which supports developmental assistance in many parts of the world. Muhammad, Karim's grandfather, was on special occasions weighed on a scale and presented with gold and precious stones in an equal amount, a practice that has since been discontinued. The Agha Khan claims descent from Isma'il through the last Grand Master of **Alamut**. *See also* NIZARIS.

AGA KHAN FOUNDATION. A nondenominational, international development agency established in 1967 by the **Aga Khan**, **imam** of the **Shi'i Isma'ili** community. Based in Geneva, Switzerland, the foundation has branches and independent affiliates in 15 countries, most in Asia and Africa. Its major areas of focus are selected issues in health, education, rural development, and the strengthening of civil society. Its principal criterion is to bring lasting benefits to project participants, and it usually intervenes "where it has a strong volunteer base to ensure knowledgeable and culturally sensitive management of its local affairs." The foundation is helping to build an endowment for Pakistan's first private university, the Aga Khan University in Karachi, and has built the first five-star hotel in Kabul, Afghanistan (it was recently attacked by a suicide bomber). A private University of Central Asia is planned with campuses in Kazakhstan, Kyrgyzstan, and Tajikistan. In 2004, the foundation provided $149 million in grants for 130 projects in 16 countries.

AGE OF IGNORANCE. *See* IGNORANCE, THE AGE OF.

AGHA KHAN (AGA, AQA). *See* AGA KHAN.

AGHLABID DYNASTY (800–909). One of a number of petty dynasties in North Africa named after Ibrahim ibn al-Aghlab. The **'Abbasid Caliph Harun al-Rashid** appointed him governor of the area of present-day Tunisia, but he proclaimed himself an independent **amir**, subject to payment of tribute to **Baghdad**. The Aghlabids quickly expanded their realm, capturing Sicily in 827 and Malta in 869, and invading the southern coast of Italy. They established their capital at Qayrawan (Keruan), where the Great **Mosque** is an architectural treasure left from their short-lived reign. The century-long reign of the **Sunni** Aghlabids was ended by the Fatimid, **Shi'i** dynasty in 909.

'AHD. Contract, treaty, pact between **caliph** and community. *See also* COVENANT.

AHKAM AL-KHAMSAH, AL-. *See* FIVE PRINCIPAL ACTS IN IS-LAMIC LAW.

AHL. Originally, those living in the same tent, but in combination with other words it denotes persons belonging to the same group. For example, Ahl al-Kitab, **Peoples of the Book**, scriptuaries.

AHL AL-BAYT. "People of the House," a term used for the family of the Prophet **Muhammad** in the **Koran** (33:33). **Shi'ites** restrict the term to Muhammad's descendants through **'Ali** and **Fatimah** and their sons **Hasan** and **Husayn**, including the Twelve Imams, and believe that they embody a special **barakah**, blessing, and authority inherited from their blood relationship to the Prophet. *See also* IMAM.

AHL AL-DHIMMA. *See* PEOPLES OF THE BOOK.

AHL AL-HADITH. "The People of **Tradition**." A Muslim reformist movement founded in the early 19th century on the Indian subcontinent and now a political movement in Pakistan and Afghanistan. Its founding fathers are Shah **Wali Allah** (d. 1762) and Sayyid Ahmad **Barelvi** (d. 1831), who demanded adherence solely to the **Koran** and Tradition (**Sunnah**), rejected **Sufism** and **Shi'ism**, and called for the right to **ijtihad**. They are commonly called Wahhabis.

AHL AL-HALL WA 'L-'AQD. "Men with the power to loosen and bind," that is, representatives of the community with the power to offer the **caliphate** to the most qualified person and to depose a sinful ruler. Once selected, the community offers an oath of allegiance (**bay'ah**). There is disagreement about the number of persons required—even one was seen as sufficient, which enabled **caliphs** to nominate their sons. The *ahl al-hall* had to be jurists versed in Islamic sciences, capable of exercising **ijtihad** (interpretation of **Islamic law**). Since the demise of the caliphate, the appointment of a ruler has become more of an inauguration ceremony, and the *ahl al-hall* have had little success in deposing an autocratic ruler. In modern days, radical

Islamists claim the right to this function for the entire community, and Muslim modernists likened their functions to that of an elected parliament.

AHL AL-HAQQ (AHL-I HAQQ). "The People of Truth." A syncretist **sect** of a number of groups found predominantly in western Iran and Kurdistan (where they are related to the **Yazidis**). They recognize the twelve **Shi'ite imams** and count seven successive manifestations of God, believing that humans must pass though a cycle of reincarnations with corresponding rewards. **'Ali**, cousin of **Muhammad**, is one of the manifestations, but the most important is a person called Sultan Sohak (15th century). The sect, also called 'Ali Illahi, is said to combine elements of Shi'ism with Jewish and **Christian** practices. Their doctrines are secret; what is known comes from the *Firqan al-Akhbar*, a publication of a former member.

AHL AL-KITAB. *See* PEOPLES OF THE BOOK.

AHL AL-SUNNAH WA AL-JAMA'AH. *See* BARELVI, SAYYID AHMAD.

AHMAD BARELVI, SAYYID. *See* BARELVI, SAYYID AHMAD.

AHMAD IBN HANBAL. *See* IBN HANBAL, AHMAD.

AHMADIS (AMADIYYAH). A messianic movement in modern Islam, which originated in British India. It is named after its founder, Mirza Ghulam Ahmad (ca. 1839–1908) of Qadian, Punjab, who declared himself the "Renewer of the Faith" in 1882. He eventually laid claim to prophethood. The **sect** divided in 1914, after the death Mirza Ghulam's successor, into the more radical Qadiani, who considered all others infidels, and the Lahori, who held Ahmad to be merely a "renewer" (**mujaddid**) of the faith. The Ahmadis conducted a vigorous missionary activity that brought them into conflict with orthodox **Sunni** regimes. After the partition of India in 1947, the headquarters of the movement moved to Pakistan. Because of **'ulama'** opposition in 1974, the government of Prime Minister Zulfiqar Ali Bhutto declared the movement to be non-Muslim. In 1984, the government of

President Zia ul-Haq made Ahmadi religious observance a punishable offense, and the head of the Qadianis, Mirza Tahir Ahmad (1982–), was forced to move to London. The Ahmadis present themselves as Muslim modernists and have been successful in winning converts in America, Europe, Asia, and Africa. They are said to number between 500,000 and one million but claim to have from 10 to 20 million followers. The sect is prohibited in Syria, Uganda, Pakistan, and several other countries.

There are also several **Sufi** orders with this name, most importantly the one of Ahmad al-Badawi (d. 1276).

AHMAD KHAN, SIR SAYYID (1817–1898). Muslim modernist who demanded reforms and called for the adoption of Western technology and education. After receiving a traditional education, he found work as a writer with the East India Company's court of justice at Delhi in 1841. He advocated coexistence between Muslims and the British, feeling that Muslim interests would be better protected under British rather than Hindu rule. In 1888, he was awarded a Knight Commander of the Star of India. Among his many publications was a commentary on the Bible and the **Koran**, pointing out the common source of the scriptures. In 1875, Sir Sayyid founded the All-India Muhammadan Anglo–Oriental College at **Aligarh**, which was eventually transformed into the Aligarh Muslim University (which supporters called the Muslim Cambridge). He sought to reconcile faith and reason and favored the adoption of Western concepts, such as science, technology, justice, and freedom. He is credited with being one of the initiators of India's Islamic renaissance and a promoter of the idea of creating a Muslim state, which was finally implemented long after his death with the creation of Pakistan. *See also* SALAFIYYAH.

AHSA'I, AHMAD AL- (1753–1826). A native of Ahsa al-Hasa (now a province of Saudi Arabia) of a **Shi'ite** family. He was self-taught, and at age 20 went to **Najaf** and **Karbala** for advanced study of Shi'ite jurisprudence (**fiqh**) and theology (**kalam**). Ahsa'i spent about 20 years at Yazd before moving to Kermanshah, where he was excommunicated when he claimed to be inspired in his dreams by the Prophet and **imams**. Denounced as an infidel in 1824, he left on a **pilgrimage** to **Mecca** and died on the way. His followers founded the

Shaykhi Shi'ite movement, which included Sayyid Ali Muhammad (1820–1850), founder of the Babi, later **Baha'i**, religion. *See also* BAB.

'A'ISHAH (AYESHA, 613–678). "Mother of the **Believers**" *(Umm al-mu'minin)*, the favorite wife of the Prophet **Muhammad** and daughter of **Abu Bakr**. She was given in **marriage** to Muhammad when she was six years old, after his wife **Khadijah** died, but the marriage was consummated a number of years later. The **Prophet** gave some household goods worth 50 (according to *Sirat*, Tr. Guillanne, 400) dirham as a dowry for **'A'ishah**. A scandal threatened the marriage, when 'A'ishah was missing on the return from an expedition. She had left her litter in search of a necklace she had lost, and the caravan left without her. Waiting to be rescued, she fell asleep and was found the next morning by a young nomad called Safwan, who brought her back to **Medina**. Rumors about infidelity finally made Muhammad consult with some of his followers, including **'Ali**, who counseled that he should **divorce** 'A'ishah. A **revelation** solved the problem in Surah 24:13, saying, "Why did they not bring four witnesses to prove it? When they have not brought the witnesses, such men in the sight of **Allah** (stand forth) themselves as liars." This established the requirement in **Islamic law** of witnesses in cases of **adultery**, unless the culprits confess.

'A'ishah did not forgive 'Ali for his advice, and she met him with the **Companions Talhah** and al-**Zubayr** during the Battle of the **Camel** in 656. The rebels were defeated, and 'A'ishah was returned to Medina, where she lived an honored life until her death in 678. A childless widow at 18, 'A'ishah outlived many of the early Companions of the Prophet and became an important transmitter of the sayings and actions (**hadith**) of the Prophet Muhammad.

According to a hadith, 'A'ishah declared the following:

> I was preferred over the wives of the Prophet by ten things: "It was asked what are they, Umm al-Mu'minin?" She said: "He did not marry any other virgin but me. He did not marry a woman whose parents were **muhajirun** except me. Allah Almighty revealed my innocence from heaven. **Jibril** brought my picture from heaven in silk and said, 'Marry her. She is your wife.' He and I used to do **ghusl** from the same vessel, and he did not do that with any of his wives except me. He used to pray while I was stretched out in front of him, and he did not do that with

any of his wives except with me. The revelation would come to him while he was with me, and it did not come down when he was with any of his wives except me. Allah took his soul while he was against my chest. He died on the night when it was my turn and he was buried in my room (Tabaqat, Muhammad Ibn Said, Tr. Aisha Bewrley, *Women of Madina* London: Ta-Ha, 1997).

AJAL. The "appointed time" of death ordained by God.

AJNADAYN. Scene of a battle on 30 July 634, about 45 kilometers southwest of **Jerusalem**, in which a united force of Arabs under **Khalid ibn al-Walid** and **'Amr ibn al-'As** defeated a Byzantine army commanded by the brother of the Greek emperor. This opened the way to the conquest of Palestine.

AKHBARIS (AKHBARIYYAH). A traditional school in **Twelver Shi'ite** jurisprudence, which holds that legal opinions should be based on the **Koran**, the Traditions (**Sunnah**) of **Muhammad** and the **imams**, rather than "derived from general principles (**usul**) by analogical reasoning." In other words, religious scholars should not exercise independent judgment (**ijtihad**) in matters of law, as maintained by the usuli school. The latter was adopted by the Shi'ite clergy in Iran in the late 17th and early 18th centuries as a justification for its role as the "guardians of the **believers**." The Akhbariyyah school was first established by Muhammad Amin Astarabadi (Akhbari, d. 1624), who rejected the teachings of most jurists after the 10th century. By the 19th century, Agha Muhammad Baqir Bihbihani (1706–1790) was instrumental in contributing to the supremacy of the **usuli school**. *See also* SHI'ISM.

AKHTAL, GHIYATH AL-TAGHLIBI AL- (640–710). Christian Arab poet and rival of his contemporaries, **al-Jarir ibn 'Atiyah** and Hammam ibn Ghalib al-**Farazdak**, who are considered among the founders of **Arabic** literary criticism. Ostentatiously Christian and not ready to renounce wine, Akhtal refused an offer of a pension of 10,000 dirhams from Caliph **'Abd al-Malik** if he converted to Islam. He was a supporter of the **Umayyad** dynasty, which used him to attack members of the pious opposition. Akhtal was devoted to his religion, but this did not prevent him from saying there was no difference between the bishop and the tail of his ass, when his wife could touch only the tail of the bishop's ass when he rode by. Akhtal was acclaimed as the first among the poets of Islam—and it was said that, if he had lived a single day before the advent of Islam, he would also have been the first of the Jahiliyyah poets.

AKHUND. A title for religious personalities and scholars. The term was first used in Timurid times (15th century) as an honorific for a great scholar, but it later denoted a simple school teacher, with a slightly pejorative connotation. In some areas, it also was the designation of theology students. A descendant of an Akhund is called Akhund-zada.

ALAMUT. A fortress in the Elburz mountain range about 45 kilometers northeast of Qazvin, captured by **Hasan al-Sabbah** (d. 1124) in 1090. He was the Grand Master of a religious order of **Isma'ilis**, subsequently called the Assassins, or *hashishin*—hashish smokers. The members of the order were initiated into successive stages of hierarchy, corresponding to their level of advancement, the lowest of which were the **fida'i**, devotees, who were sent on errands of assassination. They were said to have used hashish as part of their rituals and became a threat to the princes and crusader kings in the Middle East. **Nizam al-Mulk**, the **vizier** of the **Saljuq** ruler Alp Arslan, is said to have been one of the more famous statesmen who fell under the dagger of a fida'i of the "Old Man of the Mountain."

Hulagu, founder of the Ilkhanid state in Iran, finally captured Alamut and other Isma'ili fortifications in 1256 and ended the existence of the state, which lasted for 166 years. The word *assassin* came into Western languages as a corruption of the word *hashishiyun*. The followers of the Grand Master reckon the **Agha Khan** as their titular head.

'ALAWIS ('ALAWIYUN). A term generally applied to all **Shi'ites**, but more specifically to a religious community of several hundred thousand located in Syria, Lebanon, and southern Turkey. They are also called Nusayris after their eponymic leader ibn Nusayr (d. ca. 873), a follower of the 11th Shi'ite **Imam** Hasan al-'Askari (d. 873).

Their religious practices are secret, but they are known to have a holy book, the Book of Collection (*Kitab al-majmu'*), and are said to combine syncretist elements from Shi'ite **Isma'ili** and even Christian teachings. They observe the Zoroastrian New Year, Easter, and St. Barbara's Day and are said to believe in a holy trinity of **'Ali**, **Muhammad**, and **Salman** al-Farisi. They permit wine drinking, but prohibit drunkenness. They use candles. The 'Alawis practice **taqiyyah** (dissimulation) to protect themselves from persecution. In addition to the **Five Pillars of Islam**, they also accept **jihad** and waliyah, devotion to Imam 'Ali and hatred of his adversaries. During the French occupation of Syria, many 'Alawis joined the armed services and after independence, the Arab Socialist (Ba'th) Party. Thus they were able to gain control of the country. Hafez al-Asad, an 'Alawi, was president of Syria from 1971 to 2000.

Other communities of 'Alawis (Alevi) exist in Kurdish regions of eastern Turkey and in Arabic-speaking areas in the south near the Syrian border. An 'Alawi dynasty established itself in Morocco and continues to lead the country through the present. It was founded by Mawlay Rashid (d. 1672), who established his capital in Meknes. It derives its legitimacy from the monarch's claim as a descendant of the House of 'Ali through his son, **Hasan**.

ALBUCASIS. *See* ABU AL-QASIM.

ALCOHOL. Not expressly forbidden in the **Koran**, in which alcohol is mentioned as *khamr*, wine. The Koran says: "They ask thee concerning wine and **gambling**. Say: 'in them is great sin, and some profit for men; but the sin is greater than the profit'"(2:219). On the other hand, **believers** are promised in heaven "Rivers of wine, a joy to those who drink"(47:15). Jurists decided that it should be forbidden, including all intoxicating spirits. Alcohol was, nevertheless, produced by non-Muslim minorities and accessible even to Muslims in some countries. With independence, governments often established a monopoly in the production and sale of alcoholic beverages, including Turkey, Egypt, and Algeria, among others. But **Islamist** agitation has now resulted in restricting, or prohibiting, the consumption of alcohol in many parts of the Islamic world.

ALHAMBRA (AL-HAMRA'). "The Red One" is one of the great architectural monuments of Muslim Spain. It was named thus because of the red stucco used in construction of the palace, built in 1238–1258 under the Nasrite dynasty of Granada. The building covered an area about 740 meters in length and 205 meters at its greatest width. It was surrounded by a strong wall with 13 towers. Partially destroyed as a result of war and an earthquake, the Alhambra was periodically restored to its old glory. In 1492, an army of Ferdinand and Isabella captured Granada, the last Muslim outpost on the Iberian Peninsula.

'ALI IBN ABI TALIB (r. 656–661). The fourth of the **Rightly Guided Caliphs** and the first **imam** of **Shi'ite** Islam. He was a cousin of **Muhammad** and his son-in-law, after his marriage to **Fatimah**. One of the early converts to Islam; according to some sources the first convert after **Khadijah**, Muhammad's wife. Division in Islam into the **Sunnis** and Shi'ites resulted in a dispute over the right of succession to Muhammad after his death in 632. The partisans of 'Ali (*shi'atu 'ali*) maintained that 'Ali had a divine right to succession, to be continued through his sons **Hasan** and **Husayn**, and repudiated the first three Sunni Caliphs as usurpers. 'Ali moved his capital to Kufah, where he had the support of his troops. He was immediately challenged by **Talhah** and **Zubayr** in the Battle of the **Camel** (656), named after **'A'ishah**, the wife of Muhammad, who surveyed the battle from atop a camel to give moral support to the rebels.

Challenged by **Mu'awiyah**, the Umayyad governor of Damascus, 'Ali met him in the Battle of **Siffin** (657), which was inconclusive, and 'Ali was forced to accept arbitration. This cost him the support of part of his army, and the "Seceders," **Kharijites**, eventually turned against him. He was assassinated by a Kharijite during morning prayer in 661. His tomb in **Najaf**, in present-day Iraq, is one of the most important places of Shi'ite pilgrimage. 'Ali was described as a resolute warrior and was revered for his piety, nobility, and learning. He favored the distribution of booty among the Muslim community, and upon his death was said to have only 600 dirhams to his name. Shi'ites attribute to 'Ali and the imams divine inspiration and infallibility.

ALIGARH. A town in India, about 80 miles southeast of New Delhi, which is the location of the modernist Aligarh University. Founded by Sir Sayyid **Ahmad Khan** (1817–1898) as a boys' school and college (the All-Indian Muhammadan Anglo–Oriental College at Aligarh) to educate committed Muslims according to Western curricula. It became a university in 1920, and women were admitted in some faculties in 1938. Many of the graduates achieved positions of prominence in the early 20th century. They led the Muslim League, the **Pakistan** movement, and the new Republic of Pakistan. The first vice chancellor of Aligarh after independence was Zakir Husain, who subsequently became president of India.

'ALIM. A person who has knowledge (*i'lm*) of the Traditions, canon law, and theology. In Arabic, also the term for a secular scholar. Plural, 'ulama', is taken for the body of scholars, loosely described as clergy. *See also* 'ULAMA'.

'ALI AL-RIDHA. *See* RIDHA, 'ALI AL-.

ALLAH. "God." The Arabic name for the one and only omnipotent, omnipresent, just, and merciful God. To be a Muslim one must testify that "there is no god but Allah and that **Muhammad** is his prophet." Giving partners to Allah is an unforgivable sin. The **Koran** says: "Say: He is Allah, the One; Allah, the Eternal, Absolute; He begetteth not, nor is He begotten; and there is none like unto Him"(112). There is no trinity, or son of God; he is the Lord of heaven and earth, the Creator of the universe. He will reward and punish humankind on the **Day of Judgment**. His revelations through the medium of Muhammad are the commands of Allah, collected in the Koran. The **Koran** says: "Certainly they disbelieve who say: 'Allah is Christ the son of Mary.' Whoever joins other gods with Allah— Allah will forbid him the Garden [paradise], and the fire will be his abode"(5:72).

ALLAH, MOST BEAUTIFUL NAMES OF

1.	Al-Rahman	The Compassionate
2.	Al-Rahim	The Merciful
3.	Al-Malik	The King

4. Al-Quddus	The Pure One
5. Al-Salam	The source of Peace
6. Al-Mu'min	The Inspirer of Faith
7. Al-Muhaymin	The Guardian
8. Al-Aziz	The Powerful
9. Al-Jabbar	The Compeller
10. Al-Mutakabbir	The Greatest
11. Al-Khiliq	The Creator
12. Al-Bari'	The Maker of Order
13. Al-Musawwir	The Fashioner
14. Al-Ghaffar	The Forgiving
15. Al-Qahhar	The Subduer
16. Al-Wahhab	The Giver
17. Al-Razzaq	The Provider
18. Al-Fattah	The Opener
19. Al-'Alim	The Knowing
20. Al-Qabid	The Seizer
21. Al-Basit	The Reliever
22. Al-Khafid	The Abaser
23. Al-Rafi'	The Exalter
24. Al-Mu'izz	The Bestower of Honors
25. Al-Mudhill	The Humiliator
26. Al-Sami'	The Hearer
27. Al-Basir	The Seer
28. Al-Hakam	The Judge
29. Al 'Adl	The Just
30. Al-Latif	The Gracious
31. Al-Khabir	The All Aware
32. Al-Halim	The Forbearing
33. Al-Azim	The Magnificent
34. Al-Ghafur	The Forgiver
35. Al-Shakur	The Rewarder
36. Al-'Ali	The Highest
37. Al-Kabir	The Greatest
38. Al-Hafiz	The Preserver
39. Al-Muqit	The Nourisher
40. Al-Hasib	The Accounter
41. Al-Jalil	The Majestic

42. Al-Karim	The Generous
43. Al-Raqib	The Watchful
44. Al-Mujib	The Responsive
45. Al-Wasi'	The Wast
46. Al-Hakam	The Wise
47. Al-Wadud	The Loving
48. Al-Majid	The Majestic One
49. Al-Ba'ith	The Raiser
50. Al-Shahid	The Witness
51. Al-Haqq	The Truth
52. Al-Wakil	The Trustee
53. Al-Qawi	The Strong
54. Al-Matin	The Forceful
55. Al-Wali	The Protector
56. Al-Hamid	The Praised
57. Al-Muhsi	The Appraiser
58. Al-Mubdi	The Originator
59. Al-Mu'id	The Restorer
60. Al-Muhyi	The Giver of Life
61. Al-Mumit	The Taker of Life
62. Al-Hayy	The Living
63. Al-Qayyam	The Self-Existing
64. Al-Wajid	The Finder
65. Al-Majid	The Glorious
66. Al-Wahid	The Unique
67. Al-Ahad	The One
68. Al-Samad	The Everlasting
69. Al-Qadir	The Powerful
70. Al-Muqtadir	The Prevailer
71. A-Muqaddim	The Expediter
72. Al-Mu'akhkhir	The Delayer
73. Al-Awwal	The First
74. Al-Akhir	The Last
75. Al-Zahir	The Manifest
76. Al-Batin	The Hidden
77. Al-Wali	The Protector
78. Al-Muta'ali	The Exalted
79. Al-Barr	The Beneficent

80. Al-Tawwib	The Guide to Rependance
81. Al-Muntaqim	The Avenger
82. Al-Afu	The Forgiver
83. Al-Ra'uf	The Gentle
84. Malik Al-Mulk	The Owner of All
85. Dhu 'l-Jalali Wa-'l-Ikram	The Lord of Majesty and Bounty
86. Al-Muqsit	The Equitable
87. Al-Jami'	The Gatherer
88. Al-Ghani	The Rich
89. Al-Mughni	The Enricher
90. Al-Mani'	The Preventer of Harm
91. Al-Darr	The Creator of the Harmful
92. Al-Nafi	The Creator of Good
93. Al-Nur	The Light
94. Al-Hadi	The Guide
95. Al-Badi	The Originator
96. Al-Baqi	The Everlasting
97. Al-Warith	The Inheritor
98. Al-Rashid	The Righteous Teacher
99. Al-Sabur	The Patient

ALLAHU AKBAR. "God is most great." A formula in Islam, called the *takbir*, occurring in ritual prayers, as a call to prayer, or as a battle cry during war.

ALL INDIA MUSLIM LEAGUE. A political party founded at Dhaka in 1906 for the purpose of representing the Muslim people of India and eventually to create a Muslim state after independence from Great Britain. It was the force behind the creation of **Pakistan** and continued as a political party there. The **Agha Khan** III was appointed the first honorary president. Muhammad Ali Jinnah and Sir Muhammad **Iqbal** were early leaders, and, after independence, Jinnah (the Quaid-e-Azam Great Leader) became governor general and Liaquat Ali prime minister of Pakistan. The Muslim League continued to be a political party and, after the death of the dictator Zia-ul-Haq in 1988, Nawaz Sharif became the head of a new Muslim League, which still exists.

ALMOHADS (AL-MUWAHHIDUN, 1130–1269). A Masmuda Berber confederation and Islamic revivalist movement ruling in the Maghreb (Northwest Africa) and Spain. The Almohads (Unitarians, those who affirm the unity of God) were inspired by the teachings of Muhammad **ibn Tumart** (1077–1130), who formulated a doctrine of puritanical moral reform but eventually proclaimed himself the "**mahdi**," the "guided one" who was to appear before the **Day of Judgment**. Ibn Tumart was succeeded by Abd al-Mu'min, who proclaimed himself ibn Tumart's caliph and made his capital at Marrakesh in 1147. The Almohads put an end to the **Almoravids** and founded a dynasty, centered in Seville, that witnessed a short period of great cultural revival before the end of Muslim rule in Spain.

ALMORAVIDS (AL-MURABITUN, 1061–1147). A revivalist dynasty of Lamtuna Berber tribes, named after their fortified camps (**ribat**) on the edges of the Saharan desert, who conquered an empire in North Africa and Spain. Yahya ibn Ibrahim, a chief of the "Veiled" Sanhaja branch, returned from a pilgrimage to **Mecca** and brought with him the Berber scholar 'Abd Alla ibn Yasin. Yasin provided the ideological impetus for a series of conquests of Morocco and parts of Spain. The state reached its greatness under Yusuf ibn Tashfin (r. 1061–1106), who established his capitals at Marrakesh and Seville in Spain. The Almoravids were eventually replaced by the **Almohads**.

ALMSGIVING. "Sadaqa" alms, or "**zakat**," a tax incumbent on all Muslims. The **Koran** says: "Alms are for the poor and the needy, and those employed to administer the (funds); for those whose hearts have been reconciled (converted to truth); for those in bondage and in debt; in the cause of **Allah**; and for the wayfarer; thus it is ordained by Allah" (9:60). It is one of the obligations subsumed under the code of rituals called the **Five Pillars of Islam** and can be given in cash or in kind. Now largely voluntary, as much as 2.5 to 10 percent was customary.

According to the *Muwatta* of Imam **Malik ibn Anas**, zakat is paid on three things: the produce of cultivated land, gold and silver, and livestock. But there is no zakat obligation on fewer than five camels, on less than five awaq (200 dirhams of pure silver), or on fewer than

five awaq of dates (1,500 double-handled scoops) (17.1.1–3.).
Shi'ites look at zakat as charity rather than a religious tax.

AL SHAYKH FAMILY. Name for the descendants of Muhammad ibn
Abd al-**Wahhab** in Saudi Arabia.

'AMAL. Action for which one will be rewarded on the **Day of Judgment**.

AMAL. "Hope." A populist **Shi'ite** movement that emerged in Lebanon
in 1975 and became a major political factor in Lebanese politics. It
superseded the Movement of the Deprived, Harakat al-Mahrumin,
headed by Sayyid Musa al-**Sadr**, and marked a move to the Left
when Nabih **Berri** assumed its leadership in 1980. Also the acronym
for the Lebanese Resistance Detachment (Afwaj al-Muqawamah al-
Lubnaniyah). Amal fought Israeli occupiers but also opposed a PLO
presence in southern Lebanon. It eventually disbanded its military
arm, and Nabih Berri was elected in 1992 to the position of speaker
in the Lebanese parliament. Continued economic distress and Israeli
occupation in the south led to the emergence of **Hizbullah**, the Party
of **Allah**, a religio-political party that has since merged with the **Islamic Amal** and eclipsed the popularity of the secular Amal.

'AMIL. Until the 10th century, a provincial official responsible for the
collection of taxes. Later it was the office of the finance minister of
a prince.

AMIN, MUHAMMAD AL- (787–813). Son of **Harun al-Rashid**, and
his appointed successor (809–813). He was to be succeeded by his
brother **Ma'mun**, who served as governor of Khurasan. Amin was educated under the supervision of Fadhl ibn Yahya al-Barmaki. Amin decided to appoint his son as his successor rather than accepting Ma'mun
as the crown prince. In the succeeding war, Amin was defeated and
killed, leading to the succession of Ma'mun. According to one account, when Ma'mun's general Tahir ibn al-Husayn besieged Baghdad, he asked for permission to take care of Amin as he pleased; in
reply Ma'mun sent a shirt with no opening for the head. Thereupon
Tahir killed Amin. *See also* TAHIRID DYNASTY.

AMINAH (d. ca. 576). Mother of the Prophet **Muhammad**. She died when the Prophet was about six years old.

AMIR (EMIR). From the Arabic *amara*, meaning to command. Title of a military commander, a nobleman, chief, prince, or ruler. Amir is also a common name. During the **Umayyad** and early **'Abbasid** periods, this title was given to heads of ruling families, high Arab officials, and governors. **Islamist** groups call their supreme leader Amir.

AMIR AL-HAJJ. Leader of the pilgrim caravans, in charge of maintaining order and security while traveling and during the ceremonies. The first Amir al-Hajj was **Abu Bakr**, but the position later became an office entrusted to a notable and continued as an honorary position during the **Ottoman empire**. The amir al-hajj used to receive a part of the property of individuals who died during pilgrimages. Today, when up to two million pilgrims go on hajj, each country provides its own group leader.

AMIR AL-MU'MININ. "Commander of the Faithful," title of the caliph or **imam** who also is the commander-in-chief of the Islamic army. Abdullah ibn Jahsh first held the title as a reward for his bravery in battle, and subsequently it was adopted by Caliph **'Umar I**. Later adopted by sultans, kings, secular rulers, or military commanders. Mulla **Muhammad 'Umar**, head of the **Taliban** regime of **Afghanistan**, was given this title by his supporters.

AMIR AL-UMARA. "Amir of Amirs," title of the commander-in-chief, or governor, of a large province in the Ottoman empire. The title was first given by the **'Abbasid** Caliph al-Muqtadir (908–932) to the commander of his bodyguard. In the 10th century, the title became hereditary under the **Buyids**, but it later lost its importance.

'AMR IBN AL-'AS (ca. 575–663). A member of the **Quraysh** and conqueror of Egypt. He was originally an opponent of **Muhammad** and embraced Islam only shortly before the capture of **Mecca**. He became an important general of the Muslim armies. Together with **Khalid ibn Walid**, he defeated the Byzantines in the battle of **Ajnadayn** (634) and at **Yarmuk** (636). The 45-year-old warrior had raided into Egypt (642), when a messenger of Caliph **'Umar I** brought him a letter advising him to desist from entering Egypt, unless he had already done so. Surmising the contents of the letter, Amr did not open it until he had entered the country.

He forced Alexandria to pay tribute, established himself at Babylon in 642, and founded Fustat (later part of Cairo). In a letter to 'Umar in **Medina**, he said, "I have captured a city from the description of which I shall refrain. Suffice it to say that I have seized therein 4,000 villas with 4,000 baths, 40,000 poll-tax-paying Jews and four hundred places of entertainment for the royalty." 'Amr became governor of Egypt; he fought against **'Ali** at the Battle of **Siffin** in 657 and skillfully represented his clansman, **Mu'awiyah**, in the **Adhruh Arbitration**. He remained governor of Egypt at Fustat under Mu'awiyah, until his death in 663.

'AMR IBN AL-KULTHUM (sixth century). Pre-Islamic poet and chief of the Taghlib tribe who extolled the Bedouin values and his own nobility and bravery in one of the odes included in the **Mu'allaqat**. An anecdote states that he killed 'Amr ibn Hind, the King of Hira, when he arranged to have the poet's mother, Layla, insulted. An Arab proverb says of him: "Bolder in onset than 'Amr ibn al-Kulthum.

AMSAR. Garrison towns founded on the borders of deserts by Muslim forces in newly conquered lands. They were populated by Arab warriors and became the nuclei of the first Muslim cities, **Kufah** (638), **Basra** (635), Fustat (641 now part of **Cairo**), and Qayrawan (670).

AMULETS. "Hama'il." Dating from pre-Islamic times, amulets are widely used in the Islamic world. They consist of passages of the **Koran**, some of the 99 most beautiful names of **Allah**, or prayers written on paper or engraved in metal or stone. Small copies of the Koran are often worn around the neck in a silk or leather bag. They are fastened on arms or some other part of the body, but are also fixed on doors of houses, on animals, etc. They are to ward off the "evil eye," to protect individuals from the envy and harm of others. *See also* EVIL EYE.

ANGELS (MALA'IKA). Angels are the messengers of God. Like people, they are His servants. They record people's actions and bear witness against them on the **Day of Judgment.** **Gabriel** (*jibril*) was God's chief messenger to **Muhammad.** One angel, **Iblis,** refused to bow before Adam and tempted Eve; therefore, he was banished from paradise but given the power to lead astray all those who are not true servants of God. Other angels are **Israfil,** who trumpets in the Last Judgment, and **'Izra'il,** the Angel of Death. **Munkar and Nakir** are two guardian angels who interrogate men in the tomb about God and the Prophet. Those who cannot answer will be placed in the "tomb of torment" with snakes and scorpions. Two angels mentioned in the **Koran** (2:102), **Harut and Marut,** were sent to Earth, where they sinned and were punished for it. According to a Tradition, angels are made of light, except for Iblis, who is made of fire. **Mika'il** provides men with food and knowledge. The Koran (35:1) describes angels as "messengers with wings, two three, or four (pairs)."

ANSAR. "Helpers," the name of the people of **Medina** who converted to Islam and came to be referred to as the "Helpers of the Prophet" (*Ansar al-Nabi*), a name of honor. The Ansar participated in the Battle of **Badr** against the pagan Meccans, furnishing as many as 238 men of a force of about 300, which defeated the Meccans on 15 March 624. They became members of the "pious" opposition when a member of the **Quraysh** was elected caliph. Ansari is a patronymic, meaning descent from a Helper, and is a common name today. The **Koran** praises them as "those who before them (the muhajir), had homes (in Madinah) and had adopted the faith, show their affection to such as came to them for refuge, and entertain no desire in their hearts for things given to the (Quraysh) but give them preference over themselves, even though poverty was their (own lot)" (59:9).

ANSARI, ABD ALLAH AL- (1005–1089). Islamic theologian, commentator on the **Koran,** mystic from Herat, and author of a commentary on **Sufi** theory (*Manazil-i sha'irin*) and other works. Brilliant as a youth, he studied at Nishapur under **Shafi'ite** teachers but later adopted the more restrictive **Hanbali** school and opposed **Ash'arite** doctrines. He was born in Herat and spent most of his life in that city, a much-celebrated Sufi poet and philosopher, "mystic of love," and "mystic of tawhid" (Unity of God). The caliph gave him the title **Shaykh al-Islam**. He wrote in both Arabic and Persian; his Arabic collection is said to contain more than 6,000 couplets, and his Persian poetry is said to amount to about 14,000 verses. He went blind toward the end of his life; his tomb is in Gazargah, near Herat, amid ruins from the Timurid period.

ANTARAH IBN SHADDAT (d. ca. 615). Pre-Islamic poet and hero. Only one complete casida of his is extant, describing a battle scene, and it is part of the **Mu'allaqat** collection. The son of a black **slave** woman, Antara was freed by his father when his courage was needed to fight off Bedouin raiders. He sang, "On one side nobly born and of the best, of Abs am I my sword makes good the rest" (Nicholson, 1962 115). In modern times, novels, songs, and proverbs celebrate him as a popular hero and a protagonist of Arab union and patriotism.

APOSTASY. "Riddah." There is no agreement among the **'ulama'** about the punishment for apostasy. Some would kill an apostate; others would forgive him if he repents. At the death of the Prophet some tribes, which had accepted Islam and given their allegiance to **Muhammad**, felt free from their allegiance. They were defeated in the War of **Riddah** and were defeated by Caliph **Abu Bakr**. The **Kharijites** (seventh century) would kill the apostate and his entire family. This was explained as "political, economical, and ethnical apostasy," not an ideological act. One interpretation would declare the apostate's wife divorced (because a Muslim woman cannot be married to a non-Muslim) and his property would be divided among his heirs. He could be executed on the order of the imam. Islamic moderates refer to passages in the **Koran** that declare, "Let there be no compulsion in religion," They would declare it unlawful but not a crime. Surah 47:25 reads: Some regimes, as for example the **Taliban** of **Afghanistan**, would kill the apostate, but most modern Muslim states would try to ignore instances of conversions. A convert would leave his area of residence to avoid popular hostility.

'AQABAH. A hill near **Mecca** where, in 621, members of the **Aws** and **Khazraj** tribes of Yathrib (**Medina**) accepted Islam. *See also* 'AQABAH, PLEDGE OF.

'AQABAH, PLEDGE OF. During the time of pilgrimage in 621, a group of men of the **Khazraj** and **Aws** tribes of Yathrib (later **Medina**) secretly met with **Muhammad** and adopted Islam. They pledged: "We will not worship any god but the one God; we will not steal; nor commit adultery; nor kill our children; nor will we slander our neighbor; and we will obey the Prophet of God." This was the first pledge of 'Aqabah, also called the "Pledge of Women," because it did not require fighting in the defense of Islam. The men returned to Yathrib and converted others. A year later 73 men and two women came to **Mecca** and offered their loyalty and invited the Prophet to come to Yathrib. The city was torn by tribal disputes, and it was hoped that Muhammad's leadership would restore peace. In the second pledge of 'Aqabah, the new converts agreed to be Helpers (**ansar**) and fight for the Prophet. Muhammad thereupon made preparations for his immigration (**hijrah**) to Yathrib, where he founded the first Islamic community.

A hadith describes the event as follows:

> 'Ubaydah ibn al-Samit said: "I was present at the first 'Aqaba. There were twelve of us and we pledged ourselves to the prophet after the manner of women and that was before war was enjoined, the undertaking being that we should associate nothing with God; we should not steal; we should not commit fornication; nor kill our offspring; we should not slander our neighbors; we should not disobey him in what was right; if we fulfilled this paradise would be ours; if we committed any of those sins it was for God to punish or forgive as He pleased." (Sira, of Ibn Hisham Tr. Guillaume, *The Life of Muhammad*, 199)

'AQIDAH. *See* CREED.

'AQL. Intellect, soul, the universal mind, spirit.

AQSA, AL-. A mosque built by Umayyad Caliph **Abdul Malik** in the seventh century in Jerusalem as part of the sanctuary known as the **Dome of the Rock**. Partly destroyed in an earthquake, it was rebuilt in around 771 by 'Abbasid Caliph al-**Mansur** and restored by **Salah al-Din** (Saladin) in 1187, after his conquest of Jerusalem. It is the third holiest sanctuary (after **Mecca** and **Medina**) in Islam and the first Islamic building with a dome. The site is traditionally identified as the starting place of **Muhammad**'s **Nocturnal Journey** to heaven.

ARABI. *See* IBN AL-ARABI.

ARABIC. The language in which **Allah**'s commands were transmitted through the medium of the Prophet **Muhammad**. It was the language of the pre-Islamic Bedouin Arabs and is spoken today by some 200 million people, including non-Muslim citizens of the Arab world. It is the language of ritual **prayers** of all Muslims. God's **revelations** were collected in the **Koran**, which Muslims believe to be inimitable. Because of the sacred character of the language, it has been preserved as a classical language and serves in modified form as the written language even of present-day Arabs, whose spoken dialects vary considerably. *See also* RHYMED PROSE.

ARAB LEAGUE. A regional organization of Arab states founded in Cairo in 1945 with six members: Egypt, Iraq, Lebanon, Saudi Arabia, Syria, Jordan, and Yemen. It now includes 22 members and 3 observer states. The main goal of the League is to

> draw closer the relations between member States and coordinate collaboration between them, to safeguard their independence and their sovereignty, and to consider in a general way the affairs and interests of the Arab countries.

The League has been more successful in the cultural and social spheres than in political matters. It endorsed the principle of an Arab homeland while respecting the sovereignty of the individual member states. Palestine has been included in the membership.

'ARAFAT. A valley and a hill, about 27 kilometers southwest of **Mecca**, and the place where pilgrims (hajji) stay on the ninth day of **pilgrimage**. They rest in tents in the valley and pray and hear the **khutbah**, or sermon, from the place where **Muhammad** stood during his Farewell **Pilgrimage**. According to tradition, **Adam** and Eve met here on the Mountain of Mercy (jabal al-rahma) again, after being driven from paradise.

ARBA'AYN. "The Forty." Among **Sunnis**, the commemoration of the death of a family member 40 days later. For **Shi'as**, it is a religious observation 40 days after the Day of **'Ashura**. It commemorates the martyrdom of **Husayn**, the son of 'Ali, at **Karbala** in 680. The ceremony was prohibited in Iraq during the government of Saddam Husayn; it was held again for the first time after his overthrow in April 2003.

ARKAN. "Pillars." *See* FIVE PILLARS OF ISLAM.

'ASABIYAH. Voluntary social solidarity and unconditional loyalty and devotion to one's clan or tribe; tribal "nationalism"; also fanaticism. Islam replaced the bonds of blood with the bonds of religion and gave it its own 'asabiyah. **Ibn Khaldun** saw the decline of urban civilization in the loss of the 'asabiyah of its people. With the emergence of nation states in the Middle East, 'asabiyah also stood for Arab nationalism.

ASCENSION. *See* NOCTURNAL JOURNEY.

ASHAB. *See* COMPANIONS.

ASH'ARI, ABU 'L-HASAN AL- (873–935 [941?]). A dogmatic theologian, considered the founder of Islamic scholasticism. He was born in **Basra** of Yemeni origin and became a student of al-**Jubba'i** of the **Mu'tazilite** school. However, he adopted the teachings of **Ibn Hanbal**. Impressed by the omnipotence of God, he held that God could not be limited. He proclaimed the reality of God's eternal attributes, the **Koran** as the uncreated word of God, and the absolute sovereignty of God over human actions. His name came from the word *ashar* (the hairy), because he was born with hair on his body. One Friday he was sitting in the great mosque of Basra and shouted, "I am 'Ali ibn Isma'il al-Ashari, and I used to hold that the Koran was created, that the eyes (of men) shall not see God, and that we ourselves are the authors of our deeds; now I have returned to the truth; I renounce these opinions and I take the engagement to refute the Mu'tazilites and expose their infamy and turpitude." One scholar commented that "the Mu'tazilites went with their heads up till such time as God produced al-Ashari to the world." He died at **Baghdad**. *See also* ASH'ARITES.

ASH'ARI, ABU MUSA. *See* ABU MUSA AL-ASH'ARI.

ASH'ARITES (ASH'ARIYYAH). A school of theology founded by Abu 'l-Hasan al-**Ash'ari** (873–935). Al-Ash'ari shaped the intellectual framework for orthodox theology. He studied under the head of the **Mu'tazilites**, al-**Jubba'i**, but he seceded from the "rationalist" school, declaring that **revelation** is superior to reason. He taught that the **Koran** was the eternal and uncreated word of God, based on the Koranic **Surah** (85:21–22), which says: "Nay, this is a Glorious Qur'an (inscribed) in a Tablet Preserved!" He accepted anthropomorphisms in the Koran, and, impressed by God's omnipotence, he rejected free will but held that God created in man the power of choice that can be acquired (**kasb**) by man. He rejected all causality because it would limit the power of God and demanded that religious dogma be accepted without questioning (*bila kayfa*). A famous quote of his states:

> We believe that God created everything by bidding it "Be" [kun]. . . that nothing on earth, whether a fortune or misfortune, comes to be, save through God's will; that things exist through God's fiat; . . . and that the deeds of the creatures are created by Him and predestined by Him; . . . that the creatures can create nothing but are rather created themselves; We . . . profess faith in God's decree and fore-ordination. (Mir Zohair Husain, *Global Islamic Politics*, New York: HarperCollins, 1995. p. 91)

Ash'ari's teachings at the **Nizamiyyah** at **Baghdad** became part of orthodox **Sunni** doctrine. His *Islamic Theological Opinions* (*Maqalat al-Islamiyyin*) is a record of the doctrines of a number of **sects**. Leading Ash'arites included al-**Baqillani** (d.1013), al-**Juwayni** (d. 1086), and al-**Ghazali** (d. 1111).

ASHRAF. *See* SHARIF.

'ASHURA. "The tenth." The first 10 days of the 10th Muslim month, **Muharram**, and specifically the 10th day, on which **Shi'ite** Muslims commemorate the martyrdom of **Imam Husayn**, son of 'Ali, at **Karbala** in 680. Passion plays (ta'ziyah) are publicly performed. Processions wind through the streets, with floats reenacting the scenes at Karbala, and mourners flagellate themselves or strike their bodies with their hands, knives, or stones. For **Sunnis**, it is a day of voluntary **fasting**. According to tradition, it is the day on which God began his creation and when **Noah** left the Ark.

ASMA'I, ABU SA'ID AL- (741–828). Philologist and representative of the grammarian school of **Basra**, whose works have preserved knowledge about early Arab lexicography and poetry. His *Asma'iyyat* is a collection of some 72 pieces of pre-Islamic and early Islamic poetry. He also wrote about the customs and values of the Bedouins, as well as about animals and plants. **Ibn Khallikan** calls Asma'i "a complete master of the **Arabic** language, and able grammarian, and the most eminent of all those persons who transmitted orally historical narrations, singular anecdotes, amusing stories, and rare expressions of the language" (II, 123). Asma'i was born and died in Marw; he was said to have been quite ugly. Yahya, the **Barmakid vizier** of **Harun al-Rashid**, once asked him whether he was married, and since he was not, Yahya gave him a slave girl. Upon seeing Asma'i the girl cried, "How can you give me away to such a man as that? Do you not see how ugly he is?" Yahya relented and bought the girl back for 2,000 dinars (Khallikan, IV, 107).

ASRAFIL. *See* ISRAFIL.

ASSASSINS (HASHISHIYIN). *See* ALAMUT; NIZARIS.

ASSEMBLY OF CONSTITUTIONAL EXPERTS. A body of 85 "virtuous and learned clerics" charged by the Revolutionary Council to draft a constitution for the **Islamic Republic of Iran**. The assembly was dominated by **Shi'ite** clergy and laid the foundation for the theocratic government of Iran, establishing the supremacy of the "Guardianship of the Jurist" (*vilayat-i faqih*). It gave Ayatollah **Khomeyni** and his successors supreme authority as the representative of the **Hidden Imam**. The assembly concluded its work in October 1979, and the draft was ratified by a referendum in December. Secular forces who participated in the overthrow of the Shah of Iran were eventually eliminated, and individuals running for parliamentary elections had to be approved as to their suitability for office by a Council of **Guardians**. Article 110 of the constitution gave Ayatollah

Khomeyni sole power of appointing and dismissing the highest military and government officials, making him a virtual dictator.

ATABAT. "Threshholds." The **Shi'ite** shrine cities of Iraq—**Najaf, Karbala,** Kazimayn, and **Samarra**—containing tombs of 6 of the 12 Shi'ite **imams**. At Kazimayn the Seventh and Ninth Imams are buried, and at Samarra the Tenth and Eleventh Imams. The Twelfth went into occultation (**concealment**) from Samarra. The Tomb of Caliph 'Ali is located in Najaf, and his son **Husayn** was martyred at Karbala in 680.

ATA', WASIL IBN-. *See* WASIL IBN 'ATA'.

ATATÜRK, MUSTAFA KEMAL. *See* KEMALISM.

ATHAR. A relic, trace, or tradition—used synonymously with **hadith,** when referring to the sayings or actions of a **Companion.**

ATHIR. *See* IBN AL-ATHIR.

AVEMBACE. *See* IBN BAJJAH

AVERROES. *See* IBN RUSHD.

AVICENNA. *See* IBN SINA.

AWLIYAH. *See* SAINTS.

AWQAF. *See* WAQF.

AWS. One of two tribes at Yathrib (**Medina**) who invited the Prophet to take refuge in its town, the other being the **Khazraj**. The Aws were among the early converts to Islam, subsequently called the Helpers (**ansar**). *See also* 'AQABAH, PLEDGE OF.

AYAHS. "Signs or miracles," verses into which the 114 chapters (**Surahs**) of the **Koran** are divided. There are said to be 6,236 verses. It is also part of the title of a **Shi'ite mujtahid: Ayatollah** (Miracle of God).

A'YAN. "Notables," prominent persons.

AYA SOFIA (HAGIA SOPHIA). One of the great cathedral **mosques** of Istanbul. It was built in 537 by the Byzantine emperor Justinian and was the seat of the Orthodox patriarch of Constantinople. It was the largest cathedral in the world for almost a thousand years. After the **Ottomans** captured the city in 1453, it became a mosque, then again a cathedral during the short-lived crusader conquest of the city. It was converted into a museum under the secular government of **Kemal** Atatürk. Original wall painting, whitewashed for centuries, can again be seen.

AYATOLLAH (AYAT ALLAH). "Sign, or Miracle, of God," the title given to the most eminent **Twelver Shi'ite** legal experts. The honorific of Shi'ite **mujtahids** (jurists) in Iran, first used in the 14th century and generally adopted during the Qajar dynasty (1779–1924) (Arab-speaking Shi'ites use the title **Imam**). To qualify for the title one had to demonstrate superior learning and leadership, as well as acclamation by one's peers. The most learned of Ayatollahs were the "Sources of Emulation" (*marja-i taqlid*), who are addressed as Ayatollah al-'Uzma. In a lecture in 1970, Ayatollah Ruhollah **Khomeyni** created the concept of the **vilayat-i faqih**, political and spiritual leadership of the Islamic state, preparing the way for a theocratic regime after the Islamic Revolution of 1979. Khomeyni was proclaimed the highest of Ayatollahs; he was succeeded after his death by **Sayyid** Ali **Khamene'i**, who no longer enjoys the charisma and power of his predecessor. *See also* ISLAMIC REPUBLIC OF IRAN.

AYN. "Eye, well." *See* EVIL EYE.

AYN JALUT. "Spring of Goliath." A place in Palestine, near Nazareth, where **Baybars**, the **Mamluk** general of Egypt, defeated a **Mongol** army under the Christian Turk Kitbuga in 1260. This victory led to the reconquest of Syria and stemmed the tide of Mongol advance into the Near East. According to legend, it is the site where David killed Goliath.

AYYUBID DYNASTY. Named after Ayyub ibn Shadhi, but founded in 1174 by **Salah al-Din** (Saladin, r. 1138–1193) in Egypt. He extended his rule over Syria, Iraq, and South Arabia and destroyed the remnants of the **Fatimid** state, restoring **Sunni** orthodoxy to Egypt. Salah al-Din defeated the crusaders in the battle of **Hittin** (1187) and reconquered **Jerusalem**. Before his death, he divided the Ayyubid empire as appanages among his relatives, but by the middle of the 13th century the Ayyubid empire fell prey to their slaves, who established the **Mamluk** dynasty, with its center in Egypt.

AZAN (ADHAN). *See* CALL TO PRAYER.

AZHAR, AL-. "The resplendent," important university in **Sunni** Islam It was founded by the **Fatimid** general, Jawahar al-**Siqilli**, in 972 in **Cairo** as a **Shi'ite** college for the propagation of the **Isma'ili sect**. After the **Ayyubids** conquered Egypt, the country reverted to Sunni Islam, and Al-Azhar eventually became the dominant orthodox institution and a model for European universities. The famous historian/ sociologist **Ibn-Khaldun** lectured at Al-Azhar in the 14th century, and by the 18th century it dominated the educational scene in the Islamic world. **Shaykhs** of Al-Azhar were members of Napoleon's provincial councils, but six shaykhs were executed after a brief revolt in 1798 in Cairo.

In the 19th and early 20th centuries shaykhs of Al-Azhar were accused of acquiescing to government edicts. Muhammad '**Abduh**, member of the Supreme Council of Al-Azhar, was instrumental in initiating modern reforms in the administration and curriculum. During British colonial rule, members of the faculty and students were often in the forefront of public protests. In the 1950s, the government of Gamal 'Abdul Nasser strictly regulated the university and its shaykh-supported Arab nationalism and socialism. It became a modern university, teaching secular as well as theological subjects. **Women** were also admitted. But the majority of the faculty stood for stability rather than revolution, and the university even approved of the peace treaty with Israel.

'AZRA'IL. *See* 'IZRA'IL.

AZRAQITES. An extremist offshoot of the **Kharijite** movement in the late seventh century, named after Nafi ibn Azraq, which declared that all Muslims were unbelievers (**kafirs**) and should be killed with their **women** and children if they did not accept their radical interpretation of Islam. The Azraqites elected the warrior-poet Qatari ibn Fuja'ah as their **caliph** and invaded southern Mesopotamia and Khuzistan; for a long time they held out against superior government forces. They opposed the **Umayyads** as **apostates**. Being a small movement, their fanaticism caused their eventual destruction. Ironically, although they attacked other Muslims, they did not direct their violence against non-Muslims.

– B –

BAB. A title of varied application in **Shi'ism**, also given to **Sufi shaykhs**. Sayyid Ali Muhammad (1820–1850), a native of Shiraz, proclaimed himself the Bab, "The Gateway" to the Truth, and the initiator of a new prophetic age. In the early 1840s, he went on **pilgrimage** to **Karbala** and remained there to study with Shi'ite theologians. He became a member of the **Shaykhi** movement, which held, among others things, the view that there always existed a man who was capable of interpreting the will of the **Hidden Imam**. Upon returning to Shiraz in 1844, he announced that the mission of **Muhammad** was ended and that he was to inaugurate a new era. He published the Babi scripture, the *Bayan* (*Explanation*), which was to replace the **Koran**. He was arrested, but his teachings found wide acceptance. Eventually, he was sent to Tabriz, where he was executed. His followers saw it as a miracle that he was not killed in the first volley; he might have escaped but was found and killed in the second attempt.

The Bab's successors were two half-brothers, Mirza Yahya, the Sobh-i Azal (Eternal Dawn) and Mirza Husayn Ali (d. 1892), who headed separate factions; the latter proclaimed himself Baha Allah, the "Splendor of God," and his followers came to be known as Baha'is. Baha Allah published his teachings in the *Kitab al-Aqdas* (*The Most Holy Book*). The Baha'is greatly increased in numbers and founded communities in Europe and America. After a radical beginning, the Baha'is shed their militancy, abolished **jihad**, and advocated obedience to lawful government, universal peace and brotherhood, and recognition of all prophets.

Babi/Baha'i doctrines suggest the predominance of a commercial outlook and a progressive spirit. They permit the taking of interest—which is forbidden in Islam—and favor the emancipation of **women.** 'Abd al-Baha, eldest son of Baha Allah, visited Europe and subsequently introduced new concepts, including the equality of the sexes, the harmony of religion and science, the commonality of all religions, and progressive **revelation** (Judeo–Christian–Islamic–Babi, Baha'i), putting less emphasis on questions of reincarnation, astrology, faith healing, and spiritualism. Numerology was important, the number 19 having special mystical meaning. In 1923, Haifa in Palestine became the administrative center (the Universal House of Justice) of the Baha'is. The tomb of the Bab is in Haifa, and Baha Allah is buried in Acre (Akka), Israel. There are between 500,000 and one million Baha'is in Iran and thousands in England and America. Because the religion is an offshoot of Islam, the Baha'is in Iran have often been persecuted as heretics, and they are outlawed in Morocco, Egypt, Syria, Iraq, and other countries. *See also* BABI.

BABAK. *See* BABIK.

BABAWAYHI. *See* IBN BABAWAYHI.

BABI. Followers of the "Bab" Sayyid 'Ali Muhammad, who split into two major branches, the Azali of Mirza Yahya, who were more radical and are reduced in number to a few thousand, mostly in Iran, and the Baha'i of Baha Allah, who evolved into a world religion.

BAB-I A'LA. The Sublime Porte—name of the executive offices of the grand **vizier** in the **Ottoman empire.**

BABIK (BABAK, r. 816–837). A rebel who established himself in 816/817 in Azerbaijan and for some 20 years defied the power of Caliph al-**Ma'mun**'s armies. He founded a **sect,** called Khurramiyyah, which wanted to restore the religion of Mazdak and believed in various mystical doctrines, including the transmigration of souls. Babik was finally defeated by Caliph al-Mu'tasim's general Afshin and put to a torturous death. Babik was of humble origin, the son of an oil seller, and what we know about him and his activities comes mainly from hostile sources.

BABUR, ZAHIR AL-DIN MUHAMMAD (1483–1530). Founder of the Moghul (Mughal) empire, the "greatest soldier of his age," and a talented writer and great poet. He was a Barlas Turk who descended on his mother's side from Genghis Khan and on his father's side from Tamerlane (**Timur-i Lang**). He was ousted from his native Ferghana, the Turkic lands north of the Amu Daria, and when he could not retake his homeland, he settled in Kabul in 1504. Probing expeditions into India led to territorial conquests that became the foundation of the Moghul empire. He loved Kabul, wrote fondly about the town, and wanted to be buried in the Bagh-i Babur, a garden he had planted on the western slope of Sher Darwaza mountain. He died in Agra on 26 December 1530, and his body was transported to Kabul, where his rather modest tomb is still located.

BABUYAH. *See* IBN BABAWAYHI.

BADR, BATTLE OF. First military victory of the Muslim community of **Medina** against a superior force of Meccans. In March 624, a heavily armed Meccan caravan was attacked by a small band of some 300 Muslim raiders, who faced an army of about 950 men with 700 camels and 100 horses. In spite of the heavy odds against them, the Prophet persisted in the attack, and the Meccans were defeated. A sand storm blowing in the direction of the **Quraysh** impeded the Meccans' visibility, which was seen as a sign of **Allah**'s support.

The battle began with a "war of words" as each hurled insults at the other. Next followed single combat, in which the Muslims prevailed, and finally the forces engaged. The unity and greater morale of the Muslim forces eventually led to a rout of the Meccans. They left behind between 50 and 70 men dead, including many of their Quraysh leaders; only 14 Muslims were killed. About 50 prisoners were held for ransom. For the Muslim community, this was a sign that God was on their side and permitted the consolidation of the early Muslim community. The **Koran** says: "Allah had helped you at

Badr, when ye were helpless: then fear Allah: thus may ye show your gratitude" (3:123).

BAGHAWI, HUSAYN AL- (d. 1130 or 1136). A **Shafi'ite** traditionalist and commentator on the **Koran**, he wrote a collection of **hadith**, titled *Masabih al-sunnah*, which has been translated into English by James Robson and published in four volumes. Unlike al-**Bukhari**'s and **Muslim** ibn al-**Hajjaj**'s works, it covers a greater variety of topics and lists only the first transmitter and the text of the hadith, and is therefore more practical for use. The work was later revised and expanded under the title *Mishkat al-masabih* (*Niche for Light*) by Shaykh Wali al-Din Mahmud (d. 1342) and others. Baghawi was born near Herat, in present-day Afghanistan. He led an ascetic life, living on bread and olive oil, and refused to accept a portion of the **inheritance** after the death of his wife. Ibn Khallikan says about Baghawi: "A wife of this doctor died, and he refused to accept any portion of the inheritance left by her: he used also to live on dry bread, but having been blamed for this (as an affectation of abstinence), he ate his bread with olive oil" (Khallikan, trans. Slane, I, 420).

BAGHDAD. The "City of Peace" (*madinat al-salam*) was founded in 762 by Caliph al-**Mansur** as the capital of the **'Abbasid** dynasty. It was a circular-shaped city, located where the Euphrates and Tigris Rivers came closest, at the crossroads of trade where there was an abundance of water and fertile soil. It took four years to build the town and cost 4,883,000 dirhams. The caliphal palace and the great **mosque** were in the center, from which roads connected to the four gates. Baghdad rapidly grew and soon surpassed the older cities in splendor. Although originally named "City of Peace," Baghdad, the Persian name of a nearby village, was eventually adopted.

The city reached its cultural greatness under Caliph **Harun al-Rashid** (786–809) and during the succeeding five decades. Al-**Ma'-mun** (813–833) founded the **House of Wisdom** (*bayt al-hikma*), which became the center for translation of Greek science and philosophy. He sponsored the **Mu'tazilite** rationalists, which culminated in the controversy about the createdness, or eternal existence, of the **Koran**. Turkish influence grew as **caliphs** surrounded themselves with bodyguards who became so unruly that the caliphs moved the capital to **Samarra** in 838 for about 45 years.

In the middle of the 10th century, the **Shi'ite Buyids** captured the city and limited the helpless caliphs to an undignified existence, until the **Saljuqs** liberated the city in the 11th century. They restored **Sunni** orthodoxy and gave the '**Abbasid** caliphs their dignity, but little real power. The 'Abbasid dynasty was brought to an end when **Hulagu** captured the city in 1258. The **Ottomans** captured the city in 1638, after which it lost its importance to **Istanbul**. Baghdad is an important place of **pilgrimage** for Shi'ites who visit the tombs of the Seventh and Ninth **Imams** and for members of the **Qadiriyyah** Sufi fraternity, whose founder, 'Abd al-Qadir al-**Jilani**, is buried there.

BAGHDADI, 'ABD AL LATIF AL- (1162–1231). Encyclopedic scholar and author of numerous books, including a history of Egypt that, among others things, stated that Caliph '**Umar** ordered his general '**Amr ibn al-'As** to burn the library of Alexandria. This fact has not been corroborated by any other source. Born in **Baghdad**, he traveled widely in Syria, Egypt, and Iraq and spent a number of years at the court of **Salah al-Din** (1138–1193).

BAGHDADI, ABU MANSUR AL- (d. 1037). Ash'arite dogmatic theologian and legist who studied and taught at Nishapur. He published a systematized dogma in his *Roots of Religion* and a study of Islamic **sects**, called *al-Farq bayn al-firaq*. He died and is buried in Isfarayn in present-day Iran. Ibn Khallikan quotes from the *History of Naisapur*, saying: "He possessed great riches, which he spent on the learned (in the law) and on the Traditionists: he never made of his information a source of profit. . . . He composed treatises on different sciences and surpassed his contemporaries in every branch of learning . . . he gave lessons there (at the mosque of Akil), which were assiduously attended by doctors of the greatest eminence" (Khallikan, trans. Slane, II, 150).

BAHA'I. Follower of Baha Allah, leader of the main branch of the Babi **sect**. *See* BAB.

BAHIRAH. According to tradition, Bahira, a Nestorian Christian monk who lived near Busra on the caravan route from the **Hijaz** to Syria, recognized the sign of prophethood when he saw the 12–year-old **Muhammad**. Muhammad was traveling with his uncle, **Abu Talib**, to Syria when they came upon the monk. Bahira asked Muhammad several questions and then told Abu Talib that in Muhammad's eyes were the marks of a great prophet. A similar event is said to have happened 12 years later when Muhammad traveled on business for his wife **Khadija**; another monk called Nestor made the same prediction.

BALADHURI, AHMAD (d. 892). One of the great historians of the ninth century, a native of **Baghdad** but probably of Persian origin. Two of his historical works still extant are *The History of Muslim Conquests (Kitab futuh al-buldan)*, an abbreviated version of which has been published in English by P. K. Hitti and F. C. Murgotten under the title *The Origin of the Islamic State*. The other is the *Genealogy of Nobles (Kitab ansab al-ashraf)*, which is also important for the history of the **Kharijites**. Toward the end of his life, he became deranged, purportedly as a result of drinking the juice of the anacardia (baladhur), and he was chained to his bed in a hospital, where he died.

BALI BOMBINGS. *See* JIHADIS DECLARATION OF WAR.

BANNA, HASAN AL- (1906–1949). Founder of the **Muslim Brotherhood** (Ikhwan al-Muslimin) of Egypt in 1928 and one of the founding fathers of radical Islam. He was born in Mahmudiyya, a town about 135 kilometers from **Cairo**, and educated in his hometown and subsequently in Cairo at the Dar Al-Ulum, an Islamic teacher training college. He taught **Arabic** at an elementary school in Isma'iliya. There he founded the Society of Muslim Brethren, a religio-political organization that eventually spread to other parts of the Islamic world.

Al-Banna, an ascetic and charismatic teacher, became the "Supreme Guide" (*murshid al-'amm*), who advocated social and economic reforms, expulsion of the British from Egypt, and the establishment of an Islamic state. He blamed Egypt's social malaise of ignorance, hunger, and disease on the fact that Muslims had strayed from orthodox Islam. He called for the creation of a state that was based on the **Koran** and the Traditions (**Sunnah**) of the classical period of Islam and demanded the abrogation of secular laws and the enforcement of Islamic canonic law.

As a political party, the Ikhwan was never very successful, but it was able to mobilize the masses of lower urban and rural classes. In response to government suppression, the Ikhwan resorted to violence, and al-Banna himself became the target of assassination in 1949 (reputedly by government agents). Hasan al-Banna's teachings were carried to all corners of the Islamic world and spawned other, more radical, offshoots that agitated for the overthrow of established governments.

A Muslim Egyptian who met Hasan al-Banna' said of him:

> He talked chiefly of religious topics, but not in the accustomed manner of the preacher, with sonorous phrases and learned references. He went straight to the nub of the question, and he spoke with directness and ease. It seemed strange to me, but here was a theologian with a sense of reality, a man of religion who recognized the existence of facts. (Quoted by Wendell, 1975

BANU. Tribe. *See under tribal name, for example,* HASHIMITE; UMAYYAH.

BAQI, JANNAT AL-. "Tree Garden." Cemetery east of **Medina** where thousands of **Companions** of the Prophet are buried, including **Hasan** and **Husayn**, the sons of Caliph 'Ali, the **Shi'ite imams** Muhammad al-Baqir and **Ja'far al-Sadiq**, as well as Caliph **'Uthman** and **Malik ibn Anas**. When the **Wahhabis** conquered Medina in 1818 and again in 1925, they razed the graves and tombs, except the one of the Prophet.

BAQILLANI, ABU BAKR MUHAMMAD AL- (BAKILANI, d. 1013). **Malikite** jurist and theologian who systematized **Ash'ari** teachings, especially the dogma of atomism, according to which everything is newly created every instant by God. He rejected causality and miracles, except the miracle of the **Koran**. Baqillani gave a concise statement defining the functions of the **caliph**:

> [The caliph] need not be impeccable . . . having knowledge of the unseen, nor even every aspect of the faith . . . the Imam is [only] appointed to uphold the precepts and the limitations and the commands which the **Messenger** promulgated. For the knowledge of the Community has

precedence therein, and in everything he undertakes [the caliph] is the trustee and deputy of the Community, and the Community stand behind him guiding him and setting him right and reminding him and demanding the right from him as it is incumbent upon him, even removing and replacing him if he has committed a crime requiring his deposition. (Binder, 1961, 167)

Al-Baqillani has been called the real founder of the **Ash'arite** school. He was the first to devote an entire book, the *Kitab i'jaz al-Qur'an*, to the dogma of the inimitability of the Koran. He resided in **Baghdad** and died there.

BARAKAH. "Grace," or blessing, a vital force inherent in a person, place, or thing. Founders and heads of **Sufi** fraternities are thought to possess barakah, a spiritual power that can be transmitted from a saintly person to a disciple or devotee. A saint's barakah provides spiritual blessings, which pilgrims can obtain from shrines of venerated **pirs**. The **Hanbali** school of **Sunni** Islam rejects the veneration of saints as a sinful innovation (**bid'ah**). **Shi'ites** feel that their **imams** enjoy the special illumination or barakah and are, in fact, infallible; therefore, they are entitled to leadership of the Muslim community.

BARELVI, SAYYID AHMAD (1786–1831). Native of Rae Bareli, India, and founder of "The Way of the Prophet **Muhammad**" (Tariqah-i Muhammadiyah), a revolutionary **Islamist movement**. He called himself Commander of the **Believers** (*amir al-mu'minin*) and proclaimed a **jihad** against the Sikhs in the Punjab, India. He was defeated and killed, which postponed the dream of establishing an Islamic state in Peshawar, now Pakistan (the Pakistan government proclaimed the establishment of an Islamic state in the 1980s). The Barelvis upheld the doctrine of the unity of God (**tawhid**) and called themselves Unitarians or **Ahl al-Hadith**, while others called them **Wahhabis**. They rejected innovation (**bid'ah**) but accepted **Sufism** and believed in **intercession**, that the spirits of dead saints can be invoked for help. They used **amulets** and accepted most features of popular Islam. They are also called Ahl al-Sunna wa'l Jama'ah.

BARMAKIDS. The name *barmak*, meaning chief priest, was derived from a Buddhist monastery in Balkh. The Barmakids of Balkh (now

Afghanistan) were a family of secretaries and **viziers** in the service of **'Abbasid caliphs**. Al-Saffah (749–754) put the first Barmakid, Khalid ibn-Barmak, in charge of the divans of the army and the land tax and made him his personal adviser. Caliph al-**Mansur** (754–775) appointed him governor of Fars and Tabaristan provinces, and his grandson, Fadhl ibn Yahya, was adopted as a foster brother of **Harun al-Rashid** (786–809). Yahya, the son of Khalid, was secretary and tutor to Harun and governor of Azarbaijan, and his 17-year rule (786–803) was called the "reign of the Barmakids." His two sons, Fadhl and Ja'-far, became governors and served as military commanders.

The Barmakids amassed fabulous wealth and built beautiful palaces in **Baghdad**; they rivaled in splendor the **'Abbasid** court, which was no doubt one factor in their eventual destruction. After Harun returned from **pilgrimage** in 802, he had all of the Barmakids executed. The Barmakids were good administrators; they sponsored the arts and contributed to a revival of Iranian culture. But they had become too rich, powerful, and popular and were seen as a threat to Harun. A poet said in praise of the Barmakids: "The sons of Yahya are four in number, like the elements; when put to the test, they are found to be the elements of (which) beneficence (is formed)!" (Khallikan, IV, 105).

A memorial presented by an unknown person to Harun al-Rashid was said to have been instrumental in the destruction of the Barmakids. It stated:

> Behold, the son of Yahya has become sovereign like yourself; there is no difference between you! Your orders must yield to his, and his orders dare not be resisted. He has built a palace, of which the like was never erected by the Persian or the Indian (king). Pearls and rubies for its pavement, and the floor is of amber and aloes wood. We fear that he will inherit the empire, when you are hidden in the tomb. It is only the insolent slave who rivals his master in splendor.

Another reason given was that Harun married Ja'far to his sister al-'Abbasa, on condition that the **marriage** not be consummated. Al-'Abbasa intrigued to father a child with Ja'far, which greatly infuriated the caliph (Khallikan, trans. Slane, I, 301).

BASIJ RESISTANCE FORCE (Niru-yi Muqawamat-i Basij). A voluntary Iranian paramilitary force founded by Ayatollah Ruhollah

Khomeyni in November 1979. It was a vital factor in helping the revolutionary government consolidate its power. Also called Basij-i Mostaz'afin (The Mobilized Oppressed), the force performed the tasks of religious police, enforcing adherence to public morals as well as ideological conformity. It suppressed student protests and arrested individuals, some of whom were kept in secret prisons. The Basij takes orders from the Iranian Revolutionary Guard and, during the war with Iraq, engaged in human-wave attacks, which were costly in human casualties. It is a decentralized organization, present in virtually every Iranian town, and numbers as many as some 12 million or as few as 400,000. The force also includes **women**. It is easily mobilized in case of natural and political emergencies. *See also* IS-LAMIC REPUBLIC OF IRAN.

BASMALAH (BISMILLAH). A phrase that is invoked at the beginning of an action, translated as "in the name of God, the Merciful and Compassionate" *(bism' llah' ar-rahman' ar-rahim).* It is used at the beginning of a meal, when putting on new clothes, and when starting any new work. It occurs at the beginning of every **Surah** in the **Koran** except the ninth.

BASRA. An important Islamic city in present day Iraq, founded as a garrison town *(misr,* pl. *amsar)* in 638. It was a center of learning where renowned theologians, poets, grammarians, and historians flourished. Hasan al-**Basri** (642–728), Abu Bishr al-**Sibawayh** (d. 796), Abdullah Ibn al-**Muqaffa'** (720–757), and **Abu Nuwas** (753–813) resided in Basra. With the beginning of **Buyid** rule in the 10th century and the **Ottoman** conquest in the 16th century, the city lost much of its importance.

BASRI, HASAN AL- (HASAN-I BASRA, 642–728). A celebrated preacher, ascetic, scholar, and important traditionalist, he was born in **Medina**, the son of a slave, and was raised and educated in **Basra**. He personally met many of the **Companions** of the Prophet and was known for his uncompromising piety. He is said to have known all the branches of science and was noted for his self mortification, fear of God, and devotion. He presided over a circle of students who discussed the question of free will and **sin**. Some, later called the

Murji'ites (those who defer), felt that man had no right to judge sinners, that only God will make his merciful decision; their opponents held that a great sinner had become an unbeliever (**kafir**) and would be punished in hell. **Wasil ibn 'Ata'** stated that a grave sinner is neither an unbeliever nor a believer but occupies an intermediary position. Then he left and formed his own circle. Hasan al-Basri said Wasil withdrew (*i'tazila*), which became the name of the adherents of the **Mu'tazilite** school.

Hasan was claimed later as one of their own by the **Sufis**, orthodox **Sunnis**, and the Mu'tazilites. Hasan was quoted as saying: "I never saw a certainty of which there is no doubt, bear greater resemblance to a doubtful thing of which there is no certainty, than does death" (Khallikan, I, 370). He was described as the handsomest person in Basra until a fall from a horse disfigured his nose. Hasan died in Basra and, according to a contemporary report, "All the people followed the funeral and were so taken up with it, that no afternoon prayer was said that day in the **mosque**, for none remained in it to pray; this, I believe, was till then unexampled in Islamism" (Khallikan, trans. Slane, I, 372).

BAST. "Sanctuary." Persecuted individuals in **Iran** could escape arrest by taking refuge (*bast*) in a shrine or major **mosque**, or in the residence of a **mujtahid**. During the Iranian Revolution of 1905–1906, some 12,000 protesters took bast in the British embassy in Tehran, forcing Shah Muzaffar al-Din to grant the drafting of a constitution and the establishment of a parliament. However, on occasions a ruler has violated the sanctity of bast and has had a refugee arrested.

BATINITES (BATINIYYAH). A generic term for groups and **sects**, mostly **Shi'ites**, who distinguish the inner (*batin*) esoteric interpretation of the **Koran** and **Islamic law** from the outer (**zahir**), exoteric form. The esoteric doctrine consists of two main parts: the allegorical interpretation (**ta'wil**) of the Koran and the Traditions (**Sunnah**), and the truths (haqa'iq), a system of philosophy and science coordinated with religion. **Isma'ilis** and **Qarmatians** favored this interpretation and devised levels of initiation according to the comprehension of the believer. Among **Sunnis**, some **Sufi** orders also accept allegorical interpretation.

BATTANI, MUHAMMAD IBN JABIRE AL-HARRANI AL- (ca. 853–929).
Arab astronomer, astrologer, and mathematician who was born in Harran, near Urfa in present-day Turkey. The fihrist (catalogue) of **Ibn al-Nadim** describes him as

> one of the famous observers and a leader in geometry, theoretical and practical astronomy, and astrology. He composed a work on astronomy, with tables, containing his own observations of the sun and moon and a more accurate description of their motions than given by Ptolemy's "Almagest." In it, moreover, he gives the motions of the five planets, with the improved observations he succeeded in making, as well as other necessary astronomical calculations. . . . Nobody is known in Islam who reached similar perfection in observing the stars and scrutinizing their motions. Apart from this, he took great interest in astrology, which led him to write on this subject too: of his compositions in this field I mention his commentary on Ptolemy's Tetrabiblos. (www .groups.dcs.st-and.ac.uk/history/Biographies/Al-Battani.html)

He was a Muslim of a family of Sabian ancestry. Copernicus mentioned his indebtedness to Al-Battani. He was known in the West as Albateghius. His *Kitab al-Zij* (*On the Motion of the Stars*) was translated into Latin by Plato of Tivoli in 1116.

BATTLES. *See names of individual battles, for example,* BADR; CAMEL, BATTLE OF THE; TRENCH, BATTLE OF THE.

BATUTAH. *See* IBN BATUTAH.

BAY'AH. An oath of loyalty taken by the chiefs of tribes and notables in pre-Islamic times. It was adopted in Islam upon the election of **Abu Bakr** (632–634) and was subsequently taken upon the election of his successors. Once elected, Muslims owe obedience to the **caliph**, unless he commits a grave **sin** or becomes an **apostate**. The principle of leadership by election became accepted in **Sunni** Islam, although, in fact, dynastic succession was common. There exists no indication of the number of electors needed, and bay'ah came to be primarily a symbolic act.

BAYBARS I (r. 1260–1277). Sultan of the **Mamluk** (**slave**) dynasty, which ruled over Egypt and Greater Syria. As a commander of Amir

Qotuz, Baybars defeated the Mongol invaders in the Battle of **Ayn Jalut** in 1260 and saved the Near East from **Mongol** conquest. Sold as a slave to the **Ayyubid** sultan, he rose from the ranks because of his martial skills. He killed Sultan Qotuz and assumed supreme power. He continued the '**Abbasid caliphate** when he recognized a survivor of the 'Abbasid clan as the new caliph.

BAYHAQI, ABU'L FAZL (995–1077). Secretary to the **Ghaznavid** court and historian of the dynasty. Of his monumental work, the 30-volume *Mujalladat*, the extant portion covers the period of Mas'ud (1030–41), called *History of Masud (Tarikh-i mas'ud)*, or *History of Baihaqi*, and *Tarikh-i naseri*. Baihaqi was born in 995 in Baihaq, now Sabzawar in Farah Province of Afghanistan. He studied in Nishapur and became one of the most gifted and graceful writers of Persian prose. **Ibn Khallikan** quotes a contemporary, who said: "There was no follower of the Shafi'ite sect who was not under some obligation of al-**Shafi**, al-Baihaqi excepted; for al-Shafi was obligated to him" (Khallikan, trans. Slane, I, 57). He was imprisoned briefly for failing to pay a dowry to a former wife. For 19 years, he worked under Abu Nasr Mushkan, and he was head of the Ghaznavid secretariat for a brief time.

BAYT AL-HIKMAH. *See* HOUSE OF WISDOM.

BAZ, ABDUL AZIZ IBN ABDULLAH AL- (1911–1999). Grand mufti of Saudi Arabia and president of the Supreme Religious Council. A native of Riyadh, he went blind as a youth but continued his studies and served as a judge (1938–1952) until he became a professor of jurisprudence at the University of Riyadh (1953–1960). He advanced to the position of vice president of the University of **Medina** in 1961 and president in 1969. He was quoted as having said that the earth was flat, which he denies, saying "he only denied the earth's rotation." He opposed the stationing of non-Muslim troops in Saudi Arabia during the Gulf War, but he endorsed the Oslo peace accord between the Palestinian Liberation Organization (PLO) and Israel. He issued a **fatwa** forbidding **women** to drive and supported a petition that demanded, among other things, that Saudi Arabia end its close ties with the West. He became grand mufti in 1993.

BEARDS. According to a Tradition, the Prophet said: "Do the opposite of the polytheists, let your beards grow long and clip your mustache." This is recommended but not obligatory (**fardh**), but the neotraditionalist **Taliban** of **Afghanistan** enforced the growing of beards and other nonobligatory categories of human actions after they achieved power. *See also* FIVE PRINCIPAL ACTS IN ISLAMIC LAW.

BEKTASHI. A syncretic, heterodox **Sufi** order (*tariqa*) founded in Anatolia by Haji Bektash in 1337. According to **Ottoman** legend, Haji Bektash initiated the first contingent of the **Janissary** corps, and the order became closely associated with the Janissaries, the **pirs** serving as chaplains of its battalions. In the late 16th century, the grand master of the order became part of the force with the rank of Chorbaji (Soup Ladler), the equivalent to company commander. Although it eventually represented itself as an orthodox **Sunni** order, it was eclectic, assimilating **Christian** and **Shi'ite** elements. Its esoteric doctrines have been described thus:

> Each human soul is a portion of divinity which exists only in man. The eternal soul, saved by perishable mediums, constantly changes its dwelling without quitting the earth. Morality consists in enjoying the good things of earth without injury to any one, whatever causes no ill to a person is lawful. The wise man is he who regulates his pleasures, for joy is a science which has degrees, made known little by little to the initiated. Contemplation is the best of all joys, for it belongs to the celestial vision. (Edward Sell, *The Religious Orders of Islam.* New York: Routledge, 2000.)

It was said that members confessed their sins to their spiritual chiefs, and **women** participated unveiled in their religious rites. Celibacy was preferred by the higher ranks. In 1826, Ottoman **Sultan** Mahmud II destroyed the Janissary corps and abolished the Bektashi order. It revived in the latter part of the 19th century, to be again abolished, this time by Mustafa **Kemal** Atatürk in 1925, but it has continued to exist to the present day in Turkey, the Balkans, and especially in Albania, where it was widespread even under the communist regime.

BELIEVERS (MU'MINUN). Believers in Islam. A **Surah** in the **Koran** states: "Successful indeed are the believers, those who humble themselves in their prayers; who avoid vain talk; who are active in giving **zakat**; who guard their modesty, except with those joined to them in **marriage** bond" (23:1–6). *See also* FAITH, ARTICLES OF.

BERBERS. Indigenous population of North Africa, now primarily in Morocco and Algeria. Mostly sedentary, they now include also nomadic and seminomadic tribes. They were the dominant population in northwest Africa prior to the Arab conquest in the seventh century and resisted Arab domination for a long time. Eventually converted to Islam, they founded the **Almoravid** and **Almohad** dynasties. The Muslim invaders of the Iberian Peninsula were largely Berbers, headed by Tariq ibn Ziyad, after whom Gibraltar is named (Jabal al-Tariq, the mountain of Tariq). Conversion to Islam and cultural discrimination have led to the Arabization of some, but Berbers still make up 42 percent of the population in Morocco and 27 percent in Algeria.

BERRI, NABIH (1938–). Speaker of the Lebanese parliament since 1992 and leader of the **Shi'ite Amal** party since 1980. Born in Freetown, Sierra Leone, of Lebanese parents, Berri came to Lebanon and studied law at the Lebanese University and at the Sorbonne in Paris. In 1975, he joined the paramilitary organization of Amal, headed by Sayyid Musa al-**Sadr**. After the disappearance of Sadr in 1978, Berri advanced in the movement, and in 1980 he became chairman of Amal and the leading politician of Lebanese Shi'ites. He participated in the siege of the Palestinian refugee camps and fought **Hizbullah** in 1989, while at the same time conducting military operations into the Israeli-declared "Security Zone."

BID'AH. "Innovation," or deviation, from Islamic tradition. Anything that is new and contradicts the **Koran** and Traditions is sinful innovation. There are five categories of bid'ah. A good innovation is accepted if it is in conformity with Islamic teachings.

BILA KAYFAH. "Without questioning." The doctrine of literalism propagated by Abu 'l-Hasan al-**Ash'ari**, according to which religious dogma that has been generally approved by the leading **Sunni** schools should be accepted without further argument. This includes even seemingly anthropomorphist references to God in the **Koran**.

BILAL. A black slave who converted to Islam and was appointed by **Muhammad** to be the first **muezzin**, or caller to prayer. He was an Abyssinian slave, tortured by his master to recant his conversion but ransomed by **Abu Bakr**. He accompanied the Prophet on all his campaigns and died in the 640s. Bilal was described as tall, dark, and gaunt, with Negroid features and bushy hair. His grave in **Damascus** has become a place of **pilgrimage**.

BIN LADEN. *See* LADEN, OSAMA BIN.

BIRUNI, ABU RAYHAN AL- (973–1048). Chronicler, astrologer, astronomer, mathematician, and historian at the court of Mahmud of Ghazni. He accompanied the **Ghaznavid** ruler on his campaigns to India and studied Sanskrit and Indian philosophy there. He was one of the most profound and original scholars of medieval Islam. Born near Khiva, he was first at the court of the Khwarizm Shahs in Transcaspia and later was called to the court of Mahmud of Ghazni. He was a prolific scholar, said to have 103 finished and 10 unfinished works to his credit and, as tradition has it, his writings have exceeded a "camel-load." Translated into English are his *Chronology of Ancient Nations* (*Kitab al-athar al-baqiyah*), and *Description of India* (*Tarikh al-hind*) . Biruni died in Ghazni.

BISMILLAH. *See* BASMALAH.

BLACK MUSLIMS. *See* NATION OF ISLAM.

BLACK STONE. The Black Stone (*al-hajar al-aswad*) is a stone, possibly a meteorite, positioned in the eastern corner of the **Ka'bah**, a cubelike building that is the holiest shrine in Islam. According to tradition, the Stone was first placed in the Ka'bah by **Adam** and later again by the angel **Gabriel**. It is the object of veneration, touched by pilgrims during their circumambulations of the Ka'bah. The **Qarmatians**, a **Shi'ite** religio–political movement named after Hamdan Qarmat, invaded the **Hijaz** in 930 and carried off the Stone to their camp at al-Ahsa. It was not returned to the Ka'bah until 951. The Stone was broken into seven pieces and is now held together by a silver ring.

BLOOD MONEY. *See* DIYYAH; RETALIATION.

BOHRAS. Originally Hindus who converted to the **Isma'ili** branch of **Shi'ism** in the 11th century. They broke with the supporters of the **Agha Khan** and accepted the leadership of their "Absolute Preacher." The Bohra community of about one million is located in the Bombay area. There are also small **Sunni** Bohra communities in India and Pakistan. Another group of Bohras exists in Yemen.

BOOTY. *See* GHANIMA.

BRETHREN OF PURITY. *See* IKHWAN AL-SAFA.

BROTHERHOOD, MUSLIM. *See* MUSLIM BROTHERHOOD.

BUKHARI, MUHAMMAD IBN ISMA'IL AL- (810–870). Imam Bukhari was one of the great traditionalists who compiled one of the six books of **hadith**, titled *Sahih al-bukhari*, which has been called the most authoritative book after the **Koran**. A native of Bukhara (hence his name), he traveled to **Mecca** at age 16, spent six years in the **Hijaz**, and then visited the great cities in Syria and Iraq. He was said to have collected 600,000 hadith, but approved only 7,275. They were divided into such topics as **prayer**, **pilgrimage**, manners, commerce, medicine, and holy war (**jihad**). He was buried in Khartank, a village near Samarkand. Bukhari was described as "a lean-bodied man and of middle size"; he was quoted as having said, "I never inserted a **Tradition** in my *Sahih* till after I had made an **ablution**, and offered up a prayer of two rakas" (Khallikan, trans. Slane, II, 596).

BURAQ. The animal on which the Prophet is believed to have ridden on the **Nocturnal Journey**, called mi'raj, or ascent, from **Mecca** to **Jerusalem** and from there to **heaven**. The Archangel **Gabriel** brought **Muhammad** the white animal, the size of a mule, with a woman's head and a peacock's tail and two wings.

BURDAH. A cloak, especially the mantle of the Prophet, which, according to **Ottoman** claims, came into their possession and is now exhibited in the Topkapi Serayi.

BURIALS. *See* DEATH.

BURQA'. A veil and covering that encloses the entire body, worn by **women** in public.

BUYID (BUWAYHID) DYNASTY (932–1062). A Persian dynasty from Dailam on the southwestern shores of the Caspian Sea that ruled over Iran and Iraq from 932 to 1062. The **Shi'ite** Buyids entered **Baghdad** in 945 and dominated the **'Abbasid caliphs** for 110 years, but they did not depose them. Caliph al-Mustakfi (944–946) gave Ahmad ibn-Buwayh the title Mu'izz al-Dawlah and made him his commander (*amir a-umara'*), but Ahmad insisted on having his name mentioned in the Friday sermon (**khutbah**) and coins minted with his name as an act of his sovereignty. Under 'Adud al-Dawla (949–983), the dynasty reached its greatest power, but it was eventually eliminated by the **Ghaznavids** and **Saljuqs**, who restored orthodoxy and the dignity, if not the power, of the caliphs.

Muizz al-Dawla is said to have started the Shi'ite custom of commemorating the 10th of **Muharram** by holding a procession in Baghdad in 952. They promoted the feast of **Ghadir al-Khumm**, the appointment of **'Ali** as **Muhammad**'s successor, rebuilt Shi'ite shrines, and supported **Twelver Shi'ism** as equal to **Sunnism**. The Buyids also introduced the system of military feudalism, giving officers districts to tax in lieu of a salary. The Buyids were great patrons of the arts and sciences and contributed to a revival of Persian culture and **Mu'tazilite** doctrines. Buyid supremacy marked the low point in the 'Abbasid caliphate and contributed to a clear division in Sunnite and Shi'ite theology.

– C –

CADI (KAZI). *See* JUDGE.

CAIRO (AL-QAHIRA). The capital of Egypt (Misr), with a population of about 15 million. It is the largest city in Africa, located on the Nile River, about 170 kilometers south of the Mediterranean coast. Its general location was the site of such ancient cities as Memphis, about 5,000 years ago, and Babylon, dating back some 2,000 years. The nucleus of the modern city was Fustat, a garrison town (**amsar**) founded by **'Amr ibn al-'As** in 641. Cairo was founded slightly to the north by the Fatimid commander Jawhar in 969, and as the city grew it eventually incorporated the area of Fustat. The city became successively the capital of the **Fatimid** (909–1171) and **Mamluk** (1250–1717) dynasties, after which Egypt became part of the **Ottoman empire**. Napoleon's invasion of Egypt in 1798 brought Western influence into the area, which continued to grow under the dynasty of **Muhammad 'Ali** (1805–1848) and during the British occupation of Egypt (1882–1954). A military coup abolished the monarchy and established a government under military control, which continues to this day.

Cairo became one of the major intellectual centers of the Islamic world. The city is rich in architectural treasures, cathedral mosques, great fortresses, and Al-**Azhar**, the oldest existing university in the world. **Ibn Khaldun**, the famous Arab philosopher of history, taught there, as did Muhammad **Abduh**, the famous Muslim modernist. Under the regime of Gamal Abdul Nasser (1954–1970), Cairo became the center of Arab nationalism and, as a result of the founding of the **Muslim Brotherhood** by Hasan al-**Banna**, it became a center of the **Islamist movement**, which spread from there throughout the Islamic world.

CALENDAR. The Islamic calendar year begins with the **hijrah**, the emigration of **Muhammad** from **Mecca** to Yathrib/**Medina** on 16 July 622. It is divided into "lunar" years of about 354 days and is shorter than the Western "solar year"; therefore, the months do not coincide with the seasons. The first month, **Muharram**, is dedicated by **Shi'ites** to the commemoration of the martyrdom of **Imam Husayn**, the son of **'Ali**. It begins with the sighting of the new moon. Rabi' al-Awwal is the month of the Prophet's birthday. **Ramadhan** is the month of daylight **fasting**, and Dhu 'l-Hijja is the month of **pilgrimage**. The Muslim months have 29 or 30 days and are named as follows:

1. Muharram—the sacred month
2. Safar—the month that is void

3. Rabi' al-Awwal—the first of spring
4. Rabi' al-thani—the last of spring
5. Jamad al-Ula—the first dry month
6. Jama al-akhira—the last dry month
7. Rajab—the revered month
8. Sha'ban—the month of division
9. Ramadhan—the hot month
10. Shawwal—the month of hunting
11. Dhu 'l-Qa'da—the month of rest
12. Dhu 'l-Hijja—the month of pilgrimage

The days of the week in **Arabic** are counted from Sunday, First Day, to Thursday, Fifth Day; then comes **Friday**, the Day of Congregation (**Jum'a**), and Saturday, the Day of Sabbath (Sabt). In most Muslim countries, dates are shown using both the Islamic lunar year (qamari) and the Gregorian solar year (shamsi); for example, 1999 is equivalent to 1420/1421. *See also* FESTIVALS.

CALIPH (KHALIFAH). In **Sunni** Islam, the caliph was the successor of **Muhammad** in leadership of the Islamic community. (The **Shi'ites** use the term **imam**, and count only 'Ali as the legitimate successor of the Prophet and then count his descendants down to the Twelfth Imam.) The Sunnites accept the first four caliphs, the **Rightly Guided Caliphs** (*Rashidun*), as the legitimate successors of the Prophet. To qualify for the position, a caliph must be an adult Muslim man, sane, of sound mind and body, free, and a just person. He receives his power by nomination and election, but there is no indication of the number of electors and their qualifications. **Abu Bakr** was elected by a council of **Companions** of the Prophet, **'Umar** was nominated by the dying **Abu Bakr**, and **'Uthman** was appointed as a compromise candidate. In the beginning of the **Umayyad caliphate**, election was usually symbolic and, in fact, the dynastic principle predominated. Some scholars, like **Ibn Taimiyyah**, claimed that

with the orthodox caliphs ended the era of prophetic succession. After the prophetic caliphate there is mulk [kingship]—no longer the ideal form of government—but sovereignty belongs to the **Shari'ah**. That is cooperation of the **'ulama'** and the umara (amirs). (Qamaruddin Khan, *The Political Thought of Ibn Taymiyyah*. Islamabad, Research Institute, 1973)

But most Sunni schools accept the legitimacy of the **'Abbasid caliphate**, which ended with the **Mongol** conquest of **Baghdad**. The **Umayyad** caliphate continued in Spain during the early 'Abbasid period, and some accept the continuation of the 'Abbasid caliphate in Egypt until the capture of Egypt by the **Ottomans** in 1517. Ottoman rulers in the 19th century claimed that the last Abbasid caliph in **Cairo** had appointed Sultan Selim as his successor, and therefore, the caliphate continued until the defeat of the **Ottoman empire** in the First World War. It was abolished by the government of Kemal Atatürk in 1924.

Although usually respected and revered, the caliph had no power to make pronouncements on dogma. When caliphs made such prouncements in the middle of the ninth century, the jurists, **'ulama'**, reacted by proclaiming **Islamic law** complete and prohibited any legislation as sinful innovation (**bid'ah**). The caliphate was often weak, and during the **Buyid** occupation of Baghdad in the 9th and 10th centuries, it suffered the humiliation of being dominated by Shi'ite rulers. Eventually, the caliphs accepted the political realities and recognized secular rulers, the **sultans**, giving them the authority to legislate provided they did not infringe on the Islamic law (**shar'iah**). Some present-day **Islamist** and fundamentalist groups want to restore the caliphate and establish an Islamic state in which the shari'ah is the sole law.

CALIPHATE, CLASSICAL CONCEPT OF. Political philosophers have agreed that the caliphate is necessary and prescribed by the **shari'ah** and that the **caliph** (or **imam**) has to possess the necessary qualifications as well as the requisite military power. He is elected by those with the "power of loosening and binding" (**ahl al-hall wa 'l-'aqd**), but there is no agreement about the number of electors required. After accepting homage (**bay'ah**), the caliph assumes a contractual obligation to perform a number of functions, and Muslims are bound to obey him. According to al-**Ghazali**, even if he is a tyrant, he should be obeyed to prevent civil war.

As to the qualifications of the caliph, al-**Mawardi** gave the following: justice (*adalah*); knowledge (*'ilm*) of Islamic law and theology; sound sight, hearing, and speech; sound limbs; administrative competence (kifayah); courage and energy in war; and descent from

Muhammad's tribe, the **Quraysh**. The functions of the caliph include upholding religious orthodoxy, enforcing judicial verdicts, maintaining security, applying the **Koran**ic penalties for offenses, garrisoning the frontiers, waging holy war against infidels, collecting legally authorized tributes (*fay'*) and alms taxes (**zakat**), paying salaries and expenses, appointing trustworthy officials, and personally supervising governmental and religious business (*Nazihat al-muluk*, by Ghazali, tr. by F. R. C. Bagley). Al-Ghazali gives six physical and four moral qualifications: The former are adulthood, sanity, liberty, male sex, Qurayshite descent, and sound sight and hearing. The latter are military prowess, administrative competence, piety, and knowledge (Ibid., liii). *See also* BAQILLANI, ABU BAKR MUHAMMAD AL-; IBN TAIMIYYAH, AHMAD.

When the **'Abbasid** caliphs lost most of their power to the **sultans**, the concept of legitimate leadership was extended to include the "pious sultan," who was to have the same qualifications and functions. **Islamists**, who want to establish an Islamic state, envision the **amir** as conforming to this model.

Twelver Shi'ites consider the imams to be the only legitimate leaders of the community but accept the leadership of the highest clergy as the representatives of the **Hidden Imam**. Under Ayatollah **Khomeyni**, the concept of the guardianship of the highest Islamic jurist (*vilayat-i faqih*) was promulgated, establishing a theocratic state in Iran. *See also* 'ABBASID CALIPHATE; FATIMIDS; ISLAMIC REPUBLIC OF IRAN; UMAYYAD CALIPHATE.

CALL. *See* DA'WAH.

CALL TO PRAYER. "Adhan." The call to the five daily ritual **prayers** by the **muezzin** (*mu'adhdhin*) from the door of a **mosque** or from the top of a minaret of a large mosque. The muezzin chants the following formula, with some repetitions: "**Allah** is most great. There is no god but Allah. I testify that **Muhammad** is the apostle of Allah. Come to prayer. Come to salvation. Allah is most great. There is no god but Allah." At the morning prayer the words "prayer is better than sleep" are added. The **Shi'ites** add the words "come to the best work!" and also "I testify that Ali is the wali (protected friend) of Allah." **Bilal**, a black slave, was the first muezzin.

CALLIGRAPHY, ISLAMIC. A primary art form in the **Islamic** world due to the fact that pictorial representation is considered idolatrous and forbidden by most schools. Thus the various styles of script are used for ornamentation. In addition to the Kufic, angular script, major styles include the Naskh, Ruq'ah, and the Persian Ta'liq, Nasta'liq, and Shekasteh. There are also calligrams, figurative styles from **Shi'a** iconography, using the words "**Allah**," "**Muhammad**," "Bismillah," and others to depict various types of animals.

CAMEL, BATTLE OF THE. Named after the camel on which '**A'ishah** sat during a battle in 656 between '**Ali**, the fourth **caliph**, and a force led by 'A'ishah, wife of **Muhammad**, al-**Zubayr** ibn al-'Awwam, a cousin of the Prophet, and **Talhah** ibn 'Ubaydullah. The coalition was defeated, and Zubayr and Talhah were killed; 'A'ishah was captured and returned to Medina and restricted to honorable confinement.

CANON LAW. *See* ISLAMIC LAW.

CAPITAL PUNISHMENT. Capital punishment in Islam is in part under the principle of **retaliation** (*qisas*), equivalent of the *lex talionis* of the Mosaic law. The **Koran** says:

> O ye who believe! The law of equality is prescribed to you in cases of murder: The free for the free, the slave for the slave, the woman for the woman. But if any remission is made by the brother of the slain, then grant any reasonable demand, and compensate him with handsome gratitude. This is a concession and a mercy from your Lord. After this whoever exceeds the limits shall be in grave chastisement.

The doctrine says a life for a life and a tooth for a tooth, and is practiced especially in tribal society where the difference in blood debt is paid in blood money in various forms. In the case of individuals, the next of kin can decide to have the culprit killed or forgive the deed, with or without the payment of blood money. States have resorted to capital punishment in different ways: for treason/apostasy; terrorism; land, sea, or air piracy; rape; adultery, and homosexual behavior. Methods of punishment included beheading, hanging, stoning, and firing squads. Executions were usually held in public. In states in which the shari'ah is not enforced, only murder and treason are capital crimes.

CAPITULATIONS. An agreement of 1535 between Ottoman Sultan **Sulayman the Magnificent** and King Francis I of France, in which the sultan granted the "Franks" economic and social privileges. Ottoman citizens gained the same privileges in France, most of them Christian Armenians and Greeks. The name derives from the Latin "capitulo," chapter of the document, and not from the word "capitulation." French subjects were free to travel and trade freely in all parts of the **Ottoman empire.** French goods could be imported at low custom rates; French ships could enter Ottoman ports without paying the usual high fees; and French citizens would be subject to French, rather than Ottoman, laws. It was an agreement between equals, but eventually some 26 states gained the same preferential rights. European powers supported various sectarian and ethnic minorities and opened missionary schools. The system was greatly abused: some embassies sold passports to local merchants to enable them to avoid local taxation and gain a degree of extraterritoriality. The capitulations were one of a number of factors contributing to the bankruptcy of the Ottoman state.

CARAVANSERAI. Walled shelters on trade and pilgrimage routes to accommodate travelers, including their servants, animals, and merchandise. They were located within one-day's travel through deserts to protect the travelers from bandits or marauding tribes. They consisted of square buildings with high walls, accommodating the animals in the center and the travelers in individual rooms along the inside wall. Food, water, and other necessities could be obtained. With the construction of paved roads and motorized traffic, the need for traditional caravanserai has diminished.

CARRION. "Dead"meat, which it is unlawful to eat. *See also* FOOD.

CHADOR. "Tent," or portable dwelling. Also the traditional garment covering a **woman** from head to toe, which in some Muslim countries is obligatory. Wearing of the chador, also called chatri or **burqa'**, was prohibited in Turkey in the 1920s and in Iran in 1936, and it was discouraged in other Islamic countries, but agitation by radical elements has contributed to forcing a partial or complete reintroduction, for example in **Afghanistan**. *See also* VEIL.

CHARITIES. Almsgiving is one of the obligations for Muslims. It includes such practices as the **sadaqa** (righteousness), a voluntary donation, and **zakat** (purification), a **Koran**ic obligation, which is in effect a tax on a person's possessions. There is also the **waqf** (detention), a pious foundation, usually real estate, which is given to God in perpetuity. Like church property in the West, it is exempt from taxation.

In the 20th century, charitable foundations have been established on a worldwide basis to support the poor in the Islamic world. Oil-rich countries have contributed considerable funds for the construction of mosques and to sponsor Muslim communities in the West. Palestinians, among others, received foundation support, in addition to what they received from the United Nations and individual Western countries. Support was also given to fighters in the war against the communist regime in **Afghanistan**. As a result of the "war on terrorism," the American government declared some charity foundations fronts for terrorist organizations and banned their operation worldwide. The al-Haramain Foundation, operating internationally, was one of those banned, although charges were dropped by a federal judge.

CHILDREN. According to tradition, infants who die have a natural inclination to Islam and are therefore saved from hellfire. At the birth of a child, a **mulla** recites the adhan into the right ear of the child. The child is given a name on the seventh day after birth; and when it is able to talk, it is taught the **basmalah**. Children are exempt from **fasting** during **Ramadhan**, and they are not to be killed in battle. A mother has custody of her children in infancy, but the father has charge of them after that.

CHISHTIS (CHISHTIYYAH) (1142–1236). A **Sufi** order, named after Khwajah Abu Ishaq (d. 940) and Khwajah Muin al-Din Chishti. The latter was born in 1142 in Chisht, a village in Herat province in present-day Afghanistan, and died in Ajmir, India, in 1236. The

Chishtiyyah Order has most of its followers in India, where the tomb of the saint in Ajmir is an important place of **pilgrimage**. Originally the Chishtiyyah were a puritanical and pacific order, emphasizing the oneness of God (*wahdat al-wujud*) and invoking the names of God in their **dhikrs**.

CHRISTIANS. Islam recognizes Christianity as a revealed religion and Christ as a prophet, but not the son of God, and objects to what it considers accretions, such as the trinity and the refusal of Christians to accept Islam. The **Koran** (5:14) says: "From those too who call themselves Christians, We did take a covenant, but they forgot a good part of the Message that was sent them: so we stirred up enmity and hatred between the one and the other, to the **Day of Judgment**. And soon will **Allah** show them what it is they have done." The Koran accepts the immaculate conception of Christ by **Mary** (Maryam). **Christians** (as well as Jews and other monotheists) are **Peoples of the Book** (*ahl al-kitab*), with a revealed scripture, and they are not to be forcefully converted to Islam. A Muslim man can marry a Christian woman. In Islamic states, Christians are protected in their lives and religion, but pay a special tax (**jizyah**) and are usually exempt from military service. In the **Ottoman empire**, dhimmis, as they were called, were organized in autonomous communities (**millets**) and led by their patriarchs, bishops, or rabbis.

CIRCUMCISION, "Khitan." Practiced traditionally by the Arabs even before Islam, male and female circumcision is not mentioned in the **Koran**. The times for circumcision vary from the 7th to 40th day after birth to between 7 and 12 years of age. The **Malikite** school considers khitan meritorious, but not obligatory, whereas the **Shafi'ites** require it for both males and females. Circumcision was also considered a remedy for various diseases prevalent in the desert environment of Arabia. In parts of Africa, Southeast Asia, and the Arabian Peninsula, female circumcision is still practiced.

CIVIL LAW. *See* QANUN.

COFFEE. A beverage that was introduced into Yemen from Abyssinia and came to be widely accepted in the **Ottoman empire**. It was first the beverage of **Sufi** fraternities, who drank it as part of their ceremonies, and eventually coffee houses (*buyut al-qahwah*) were established in major towns and even in **Istanbul**, in spite of **'ulama'** opposition. When the Ottoman army had to withdraw from Vienna after an unsuccessful siege in 1529, they left some sacks of coffee beans behind. The Viennese experimented with the beans and eventually brewed a decent cup, which could be relished in the proliferating cafés of the city. Today, to offer coffee is part of Middle Eastern hospitality, but from Iran eastward, tea is the most common beverage.

COMMANDER OF THE FAITHFUL. *See* AMIR AL-MU'MININ.

COMMENTARIES ON THE KORAN. *See* EXEGESIS OF THE KORAN.

COMPANIONS. "Ashab" or "sahaba." The Companions of the Prophet were close associates of the Prophet, most importantly the first four **caliphs**, the contemporaries, and those who had seen him. Eventually anyone who had seen the Prophet or had come in contact with him came to be called a Companion; according to some biographers there were as many as 144,000. They are the transmitters of **hadith** who recorded the actions and sayings of the Prophet, constituting, together with the **Koran**, the core of **Islamic law**. Works listing the names and biographies of Companions were compiled to serve the task of evaluating the quality of a hadith. **Shi'ites** (except for **Zaydis**) do not recognize the legitimacy of the first three caliphs and accept only hadith from the Prophet and the **imams**.

CONCEALMENT. In **Shi'ite** Islam, discretion or concealment (*taqiyya* or *kitman*) is permitted under compulsion, threat, or fear of injury. The **Koran** allows denial of faith as long as one keeps believing in one's heart. **Surah** 16:106 says: "Any one who, after accepting faith in **Allah**, utters unbelief, except under compulsion, his heart remaining firm in faith—but such as open their breasts to unbelief on them is wrath from Allah, and theirs will be a threatful chastisement." Therefore, it is permissible also for **Sunnis**. *See also* GHAYBAH.

CONCUBINAGE. "Surriyah." As a result of war, **slavery** existed, and **women** were part of the spoils. Concubinage was inferred as permissible on the basis of **Surah** 23:5–6: "(The **Believers**) who guard their modesty, except with those joined to them in the **marriage** bond, or (the captives) whom their right hands possess, they are free from blame." Modernists maintain that it is forbidden because of the injunction that all males and females must be married. *See also* 'ABD.

CONSTITUTION OF MEDINA. *See* MEDINA, CHARTER OF.

CONSTANTINOPLE. *See* ISTANBUL.

CONVERSION. One converts to Islam by testifying before two witnesses that one believes there is only one God and that **Muhammad** is the Prophet of God. Orthodox consensus requires that six conditions be met to recite the word "kalima": It must be repeated aloud, it must be perfectly understood, it must be believed in the heart, it must be professed until death, it must be recited correctly, and it must be professed and declared without hesitation. The convert is then committed to the obligations of performing the five daily **prayers**, paying the poor tax (**zakat**), **fasting** during **Ramadhan**, and performing a **pilgrimage** to **Mecca** if he can afford it during his lifetime. The convert no longer pays the poll tax (**jizyah**); he usually adopts a Muslim name and enjoys all the privileges granted to Muslims.

A **hadith**, narrated by Abu Sa'id, says:

> If any person embraces Islam sincerely, then **Allah** shall forgive all his past sins, and after that starts the settlement of accounts: the reward of his good deeds will be ten times to seven hundred times for each good deed and a bad deed will be recorded as it is. (Bukhari, II, 1951, 32)

COPTS (QUPTI). Copts are the largest **Christian** community in the Middle East. They were the original Egyptians before the Muslim conquest in the seventh century and, although Arabized, they adhered to their Christian beliefs. They disagreed with the Byzantine church after the Council of Chalceton in 451 proclaimed the doctrine that Jesus had two natures, one human and one divine, and adhered to a monophysite interpretation that Jesus had only one divine nature. They have preserved Coptic, the original language of Egypt, as their liturgical language. Persecuted by the Byzantine church, they did not fight the Arab conquest and enjoyed a measure of religious freedom thereafter. Although they often held high government offices, they were at times subject to discriminatory treatment, and in recent times have suffered from attacks by **Islamist** groups. Boutros Boutros-Ghali, Egypt's acting foreign minister (1978–1979) and United Nations Secretary General (1992–1997), is a Copt.

CORDOVA. Capital of the **Umayyad caliphate** of al-Andalus, which reached the zenith of its greatness under Caliph **Abd al-Rahman** III (912–961). It was described as the most cultured city in Europe and, with **Constantinople** and **Baghdad**, one of the three cultural centers of the world. With its 113,000 homes; 21 suburbs; 70 libraries; and numerous bookshops, mosques, and palaces, it acquired international fame and "inspired awe and admiration in the hearts of travelers" (Hitti, 1964, 526). The Cordovan caliphate eventually collapsed in 1016 and was followed by petty states, a period that ended with the **Reconquista** of the Iberian peninsula.

COUNCIL OF EXPERTS. *See* ASSEMBLY OF CONSTITUTIONAL EXPERTS.

COVENANT. "Mithaq." The dominant opinion of commentators accepts that there is an implied covenant taken from the posterity of **Adam**, that is, humanity, which creates a spiritual obligation of obedience to God's commands. It is based on a **Koranic** passage (7:172) that says, "When the Lord drew forth from the children of Adam—from their loins—their descendants, and made them testify concerning themselves (saying) 'Am I not your Lord (who cherishes and sustains you)?' They said 'Yeah! We do testify! (This) lest ye should say on the **Day of Judgment**: Of this we were never mindful.'" According to tradition, the souls of **Muhammad**, **Noah**, **Abraham**, **Moses**, and **Jesus** were present at the Covenant.

A document called the "Covenant of 'Umar," in fact, an abstract of many letters, gives a description of the situation at about 800 CE of the **Peoples of the Book**. They were monotheists with a scripture and prophets recognized in Islam, like Moses and Jesus, and were in possession of a protective treaty, dhimma, which guarded their personal safety, property, and religion. They were relegated to second-class status and under obligation to pay a poll tax (**jizyah**). Dhimmis were not to be ostentatious in performing their religious performances, and not to be armed. In most parts of the Islamic world, non-Muslims now have equal citizen rights.

CREATEDNESS OF THE KORAN. Controversy over this issue led to acceptance in **Sunni** Islam that the **Koran** is uncreated and existed with God. *See also* ASH'ARITES; IBN HANBAL; MU'-TAZILITES.

CREATION. "Khalqa." Muslims believe that God created **heaven** and earth and all that is between them. According to Traditions, God created the earth on Saturday, the hills on Sunday, the trees on Monday, all unpleasant things on Tuesday, the light on Wednesday, the beasts on Thursday, and **Adam**, the last of Creation, after the afternoon prayer on Friday. **Surah** 41:9 reads:

> Say: is it that ye deny Him who created the earth in two days? And do ye join equals with Him? He is the Lord of (all) the worlds. He set on the (earth), mountains standing firm, high above it, and bestowed blessings on the earth, and measured therein its sustenance in four days, alike for (all) who ask. Then He turned to the sky, and it had been (as) smoke: He said to it and to the earth: come ye together, willing or unwillingly. So, He completed them as seven firmaments in two days, and He assigned to each heaven its duty and commands.

CREED. Aqida" (pl. Aqa'id). Belief in God, **angels**, **prophets**, **scripture**, and the **Day of Judgment**. Muslims believe in one God, **Allah**, who is the Creator, Supreme Power, Judge, and Avenger but is also the Compassionate and Merciful One. Angels are Allah's messengers and, like humans, his creatures and servants. **Surah** 4:136 says: "O ye who believe! Believe in Allah and His **Messenger**, and the scripture which He hath sent to His Messenger and the scripture which He sent those before (him). Any who denieth Allah, His Angels, His Books, His Messengers, and the Day of Judgment, hath gone far, far astray."

CRUCIFIXION. The **Koran** denies the crucifixion of **Jesus**: "That they said (in boast), 'We killed Christ Jesus the son of **Mary**, the

Messenger of **Allah'**; But they killed him not, nor crucified him. Only a likeness of that was shown to them" (4:157).

CRUSADES. A series of confrontations between the Christian West and the Islamic world that had a greater impact in the West than in the East. Historians have divided the confrontations into a period of conquest from the end of the 11th century to 1144; a period of Muslim reaction culminating in the victory of **Salah al-Din** (Saladin) in the Battle of **Hittin** (Hattin) in 1187; and a period of petty wars, ending in 1291, during which the crusaders were expelled from the Syrian mainland. It was a coastal affair that had little impact on the interior of the Islamic world. The First Crusade, proclaimed by Pope Urban II in 1095, was to liberate Jerusalem, which was accomplished by the end of the century. It was accompanied by a general massacre of the Muslim population, and the Kingdom of Jerusalem was created. The sacking of **Constantinople** in the Fourth Crusade (1204) contributed to weakening the Byzantine empire for Muslim conquest. Both the crusaders and the Muslims were divided into competing factions, and after local wars with not much impact, the 200-year Crusades came to an end.

– D –

DAHNA. The 10 days of **Muharram**, during which **Shi'ites** mourn the assassination of **Husayn**.

DAHRI. "Atheists;" or materialists, characterized in the **Koran** as saying: "What is there but our life in this world? We shall die and we live, and nothing but time (*dahr*) can destroy us" (14:24).

DA'I. Literally, "he who summons." The term was applied to **Shi'ite** missionaries or propagandists during the latter part of the **Umayyad** and **Fatimid** periods. The **Druzes** are named after Darazi, one of their da'is.

DAJJAL, AL-. "The deceiver." A false messiah or Antichrist who will come before the appearance of Christ to lead people into disbelief.

Sunnis believe that **Jesus** will destroy the Dajjal, and the **Day of Judgment** will follow. **Shi'ites** link his appearance as a precursor to the **Mahdi**. The Dajjal was described as a plump, one-eyed man with a ruddy face and curly hair and the letters k-f-r (kufr—unbelief) on his forehead.

DAMASCUS (DIMASHQ). Said to be the oldest inhabited settlement in the world and at present the capital of Syria. It was the seat of the **Umayyad caliphate** from 661 to 750. The city surrendered in 635 to Muslim forces under **Khalid ibn al-Walid** after a six-month siege. Khalid promised the residents protection (dhimma) and security for their lives, property, churches, and the walls of the city upon payment of a poll tax (**jizyah**). According to some sources, the Great Mosque of Damascus was for a time shared with the **Christians**. **Mu'awiyah** was appointed governor of the city, and in 661 he became the first Umayyad ruler at Damascus. With the establishment of the **'Abbasid caliphate**, **Baghdad** became the capital of the Islamic empire. Some **Sunnis** rank the city as the fourth holiest after **Mecca**, **Medina**, and **Jerusalem**.

DANCING. "Raqs." Dancing in Islam is a reprehensible act, *makruh*, but not expressly forbidden, *harram*, in the **Koran** or Traditions (**Sunnah**). In many countries, dancers are a caste, usually young men, who are often not native to the area in which they perform. Tribal and folk dances are performed in public on special occasions, such as weddings, when the participating men dance to the accompaniment of drums and various instruments. Female belly dancers perform in metropolitan areas in many parts of the Arab world. Only among the most Westernized do men and **women** dance together. Mystical orders perform ecstatic dances as part of their rituals. Radical **Islamists** or neofundamentalists, such as the **Taliban** rulers of Afghanistan, forbid dancing and **music**. This prohibition is deduced from a passage in the Koran that says: "Nor walk on the earth with insolence" (17:37). *See also* MEVLEVIS.

DAR AL-HARB. The "abode of war" is that part of the world in which Islam does not prevail. It can also be applied to a Muslim state that is under non-Muslim control, if the edicts of Islam are suppressed. After World War I, a movement in India proclaimed the state dar al-harb, and some 50,000 Muslims made the "**hijrah**" (emigration) to **Afghanistan**, which was an independent Muslim state. Muslim modernists do not accept this classification by the jurists, saying it has no basis in the **Koran** or Traditions. *See also* DAR AL-ISLAM; DAR AL-SULH.

DAR AL-HIKMAH. "House of Wisdom." A foundation established by the **Fatimid** ruler of **Cairo**, al-**Hakim**, in 1005 for the purpose of teaching and propagating **Shi'ite** doctrine. The dar al-hikmah, also called dar al-'ilm, House of Wisdom and Science, included a library with some 6,500 volumes, lecture rooms, and rooms for translation of manuscripts. It was connected to the palace. In addition to the Islamic sciences, its curriculum included astronomy and medicine. The library was headed by the Fatimid chief missionary (*da'i al-du'at*). The institution survived until the conquest of Egypt by the **Ayyubids** under **Salah al-Din** (Saladin, 1169–1193).

DAR AL-ISLAM. The "abode of Islam" defines that part of the world ruled by a Muslim and where the edicts of Islam have been fully promulgated. Non-Muslim monotheists were protected subjects (dhimmis), but not full citizens. They were protected in life and property and permitted to worship God according to their own customs. Certain restrictions applied to them, for example, the paying of a poll tax (**jizyah**). The Dar al-Islam is territorial, whereas the community of **believers** (**ummah**) is universal; it includes individual Muslims wherever they may be. *See also* DAR AL-HARB; DAR AL-SULH.

DAR AL-SULH. The "abode of truce" is that part of the world that is in a treaty or tributary relationship with the Islamic world (**dar al-Islam**). It originally applied to areas whose inhabitants had voluntarily surrendered to Muslim conquerors on the condition that they be allowed to retain their lands and practice their religion and customs. This category is not accepted by some schools, but Muslim modernists would apply this term to the entire non-Muslim world, implying an end to the obligation of perpetual warfare against the "abode of war" (**dar al-harb**).

DARAZI, MUHAMMAD IBN ISMA'IL AL- (d. 1019). Isma'ili missionary whose followers came to be known as the **Druzes**. Darazi was a Persian who entered the service of the **Fatimid Caliph al-Hakim** in 1017. He preached that the divine spirit, transmitted through '**Ali** and the **imams**, had become incarnated in al-Hakim. This caused a public riot, and Darazi had to flee from **Cairo** to Syria, where he was killed in battle (or was assassinated at the instigation of a rival). His teachings found acceptance in the mountains of Lebanon, leading to the creation of the Druze community.

DARWISH (DERVISH). A **Sufi**, religious mendicant, the Persian equivalent of a **faqir**.

DAUGHTERS OF THE PROPHET. *See* FATIMAH; RUQAYYAH; UMM KULTHUM; ZAYNAB BINT KHADIJAH.

DA'WAH. "Call." Appeal to conversion by missionary activity rather than by **jihad**. In modern times, **Islamists** call Muslims to accept their **fundamentalist** beliefs based on the **Koran** and early Traditions.

DA'WAH, HIZB AL-. "Islamic Call" Party founded in Iraq in 1969 in response to government suppression of **Shi'ite** political activity. A religious procession in 1974 resulted in political demonstrations, which were severely suppressed, and five of its leaders were executed. Da'wah militants tried to assassinate Tariq Aziz, the deputy premier, and, with the start of the Iran–Iraq War in September 1980, they began a campaign of sabotage and armed attacks. Eventually, Saddam Husayn's government was able to destroy them as a fighting force.

DAY OF JUDGMENT. "al-Yaum al akhir." Muslims believe in the resurrection of the body and the Day of Judgment, when God will reward or punish men according to their deeds. **Surah** 18:49 states: "And the book (of deeds) will be placed (before you); and thou wilt see the sinful in great terror because of what is (recorded) therein; they will say, 'Ah! woe to us! What a book is this! It leaves out nothing small or great, but takes account thereof!' They will find all that they did, placed before them: and not one will thy Lord treat with injustice." There will be a number of signs preceding the **Last Day**: the Antichrist (**Dajjal**) will appear, faith on earth will decline, there will be tumults and sedition, there will be commotion in heaven and earth, the sun and moon will be darkened, and Christ will appear to fight the Dajjal.

DEATH. Burial ceremonies include the ritual washing of the corpse, which is then enveloped in a shroud (**Shi'ites** permit a coffin); a ritual prayer is said for the dead, and the funeral service is performed. The corpse is buried with the head in the direction of **Mecca**. The **Koran** says: "Every soul shall have a taste of death: and only on the **Day of Judgment** shall you be paid your recompense. Only he who is saved far from the fire and admitted to the garden will have succeeded: For the life of this world is but goods and chattels of deception" (3:185). The Koran is silent about funerals, but according to **Tradition**, the dead are to be handled with respect and buried swiftly, and mourners are to refrain from excessive lamentation. According to a **hadith** transmitted by **Abu Bakr**, **Muhammad** said: "No prophet was ever buried except in the place where he died." Therefore, a grave was dug at the spot where Muhammad died" (*Muwatta*, trans. Doi, 16.10.27).

DELUGE. "Tufan." The story of the deluge is given in the **Koran**: "We, when the water (of **Noah**'s Flood) overflowed beyond its limits, carried you (mankind) in the floating (Ark), that We might make it a reminder unto you, and that ears (that should hear the tale and) retain its memory should bear its (lesson) in remembrance" (69:11–12).

DEOBAND. An Islamic college (*dar al-ulum*, later **madrasah**) was founded in 1866 in Deoband, a town near Delhi, India, by the Hanafi mystic Muhammad 'Abid. The Deobandis are strictly orthodox but accept the dogma of **intercession** and permit **prayer** at the tombs of prophets and saints to appeal for God's assistance. They are traditionalists and insist on following the law (**taqlid**), and reject independent reasoning (**ijtihad**) of the jurists to interpret **Islamic law**. The Deobandis were hostile to the modernism of **Aligarh** and, because many graduates supported the Shah **Wali Allah** reformist movement, they were called **Wahhabis** by their critics. They founded a political party, the Jami'at-i 'Ulama-i Islami, in Pakistan, which established hundreds of madrasahs in the tribal belt of the Afghan frontier. The students of these schools, many of them orphans, were provided free education, food, shelter, and military training during the war against the communist government of **Afghanistan** in the 1980s. These students later became the core of the **Taliban** forces that conquered most of Afghanistan. The Jami'at-i 'Ulama-i Islami and their Taliban brothers have now won followers in neighboring countries, who are spreading their **Islamist** ideology.

DEPUTATIONS, YEAR OF (630–631). After the fall of **Mecca** and the conversion of the **Quraysh**, tribal deputations from all over Arabia came to **Medina** to submit to the new predominant power and accept Islam.

DEVIL. The devil, Iblis, or Shaytan, in Islam is a fallen **angel** who refused to bow before **Adam** when commanded by God. For this he was expelled from **heaven** until the **Day of Judgment**, to be the "Adversary," tempting human beings to sin. *See also* IBLIS.

DEVOTEES OF THE PEOPLE. *See* FIDA'IYAN-KHALQ.

DEVSHIRME. A system of levying Christian boys in the **Ottoman empire** in the form of taxation for service in the Ottoman army and government administration. Boys 8 to 10 years old were periodically levied from Christian subjects in the Balkans, converted to Islam, and divided into two groups. The larger group was destined for military service, and the best intellectual and physical specimens were trained to be the **sultan**'s pages or to head administrative positions, including those of provincial governors and ministers (**viziers**) of government departments. This prevented the development of a hereditary aristocracy, as each generation of the sultan's slaves became members of the Ottoman ruling class. It was a practice contrary to the **shari'ah**, which considered monotheists protected citizens, dhimmis, who enjoyed a measure of cultural autonomy on payment of a special capitation tax (**jizyah**).

The Ottomans tried to rationalize the system by claiming that children have a natural inclination to Islam, and thus conversion was leading them to the true religion and salvation. Sons of the sultan's slaves were born Muslims and not qualified for service in the positions of their fathers. Because it was an avenue to social advancement, Christian boys became loyal protectors of the sultan. When, in the 17th century, Muslims were admitted to the administration, the devshirme system gradually declined. *See also* SLAVERY.

DHIKR (ZIKR). "Remembrance." In **Sufism**, dhikr is the remembrance of God, his commands, death, and the **Day of Judgment**. It is the recitation of a litany consisting of the glorification of the names of God, selections from the **Koran**, and special **prayers**. Dhikr may be performed in private meetings or mosques and involve rhythmical body movements and breathing techniques, while uttering the various formulas and names. Dhikr Allah, the Remembrance of **Allah**, is a striving for union with God, performed under the supervision of a master; it also includes dancing, in which the practitioners reach a state of ecstasy. Dhikr can be performed in a loud voice, or silently, when a person shuts his eyes, closes his lips, and fixes his attention on inhalations and exhalations, thinking *la ilaha* "there is no god" upon exhalation and *illa Allah* "except God" upon inhalation.

DHIMMI (ZIMMI). *See* PEOPLES OF THE BOOK.

DHU 'L-QA'DAH. "The master of truce" The 11th month of the Muslim year, because it was the month in which the Arabs abstained from warfare during the Jahilyya period.

DIN. "Religion." Muslim theologians distinguish between religious belief (iman) and acts of worship and religious duties (**'ibadat**), all of which are included in the term din.

DINAR. From *denarius* (Greek/Latin). The gold coin of the early Islamic period, weighing until the 10th century 4.25 grams. It was divided into 10 **dirhams** and later into 12. First copied by the **Umayyads**, the dinar was struck as an Islamic coin during the reign of Caliph 'Abd al-Malik (d. 705). The dinar is still the currency of some Middle Eastern countries.

DINAWARI, ABU HANIFA AL- (828–896). Botanist, historian, geographer, and mathematician, whose most famous work is the *Book of Plants* (*Kitab al-nabat*). He also pioneered a book on the ancestry of the Kurds (*Ansab al-akrad*), his own ethnic background. He was born in Dinawar, in present-day western Iran, and studied in Isfahan, **Kufah**, and **Basra**. His book on history, *Akhbar al-tiwal*, was translated into French.

DIRHAM. Monetary unit named from *drachme*, the currency in use in Greece, until it was replaced by the euro. It is a silver coin, originally of 2.97 grams (or 50 grains of barley with cut ends), later of varying value. Ten or 12 dirhams equaled the value of one gold **dinar**.

DITCH, BATTLE OF THE. *See* TRENCH, BATTLE OF THE.

DIVORCE. "**Talaq**." According to tradition, "with **Allah** the most detestable of all things is divorce" (Bukhari, VIII, 63). The various orthodox schools and **sects** disagree on the details, but generally a man can divorce his wife by repudiation, repeating three times, "I divorce thee," and a **woman** has the right to divorce under certain conditions that require dissolution by a court. If a husband is missing for four years, a woman can sue for divorce according to the **Malikite** and **Shafi'ite** schools of jurisprudence; **Shi'ites** agree with this period of time, but the Hanbali school favors a waiting period of 100 years, making divorce impossible. Divorce by mutual consent is immediately effective, and courts accept such grounds against the husband as impotence, **apostasy**, madness, and dangerous illness.

After repudiation, the man must wait for three menstrual periods to be certain that there is no pregnancy before the divorce is legal. During this waiting period, *'idda*, the man can relent his decision and his **marriage** remains legal. If a man divorces his wife three times, she has to be married to another man before he can marry her again: "So, if a husband divorces his wife (irrevocably) he cannot, after that, remarry her until after she has married another husband and he has divorced her" (2:230). Part, or all, of the dowry must be given the woman upon divorce, and women get custody of the children, in some cases until the age of seven and in others until puberty. In a number of countries in the Islamic world, divorce is possible only in a court of law (e.g., Turkey and Albania), but in most countries personal law is still under the jurisdiction of **Islamic law**, modified more or less to give women protection from certain abuses. Divorce is relatively rare, because marriage is often concluded within a clan; marriages of cousins are frequent, and alliances are formed through marriage. Therefore, a certain stigma attaches to divorce. *See also* LI'AN.

DIWAN. A word adopted from Persian for an anthology, financial register, or government department. The French word *douane*, customs, is derived from it. Under **'Umar** I (634–644), it was a register for the distribution of state income in the form of pensions paid to members of the early community according to closeness to the Prophet and early conversion to Islam. The allocations were as follows:

Those who fought at Badr (Dirhams)	5,000 Dirham
Those who were Muslims before al-Hudaybiyah	4,000
Muslims in the reign of Abu Bakr	3,000
Fighters at Qadisiyyah and in Syria	2,000
Muslims after Qadisiyyah and the Yarmuk	1,000
Various minor groups	500, 300, 250, 200
Muhammad's widows	10,000
Wives of men at Badr	500
Wives of next three classes	400, 300, 200
Wives of others and children	100
(Watt, 1974, 49)	

Under the **'Abbasids**, the term "diwan" was used for government departments, and under the **Ottomans**, it designated a council of court and eventually an administrative department of government. In literature, it means a collection of poetry of an individual.

DIYYAH. "Blood money." In pre-Islamic Arabia, blood money was to be paid in retaliation for injury or death. The principle became part of **Islamic law** as **retaliation** (*qisas*). The **Koran** says: "Life for life, eye for eye, nose for nose, ear for ear, tooth for tooth, and wounds equal for equal." But if anyone remits the retaliation by way of charity, it is an act of atonement for himself (5:45). This amounted to a recommendation for mercy, which did not exist in pre-Islamic times. Blood money is still demanded, especially in tribal areas of some parts of the Middle East. During their occupation of India, the British Indian government codified tribal law, including the blood money to be paid for injury or death. Examples are that the compensation for murder of a man was 3,000 rupees, half that amount for a woman; accidental death of a man was 1,550 and half for a woman. Cutting off a hand or a foot demanded a compensation of 1,000 rupees; breaking a hand or a foot or rendering an eye blind cost 500 rupees. Facial wounds demanded greater compensation than wounds covered by clothing.

In a tribal war, peace was possible when the casualties were equal; otherwise, the party with a blood debt had to pay the difference. Retaliation for murder could be forgiven if the next of kin agreed to accept blood money. This was often seen as dishonorable; therefore, blood money had to be paid secretly, and, if refused, the next of kin was permitted to kill the culprit. The amount of blood money also varied with the importance or wealth of a person, tribe, or community. In Afghanistan, the state had extended its jurisdiction into criminal law, but the **Taliban** regime enforced qisas as a public event.

Some **Shi'ite** schools counted six types of compensation: 100 camels, 200 cows, 1,000 sheep, 100 two-piece garments, 100 **dinars** in gold coinage, or 10,000 dinars in silver. The diyyah for a dhimmi or **slave** was less.

DOGS. Dogs are unclean animals, but hunting dogs are all right, and the game they catch becomes lawful food. There is some disagreement about this between various legal schools.

DOME OF THE ROCK. A shrine that stands on the rock of the Temple Mount in **Jerusalem**, from which the Prophet ascended to heaven in the **Nocturnal Journey** (*mi'raj*). The sanctuary was built during the period of **Umayyad Caliph 'Abd al-Malik** in the late seventh century and is part of the Al-**Aqsa** Mosque complex.

DÖNME. The followers of Shabbetai Tsevi (1626–1676), who proclaimed himself the messiah of Muslims and Jews. He went to **Istanbul** in 1666 to overthrow the **Ottoman sultan** and inaugurate his kingdom. Forced to convert, he adopted the name Mehmet 'Aziz Effendi, and many of his followers also adopted Islam, but they seemed to have secretly continued practicing Judaic rites. Their descendants were largely concentrated in Salonika, which had the largest Jewish community in the **Ottoman empire**. There is no evidence that they maintained their beliefs and practices. Many of the Young Turk leadership who fought **'Abd al-Hamid**'s absolutism were Dönmes, but they had assimilated with the Muslim Turks and rejected a return to Judaism.

DOWRY. *See* MAHR; MARRIAGE.

DRUZES. A religious community with a worldwide population of about one million, found primarily in Lebanon, Syria, and in smaller numbers in the Israeli-occupied Golan Heights. The Druzes are named after one of their early missionaries, Muhammad al-**Darazi** (d. 1019), who converted the early communities on Mount Lebanon, where most of them are still settled. They call themselves Unitarians (*muwahhidun*). The religion recognizes **Fatimid Caliph** al-Hakim ibn Amr Allah (r. 996–1021) at **Cairo** as a manifestation of God. Other missionaries included **Hamza ibn 'Ali**, who announced that al-Hakim had temporarily withdrawn from the world when he mysteriously disappeared. Baha al-Din al-Samuki succeeded after the disappearance of Hamza; he codified the new religious teachings in the six books known as *The Noble Knowledge* (*al-Hikma al-sharifa* or *rasa'il al-hikma*).

The Druze faith is exclusive and secret; therefore, accounts of the rites are unclear. Druzes do not accept two of the **Five Pillars of Islam**, **fasting** during **Ramadhan**, and **pilgrimage** to **Mecca**. In 1043, the "door of conversion" was shut, and no new converts were admitted. Although monotheistic like their Islamic origins, Druzes believe in the transmigration of souls, prohibit **polygamy** and temporary **marriage** (*'mut'ah*), practice dissimulation (taqiyya), and are known for their strict morality. They are divided into the "sages, *'uqqal*," who are initiated into the faith and are the leaders of the community, and the "ignorant, *juhhal*." Although at times considered heretics, they are accepted as **Peoples of the Book** by Muslims. In Syria and Lebanon, they have supported Arab nationalism and Palestinian rights and profess themselves to be Muslims. Druzes in Israel have served in the Israeli military. During its invasion of Lebanon, Israel missed a chance to win the support of the Druzes and **Shi'ites** in Lebanon.

DU'A. "Call." The individual, informal **prayer** that is offered on special occasions, for example, at the birth of a child or a visit to a grave. The Prophet described du'a as "the kernel of worship." According to a **hadith** transmitted by **'A'ishah**, the Prophet abstained from performing the du'a because of fear that the people would do the same and it would become obligatory (**fardh**) (*Muwatta*, trans. Doi, 9.8.32).

– E –

EDEN. "'Adn." Paradise. *See* HEAVEN.

EDUCATION. Classical Islamic education consisted of two levels: elementary (kuttab or maktab) and secondary (**madrasah**, "a place to study"). Education was informal, conducted at home, in a **mosque**, or in a building attached to a mosque. Elementary schools taught reading and writing skills; the textbook was usually the **Koran**, but writing was practiced from secular works, so as not "to dishonor the sacred book." Teaching included the **prayers** and rituals and simple arithmetic. Some students memorized the Koran and thus earned the title **hafiz**. In non-Arab areas, some Turkish and Persian poetry was memorized. Secondary education included the study of the Islamic sciences, the Koran, **hadith**, jurisprudence (**fiqh**), and ancillary fields, such as **Arabic** grammar, philology, etc. Philosophy and the rational sciences were not included, and medical studies were by apprenticeship. Students attended the lectures of a teacher, who would certify that a certain course had been completed, and he could then teach the subjects he had mastered. He would have a license (*ijaza*) to answer juridical questions. It would read like the following:

> The most eminent, unique, learned lawyer . . . read with me the whole of *al-muhadh'dhab* in law with all proofs from the Koran and Sunna and, where there are no proofs, the meaning, correct reading, and implications of the text, the agreement, the adductions and extension of it so that he is worthy that advantage may be taken of him and may be handed on by his teaching. (Szyliowicz, *Education and Modernization in the Middle East*, 1973, 61)

Graduates would travel to various cities to collect hadith and to study with noted Islamic scholars. Higher education produced the **'ulama'**, Islamic functionaries, the **judges**, **muftis**, etc. A distinction was usually made between the Islamic and foreign sciences. The former consisted of Koranic **exegesis** (*'ilm al-tafsir*), the science of hadith (*'ilm al-hadith*), jurisprudence (*fiqh*), scholastic theology (*ilm al-kalam*), grammar (*nahw*), lexicography (*lugha*), rhetoric (*bayan*), and literature (*adab*). Foreign sciences included philosophy (*falsafa*), geometry (*handasa*), astronomy (*ilm al-nujum*), music (*musiqi*), medicine (*tibb*), and magic and alchemy (*al-sihr wa 'l-kimiya*).

Special buildings for education, madrasahs, were first erected in the 10th century; they included living quarters for students. Education was free and informal. The first Islamic universities were the Fatimid Al-**Azhar** at **Cairo** (972) and the 11th-century **Sunni Nizamiyyah** at **Baghdad**, which became models for educational institutions elsewhere. During the **Ottoman** period, the classical system continued, reaching its height by the 17th century. The medieval secretary (*katib*) needed, in addition to a natural gift for expression and a general knowledge of everything (*adab*), eight kinds of tools: "1) a thorough knowledge of Arabic, accidence and syntax, and 2) of lexicography and the distinctions between eloquent, obsolete, unusual, etc., expression; 3) an acquaintance with proverbs and *ayyam* (war) tales of the Arabs and with other incidents current among the people; 4) a wide reading in prose and poetry of early authors and a memorization of a great deal of their work; 5) a solid knowledge of political theory and the science of administration, 6) knowledge by heart of the Koran and 7) of the traditions issuing from the Prophet; and 8) command of prosody and poetics" (Von Grunebaum, 1956, 253–254).

Modern reforms in the Islamic world began as a reaction to Western imperialism. **Muhammad 'Ali** of Egypt and Ottoman **sultans** felt a need to modernize their armies and began to introduce reforms along European lines. In the early 19th century, foreign teachers were imported and native students were first sent abroad to study in Europe. Military academies and medical and administrative colleges were established, resulting in the beginning of a dual educational system: the traditional and the modified modern system, which trained different elites competing for government positions. This educational dualism exists in most parts of the Islamic world today.

In the 18th and 19th centuries, missionary schools were established in the Middle East that provided education in Arabic and local languages. Some of their textbooks and curricula were gradually adopted by local schools. American missionaries founded the Syrian Protestant College in 1866, which eventually became the American University of Beirut, and French Jesuits founded the St. Joseph University in Beirut in 1875. Other European powers established schools. Local authorities established schools and teachers' colleges (*dar al-ulum*), but by 1939 there were fewer than a dozen colleges in the Middle East. Only after World War II did higher education, patterned after Western models, greatly expand. By the 1980s, there were about 100 colleges and universities in the Middle East.

EGYPT. *See* CAIRO.

ELIJAH MUHAMMAD (1897–1975). Leader of the **Nation of Islam**, which transformed itself into one of the most powerful Afro-American organizations. Born Paul Robert Poole in 1897 in Georgia, Elijah Muhammad moved to Detroit in the 1920s, where he came under the influence of Fard Muhammad and succeeded him in the leadership of the early Muslim community. He successfully reformed thousands of Afro-Americans in the ghettos and won notable converts in the persons of Malcolm X and Muhammad Ali. Wallace (Warith) Deen Muhammad, son of Elijah, assumed leadership of the movement and made the transition to orthodox Islam, calling the movement "The American Muslim Mission."

EMIGRANTS. *See* MUHAJIRUN.

EMIGRATION. "Hijrah." The flight of **Muhammad** from **Mecca** to Yathrib (**Medina**) on 16 July 622. It marks the date from which Muslims count the Islamic **calendar**.

EMIR. *See* AMIR.

ENJOINING THE GOOD AND FORBIDDING EVIL. One of the obligations of every Muslim, based on the **Koran** (22:41, *al-amr bi 'l-ma'ruf wa an'n-nahy 'an al-munkar*), which became institutionalized in offices like the **Muhtasib**. In some Arab Gulf countries, this institution is still practiced, and in the newly established "Islamic states," such as Iran and **Taliban Afghanistan**, a ministry employs guardians who ensure that **women** are properly attired, people attend ritual prayers, and public morality is enforced. *See also* ISLAMIC REPUBLIC OF IRAN.

ERBAKAN, NECMETTIN (ARBAKAN NAJM AL-DIN, 1926–). Turkish **Islamist** and prime minister (1996–1997), who led his Refa party to victory in municipal elections in 1994–1995 and won the position of prime minister in parliamentary elections in 1996. Because of his policy of re-Islamization, which went counter to **Kemalist** principles, he was forced to resign. *See also* ERDOGAN, RECEP TAYYIP.

ERDOGAN, RECEP TAYYIP. Prime minister of Turkey since March 2003, he is an **Islamist** turned pro-Western conservative. He showed himself a good administrator and was responsible for improving **Istanbul**'s infrastructure and beatifying the city. When his Justice and Development Party gained power in November 2002, a stand-in prime minister had to serve until legislation permitted him to assume the position. He was barred from standing in elections because of a conviction in 1998 for "inciting religious hatred" when he recited a poem stating "The mosques are our barracks, the domes our helmets, the minarets our bayonets, and the faithful our soldiers." Once elected prime minister, he claimed to be in favor of membership in NATO and desirous of entering the European Union (EU). He visited Greece in May 2004 and won a promise from his Greek counterpart that Greece would support aTurkish bid for European Union membership. Erdogan was born in a village in northern Turkey and went with his family to Istanbul in 1967. He attended an Islamic school before graduating in management from Istanbul's Marmara University. He is a charismatic politician from a poor background and enjoys great popularity among the masses, although secularists still do not quite trust him.

EVE (HAWWA). Wife of **Adam**, created from his rib. She is the mother of Cain, Abel, and Seth. When driven from paradise, according to tradition, Eve was united with him in the valley of **'Arafat** near **Mecca**.

EVIL EYE. "Isabat al-'ayn." The common belief that certain individuals have the power of looking at people, animals, and inanimate objects to cause harm. It has existed since pre-Islamic times, and the **Koran** warns to seek refuge "from the mischief of the envious one as he practices envy" (113:5). Talismans and images with an eye are used to ward off the evil eye. An **amulet** may read as follows: "O **God**, tear forth his eye who would curse therewith, snatch the evil thought from his forehead and the word from his tongue. Let his mischief fall upon his own head, upon his goods and on those most dear to him" (Canon Sell, 64). According to a **hadith**, the Prophet permitted the use of talismans to ward off the evil eye (Muwatta, trans. Doi, 50.2.3)

EXCOMMUNICATION. "Takfir." Modern radical revivalist movements demand excommunication of Muslims who have been lax in the performance of the ritual obligations of **Islam** and have accepted a measure of secularism. They oppose Muslim rulers as **apostates** because they have permitted Islamic lands to fall into a condition of jahiliyyah (ignorance of the true mission of Islam). The movement calls for the establishment of an Islamic state in which all manifestations of Westernization are abolished and the **Islamic law** (Shari'ah) is the only law of the state. It tries to mobilize the masses to accept its purist concept of Islam and proclaims holy war (**jihad**) against its enemies. Some **Islamist** movements, for example, **Takfir wa al-Hijrah**, demand that the **believers** make the migration to an Islamic community or state. In their radicalism and **fundamentalist** beliefs they resemble the **Kharijites**, who proclaimed that all Muslims who did not make the migration (**hijrah**) to their camp were infidels.

EXEGESIS OF THE KORAN. "Tafsir." Abdallah ibn al-'Abbas (d. 686) is said to have been the first to write a commentary on the **Koran**, but **Muhammad** had already provided verbal explanations. As time passed, difficulties had to be explained, and eventually commentaries examined philological, historical, and juridical questions. In addition to literal interpretation, some **Shi'ites** (and **Sufis**) focused on an allegorical interpretation. An extensive **Sunni** tafsir literature exists, produced by such scholars as Al-**Tabari** (d. 923), Fakhr al-Din Radhi (**Razi**, d. 1209), Ibn Kathir (d. 1373), Al-**Suyuti** (d. 1505), and the Shi'ite al-Tabarsi (d. 1153). Modern authors who published exegetic works are Muhammad **Abduh** (d. 1905), Rashid **Ridha** (d. 1935), and the **Islamist** Sayyid **Qutb** (d. 1966). Recent authors have tried to show that even the most recent technical innovations were predicted in the Koran.

EXTINCTION. *See* FANA'

– F –

FADLALLAH, MUHAMMAD HUSAYN (FAZL ALLAH, 1935–). **Shi'i** religious scholar and spiritual leader of the Lebanese **Hizbullah** (Party of God). Born of a Lebanese family in **Najaf**, Iraq, he was educated at the Shi'ite university at Najaf. He went to Lebanon in 1966 and established cultural youth clubs, free clinics, and community centers to attract youth to religion. He was inspired by the Islamic revolution in Iran and in 1982 became Hizbullah's spiritual leader. He participated in a council that drafted the Lebanese Islamic Constitution, but he had reservations about giving autocratic power to an individual. Nor did he want to reestablish the **caliphate**. Although not participating in any violent actions, he did not rule out the possibility of violent revolution and was suspected of supporting military activities. He supports equal rights for **women** but favors Islamic dress, which leaves only the face and hands free. An assassination attempt on 8 March 1985 did not kill him, but leveled an apartment building and a cinema and killed 80 people. Fadlallah is married, with 11 children.

FAITH, ARTICLES OF. "Iman." The doctrine in Islam that includes: the belief in God (**Allah**), **angels**, **prophets**, **scripture**, the **Last Day**, and the Divine Decree. A passage in the **Koran** says: "O ye who believe! Believe in Allah and his **Messenger**, and the scripture which He hath sent to his messenger and the **scripture** which he sent to those before (him). Any who denieth Allah, His angels, His books, His messengers, and the **Day of Judgment**, hath gone far, far astray" (4:136).

Belief in Allah is expressed in the shahada, or profession of faith: "There is no god, but Allah" (*la ilaha illah llah*). Allah has 99 "**beautiful names**," most important of which are *al-rahman al-rahim*, "The Compassionate, The Merciful." All **Surahs** of the Koran, except the ninth, begin with the **basmalah**, "In the name of Allah, Most Compassionate, Most Merciful." Allah has neither beginning nor end, he has knowledge of all things, he is almighty, he has hearing, sight, and speech. Most important is the oneness of God; it is a great offense to give partners to God. God is eternal, and everything from the seven heavens downward is created by him. God reveals himself in the Koran, and to understand Him, one must ponder the Koran in its entirety. He is utterly transcendent and yet nearer to man "than his jugular vein."

Angels have specific activities. They praise Allah and are His messengers, guardians of the Koran in **heaven**, guardians of man, recorders of man's deeds, receivers and punishers of sinners, and guardians of **hell**. They are made of fire. The jinn are like man, good and evil, and will be judged like man. They differ from man in that they are created of fire rather than clay. The rebellious jinn are **devils** (*shaytan*), and the fallen angel (**Iblis**) is their chief.

Great Prophets include **Adam**, God's chosen one; **Noah**, God's preacher; **Abraham**, God's friend; **Moses**, speaker with God; **Jesus**, God's spirit; and **Muhammad**, God's messenger and last prophet. Muhammad is merely a man and has no superhuman powers. The **Shi'ites** believe that he had a special **barakah**, and that his descendants, the **imams**, were infallible.

Scripture (*kitab*) comes to man through his messengers. The Koran is the word of Allah to Muhammad; Moses received the Torah (*tawrat*), David the Psalms (**zabur**), and Jesus the Gospel (**injil**).

Resurrection and the Last Day are preceded by a number of signs: the **Dajjal** (Antichrist) will appear; faith on earth will decline; tumults and sedition will occur; there will be commotion in heaven and earth; and the sun and moon will be darkened, leading to the second advent of Christ. The archangel **Israfil** will sound the trumpet, and Allah will appear. Then follows the weighing of the deeds, at which the archangels **Gabriel** and Michael will preside, and everyone crosses a narrow bridge from which the infidels will fall into hell. The only sure way of going to paradise is to be a **martyr** for the faith. Others must repent and believe and be righteous in their actions.

The fifth article of belief is the "divine decree and predestination" (*al-qadha wa 'l-qadar*), which recognizes the absolute power of God but does not exclude a measure of free will. Al-**Ash'ari** has tried to resolve this question with the mechanism of "acquisition" (**kasb**), according to which God creates the actions of his creatures, but they are then acquired by the individual. *See also* FIVE PILLARS OF ISLAM.

FAKIR. *See* FAQIR.

FANA'. "Extinction," when everything will perish on the **Last Day**. In Islamic mysticism, it is the last stage of the journey, the passing away from the self, the union with God. *See also* SUFI(ISM).

FAQIH. A jurist (pl. fuqaha), interpreter of Islamic jurisprudence (**fiqh**). The *fuqaha* function as **judges**, jurisconsults, and **muftis**, giving legal opinions (**fatwas**). The institution of the faqih became important in the 10th century, but it later lost its importance in parts of the Islamic world, where the traditional system was supplanted by European codes and courts. In the **Islamic Republic of Iran**, the principle of the guardianship of the jurisprudent (**vilayat-i faqih**) over all spiritual and temporal authority of the state was proclaimed by Ayatollah **Khomeyni**.

FAQIR. "Poor." In **Arabic**, it is the designation of a religious mendicant, also called **darwish**. In the West, the term has been applied to a public performer or magician.

FARABI, ABU NASR MUHAMMAD AL- (ca. 870–950). One of the greatest Muslim philosophers, who published in the fields of logic, politics, ethics, natural science, psychology, mathematics, music theory, and other subjects. He was of Turkic origin, born in Farab, Turkestan, and studied in **Baghdad** and other cities of the Islamic world, finally settling in Aleppo, Syria. He tried to create a synthesis of Platonic and Aristotelian philosophy and **Sufism** and aimed at the reconciliation of philosophy and religion. Called the "Second Master" (next to Aristotle), his major works include the *Epistles on the*

Gems of Wisdom (Risalat fusus al-hikam), *Opinions of the People of the Model State (Risalat fi ara ahl al-madinah al-fadhila)*, and *Political Economy (al-Siyasah al-madaniyah)*, among others.

Ibn Khallikan writes of him that

> he excelled all the people of Islamism and surpassed them by his real acquirements in that science; he explained its obscurities, revealed its mysteries, facilitated its comprehension and furnished every requisite for its intelligence, in works remarkable for precision and style and subtlety of elucidation. (III, 308)

FARAJ, ABU AL-. *See* ISFAHANI, ABU AL-FARAJ AL-.

FARAZDAK, HAMMAM IBN GHALIB AL- (640–728). A native of **Basra** and one of the great poets of the **Umayyad** period. A contemporary of al-**Jarir** and al-**Akhtal**, he was a bitter rival of Jarir and tended to be supported by Akhtal. He was described as "reckless, dissolute, and thoroughly unprincipled," and apart from his gift of vituperation, "there was nothing in him to admire" (Nicholson, 1962, 243). His panegyrics of the 'Alids and lampoons of important individuals resulted in his banishment and flight. Farazdak tricked Nawar, his cousin, into **marriage**, only to **divorce** her soon afterward, a step he bitterly regretted, and "the repentance of Farazdak" became a proverbial expression.

FARDH (FARZ). A religious duty (pl. *fara'idh*) enjoined in the **Koran**, the performance of which is incumbent on all Muslims. Fulfillment of such a duty is rewarded and neglect is punished. In the Hanafi school, a distinction is made between fardh as a "duty on the basis of cogent arguments" and **wajib**, necessity, on the grounds of probability. *Fardh al-'ayn* is an individual duty, binding on all adult Muslims, such as **prayer** and **fasting**. *Fardh al-kifaya* is a communal duty, binding on the Muslims as a group, which is fulfilled if a sufficient number perform it, for example, making a **pilgrimage**, visiting the sick, and returning a greeting.

FAREWELL PILGRIMAGE. *See* PILGRIMAGE, FAREWELL.

FARRAKHAN. *See* NATION OF ISLAM.

FASTING. "Sawm." Daylight fasting is obligatory during the 30 days of the month of **Ramadhan**. The **Koran** enjoins: "[Fasting] for a fixed number of days; but if any of you is ill, or on a journey, the prescribed number (should be made up) from days later" (S.2:184). Voluntary fasting is recommended on various occasions, especially on the 10th of the month of **Muharram**, the month of Sha'ban, on alternate days, etc. According to a **Tradition**, the Prophet said: "Every good act that a man does shall receive from ten to seven hundred rewards, but the rewards for fasting are beyond bounds, for fasting is for God alone, and He will give the rewards." Fasting includes refraining from drink or sexual intercourse, the inhaling of tobacco smoke, and swallowing of spittle that could have been ejected. It begins at daybreak, when one can distinguish a white from a black thread. The end of fasting is generally announced by the firing of a cannon.

FATALISM. Impressed by the omnipotence of God, al-**Ash'ari** rejected free will and all causality as limiting the powers of God, hence contributing to a tendency toward fatalism in Islam. He quotes the **Koran**ic saying: "Nothing will happen to us except what **Allah** has decreed for us" (9:51). But another **Surah** says: "Whatever good (O man!) happens to thee is from Allah; but whatever evil happens to thee, is from thyself " (4:79). Al-Ash'ari reconciled this with the doctrine of acquisition (**kasb**). *See also* KISMET; PREDESTINATION.

FATIHA. The "opener," or first **Surah** in the **Koran**, is part of the Muslim **prayer**. It can be translated as follows: "In the name of **Allah**, Most Gracious, Most Merciful, Praise be to Allah the Cherisher and Sustainer of Worlds: Most Gracious Most Merciful; Master of the **Day of Judgment**. Thee do we worship, and Thine aid we seek. Show us the straight way, the way of those on whom Thou hast bestowed Thy Grace, those whose (portion) is not wrath. And who go not astray" (1:1–7).

FATIMAH. Daughter of the Prophet and **Khadijah**, she married **Muhammad**'s cousin **'Ali ibn Abi Talib** at Medina in 624. Because he was poor, 'Ali gave his coat of mail (or a sheepskin) as a dower; it was worth four **dirhams**. They had two daughters and three sons, **Hasan**, **Husayn**, and Muhsin; the latter died in infancy. Their descendants through Husayn are revered by **Twelver Shi'ites** as infallible **imams**, whereas Sunnites count 'Ali as the fourth of the **Rightly Guided Caliphs**. For Muslims, Fatimah is the example of the virtuous **woman**; she died around 633 at age 29. The founders of the **Fatimid** caliphate claimed descent from 'Ali and Fatimah.

FATIMIDS (909–1171). An **Isma'ili Shi'ite** dynasty, claiming 'Alid descent through **Fatimah**, which ruled **Egypt** and parts of North Africa, as well as Syria, the Holy Places of **Mecca** and **Medina**, and for a short time even extended their power to **Baghdad** and Sicily. **Sunni** opponents deny their link to Fatimah and call them 'Ubaydiyun, the descendants of 'Ubaydallah al-Mahdi (909–934), the first of the Fatimid rulers. They established their capital at **Cairo** in 969 and founded **Al-Azhar** University as an Isma'ili research center. Under the rule of al-**Hakim** (996–1021), the Fatimids sent their missionaries to distant lands. One of them, Muhammad al-**Darazi**, converted the **Druze** community in Lebanon, which still carries his name. A Persian Isma'ili, **Hasan al-Sabbah**, visited Cairo and then established a base in **Alamut**, founding the Order of the Assassins. The Fatimids were finally replaced by the Sunni **Ayyubid** dynasty of **Salah al-Din** (Saladin).

The Fatimid dynasty included the following members:

909 Ubaydullah al-Mahdi	1036 Al-Mustansir
934 Al-Qaim	1094 Al-Must'ali
946 Al-Mansur	1101 Al-Amir
953 Al-Mu'izz	1130 Al-Hafiz
975 Al-'Aziz	1149 Al-Zafir
996 Al-Hakim	1154 Al-Fa'iz
1021 Al-Zahir	1160–71 Al-Adid

FATWA (FETVA). A formal legal opinion by a **mufti**, or canon lawyer, in answer to a question of a **judge**, *kadhi*, or private individual. Fatwas cover legal theory, theology, philosophy, and creeds, which are not included in **fiqh** books. Fatwas are informational and advisory and generally are not enforced by the state. Until the 19th century, the **Ottoman empire** maintained a hierarchy of muftis, headed by the grand mufti of **Istanbul**, who held the title **Shaykh al-Islam**. He had the function of certifying the legality of secular laws, *qanun*, issued by the government, and appointed muftis to the major towns in the empire. **Muhammad Abduh**, grand mufti of Egypt, issued a number of liberal fatwas, and the grand mufti of **Jerusalem**, Amin al-**Husayni** (b. 1890s) issued fatwas opposing the British mandatory power over Egypt and the Zionist movement. In most Muslim countries, fatwas were relegated to personal law, such as **marriage** and **divorce**, when the state extended its jurisdiction into criminal and civil law. Famous fatwas from **Shi'ite** Iran were the prohibition of smoking, which led to the "Tobacco Revolt" of 1891, and the fatwa issued by Ayatollah Ruhollah **Khomeyni** in 1989, calling for the execution of Salman Rushdie for blasphemy for publishing the book *The Satanic Verses*.

FAY'. *See* GHANIMA.

FESTIVALS. Islamic festivals include **Shi'ite** and **Sunni** observances of **'Ashura**, the 10th of the month of **Muharram**, the Prophet's birthday ('id al-milad al-nabi), the Breaking of the Fast (**'id al-fitr**) in the month of **Ramadhan**, **Muhammad**'s Ascension (laylat al-mi'raj), fasting (sawm) during the month of Ramadhan, and the Feast of Sacrifice (**'id al-adha**). Muslims exchange presents and give gifts to their servants and the poor.

FIDA'I (pl. FIDA'IYAN). One who sacrifices his life, a guerrilla soldier. Various religio–political movements adopted this designation, such as the devotees of the grand master of the **Assassins**, the **Fida'iyan-i Islam**, and the **Fida'iyan-i khalq** of Iran. In the 1950s, the term designated guerrilla fighters against the British forces in Egypt and later Palestinian guerrilla fighters who conducted raids against Israel.

FIDA'IYAN-I ISLAM (FIDA'IYYUN). A **Shi'ite** religio–political movement founded in 1945 in Tehran by Sayyid Mujtaba Navvab Safavi (1923–1956). The Fida'iyan (Devotees) were a radical movement that wanted to establish a government guided by **Islamic law**. Navvab had the support of Ayatollah Abu 'l-Qasem **Kashani** in his fight against the Iranian monarchy. The Feda'iyan assassinated high government officials, including the court minister, Abd al-Husayn Hazhir, and the prime minister, Husayn 'Ali Razmara, both in 1949. During the National Front government of Muhammad Musaddiq (1951–1953), Navvab broke with Kashani, and many of the Fida'iyan were arrested.

In 1955, Navvab and three of his comrades were sentenced to death and executed. The movement supported the Palestinian Arabs and opposed Iranian membership in the **Baghdad** Pact. It favored an increased role for the **'ulama'** in the state, Islamic **education**, and the introduction of **Koran**ic punishments, including mutilation for theft and stoning for **adultery**. The movement considered the **Baha'is** heretics. Its violence led to increased suppression by the state, but many of its demands were realized after the Islamic Revolution of 1979. *See also* ISLAMIC REPUBLIC OF IRAN.

FIDA'IYAN-I KHALQ. "Devotees of the people." A movement of university students and intellectuals founded in 1970 by the merger of two leftist groups, which started guerrilla activities against the regime of the shah of Iran. They attacked official buildings, especially police stations and banks, trying to rouse the Iranian people to revolt. After the Iranian revolution of 1979, they cooperated with the regime of Ayatollah Ruhollah **Khomeyni**, but they were eventually destroyed by the revolutionary government and disbanded in 1987. *See also* ISLAMIC REPUBLIC OF IRAN.

FINES. *See* DIYYAH.

FIQH. "Understanding; jurisprudence." The science of knowledge and interpretation of law, both civil and religious; it encompasses all branches of Islamic studies. It is the core of Islamic **education**. The books of fiqh provide details about the obligations of the individual in **Islamic law** (shari'ah). The **faqih** (pl. *fuqaha*), canonic lawyer, must be a learned and pious scholar. He interprets the law on the basis of the **Koran** and the Traditions (**Sunnah**), and depending on the school, on consensus of the scholars (**ijma'**), and analogical reasoning (**qiyas**). The Book of Great Fiqh (*Kitab al-fiqh al-akbar*) by **Abu Hanifah**, founder of the Hanafite **school of law**, is a treatise on theology rather than on fiqh. **Sunnis** recognize four schools, or rites of fiqh, and **Shi'ites** adhere to the Ja'farite school, named after the sixth **imam, Ja'far al-Sadiq** (d.765). Shi'ites also permit **ijtihad**, independent reasoning and judgment by learned theologians (**mujtahids**).

FIRDAUSI, ABU'L QASIM MANSUR (934?–1020?). Author of the great national epic, the *Book of Kings (Shahnama)*, which contains all the legends and history of Persia and ancient Afghanistan known to him. Born in Tus, **Khorasan**, he began work on the *Shahnama* there and at age 71 presented it to Mahmud of Ghazni (r. 988–1030), at whose court he had completed the work. His work is the most voluminous collection of early Persian poetry and therefore an important source for linguistics and literary studies. He felt not properly rewarded and was forced to flee Mahmud's domain after he made his discontent known.

FITNAH (pl. FITAN). "Trial, revolt." In Islamic history, a period of dissension or civil war. Also the period preceding the Day of Resurrection. It shall precede the resurrection.

FIVE PILLARS OF ISLAM (ARKAN AL-DIN). The belief and actions required of a Muslim can be summarized as follows: profession of faith, performance of ritual **prayers, almsgiving, fasting,** and **pilgrimage**. The profession of faith (**shahada**) consists in testifying that "there is no god but **Allah** and that **Muhammad** is the **Messenger** of Allah." To become a Muslim, six conditions must be fulfilled: The shahada must be repeated aloud, it must be perfectly understood, it must be believed in the heart, it must be professed until death, it must be recited correctly, and it must be declared without any hesitation.

The ritual prayer (salat) is performed five times during a day: at dawn before sunrise, after the sun passes the zenith, in the late afternoon, immediately after sunset, and between sunset and midnight. Prayers can be performed anywhere, but on **Fridays** preferably in a **mosque**. The person turns in the direction of **Mecca** (**qiblah**) and performs the bowings (ruku') on a mat or carpet. **Women** pray at home or in a separate area of a mosque.

Fasting (sawm) during the day is obligatory in the month of **Ramadhan**. It begins on the eve of Ramadhan, that is, on the 29th of the month of Sha'ban and ends at sunset on the last day of Ramadhan. **Believers** are to avoid all sins and abstain from eating, drinking, or having sexual intercourse.

Almsgiving (**zakat**) is enjoined to help the poor, destitute, those in debt, travelers, those who are fighting in the cause of Islam, **slaves** to buy their freedom, and those who perform a public service. It is a tax on savings, not on income. In many countries, it has become a voluntary tax.

Pilgrimage (**hajj**) is an obligation only for those who can afford the expense. It can also be performed for a person by a substitute.

Some consider holy war (**jihad**) a sixth pillar of Islam, which is satisfied if a "sufficient number" of Muslims perform it, but most schools now justify it only as a war of defense against aggression.

FIVE PRINCIPAL ACTS IN ISLAMIC LAW. Human acts are divided into five categories (*al-ahkam al-khamsa*), as follows: (1) Obligatory (**fardh** or **wajib**) duties whose performance is rewarded and whose omission is punished. This includes such acts as **prayer**, **almsgiving**, **fasting**, etc.; (2) Recommended (sunnah, masnun, **mandub**, and mustahabb), whose performance is rewarded but whose omission is not punished, for example, supererogatory prayers; (3) Indifferent (**mubah** or ja'iz), actions whose performance or omission is neither rewarded nor punished; (4) Reprehensible (**makruh**) actions that are not forbidden and will not be punished, for example certain dietary rules; and (5) Forbidden (**haram**), actions that are forbidden and punishable, for example, **adultery**.

FIVERS. Shi'ite followers of the Fifth **Imam** Zayd ibn 'Ali (ca. 698–740). *See* ZAYDIS.

FOOD. Food must be lawful (**halal**) and earned lawfully. No animal, except fish and locust, is lawful unless it is ritually slaughtered by cutting the throat. Meat of all quadrupeds that seize their prey with their teeth and all birds that seize it with their talons is forbidden. The **Koran** enjoins **believers**: "O ye who believe! Eat of the good things that We have provided for you. And be grateful to **Allah**, if it is Him ye worship. He hath only forbidden you dead meat, and blood, and the flesh of swine, and that on which any other name hath been invoked besides that of Allah. But if one is forced by necessity, without willful disobedience, nor transgressing due limits—then is he guiltless" (2:172–173). The prohibition against wine also includes all intoxicating beverages as well as opium and similar drugs. Muslims are permitted to eat in the company of **Peoples of the Book** (ahl al-kitab), which includes **Christians** and Jews; the golden rule is to eat in moderation. *See also* ALCOHOL.

FORGIVENESS. God is Merciful; He forgave **Adam** and Eve the sin of eating from the forbidden tree, and He wants men to also be forgiving. He never forgives **shirk**, idolatry, and those who disbelieve or commit repeated acts of unbelief. The **Koran** says: "Those who disbelieve and hinder (men) from the path of **Allah**, then die disbelieving—Allah will not forgive them" (47:34). According to one **hadith**, "anyone who does **wudhu**, and makes sure he does it correctly, and then does the **prayer**, will be forgiven everything that he does between then and the time when he prays the next prayer" (*Muwatta*, trans, Doi, 2.6.30).

FORNICATION. "Zina." Fornication is prohibited in Islam. Like **adultery**, it must be established by proof provided by four witnesses or by confession. The confession can be retracted. The punishment for fornication is 100 lashes, which should be given with moderation and not aimed at the same location. The law is based on the passage in the **Koran** that says: "The **woman** and the man guilty of fornication—flog each of them with a hundred stripes: let not compassion move you in their case, in a matter prescribed by **Allah**, if ye believe in Allah and the **Last Day**: and let a party of the **believers** witness their punishment" (24:2). Any person who wrongfully accuses a chaste woman of fornication must be punished with 80 lashes.

FOUR BOOKS. The four principal collections of **hadith** are *When No Theologian Is Present* (*Man la yahdururhu al-faqih*) by Muhammad **Ibn Babawayhi**; *Compendium of the Science of Religion* (Al-Kafi) by Muhammad Yaqub al-**Kulayni**; and *The Perspicacious* (al-Istibsar) and *The Confirmation of Decisions* (Tahdhib al-ahkam) by Muhammad al-**Tusi**.

FREE WILL. *See* ASH'ARITES; FATALISM; KISMET; PREDESTINATION.

FRIDAY. "Jum'ah." Friday, rather than Sunday, is the Islamic holiday. It is the Day of the Assembly, when Muslims are enjoined to attend midday prayer at a congregational **mosque**. A preacher (**khatib**) delivers a sermon (**khutbah**), in which the name of the legitimate ruler is invoked. Therefore, the khutbah also had political importance as, at the outbreak of a rebellion, the name of the ruler is omitted, or a challenger has his name proclaimed. In some countries, for example in Saudi Arabia and in **Afghanistan** under the **Taliban** regime, attendance at the Friday prayer is obligatory, and no one may loiter in the streets or conduct business at prayer times. According to tradition, Friday is the day on which the **Creation** was finished, or when **Adam** entered paradise and was again expelled, **Muhammad** came to **Medina** on a Friday, and Friday will also be the **Day of Judgment**.

FUNDAMENTALISM. "Usuliyya." Fundamentalism is a term that was originally applied to conservative Protestant movements in the United States. It has subsequently been applied to any major religion with tendencies such as authoritarianism, messianic spirit, subordination of secular politics to religious beliefs, belief in the infallibility of holy scripture, charismatic leadership, and enforced moralism. The designation "fundamentalist" has been applied to puritanical Islamic revivalist movements such as those promoted by Muhammad ibn Abd al-**Wahhab** (1703–1792), Hasan al-**Banna** (1906–1949), Sayyid Abu'l A'la **Maududi** (1903–1979), Ayatollah Ruhollah **Khomeyni** (1900–1989), and Mulla Muhammad 'Umar (b. ca. 1960) of Afghanistan. Supporters of Muslim "fundamentalism" have come to be called **Islamists**.

FUNERALS. *See* DEATH.

FURQAN. "Criterion." A name for the **Koran**, because it divides or makes a distinction between good and evil. **Surah** 25, named al-

Furqan, states that God's highest gift to humanity is the criterion for judgment between right and wrong, and those who do not heed it will be "full of woe on the **Day of Judgment**."

FUSTAT. *See* CAIRO.

– G –

GABRIEL (JIBRIL). The archangel Gabriel is believed to be the **angel** of revelation. He led **Adam** from paradise to Mount **'Arafat**, where he found Eve, and he accompanied the Prophet on **Muhammad**'s **Nocturnal Journey** (*lailat al-mi'raj*) from Jerusalem to **heaven**. He (and the angel Michael) will supervise the weighing of good and bad deeds. The **Koran** is believed to have been communicated to Muhammad by means of the angel Gabriel.

GAILANI, SAYYID AHMAD (GILANI, JILANI, 1932–). Descendant of the Muslim Pir Baba Abdul Qadir Gailani (1077–1166) and hereditary head of the Qadiria **Sufi** fraternity. He succeeded to his position upon the death of his older brother, Sayyid Ali, in 1964. Born in Kabul, the son of Sayyid Hasan **Gailani**, he was educated at Abu Hanifa College and the faculty of theology of Kabul University. He left **Afghanistan** after the Saur Revolt and founded the National Islamic Front of Afghanistan (NIFA, Mahaz-i Milli-yi Afghanistan) in Peshawar. His movement was part of the seven-member alliance that formed the "Afghan Interim Government" in 1989. Although Sayyid Gailani did not want any position in the Interim Government, he later accepted the post of supreme justice (qadhi al-qudhat). After the fall of the **Taliban** regime, Gailani returned to Kabul as a supporter of the Loya Jirga process of democratic elections.

GAILANI, SAYYID HASAN (GILANI, JILANI, 1862–1941). Born in **Baghdad**. Sayyid Hasan Gailani is the son of Sayyid Ali Gailani, the son of Sayyid Salman Gailani, descendant of al-Imam Hasan, son of Caliph Ali, son of Abu Taleb. A member of the family of the Naqib al-Ashraf of Baghdad, Sayyid Hasan Gailani went to **Afghanistan** in 1905. He was welcomed warmly by the king and the *qadirites* of

Afghanistan. Amir Habibullah paid him an allowance of Rs. 3,500 per month and built him a winter residence at Chaharbagh, near Jalalabad. Thus he became known as the Naqib Sahib of Charharbagh, as well as the Pir Naqib of Baghdad, the place where his ancestor's tomb is located. His reason for leaving Baghdad and going to Afghanistan was primarily a disagreement with his older brother, Sayyid Abdul Rahman Gailani, who was the oldest in the family and was Naqib al-Ashraf of Baghdad. He wanted to get married against the wishes of his brother, and Sayyid Hasan Gailani—wherever he would have gone—would have been sent back because of the influence of his brother. So he went to Afghanistan, which was not a part of the **Ottoman empire**. Furthermore, Afghanistan is a Hanafite Islamic country, having many Qadiri followers. In 1941, he died of a brain hemorrhage and was buried in his Chaharbagh garden in Jalalabad.

GALIEV. *See* SULTAN-GALIEV, MIRZA.

GAMA'AT AL-ISLAMIYYAH (JAMA'AT). An **Islamist** movement founded with the support of the Egyptian government of President Anwar Sadat in 1971 as a check on the Marxist movements in schools and universities. The Islamists grew in numbers and in 1978 gained 60 percent representation in the university student union election. As a result of the Egypt–Israeli peace treaty of 1979, they turned against the government. They applauded the assassination of Sadat in 1981 and continued their activities against the regime of Husni Mubarak. Under the guidance of Shaykh Muhammad Abu Nasr, they set up a network of private **mosques** that provided, among other things, health, welfare, and **educational** facilities. Augmented by Egyptians, who had been fighting the communist government in **Afghanistan**, the movement eventually tried to destabilize the country by attacking foreign tourists and the economic benefits derived from tourism. The government responded with mass arrests, but it has not succeeded in crushing them.

GAMBLING. Gambling is forbidden in Islam. **Surah** (2:219) says: "They ask thee concerning wine and gambling. Say: 'In them is great sin, and some profit for men; But the sin is greater than the profit.'"

Another (5:90) says: "O ye who believe! Intoxicants and gambling, sacrificing to stones, and (divination by) arrows, are an abomination—of Satan's handiwork: eschew such (abomination) that ye may prosper." According to tradition, the evidence of a gambler is not admissible in a court of law. However, in most Muslim countries various types of gambling have been tolerated. The **Taliban** regime in Afghanistan, which desired to establish an Islamic state in which the **shari'ah** is enforced, has forbidden all games of chance and betting on pigeons and quails, among other things.

GARDEN. *See* HEAVEN.

GARRISON TOWNS. *See* AMSAR.

GENGHIS (CHINGIZ) KHAN. *See* MONGOL INVASION.

GENIE. In **Arabic** "jinn." They are said to be spirits who enjoy a certain amount of free will and will therefore be called to account on the **Day of Judgment.** They are created of fire, unlike man, who is created of clay, as stated in the **Koran:** "We created man from sounding clay, from mud molded into shape; and the jinn race, We had created before, from the fire of a scorching wind" (15:26–27).

GHADIR AL-KHUMM. "The Pool of Kumm." A small lake near **Mecca** where, according to **Shi'ite** belief, **Muhammad** had promised **'Ali** "as much power as he held." This was taken as 'Ali's appointment to succeed the Prophet after his death. Shi'ites celebrate this event each year in the Islamic month of Dhu 'l-Hijjah.

GHANIMA. "Booty" in the early wars of conquest, which consisted of movable property. The soldiers traditionally received four-fifths, and one-fifth went to **Muhammad**, the **caliphs**, or, later, the heads of state to defray the costs of government. When an area, or city, surrendered peacefully (*sulhan*), no plunder was permitted, and the new subjects paid only their taxes but, if an enemy resisted until defeat (*anwatan*), leaving the decision to God, even the population could become *ghanima*. The spoils of war acquired without fighting, called *fay'*, are divided into five equal shares: for God (missionary activity), for the Prophet's institutional use for kinsmen in need for orphans, the needy, and wayfarers. The **Koran** says: "And know that out of all the booty that ye may acquire (in war), a fifth share is assigned to **Allah** and to the **Messenger**, and to near relatives, orphans, the needy, and the wayfarer" (8:41). Subsequently, the state took four-fifths of the booty and provided pensions to the soldiers. *See also* GHAZWAH.

GHANNUSHI, RASHID AL- (b. 1941–). Tunisian **Islamist** leader and one of the founders of the Renaissance Party (Harakat al-nahda al-Islamiyya). He was born in Balhamah, Tunisia, in 1941, and educated at the University of Damascus and at the Sorbonne, but did not finish his doctoral degree. Originally a socialist, he turned Islamist, devoted to reforming Tunisian society along Islamic principles. He became a professor of philosophy in Tunisia in 1969 and published articles in Islamist publications. His activities resulted in a prison term of 11 years in 1981 and a life sentence in 1987, but he was released after serving only short terms.

GHASSANIDS. An Arab kingdom of Monophysite **Christians** in the Syrian desert, which served as an auxiliary force of the Byzantine empire. It acted as a buffer state to protect the Byzantines from Bedouin raids. The state came to an end when Persia captured **Jerusalem** and **Damascus** in 613/614. The Ghassanids fought on the side of the Byzantines at the battle of **Yarmuk** (636), **Labid**, one of the seven poets of the **Mu'allaqat**, flourished in the Ghassanid state.

GHAYBAH. "Occultation." Meaning also absence or concealment. The **Twelver Shi'ites** believe that the Twelfth **Imam**, Muhammad al-**Muntazar** (878), did not die but went into concealment to guide the community and to reappear as the messianic **Mahdi**. He then will restore justice and equity after a long reign of injustice and oppression. There are two periods of ghaybah, the lesser and the greater concealment. The lesser occultation lasted for 60 years, during which the Imam guided the community through four intermediaries. After the death of the fourth intermediary in 940, the greater occultation began, which has lasted until the present. In the absence of the imam, the **'ulama'** is collectively responsible for the interpretation of **Shi'ite** doctrine.

GHAZALI, ABU HAMID MUHAMMAD AL- (1058–1111). Jurist of the **Shafi'ite** school, philosopher, theologian, mystic, and one of the most influential thinkers. He was born at Tus, near the present-day city of **Mashhad** in eastern Iran, and educated in Nishapur. When still a child, he memorized the **Koran** and subsequently studied the Traditions and **Islamic law** under the famous theologian **Imam** al-Haramayn al-**Juwayni**. In his works *Deliverance from Error (al-Munqidh min al-dalal)* and *The Incoherence of the Philosophers (Tahafut al-falasifa)*, al-Ghazali attacked the philosophers and **batinites** who advocated an esoteric, inner *(batin)* interpretation of the Koran. He served as chief teacher at the **Nizamiyyah** in **Baghdad** from 1091 to 1095, when he suffered a spiritual crisis and dedicated himself to **Sufism**. Ghazali said about his conversion: "This did not come about by systematic demonstration or marshaled argument, but by a light which God Most High cast into my breast" *(Deliverance from Error*, from Denny, 1994). He traveled widely and eventually settled down to compile his encyclopedic work, *The Revival of the Religious Sciences (Ihya ulum al-din)*. He was instrumental in reconciling Sufism with orthodox Islam.

GHAZALI, ZAYNAB AL- (1917–2005). Egyptian **Islamist** leader and, in 1936, founder of the Muslim Women's Association (Jama'at sl-sayyidat al-Muslimat), affiliated with the **Muslim Brotherhood** of Hasan al-**Banna**. The daughter of an Al-**Azhar**-educated merchant, she was a feminist, but at age 18 she founded the **women**'s organization, which eventually attained a membership of about three million. She believed that Islam guaranteed women's freedom, and economic, political, and social rights. Although a woman's first duty is to her family, she can devote her time to public affairs. She was divorced from her first husband, but she nevertheless considered **divorce** a crime. Her organization was able to cooperate with the Muslim Brotherhood when the government of Gamal Abdul Nasser imprisoned many of its members. In 1965, she was sentenced to 25 years, but she was freed in 1971 by the Anwar Sadat government. A prolific writer, contributing to Islamist publications, she published an autobiographical book called *Days of my Life (Ayyam min hayyati)*, in which she reports on her prison experience. An activist rather than Islamic scholar, she would postpone the full implementation of

shari'ah rule until at least 75 percent of Egyptians are ready to accept Islamic rule.

GHAZI. Originally "one who conducts a raid" (*ghazw*); also a veteran, or hero, in a religious war. Ghazi became a title for a victorious leader in war, but it was also adopted as a family name. It is synonymous with **mujahid**, a fighter in a holy war (**jihad**).

GHAZNAVID DYNASTY (977–1186). A dynasty of Turkish origin founded by Nasir al-Dawla Sebuktegin (r. 977–997), with its administrative capital in the city of Ghazni. During the reign of Sultan Mahmud of Ghazni (r. 998–1030), the Ghaznavid empire extended from the Tigris River to the Ganges River and from the Indian Ocean to the Amu Darya. **Ibn Khallikan** put it thus: "he [Mahmud] continued to pursue his conquests in India, and he carried his arms into regions which the banner of Islamism had never yet reached, and where no surat or verse of the **Koran** had ever been chanted before" (III, 332). Ghazni experienced a period of enormous wealth, most of it amassed by Mahmud during some 17 campaigns into the Indian subcontinent. He attracted some 400 scholars and poets to his capital, including Abu al-Qasim Firdawsi and Abu Rayhan al-**Biruni**. Although the dynasty counted 19 rulers over a period of two centuries, the empire began to disintegrate soon after Mahmud's death.

GHAZWAH (GHAZW). "Raiding." Originally a Bedouin raid for booty in which camels were used to cross the desert and horses were used for a lightning attack on the object of prey. After Islam, it designated forays into hostile territory, the no-man's land between the **dar al-Islam** and the **dar al-harb**. The word "razzia" in some Western languages is derived from ghazwah, meaning a police raid. One **Umayyad** poet said about ghazwah: "Our business is to make raids on the enemy, on our neighbour and on our own brother, in case we find none to raid but a brother" (Hitti, 1964, 25). *See also* GHANIMA.

GHULAT. "Exaggerators." Sects of religious extremists, mostly **Shi'ites**, who ascribe sainthood to members of the Prophet's family and differ from orthodox practices in various ways. They are a peaceful people, situated in the borderlands between Iran, Iraq, Turkey, and

Syria. They go by different names and avoid persecution by keeping their practices secret.

GHUSL. Ritual washing, which is obligatory before **prayer** after a major impurity caused by orgasm, menstruation, childbirth, etc. It is also obligatory on Fridays, and during the two **festivals**, the **'Id al-Fitr** and the **'Id al-Adha**. A pilgrim to **Mecca** will perform ghusl before entering the sanctuary. It requires that the entire body be washed, beginning with the head, then going on to the body, starting from the right side, and finally cleaning the interstices of the body. The water must moisten every part of the body. If there is no water, a symbolic washing (**tayammum**) can be made by wiping with sand the face and arms. *See also* ABLUTION.

GOD. *See* ALLAH.

GRANADA. Muslim kingdom in southern Spain, which was the longest lasting Muslim dynasty in the Iberian peninsula, ruled by the Nasrid dynasty from 1232 to 1492. The state became the Kingdom of Granada in 1238, and its rulers started the building of the **Alhambra**. Eventually the kingdom was weakened and the Nasrid kings became vassals of the Christian kingdom of Castile, until they were finally destroyed by the Reconquista in 1492. Persecutions eventually forced Muslims and Jews to flee and settle in the cities of the Islamic world. Some Jews continue to speak Latino, a Spanish dialect, to this day.

GRAVE. *See* DEATH.

GUARDIAN COUNCIL. As a result of the Iranian Revolution in 1979, a council of 12 guardians was set up to pass on the legitimacy of all laws and regulations of government. Six of the members were jurists, appointed by Ayatollah Ruhollah **Khomeyni** and, subsequently, by a Leadership Council, and six were nominated by the head of the judiciary and approved by parliament for a six-year term. Together they certified that all parliamentary legislation was in conformity with the Iranian constitution and **Islamic law**. In the parliamentary elections of 1992 and 1999, large numbers of reformist candidates were disqualified. In the 2005 elections, most of the reformists were eliminated, and

Mahmud Amadinejad, a hard-liner, was elected president. *See also* IS-LAMIC REPUBLIC OF IRAN.

– H –

HABIBAH. Wife of **Muhammad**. *See* UMM HABIBAH BINT ABI SUFYAN.

HADD (HUDUD). "Obstruction." Mandatory punishments imposed in classical **Islamic law** in cases of **adultery**, **fornication**, and false accusation of adultery, as well as for theft, highway robbery, **apostasy**, and drunkenness. For these offenses, punishments are fixed and details as to their execution are specified in the Traditions or the **Koran**. For example, the punishment for adultery is stoning or 100 lashes for fornication, but strict rules of evidence require either a confession from the culprits or the testimony of four male witnesses. The amputation of a hand for theft requires either a confession or two witnesses. Furthermore, the stolen property has to exceed a certain value, and the theft must not be between relations. The punishment for wine drinking, not mentioned in the Koran, is 80 lashes, according to the Traditions. Because of the severity of hadd punishments, they have not been imposed in most parts of the Islamic world. Only in Saudi Arabia and in the self-described "Islamic States" of **Pakistan** and Sudan, and, during the **Taliban** regime, in **Afghanistan**, have hadd punishments been exacted.

HADITH. It has been defined as "the story of a particular occurrence, and Sunnah as the rule of law deduced from it. It is the practice of the Prophet, his model behavior" (Fyzee, 1967, 19). Next to the **Koran**, the **Sunnah**, Tradition, is the second source of the doctrine and ritual of Islam, political theory, and **Islamic law**. During the life of the Prophet **Muhammad**, stories about his actions and sayings were collected by eyewitnesses and then told to others. These stories were transmitted by word of mouth. A chain (**isnad**) of credible transmitters was produced that preceded the text (**matn**), which went something like this: "Muhammad bin Abdullah said to us that Abu Khalid said that Abu Malik said that Sa'd bin 'Ubaydah said that the son of 'Umar said that the Prophet said 'Islam is founded on five things'."

The hadith were eventually recorded in writing, and a science of hadith criticism classified hadiths as Sound (*sahih*), if there was no weak link in the chain of transmitters and corroboration existed from others; Good (*hasan*), if there was a weak link or the character of the transmitter was doubtful; and Weak (*dha'if*), if there were several weak links or the narrator was unreliable. This resulted in the production of biographical works that described the qualifications and character of transmitters.

Six major collections of hadith were eventually compiled, which were accepted by all **Sunni** Muslims. They included those of al-**Bukhari** (d. 870), **Muslim ibn al-Hajjaj** (d. 875), **Ibn Majah** al-Qazvini (d. 886), Abu Dawud al-**Sijistani** (d. 888), Abu 'Isa al-**Tirmidhi** (d. 892), and Abu Abd al-Rahman al-**Nasa'i** (d. 915). The collections of al-Bukhari and al-Muslim are considered the most reliable. **Malik ibn Anas** (d. 795) and Ahmad **ibn Hanbal** (d. 855), the founders of two orthodox schools, also produced collections. One collection by Husayn al-**Baghawi**, titled *Niche for Lights* (*Mishkat al-masabih*), has been translated into English by James Robson and published in four volumes. In addition to the hadith of the Prophet, **Shi'ites** also use those of their **imams**. Authoritative collections of the Shi'ites were compiled by Muhammad ibn Yaqub al-**Kulayni** (d. 939), **Ibn Babawayhi** (Babuya, d. 991), and Muhammad al-**Tusi** (d. 1067).

The hadith provide a wealth of information regarding the personality, family, and activities of the Prophet and serve as examples for emulation, providing guidance in matters of jurisprudence not stipulated in the Koran. A Western, revisionist school supports the Goldzieher-Schacht thesis that the majority of hadith were "back-projected as the sayings of the Prophet only at a much later date." Another view holds that the Sunnah is actually the local practice of the people of **Medina**; but this interpretation is not likely to find acceptance in the Islamic world.

HAFIZ. One who has memorized (*hafaza*) the **Koran**. As part of Islamic **education**, many scholars memorized the Koran in early youth, before progressing to higher education. One who has memorized the Koran carries the title "Hafiz." Encouragement for this task is found in the Koran, which says: "And we have indeed made the Qur'an easy to understand and remember" (S. 54:17). Hafiz and Hafiza are also male and female names.

HAFIZ SHIRAZI, KHWAJAH SHAMS AL-DIN MUHAMMAD (1319–1389). Persian mystic and poet, "one of the three greatest poets of the world." Said to have produced some 500 ghazals, 42 rubayat, and a number of **qasidahs.** As a child he memorized the **Koran,** hence his name and title, "Hafiz." He became a poet at the court of Abu Ishaq in Shiraz and subsequently of Shah Shuja of the Muzaffarid dynasty. He is said to have met the nomadic conqueror Timur-i **Lang** to defend himself against charges of blasphemy. Hafiz's tomb is located in the Musalla Gardens of Shiraz. His poetry was compiled only some 20 years after his death.

HAFSAH. Daughter of Caliph **'Umar ibn al-Khattab** and one of the wives of **Muhammad.** Hafsah was the widow of a man killed in the battle of **Badr.** Her father offered her to **'Uthman** and **Abu Bakr** in **marriage,** and when they did not accept her, the Prophet married her, giving her a **dowry** of 400 **dirhams.** According to tradition, Hafsah was the custodian of the first official copy of the **Koran,** compiled during the **caliphate** of Abu Bakr (632–634) or 'Umar. The version accepted as definitive by Muslims was, however, compiled during the period of Caliph 'Uthman (644–656). Hafsah enjoyed considerable influence and recorded a number of Traditions of the Prophet. She died at age 60 in 667.

HAGAR (HAJAR). Slave wife of **Abraham** and mother of his son Isma'il. When Abraham built the foundation of the **Ka'bah,** he abandoned Hagar and Isma'il in the desert, and their search for water led them to discover the **Zamzam** well. According to tradition, Hagar's descendants were the Arabs and Sarah's were the Jews.

HAJAR AL-ASWAD. *See* BLACK STONE.

HAJJ. *See* PILGRIMAGE.

HAJJAJ, IBN YUSUF AL- (661–714). A schoolmaster of Ta'ef in **Hijaz** who became an important general in the service of the **Umayyad**

caliphs 'Abdul Malik (685–705) and al-**Walid** (705–715). He besieged **Mecca** for seven months and defeated and killed the anti-caliph 'Abd Allah ibn **Zubayr** in 692. He pacified Arabia and Iraq, where he served as governor for about 20 years, until his death. He arrived at **Kufah** with an escort of only 12 cameleers and proclaimed from the city **mosque**: "O people of al-Kufah! Certain am I that I see heads ripe for cutting, and verily I am the man to do it. Methinks I see blood between the turbans and the beards" (Hitti, 207). He is said to have sacrificed some 120,000 lives before he was able to establish his tyrannical control over Persia and Iraq. Under his direction, vowel markings were introduced into the **Arabic** script to make the pronunciation of the **Koran** more precise. Hajjaj was buried in Wasit (middle), the city he founded between **Kufah** and **Basra**.

HAKIM, ABU'L 'ALI AL-MANSUR AL- (r. 996–1021). The sixth **Fatimid caliph** at **Cairo**, described as a whimsical tyrant who promoted **Isma'ili** propaganda in a predominantly **Sunni** country. He enforced discriminatory restrictions on **Christians** and Jews who had attained high positions at court during the reign of his father, and he instituted puritanical reforms, prohibiting **women** from appearing in the streets. At one time he ordered all the dogs in the city to be killed, then he forbade the sale of grapes and ordered all the jars of honey broken and the contents poured into the Nile. He founded "A House of Wisdom" (**dar al-hikmah**) in 1004 for the training of Isma'ili missionaries. Two of his missionaries (**da'is**), **Hamza** al-Zuzani and **Darazi**, urged him to proclaim his divinity, which led to civil war and the flight of Darazi, who founded the **Druze** community in Lebanon. Al-Hakim disappeared during one of his nocturnal wanderings about the city; the Druzes expect him to return at the end of time as the **Mahdi**. **Ibn Khallikan** said of him: "He was prodigal of wealth and fond of shedding blood: a great number of persons holding eminent stations in the administration of the state were put to death by him in an arbitrary manner" (III, 449).

HALAL. "Permissible." That which is lawful and allowed, as compared to that which is forbidden (**haram**). It includes proper behavior in law as well as the consumption of **food**. Halal food includes meat of animals that have been ritually slaughtered, game over which the name of **Allah** has been pronounced, and various types of seafood. *See also* FIVE PRINCIPAL ACTS IN ISLAMIC LAW.

HALIMAH. A Bedouin woman who acted as wet nurse of **Muhammad** during his early childhood. It was the custom of city nobility to temporarily leave their infants with Bedouins in the desert, away from the unhealthy conditions of urban life.

HALLAJ, HUSAYN IBN MANSUR AL- (857–922). A Persian **Sufi** poet who was born in Tus (or Bayza in Fars?) and executed as a heretic. A cotton carder by trade, he traveled as far as Turkestan and northern India and was able to win many disciples, who ascribed to him supernatural powers. He stressed a spiritual relationship between human beings and God, denied the necessity of **pilgrimage**, and suggested that saved funds ought to be spent on the support of orphans. An **'Abbasid** inquisition had him flogged and tortured, then decapitated and burned, because of his ecstatic utterance: "I am the Truth"(*ana al-haqq*), that is, God. One of his verses states: "I am He whom I love, and He whom I love is I, We are two souls dwelling in one body. When thou seest me, thou seest Him: And when thou seest Him, thou seest us both" (Hitti, 436).

Ibn Khallikan said of Hallaj "some (are) extolling him to the utmost, whilst others treat him as an infidel" (I, 423). Members of the **'ulama'** said he merited death, and he was handed over to the police guards with instructions to administer a flogging of 1,000 strokes and "If al-Hallaj does not expire under the bastonnade, cut off one of his hands, then one of his feet, then the other hand, then the other foot; then strike off his head and burn his body" (I, 425). "Hallaj and I believe the same thing," said Shibli, "but my madness saved my life, and his intelligence led him to his death" (Schroeder, 521).

HAMAS. Acronym, for a Palestinian Islamist revivalist movement, the Movement of Islamic Resistance (Harakat al-Muqawamah al-Islamiyah). It was established in December 1987, at the beginning of the *intifadah*, the Palestinian uprising against Israeli occupation of the West Bank and Gaza Strip. It rose out of the **Muslim Brotherhood** and combined a network of social welfare activities with political and military action. Its military wing, the Qassim Brigade

(Kata'eb 'Izz al-Din al-Qassam), conducted armed attacks against Israeli targets. Unlike the nationalist Palestinian Liberation Organization (PLO), Hamas wants to "re-Islamize" society with the objective of creating an Islamic state.

Israel originally welcomed the emergence of Hamas "in order to help create a force that would stand against the leftist forces which support the PLO" (Gen. Yitzhak Segev, quoted in Graham Usher, *What Kind of Nation?*). But it embarked on armed actions against Israeli targets in retaliation for the al-**Aqsa** mosque massacre in **Jerusalem** in 1990, in which 18 Palestinians were killed. In the ensuing conflict, Israel sentenced Shaykh Ahmad Yasin, the "spiritual guide" of Hamas, to life imprisonment; assassinated 'Imad 'Aql, leader of the Brigade; and attempted to assassinate Khalid Mash'al, head of the Hamas political bureau in Amman, Jordan (King Husayn demanded the freeing of Shaykh Yasin after the Mossad assassination attempt). According to Efraim Halevy, one-time head of Mossad, Israeli's foreign intelligence service, Hamas offered a 30-year truce to Israel in 1997, but Israel was not interested. This offer, repeated several times, constitutes de facto recognition of Israel, contingent on Israel ending its occupation of the West Bank and Gaza Strip. In the parliamentary elections of January 2006, Hamas won a landslide victory. It gained 30 out of 66 national seats, compared to 27 for Fatah and 9 others, and 76 seats out of 132 national and district seats, reducing Fatah to 43 seats. This appears to be as much a protest vote against perceived Fatah corruption as a vote to demonstrate the Palestinian plight to the world. Israel and the United States have announced that they will not deal with the new government. In July 2008, Israel and Hamas agreed to an exchange of prisoners and a general truce in Gaza.

HAMDAN QARMAT. *See* QARMATIANS.

HAMZA IBN ALI IBN AHMAD. An **Isma'ili** missionary (**da'i**) of the **Fatimid Caliph al-Hakim.** He promoted the idea that Hakim was a manifestation of God, a doctrine eventually accepted by the **Druzes.** He disappeared or was assassinated in 1021.

HANAFI. *See* ABU HANIFAH; SCHOOLS OF LAW.

HANAFIYYAH, MUHAMMAD IBN AL- (637–701). Son of Caliph 'Ali by a woman of the Hanifa tribe and therefore not a descendant of the Prophet. He was not politically active and reluctantly carried the banner of his father 'Ali at the Battle of the **Camel**. As 'Ali's only surviving son, he was recognized by the **Kaysaniyyah** as their **imam**. Al-**Mukhtar** revolted in **Kufah** in 685–687, in the name of al-Hanafiyyah, proclaiming him the expected **Mahdi** in occultation (**concealment**) on Mount Radwa. Hanafiyyah eventually declared his allegiance to Caliph **Mu'awiyah** and retired to **Medina**.

HANBAL, AHMAD IBN. *See* IBN HANBAL, AHMAD,

HANBALI. *See* IBN HANBAL, AHMAD; SCHOOLS OF LAW.

HAND. Muslims traditionally use the right hand for "honorable purposes" and the left hand for necessary but unclean actions. When eating with one's fingers, as is customary in many parts of the world, one is supposed to eat with the right hand.

HAND OF FATIMAH. A charm or **amulet**, also called the Eye of Fatimah, referring to **Fatimah**, the daughter of **Muhammad**. The symbol is painted at the entrance of homes to fend off the **evil eye**, or fashioned of metal or ceramics and carried as an adornment. Orthodox **'ulama'** object to its use as idolatry, but it's widespread in the Islamic world.

HANIF. "One who is inclined to Islam," the term for a monotheist in pre-Islamic Arabia. **Abraham**, the biblical ancestor of Muslims and Jews, is a hanif. The **Koran** says, "They say: 'Become Jews or **Christians** if ye would be guided (to salvation).' Say thou: 'Nay! (I would rather) the religion of Abraham the True, and he joined not gods with **Allah**" (S. 2:135). A Hanif rejects idolatry and worships God with complete devotion and undivided loyalty. It was the religion of Abraham (*hanifiyya*), who was neither Jew nor Christian.

HANIFA, ABU. *See* ABU HANIFAH.

HANIFITES. *See* SCHOOLS OF LAW.

HAQQANIYYA, DAR AL-ULUM. Dubbed "University of Jihad," it is a **madrasah** in Akora Khattak, about 35 miles east of Peshawar, **Pakistan**, which trained many of the **Islamist** and **Taliban** leadership. Its graduates supported the war against the communist regime in **Afghanistan** and, on occasion, schools were closed to assist the Taliban in major campaigns. Some 2,500 students, aged from 8 to 30 years, enjoy free tuition and board, and some 600 of the older students are enrolled in mufti (canon law) courses. (A World Bank study shows that the number of "jihadi" schools has been greatly exaggerated.) Most students are from Pashtun areas in Afghanistan and Pakistan, but there is also a sizable international student body. Maulana al-Haq, the principal of the madrasah, is also a head of the Jam'iat i Ulama Islami, a Pakistani religio political party. Notable alumni include Amir Khan Muttaki, minister of information and culture; Abdul Latif Mansur, minister of agriculture; Maulawi Ahmad Jan, minister of mines and industries; and Mulla Jalaluddin Haqqani, minister of frontier affairs in the former Taliban government. The government of former President Pervez Musharraf was not able to force the school to abandon the martial aspect of its education.

HARAM. "Sanctuary." The areas of **Mecca** and **Medina**, the *Haramayn*, which are sacred and forbidden to non-Muslims. Haram is that which is forbidden and sinful and will be punished on the **Day of Judgment**. In jurisprudence, it is an unlawful act, subject to punishment by an Islamic **judge** (kadhi). *See also* FIVE PRINCIPAL ACTS IN ISLAMIC LAW.

HARIM (HAREM). The **women**'s quarters of an apartment that any unrelated men were forbidden to enter. Muslim rulers maintained special quarters in which their wives and female servants were kept. The custom is based on the injunction of the **Koran**, which says: "There is no blame (on those ladies if they appear) before their fathers or their sons, their brothers, or their brothers' sons, or their sisters' sons, or their women, or the (**slaves**) whom their right hand possess" (33:55). As an institution, the harim was taken from Byzantine practices and continued by **caliphs** and secular rulers down to the **Ottoman empire**, when it included several hundred women. Only a few were the actual wives of the **sultan**; the majority were servants and slaves. The mother of the reigning sultan was the queen of the harim, which was organized in a highly hierarchical system. The harim system ended in 1909 with the Young Turk revolution and the removal of Sultan Abdul Hamid.

HARIRI, ABU MUHAMMAD AL-QASIM IBN ALI AL-(1054–1122). Scholar of Arabic language and literature, born in **Basra** in the street of the Banu Haram, from which he got the surname Hariri. He was of a wealthy family that possessed 18,000 palm trees. Hariri was described as

one of the ablest writers of his time, and obtained the most complete success in the composition of his Makamat (Stations), wherein is contained a large portion of the language spoken by the Arabs of the desert, such as the idioms, its proverbs, and its subtle delicacies of expression. Any person who acquires a sufficient acquaintance with this book to understand it rightly, will be led to acknowledge the eminent merit of this man, his extensive information and his vast abilities." (Khallikan, trans. Slane, II, 490)

HARUN AL-RASHID (r. 786–809). The fifth 'Abbasid caliph, whose reign was the high point of 'Abbasid rule in **Baghdad**. A contemporary of Charlemagne in the West, Harun exceeded the European rulers in power and territorial possessions. He was served by the Persian **Barmakid** family of **viziers**, but he eventually eliminated them when they began to rival his power and wealth. Harun repeatedly fought Kharijite revolts and could not prevent the emergence of the **Idrisids** (789–926) and Aghlabids (800–909) in North Africa as independent states. As a youth, Harun led an army against the Byzantines, forcing Constantine VI to pay a tribute of some 70,000 **dinars**. In the West, he came to be known from the tales of *A Thousand-and-One Nights*.

HARUT AND MARUT. Two **angels** who deplored sinful humanity and were sent by God to earth, where they became sinful themselves. They taught magic to people without warning them of its evil uses; therefore, they were punished. "They learned from them (the angels) the means to sow discord between man and wife" (2:102).

HASAN AL-BANNA. *See* BANNA, HASAN AL-.

HASAN AL-BASRI. *See* BASRI, HASAN AL.

HASAN IBN 'ALI (625–670). Son of **'Ali** and **Fatimah** and grandson of the Prophet **Muhammad.** Hasan was politically inactive and surrendered his rights to the **caliphate** to the first **Umayyad caliph, Mu'awiyah.** The **Shi'ites** count him as the second **imam.**

HASAN AL-SABBAH (HASAN-I SABBAH, 1055–1124). A propagandist (**da'i**) of the **Isma'ili sect** who established his base in the fortress of **Alamut,** and as grand master sent his devotees (**fida'i**) on errands of assassination. The members of the **sect** are said to have used hashish in their ceremonies and therefore came to be known as the *hashashiyun,* from which the word *assassin* derives.

HASHIM, BANU. *See* HASHIMITE CLAN.

HASHIMITE CLAN. The noble, but small, clan of the Prophet, named after its eponymic ancestor, Hashim Ibn al-Manaf (d. 540). The Hashimites were part of the **Quraysh** tribe and were able to protect **Muhammad** from Meccan persecution. It was only when his grandfather, 'Abd al Muttalib, and his uncle, **Abu Talib,** died, that Muhammad was forced to flee to **Medina.** The rulers of Jordan (1922–present) claim Hashimite descent and designate their state the Hashimite Kingdom of Jordan.

HASHISHIN. *See* ALAMUT; NIZARIS.

HATIM AL-TA'I (d. ca. 605). A man who personifies the Bedouin ideal of generosity and hospitality. He was in charge of his father's camels when he encountered three travelers and slaughtered three camels for them when they only asked for some milk. Then he divided the camels among the travelers. *See also* HOSPITALITY.

HAYTHAM, IBN AL- (ALHAZEN, 965–1039). Arab mathematician, astronomer, and physicist from **Basra.** In his *Opticae Thesaurus (Kitab al-manazir),* he rejected the theories of Euclid and Ptolemy that visual rays travel from the eye to the object. In what came to be known in the West as "Alhazen's problem," he solved an equation of the fourth degree. Al-Haytham was invited to **Cairo** by the **Fatimid Caliph** al-**Hakim** to study the feasibility of controlling the flooding of the Nile.

HEAD SCARVES. *See* HIJAB; VEIL.

HEAVEN. "Jannah." Heaven is the abode of the virtuous in the next life. The **Arabic** word *jannah* means garden; another term, *firdaws* (probably of Persian origin), means paradise. Heaven is described as a garden with flowing streams, a place of bliss and perpetual happiness (2:25). **Surah** 3:15 reads: "Say: Shall I give you glad tidings of things far better than those (wealth)? For the righteous are gardens in nearness to their Lord with rivers flowing beneath; therein is their eternal home; with spouses purified and the good pleasure of **Allah**. . . . And he will be in a life of bliss, in a garden on high, the fruits whereof (will hang in bunches) low and near. 'Eat ye and drink ye, with full satisfaction; Because of the (good) that ye sent before you, in the days that are gone!'" (69:21–24).

There are several types of heaven, including the Seventh Heaven. "But for such as fear the time when they will stand before (the Judgment Seat of) their Lord, there will be two gardens . . . abounding in branches . . . in them (each) will be two springs flowing (free) . . . in them will be fruits of every kind two and two. . . . They will recline on carpets, whose inner linings will be of rich brocade: the fruit of the garden will be near (and easy to reach) . . . in them will be (maidens), chaste, restraining their glances, whom no man or jinn before them has touched" (55:46–56). While some Muslims tend to take the descriptions of the joys of paradise literally, others see them as metaphors.

HEKMATYAR, GULBUDDIN (1947–). Amir of the **Hizb-i Islami-**yi Afghanistan (Islamic Party of Afghanistan), one of the seven **mu-jahidin** groups formed in Peshawar. His party is radical **Islamist** and fights for the establishment of an Islamic republic, to be governed according to its interpretation of **Islamic law**. Born in Imam Sahib, Kunduz, a Ghilzai Pashtun, Hekmatyar studied engineering at Kabul University for two years and became involved in campus politics. He became a member of the "Muslim Youth" movement in 1970 and was elected to its executive council (*shura*). He was imprisoned in Dehmazang jail in Kabul, from 1972 to 1973, and, after the Muhammad Daud coup of 1973, fled to **Pakistan**. In 1975, he became leader of the Hizb-i Islami and began armed attacks from bases in Pakistan with clandestine support from the Zulfikar Ali Bhutto government. Isolated raids developed into modern guerrilla warfare after the communist coup of April 1978. The party adopted from the Muslim Brotherhood such features as a centralized command structure, secrecy of membership, organization in cells, infiltration of government and social institutions, and the concept of the party as an Islamist "vanguard" in Afghan society.

Being Islamist rather than nationalist, the party enjoyed considerable support from like-minded groups in Pakistan and the Gulf. Hekmatyar surprised friends and foes alike when he allied himself with Lieutenant General Shahnawaz Tanai, a radical Khalqi, in a coup against the Kabul government of Dr. Najibullah. Expelled by the **Taliban**, Hekmatyar fled to Iran, returning to **Afghanistan** in spring 2002 to continue his **jihad** against the American forces.

HELL. "Jahannam," the abode of polytheists and sinners. There is disagreement about who will be condemned to eternal hell fire. Some theologians believe that Muslims who sinned, but repented, will be only temporarily in hell, while others would assign Muslims who committed a great **sin** forever to hell. According to tradition, there are seven gates of hell: one a purgatory for Muslims, and individual sections for **idolaters**, **hypocrites**, **Christians**, Jews, and others (15:44). The sinners will neither live nor die and will be tormented forever. Their food will consist of thorny bushes and the fruit of the *zaqqum* tree: "In front of such a one (sinner) is hell, and he is given, for drink, boiled fetid water. In gulps, will he sip it, but never will he be near swallowing it down his throat; death will come to him from every quarter, yet will he not die; and in front of him will be a chastisement unrelenting" (14:16–17).

HELPERS. *See* ANSAR.

HENNAH (HINNAH). The leaves of a bush widely grown in the Middle East that are ground and mixed with various ingredients to make a paste used as a cosmetic for **women**. They dye their palms, soles of the feet, fingertips, nails, or face a bright red color. With certain admixtures it is used to dye men's hair and beards. Originally hennah was believed to have magical powers, for example, protection from the "**evil eye**."

HEREAFTER, THE. The concept of life after death, *akhirah*, resurrection, judgment, and reward or punishment on the **Day of Judgment**. God has created humankind and will re-create man a second time: "Say, He will give them life Who created them for the first time! For He fully knows all creation." **Abraham** was shown how God will revive the dead in the hereafter: "He (Abraham) said: 'Oh! How shall **Allah** bring it (ever) to life, after this (its) death?' But Allah caused him to die for a hundred years, then raised him up (again). He said: 'How long didst thou tarry (thus)?' He said: '(Perhaps) a day or part of a day.' He said: 'Nay, thou hast tarried thus a hundred years: But look at thy food and thy drink; they show no signs of age: and look at thy donkey: and that we may make of thee a sign unto the people. Look further at the bones, how We bring them together and cloth them with flesh.' When this was shown clearly to him, he said: 'I know that Allah hath power over all things'" (2:259). Belief in the hereafter is one of the basic tenets of Islam. *See also* HEAVEN; HELL.

HIDDEN IMAM. The Twelfth **Shi'ite Imam**, Muhammad al-Muntazar, who disappeared in 878, is believed to be in occultation (**concealment**), and is expected to return at the end of time. During the first stage, the Lesser Occultation (878–940), the Hidden Imam was represented by four intermediaries, who had the authority to speak on his behalf. After this, the Greater Occultation began, and the **'ulama'** are believed to act as his representatives.

HIJAB. "Cover, veil." One of a number of terms for the **veil** and the seclusion of **women**. In the **Koran**, the term is taken for seclusion: "O ye who believe! Enter not the Prophet's houses—until leave is given you . . . and when ye ask (his ladies) for anything ye want ask them before a screen: that makes for greater purity for your hearts and for theirs" (33–53). The veil existed in the Hellenistic–Byzantine and the Sassanian empires and was worn by aristocratic ladies in urban environments. Adopted in Islam, the veil became obligatory for women, but the type of veil varied in different parts of the Islamic world. Nomad and peasant women would wear a kerchief that did not interfere with them working. In cities, women would wear the burqa', also called **chador** or chatri, which covers the head and the entire body. As a result of Westernization, women began to appear on the streets without a veil, and modernizing reformers tried with varying success to abolish the veil. The Islamic revival, beginning in the 1970s, led to the adoption of the "Islamic" dress as a political statement in many parts of the Islamic world and even among Muslims in the West.

HIJAZ. "Barrier." A province in west-central Saudi Arabia in which the holy cities of **Mecca** and **Medina** are located. Pilgrims from all over the world visit the two cities, which are off limits to non-Muslims. Hijaz means "barrier," named after a range of high mountains, which rises parallel to the Red Sea coast and in the east gradually declines to form the Arabian plateau.

HIJRAH (HEJIRA). "Emigration." The beginning of the Islamic **calendar** was determined to be 16 July 622, when **Muhammad** and a small group of his followers fled from **Mecca** to Yathrib (**Medina**). It was during the month of **Muharram**, the first month of the Islamic lunar year. Muhammad's teachings had aroused the hostility of the powerful **Quraysh**, who feared the new Islamic community as a threat to their social and economic interests. When **Abu Lahab** became head of the **Hashimite clan**, Muhammad lost the protection of his clan, and his enemies conspired to kill him. Once established in Medina, the Muslim community grew to the extent that it recaptured Mecca and unified Arabia under Islam. Hijrah also means "fleeing from sin" and the act of leaving a country under infidel rule.

HIJRAT MOVEMENT. "Emigration Movement," also called Khilafat movement (of 1920), which originated in the North-West Frontier Province of India to protest the destruction of the **Ottoman empire** by Britain and its allies. Indian Muslims recognized the Ottoman claims to the **caliphate** and spiritual leadership of the (**Sunni**) Islamic world. Muhammad 'Ali and other leaders of the movement proclaimed it the "Islamic duty" of Indian Muslims "to abandon a country ruled by a sacrilegious government," the Abode of War (**dar al-harb**), and migrate to the Abode of Peace (dar al-Islam), an Islamic state. Encouraged by King Amanullah, who had just won the independence for his country, some 18,000 Muslims went to **Afghanistan**. The Afghan king hoped to attract professional and skilled manpower, but most of the immigrants (*muhajerun*) were unskilled and poor and could not adapt to the new environment. Some Pashtuns from Peshawar were settled in the area of Kunduz and some Sindhis in the area of Balkh, and a few went on to the Soviet Union and Europe, but most of the *muhajerun* eventually returned to India. *See also* DAR AL-ISLAM.

HILA (pl. HIYAL). "Evasion," or subterfuge, used to circumvent the dictates of law, for example, to permit the taking of interest. The transaction is represented as the sale of an item, repurchased for a smaller amount, or making the transaction a partnership. Such stratagems came into use during the **'Abbasid** period, mainly in the Hanafi **school of law**, but they were also adopted by others.

HILAL. "Crescent." A symbol on Muslim banners. The Red Crescent (*al-hilal al-ahmar*) is the Muslim equivalent of the Western Red Cross. The appearance of the crescent marks the beginning of the Muslim month and the beginning of the sacred seasons.

HILLI, ALLAMAH IBN AL-MUTAHHAR AL- (1250–1325). An Islamic scholar and jurist of the **Twelver Shi'ite** school, known as the "wise man of Hilli." Born in Hilla, Iraq, and educated in **Baghdad**, he became famous for his works on grammar, logic, **hadith**, **tafsir** (commentary on the **Koran**), and biography. He was a supporter of the **usuli school**, which favored the use of independent judgment (**ijtihad**) in matters of law. His treatise, the *Principles of Shi'ite Theology (al-Bab al-hadi 'ashar)*, is still used by Shi'ites today. Hilli is buried in **Mashhad**.

HIRAH AL-. Capital of the **Lakhmid** buffer state between the nomads of Arabia and Sassanian Persia that flourished under its king, Imru' al-Qays (d. 328). Three of the seven authors of the **Mu'allaqat** enjoyed the patronage of the al-Hirah courts, which were famous for sponsoring prize-winning competitions. The population was largely Christian and spoke **Arabic**, but used Syriac in writing. The Muslim general, **Khalid ibn al-Walid**, conquered al-Hirah in 633.

HISBAH. The state institution that promotes virtue and forbids vice: *al-amr bi al-ma'ruf wa-al-nahy 'an al-munkar.* Although every Muslim has the obligation to admonish fellow Muslims to good conduct, the hisbah has a function in public law. The **muhtasib**, the person responsible for the hisbah, has been a combination of market inspector and overseer of public morals, who can investigate and judge an offender and administer punishment, usually a number of lashes. In most Islamic countries, the urban police have taken over this function, but in some, such as Afghanistan under the **Taliban**, the hisbah institution has been reintroduced.

HISHAM, ABD AL-MALIK IBN. *See* IBN HISHAM, ABU MUHAMMAD 'ABD AL-MALIK.

HITTIN (HATTIN). A place in Palestine where **Salah al-Din** (Saladin) defeated the crusaders in 1187. The battle prepared the way for the conquest of **Jerusalem** three months later.

HIZB. A part or division, such as a part of the **Koran**; also a political party.

HIZB AL-DA'WAH. *See* DA'WAH, HIZB AL-.

HIZB-I ISLAMI. "Islamic Party." Two **Islamist** parties with this name in **Afghanistan**, headed by Gulbuddin **Hekmatyar** and Yunus Khalis, fought against the Marxist government in the 1980s with considerable assistance from the United States, **Pakistan**, and governments from the Gulf states. As radical Islamists, they were ideologically trusted to be implacable enemies of the communists. Many Arab **mujahidin** favored these parties and fought on their side; the skills they acquired in weaponry and guerrilla warfare were later employed in fighting the governments in their countries of origin. Some, such as **Osama bin Laden**, stayed in Afghanistan and supported the

Taliban regime, which for four years controlled most of the country. *See also* AFGHANIS.

HIZBULLAH (HIZB ALLAH). The Party of God (**Allah**), a term that was adopted by **Shi'ite Islamist** parties in Iran and Lebanon. In Iran, Hizbullah rose as a revolutionary movement in the late 1970s, when it contributed to the downfall of Muhammad Reza Shah and became a vanguard of the Islamic Republican Party. It contributed to the consolidation of the new regime, but it did not emerge as a separate party. The movement established links with the Lebanese forces and contributed to their training and financial support.

In Lebanon, the Hizbullah emerged in the late 1970s among Shi'ites with support from Iran. Its spiritual leader was Sayyid Muhammad Husayn **Fadlallah**, and Shaykh 'Abbas Mussavi was secretary general until his assassination by Israeli agents in 1992. Supported by volunteers from Iran, the party opposed the Maronite regime of President Amin Gemayel and cooperated with like-minded Islamist parties. It proclaimed its objective to fight American and French influence in Lebanon, eliminate Israeli occupation of Lebanese territory, and establish an Islamic system of government. It staged assassinations and suicide attacks on the American and French embassies and peacekeeping forces, including the attack in 1983 on the U.S. Marine barracks that resulted in the death of 241 American soldiers.

Hizbullah became a major force in the struggle against Israeli occupation in southern Lebanon, exacting a continuing toll in lives that the Israeli government could not stop. In 1992 and 1996, Hizbullah participated in the Lebanese elections and obtained a minority of 27 parliamentary seats allotted to the Shi'ite community. The successes of the Lebanese Hizbullah against the South Lebanon Army and its Israeli supporters resulted in increasing appeals for unilateral withdrawal of Israeli forces from its self-declared security zone, which was completed in 2000. Hizbullah's secretary general, **Shaykh** Hasan **Nasrallah**, was elected in 1992, after the Israelis assassinated his predecessor, Shaykh Abbas Musawi. A number of splinter groups, the **Islamic Amal**, **Islamic Jihad**, and Islamic Resistance, were either part of Hizbullah or merged with the movement. The Party of God prevailed when Prime Minister Ehud Barak pulled out all Israeli troops in June 2000, and it fought Israel to a stalemate in the "Second" Lebanon War (12 July–8 September 2006). *See also* ISLAMIC REPUBLIC OF IRAN.

HOJJATIYEH. *See* HUJJATIYAH SOCIETY.

HOLIDAYS. *See* CALENDAR; FESTIVALS.

HOLY WARRIOR. *See* MUJAHID.

HOSPITALITY. "Dhiyafah." A virtue obligatory by **Tradition** and enjoined in the **Koran**: "And do good to parents and kinfolk, orphans, those in need, neighbors who are of kin, neighbors who are strangers, the companion by your side, the way-farer (ye meet)"(4:36). Pre-Islamic poetry extolls the virtue of **Hatim al-Ta'i**, who slaughtered three camels to entertain three travelers who only asked for a little milk. Hospitality is one of the obligations of the code of manly virtue, **muruwwa**, which demands courage, loyalty, and generosity. Originally the code of the Bedouin Arabs and an act that permitted survival in a hostile environment, hospitality is an obligation observed throughout the Islamic world.

HOUSE OF WISDOM. An academy with a library and translation bureau, founded in **Baghdad** in 830 by Caliph al-**Ma'mun** (r. 813–833), which became the most important educational institution in the **'Abbasid** period (749–1258). Scholars translated Greek works in medicine by Galen (d. ca. 200), mathematics by Euclid and Ptolemy, and philosophy by Plato and Aristotle at a time when Europeans were almost totally ignorant of Greek thought and science.

HUDAYBIYAH. A valley on the road from Jeddah to **Mecca** where **Muhammad** concluded a treaty with the **Quraysh** in February 628. Muhammad moved from **Medina** to Mecca, accompanied by a force of 1,400 of his followers. He halted at Hudaybiyah and stated that he wanted to perform the **pilgrimage** to the **Ka'bah**. After some negotiation, Muhammad agreed to postpone his entry into Mecca for a year and to conclude a truce for 10 years. He also agreed to return subjects of the Quraysh who had accepted Islam, although Muslims who defected were not to be extradited. In the following year, the Muslims performed their pilgrimage, and in 630, they took Mecca, claiming a violation of the treaty by the Quraysh.

HUDUD. *See* HADD.

HUJJATIYAH SOCIETY (SAZMAN-E HOJJATIYEH). A Shi'ite religio-political school founded in the early 1950s by Shaykh Mahmud Halabi in **Mashhad**, Iran. Hujjat, meaning proof, refers to a person who is an intermediary to the **Hidden Imam**. The Society organized campaigns of intimidation of **Baha'is** as heretics, and after the Iranian Revolution it was suspected of rejecting the concept of the **vilayat-i faqih**, the rule of the jurisconsult Ayatollah Ruhollah **Khomeyni**. Therefore, it was eventually forced to suspend its activities.

HULAGU (1217–1265). Grandson of the **Mongol** conqueror Genghiz Khan and founder of the Ilkhanid dynasty of Iran. He invaded Iran and captured the fortress of **Alamut** of the Assassins in 1256 and took **Baghdad** in 1258. He ordered the execution of the **'Abbasid** caliph Al-Musta'sim and members of his family and thus ended the classical **caliphate**. One member of the 'Abbasid family managed to escape and established himself as caliph under **Mamluk** protection in **Cairo**. Hulagu invaded Syria and took Aleppo and Hama, but he could not capture **Damascus**. The Mongols were finally stopped by the Mamluks under Qotuz at **Ayn Jalut** in 1260. Although largely shamanist by religion, the Ilkhanids eventually adopted Islam and assimilated with the local population.

HUNAYN, BATTLE OF. A battle that took place in a valley on the road from **Mecca** to Tayef. **Muhammad** fought the tribes of Hawazin and Thaqif, which planned to recapture Mecca, in 630. The tribes attacked Muhammad's forces and after some initial success were decisively defeated. According to the Prophet's biographers, some 6,000 **women** and children and large herds of camels were taken as **booty**. Many of the survivors embraced Islam, and the prestige of the Muslim community was greatly enhanced. The **Koran** related that an unseen army of **angels** supported the Muslims: "Assuredly **Allah** did help you in many battle fields and on the day of Hunayn: Behold! Your great numbers elated you, but they availed you nought; the land for all that it is wide did not constrain you, and ye turned back in retreat. But Allah did pour His calm on the **Messenger** and on the **believers**, and sent down forces which ye saw not: He punished the unbelievers: thus doth he reward those without faith" (9:25–26).

HUR. The **women** of paradise, described in the **Koran**: "We shall wed them to maidens with beautiful, big, and lustrous eyes" (44–54). Commentaries explain the word hur as connoting the idea of purity, beauty, and truth.

HURAYRAH, ABU. *See* ABU HURAYRAH.

HURUFIYYAH. A mystical, esoteric Sufi sect founded by Fazlallah Astarabadi (1340–1394). It is the mystical science of letters and words as a key to the "seventh sealed book," the **Koran**. The Hurufis staged an uprising in Azerbayjan that was crushed, and Fazlallah was executed in 1394. It existed primarily in the area of present-day Iran and Turkey and became extinct within a decade of its foundation.

HUSAIN, TAHA (1889–1973). Egyptian modernist and reformer who, although blind, studied at Al-**Azhar** University in Egypt and obtained a doctorate from the Sorbonne in Paris. He rose from humble beginnings to become a university professor, provost, rector, and minister of education. Praised as the "conqueror of darkness," he advocated modernization of **education** at both traditional and secular institutions. He produced works of both literature and literary criticism. He wanted Muslims to learn from the West but continue to be inspired by their own traditions. He believed the **Koran** and **Sunnah** are for all times, but should inspire later generations in a more flexible manner. He became a member of UNESCO's Executive Board and vice president of the General Conference in 1950–1951.

HUSAYN IBN 'ALI (626–680). Second son of **'Ali ibn Abi Talib** and **Fatimah** and grandson of the Prophet **Muhammad**. Muhammad had no male heirs, therefore Husayn and his brother, **Hasan**, were considered by the partisans of 'Ali to be the rightful successors to the leadership of the Islamic community. When 'Ali was assassinated in 661, Iraq opted for Hasan, but he abdicated in a deal with **Mu'awiyah**, which gained him a considerable pension and retirement in **Medina**. Husayn refused to acknowledge Mu'awiyah and, following a call by the people of Iraq, he set out for **Kufah**. Deserted by most of his followers, he was confronted at **Karbala** by an army of some 4,000 troops, headed by Sa'd ibn Abi **Waqqas**, and he was killed with his family and companions. The 10th of **Muharram** (680) has since been mourned by **Shi'ites** with passion plays, reenacting the scenes at Karbala (*see* 'ASHURA). Shi'ites consider him the second infallible **imam**, and **Sunnis** respect him as the grandson of the Prophet.

HUSAYNI, AMIN AL- (1895–1974). Grand **mufti** of **Jerusalem** (1926–1937) and head of the Arabic High Command in Palestine (1936). Educated at Al-**Azhar** University in **Cairo** and the School of Administration in **Istanbul**, he became a major force against the British mandatory power of Palestine and was eventually forced to flee in 1937. He spent the Second World War in Italy and Germany, from where he conducted anti-Allied propaganda. He was a leading member of the Palestinian Nationalist Movement.

HUSAYNIYYAH. A special site for ritual commemoration of the martyrdom of **Imam Husayn**. Husayniyyahs exist in every **Shi'ite** community in Iraq, Iran, and Lebanon and, with different names, also in Bahrain, Oman, and India. First introduced in **Baghdad** by the **Buyyids** (932–1055) and eventually institutionalized under the **Safavid** dynasty (1501–1722), the practice of commemoration spread throughout the Shi'ite world and has become a common feature in every community.

HYPOCRITES, THE. "Munafiqun." Medinans and members of tribes who adopted Islam but deserted **Muhammad** before the Battle of **Uhud** in 625. They wanted to ally themselves with the growing strength of Islam but were ready to desert or intrigue against the early Islamic community. By extension, the term *hypocrites* has come to refer to opportunists who did not become Muslims by conviction. The **Koran** says: "When the hypocrites come to thee, they say, 'We bear witness that thou art indeed the **Messenger** of **Allah**.' Yea, Allah knoweth that thou art indeed His Messenger. And Allah beareth witness that the hypocrites are indeed liars. They have made their oaths a screen (for their misdeeds): Thus they obstruct (men) from the path of Allah: Truly evil are their deeds" (63:1–2).

– I –

'IBADAT. God's commands concerning worship and ritual. They include ritual **prayer** (salat), **fasting** (sawm), **almsgiving** (zakat), and **pilgrimage** (hajj), and they constitute part of the **Five Pillars of Islam**, the first of which is the profession of faith (shahada). *See* FAITH, ARTICLES OF; FIVE PILLARS OF ISLAM.

IBADITES (ABADITES). Followers of the Ibadiyya, a **Kharijite** offshoot named after its eponymic ancestor, Abdallah Ibn Ibad (d. 680), who lived in **Basra** in the second half of the seventh century. They rejected the intolerance of other Kharijites and did not consider Muslims of other **sects** to be unbelievers (**kafirs**). They opposed political assassinations and believed in the election of their **imam**. Unlike the orthodox schools, they believe that the **Koran** is created. They live in parts of northwest Africa as well as in Oman and the United Arab Emirates. The head of the Ibadites established his center at Nazwa in the Sultanate of Oman.

IBLIS. "Shaytan." A **devil** and a fallen **angel** (or rebellious jinn) who refused to bow before **Adam** and tempted Eve to eat from the tree of immorality; therefore, he was expelled from paradise and given the power to lead astray all those who are not true servants of God. He is made of fire, whereas man is made of clay, and he will exist until the **Day of Judgment**, when he will be destroyed. The **Koran** says: "And behold, We said to the angels: 'Bow down to Adam:' and they bowed down: Not so Iblis: he refused and was haughty: he was of those who reject faith" (2:34). Also, "(**Allah**) said: 'What prevented thee from prostrating when I commanded thee?' He said: 'I am better than he: Thou didst create me from fire, and him from clay'," and "(Allah) said: 'get thee down from it: it is not for thee to be arrogant. Here: get out for thou art of the meanest (of creatures)'" (7:12–13).

IBN AL-'ABBAS, 'ABDALLAH (619–687). Son of 'Abbas ibn 'Abd al Muttalib, the uncle of the Prophet. He was a **Companion** of the Prophet and Islamic scholar, the first to produce a commentary on the **Koran**. Originally a partisan of **'Ali**, who appointed him governor of **Basra**, he made peace with the **Umayyads**. He participated in many campaigns, acted as an adviser to **caliphs**, and retired to Tayef, where he died.

IBN ABIHI. *See* ZIYAD, IBN ABIHI.

IBN AMAJ, AL-QAZVINI (d. 886). Author of one of the six "sound" collections of **hadith**.

IBN AL-ARABI, ABU ABDULLAH (767–846). Philologist and genealogist of the highest reputation, who transmitted orally the poems composed by the Arab tribes. Son of Ziad, a slave from Sind, he was raised by al-**Mufadhdhal** Ibn Muhammad al-Dabbi, author of the *Mufaddaliyat*, who had married his mother. **Ibn Khallikan** reports that up to 100 persons attended his sittings, one commenting: "I followed his lessons upwards to ten years, and I never saw him with a book in his hand; and yet he dictated to his pupils camel-loads of (philological) information." (III, 24). He died in Samara (*surra man raa*) in 846.

IBN AL-ARABI, MUHYI AL-DIN (1165–1240). Mystic, philosopher, and poet known as the "Greatest Master" (Shaykh al-Akbar) of the Ta'i tribe. He was educated in Seville, Spain, where he lived for 30 years. He traveled widely in the Middle East and settled in Malatya, near **Damascus**, where his tomb is a much-visited shrine. Some 150 of his numerous works are still extant, most famous of which are his *Meccan Revelations (Futuhat al-makkiyah)* and *Gems of Wisdom (Fusus al-hikam)*. In these works, he expounded his ideas as a fusion of literal belief and belief submerging into spiritual illumination and divine inspiration. His concept of the "Perfect Man" (*al-Insan al-kamil*) shows man as the image of God, whose mission is to reveal the perfection of God. Condemned as a pantheist by **Ibn Taimiyyah** and **Ibn Khaldun**, he was defended by Firuzabadi (d. 1414), al-**Suyuti** (1445–1505), and al-**Sha'rani**.

IBN ATA, WASIL. *See* WASIL IBN 'ATA'.

IBN AL-ATHIR, 'IZZ AL-DIN (1160–1234). Arab historian and biographer, born in southeastern Turkey and educated at Mosul, **Baghdad**, and **Jerusalem**. He was with **Salah al-Din**'s (Saladin) army in Syria and served as minister at various princely courts. He published the *Complete History of the World* (*Kitab al-kamil fi 'l-tarikh*), starting with **Adam**, and a work on Traditions, *Lion of the Jungle* (*Usd al-ghaba*), which contains biographies of some 7,500 **Companions** of the Prophet. **Ibn Khallikan** placed him in the first rank of traditionalists, historians, and genealogists. Considered arrogant and conceited by some, he was appreciated by others for his independent and original mind.

IBN BABAWAYHI (BABUYAH, 923–991). Most eminent of traditionalists and jurist of the school of Qom. His *Kitab al-Tawhid* tries to show the compatibility of the imamat traditions with God's unity and justice. He held a position between the **Ghulat** and **Mu'tazilites** and was a **Shi'ite** collector of **hadith**. Educated by his father, he continued his studies at Rayy with noted scholars and traveled widely in the Islamic world. Author of one of the Shi'ite *Four Books* of hadith (*Kutub al-arba'a*), he was the last prominent member of the Shi'ite traditionalist school of **Qom**. His *Shi'ite Creed* (*Risalat al-i'tiqadat*) shows the doctrinal development of Shi'ism. Most of his 200 publications are lost.

IBN BAJJAH, IBN AL-SA'IGH (AVEMBACE, ca. 1095–1138). Spanish–Arab philosopher, natural historian, music theorist, composer, and musician. He spent some 20 years as **vizier** of the governor of Murcia and Zaragoza, until the region was captured by King Alphonso. He wrote, among others, commentaries on the writings of Aristotle. He tended to a pantheistic-materialistic philosophy, which exposed him to the accusation of heresy. Khakan, a Muslim contemporary, called him an infidel and atheist, saying: "Faith disappeared from his heart and left no trace behind; his tongue forgot (the praises of) the Merciful, neither did (the holy) name cross his lips" (Khallikan, trans. Slane, III, 131).

IBN BATUTAH, MUHAMMAD IBN 'ABD ALLAH (1304–1368 [1377?]). A native of Tangiers who started out on a **pilgrimage** to **Mecca** in 1325/1326 and went on to visit most countries in the Islamic world. He had a traditional education and later studied with noted Islamic scholars and wrote about his travels to the **Ottoman empire**, the steppes of the Golden Horde, India, East Asia—including China—and East and West Africa. After his return to Tangiers 24 years later, he set out for Spain and then crossed the Sahara into Black Africa. It is doubtful whether the "Arab Marco Polo" actually visited the Volga regions, but he included descriptions of all these areas in his travel account, entitled *Tuhfat al-nuzzar fi ghar'ib al-amsar wa-'aja'ib al-asfar.* It has been translated into French, and parts appeared in English under the title *The Travels of Ibn Batuta.* His rule was, "never travel the same road a second time," and he seems to have adhered to it.

IBN BAZ. *See* BAZ, ABDUL AZIZ IBN ABDULLAH AL-.

IBN HAJAR AL-ASQALANI (1372–1448). Author of some 50 works on **hadith**, history, biography, **tafsir**, poetry, and **Shafi'ite** jurisprudence. He compiled the most valued commentary of the Sahih of **Bukhari**, the completion of which in 1428 was marked as "the greatest celebration of the age" in Egypt. Ibn Hajar's funeral was said to have been attended by 50,000 people, including the sultan and the caliph.

IBN HANBAL, AHMAD (780–855). Islamic scholar and eponymous founder of the Hanbali **school of law**. He was a student of al-**Shafi'i**, founder of the Shafi'ite school of law. His is the most conservative, but smallest, of the four **Sunni** schools. It limits the jurists to only the **Koran** and the **Sunnah** for a decision of law. Ibn Hanbal was born in **Baghdad** and traveled widely in the Arab world in search of Traditions of the Prophet. His *Musnad* is a collection of some 28,000 Traditions. Ibn Hanbal resided in Baghdad, where he was an opponent of the **Mu'tazilite** school, which held that the Koran was created. During the inquisition, *mihna*, he refused to recant and was imprisoned during the reigns of the caliphs al-**Ma'mun** and al-Mu'tasim. Vindicated under the rule of Caliph al-Mutawakkil, Ibn Hanbal saw Sunni Islam accept the dogma of the uncreatedness of the Koran. He was described as "a handsome man of middle size, having his hair dyed of a light red color with hinna, and a few black hairs appearing in his (white) beard." (Khallikan, trans. Slane, I, 44). Imam Shafi'i said of him: "I went forth from Baghdad and left not behind me a more pious and a better jurisconsult than Ibn Hanbal" (Ibid).

Historians relate that his funeral was attended by 800,000 men and 60,000 **women** and that 20,000 **Christians** and Jews converted to Islam on that day. The **Wahhabis** (Unitarians) of Saudi Arabia are followers of the Hanbali school. *See also* CREATEDNESS OF THE KORAN.

IBN HAWQAL, ABU 'QASIM MUHAMMAD (HAUKAL) (d. 1990). Arab writer, geographer, and chronicler, who traveled widely and visited most parts of the Islamic world and remote parts of Asia and Africa between 943 and 969. He described countries in gazetteer form in his *The Face of the Earth (Kitab surat al-ardh)*, which included a map of the world and a detailed description of Muslim Spain, southern Italy, the Byzantine empire, the Caucasus, and north to Kiev. His book was first published in the West by M. J. de Goeje in Leiden in 1873 and most recently by Wiet in 1964. Ibn Hawqal was born in Nisibis, in present-day Iraq. He was suspected by some to be a Fatimid agent.

IBN HAZM, ABU MUHAMMAD 'ALI (994–1064). He is said to have been the greatest scholar and most original genius of Muslim Spain. He was a literalist (**zahirite**) and so virulently critical of other scholars that it was said, "The tongue of Ibn Hazm and the sword of al-**Hajjaj** ibn Yusuf were brothers." Born in Cordoba of a family of Christian converts, he held high offices at princely courts but retired to devote himself to the writing of poetry, biographies, and history. He was said to have produced some 400 works; the best known in the West is *The Dove's Neck Ring: On Love and Lovers (Tawq al-hamamah fi al-ulfa wa al-ullaf)*. Because of his unorthodox beliefs, he was several times imprisoned, and most of his works were burned.

Ibn Khallikan called him a man of "profound humility equal to the greatness of his talents," and quotes one ibn Bashkuwal as saying: "Of all the natives of Spain, Ibn Hazm was the most eminent by the universality and depth of his learning in the sciences cultivated by the Muslims; add to this his profound acquaintance with the (**Arabic**) tongue, and his vast abilities as an elegant writer, a poet, a biographer, and a historian" (II, 268).

IBN HISHAM, ABU MUHAMMAD 'ABD AL-MALIK (767–833/834). Arab Islamic scholar of south Arabian origin and a native of **Basra**, who lived in Egypt, where he edited **Ibn Ishaq**'s *Biography of the Prophet (Sirat rasul Allah)*. Only Ibn Hisham's recension is extant. It has been translated into German by G. Weil under the title *Das Leben Mohammeds* (Stuttgart, 1894) and into English by A. Guillaume under the title *The Life of Muhammad*.

IBN ISHAQ, MUHAMMAD (704–767). Author of the first biography of **Muhammad** (*Sirat rasul Allah*), which is extant only in the recension of **Ibn Hisham**. Ishaq was born in **Medina** and died in **Baghdad**. He studied with his father and with Medinan scholars and moved to Hira and **Kufah** to teach and write, later spending the rest of his life in Baghdad. The traditionalist Ibn Shihab al-Zuhri said of him: Medina would never lack *'ilm* (knowledge) as long as Ibn Ishaq is there.

IBN KATHIR, ISMA'IL BIN UMAR BIN- (1301–1373). A **Shafi'ite judge**, master scholar of history, and commentator on the **Koran**. Born in Busra, Syria, he was a student of **Ibn Taimiyyah** in **Damscus** and held various positions, including a professorship of Koranic commentary at the Great Mosque of Damascus. His *Tafsir ibn-Kathir* is one of the most widely used explanations of the Koran. He eventually became blind. When he died he was buried next to the grave of ibn-Taimiyyah.

IBN KHALDUN, 'ABD AL RAHMAN IBN MUHAMMAD (1332–1406). Arab philosopher of history and "Father of Sociology," born in Tunis, where he worked as a secretary. In Fez, he was secretary and chief judge. In Oran, he wrote the famous *Muqaddimah*

(*Prolegomena*), the introduction to his book on the origins of the Arabs, Berbers, and Persians. He held that history is subject to universal laws and presented a theory of cyclical change of humanity, from barbarism to rural and urban culture. He coined the term 'asabiyah as the binding element of society, which is strong among the nomadic conquerors who founded kingdoms. Gradually it weakened, leading to decay within a few generations, and fell prey to new nomad conquerors. At that time the cycle of evolution began anew. Ibn Khaldun served a number of princes, in Tunis, Fez, and Egypt. He was imprisoned and forced to escape to **Cairo**, where he became chief judge in **Mamluk** Egypt in 1384. He taught at Al-**Azhar** University and had an encounter with **Timur-i Lang** (Tamerlane) at **Damascus**. The nomad conqueror permitted him to return to Cairo in 1401, where he died in 1406.

IBN KHALLIKAN, SHAMS AL-DIN (1211–1282). Born at Arbela in Iraq of a family descended from the **Barmakids.** He was educated at Aleppo and **Damascus**, where he achieved the position of chief **judge** in 1261 and, after a short assignment in Egypt, again in 1278. Ibn Khallikan was described as "a pious man, virtuous, and learned; amiable in temper, in conversation serious and instructive. His exterior was highly prepossessing, his countenance handsome and his manners engaging." Ibn Khallikan was the first Muslim writer to compile a biographical dictionary in alphabetical order of some 800 great men; it is entitled *Deaths of Eminent Men (Wafayat al-'ayan)*. The British scholar Reynold A. Nicholson called it the "best general biography ever written" (Nicholson, 1962, 452). It was translated by M. de Slane, (1842–1874), with the title *Ibn Khallikan's Biographical Dictionary* (De Slane, IV, xv).

IBN MAJAH, ABU ABDULLAH MUHAMMAD (824–886). A Persian from the town of Qazwin. He ranked as a high authority in the Traditions, and was versed in all the sciences connected with them. He was a famous traditionalist and compiler of the *Book of Traditions (Kitab al-sunnan)*, one of the six canonical collections of **Sunni hadith.** Ibn Majah traveled widely in the Islamic world, collecting traditions from outstanding scholars. He is also known for his commentary on the **Koran.**

IBN AL-MUQAFFA'. *See* MUQAFFA', IBN AL-.

IBN AL-NADIM, MUHAMMAD IBN ISHAQ (936/937–995).
Twelver Shi'i scholar and bibliographer and author of the *Kitab al-Fihrist*, an index of all books written in Arabic up to his time. He was a bookseller and made a living also by copying manuscripts for sale; therefore he was also known as al-Waraq ("the manuscriptist"). The *Fihirist* contains 10 discourses on such topics as the Holy Scriptures; grammar and philology; history, biography, and genealogy; poetry; **kalam**; **fiqh**; philosophy; legends; doctrines of nonmonotheist creeds; and alchemy. Its author explains that the *Fihrist* is

> an Index of the books of all nations, Arabs and foreigners alike, which are extant in the Arabic language and script, on every branch of knowledge; comprising information as to their compilers and the classes of their authors, together with the genealogies of those persons, the dates of their birth, the length of their lives, the times of their death, the places to which they belonged, their merits and their faults, since the beginning of every science that has been invented down to the present epoch: namely the year 377 of Hijra. (Nicholson, 1962, 362)

IBN QUTAYBAH. *See* QUTAYBAH, MUHAMMAD IBN MUSLIM AL-DINAWARI AL-.

IBN RUSHD, ABU AL-WALID MUHAMMAD (AVERROËS, 1126–1198). Arab philosopher, theologian, jurist, physician, and great authority on Aristotle's philosophy. He was born in Cordoba, Spain, and later served as chief **judge** in his hometown, until he was banned as a heretic in 1195. He died in Marrakesh. Ibn Rushd wrote a refutation of Abu Muhammad al-**Ghazali**'s *Refutation of the Philosophers (Tahafut al-falasifa)*, and he was accused of denying the immortality of the human soul and the resurrection of the body after death. He held that only spirits, not bodies, would be resurrected and felt that God knows only universals, not particulars. Ibn Rushd separated religion from philosophy and favored an allegorical interpretation of the **Koran**. In the West, he became famous as Averroës for his *Commentaries on Aristotle.*

IBN SA'D, ABU ABDULLAH MUHAMMAD (764/765–845). One of the great Islamic biographers. His *Great Book of Classes (Kitab al-*

tabaqat al-kabir) is one of the earliest collections and an important source for the Prophet's biography and for early Islamic history. He was born in **Basra** and educated at **Baghdad**. He was secretary of Umar al-**Waqidi**, the Arab historian. Volume 8 of the *Tabaqat* was translated into English by Aisha Bewley under the title *The Women of Medina.*

IBN SA'UD, 'ABD AL-AZIZ IBN 'ABD AL-RAHMAN AL-FAISAL AL- (1880–1953). Great-grandson of Muhammad ibn Saud (r. 1747–1765), the founder of the Saudi dynasty and of modern Saudi Arabia. Driven from his native Najd in 1891, he lived in exile in Kuwait. With a band of only 40 men, Ibn Saud was able to recapture the castle of the Rashidi governor in Riyadh in 1902. Supporters flocked to his banner, and he took Hasa on the Gulf in 1913. Neutral during the First World War, he had conquered the **Hijaz** by 1925 and, in the Treaty of Jidda, Great Britain recognized the independence of the new state. It was renamed the Kingdom of Saudi Arabia in 1932. In 1933, Saudi Arabia signed the first agreement with the American Oil Company, which struck oil in 1938, and by 1953 the kingdom was making £5,000 ($2.5 million) a week in royalties.

Ibn Saud founded the tribal Brotherhood (Ikhwan) in 1912, which was formed into an effective army. He wanted his followers to become sedentary and settle in camp communities. Disagreements about raiding into neighboring countries led Ibn Saud to destroy the Ikhwanis in the Battle of Sibilla (1929). He restored the puritanical **Wahhabi** (Unitarian) creed to much of his realm, which accepts only the **Koran** and early Traditions (**Sunnah**) and rejects later developments of the classical period as innovations (**bid'ah**) and sinful. It forbids intercession and the veneration of tombs. Saudi kings draw their legitimacy as the "pious sultans" who perform all the functions formerly performed by the Rightly Guided Caliphs. Ibn Sa'ud had several wives and over 40 sons and an equal number of daughters. The dynasty continued under Sa'ud (1953–1964), Faisal (1964–1975), Khalid (1975–1982), Fahd (1982–2005), and Abdullah (2005–).

IBN SA'UD, 'ABD AL-'AZIZ IBN MUHAMMAD (1721–1803). Son of Muhammad Ibn Sa'ud (r. 1747–1765). He was the amir of the **Wahhabis**, who captured Riyadh in 1773 and in 1786 founded the first Sa'udi state in the Najd. After the death of **'Abd al-Wahhab** in 1792, he held both spiritual and temporal powers. His army sacked

Karbala in 1801 and captured **Mecca** and **Medina** in 1803, but his grandson, Abdullah ibn Sa'ud (1814–1818), was defeated by the army of **Muhammad 'Ali** of Egypt. The House of Sa'ud was able to recover from the disaster, and **Ibn Sa'ud** (1880–1953) was able to conquer most of the Arabian Peninsula.

IBN SINA, ABU 'ALI AL-HUSAYN IBN 'ABD ALLAH (AVICENNA) (980–1037). Born near Bukhara of Persian parents, Ibn Sina traveled to study with famous doctors. "At the age of ten years, he was a perfect master of the **Koran** and general literature, and had attained a certain degree of information in dogmatic theology, the Indian calculus (arithmetic), and algebra. . . . In the sixteenth year of his age, physicians of the highest eminence came to read, under his tuition the works which treat of the different branches of medicine and learn from him those modes of treatment which he had discovered by his practice" (Khallikan, trans. Slane, I, 440).

Known in the West as Avicenna, he was a philosopher, physician, and author of the *Great Book of Classes Canon of Medicine (al-Qanun fi tibb)*, which made him famous in Europe. He also wrote the *Book of Healing (Kitab al-shifa)*, a philosophical encyclopedia that earned him the title "Prince of Physicians." Translated into Latin, it served as a major medical text in medieval Europe and is still studied in the East today. He combined Islamic mysticism with Platonic idealism and asserted man's free will. Because he denied predestination, Ibn Sina was declared an unbeliever (**kafir**), and Caliph Mustanjid ordered his books to be burned. Ibn Sina died in Hamadan.

IBN TAIMIYYAH, AHMAD (1263–1328). Born in Harran in northern Syria and educated in **Damascus**, he became a jurist of the Hanbali **school of law**, teaching at Damascus and **Cairo**. His father and grandfather were famous authorities of the Hanbali school. A strict traditionalist and opponent of **Sufism**, **Shi'ism**, saint cults, shrines, and philosophy, Ibn Taimiyyah was a "literalist," accepting anthropomorphic references in the **Koran**. He held that the Koran must be interpreted according to the letter, not understood through reason; **revelation** is the only source of knowledge, and the Koran and **Sunnah** are the only authentic guides in all matters. Ibn Taimiyyah denied the legitimacy of theology and the obligation to follow the decisions of the early schools of jurisprudence. He condemned many practices of popular Islam as sinful innovations (**bid'ah**), was repeatedly imprisoned, and died in jail. One of his major works is *Book of the Refutation of the Logicians (Kitab al-radd 'ala al-mantiqiyyin)*. His teachings have inspired revivalist movements, including 19th-century **Wahhabism** and present-day **Islamists**. A chief of the **Shafi'ite** school in Syria said of Ibn Taimiyyah:

> If he were asked a question in any of the sciences, it would appear as though he knew that science masterfully, to the exclusion of other sciences; and it would be judged that no one knows it as well as he. The jurists of all schools would benefit from his knowledge in their own schools, and would learn about them what they would not have known before. . . . It is not known that any scholar could win a debate against him. . . . He was master at interpretation, expression, organization, categorization and clarification. . . . (Victor E. Makari, *Ibn Taymiyyah's Ethics: The Social Factor*, 26–27)

IBN TUFAYL, ABU BAKR MUHAMMAD (d. 1185). Spanish philosopher of Arabic descent and author of *Hayy ibn Yaqzan*, a philosophical novel that describes how a youth, growing up on an isolated island, arrives at the truth of revelation through introspection. He also had a great reputation as a mathematician and physician and entered the service of the Almohad Sultan Abu Yaqub Yusuf. He was born in Guadix and died in Morocco. His book was translated into Latin in 1671 under the title *Philosophicus Autodidactus*.

IBN TUMART, ABU 'ABD ALLAH MUHAMMAD (1077–1130). A Berber native of Morocco and ideologue of the **Almohad** dynasty, who eventually proclaimed himself the **Mahdi**. A member of the Masmuda tribe, he was educated at Alexandria and **Baghdad** and subsequently organized the Masmuda in a campaign against the **Almoravids** (1061–1147). He emphasized the unity of God and demanded puritanical moral reform based on the **Koran** and Traditions. Ibn Tumart's creed has been described as a mixture of messianic **Shi'ism**, **Ash'arite** dogmatics, **Zahirite** legal theory, some **Mu'tazilite** ideas, and **Kharijism**. His writings on theology, philosophy, and law were translated from Berber into Latin. Ibn Tumart was described as

> pious and devout, he lived in squalid poverty, subsisting on the coarsest fare and attired in rags; he generally went with downcast eyes; smiling whenever he looked a person in the face, and ever manifesting his propensity of devotion. He carried with him no other worldly goods than a staff and a skin for holding water; his courage was great; he spoke correctly the **Arabic** and the Maghrib (Berber) languages; he blamed with extreme severity the conduct of those who transgressed the divine law, and not content with obeying God's commandments, he labored to enforce their strict observance. (Khallikan, trans. Slane, III, 206)

IBN ZUHR, ABU MARWAN ABD AL-MALIK (1091–1161). Father of experimental surgery, expounded in his famous work *al-Taisir*, and one of the greatest Arab physicians. Known in the West as Avenzoar, he was born in Seville and studied at the University of Cordova. He was the first to perform human dissections and postmortem autopsies and to reject the theory of "four humors." He established surgery as an independent field of medicine.

IBRAHIM. Arabic for Abraham. *See* ABRAHAM.

'ID. "Festival." *See* FESTIVALS.

'ID AL-ADHA. The Feast of Sacrifice on the 10th of the month of Dhu al-Hijja of the Islamic **calendar**. It is an Islamic holiday in Muslim countries, also called the Greater Bairam in Turkey (or 'Id al-Kabir or Bakr-i 'Id), which marks the end of the month of **pilgrimage**. Pilgrims and Muslims throughout the world slaughter a sheep, or camel, or purchase meat from a butcher, as a sacrifice and distribute most of it to the poor. Large quantities of meat are shipped every year from Saudi Arabia to Afghanistan and other countries for distribution to the poor. Major purification, **ghusl**, is obligatory before prayer at a **Friday mosque**. This dates back to the tradition of **Abraham** attempting to sacrifice his son at the command of God.

'ID AL-FITR. The Feast of Breaking the Fast, celebrated on the first of the month of Shawwal, the day following the **fasting** month of **Ra-**

madhan. The celebration begins with the appearance of the new moon, and the following day people pay their poor tax, *zakat al-fitr*, before attending prayer at a **Friday mosque**. It is a joyful celebration, as it marks the end of the hardships of fasting for an entire month. New clothing is traditionally purchased on this occasion for family and servants, making it an occasion of gift giving. The holiday is also called Lesser Bayram (*'Id al-Saghir*) or the Minor Feast, or the Feast of Alms (*'Id al-Sadaqah*).

'IDDAH. "Number." The number of days a **divorced** or widowed **woman** must wait before she can remarry. *See also* WAITING PERIOD, THE.

IDOLATRY. "Shirk." Islam demands a strict monotheism; giving "partners to God" is idolatry (shirk) and an unforgivable sin. The Hanbali school, unlike the other orthodox **Sunni schools of law**, prohibits any intermediaries between God and mankind, forbidding the cult of **saints**, soothsayers, the healing properties of **amulets**, and the worship of holy shrines. All Sunni schools prohibit representational art—whether statues or images of living things (although this is no longer enforced in many parts of the Islamic world). Therefore, floral motifs and the **Arabic** script are used for ornamentation. The **Koran** says: "They disbelieve who say: 'Allah is one of three (in a Trinity) for there is no god except One God' (5:73). . . . Say, to Allah belongs exclusively (the right to grant intercession . . .)" (39:44). The **Twelver Shi'ites**, on the other hand, permit even portraits of **Imam 'Ali**.

IDRISI, AL-SHARIF AL- (1100–1165). Arab geographer who traveled widely in Europe, Africa, and Asia. At the court of the Norman king Roger II in Sicily, he produced a geographic work that summed up all the previously known features of the world and made original contributions in his work entitled *The Recreation of Him Who Yearns to Traverse the Lands (Nuzhad al-mushtaq fi ikhtiraq al-afaq)*.

IDRISID DYNASTY (788–985). First **Shi'ite** dynasty in Islamic history, founded by Idris ibn Abdullah (d. 793), a grandson of **Hasan**, the son of 'Ali. He escaped to northern Morocco after an unsuccessful uprising in **Medina**, and the Berbers recognized him as their **imam**. He was poisoned at the instigation of **Harun al-Rashid** (786–809), the **'Abbasid caliph** at **Baghdad**. His son Idris II founded his capital in Fez, Morocco, but the state disintegrated soon thereafter as a result of attacks from the **Fatimids** in the east and the Spanish **Umayyads** in the west. The Idrisids' major contributions included converting the Berbers and helping to maintain **Sunni** predominance by fighting their **Kharijite** neighbors. They founded the Sharifian dynasty in Morrocco, which still rules the country.

'IFRIT (EFRIT). Powerful, malevolent jinn. They are giants and have also been called the ghosts of the wicked dead.

IFTAR. "Breaking." The breaking of the fast at sunset during the month of **Ramadhan**. Cannon shots usually announce the time when it is permissible to eat, and people in the streets, bazaars, and homes begin their evening meal. Shortly before dawn, people eat once more to last them during the daylight **fasting**, which can be quite long during the hot summer months.

IGNORANCE, THE AGE OF. Muslims call the pre-Islamic period the "Age of Ignorance" (*jahiliya*). It was the age of tribalism and is reckoned to cover about a century before the advent of Islam. It is also the heroic age of the great Bedouin poets, who extolled the virtues of Bedouin life: courage, loyalty, and generosity. The *Seven Odes* (**Mu'allaqat**) and similar collections of this period are considered superior to any poetry composed thereafter.

IHRAM. "Prohibiting." The state of ritual purity before **prayer**; also during **pilgrimage** (hajj) before entering the perimeter of the city of **Mecca** (haram). The pilgrim (hajji) performs the **ablution** (ghusl) and puts on a dress, consisting of two unsewn sheets or, in the case of **women**, a long robe. Women do not veil their faces during ihram. In the state of consecration, all Muslims are manifestly equal before God.

IJMA'. "Collecting." The consensus of the community, but subsequently only of the competent jurists on a point of theology or law, expressed in words or deeds, as well as in silent agreement. In the early **Umayyad** period, the Caliph **'Umar** II instructed his governors in the provinces that cases should be decided by consensus of the jurists in each region. Together with the **Koran**, Traditions (**Sunnah**), and reasoning by analogy (**qiyas**), ijma' is one of the four pillars of **Sunni Islamic law** (**shari'ah**). Ijma' is based on a saying of the Prophet: "My people will never agree in an error." The number required to validate a practice or belief varied among the four orthodox schools of jurisprudence, ranging from the entire community (**ummah**) to local groups or the **Companions** of the Prophet. Limited at first to the Companions of the Prophet, ijma' came to designate the agreement of the learned and had to be determined by retrospection. Ijma' permitted the acceptance of **Sufism** and other innovations that were at first thought to be sinful.

IJTIHAD. "Exertion." The exercise of personal reasoning and private judgment or "informed opinion" (**ra'y**) and reasoning by analogy (**qiyas**) in questions of **Islamic law** not expressly provided for in the **Koran** and the Traditions (**Sunnah**). An example of this is the prohibition against all intoxicants, not just wine, mentioned in the Koran. Eventually, it came to be accepted by the four **Sunni schools of law** but exercised by those qualified to make a decision, the **mujtahids**, whose agreement became law on the basis of consensus (**ijma'**).

Eventually, the four orthodox schools declared the "gate of ijtihad" closed and demanded imitation or emulation (**taqlid**) and condemned any further employment of ijtihad as sinful innovation (**bid'ah**). Muslim modernists and their radical opponents, the **Islamists**, favor the reopening of the "gate of ijtihad" for different reasons. The modernists feel that it is necessary to reinterpret the bases of Islamic religion and law in light of modern developments, whereas many Islamists reject much of what was produced during the period of classical Islam as innovation and want to establish an Islamic state on the model of **Muhammad**'s community. **Shi'ites** have always accepted the ijtihad of the qualified doctors (mujtahid). *See also* MU'ADH IBN JABAL.

IKHSHIDID DYNASTY (935–969). A dynasty founded by Muhammad ibn-Tughj (d. 496) in Egypt. He was a Turk from Ferghana who was made governor of Egypt by the **'Abbasid caliph** al-Radhi (r. 934–940). He made himself independent and annexed Syria and Palestine and, eventually, also the holy cities of **Mecca** and **Medina** to his domains. After his death, al-Misk **Kafur** (Musky Camphor), an Abyssinia eunuch, became the de facto ruler (946–968). The dynasty ended in 969 as a result of **Fatimid** attacks.

IKHWAN. "Brethren." **Wahhabi** Bedouin followers of Abd al-Aziz **Ibn Sa'ud** who formed armed militias and settled in village camps in 1912. They were an important factor in establishing their **imam** as king of Saudi Arabia, but they proved to be hostile to reforms promoting modernization and at times resisted attempts at limiting their political influence.

IKHWAN AL-MUSLIMIN, AL-. *See* ISLAMIST MOVEMENT; MUSLIM BROTHERHOOD.

IKHWAN AL-SAFA (BRETHREN OF PURITY). A secret organization of philosophers, probably of **Isma'ili** background, which flourished in **Basra** and **Baghdad** in the 10th and 11th centuries. It was a religio–political organization aiming at the overthrow of the political system. The members were organized in four ranks by age: the Craftsmen, at least 15 years old; the Political Leaders, at least 30 years old; the Kings, at least 40 years old; and the Prophets and Philosophers, above 50 years of age. Their teachings are collected in the *Encyclopedia of the Brethren of Purity* (*Rasa'el ikhwan al-safa*), consisting of 52 epistles dealing with mathematics, astronomy, geography, music, ethics, and philosophy.

ILHAD. "To turn away." Denying the attributes of knowledge from **Allah**.

ILKHANIDS (1256–1353). One of the **Mongol** hordes that, under Hulagu (1253–1265), conquered Iran in 1256 and founded a dynasty. At its height it also ruled parts of Syria, eastern Anatolia, and the Caucasus. The dynasty eventually assimilated and accepted **Islam** under Ghazan (1295–1304). In the mid-fourteenth century, the Ilkhanid state disintegrated into a number of smaller entities.

'ILM ('ELM). Knowledge, especially that of the Islamic sciences. An *'alim* is a doctor of Islamic sciences, and the plural of the word, **'ulama'**, is applied to the body of Islamic jurisconsults and theologians.

'ILM AL-FIQH. *See* FIQH.

'ILM AL-HADITH. *See* HADITH.

'ILM AL-TAFSIR. *See* EXEGESIS OF THE KORAN.

IMAM. A leader who stands in front (*amama*) of the congregation at **prayer**. The term is also the title of the first four **Sunni caliphs** and the founders of the four orthodox schools of jurisprudence. **Shi'ites** use the term for the descendants of Ali and **Fatimah**, whom they consider the rightful successor to the Prophet **Muhammad** in leadership of the Islamic community. Shi'ites are divided between those who accept, respectively, **Zayd**, the son of 'Ali (d. 740), the Fifth Imam; **Isma'il** (d. 760), the Seventh Imam; and Muhammad al-**Muntazar** (disappeared in 878), the Twelfth Imam. The imams are the descendants of the Prophet and considered free of sin, infallible, and intermediaries with **Allah**. The **Twelver Shi'ite** (or Imamis) believe that Muhammad al-Muntazar, who disappeared as an infant, went into occultation and will return as the Messiah (**Mahdi**) on the **Day of Judgment**. In the meantime, the Twelver Shi'ite jurist/ theologians rule on the imam's behalf. The Shi'ite imams include the following:

'Ali ibn Abu Talib (d. 661)	Ja'far al-Sadiq (d. 765)
al-Hasan (d. 669)	Musa al-Kazim (d. 799)
al-Husayn (d. 680)	'Ali al-Radhi (d. 818)
'Ali Zayn al-'Abidin (d. 712)	Muhammad al-Jawad (d. 835)
Muhammad al-Baqir (d. 731)	Ali al-Hadi (d. 868)
Zayd ibn 'Ali (d. 740)	al-Hasan al-Askari (d. 874)
Isma'il (d. 760)	Muhammad al-Muntazar (878)

See also HIDDEN IMAM; ISMA'ILIS; KHOMEYNI, AYATOLLAH RUHOLLAH AL-MUSAVI AL-; VILAYAT-I FAQIH; ZAYDIS.

IMAMIS. Referring to **Twelver Shi'ites**. *See also* SHI'ISM.

IMAN. "Faith." The six articles of Islamic faith include belief in God, the **angels** of God, the book of God (**Koran**), the **prophets** of God, the **Day of Judgment**, and the Divine Decree. **Shi'ites** must also believe in the infallible **imams**. **'Amal**, actions, are summarized under the term the **Five Pillars of Islam**, as follows: (1) profession of faith (shahada), (2) **prayer** (salat), (3) **fasting** (sawm), (4) **almsgiving** (zakat), and (5) **pilgrimage** (hajj). To become a Muslim, one has to testify that there is no god but **Allah** and that **Muhammad** is the **Messenger** of Allah (*La ilaha illa' llah wa Muhammad Rasul Allah*). *See also* CREED; FAITH, ARTICLES OF.

IMITATION. *See* TAQLID.

IMMACULATE CONCEPTION. *See* MARY, MOTHER OF JESUS.

IMMORALITY. Immorality is forbidden by God and encouraged by **Iblis** (Satan). It is immoral to commit **adultery** (4:19, 25; 17:32), engage in homosexuality (7:80, 27:54, 29:28, 33:30 and 65:1), marry the wife of one's father (4:22), and commit slander (24:16, 17). A sinner must ask God's forgiveness and resolve not to commit such an act again.

IMRU 'L-QAYS (ca. 500–540). Grandson of the last king of Kindah, who was rejected by his father because of his dissolute life. He was to avenge the murder of his father and sought the support of the Emperor Justinian at Constantinople, but was reputedly poisoned by the emperor. Known as the "Vagabond Prince," wandering from tribe to tribe, he is recognized as the greatest of pre-Islamic poets. Nicholson says of him: "**Muhammad** described him as 'their [poet's] leader in Hell-fire,' while the Caliphs **'Umar** and **'Ali**, . . . notwithstanding, extolled his genius and originality" (1962, 105). Hailing a starved wolf as a comrade, he said: "Each of us what thing he finds devours: Lean is the wretch whose living is like ours" (ibid.). His prized poems are part of the **Mu'allaqat**.

INHERITANCE, LAW OF. The purpose of the law of inheritance is to prevent the possibility of concentration of wealth. In the tribal society of pre-Islamic Arabia, **women** possessed no right of inheritance; in fact, they were often part of the objects to be inherited. The **Koran** said: "From what is left by parents and those nearest related there is a share for men and a share for women, whether the property be small or large—a determinate share (4:7). . . . O ye who believe! Ye are forbidden to inherit women against their will. Nor should ye treat them with harshness, that ye may take away part of the dower" (4:19). The law of inheritance is complex; generally a female inherits half the share that a man does. The property is to be distributed among ascending as well as descending relatives. No more than a third of the estate can be willed to a designated heir after all outstanding debts have been paid. In certain tribal societies, such as some on the Afghan frontier, women do not receive their inheritance, and a brother, or nearest male relative, marries the wife of the deceased.

INJIL. Gospel, referred to in the **Koran** and Traditions 12 times as "original Gospel which was promulgated by Jesus." The Koran says, "It is He who sent down to thee (step by step) in truth, the Book, confirming what went before it; and He sent down the Tora (of Moses) and the Gospel (of Jesus)" (3:3).

INQUISITION. *See* MIHNA.

INSHALLAH (IN SHA'A ALLAH). A phrase meaning "if God wills," is used when talking about the future. It recognizes the supreme power of **Allah**, who alone decides the events of the future. Westerners who expect a firm commitment wrongly interpret the saying as evasive and tantamount to meaning "perhaps." It is based on an injunction in the **Koran** that says, "Nor say of anything 'I shall do so and so tomorrow'—except if Allah so wills" (18:23–24).

INTERCESSION. "Tawassul." According to several verses in the **Koran**, the concept of intercession on the **Last Day** to save a sinner from punishment is not accepted. There are, however, some verses that hint at the possibility of intercession (43:86), which some have interpreted to mean that it is possible if good and bad deeds are evenly matched. According to one tradition, the Prophet **Muhammad** would intercede on the **Day of Judgment** "until all his community had gone to paradise before him." **Shi'ism** accepts the intercession of the **imam**. **Sufism** and popular Islam accept the cult of **saints** and intercession, but it is forbidden by the Hanbali **school of law**.

INTEREST. "Riba'." Taking of interest is forbidden in Islam (2:275). The prohibition has been evaded by legal subterfuge (**hila**, pl. hiyal), for example, when the moneylender buys something and later sells it back for a lower amount. Islamic banks do not pay interest but do charge fees or make a person who opens an account a partner, who shares in the profits (and theoretically in the losses) of the bank.

INTERNATIONAL COALITION AGAINST "TERROR." A largely American–British force engaged in hunting down **Islamist** guerrilla forces in **Afghanistan**. As a result of the terrorist attack on the World Trade Center on 11 September 2001, the United States invaded Afghanistan and with the help of local militias was able to destroy the **Taliban** government and drive al-**Qaeda** forces from its bases. The campaign, dubbed Operation Enduring Freedom, at first involved only American troops, which were quickly reinforced with British contingents. The United States appealed to the North Atlantic Treaty Organization, invoking Article 5 of its charter, which says, "an attack on one NATO nation is an attack on all," obligating the members to provide material assistance. The U.S. State Department has released a list of 37 countries providing some type of assistance, claiming that there are others who for "internal political reasons choose not to broadcast their participation." Most members of the coalition have given nonmilitary support; for example, **Pakistan** and Uzbekistan provided bases and overflight permission; Italy and France sent naval forces into the Arabian Sea and the Persian Gulf; Estonia, Norway, Jordan, and Denmark contributed demining units; and others supplied food, clothing, and medical aid for Afghanistan.

IQBAL, SIR MUHAMMAD (1877–1938). Poet in Persian and Urdu, philosopher, and a founding father of the state of Pakistan. He was the product of a traditional and Western education, with a doctorate from Munich, Germany, and he taught **Arabic**, history, and economics at the Oriental College at Lahore. Iqbal was a Muslim modernist who favored the reinterpretation of Islam on the basis of **ijtihad** to reflect the interests of society. He held that

> Islam properly understood and rationally interpreted is not only capable of moving along with the progressive and evolutionary forces of life, but also of directing them into new and healthy channels in every epoch. (Mir Zohair Husain, 1986, 105)

He favored the partition of India to protect the culture of Muslims in what would have been a predominantly Hindu state. In Urdu and, primarily, Persian, he called for reforms and the creation of a sound and prosperous Muslim nation.

IRAN. *See* ISLAMIC REPUBLIC OF IRAN.

IRTIDAD. *See* APOSTASY.

ISFAHANI, ABU AL-FARAJ AL- (897–ca. 967). Arab literary historian and critic who won fame for his *Book of Songs (Kitab al-aghani)*, which contained about 2,000 favorite songs of his time, annotated with anecdotes, biographical information, and excerpts from poetry. He was born in Isfahan, a direct descendant of the **Umayyad caliphs**, and educated at **Kufah** and **Baghdad**. One of his teachers was **Tabari**, the grammarian and **hadith** scholar. Criticized for his dirty appearance, drunkenness, and **Shi'ite** tendencies (he is said to have been a **Zaydi** Shi'ite), he was nevertheless one of the most widely quoted authorities on **Arabic** culture. It was at the Hamdanid court of Prince Sayf al-Dawlah at Aleppo that he wrote the *Book of Songs*. **Ibn Khaldun** says of the work:

> [It] is the Register of the Arabs. It comprises all that they had achieved in the past of excellence in every kind of poetry, history, music, et cetera. So far as I am aware, no other book can be put on a level with it in this respect. It is the final resource of the student of belles-lettres, and leaves him nothing further to desire. (Nicholson, 1962, 32)

ISFAHANI, ABU NU'IM AL- (948–1038). **Shafi'ite** jurist and mystic of Isfahan, who published *The Jewel of the Saints (Hilyat al-awliyah)*, a biographical dictionary of **Sufism**.

ISHAQ, MUHAMMAD IBN (704–767). *See* IBN ISHAQ, MUHAM-MAD.

ISLAM. "Submission." A monotheistic religion that continues the prophetic Judeo–Christian tradition and recognizes **Muhammad** as the last of the **prophets**. It is the religion of about 800 million people, living predominantly in Asia, with minority populations all over the world. There are more than 2 million Muslims in the United States. The word Islam is **Arabic** and means submission, the obligation to "submit" to the commands of Allah, the Omniscient and Omnipotent God. Theologians distinguish among religious belief, or faith (iman); acts of worship and religious duty (**'ibadat**); and rightdoing (ihsan)—all of which are part of the term **din**, religion.

Muslims believe in one God, **Allah**, who is the Creator, Supreme Power, Judge, and Avenger, but who is also the Compassionate and Merciful One. **Angels** are Allah's messengers and, like humans, His creatures and servants. They record men's actions and bear witness against them on the **Day of Judgment**. The Angel **Gabriel** is God's chief **messenger**. There are also jinn, spirits, who are good or evil like men. The fallen, or evil, jinn are called shaytans, **devils**, whose leader is **Iblis** (Satan). He is given "authority over those who should be seduced by him." God sends His prophets to bring His message. The major messengers include **Adam**, **Noah**, **Abraham**, **Moses**, and **Jesus**, but Muhammad is the last of the prophets, and the **Koran** is the last message, superseding the Torah (Tawrah) of Moses, the Psalms (**Zabur**) of David, and the Gospel (Injil) of Jesus. Muslims believe in a Day of Judgment, when the good will enter paradise and the evil will be condemned to eternal hellfire. Personal responsibility before God is important in Islam, and there is no belief in atonement.

Religious duties ('Ibadat) can be summarized under a code of rituals called the **Five Pillars of Islam**, as follows:

The profession of faith (**shahada**). A Muslim says: "I testify that there is no god but Allah and I testify that Muhammad is the **Messenger** of Allah." Anyone who sincerely testifies to that is a Muslim.

Prayer (salat), which is to be performed five times a day, facing the prayer direction (**qiblah**), the location of the **Ka'bah** a cubelike building in **Mecca** (built by Abraham, according to the Koran). Prayers include recitation of the Arabic text accompanied by rhythmical bowings (rak'ah) and can be performed in public or private. A ritual washing (**wudhu**) is required before prayer. If there is a congregation, one person is the leader (**imam**), and the rest perform their prayers in unison. The muezzin (mu'adhdhin) sounds the call to prayer (adhan), often from the top of a minaret. The Friday sermon (**khutbah**) also has political significance because the name of the ruler is invoked, indicating the political loyalty of the congregation.

Almsgiving (**zakat**) is the requirement to give a percentage of either one's wealth or one's yearly income to the poor. This obligation is not uniformly enforced in the Islamic world.

Fasting (sawm) is enjoined during the Muslim month of Ramadhan, "the month during which the Koran was sent down." From sunrise to sundown, the believer is to abstain from food or drink, which poses considerable hardship when the fast occurs during the long, hot summer months. Children, the ill, pregnant **women**, travelers, and soldiers in war are exempt, but those prevented from fasting must make up this obligation at a later time.

Pilgrimage (hajj) is a legal obligation of every adult Muslim of either sex to travel at least once in a lifetime to **Mecca**, provided the person is economically able to do so, and one who has performed pilgrimage carries the honorific title of "hajji."

"Striving in the Way of God" (**jihad**) is considered by some to be one of the Pillars of Islam. It is now interpreted as a war in defense of Islam, or any effort in a good cause. The fallen **martyr** is assured of immediate salvation and **heaven**.

Duties to one's fellow men (mu'amalat) and right-doing (ihsan) demand private and public morality, the avoidance of actions that are forbidden (**haram**) or reprehensible (**makruh**). Minor differences exist in the performance of these obligations within the four orthodox **Sunni** schools. Sunni Islam does not recognize a central church with power to make decisions on dogma, nor are its practitioners clergy who stand between mankind and God. They are members of the **'ulama'**, a body of scholars of the Islamic sciences who constitute the teachers, judges, **muftis**, and jurists of the Islamic world. They find the law on the basis of the four **schools of law** but do not legislate. The **Shi'ite** school of jurisprudence is based on the Ja'farite school, named after the Sixth Shi'ite **Imam, Ja'far al-Sadiq** (699–765).

ISLAMBULI, KHALID (1955–1982). Member of the Egyptian **Islamic Jihad**, who is said to have planned and participated in the assassination of Anwar Sadat on 6 October 1981. On the occasion of the "6 October 1973 Victory Parade," he and three of his supporters jumped from their truck and rushed to the stand where leading Egyptian government officials and their foreign guests were assembled. Islambuli emptied his assault rifle into Sadat's body, shouting "I have killed the Pharaoh." He and his three coconspirators were executed by firing squad on 15 April 1982.

ISLAMIC AMAL. A movement established in 1982 by Husain Musawi, who left **Amal** and allied himself with the Iranian Revolutionary Guards in the Baalbek Valley of Lebanon. The movement merged with **Islamic Jihad** and **Hizbullah** to fight Israeli occupation forces, but eventually lost its influence to Hizbullah.

ISLAMIC CALENDAR. *See* CALENDAR.

ISLAMIC CALL SOCIETY. "Jami'at al-Dawah al-Islamiyyah," a Libyan missionary society, founded in 1972, to train preachers and missionaries for worldwide service. Its organizational structure is headed by a secretary general, assisted by a 5-member executive committee and a 36-member executive council. Members meet in a general congress every four years to discuss the society's activities and work programs in the religious, cultural, social, and educational fields. The society maintains a college, which attracts students primarily from Asia and Africa. Islamic Call Society's activities have aroused hostility from Islamic orthodox sources and from some who see it as a vehicle of political power of the Libyan leader Muamar al-Gadhafi.

ISLAMIC CONFERENCE ORGANIZATION. *See* ORGANIZATION OF THE ISLAMIC CONFERENCE.

ISLAMIC DRESS. A dress for **women**, which covers most of the body and head but leaves the face free. It is worn in areas where the **veil** is not obligatory by **Islamist** women as a political statement and as a sign of orthodoxy. The **Koran** says: "And say to the believing women that they should lower their gaze and guard their modesty; that they should not display their beauty and ornaments except what (ordinarily) appear thereof; that they should draw their veils over their bosoms and not display their beauty except to their husbands, their fathers, their husband's father, their sons, their husband's sons, their brothers and their brothers' sons" (24:31). *See also* CHADOR.

ISLAMIC JIHAD. A pro-Iranian **Shi'ite** group, founded in Lebanon in 1982, which declared war on the American and Western presence in Lebanon. It is held responsible for the 1983 bombing of the U.S. Embassy in West Beirut and the attack on the U.S. Marine headquarters, which cost the lives of 241 soldiers. In 1982, the group took the vice president of the American University of Beirut hostage in retaliation for the kidnapping of four Iranian diplomats by Maronite militias. It facilitated a hostages-for-arms deal between the United States and Iran, and eventually an exchange of Israeli, Lebanese, Palestinian, and Western detainees and hostages. It appears to have ceased its activities, and some of its members merged with **Hizbullah**.

ISLAMIC JIHAD. An offshoot of the **Muslim Brotherhood** of Egypt, which claimed to have been a major force in the *intifada*, the resistance to Israeli occupation of Palestine. It opposed the accord of September 1993 between Israel and the Palestinian Liberation Organization (PLO) and continued armed attacks on Israeli targets. It has considerable support in the Gaza Strip, where Jihad publishes a weekly newspaper.

ISLAMIC LAW. Islamic law (shari'ah, from *shar'*, the path leading to the water hole) is God-given and a prescription for the right life in this world and for salvation in the world to come. During his lifetime, the Prophet **Muhammad** transmitted **Allah**'s commands. These were eventually collected in the book of readings, or recitations, the **Koran**. The Koran is the basis of law for all Muslims, although various **sects** and schools have differed in its interpretation. When no conclusive guidance was found in the Koran, the Traditions (**Sunnah**), or practice of the Prophet, were consulted. There are six "correct" books of **Sunni** Traditions, compiled by al-**Bukhari**, **Muslim ibn al-Hajjaj**, Abu Dawud al-**Sijistani**, Muhammad ibn 'Isa al-**Tirmidhi**, Abu 'Abdullah Muhammad **ibn Majah**, and Ahmad al-**Nasa'i**.

Four **schools of law** eventually developed in Sunni Islam, named after early legal scholars: the **Malikite**, named after **Malik ibn Anas** (d. 795); the Shafi'ite, named after Muhammad ibn Idris al-**Shafi'i** (d.819); the Hanbalite, named after Ahmad **ibn Hanbal** (d. 855); and the Hanafite, named after **Abu Hanifah** (d. 767). The Hanafite school has the largest number of adherents. It recognizes as a basis of jurisprudence, in addition to the Koran and the Sunnah, consensus of the scholars (**ijma'**) and reasoning by analogy (**qiyas**). Legal reasoning is called **ijtihad**, the struggle, or effort, in arriving at a legal decision. By the 10th century, Muslim jurists had decided by consensus that Islamic law was complete and that independent interpretation, ijtihad, was no longer permissible. Henceforth, Sunni Muslims were to follow, or imitate (**taqlid**), the existing body of law. Muslim modernists as well as radical **Islamists** want to reopen the "Gate of Ijtihad" to permit a reinterpretation of Islamic law to meet new, modern requirements.

Judges (qadis) in **shari'ah** courts are to apply the law, subject to consultation with legal experts (**muftis**), who issue legal decisions (**fatwas**). A jurist (**faqih**) is trained in an Islamic college (**madrasah**) to serve as lawyer, teacher, judge, and mufti. Punishments include the penalties for major offenses prescribed in the Koran or Traditions (**hadd**, pl. hudud), discretionary and variable punishments (**ta'zir**), and **retaliation** (qisas). There are five religious injunctions (*al-ahkam al-khamsa*): (1) obligatory (**fardh** or wajib) duties, whose performance is rewarded and whose omission is punished; and (2) forbidden (**haram**) actions, which are forbidden and punishable; (3) meritorious (**mandub**, also called sunnah, masnun, and mustahabb) actions, whose performance is rewarded but whose omission is not punished; (4) reprehensible (**makruh**) actions, which the believer is advised to refrain from; and (5) indifferent (**mubah** or ja'iz) actions, whose performance or omission is neither rewarded nor punished. *See also* FIVE PRINCIPAL ACTS IN ISLAMIC LAW.

Shi'ites of the **Twelver** Usuli school of jurisprudence find their sources of law in the Koran and the Traditions (Sunnah), the statements, deeds, and tacit consent of the Prophet and the **imams**, as well as the consensus (ijma') of the Shi'ite jurists, and the application of reason (*'aql*). Aql follows from the principle that "whatever is ordered by reason is also ordered by religion (*kull ma hakam bih al-'aql, hakam bih al-shar'*). The most important sources for Shi'ite law are the Four Books *(al-Kutub al-arba'a)*. In the absence of the **Hidden Imam**, the qualified scholars (**mujtahid**) of the Twelve Shi'ites are permitted to legislate on the basis of ijtihad.

Islamic law is an ideal law because it includes man's obligation to God (*'ibadat*), ritual worship, as well as matters of hygiene and etiquette and man's obligations to his fellow men (*mu'amalat*). There has always existed a dichotomy between "God's law" and the "King's law," and customary practices continued, provided they did not conflict with Islamic law. Rulers and governments enacted statutes according to the needs of the day. Police courts existed, and judges based their decisions on local custom. Toward the end of the 19th century, Islamic law was increasingly relegated to matters of personal status. Great Britain introduced "Anglo–Muhammadan" law, and the French employed their civil, criminal, and commercial codes. After the demise of the **Ottoman empire** as a result of the First World War, independent Muslim states continued this process. But no Muslim country went as far as Turkey, which abolished all aspects of Islamic law and established a secular republic in the 1920s. Saudi Arabia, Oman, Sudan, Yemen, and Afghanistan are the only countries that rely predominantly on the shari'ah.

ISLAMIC MODERNISM. *See* SALAFIYYAH.

ISLAMIC REFORM MOVEMENTS. *See* SALAF; SALAFIYYAH.

ISLAMIC REPUBLIC OF IRAN. The Islamic Republic of Iran was established in 1979 when a national revolt resulted in the overthrow of the Pahlavi monarchy. Soon the **Shi'ite** clergy, under the leadership of Ayatollah Ruhollah **Khomeyni**, were able to prevail, gradually eliminating all secular parties. Khomeyni proceeded to realize his concept of the Islamic state, which was to be governed under the principles of **Islamic law**. Although permitting such modern institutions as a representative government and parliament, he claimed for himself the governance of the supreme jurist (**vilayat-i faqih**). He was to rule in the absence of the **Hidden Imam**. Khomeyni was assisted by a 12-member **Guardian Council**, which had veto power over all legislation and political appointments. The **Revolutionary Guards** were established as the military arm of the new regime.

It took some time for the regime to consolidate its power, confronted by armed resistance by political groups, primarily the **Fida'iyan-i Khalq**, a leftist **Islamist** party. Relations with the United States, characterized as the "Great Satan," deteriorated in November 1979 when young supporters of Khomeyni occupied the U.S. embassy and took its staff hostage for 444 days. In late 1980 Iraq invaded Iran in an indecisive but very bloody war, which lasted until August 1988. When Khomeyni died in June 1989, he was succeeded as the supreme jurist by Ayatollah Ali **Khamene'i** who had similar powers but did not enjoy the charisma of his predecessor. When Sayyid Muhammad **Khatami** was elected president in a landslide election on 23 May 1997, there was hope that a liberalization in policies was imminent. But the conservatives continued to control all levers of power and prevented any political or social reforms. In the 2000 and 2005 elections, the council of guardians blocked thousands of candidates, including most reformers. Voter turnout was greatly reduced, to about 40 percent of the eligible voters, and the hard-liner Mahmud Ahmadinejat was elected president.

ISLAMIC SALVATION FRONT (FRONT DE SALUT ISLAMIQUE, FIS). A radical Algerian Islamist movement founded in 1998 that resorted to terrorism after being denied victory in the general elections of December 1991. In the first free election in Algeria, the FIS called for the establishment of an Islamic state in which **Islamic law** would replace secular law. The FIS won 55 percent of the vote in regional elections in 1989 and 49 percent in the first round of general elections on 26 December 1991. To prevent an FIS victory, the military took control of the government in mid-January 1992, prohibited all parties, and arrested **Islamist** leaders. As a result, the FIS has since conducted a reign of terror, which has destabilized the political process and cost many thousands of lives.

ISLAMIC SCIENCE. *See* EDUCATION.

ISLAMIC SOCIETY OF NORTH AMERICA (ISNA). An umbrella group of Muslim organizations and individuals that endeavors "to be an exemplary and unifying Islamic organization in North America that contributes to the betterment of of the Muslim community and society at large." It claims to be the largest **Sunni** Muslim organization in America and aims "to provide a common platform for presenting Islam, supporting Muslim communities, developing educational, social and research programs, and fostering good relations with other religious communities and civic and service organizations." It publishes *Islamic Horizons*, a bimonthly journal, and holds an annual convention in Chicago. It was one of a number of Muslim groups investigated for "possible funding" of terrorist organizations, but "nothing alarming enough" was found. Liberal Muslim groups have accused ISNA of promoting a **Wahhabi** interpretation of Islam.

ISLAMIC WORLD. *See* ORGANIZATION OF THE ISLAMIC CONFERENCE.

ISLAMIST MOVEMENT. The movement, also called "political" Islam, was born in large measure as a reaction to the process of Westernization in the Islamic world and the growth of secular, liberal, and Marxist ideologies among Muslim youth. The movement owed much of its organization and ideology to the influence of the **Muslim Brotherhood** of Egypt. Egyptians and foreign Muslims studying at Egyptian institutions spread the message of revolution throughout the Islamic world. They studied the works of Islamic thinkers, such as Hasan al-**Banna** (1906–1949), the "Supreme Guide" of the Ikhwanis; Sayyid **Qutb**, executed in **Cairo** in 1966; and Abu'l A'la **Maududi** (d. 1973), founder of the Pakistani **Jama'at-i Islami** and author of religio-political treatises. They staged demonstrations protesting government policies, Zionism, and the war in Vietnam. They also honed their oratorical and martial skills in confrontations with Marxist students on campuses throughout the Islamic world and soon won the majority of offices in student elections.

Many of the Islamist leaders are the product of secular, rather than religious, educational institutions. Many are graduates of technical and medical schools. They share the basic beliefs of the **'ulama'**, but their philosophies are derived through contact with Western ideologies.

They see themselves as a vanguard of a revolutionary revivalist movement and preach political sermons to mobilize the masses. They build neighborhood **mosques**, provide soup kitchens for the poor, and aid the families of **martyrs**. They are missionaries who want to make "true" Muslims of the people. Ideologically, they reject the Traditions of classical Islam and call for the **ijma'** of the community, not the **'ulama'**, and the reopening of the "gate of **ijtihad**."

The Islamists are not a monolithic movement, but rather a collection of numerous organizations that want to establish a "true" Islamic state in which sovereignty belongs to God, and the **shari'ah** is the law and constitution. In such a state, they would enforce all the Islamic punishments, including prohibitions on taking **interest**, playing music, showing television, and playing games, and would enforce traditional **dress** and attendance at **prayers**. They want to turn a Muslim state into an Islamic state. *See* also JIHADIS DECLARATION OF WAR.

ISLAMIST PARTY IN TURKEY. *See* WELFARE PARTY.

ISM. Personal name. *See also* NAMES AND NAMEGIVING.

ISMA'IL (d. 760). Son of the Sixth **Imam, Ja'far al-Sadiq**, imam of the **Isma'ilis**, or Sevener **Shi'ites**. He was designated by his father to succeed him, but he died before his father. Therefore, Ja'far al-Sadiq appointed Musa al-Kazim as imam. This led to schism in the Shi'ite movement, and the followers of Isma'il proclaimed him the last and Seventh Imam, whereas the Twelvers continued to count six successors. *See also* ISMA'ILIS.

ISMA'IL, SHAH (1487–1524). *See* SAFAVID DYNASTY.

ISMA'ILIS. A **Shi'ite sect** that recognizes **Isma'il**, son of **Ja'far al Sadiq**, as the Seventh and last **imam**; therefore, they are also called the Seveners (*sab'iya*). They hold that Isma'il will return as the **Mahdi** at the end of time, and they also believe in the exoteric (**zahir**) interpretation of the **Koran** and in an esoteric (batin) doctrine. The esoteric doctrine consists of two parts: an allegorical interpretation (**ta'wil**) of the Koran and the **shari'ah**, and truths (haqa'iq), a system of philosophy and science, coordinated with religion. This doctrine is only known to the initiated, who pass through stages of enlightenment according to their intellectual capacity. They try to explain all cosmic and historical developments by the number seven: seven prophets have legislative functions (**Adam, Noah, Abraham, Moses, Jesus, Muhammad**, and Muhammad ibn Isma'il). Between each of them are 7 or 12 silent legislators. Regarding the **imam**, some believe him to be merely the lieutenant of the Prophet; others regard him as embodying God's will. The Isma'ilis are divided into subgroups, including, among others, the Assassins, **Bohras, Druzes, Fatimids, Khojas**, Nusairis, and **Qarmatians**.

ISNAD (SANAD). The chain of trustworthy persons, beginning with an eyewitness, who report a saying or action of the Prophet. *See also* HADITH.

ISRAFIL (ASRAFIL). One of the four archangels, who trumpets the beginning of the **Day of Judgment**. On the first blow of the trumpet, "all bad things are lifted and taken away from the earth;" on the second sounding "all beings in the heavens and on earth will enter a state of perplexity;" and on the third sounding of the trumpet, "God will dress and adorn all human beings with angelic power and send them into the throng of His servants." *See also* ANGELS.

ISTANBUL. Capital of the **Ottoman empire** since its capture in 1453 by Muhammad the Conqueror (1451–1481). The city, named Constantinople after its founder, Emperor Constantine, in 330, is strategically important because it is located at the divide of two continents and at an important crossroads of trade. It was the seat of the **Ottoman sultan/caliph** until 1923. The name Constantinople was used interchangeably with Istanbul until 1930, when the government had it officially changed.

ISTIHSAN. "Seeking the good" is a principle in the Hanafite school of jurisprudence, which permits the judge to make a decision on the basis of equity and justice.

ISTISLAH. Employed especially in the **Malikite** school of jurisprudence, which permits the judge to make a decision on the basis of what is good for the general welfare of the community.

ITHNA 'ASHARIYYAH. *See* TWELVER SHI'ITES.

'IZRA'IL. "Angel of death." 'Izra'il is not mentioned by name in the **Koran**, which states: "Say: 'The Angel of Death put in charge of you, will (duly) take your souls: Then shall you be brought back to your Lord'" (32:11). *See also* ANGELS.

IZZ AL-DIN AL-QASAM BRIGADES. The military wing of the Palestinian **Hamas**, founded in 1992 in reaction to the al-Aqsa massacre in 1990, in which 18 Palestinians were killed. It embarked on attacks on Israeli targets, at times to retaliate for aerial assassinations or to capture Israeli soldiers for a prisoner exchange deal. After the withdrawal of Israeli occupation of the Gaza Strip, it became the dominant force in the area. In June and July 2006, Hamas conducted a raid that led to the capture of the Israeli soldier Gilad Shalit for the purpose of trading him in exchange for Palestinians imprisoned in Israel. No deal has as yet been concluded. The Brigades are well armed with modern weapons, including long-range rockets as well as guided anti-tank and anti-aircraft missiles. In addition to smuggled supplies, missiles of local manufacture have been used. The Israeli government has killed many Hamas leaders in aerial attacks, and an occasional truce has been concluded to try to end the cycle of violence.

– J –

JABARTI, ABD AL RAHMAN AL- (1753–1825). Egyptian historian and biographer who wrote a modern history of Egypt, covering the period of French occupation (1798–1803) and its aftermath, which is one of the primary sources for the period. He rejected French materialism and unbelief, but he was impressed by French civic honesty and diligence, which he contrasted with the shortcomings of Egyptian society. He was a pioneer whose ideas found acceptance among Muslim modernists.

JABRITES (JABARIYYAH). A school of the **Umayyad** period that denied man's free will and asserted that man in all of his actions is subject to the compulsion (*jabr*) of God's sovereignty. Most important of the Jabrites was Jahm ibn Safwan (d. 746), who held that salvation was predetermined. Orthodox Islam accepts a measure of free will with the **Ash'arite** concept of "acquisition" (**kasb**). Popular Islam tends to a fatalistic acceptance of man's fate (**kismet**). For a school that accepts man's free will, *see* QADARIYYAH.

JA'FAR AL-BARMAKI (d. 803). Member of the **Barmakid** family of **viziers**, tutor of Caliph al-**Ma'mun** (813–833), and adviser to **Harun al-Rashid**.

JA'FAR AL-SADIQ (699?–765). Sixth **Shi'ite Imam** and founder of the Ja'farite school of jurisprudence of **Twelver Shi'ism**. He was named "Sadiq" (The Truthful) for his veracity and was also known for his treatise on alchemy, augury, and omens. He lived in **Medina**, where two of his students, **Malik ibn Anas** and **Abu Hanifah**, became founders of **Sunni schools of law**. Ja'far al-Sadiq appointed his son **Isma'il** as the Seventh Imam, but subsequently he chose another son, Musa al-Kazim. The supporters of Isma'il, the **Isma'ilis**, consider Isma'il the Seventh and last imam (except for the **Khojas**, who recognize the **Agha Khan**), whereas the Twelvers continued to count their imams from Musa al-Kazim. Ja'far was buried at the al-**Baqi** cemetery in Medina. See also SHI'ISM.

JAHANNAM. *See* HELL.

JAHILIYYAH. *See* IGNORANCE, THE AGE OF.

JAHIZ, AMR IBN BAHR AL- (776–868). Member of the **Mu'-tazilite** school who formed his own sub**sect** supporting the doctrine of free will, named, after him, *al-Jahiziyyah*. Al-Jahiz, the "Goggle Eyed," was born and educated in **Basra** and spent several years at the caliphal court in **Baghdad** and Samarra. Called a freethinker, Jahiz was a prolific writer with more than 200 publications to his name, of which about 30 (or 75? sources differ) are still extant. His most important work is the seven-volume *Book of Animals (kitab* *al-hayawan*), which presents much scientific information. He published in a variety of fields, including theology, philosophy, linguistics, history, literature, ethics, astronomy, geography, botany, zoology, mineralogy, and music. His *Book of Eloquence and Exposition (Kitab al bayan wa al-tabyin)* is a treatise on rhetoric, which is still used as a text today.

JALAL AL-DIN RUMI, MAULAWI (JALALUDDIN RUMI, 1207–1273). Held to be the greatest of all **Sufi** poets, called Shaykh al-Akbar, the "Greatest Master" (or mawlana) by his supporters. Born in Balkh, in present-day Afghanistan, he moved with his father to Konya in Turkey, called Rum at the time; hence his name, Rumi. He received a traditional **education**, and at age 15 he experienced his mystical "unveiling." He studied at the **Nizamiyyah** in **Baghdad** and traveled widely in the Islamic world. His masterpiece, the *Masnawi*, written in Persian, is a six-volume work of spiritual teachings. He is the founder of the **Mevlevi** order, also known as the "Whirling Dervishes." Jalal al-Din is buried in Konya.

JAMA'AT-I ISLAMI. Name of a Pakistani political organization founded by Maulana Abu'l-'Ala **Maududi** (1903–1979) in 1941, which advocates the establishment of an Islamic state patterned after the early Islamic community. It is **pan-Islamic** in nature and looks at the Muslim community as one nation (**ummah**), rejecting nationalism as contrary to Islam. The party opposes capitalism and socialism forbids the taking of **interest, gambling**, prostitution, consumption of **alcohol**, speculation, and hoarding; and demands the promotion of social welfare. It is organized with a 50-member executive committee (Markaz-i majlis-i shura), elected for three-year terms and responsible for making policy decisions. It is headed by an **amir**, who nominates a working committee of 12 men and a secretary general. Banned in 1953 for its involvement in the Punjab riots against the Ahmadiyyah movement, the party gained new prominence when President Zia ul-Haq proclaimed Pakistan an Islamic state in the late 1970s. It has not been very successful in winning votes because of ethnic and sectarian differences in Pakistan and resistance from secular and feudal forces. The party has supported like-minded groups in Afghanistan and elsewhere.

JAMI, NUR AL-DIN ABD AL-RAHMAN (1414–1492). The last great poet of classical Persian, a scholar and mystic who was born in Jam and educated in Herat and Samarkand. He settled in Herat, where he enjoyed the support of Ali Shir Nawa'i, **vizier** at the court of Sultan Bayqara. His works deal chiefly with moral philosophy and mysticism.

JANABAH. A state of major impurity that requires the purification of greater ablution (**ghusl**). Such impurity is caused by orgasm, copulation, menstruation, and other bodily discharges.

JANISSARY (YENIÇERI). Ottoman infantry army, composed largely of Christian levies, founded in the early Ottoman period, when wars were still fought on horseback. They were the first standing army, equipped with firearms. They were the personal slaves of the sultan, and to inspire an esprit de corps, **Sulayman the Magnificent** paid them the compliment of enrolling in their ranks as a corporal. He collected his pay as a low-ranking member of the corps. The janissaries were drafted in the **devshirme** process, converted to Islam, and sworn in by Haji Bektash, who became the patron saint of the Janissaries and whose **Bektashi** order still exists. They were not permitted to marry and wear beards and therefore were compensated by sporting huge "handlebar" mustaches. They made possible the extraordinary Ottoman conquests, defeating the Mamluk and Safavid armies, leading to the conquest of territories up to the gates of Vienna. Eventually the system declined. Muslims were permitted to enter the forces, and the Janissaries became a force of reaction. Therefore, Sultan Mahumd II provoked them to revolt and eliminated them in an action called the "Auspicious Event" (1826). The way was now free for needed military reforms.

JANNAH. "Garden." *See* HEAVEN.

JARIR, IBN 'ATIYAH (ca. 650–729). A native of the Banu Tamim of Iraq, known as the greatest satirist of the **Umayyad** period and court poet of Ibn Yusuf al-**Hajjaj**, the governor of Iraq. A Bedouin poet and rival of Hammam ibn Ghalib al-**Farazdak** and Ghiyath al-Taghlibi al-**Akhtal**, his fame was so great "that to be worsted by him was reckoned a greater distinction than to vanquish anyone else" (Nicholson, 245). In addition to his satires, several elegies, and panegyrics in honor of the Caliphs 'Abd al-Malik and 'Umar II have been preserved. **Ibn Khallikan** said, "of the four kinds of verses—boasting, laudatory, satirical, and amatory—al-Jarir excelled in all" (I, 295).

JERUSALEM (AL-QUDS). A holy city to Jews, **Christians**, and **Muslims** and site of the oldest Muslim archeological treasures, the **Dome of the Rock** and Al-**Aqsa Mosque**, built by Caliph **'Abd al-Malik** in the seventh century. It is the site of **Muhammad**'s **Nocturnal Journey** to heaven in 619. Caliph **'Umar ibn al-Khattab** accepted the surrender of the city in 638, and the inhabitants were given protection and allowed to live autonomously under their own laws and religion in exchange for payment of a poll tax (**jizyah**). In 1099, the crusaders captured the city and founded the Kingdom of Jerusalem, but in 1187 **Salah al-Din** (Saladin) recaptured the city. The crusaders gained it again from 1229 to 1244, but then it remained in **Mamluk** and **Ottoman** hands, until it became part of the British mandate of Palestine in 1920. After the United Nations decided to partition Palestine, and the resulting war of 1948, the old part of the city remained in Arab hands until Israel occupied it in 1967; it still holds Jerusalem today.

JESUS ('ISA). Recognized in Islam as a **prophet** (19:30, 34), **messenger** (4:171), messiah, and the only creature, besides **Adam**, who has no father (3:52, 59). He is an apostle, but not God (5: 72). He will bear witness on Resurrection Day (4:157). The **Koran** says: "Such (was) Jesus the son of **Mary**: (it is) a statement of truth, about which they (vainly) dispute (19:34); . . . O **People of the Book!** Commit no excesses in your religion: nor say of **Allah** aught but the truth. Christ Jesus the son of Mary was (no more than) a messenger of Allah, and His word which He bestowed on Mary and a spirit proceeding from Him: so believe in Allah and His Messengers. Say not 'Three:' desist: it will be better for you: for Allah is one God: Glory be to Him: (far exalted is He) above having a son" (4:171). Muslims believe that Jesus was not crucified: "That they said (in boast), 'We killed Christ Jesus the son of Mary, The Messenger of Allah;' But they killed him not nor crucified him. Only a likeness of that was shown to them. . . .

Nay, Allah raised him up unto Himself, and Allah is Exalted in power Wise" (4:157–158). Jesus is believed to have had the power to raise the dead, heal the sick, and breath life into clay birds.

JEWS. *See* JUDAISM.

JIBRIL (JABRA'IL). The archangel Gabriel. *See* ANGELS.

JIHAD. "Striving." An "effort in the way of God" was originally an obligation to wage war against unbelievers until they accepted Islam or submitted to Islamic rule. A Muslim who dies in jihad is a **martyr** (*shahid*) and directly enters paradise. Monotheists with a sacred book, like **Christians** and Jews, are not forced to convert and enjoy the status of protected subjects. In battle, an enemy is given three choices: accept Islam and enjoy rights of equality with Muslims; submit and become a tribute-paying subject with religious freedom and protection of one's property; or fight and leave the judgment to God, in which case a defeated enemy becomes part of the booty.

These options were historically offered in the siege of a fortified city to encourage the enemy to surrender. In large conquests, as for example in India, Muslim rulers accepted even polytheistic "idol worshippers" as **Peoples of the Book** and therefore not subject to annihilation. Muslim modernists quote a **Koran**ic passage: "Fight in the Way of God against those who fight against you, but do not commit aggression" (2:190), maintaining that the obligation of jihad was binding only for the early Islamic period and that jihad also means inwardly waging war against the carnal soul—a kind of moral imperative. The latter is called "The Great Effort" (*jihad akbar*) and is more important because it strives to achieve man's personal perfection; jihad within the **ummah** addresses wrongs within the community of Muslims. The "martial jihad" is called "The Small Effort"; it is promoted by jihadi groups, such as al-**Qaeda,** who have declared war on the West and Muslim states and were responsible for suicide attacks on the World Trade Center in New York and the Pentagon in Washington, D.C., as well as the bombings in Bali, Madrid, and London.

JIHADIS DECLARATION OF WAR. Radical Islamists who declared holy war (jihad) on Muslim rulers and their "supporters" in the

West. They are accused of terrorist bombings in the United States, Britain, Spain, the Philippines, Kenya, Tanzania, and other countries. They are of many nationalities, including European and American. Some of the most spectacular attacks are listed below:

The Bali bombings on 12 October 2002, of two popular night clubs, resulted in the death of 202 people and wounded more than 100 others. Many of the dead and wounded were Australians, but Indonesian, German, French, British, and Americans were also among the casualties. American sources attributed the attacks to Jemaa Islamiah, a group purportedly linked to al-**Qaeda**. A radical cleric, Abu Bakr Basyr, was cleared of direct involvement in an attack on the JW Marriott Hotel in Jakarta in 2003, but was convicted on charges of incitement.

The Madrid bombings on 11 March 2004 killed 200 people and wounded about 1,500. Ten bombs ripped through rush-hour trains packed with commuters heading for the city center. Spanish authorities at first suspected Eta, the Basque separate group, but police soon identified two Moroccans and two Indians as the perpetrators. As a result, the conservative government of Prime Minister José Maria Aznar, which had supported the American war in Iraq, lost the elections.

The London bombings on 7 July 2005, in which four bombs exploded on three London subway trains and a bus, killing 52 commuters and four of the bombers. Three of the bombers were British-born Muslims of Pakistani descent; the fourth was Jamaican. On 21 July, exactly two weeks later, a team of four men attempted a similar attack, but the bombs did not detonate and all were arrested. Two-thirds of Britons believe the attacks are linked to the war in Iraq. Ayman al-**Zawahiri** is said to have claimed responsibility for the massacre.

In response to the attacks of 11 September 2001, the U.S. government established the Department Homeland Security. Its mission is to prevent terrorist attacks within the United States; reduce America's vulnerability to terrorism; and minimize the damage from potential attacks and natural disasters. Britain followed suit, passing the Antiterrorism, Crime and Security Act of 2001, which after the London bombings was modified by the Prevention of Terrorism Act of 11 March 2005. Although the laws were primarily intended to allow the potentially unlimited detention of noncitizens, they also increased the investigative powers of the state, calling into question such notions as habeas corpus. Other European states followed with measures to protect themselves from terrorist attacks, but human rights and other organizations in the United States and Europe are opposed to certain provisions of recent legislation.

JILANI, 'ABDUL QADIR AL- (1077–1166). Theologian, preacher, mystic, and founder of the **Sufi** order that bears his name. Born in Gilan in Persia, he lived in **Baghdad**, where his tomb is the object of much veneration. Introduced to Sufism late in life, he became one of the first Sufi **saints** and won great fame for his collection of exhortations, called the *Revelations of the Unseen (Futuh al-ghayb)*. He called for **jihad** against the self to conquer worldliness and submit to God's will. The **Qadiriyyah** is the first and largest of Sufi fraternities, with devotees throughout the Islamic world. 'Abdul Qadir is said to have had 49 sons.

JINN. *See* GENIE.

JIZYAH. Poll tax levied formerly on non-Muslim monotheists who were possessors of a scripture, the **Peoples of the Book** (*ahl al-kitab*, such as **Christians** and Jews). Only adult males of sound mind and body and financial means were to be so taxed. **Women**, children, the aged, beggars, monks, and **slaves** were exempted. In exchange, they enjoyed freedom of life, liberty, and property and were not drafted into the military. In modern days, this discriminatory tax is no longer levied.

JUBBA'I, ABU ALI MUHAMMAD AL- (849–915). A celebrated scholastic theologian. He was one of the leading **Mu'tazilites** and an antagonist of his former student, Abu 'l-Hasan al-**Ash'ari**. Juba'i's numerous works were frequently cited but are no longer extant. His son, Abu Hashim 'Abd al-Salam, continued his father's work and tried to reconcile his doctrines with orthodox teachings. Jubba'i was born in Jubba, near **Basra**, and died in **Baghdad**.

JUDAISM. Jews are mentioned in the **Koran** and Traditions, called Yahudi (pl. Yahud) and Banu Israel, the Tribe of Israel. They are a

People of the Book, monotheists with a **scripture**, whose validity was to be corrected with the message of the **Prophet Muhammad**. Virtually all major characters of the Old Testament are mentioned in the Koran and the Traditions. Abraham is recognized as the ancestor of the Arabs and Jews; **Moses** (Musa) is the Law-Giver of the Jews. The Koran appeals to the Jews, saying "O Children of Israel! Call to mind the (special) favour which I bestowed upon you, and that I preferred you to all others" (2:47). It appeals to the Jews to accept Muhammad's message, saying: "It was We who revealed the Torah (to Moses), therein was guidance and light" (5:44), and "We sent Jesus the son of **Mary**, confirming the Torah that had come before him: We sent him the Gospel, therein was guidance and light" (5:46). But the books were corrupted with time, and **Allah** "sent the Scripture in truth [the Koran], confirming the scripture that came before it, and guarding it in safety: so judge between them what Allah hath revealed." When the Jews did not accept Muhammad's invitation to accept the new **revelation**, the Koran warned Muslims not to make them their friends (5:78, 80).

However, Jews lived throughout the centuries in the Islamic world, and some 200,000 fled from Granada after the Christian conquest in 1492 and settled in the major cities of the Islamic world. They continue to speak Latino, their Spanish dialect, to this day. It was only with the establishment of Israel that most Jews left, to live in the new state of Israel.

JUDGE. "Qadhi." A person of good reputation who is versed in Islamic jurisprudence and acts as a judge in civil and criminal matters. As an institution, it dates from the time of **'Umar** II (r. 717–720), who appointed the first judges for Egypt and Syria; subsequently, governors appointed judges in the provinces. Since the late ninth century, judges have been organized in a hierarchical manner, with a chief judge (*qadhi al-qudhat*) at the **'Abbasid** capital. **Islamic law** is God-given, and cases are decided by precedent according to a particular school of jurisprudence. A judge could seek the advice of a professional jurist (**mufti**), the litigants appeared personally in court, and written or circumstantial evidence was not admitted. Judges were primarily confined to the cities, and non-Muslims were left under the jurisdiction of their own ecclesiastical courts. Qadhis also acted as guardians of orphans, lunatics, and minors, and administered the pious foundations (**waqf**).

In modern times, states have increasingly secularized the courts, leaving only matters of personal status under the jurisdiction of the **shari'ah**. Special police courts (*mazalim*) have existed since classical times. Military courts and courts set up according to Western models eventually evolved. But recent revivalist movements want to return legal jurisdiction to the traditional system.

JUM'A. The day of "general assembly." *See* FRIDAY.

JUNAYD, AL BAGHDADI (d. 909/910). (Full name Junayd ibn Muhammad Abu al-Qasim al-Khazzaz al-Baghdadi.) One of the early **Sufi shaykhs**, "the Imam of the World" in his time. His family was from Nahawand (in present-day Iran), and he was born and raised in Iraq. He taught in Baghdad and was an important figure in the development of Sufi doctrine. As the name Khazzaz suggests, he was a silk merchant and kept a shop in **Baghdad**. Ibn Khallikan quotes an eyewitnesss who said "that the Katibs of Baghdad went to hear al-Junaid for his choice of words; the philosophers for the subtilty of his discourse; the poets for the elegance of his language, and the dogmatic theologians for his profound ideas." (I, 340)

JUWAYNI, 'ABD AL-MALIK AL- (1028–1085). Imam of the Holy Places (*Imam al-Haramayn*), a **Shafi'ite** jurist and **Ash'arite** theologian who taught in **Baghdad, Mecca, Medina**, and Nishapur, where his activities were sponsored by the **Saljuq vizier** Hasan ibn 'Ali **Nizam al-Mulk**. Al-Juwayni was a teacher of al-**Ghazali** and al-**Ansari**. As a Persian, he held the view that the **caliphate** need not be held by a member of the **Quraysh**. Historians tell us that after his death, some 400 of his students broke their pens and refused to study for an entire year.

JUWAYNI, ALA AL-DIN ATA MALIK Al- (1226–1283). Born in Juwayn, Khorasan, he received a traditional **education** and traveled widely, visiting the **Mongol** Great Khan in Karakorum. One of the great Persian historians, he accompanied the Mongol founder of the Ilkhanid dynasty, **Hulagu** Khan, on his invasion of Persia. He was governor of **Baghdad** for 24 years and is the author of the *Tarikh-i Jahan Kusha*, translated into English by J. A. Boyle under the title *The History of the World Conqueror*. It is an important source also on the state of the Khwarizm Shahs and the **Isma'ilis** at **Alamut**. He is buried in Tabriz.

JUWAYRIYYAH BINT AL-HARITH. Wife of the Prophet. Captured by Muslim forces, she asked to be ransomed, but **Muhammad** married her and released 100 of her relatives. He provided a dowry of 400 **dirhams**. 'A'ishah was said to have said of her: "No woman was ever greater blessing to her people than this Juwayriyyah."

– K –

KA'BAH. "Cube." A cubelike building, the most holy shrine of Islam, located in the center of the Grand **Mosque** in the holy city of **Mecca**. The building is about 12 meters long, 10 meters wide, and 15 meters high, made of grey stone with a small entrance on the northern side. On the eastern corner the **Black Stone** is attached at the height of 1.5 meters. Muslims believe that the Ka'bah was erected by **Adam** and rebuilt by **Abraham** after the Flood; a small shrine marks the place where Abraham was said to have stood. The building is covered with a black (during **pilgrimage**, white), gold-embroidered brocade curtain (*kiswa*), which is changed every year. It is cut up into pieces and sold to pilgrims. The Ka'bah is the prayer direction (**qiblah**) toward which Muslims all over the world bow. The surrounding area is sacred territory, forbidden to non-Muslims and in which no animals are to be killed. The **Koran** says: "And remember Abraham said: 'My Lord, make this a city of peace, and feed its people with fruits, such of them as believe in **Allah** and the **Last Day**.'" The Ka'bah was repeatedly destroyed and rebuilt, and the Black Stone was carried off by **Qarmatian** invaders in 930. The Grand Mosque surrounding the Ka'bah was enlarged and renovated in the 1950s to accommodate up to two million pilgrims to perform the ritual circumambulation of the shrine.

KADHI (KAZI). *See* JUDGE.

KAFIR. "Coverer." One who hides, or covers up the truth. An unbeliever, polytheist, and idol worshiper, who is condemned to eternal hellfire. Heretics and apostates from Islam were at times killed. **Christians** and Jews, as well as other monotheists and peoples of a revealed **scripture**, are not kafirs. They are protected subjects who, upon payment of a poll tax, enjoy freedom of religion and property, although in popular terminology they are often included in the term kafirs. *See also* RIDDAH.

KAFUR, ABU AL-MISK (d. 969). "Father of the Muski Camphor." Abyssinian eunuch who became virtual ruler of Egypt and Syria in the second half of the **Ikhshidid dynasty** (935–969). He was tutor of Muhammad al-Ikhshid's sons, Unjur and 'Ali, and after the latter's death in 966, he took the reins of government and held the state together until his death in 969. Kafur was said to have been repellently ugly (described as a negro of deep black color with a smooth shining skin), a man who loved the society of virtuous men and treated them with marked honor. He was praised as a great sponsor of the arts and sciences.

KAHIN. Pre-Islamic soothsayer, usually the guardian of a sanctuary. He was said to have supernatural powers and was consulted in personal matters or to settle disputes. In his pronouncements, the Kahin would speak in **rhymed prose**, called saj. Some of his opponents called the Prophet **Muhammad** a kahin. The **Koran** says the Message is "not the word of a poet . . . nor is it the word of a soothsayer"(69:41–42).

KALAM. "Word." The scholastic theology of Islam (from *kalam*, speech, or the Word of God). During the **Umayyad** period, no true orthodoxy prevailed in the Islamic world. The **'Abbasid** period marks the creation of a systematic theology. Schools appeared in which new ideas were broached, but most of them disappeared. Gradually four **Sunni** theological schools emerged in **Medina**, **Damascus**, **Basra**, and **Kufah**. In each of these towns, pious men gathered, usually in **mosques**, to discuss religious questions. They debated such questions as sin and the sinner, free will and **predestination**, reason versus **revelation**, etc.

The **Kharijites** (or those who went out) were the first Islamic **sect**. Originally partisans of **'Ali**, they broke with him over his submission to arbitration at **Adhruh** in his controversy with **Mu'awiyah**, proclaiming that judgment belongs to God alone (*la hukma illa li-llah*). A radical subgroup, the **Azraqites** (named after their leader, Nafi' ibn al-Azraq), proclaimed 'Ali a sinner and therefore an unbeliever (**kafir**) who had to be destroyed. They held that any pious Muslim is qualified for the position of **caliph**, even an Abysinian **slave**. A quietist group, the **Murji'ites** held, in reaction to the Kharijites, that a sinner is still a Muslim, and judgment of a sinner should be left (*irja'*) to God. Sins are offset by faith and a believer will not be condemned to eternal hellfire. In political terms, the Murji'ites would give tacit support even to a sinful ruler, and they acquiesced in **Umayyad** rule.

An important dogma in Islam is God's omnipotence—from this would follow that nothing happens without God's will—reducing the believer to **fatalistic** resignation. One group, the Qadarites (from *qadar*, power), postulated that God is just and therefore leaves man to decide between good and evil. They were influenced by the rationalist **Mu'tazilite** (seceders, from *'itazala*) school, which stood for free will and human responsibility. **Wasil ibn 'Ata'** withdrew from a discussion between Murji'ites and Kharijites, in which the former declared the sinner a believer while the latter held that he had become an unbeliever. The Mu'tazilites became important under the rule of Caliph **Ma'mun**, who enforced their view that the **Koran** was created, rather than eternal. One group, the **Jabrites**, proclaimed man's compulsion (*jabr*) and denied man's free will, saying that man is necessarily constrained by the force of God's eternal and immutable decree.

Orthodox Sunni belief took shape finally under the influence of al-**Ash'ari** (873–935). Al-Ash'ari was originally a Mu'tazilite who for various reasons broke with his circle and used rational methods to espouse a rigid **fundamentalist** view. He favored a literal interpretation of the Koran and was impressed with God's omnipotence—as the creator of good and evil. He held that nothing can infringe on the power of God and denied the existence of all causality. If day follows night, it is only because God in his mercy permits repetition. There is no continuity; God creates the world anew every moment. Although he accepted predestination, he adopted the concept of "acquisition" (**kasb**), which would make man responsible for his deeds. The Ash'arite school became the foundation of orthodox scholasticism. It was left to al-**Ghazali** to provide a synthesis of philosophy, theology, and mysticism. For **Shi'ite** Kalam, *see* SHI'ISM.

KALBI, ABU 'L-MUNDHIR HISHAM IBN MUHAMMAD AL-(d. 819).
Genealogist and native of **Kufah**, called "the most learned of men." His *Collection of Genealogies* (*Jamhara al-Nisab*) was characterized as "one of the best works ever composed on the subject." His *Book of Idols* (*Kitab al-asnam*) is a record of Jahiliayyah idolatry. He produced upward of 150 works, only a few of which have survived, and was severely attacked by some scholars for his interest in the pre-Islamic period.

KARAMAH. God's manifestation of His Grace; supernatural powers to perform miracles, which God has bestowed upon **saints**. In popular belief, they are miracles performed by saints.

KARBALA (KERBALA). A town in present-day Iraq where **Imam Husayn** was martyred in 680. It is a holy city for **Shi'ites** and a place of **pilgrimage**. Husayn's body is buried there (his head is buried in the Husayn Mosque in **Cairo**).

KARUBIYUN. "Cherubim." Archangels, namely Jibril (**Gabriel**), **Mika'il**, and **'Izra'il**. *See* ANGELS.

KASB. "Acquisition," the doctrine introduced by al-**Ash'ari** that permits humans a measure of free will. According to the doctrine, God wills both good and evil; that is, God produces the act, but it is "acquired" by the individual to win salvation. In this way, al-Ash'ari was able to reconcile the contradiction seemingly posed by God's omnipotence and man's free will.

KASHANI, AYATOLLAH ABU 'L-QASEM (GHASEM 1884–1961).
Shi'i alem and member of the Iranian parliament who called for the creation of an "Islamic State" and an end to "oppression, despotism, and colonization." Exiled by the British/Soviet occupation forces during the Second World War, he returned to Iran in 1950 and joined

Prime Minister Muhammad Mosaddeq in calling for the nationalization of the Anglo–Iranian Oil Company. He broke with Mosaddeq in 1953 when the latter called for a National Front government, which was to include the communist Tudeh Party. Kashani was a precursor of the Khomeyni revolution of 1979.

KAYSANIYYAH. A **Shi'ite sect**, probably named after Kaysan Abu 'Amr, the cruel chief of police of Caliph **'Ali** at **Kufah**, Kaysan joined the revolutionary movement headed by al-**Mukhtar**, which supported the **caliphate** of Muhammad ibn al-**Hanafiyyah**, the Caliph Ali's son by a Bedouin woman. It was one of the first **sects** in Islam, supported primarily by the newly converted, who aimed at avenging the assassination of al-**Husayn** at **Karbala** in 680. After the death of al-Mukhtar, the sect splintered into small groups, which eventually disappeared or merged with the **'Abbasid** revolt.

KEMALISM. Policy of secular reforms in the Turkish Republic, named after Mustafa Kemal Atatürk (1881–1938). The policy can be summarized under six principles that became part of the Turkish constitution: nationalism, secularism, revolutionism, republicanism, populism, and statism. Atatürk and his reformers abolished the **sultanate** in 1922 and the **caliphate** in 1924 and established the Turkish republic. They tried to instill in the people pride as the descendants of "the world's greatest conquering race," rooted in Anatolia from time immemorial. Although the reformers claimed not to be hostile to religion, they abolished **polygamy**, outlawed all religious orders, and adopted the international time and calendar in 1925. Religious laws and courts were abolished, and Western civil, penal, and commercial laws were adopted. In 1928, Latin numerals and the Latin alphabet were adopted, and the use of the **Arabic** script was forbidden. Arabic and Persian vocabulary were replaced with Turkish words, and the metric system was adopted. In 1934, **women** got the right to vote and, a year later, all citizens had to adopt family names. Finally, Sunday was adopted as the day of rest.

Atatürk was elected president for life, and although many of these reforms were repugnant to devout **believers**, he was able to implement them. The Turkish people saw him as having saved the country from dismemberment after the First World War and therefore accepted his reforms. Since the 1960s, there has been a gradual erosion of Kemalism: **madrasahs** have been reopened and the great cathedral **mosques** of **Istanbul** are again houses of worship. The movement of Islamic revivalism in the Islamic world has spread also to Turkey: women can be seen in "Islamic dress," something previously forbidden, and an **Islamist** prime minister was elected but subsequently forced to resign through military intervention in 1997. In March 2003, Recep Tayyip Erdogan, an Islamist turned moderate, was elected prime minister and has remained unchallenged.

KERBELA. *See* KARBALA.

KHADIJAH (d. 619). First wife of the Prophet **Muhammad.** She was a wealthy lady, about 15 years his senior, who conducted her deceased husband's business and employed Muhammad for some time before she married him. Muhammad gave her 20 she-camels as a dowry. She bore Muhammad seven children, of whom only the girls survived. The girls were **Zaynab,** who married Abu al-'As; **Ruqayyah,** who married the third **caliph, 'Uthman; Fatimah,** who married the fourth caliph, **'Ali;** and **Umm Kulhthum,** who married 'Uthman. Khadijah encouraged Muhammad in his mission and became his first convert. Muhammad did not take another wife as long as Khadijah was alive.

KHALID IBN AL-WALID (d. 641). Early Islamic general of the Makhzum clan of **Quraysh,** who contributed greatly to the early conquests. He fought **Muhammad** at the Battle of **Uhud** (625) but converted to Islam in 629. After the death of Muhammad, Khalid defeated a number of false prophets, including **Musaylimah** in 633. He conquered Hira in Iraq, and, together with **'Amr ibn al-'As,** he defeated a Byzantine army at **Ajnadayn** in 634. Temporarily dismissed, he led a contingent in the Battle of **Yarmuk** (636). For his services he was given the title Sword of Islam (*sayf al-Islam*). He was rewarded for his service with the governorship of Syria and is buried in the city of Homs.

KHALIFA. *See* CALIPH.

KHALIL IBN AHMAD, AL (718–791). Arab philologist and compiler of the first **Arabic** dictionary, the *Book of the Letter 'Ayn (Kitab al-'ayn)*. It was arranged in alphabetical order according to pronunciation, beginning with the letter 'ayn. A book of his on prosody is lost. Al-Khalil was born in Oman and moved to **Basra**, where he lived in very modest circumstances. Abu 'l Faraj al-**Isfahani** said: "It must be observed that Islamism never produced a more active spirit than al-Khalil for the discovery of sciences which were unknown, even in their first principles, to the learned among the Arabs" (Khallikan, trans. Slane, I, 494). Khalil died of an accident when, engrossed in thought, he walked into a pillar when entering a **mosque**.

KHALWATIYYAH. A Sufi order, founded in 14th-century Persia and spread into Anatolia and subsequently into Egypt and Africa. Its founding heads (**shaykhs**) were Umar al-Khalwati (d. 1397) and Yahya Shirwan (d. 1464). Its practices include voluntary hunger, silence, vigil, seclusion, meditation, permanent ritual cleanliness, and complete devotion to one's spiritual master. Kemal Atatürk suppressed all Sufi orders, but they continued clandestinely and, like the Bektashi order, were strong in the Balkans even during the communist regimes.

KHAMENE'I, AYATOLLAH SAYYIOD ALI HUSAYNI (b. 1939). Elected as spiritual leader of Iran, after the death of Ayatollah Ruhollah **Khomeyni** in 1989. He was born in **Mashhad** in 1939 and educated in **Qom** and **Najaf**, where he was a student of Khomeyni. Arrested several times during the period of the monarchy, he became a member of Khomeyni's Revolutionary Council and commander of the **Revolutionary Guards**. He became president of Iran in 1981 and was reelected in 1985, until he succeeded Ayatollah Khomeyni in 1989. Khamene'i is said to be relatively moderate—he opposed absolute rule by the theologians and agreed to pardon Salman **Rushdie**—but he has never enjoyed the power or charisma of his predecessor.

KHAMR. *See* ALCOHOL.

KHAN, SIR SAYYID AHMAD (1817–1898). Muslim modernist who demanded reforms and the adoption of Western technology and education. After receiving a traditional **education**, he found work as a writer at the East India Company's court of justice in Delhi in 1841. He advocated coexistence between Muslims and the British, feeling that Muslim interests would be better protected than under Hindu rule. Among his many publications was a commentary on the Bible and the **Koran**, pointing out the common source of the **scriptures**. In 1875, Sir Sayyid founded the All-India Muhammadan Anglo–Oriental College at **Aligarh**, which was eventually transformed into Aligarh University. He sought to reconcile faith and reason and favored the adoption of Western concepts, such as science, technology, justice, and freedom. He is credited with being one of the initiators of India's Islamic renaissance and a promoter of the idea of creating a Muslim state, which was implemented long after his death with the creation of Pakistan.

KHANAQAH (KHANQAH). **Sufi** lodge, or monastery, where the devotees live under the direction of a Sufi master. It is often connected with a **mosque** or **madrasah**, and it is most commonly found in Iraq and Iran. The lodges are also called *tekke* and in North Africa *zawiyah* ("corner").

KHANDAQ. *See* TRENCH, BATTLE OF THE.

KHARAJ. Land tax, adopted from the Byzantines. It was originally levied on non-Muslim subjects, together with the poll tax (**jizyah**). When farmers converted to Islam and Muslim conquerors also acquired land in the early eighth century, the kharaj was levied on all landowners. Originally the income of the kharaj, often paid in kind, served to defray the cost of the military and administration. Muslims also had to pay the poor tax (**zakat**). **Shi'ites** dispute the legitimacy of kharaj, because it was introduced by the **Sunni caliph 'Umar ibn al-Khattab**.

KHARIJITES (KHAWARIJ). Originally followers of Caliph **'Ali**, who deserted him when he agreed to arbitration in the caliphal dispute with **Mu'awiyah** at **Adhruh**. They went out (*yakhraju*) from 'Ali's camp (hence their name) at **Kufah** and settled at Harura. They turned against 'Ali and became a source of rebellions during the

Umayyad and early **'Abbasid** periods. The Kharijites (pl. *khawarij*, self-designation "the People of Paradise") found their supporters primarily among the reciters (*qurra'*) of the **Koran**, the newly converted, as well as among Arab nomadic tribes that did not benefit from the early conquests. 'Ali defeated the Kharijites decisively at **Nahrawan** in 658, but he was assassinated by a Kharijite in 661.

The Kharijites claimed the right to chose a **caliph** and depose him if he had become a sinner. They recognized **Abu Bakr**, **'Umar**, the first six years of the **'Uthman caliphate**, and the period of 'Ali until the battle of **Siffin** (657). They held that the caliphate is elective and that any pious Muslim is entitled to the caliphate, even if he were an Abyssinian slave. Contrary to other **sects**, they held that a Muslim who had committed a grave **sin** had become an unbeliever (**kafir**). The most radical of the Kharijite **sect** (the **Azraqi**) held that such a sinner was an apostate and had to be killed together with his wives and children. Because of their radicalism, most of them were eventually wiped out. A reaction to their radical views appeared with the rise of the **Murji'ites**, who deferred judgment of sinners to God. A more tolerant group, the **Ibadites**, named after their leader Abdullah ibn Ibad, disassociated itself from the radicals in the second half of the eighth century. They are close to mainstream **Sunni** Islam and have survived until this day in Oman and in East and North Africa.

KHATAM. Meaning "seal," and referring to **Muhammad** as Seal of the Prophets *(khatam al-nabiyun)* the last, or final, prophet until the **Day of Judgment**.

KHATAMI, SAYYID MUHAMMAD (1943–). A moderate, he was elected president of Iran in May 1997 with 69 percent of the vote and reelected in 2001–2005 with some 70 percent. Largely opposed by the conservatives, his election has been interpreted as the popular desire for a more liberal policy. He was accused by his supporters of failing to stand up to the hard-liners and was not able to implement his idea of "Islamic democracy" in Iran. Khatami was born in Yazd and educated at home and in theology at **Qom**. Subsequently, he earned a doctorate at Tehran University and spent several years as head of the Islamic Center of Iran in Hamburg. After the Iranian Revolution of 1979, he served as a member of the Supreme Council of the

Cultural Revolution. He became a member of parliament in 1980 and minister of education in 1982, and acted as an adviser to Ali Akbar Rafsanjani. As president, he supported freedom of the press and tried to protect liberals from conservative attacks. He usually kept a smiling face and was therefore nicknamed "the laughing Sayyid."

KHATIB. A religious functionary who delivers the **Friday** sermon (**khutbah**) in a major **mosque**. Originally, the khatibs were tribal spokesmen and intellectual leaders. After the advent of Islam, the **caliph** and his governors in the provinces performed the functions of the khatib, but, eventually a preacher was assigned to every major mosque. Because it was customary to invoke the name of the caliph (or ruling **sultan**) in the sermon, the khutbah gained an important political aspect. Rebellions started when a challenger had his own name mentioned in the sermon.

KHAWARIJ. *See* KHARIJITES.

KHAYYAM, OMAR (1048–1131). Eminent Persian poet, astronomer, mathematician, and philosopher. He is best known for his quatrains, first translated into English by Edward Fitzgerald in the 19th century under the title *The Rubaiyat of Omar Khayyam*, then later into other European languages. Born into a family of "tent makers" (khayyam) in Nishapur in present-day northeastern Iran, he was educated in Balkh (in present-day **Afghanistan**) and Nishapur. His *Treatise on Demonstration of Problems of Algebra* was a significant contribution to mathematics, and he participated in a project of reforming the Persian calender. As an astronomer, he favored a heliocentric theory before Copernicus. Because of his unorthodox views of Islam, he repeatedly got into trouble with the authorities. One of his quatrains says: "Enjoy wine and women and don't be afraid, God has compassion."

KHAZRAJ. A south Arabian tribe that settled in **Medina**, who together with the **Aws** became the Helpers (or **Ansar**) of the first Muslim community. Engaged in internecine warfare with the Aws and members of the three Jewish tribes in Medina, they accepted **Muhammad** as an arbiter and head of the first Judeo–Arab community. After the

Muslim conquest of **Mecca** in 630, the Ansar were second in rank among converts, after the **Muhajirun**, those early converts who followed Muhammad from Mecca to Medina. *See also* 'AQABAH, PLEDGE OF.

KHILAFAT MOVEMENT (1919–1924). A religio-political movement, headed by the brothers Muhammad Ali and Shaukat Ali, which rose in 1919 in India in response to the defeat of the **Ottoman empire** in the First World War. Although under British control, Indian Muslims continued to recognize the Ottoman **sultan/caliph** as the legitimate head of the **Sunni** Muslim community. The danger of division of the Ottoman empire and the possibility of occupation of the Holy Places by non-Muslims convinced many that they could no longer live in the Abode of War (**dar al-harb**) under British control. King Amanullah of Afghanistan, who had just secured his country's independence from Great Britain, invited the emigrants (**muhajirun**) to come to his country. Some 18,000 followed his invitation, but most were poor and unskilled people who could not contribute to the development of Afghanistan. When the Turkish government abolished the **caliphate** in 1924, and the Afghan ruler began his secular policies of reform, the Khilafat Movement gradually lost support. Many of the muhajirun returned to India to join the Pakistan movement or moved on to the Soviet Union and Turkey.

KHIRQAH. A **Sufi**'s woolen robe, bestowed on a disciple by his master.

KHITAN. *See* CIRCUMCISION.

KHOJAS. A community of Hindus of the Lohana caste that was converted by **Isma'ili** missionaries in the 14th century and adopted the **Nizari** branch of the Isma'ili **sect**. Most recognize the **Agha Khan** as their spiritual leader. They have their own **scriptures** and consider their **imams** god incarnate. There are, however, **Sunni** and **Twelver Shi'ite** Khojas who follow their own respective rites.

KHOMEYNI, AYATOLLAH RUHOLLAH AL-MUSAVI AL- (ca. 1900–1989). Born in Khomeyn, a town about 270 kilometers south of Tehran, Khomeyni received a traditional **madrasah education**. At the age of 27, he taught at Isfahan and later at **Qom**, lecturing on Islamic philosophy, law, mysticism, and ethics. He was quickly involved in political activism, opposing the governments of Reza Khan and his son Muhammad Reza and the growing secularization in Iran. His book, *Unveiling the Secrets (Kashf al-asrar)*, published in 1942, condemned the shah's tyranny, and he made himself the leader of a movement of political protest, which led to his brief imprisonment in 1963. Exiled to Turkey in 1964, Khomeyni went to **Najaf** in Iraq a year later, where he taught for the next 14 years. In his lectures, published under the title *Guardianship of the Islamic Jurists*, he advocated the establishment of an Islamic state under the leadership of the supreme jurisconsult (**vilayat-i faqih**). Khomeyni next moved to France, but his speeches were reproduced on cassettes and broadcasts from **mosques** throughout the country and made him the major spokesman of the Iranian Revolution.

In February 1979, Khomeyni returned to Iran to implement his political ideas. The function of government, he felt, is to enforce the **shari'ah**, to combat oppression, corruption, heresies, and "errors legislated by false parliaments." A reign of terror, the occupation of the American embassy in Tehran, and his proclamation of the export of the revolution led to the increasing isolation of Iran. An indecisive war with Iraq broke out in 1982 that was costly in human and financial resources and weakened the state. Khomeyni's **fatwa** of 1989, calling for the assassination of Salman Rushdie for writing *The Satanic Verses*, has left an issue that has contributed to preventing the normalization of relations with the West. Khomeyni's revolution stimulated revivalist movements elsewhere in the Islamic world that oppose Westernization and demand establishment of a purist Islamic state based on the model of the state under the Prophet **Muhammad**.

KHORASAN. The East or "Land of the Rising Sun," the name of a province in northeastern Iran and the historical name of an area that roughly corresponds to eastern **Iran** and **Afghanistan** at the time of Ahmad Shah (r. 1747–1773). It was part of the Achaemenid and Sassanian empires, then conquered by the Muslim Arabs in 651–652 CE. Abu Muslim raised the "Black Banner" of the house of Abbas and with his Khorasanian army defeated the **Umayyads**, bringing the

Abbasid **caliphs** to power. Khorasan was virtually independent under the **Tahirid**, Saffarid, and **Samanid** dynasties (821–999) and part of the **Ghaznavid**, **Saljuq**, and Khwarizm empires. The **Mongols** controlled the area, and the **Safavids** fought the Uzbeks over Khorasan before it became the heartland of Ahmad Shah's empire. Khorasan was called the "cradle of classical Persian culture."

KHUMS. A fifth (*khums*) of the booty (**ghanima**) of the early Islamic wars, reserved for the institutional use of the government. In **Shi'ism**, it was the religious tithe collected by the **'ulama'**, which gave them a measure of independence.

KHUTBAH. **Friday** sermon delivered at noon at a congregational **mosque** (*jam'ah masjid*) and during **pilgrimage** and at the time of special festivities. It has political significance because the **khatib** (preacher) traditionally invokes the name of the recognized ruler. Under colonial rule, the khutbah was often read in the name of the "Ruler of the Age," the **Ottoman caliph**, or even, in Algeria, in the name of the French president. The khutbah was initially read by the Prophet, later by the **Rightly Guided Caliphs**, and under the **Umayyads** by provincial governors. Only in the **'Abbasid** period were khatibs appointed.

KHWARIZMI, MUHAMMAD IBN MUSA AL- (ca. 800–846). Mathematician, geographer, and astronomer from Khwarizm, the present-day Khiva in Uzbekistan, Khwarizmi was the first to compose works on arithmetic and algebra. His *Calculation of Integration and Equation (Hisab al-jabr wa'l muqabalah)* was translated into Latin in the 12th century and became the principal text at European universities. The word "algebra" is derived from the title of his book. He was a pioneer in pointing out the importance of "Arabic" numerals and zero instead of the roman numerals used at the time. As court astronomer to the Caliph al-**Ma'mun** at **Baghdad**, al-Khwarizmi compiled the oldest astronomical tables, which were important because they laid the groundwork for the beginning of European astronomy. The mathematical term "algorithm" is derived from his name.

KINDI, YA'QUB IBN ISHAQ AL- (801–873). The first important Muslim philosopher, who connected Greek philosophical doctrines with the rationalist school of the **Mu'tazilites**. Al-Kindi was born in **Kufah** and became a calligrapher at the caliphal court at **Baghdad**. An adviser at the court of the Caliph al-Mu'tasim (r. 833–842) and a tutor of princes at **Samarra**, al-Kindi faced hostility from courtiers. He believed in the theory of creation out of nothing (*creatio ex nihilo*) and called for the allegorical interpretation (**ta'wil**) of the **Koran**. Of some 270 publications on medical topics, alchemy, and mathematics, about 40 are extant. He held the title "Philosopher of the Arabs."

KISMET. In popular Islam, the fatalistic acceptance of what God has preordained as one's lot. The **Ash'arite** school of **Sunni** Islam accepts the idea of acquisition (**kasb**), which permits humans free will to win salvation, while at the same time maintaining that God produces all acts. *See also* FATALISM.

KISWAH. "Robe." The black gold-embroidered brocade that covers the **Ka'bah**, except for the area of the **Black Stone**. It is changed each year and cut up and sold or given to pilgrims. To furnish the Kiswah each year was the privilege of the **caliphs**, later of the **Mamluk** and **Ottoman sultans**. At present, the Kiswah is woven in Egypt and carried to **Mecca** in a special procession. After the **Wahhabi** conquest of the **Hijaz** in the early 19th century, the Kiswah procession was prohibited, but it was resumed after a hiatus of 10 years.

KITAB. "The Book." Muslim designation for the **Koran**, but also for the scriptures (Bible) of the **Christians** and Jews, who are **Peoples of the Book** (*ahl al-kitab*).

KIZILBASH. "Red Heads." Members of seven Turkoman tribes who formed a military and governmental elite under Shah Isma'il (r. 1499–1524), whom they regarded as a **saint** and king. They derived their name from the fact that they wore 12 red stripes on their turbans, each for one of the **Twelver Shi'ite imams**. The Kizilbash were believed to be invincible until they were defeated by **Ottoman** Sultan Selim at the Battle of Chaldiran in 1514. They remained a force until the 18th century, when they accompanied Nadir Shah Afshar (r. 1736–1747) on his invasions of India and manned fortified bases of occupation in Iran, Afghanistan, and India.

KORAN (QUR'AN). The Koran is the sacred book of Islam, containing God's direct revelations through the medium of the Prophet **Muhammad**. According to dogma, it is a miracle, divine in origin, and the uncreated word of God. **Revelation** began in 610 during the holy month of **Ramadhan** when the angel **Gabriel** called to Muhammad: "Recite! (or Read) in the name of thy Lord." A **hadith** transmitted by **'A'ishah** quotes the Prophet telling the story of his first revelation as follows:

> The angel caught me (forcibly) and pressed me so hard that I could not bear it anymore. He then released me and again asked me to read and I replied "I do not know how to read." At the third time the angel said: "Read in the name of your Lord, who created, created man from a clot. Read! And your Lord is most generous." Then **Allah**'s apostle returned with the inspiration and with his heart beating severely. Then he went to **Khadijah** bint Khuwailid and said, "Cover me! Cover me!" They covered him till his fear was over and after that he told her everything that had happened and said, "I fear that something may happen to me." Khadijah replied, "Never! By Allah, Allah will never disgrace you. You keep good relations with your kith and kin, help the poor and the destitute, serve your guests generously and assist the deserving calamity-afflicted ones." (Bukhari, I,1, 1951, Muhsin)

The revelations were collected into one volume. The Koran is divided into 114 chapters (**Surahs**), 6,236 verses (**ayahs**), 77,934 words (*harf* pl. *huruf*), and 323,621 letters. The Surahs are arranged roughly according to length, beginning with the longest. An exception is the *Fatiha*, or "Opener," which is a short one. The Koran is possibly the most widely read book ever written. Besides serving for worship, it is the textbook from which generations of Muslims have learned to read **Arabic**. Orthodox Muslims believe that the Koran is inimitable (2:23–24), and no authorized translation exists (although the **Ottoman 'ulama'** recognized the Turkish translation as authoritative). The word Qur'an means recitation (or reading), and the book is clearly meant for recitation. The language of the Koran is the written language from which modern standard Arabic is derived.

European Orientalists have attempted to establish a chronology, according to which the Meccan Surahs are usually shorter and reflect the period of struggle with the **Quraysh**. Muhammad is the one who warns of the impending **Day of Judgment**, whereas in the Medina period he is a statesman and head of the Islamic community. Passages of the Koran were at first memorized, but already under Caliph **Abu Bakr** (632–634) collection began, and in the period of **'Uthman** (644–656) a definitive version was compiled. (Some European scholars [e.g., Wansbrough] maintain that the Koran was generated at a much later date.) A science of **exegesis** eventually evolved, which examines hadiths and grammatical and lexicographical factors; **Shi'ites** permit an allegorical interpretation (**ta'wil**). Schools were established early in Islam in which pupils would memorize passages of the Koran; a person who has memorized the Koran holds the honorific title of **Hafiz**. Together with the **Sunnah**, the deeds and pronouncements of Muhammad, the Koran is the basis of **Islamic law (shari'ah)**.

KORANIC SCHOOLS. *See* EDUCATION.

KUFAH. One of the garrison towns (**amsar**) founded in 638 by **'Umar I** on the west bank of the Euphrates River to keep the conquering Arabs apart from the sedentary population. It became the capital of **'Ali ibn Abi Talib** from 657 to 661. In the early **'Abbasid** period (749–762), it was an important cultural center but lost its importance in the 10th century because of **Shi'ite**, **Kharijite**, and **Qarmatian** revolts and because of the transfer of the capital to **Baghdad**. The "kufic" script of **Arabic** was pioneered at Kufah.

KUFR, AL-. "Unbelief." A **kafir** is an infidel, one who denies the existence of God or gives partners to God (a polytheist). Surah 109:1–5, titled Al-Kafirun, says: "Say: O ye that reject Faith! I worship not that which ye worship, Nor will ye worship that which I worship."

KULAYNI, MUHAMMAD YAQUB AL- (KULINI, d. 940). Shi'ite scholar at **Baghdad** and author of one of the four canonical Shi'ite collections, the *Kitab al-Kafi*, containing more than 15,000 **hadith**. Unlike the **Sunnis**, the **Shi'ite** include their **imams** in the chain (**isnad**) of transmitters of a hadith to guarantee its soundness.

KUNYAH. The formal name of a person, indicating the relationship of the name bearer to another person, for example, Abu Qasim, the father of Qasim. It may also describe a metaphorical relationship or be a nickname, for example, Abu 'l-Fadhl, father of merit. It is a surname in addition to the *ism*, personal name, to provide additional information; for example, Muhammad Abu al-Qasim (Muhammad the father of Qasim). A surname of honor or nickname is called *laqab*, for example, Nur al-Din, "The Light of Religion," and the *nisbah*, referring to a place, **sect**, and trade, for example, al-Baghdadi (the one from **Baghdad**). The patronymic *nasab* list the names of ancestors with the word *ibn* (son), for example, Qasim ibn Muhammad—Qasim the son of Muhammad. *See also* NAMES AND NAMEGIVING.

– L –

LABID IBN RABI'A (ca. 560–661). Arab poet and composer of one of the prizewinning poems in the **Mu'allaqat**. He adopted Islam in 630, together with his tribe, and he lived in **Kufah**. Labid then abjured poetry, saying "God has given me the **Koran** in exchange for it" (Nicholson, 119). He was a true Bedouin, extolling the Arab virtues of hospitality, generosity, and bravery.

LADEN, OSAMA BIN (1957–). Citizen of Saudi Arabia, born in Jeddah, the 17th son of Osama bin Muhammad bin Awad bin Laden, a Yemeni construction tycoon, and a Syrian mother. He graduated from King Abdul Aziz University in Jeddah in 1979 with a degree in economics and public administration and worked in the family business. In 1984, bin Laden moved to Peshawar, **Pakistan**, to support the war against the communist government. He is said to have fought only at one battle, and his contribution was primarily as a fund-raiser. He is said to own the al-Hijrah Construction Company, an Islamic Bank, an import–export company, and an agricultural products firm. In 1989, he returned to Jiddah and worked in the family construction business, but in 1991 he was expelled from Saudi Arabia and moved to **Afghanistan** and a year later to Sudan. He protested the presence of American troops on Saudi soil and supported militant **Islamist** groups in addition to his own al-**Qaeda** organization, founded in 1988.

Forced to leave Sudan in May 1996, he went to Afghanistan, where he established training camps for Islamist fighters to support the **Taliban** regime and Muslim fighters in Kashmir, Chechnya, Bosnia, and elsewhere. The U.S. government accused him of the attacks on U.S. embassies in Kenya and Tanzania and demanded his extradition from Afghanistan. In retaliation for the embassy attacks, American cruise missiles bombarded the al-Shifa chemical plant in Sudan and three Islamist bases in Afghanistan. The refusal of the Taliban government to extradite bin Laden resulted in a United Nations boycott of Afghanistan, severely restricting Taliban movements. A U.S. "fact sheet," issued by the Office of Public Affairs of the American embassy in Islamabad, listed "criminal charges" against bin Laden, including repeatedly declaring war against the United States; being a **terrorist** and leader of the terrorist organization al-Qaeda; being responsible for the 7 August 1998 bombing of the U. S. embassies in Nairobi, Kenya, and Dar es-Salaam, Tanzania; and in August 1996 inciting Muslims to commence a "jihad against the Americans occupying the Land of the Two Holy Mosques" and ordering them to "expel the heretics from the Arabian Peninsula." In February 1998, a **fatwa** endorsed by bin Laden called on Muslims "to kill Americans—including civilians —anywhere in the world where they can be found."

When on 11 September 2001, suicide teams attacked the World Trade Center in New York and the Pentagon in Washington, D.C., the American government retaliated with war against al-Qaeda and its Taliban protectors. On 7 October 2001, American forces began their attack, which quickly eliminated the Taliban regime, but bin Laden and Muhammad Omar managed to escape. Although dispersed in Afghanistan, reputed al-Qaeda remnants still carry out attacks. Some units were collaborating with Abu Musab al-**Zarqawi** in Iraq, where they have been responsible for a number of suicide attacks.

All attempts to find bin Laden have so far failed. A new effort has been made in the United States at the initiative of two Republican Party legislators. About $100,000 has been spent by an advertising agency on ads on Pakistani radio and in newspapers. Legislation has been passed permitting President George W. Bush to increase the reward for the capture of bin Laden to $50 million. To make the value of the reward comprehensible to potential informants, one legislator suggested that payments be made also in farm equipment and live-stock, for "people understand what a herd of cattle is worth."

A tape released on 18 January 2006 purported to be from bin Laden seemed to indicate that he was ready for peace. It stated

We know that the majority of your people want this war to end and based on the substance of the polls, which indicate Americans do not want to fight Muslims on Muslim land, nor do they want Muslims to fight them on their land, we do not mind offering a long term truce based on just conditions that we will stand by . . . a truce that offers security and stability and the rebuilding of Iraq and Afghanistan that war has destroyed. . . . And there is nothing wrong with this solution except that it deprives the influential people and warlords in America from hundreds of billions of dollars—those who supported [President George W.] Bush's election campaign with billions of dollars.

See also JIHADIS DECLARATION OF WAR; QAEDA, AL-, INTERNATIONAL COALITION AGAINST 'TERROR'; TORA BORA, BATTLE OF.

LAHAB, ABU. *See* ABU LAHAB.

LAKHMIDS. A dynasty of the Tanukh tribes in southwest Iraq that ruled a buffer state, blocking Arab nomadic expansion to the northeast. The Tanukh established their capital at al-Hira (near the subsequent town al-**Kufah**) in the latter part of the third century. One of their first kings was **Imru 'l Qays** (r. 200–320), whose epitaph is the oldest proto-**Arabic** inscription yet discovered. Under al-Mundhir III (ca. 505–554), the Lakhmid state was at its height. Some among the Tanukh were Nestorian **Christians**, and the first and only Christian king was al-Nu'man III (r. ca. 580–602). After his time the kingdom began to decline and was vanquished in the first Muslim conquests. Three of the seven reputed authors of the "Golden Odes" (**Mu'allaqat**) flourished at the Lakhmid court.

LAQAB. An honorific title or nickname, added to the name (*ism*), for example, *Nur al-Din*, the Light of Religion. *See also* NAMES AND NAMEGIVING.

LAST DAY. The **Koran** describes the "folding up" preceding the **Day of Judgment**, saying:

When the sun (with its specious light) is folded up; when the stars fall, losing their lustre; when the mountains vanish (like a mirage); when the she-camels, ten months with young, are left untended; when the wild beasts are herded together (in human habitations); when the oceans boil over with a swell; when the souls are sorted out (being joined like with like); when the female (infant), buried alive, is questioned—for what crime she was killed; when the Scrolls are laid open; when the sky is unveiled; when the blazing Fire is kindled to fierce heat; when the Garden is brought near; (then) shall each soul know what it has put forward. (81:1–14)

According to a **hadith**, the Prophet was asked what are the signs of the hour (last Day), and he replied. "They are the disappearance of (religious) knowledge. The appearance of (religious) ignorance. The taking of alcoholic drinks. The prevalence of open illegal sexual intercourse."

LAUH AL-MAHFUZ, AL-. "The preserved tablet." It denoted the tablet on which the decrees of God regarding mankind are written. Referred to also as the "Mother of the Book," it records the destiny of humankind, and the expression "it is written" is indicative of a fatalistic trend in Islam. The **Koran** says: "This is the Glorious Qor'an, (inscribed) in a Tablet Preserved."

LAW. *See* ISLAMIC LAW.

LAYLAT AL-QADR. "The Night of Power or Destiny" is a sacred period that fell on the last 10 days of the month of **Ramadhan** of the year 610. According to tradition, the **Koran** came down from the lowest **heaven** on the night of the 27th (or 29th?), when the Angel Gabriel first spoke to **Muhammad**. The fate of a person for the coming year is predestined at that time. The Koran says: "We have indeed revealed this (Message) in the Night of Power: and what will explain to thee what the Night of Power is? The Night or Power is better than a thousand months. Therein came down the angels and the spirit by **Allah**'s permission, on every errand: Peace! . . . This until the rise of Morn! (97:1–5).

LI'AN. "Mutual cursing." An oath taken by the wife and the husband when the latter accuses his wife of **adultery**. He makes three oaths that he is truthful and a third time he invokes the curse of **Allah** on himself if he has lied. The wife can free herself of guilt by performing the same oath, and as a result, the couple is irrevocably **divorced** (24:6–9).

LINDH, JOHN WALKER. The first American prosecuted for contributing his "services" to the **Taliban**. The then 20-year-old American was accused of complicity in the death of the Central Intelligence Agency officer who was killed in a Taliban uprising in the Qala-i Jang fortress in **Afghanistan**. Eventually the government dropped nine of the charges, and in a plea agreement Lindh was sentenced to 20 years in prison. A native of California, Lindh converted to Islam during high school and went to Yemen to study Arabic. He joined the Pakistani Harakat al-Mujahidin to fight against Indian forces in Kashmir, but then underwent military training at al-Faruq camp in Afghanistan to fight against the Northern Alliance. Lindh presents himself as a devout Muslim who wanted to "liberate" Indian-held Kashmir and help establish a "pure Islamic state" in Afghanistan. He claimed not to have been a **terrorist** or a member of al-**Qaeda**, and denied having had foreknowledge of the attack on the World Trade Center in New York.

LONDON BOMBINGS. *See* JIHADIS DECLARATION OF WAR.

LONDONISTAN. A pejorative term coined by French counter**terrorism** officers to refer to the shelter wanted **Islamists** or opponents of Middle Eastern regimes, enjoyed in London. In the days before 11 September 2001, numerous individuals and groups who were wanted in their home countries for political offenses were able to find asylum in Great Britain, where they published pamphlets and newspapers attacking Middle Eastern regimes. Britain's judicial system permitted appeals for **jihad** against the West by radical leaders as expressions of freedom of speech. The policy saw "watchful tolerance" as the "best way of keeping tabs on the mosques," rather than muzzling radical **imams**. After all, Western governments encouraged Islamist groups based in their countries to foment unrest and help to arm the struggle against communism. Foreign pressure and 11 September changed this. The Terrorism Act of 2000 and the Anti-Terrorism, Crime and Security Act of 2001 permit the government to detain people without charge if their presence in the United Kingdom is deemed "not to be conducive to the public good."

LUNATIC. "Majnun." Popularly considered an "inspired" person, a lunatic is not responsible for his deeds, including murder and robbery. He is not to be killed in war and does not pay the alms tax (**zakat**).

– M –

MA'ARRI, ABU 'L-'ALA AL- (973–1057). Poet, philosopher, and man of letters. He was born in Syria, about 30 kilometers south of Aleppo, and educated in his hometown. Blind as a result of smallpox since early childhood, he was gifted with an extraordinary power of memory. After a short stay in **Baghdad**, he retired to Ma'arra, his hometown, and spent the rest of his life in seclusion. He seemed to deny the resurrection of the dead when he said: "We laugh, but inept is our laughter; We should weep and weep sore, Who are shattered like glass, and thereafter Re-moulded no more!" And he seemed to consider Islam no better than other creeds, saying:

Hanifs are stumbling, Christians all astray,
Jews wildered, Magians far on error's way
We mortals are composed of two great schools—
Enlightened knaves or else religious fools. (Nicholson, 317, 1962, 318)

MADHHAB. "Direction." A school or rite of Islamic jurisprudence, the Hanafi, Hanbali, **Shafi'i**, and **Maliki schools of Sunni law**. Divergences among the four orthodox schools are based on different Traditions or on different interpretations of the same Tradition. Generally, **Sunni** Muslims are under the jurisdiction of one of the schools, except some Muslim modernists and **Islamists**. **Shi'ite** schools include the **Zaydis** or Fivers, and the **Twelvers** adhere to the **Ja'fari** school of jurisprudence. *See also* ISLAMIC LAW.

MADRASAH. "Place of study." General name for a secondary school that functions as a theological seminary, a law school, and a **mosque** and trains religious functionaries in Islamic sciences and law. Usually attached to a mosque, with accommodation for students and teachers, the madrasah provides free **education** and, if necessary, support for needy students. The curriculum generally includes the sayings and actions of the Prophet (**hadith**), jurisprudence (**fiqh**), scholastic theology (**kalam**), and **Kora**nic exegesis (**tafsir**), as well as such fields as grammar, logic, lexicography, rhetoric (*balagha*), and literature (*adab*). Some of the most famous madrasahs were Al-**Azhar**, founded as an **Isma'ili** institution at **Cairo** in the 10th century, and the **Nizamiyyah**, founded by the **Saljuq sultans** in 1065–1067 in **Baghdad**. They became the models for Eastern and European universities. In the 19th and early 20th centuries, secular courses were added to the curriculum, and governments regulated such matters as accreditation and curriculum. In many parts of the Islamic world, private madrasahs continue to coexist with state-supported institutions.

MADRID BOMBINGS. *See* JIHADIS DECLARATION OF WAR.

MAGHREB. "Lands of the Sunset, the West." The area of northwestern Africa, including primarily Morocco, Algeria, and Tunisia, but also Mauritania and Libya. Arabs brought Islam and the Arabic language to the area, inhabited primarily by Berbers. In the 16th century, the area became part of the **Ottoman empire**; in the 19th century, the French became the dominant colonial power. Italy took control of Libya in the 20th century.

MAHDI, AL-. The "guide," who will appear at the end of time to fight against evil, restore justice, and unify the world under Islam before the advent of the **Day of Judgment**. A title, first attributed to Muhammad ibn al-**Hanafiyyah**, a son of 'Ali, and later part of the doctrine of the **Hidden Imam** (Imam Mahdi) of the **Twelver Shi'ites**. The **Tradition** that the Mahdi is preceded by a "Shedder of Blood" (al-Saffah)—a name the founder of the '**Abbasid caliphate** adopted, followed by the name al-Mahdi, a name adopted by his grandson—may very well have had the political purpose of legitimizing the revolt against the **Umayyad** caliphate. A number of individuals have laid claim to being the Mahdi, including 'Ubayd-ullah (909–934), founder of the **Fatimid** dynasty, **Ibn Tumart** (1077–1130) the **Almohad caliph**, and Muhammad ibn 'Abdullah, who appeared in the Sudan in 1883 and defeated a British expeditionary force. *See also* MAHDI OF THE SUDAN.

MAHDI OF THE SUDAN. Title of Muhammad ibn 'Abdullah (1844–1885), who became the head of a theocratic regime in the Sudan when he pronounced himself the "Mahdi." He won a wide following and was able to capture most of the Sudan, including the capital, Khartoum. He conducted a **jihad** against the British occupation forces and defeated General Charles Gordon at Khartoum in 1885. After his death in the same year, his disciple 'Abdullahi continued to rule for some 14 years, until he was defeated and killed in battle by Lord Kitchener in 1899. The Mahdi was born in 1844 in Dongola on the Red Nile. Claiming descent from **Caliph 'Ali**, he advocated a reformist Islam, with emphasis on the teachings of the **Koran**. A **Sufi shaykh** and head of the Samaniyyah order, the Mahdi was able to mobilize the masses, and it was only due to the superior firepower of the British that the Mahdist revolution was finally suppressed. *See also* MAHDI, AL-.

MAHMUD OF GHAZNI. *See* GHAZNAVID DYNASTY.

MAHR. The dowry, in pre-Islamic times a bride price given to the father or oldest male relative. In the Islamic period, the mahr was given to the bride, and a **marriage** was not legal without it. Surah 4:4 says: "And give the **women** (on marriage) their dower as an obligation; but if they, on their own good pleasure, remit any part of it to you, take it and enjoy it with right good cheer." The gift remains the property of the woman if the marriage is dissolved "But if ye decide to take one wife in place of another, even if ye had given the latter a whole treasure for dower, take not the least bit back" (4:20). Customs vary in the Islamic world, from giving only a symbolic amount to considerable sums that often pose severe hardships on the groom or his family. Therefore, various governments have attempted (usually with little success) to limit the amount of the dowry. In some countries, the mahr has amounted to a bride price, paid to the father of the bride. *See also* DIVORCE.

MAHSUD. *See* MEHSUD, ABDULLAH.

MAJAH. *See* IBN MAJAH, ABU ABDULLAH MUHAMMAD.

MAJLIS. A tribal council (sitting) in pre-Islamic Arabia in which the male members participated in making decisions of common interest. The council was presided over by the chief (**shaykh**), who was essentially an arbiter, rather than a dictator. Although it was a democratic institution, the votes were not counted, but weighed, and the elders, or more prosperous members, carried greater clout. The members of the clan, or tribe, voluntarily submitted to the decision of the council. The concept was continued into the Islamic period in the obligation of the ruler to seek council (**shurah**). The first four **caliphs** were elected by a majlis of **Companions** of the Prophet. Even today, majlis is the name of the parliament in a number of Muslim states.

MAJUSI, AL- (d. 994). Persian physician and psychologist who won fame for his *Complete Book of Medical Art* (*Kitab kamil al-sina'a al-tibbiyyah*), a concise encyclopedia dealing with the theory and practice of medicine. It was translated into Latin and widely consulted in the West. Majusi was born in Ahwaz, in present-day Iran, but he conducted his research in **Baghdad**.

MAKRUH. Behavior in law that is reprehensible, but not forbidden (**haram**) and therefore not punishable. *See* FIVE PRINCIPAL ACTS IN ISLAMIC LAW.

MAKTUB. "It is written," the fatalistic acceptance that the destiny of every individual is preordained and preserved in a book. The **Koran** says: " Nothing will happen to us except what **Allah** has decreed" (9:51). *See also* KISMET.

MALAK. *See* ANGELS.

MALIK. Title of ancient Arab kings, later of secular Arab rulers. A notable, landowner, or chief; also a personal name.

MALIK IBN ANAS, ABU 'ABD ALLAH (ca. 710–795). Arab Islamic scholar of the Hijazi school and nominal head of the **Malikite** school of Islamic jurisprudence. He taught at **Medina** and stressed the importance of **hadith**, supplementing the Traditions with the practice of the community at Medina. His **school of law** (madhhab) bases its decisions on the consensus (**ijma'**) and permits opinion (**ra'y**) of the doctors of Islamic law, if there is no clear indication in the sources. His work *The Beaten Path (al-Muwatta)* was the first attempt to codify Islamic law and is the basis of the Malikite school of jurisprudence. It gives a survey of law and justice, ritual and practice of religion, based on the consensus of the Medina community. Malik was given 70 lashes because of a legal opinion that did not please the **amir**. Mus'ab al-Zubayri described Malik as "one of the most handsome people in his face and the sweetest of them in eye, the purest of them in whiteness and the most perfect of them in height and the most excellent in body" (Bewley, *Islam: The Empowering Women.* London: Ta-Ha, 1989, xxviii).

MALIKITE. Sunni school of law (madhhab), named after **Malik ibn Anas**. It advocates the use of **ra'y** (informed opinion) and **ijma'** (consensus), but is ambivalent about **istislah**, which permits making the welfare of the community (**umma**) a consideration in a legal decision. Major Malikite scholars include 'Abd al-Salam ibn Sa'id al-Tanuhi Sahnun (776–854), Abu Bakr Muhammad al-**Baqillani** (d. 1012), 'Abd al-Wahhab 'Ali al-Baghdadi (d. 1030), Ahmad Muhammad al-Ma'afiri (1037), and 'Ali **ibn Hazm** (1063). Members of this school predominate on the east coast of the Arabian Peninsula, in Upper Egypt, in the Maghreb, and in Mauritania.

MAMLUK DYNASTY (1250–1517). A dynasty of Turkic **slaves** (*mamluk*—one possessed) who rose from being a slave force of the **Ayyubid** rulers of Egypt to establish their own kingdom. Initially, a woman, Shajar al-Durr (Tree of Pearls), ruled, followed by Aybak, whom she married and subsequently killed. The first line were called the Bahri (or River) Mamluks, who ruled from 1250 to 1390, followed by the Burji (or Citadel) Mamluks, who ruled from 1382 until the **Ottoman** conquest of Egypt in 1517. The former were largely Qipchaq Turks from southern Russia, the latter Circassians from the Caucasus. To be a member of the ruling class, one had to be purchased as a slave. Some, like **Sultan** Qala'un, called himself Al-Alfi (the Thousander), to indicate the amount for which he was originally purchased.

Baybars defeated the **Mongols** at **Ayn Jalut** in 1260, and Nasir defeated them at Marj Soffar in 1303, thus stemming the Mongol advance into Syria. The Mamluks supported **Sunni** orthodoxy and expelled the crusaders from Syria. They controlled the spice trade with India and East Asia until the circumnavigation of Africa by the Portuguese. Eventually they were weakened and were easily defeated by the Ottomans. Mamluk, or slave rulers, existed also in India (1210–1290) and elsewhere.

MA'MUN, ABU AL-'ABBAS 'ABD ALLAH AL- (786–833). '**Abbassid caliph** who succeeded his father, **Harun al-Rashid**, in 813 He was governor of the eastern provinces at Merv, from which base he sent an army against his half-brother al-**Amin**, and he eventually established himself on the caliphal throne in **Baghdad**. To heal the schism in Islam, al-Ma'mun appointed the **Shi'ite imam**, 'Ali ibn Musa al-**Ridha**, as his successor in 817. But 'Ali died a year later, and is buried in **Mashhad**. Al Ma'mun waged successful wars against Byzantium, but he faced numerous revolts. His general, Tahir ibn al-Husayn, established the **Tahirid dynasty** (821–873) in Khurasan. Al-Ma'mun supported the **Mu'tazilite** doctrine of the createdness of the **Koran** and started an inquisition (**mihna**) to force its acceptance. He supported science and art and in 830 founded the famous **House of Wisdom** (*bayt al-hikmah*), where works of Greek learning were translated into **Arabic**.

MANDEANS. Originally a heretical **sect** of **Judaism** whose members probably migrated in the first century from Palestine, southeastern Iraq, and Khuzistan in Iran. Persecuted under the Sassanians, the Mandeans became protected subjects (dhimmis), being considered scriptuaries (**Peoples of the Book**). Their language is part of the east Aramaic group and is still the cultural language of the Mandeans today. The **Koran** seems to call them Sabians.

MANDUB. "Recommended." A religious duty that is recommended but not essential and fulfillment of which is rewarded. It may be neglected without punishment. Terms synonymous with mandub are **Sunnah**, *mustahabb*, and *masnun. See also* FIVE PRINCIPAL ACTS IN ISLAMIC LAW.

MANICHAEISM. A gnostic religion named after its **messenger**, Mani (216–277), which emerged in Mesopotamia and quickly spread to North Africa and East Asia. It was to replace all religions before the end of the world. Mani proclaimed the dualism of lightness and darkness, and body and spirit. The scriptures of Manichaeism are the Seven Books of Mani. Mani was imprisoned and died in jail.

MANSUR, ABU JA'FAR 'ABD ALLAH IBN MUHAMMAD (714–775). Second **'Abbasid caliph**, who consolidated the new dynasty by eliminating all potential rivals to his power. He defeated his uncle, 'Abd Allah, in 754 and had him assassinated. He summoned his general **Abu Muslim**, who had helped him to attain power, and had him treacherously killed. Mansur suppressed numerous revolts. In 762, he ordered the building of **Baghdad**, initially called The House of Peace (*dar al-salam*), which subsequently served as the new capital of the empire. During his time Persian influence began to grow, and the **Barmakids**, a family of **viziers**, served until their destruction under **Harun al-Rashid** in the early ninth century. Mansur was given the nickname "Father of the Penny" (or Penny Pincher, *Abu Dawaniq*) because of his parsimoniousness.

MAQAM IBRAHIM. The spot near the **Ka'bah** where **Abraham**'s footprint was preserved from the time he built the Ka'bah. The **Koran** says: "In it [the Ka'bah] are signs manifest; the Station of Abraham; whoever enters it attains security."

MAQRIZI, TAQI AL-DIN AL- (1364–1441). Historian and geographer who served as a judge in **Cairo** and subsequently taught theology at **Damascus**. He wrote, among other works, a history of the **Ayyubids** and the **Mamluks** (*al-Suluk li-ma'rifati duwali al-muluk*) and a description of Egypt, called *The Districts* (*al-Mawa'iz*). He collected much information that would have been otherwise lost and was characterized as "generally painstaking and accurate, and always resorting to contemporary evidence if it is available" (Nicholson, 453).

MARABOUT. The designation of a **saint** or his descendants, who are called upon to dispense blessings (**barakah**), and whose tombs are places of **pilgrimage**. The term is used primarily in North Africa.

MA'RIB. In ancient times, the largest city in southern Yemen and the capital of a Sabean state that lasted from the 10th century BCE to the 6th century CE. It was a rich area, benefiting from the trade in incense and agriculture, made possible by a network of irrigation. When the Ma'rib dam burst in 575, the area quickly declined. The **Koran** says: "But they (Saba) turned away (from **Allah**), and We sent against them the flood (released) from the dams, and We converted their two gardens (rows) into 'gardens' producing bitter fruit" (34:16).

The *Sirah* tells the story of how one 'Amr ibn Amr escaped the catastrophe:

> 'Amr saw a rat burrowing in the dam at Marib where they used to hold back the water and then direct it where it was most needed. He perceived that the dam could not last and he determined to leave the Yaman. He proposed to deceive his people in this wise. He ordered his youngest son to get up and hit him in retaliation for his rough treatment; and when he did so 'Amr said publicly that he would not go on living in a land where the youngest son could slap his fathers face. (*Sira*, Guillaume, *The Life of Muhammad*. New York: Oxford University Press, 1924.)

He left, and God "sent a torrent against the dam and destroyed it," making the country uninhabitable.

MA'RIFAH. "Knowledge." In **Sufism**, experiential knowledge that, through illumination (kashf) leads to union with God. This knowledge is reached in stages: the devotee (**murid**) passes on the path (tariqa) from the stage of common humanity to the stage of purity, then to the stage of power, and finally to the stage of absorption in God.

MARJA' AL-TAQLID. A "source for emulation," the title of a top **mujtahid** of the **Usuli school** of **Shi'ism**. Shi'ites must find religious truth either by imitation (**taqlid**) or by seeking guidance from a living mujtahid (a religious personage who, through learning, is capable of making independent judgments). A Marja' al-Taqlid has a following and has to have published a book expounding his views. The highest of the mujtahids holds the position of **Ayatollah** al-Uzma. Ayatollah **Khomeyni** held this position.

MARJ RAHIT. Place in Syria where a tribal federation led by the Banu Kalb, allied with the forces of the **Umayyad caliph** Marwan, defeated the followers of the anti-caliph 'Abdallah ibn al-**Zubayr** in 684. This battle served as an important event in consolidating the power of the Umayyad dynasty.

MARONITES. A **Christian sect**, named after its patron saint Maron (d. 410), which is found largely in Lebanon. They were originally Monophysites who were persecuted by the Byzantine church and, therefore, accepted union with Rome in 1495. They were autonomous under the **Mamluk** and **Ottoman empires** and came under French protection in 1516. The Maronite community became increasingly Frenchified and enjoyed French protection after a bloody civil war with the **Druze** community in 1860. After World War I, the French became the mandatory power of Syria, and they established the state of Lebanon, in which **Christians** were a small majority. After Lebanon's independence in 1944, the office of the president of the republic was reserved for a Maronite, but the changing demographics in Lebanon—in which the **Shi'ites** became the largest community—led to a bloody civil war (1975–1985), which was stopped only by Syrian intervention. The Taif Accord of 22 October 1994 transferred power from the Maronite presidency to a cabinet in which Muslims and Christians were equally represented.

MARRIAGE. "Nikah." Marriage according to Muslim law is a civil contract rather than a religious sacrament. Its legality depends on consent of the parties, expressed in the "declaration and acceptance" (*i'jab-o-qabul*). Two male witnesses are required (two **women** equal the testimony of one man), and the amount of a dowry has to be determined. A Muslim man can legally marry four women, which Muslim modernists want to restrict because of the obligation that a man has to treat all his wives equally.

Shi'ites are permitted temporary marriage (**'mut'ah**), which has been explained as a necessity in olden times when a merchant had to travel long distances and be separated from home for months or even years. It is forbidden to marry a blood relation. The **Koran** says: "Prohibited to you are: Your mothers, daughters, sisters; father's sisters, mother's sisters; brother's daughters, sister's daughters; foster mothers, foster sisters; your wives' mothers; your step-daughters under your guardianship, and two sisters in wedlock at one and the same time" (4:23).

MARTYR. "Shahid." Originally a person who is killed in a holy war (**jihad**) against unbelievers or in performing a religious duty. The martyr is freed of all **sin** and goes directly to paradise to sit in the nearness of God. The **Koran** says: "Think not of those who are slain in **Allah**'s way as dead. Nay, they live, finding their sustenance from their Lord" (3:169). A **hadith** quotes the Prophet, saying: "There are seven kinds of martyr other than those killed in the way of Allah. Someone who is killed by the plague is a martyr, someone who drowns is a martyr, someone who dies of pleurisy is a martyr, someone who dies of a disease of the belly is a martyr, someone who dies by fire is a martyr, someone who dies under a falling building is a martyr and a woman who dies in childbirth is a martyr" (*Muwatta*, trans, Doi, 16.12.36). *See also* MARTYR; SUICIDE AND SUICIDE BOMBING.

MARY, MOTHER OF JESUS. Mentioned in the **Koran** and especially respected in Islam, Mary (Maryam) is the head of the **women** in paradise. Muslims believe in the virgin birth of **Jesus**, but they reject the appellation "Mother of God." The Koran says: "And (remember) her who guarded her chastity: We breathed into her from our spirit, and We made her and her son a sign for all peoples" (21:91).

MARY THE COPT (MARIAT AL-QIPTIYAH). Christian concubine of the Prophet **Muhammad** who was a gift from the Christian governor of Egypt in 629. She bore him a son, Ibrahim, who died in infancy. *See also* COPTS.

MASHHAD (MESHED). Tomb of a **saint**, a place of martyrdom, which emanates from the spiritual power of the saint and is visited by pilgrims. Also the name of a city in eastern Iran where the Eighth **Imam** 'Ali ibn Musa al-**Ridha** (Reza) is buried. It is the most important shrine of the **Twelver Shi'ites** in Iran after **Karbala**, where

Imam **Husayn** was martyred in 680, and **Najaf**, where Imam 'Ali was buried. In 1911, Russian troops, trying to restore Muhammad 'Ali (1907–1909) to the Qajar throne, bombarded the city and damaged the golden dome of the shrine.

MASJID. "Place of prostration." *See* MOSQUE.

MASLAHA. In **Islamic law** (**shari'ah**), the legal principle that permits or prohibits some act if it serves a useful purpose in advancing the public welfare. It would permit a ruler to levy special taxes in an emergency, or allow such innovations as blood transfusions. Of the four orthodox **schools of law**, only the **Shafi'ite** school accepts this principle, with some reservations. Maslaha permits overriding reasoning by analogy (**qiyas**) when a decision is considered harmful or undesirable. The Hanafite and **Malikite** schools use the term **istihsan**, an equitable preference to find a just solution, and the Hanbalis use the term **istislah**, seeking the best solution for the general interest. *See also* ISTIHSAN.

MASNAWI. *See* JALAL AL-DIN RUMI, MAULAWI.

MASRI, ABU HAMZA AL- (1958–). Called one of the most radical spiritual leaders in Great Britain and wanted by the authorities in Yemen and the United States, he was arrested by British police in August 2004 and charged with 16 crimes, including "encouraging the murder of non-Muslims, and intent to stir up racial hatred." He served as **imam** of the Finsbury Park Mosque in north London but was suspended and later dismissed from his position at the mosque. He continued to preach in the streets to large crowds outside the mosque. Abu Hamza was born Mustafa Kamel Mustafa in Alexandria, Egypt. In 1979, he went to England and studied in Brighton. He married and became a British citizen. Dubbed "The Hook" by British tabloid newspapers because he uses a hook as his right hand, Abu Hamza claims to have lost the use of his hands and was blinded in his right eye as a result of clearing mines in **Afghanistan**. He was held in Belmarsh Prison until his trial on 6 February 2006, and was sentenced to seven years for "inciting murder and racial hatred." The United States asked for his extradition.

MASTS, BATTLE OF THE. A sea battle off the Anatolian coast between the new Arab and the Byzantine fleets in 655 that resulted in a great victory for the Arabs.

MAS'UDI, ALI IBN HUSAYN (ca. 895–956). Arab historian and geographer from **Baghdad**. A **Muta'zilite**, Mas'udi was called the "Herodotus and Pliny" of the Arabs. He traveled widely from Black Africa to China and settled in Fustat (**Cairo**), where he compiled his 30-volume encyclopedic history. Part of the work was published under the title *Meadows of Gold* (*muruj al-dhahab*). The work begins with the Creation and ends with the reign of **Caliph** Muti' (946–974). In another work, *Book of Admonition and Recension* (*Kitab al-tanbih wa al-ishraf*), he summarized his philosophy of history. About his voyages, he said: "My journey resembles that of the sun, and to me the poet's verse is applicable." He wrote further:

> We turn our steps toward each different clime,
> Now to the Farthest East, then West once more;
> Even as the sun, which stays not his advance
> O'er tracts remote that no man durst explore. (Nicholson, 352.)

MATN. The text of a **hadith**, a report, supported by a chain of transmitters (**isnad**). It relates an action or pronouncement of the Prophet.

MATURIDI, ABU MANSUR AL- (d. 944). A theologian from Samarkand who founded his own orthodox school, the *maturidiyyah*, in a dispute with the **Mu'tazilites**. He accepted man's free will and assurance of salvation; in legal matters he followed Hanafite law. He led an ascetic life and was believed to have performed miracles. Maturidi died in Samarkand, where his school is still dominant.

MAUDUDI, SAYYID ABU'L A'LA (1903–1979). Founder of the **Jama'at-i Islami** in India (1941) and one of the ideological fathers of the **Islamist movement**. Born in Aurangabad, India, he was educated in Islamic studies at a **madrasah** and later at the Dar al-Ulum of Heyderabad. His formal **education** was ended at age 16 when his father died, and Maududi started a career in journalism. He founded his own journal, *The Translator of the Koran* (*Tarjoman al-Koran*) in 1935 and became a prolific writer, opposing Westernization as well as the creation of **Pakistan**. After partition of India in 1947, he settled in Pakistan and promoted his ideas of an Islamic state, which led to the drafting of a constitution that was, however, never implemented. His conditions for the establishment of an Islamic state included affirmation of the sovereignty of **Allah**, acceptance by the government that it would exercise its powers within the boundaries laid down by Allah, approval that all existing laws that were contrary to the **shari'ah** would be repealed, and agreement that all laws would be in accordance with the teachings of Islam. His ideas had a considerable impact on the political life of Pakistan, and the Jama'at-i Islami continued to agitate as a vanguard of Islamist causes. General Zia-ul-Haq staged a military coup against an elected government in 1977, seeking to make Pakistan an Islamic state. Many, but not all, of Maududi's ideas were finally realized. The war against the communist regime in Afghanistan contributed to the growth of an international **Islamist** movement, which has since become a destabilizing factor in a number of Muslim countries.

MAWALI. *See* MAWLA.

MAWARDI, ABU AL-HASAN AL- (974–1058). Jurist and moralist, famous for his *Book of the Principles of Government* (*Kitab al-ahkam al-sultaniyyah*), which is a valuable source on the organization of civil administration in the **caliphate**. It was the earliest and most important treatise on Islamic government at a time when the **'Abbasid** caliphate was under **Shi'ite Buyid** control. Al-Mawardi defined the functions of the **caliph** as safeguarding Islam from innovation, providing justice, protecting the borders of Islam, executing the penalties of the **shari'ah**, garrisoning the borders, compelling unbelievers to convert or submit and pay the poll tax (**jizyah**), levying taxes according to the **Koran**, regulating the expenditures of the state, appointing the right people to offices, and supervising the administration.

Jurists, philosophers, and Islamic thinkers like al-Mawardi, **Ibn Taimiyyah**, al-**Baqillani**, and **Ibn Khaldun** have greatly influenced Islamic political theory. Educated in **Baghdad** and **Basra**, al-Mawardi served as a judge in a number of towns before settling in Baghdad as a juridical expert at the court of the caliph. Writing at a time of Buyid hegemony, he wanted to strengthen the power of the orthodox caliph. Al-Mawardi also wrote handbooks for judges and for guidance in the worldly and religious life, such as *Instructions for This World and the Next* (*Adab al-dunya wa al-din*), as well as a number of treatises on morals and ethics. However, it was only when al-Mawardi (the name means "seller of rose-water") lay on his deathbed that he consented to have his works published.

MAWDUDI. *See* MAUDUDI.

MAWLA (MAWALI). Freed **slaves** and early converts to Islam who were, according to Arab custom, attached as clients (mawali) to a tribe. They were not fully accepted as equals and were initially taxed like **Peoples of the Book**. The Berbers in North Africa were kept in this inferior position, as were non-Arab converts in the eastern part of the empire. This led to resentment and eventual revolt against the **Umayyads**.

MAWLAWIYYA (MEVLEVI). *See* MEVLEVIS.

MAWLID AL-NABI (MAULID AN-NABI). Birthday of the Prophet on the 12th of Rabi' al-Awwal of the Muslim **calendar**, which began to be celebrated in the 12th century. Muslims hold special meetings and recite poems, describing the excellence and achievements of the Prophet **Muhammad**.

MAYMUNA BINT AL-HARITH (d. 683). A wife of **Muhammad** who was **divorced** from her first husband and widowed by her second. She married the Prophet in 629, when she was a "comely widow," 26 years old. Muhammad gave her a dowry of 400 **dirhams**. Maymuna was the aunt of the famous general **Khalid ibn al-Walid**; she bore no children and died at about age 80.

MAZAR. A tomb, or shrine of a **saint** or **imam**, and a place of **pilgrimage**.

MAZAR-I SHARIF. The capital of Balkh province in northern Afghanistan, with a population of about 70,000. According to local belief, the town is built around "The Noble Tomb" of **Caliph 'Ali** (r. 656–661), whose body was brought to this place in the early 15th century. This conflicts with the claim that 'Ali was buried in **Najaf**, now a holy city to **Shi'ites**.

MECCA (MAKKA). Holy city of Islam with a population of about 1.4 million, located about 60 kilometers from Jiddah. In the seventh century, the **Quraysh** tribe, to which the Prophet **Muhammad** belonged, made it its commercial center on the trade routes north to Syria. It was a place of **pilgrimage** even before the advent of Islam. Muhammad had his first **revelations** there in 610, but he was opposed by the pagan Quraysh and emigrated to **Medina** (Yathrib) in 622. In 630, the Muslims were able to capture the city and make it their capital and establish the **Ka'bah** as the most holy shrine of Islam. It has been a place of Muslim pilgrimage ever since.

In 930, the **Qarmatians** plundered the city and carried the **Black Stone** away with them; it was returned to the Ka'bah in 951. Mecca lost some of its importance when the Islamic capital was successively moved to **Medina, Kufah, Damascus,** and **Baghdad** and was administered by **sharifs** (descendants of the Prophet). In the First World War, Husayn, the sharif of Mecca, revolted against the **Ottoman sultan** and became king of the Hijaz, until the city was conquered by King Abd al Aziz (**Ibn Sa'ud**), who founded the Kingdom of Saudi Arabia. Mecca is sacred territory and off limits to non-Muslims.

MEDINA (AL-MADINA). A city of some 1.3 million inhabitants, located in a fertile oasis north of **Mecca**. The city, called Yathrib in pre-Islamic days and "City of the Prophet" (*Madinat al-Nabiy*) thereafter, sheltered the first Islamic community. When **Muhammad** came to Medina in 622, the town was inhabited by three Jewish and two Arab tribes. He became the head of this community, and from this base he captured Mecca and unified Arabia under Islam. The tombs of Muhammad and his daughter **Fatimah**, as well as a number of **Companions**, are located in Medina. It was the Islamic capital from 622 until the death of the Prophet in 632. Although it lost some of its former importance, Medina remained a cultural center and, together with Mecca, sacred territory. According to a **hadith**, the Prophet said: "There are **angels** at the entries of Madina, and neither plague nor the

Dajjal will enter it" (*Muwatta*, trans, Doi, 45.4.16). After the **Ottoman** conquest of Egypt in 1517, the entire **Hijaz** came under Ottoman administration until the end of the empire as a result of the First World War. *See also* MEDINA, CHARTER OF.

MEDINA, CHARTER OF. The Charter regulated the coexistence of the early community and can be seen as the prototype of an Islamic constitution. When **Muhammad** moved to Medina, he took with him some of the early converts, his **Meccan** emigrants (**muhajirun**), who together with the Helpers (**ansar**) were the first **believers** (mu'min). The Ansar were members of the Arab tribes, **Aws** and **Khazraj**, who considered Muhammad their Prophet and leader, but there were also three Jewish tribes, the **Qaynuqah**, **Nadir**, and **Qurayzah**, for whom Muhammad was a statesman and commander-in-chief.

The Charter of Medina constitutes the precedent for coexistence of Muslims and non-Muslims to this day. The preamble of the document states: "From the Apostle of God, for those of the **Quraysh** and the inhabitants of Medina who accept Islam and adopt the Faith; and for those who are subservient to them in war and alliance." It had political, civil, and religious sections, stating that Muslims and Jews constitute one political entity, with Medina as their sanctuary. God is the sovereign and Muhammad the head, and both should make war or peace together. Each community was responsible for blood money (**diyyah**) of its own, and everyone had the right to retaliation in self-defense. The Muslims are brothers and constitute one unit against the entire world; if a Jew becomes a Muslim, he will be treated as an equal, and both Jews and Muslims are to offer reciprocal respect and tolerance for the two religions. It set the precedent for the status of **Christians** and Jews as protected subjects (dhimmis), who were permitted to live in peace and practice their own religions. Because Islamic law applies only to Muslims, dhimmis were subject to their own religious traditions. The **millet** system of the **Ottoman empire** continued the autonomy of its subjects until the end of the 19th century, and traces of the system can still be found in Lebanon. *See also* PACT OF UMAR.

MEHSUD, ABDULLAH (MAHSUD) (1970s–). "Unofficial amir" of South Waziristan in the autonomous tribal area of **Pakistan**. He is a powerful leader of the Mahsud tribe, who has been accused of complicity in the assassination of Benazir Bhutto, a charge he strongly denies. He has supported **Taliban** fighters in **Afghanistan** and Pakistan, and, although there is a price on his head, the Pakistan government was forced to conclude a peace treaty with him at Sarogha in February 2005. Mehsud claimed that Pakistan violated the agreement and, in August 2007, he captured 200 regular troops, whom he exchanged for 25 of his fighters held by Pakistan. The Afghan government protested that the Sarogha agreement led to increased Taliban and al-**Qaeda** attacks in their country. One of Mehsud's clansmen, or a relative according to some sources, was held in Guantanamo, but was subsequently freed. Mehsud was born in the district of Banu of Dera Ismail Khan, North-West Frontier Province of Pakistan.

MESSENGER. The belief in a Messenger of God is one of the basic dogmas of Islam. The **Koran** says: "The messenger believeth in what hath been revealed to him from his Lord, as do the men of faith, each one (of them) believeth in **Allah**, His **angels**, His books, and His messengers" (2:285). According to Tradition (**Sunnah**), the Prophet is believed to have said that there were 124,000 prophets and 315 apostles or messengers. But there are only 25 mentioned in the Koran, 6 of whom are honored with special epithets: **Adam**, God's chosen one; **Noah**, God's preacher; **Abraham**, God's friend; **Moses**, speaker with God; **Jesus**, God's spirit; and **Muhammad**, God's Messenger. Muhammad is the last, the "seal of the prophets." He is a witness, a bearer of good tidings, and a warner of impending doom. His message is the culmination of all previous messages. **Prophets** are to guide mankind on the right path to the good life in this world and for salvation in the world to come.

MEVLEVIS (MAULAWIYYA). Mystical order named after its founder, Mawlana (Master) **Jalal al-Din Rumi**, who are known in the West as "Whirling Dervishes" because of their ecstatic **dances**, which form part of their spiritual exercises. The order flourished in Anatolia, in present- day Turkey, but was forbidden, as were all **Sufi** lodges, by the secular government of Mustapha Kemal Atatürk in 1928. Like the **Bektashi** order and others, it went underground and reappeared when government restrictions were relaxed after World War II.

MIHNA. "Trial." An inquisition, set up during the **'Abbasid** period (827–848) to force the acceptance of the **Mu'tazilite** dogma of the "**createdness of the Koran**." Al-**Ma'mun** issued a proclamation in 827, declaring that the Koran was created and demanded that all his officials accept his edict. He set up a tribunal. One of its most prominent victims was Ahmad **ibn Hanbal**, founder of the Hanbali school of jurisprudence, who refused to accept the decree. He was beaten but set free because of his popularity. Eventually, **Caliph** Mutawakkil (833–849) restored the old dogma, namely, that the Koran was not created, which is the orthodox view today.

MIHRAB. A niche in the wall of a **mosque** indicating the direction (**qiblah**) of the **Ka'bah** in **Mecca**, which Muslims all over the world must face during **prayer**. The mihrab is often richly ornamented, adorned with tiles with floral design or **Koran**ic inscriptions. The oldest preserved mihrab is said to be in the **Umayyad** Mosque in **Damascus** (720).

MIKA'IL (MIKAL). One of the archangels. *See also* ANGELS.

MILLET (MILLAT). A religio–political community and a system of administrative division under the **Ottoman empire**. Subjects were autonomous under their respective confessional leaders, who had civil and criminal jurisdiction over their flocks. The leaders, usually the patriarchs, bishops, or chief rabbis, were responsible for taxation and maintenance of law and order in their communities. Eventually European powers became protectors of various millets: the Russians favored the Orthodox, the French the Catholics, the British the Protestants and certain **Shi'ites**, etc. The system ended with the defeat of the Ottoman empire in the First World War, but traces of confessional autonomy still remain in Lebanon and other countries in the Middle East, where matters of family law are still reserved for the jurisdiction of sectarian communities. The terms *millet* and *milli* also mean nation and national, respectively.

MINA. A station on the second day of **pilgrimage** (hajj) to **Mecca**. Pilgrims sacrifice an animal, then throw seven pebbles each at "satan's three pillars" while proclaiming "**Allah** is most Great." The pilgrims spend the night at Mina and then proceed to Mecca.

MINARET. A round, square, or octangular tower of a **mosque** from which the **muezzin** (mu'adhdhin) calls to **prayer**. It either stands separately or is part of the building and has an interior stairway that leads to a balcony for the muezzin. The minaret is ornamented with brickwork or tiles with floral designs or inscriptions in **Arabic**. Some of the **Ottoman** cathedral mosques have as many as four or six minarets.

MINBAR (MIMBAR). The raised pulpit in a **mosque** from which the preacher (**khatib**) delivers his Friday sermon (**khutbah**). Originally it was the chair of the ruler or judge, located on the right side of the prayer niche (**mihrab**). The minbar was first introduced by the **'Abbasid caliphs** in the eighth century. It is a wooden structure with several steps, often richly ornamented.

MI'RAJ. *See* NOCTURNAL JOURNEY.

MISKAWAYH, AHMAD IBN MUHAMMAD (932–1030). A native of Ray, Iran, he acted as secretary and librarian to the **Buyid** ruler in Ray and **Baghdad**. His writings included the fields of philosophy, medicine, and alchemy as well as a history of the world through the year 980 (*kitab al-tajarib al-umam wa ta'aqub al-himam*). It was translated by D. S. Margoliouth under the title *The Eclipse of the Abbasid Caliphate.*

MISR. *See* AMSAR.

MOGUL (MUGHAL) EMPIRE. *See* BABUR, ZAHIR Al-DIN MUHAMMAD.

MONGOL INVASION. The Mongol invaders of the Islamic world caused terror and wreaked destruction from which it took centuries to recover. According to some sources, the **'Abbasid caliph** sought the help of Genghis Khan against the neighboring state of the Khwarizm Shahs, and for a short time **Baghdad** was safe. But after the death of Genghis in 1241, his grandson **Hulagu** moved west. He defeated the **Isma'ili** Assassins in 1256, and in 1258 captured Baghdad and established the Ilkhanid dynasty, which ruled much of the Middle East from 1256 to 1353. The Mongols were eventually stopped by the **Mamluks** of Egypt under Qotuz in the battle of **Ayn Jalut** in 1260. Most members of the 'Abbasid family were killed, but an uncle of al-Musta'sim (1242–1258) escaped and continued the 'Abbasid line in Mamluk Egypt until the conquest of **Cairo** by the **Ottomans** in 1517.

MONTAZERI, HUSAYN 'ALI (1921–). Chairman of the **Assembly of Constitutional Experts** of the Iranian revolutionary government and nominated as a successor to Ayatollah Ruhollah **Khomeyni**. He was born in Najafabad, Iran, and educated in Isfahan and **Qom**, where he was a student of Khomeyni. In the 1960s, he taught at Qom and became involved in antigovernment agitation. Jailed in 1975–1978, he was appointed **khatib** of Qom by Khomeyni and given a seat on the Islamic Revolutionary Council in 1979. In 1989, he fell out of favor with Khomeyni and was no longer considered in line for succession. *See also* ISLAMIC REPUBLIC OF IRAN.

MOORS. "Blacks." A term designating the Muslims of the **Maghreb** and Spain. Muslims who outwardly converted to **Christianity** after the fall of **Granada** were called Moriscos. They originated from ancient Mauri, the present Mauritania. Subsequently the term was employed to designate Muslims in general. Derived from the Latin *maurus*, meaning "dark complexioned."

MORABITUN. Inhabitants of a religio–military outpost in the desert (**Ribat**) who started a **jihad** that led to the establishment of the **Almoravid** dynasty in North Africa.

MOSES (MUSA). One of the great prophets recognized in Islam and the one most mentioned in the **Koran**. His title is "Speaker with God" (*Kalim Allah*). He is a lawgiver and nation-builder who delivered the Israelites from oppression. According to the Koran "(Allah) said: 'O Moses! I have chosen thee above (other) men, by the messages I (have given thee) and the words I (have spoken to thee); take then the (**revelation**) which I give thee, and be of those who give thanks'"(7:144). Moses performed miracles: "And remember Moses prayed for water for his people; We said: 'Strike the rock with thy staff.' Then gushed forth therefrom twelve springs" (2:60).

MOSQUE (MASJID). A place where one prostrates oneself (*sajadah*) five times a day in **prayer**. The mosque has been a center for social as well as political life. It has been a court of law, a center of **education**, and a place where social services are provided to the poor. Major mosques were centers of refuge where the authorities would not arrest an individual. This practice continues the tradition of the Prophet **Muhammad**, who took care of religious as well as political affairs in his home or a yard outside. Eventually cathedral mosques were built where a preacher, **khatib**, delivers the **Friday** sermon (**khutbah**).

Each mosque has a prayer niche (**mihrab**), which indicates the prayer direction (**qiblah**), and a pulpit (**minbar**) for the preacher. A fountain in the yard provides water for **ablutions**, necessary before prayer. A **madrasah**, an Islamic secondary school, is usually part of the Friday mosque, with accommodation for pupils. Major mosques are provided with a **minaret** from which the call to prayer (adhan) is broadcast. The mosque and its services are supported by pious foundations (**waqf**, pl. auqaf), but in modern times the state has increasingly taken control of funding, certification of diplomas, and other matters. Although Friday prayers are to be performed preferably in a cathedral mosque, Muslims may pray at home, in their offices, in prayer rooms, and in areas set out for prayer. After ablution, prayers, including bowings, kneelings, etc., are performed on a rug. People enter the mosque without shoes or with slippers over their shoes. **Women** do not usually attend mosques, or they are provided a special area for praying.

One Muslim scholar defined the role of the mosque as a base for establishing closer ties to God; a place for scientific and theological sessions; a court for resolving people's differences; a base for military training; a place for concluding contracts and political treaties; a weekly meeting place for rulers to deliver their address to the people; a place for bringing up current political issues; a place for marriage; a place for refugees and helpless people; a gathering place for Muslim combatants before going to battle; and a sanctuary for Muslims as a political means to exert pressure on their tyrannical rulers (Anonymous, "The Role of the Masjid," *Echo of Islam* 1, no. 7 [October 1981] and no. 8 [November 1981]).

MOUSSAOUI. *See* MUSAWI, ZACARIAS.

MU'ADH IBN JABAL. A **Companion** of the Prophet of the Khazraj tribe, who, according to tradition, was the first to use opinion (**ra'y**) as a judge. He was sent to be judge in Yemen and, before he departed, the Prophet asked him on what grounds he would judge. He responded, "According to the scriptures of God." He was then asked, "And if thou findest nought therein?" to which he answered, "According to the **Tradition** of the **Messenger** of God." And when asked "And if thou findest nought therein?" he responded, "Then I shall interpret with my reason" (Fyzee, 1967, 17–18). The Prophet approved his use of independent judgment.

MU'ALLAQAT. The oldest collection of pre-Islamic poetry, called "the suspended ones" because they were believed to be suspended at the **Ka'bah** as prizewinning examples (some scholars say it refers to a necklace). The *Seven Odes*, collected by Hammad al-Rawiyah (d. ca. 772), are samples of poetry from **Imr 'l-Qays** (d. ca. 540), Tarafa ibn al-'Abd (d. 564), Zuhair Ibn Abi Sulma (d. ca. 627), **Labid ibn Rabi'a** (d. 661), **'Amr ibn al-Kulthum** (d. ca. 600), **Antarah ibn Shaddat** (d. 615), and al-Harith ibn Hilliza (d. ca. 570). They extol the Bedouin virtues of honor, courage, generosity, and loyalty, as well as vengeance and romance. The *Seven Odes* (there may have been nine, and only five are accepted by all) and other collections, like the *Mufadhdhaliyat* of 120 odes, are invaluable sources for pre-Islamic Bedouin life, and the poetry is still appreciated today. *See also* MUFADHDHAL, AL-DABBI AL-.

MU'AWIYAH (ca. 605–680). First **Umayyad caliph**, who disputed the election of 'Ali ibn Abi Talib and, after the arbitration of **Adhruh**, proclaimed himself caliph in 659. After 'Ali's death in 661, his claim was no longer challenged, and he established his capital in **Damascus**, where he had earlier served as governor. He continued the Arab conquests in North Africa and Central Asia and built the first Islamic navy. He stressed capacity as the primary qualification for the office of caliph and started the dynastic principle by appointing his son **Yazid** as his successor. When reproached about this, he asserted that Yazid was the most suitable and offered to cancel his appointment if the community could decide on someone more worthy. Mu'awiyah eliminated **Hasan**, son of 'Ali, as a contender by providing a handsome pension for his retirement. Another of 'Ali's sons, al-**Husayn**, refused to acknowledge Mu'awiyah's son and moved from **Medina** to Iraq, where he and his small following were massacred at **Karbala** in 680.

Mu'awiyah was the first Islamic ruler to set up an office of registry. He appointed **judges** (qadhis) to major cities, issued the first coins—patterned after Byzantine and Persian examples—and began a postal service; he also reorganized the army, which included Christian mercenaries, into an excellent fighting force and proved himself to be a competent administrator. He cherished **Arabic** poetry, and one of the Umayyad's most favored poets was **Akhtal**, a Christian. Later historians characterize Umayyad rule as constituting an Arab kingdom rather than a caliphate. Some felt that the caliphate had come to an end and the institution of worldly dominion had begun.

MUBAH. An action that is neutral, neither recommended nor disapproved, and that may be left undone without fear of divine punishment. *See also* FIVE PRINCIPAL ACTS IN ISLAMIC LAW.

MUBARRAD, ABU AL-'ABBAS AL- (826–898). Arab philologist and one of the major representatives of the Basran school of grammarians. Mubarrad was born in **Basra** and went to the caliphal court at **Baghdad**, where he remained until his death. His major work, *The Perfect in Literature* (*Kitab al-kamil fi al-adab*), has been called the classical **adab** work par excellence. It includes examples of pious sayings, proverbs, poems, and grammatical and lexicographical commentaries. Al- Mubarrad and Abu l'-'Abbas Tha'lab, his rival at **Kufah**, were praised by a contemporary as follows:

> Turn to Mubarrad or to Tha'lab, thou
> That seek'st with learning to improve the mind!
> Be not a fool, like mangy camel shunned:

All human knowledge thou with them wilt find.
The science of the whole world, East and West,
In these two single doctors is combined. (Nicholson, 344)

MUEZZIN (MU'ADHDHIN). Islamic functionary who delivers the call for **prayer** from either a **minaret** or the door of a **mosque**. He calls for five prayers: a few minutes after sunset; at night, when the sky is quite dark; at daybreak; a few minutes after noon; and in mid-afternoon. Two additional, but not obligatory, prayers are announced after midnight and an hour before dawn. The first muezzin in Islam is said to have been **Bilal** (d. 640s), an Abyssinian slave who converted to Islam.

MUFADHDHAL, AL-DABBI AL- (d. ca. 786). Arab philologist of **Kufah** who was an authority on pre-Islamic poetry. Imprisoned for involvement in a revolt against **Caliph** al-**Mansur**, he was pardoned and became tutor to the caliph's son, al-Mahdi (775–785). He compiled an anthology of 128 odes (*qasidah*) for his pupil, which is named after him, the *Mufadhdhaliyat*, and he wrote a number of treatises on prosody and proverbs. The *Mufadhdhaliyat* was translated into English by Lady Ann Blunt and put into English verse by Wilfrid S. Blunt (*The Mufadhdhaliat*, London, 1903).

MUFTI. A canon lawyer of reputation who gives a formal legal opinion (**fatwa**) in answer to a question submitted to him by either a judge or a private individual. During the Ottoman empire, which controlled much of the **Sunni** Islamic world from the 14th to the 20th centuries, the Grand Mufti was given the title **Shaykh al-Islam**. He appointed all the muftis in the empire and had the authority to declare legislation by the **sultan/caliph** in conformity with **Islamic law**. After the disintegration of the empire, Muslim countries appointed a Grand Mufti or a council of **'ulama'**, which issues fatwas on legal issues. In the **Twelver Shi'ite** tradition, the **mujtahid**, who was also at times called Shaykh al-Islam, performed a similar role.

MUHAJIRUN. "Exiles," or "emigrants." Designation for the early converts who followed **Muhammad** from **Mecca** to **Medina** or joined him there until the capture of Mecca. Since they were the earliest Muslim converts, they enjoyed a special status in the Muslim community and received a preferential share of the booty. Next to them in status were the **ansar** (Helpers), Medinan converts who rivaled the influence of the muhajirun, until they all merged and came to be called the **Companions** (ashab) of the Prophet. Modern Islamist groups summon Muslims to make the migration (**hijrah**) to their camp, that is to say, convert to their concept of Islam.

The **Koran** says "Those who believe, and emigrate and strive with might and main in **Allah**'s cause, with their goods and their persons, have the highest rank in the sight of Allah: They are the people who will achieve (salvation)" (9:20).

MUHAMMAD 'ABDUH. *See* 'ABDUH, MUHAMMAD.

MUHAMMAD 'ALI (1769–1848). Viceroy of Egypt and founder of a dynasty that lasted until 1953. Muhammad 'Ali, perhaps of Albanian origin, came to Egypt with an **Ottoman** army, which expelled the French invaders from Egypt in 1801. He headed an Albanian contingent that enabled him to eliminate all rivals to his power to become the unchallenged ruler of Egypt from 1805 to 1848. Benefiting from the example of French administration, he initiated modern reforms in the military, administration, and economy of his state. Ably assisted by his son, Ibrahim, he annexed large areas of the Sudan, eliminated the threat of the unruly Bedouins, destroyed the power of the **Mamluks,** and served the Ottoman **sultan** by defeating the **Wahhabi** uprising in Arabia. Eventually, he even challenged the power of the Ottoman sultan, invading Syria and defeating the Ottoman forces in 1832 and 1839. It was only because of European intervention that he was compelled to withdraw his forces from Syria.

During the reign of his son, Sa'id (1854–1863), the Suez Canal project was started. It was finished under Isma'il (1863–1879). The enormous cost of the construction resulted in the country's bankruptcy and the British invasion of Egypt in 1882. Thereafter, Egyptian kings had to heed British "advice" in the conduct of their domestic affairs.

Faruq inherited the throne in 1936, when he was still a minor, and was subject to the guidance of his regents until July 1937. In 1942, the British ambassador and the commander-in-chief of the British forces in Egypt, accompanied by armored units, forced Faruq to appoint an enemy of his as prime minister. This "humiliation of Faruq" was seen by some as the cause of his subsequent life as a "voluptuary" and habitué of nightclubs, neglecting the affairs of state. He was overthrown by a revolt of military officers, some of whom still control Egyptian affairs today.

The line of Muhammad 'Ali included the following members:

Muhammad 'Ali (1805–1848)	Abbas II Hilmi (1892–1914)
Abbas I (1848–1854)	Husayn Kamil (Sultan) (1914–1917)
Sa'id (1854–1863)	Ahmad Fu'ad (King) (1917–1936)
Isma'll (1863–1879)	Faruq (1936–1952)
Tawfiq (1879–1892)	Fu'ad (1952–1953)

MUHAMMAD, MESSENGER OF GOD (ca. 570–632). He was born in **Mecca** in the "Year of the Elephant," the son of Abdallah, of the **Hashimite clan** of the **Quraysh**, and Amina, of the Zuhra clan. His father died four months before his birth and his mother about six years later. He was nursed by **Halimah**, a Bedouin **woman**; his grandfather, 'Abd al-Mutalib, and later his uncle **Abu Talib**, acted as his guardians. In about 586, he entered the service of **Khadijah**, a widow some 15 years his senior, whom he married in 595. Khadijah bore him two sons and four daughters, but all except the last born, **Fatimah**, died early. He made several trips to Syria, and in 610, when he was 40 years old, he confessed to Khadijah that he was hearing voices speaking to him. One Monday in the month of **Ramadhan** of the year 610, he had his first **revelation**. Muhammad soon gained a small number of converts. After Khadijah, his cousin and son-in-law **'Ali** was one of the first male converts, followed by **Abu Bakr**. Most of the early converts were young men who did not enjoy powerful protectors.

At the time, Mecca was in a stage of transition from a pastoral, nomadic economy to a mercantile one, but the traditional Bedouin values continued. Muhammad's new religion was to substitute the bonds of religion for the bonds of blood. The Meccan **Quraysh**, who were the predominant power, were opposed to Muhammad's message. The new religion constituted a revolution that threatened their economic position and their way of life. Pagan shrines, which brought income from **pilgrimages**, were to be replaced, and the illustrious ancestors of the Quraysh, born before Muhammad's message, were to be condemned to eternal hellfire. Quraysh hostility forced many early converts, who did not have powerful protectors, to emigrate to Abyssinia. When Muhammad's uncle and protector died in 619, **Abu Lahab** became the chief of the **Hashimite** clan and promptly withdrew his protection from Muhammad.

Following an invitation from some tribesmen in Yathrib (**Medina**), Muhammad fled with a small retinue of emigrants (**muhajirun**) and established himself as leader of the early community. This flight (**hijrah**) in 622 marked the beginning of the Islamic **calendar**. In addition to the muhajirun and the early converts of Medina, the **ansar** (Helpers), there were also three major Jewish tribes who formed an alliance against the Meccan Quraysh. There was no room for two powers in the **Hijaz**, and it was inevitable that Medina and Mecca would have to fight for dominance. Three battles, at **Badr** (624), **Uhud** (625), and a defensive battle of the **Trench** (627), convinced the Meccans that they could not prevail, and they made peace in the Treaty of **Hudaybiyah** (628). Two years later, the Muslim forces took Mecca, and by the time of Muhammad's death in 632, most of the Arabian Peninsula was united under Islam.

Muhammad continued to have revelations until his death; they were eventually collected and embodied in the sacred book, the **Koran**. His model behavior and the actions of the early community served as the basis of the **Sunnah** (Traditions), which, together with the Koran, serve as the two major pillars of Islamic law. 'Ali, Muhammad's son-in-law, described the Prophet as follows:

[He was] neither very tall nor excessively short, but was a man of medium size, he had neither very curly nor flowing hair but a mixture of two, he was not obese, he did not have a very round face, but it was so to some extent, he was reddish-white, he had black eyes and long eyelashes, he had protruding joints and shoulder-blades, he was not hairy but had some hair on his chest, the palms of his hands and feet were calloused, when he walked he raised his feet as though he were walking on a slope, when he turned [for example to someone] he turned completely. (Miskat, quoted in Denny, 1994, 80)

MUHAMMAD 'UMAR, MULLA. *See* UMAR, MULLA MUHAMMAD.

MUHARRAM. "That which is forbidden" or "that which is sacred." The first month of the lunar Islamic **calendar** and a sacred month to **Sunnis** and **Shi'ites**. Sunnis celebrate the new year and fast on the 10th of Muharram, and Shi'ites commemorate the martyrdom of **Imam Husayn**, the son of **'Ali**, at **Karbala** in 680. The day, called **'Ashura**, is the climax of 10 days of mourning for the **Twelver Shi'ites**, in which they conduct processions in communal lamentation with self-flagellations and passion plays, called **ta'ziyahs**, that reenact the events at Karbala. At a time of heightened passions, religious observances often turned into revolts, for example, during the Islamic Revolution of 1979, when they contributed to the downfall of the Shah of Iran.

MUHTASIB. "Censor." A market inspector and overseer of public morals, fulfilling the community's obligation to command the good and forbid the evil (*al-amr bi al-ma'ruf wa-al-nahy 'an al-munkar*). He was to discourage sinful behavior, encourage attendance at **prayers**, check measures and weights in the bazaars, and ascertain that foodstuffs were not adulterated. He was usually a jurist (**faqih**), appointed by a **judge** (qadhi) and paid from the public treasury. He was empowered to administer whippings for minor offenses. Since the mid-19th century the urban police have taken over these functions in most parts of the Islamic world. Muhtasib has been reintroduced in the **Islamic Republic of Iran** and Afghanistan, where revolutionary guards (**Basij**), or **Taliban** activists, have patrolled the streets of major towns to enforce religious edicts. *See also* HISBAH; MUTATAWI'AH.

MUJADDID. "Reformer" or "renewer." According to **Tradition**, at the turn of each century a reformer would appear in Islam. Various individuals have claimed this mission, including a **Sufi shaykh**, Ahmad Sirhindi (1564–1624). He was called the Renewer of the Second Millennium (*Mujaddid Alf-i Thani*), and his descendants carry the name Mujaddidi and continue to be public personalities. Another person who claimed this title was Mirza Ghulam Ahmad, founder of the **Ahmadi sect** in British India.

MUJAHID (pl. MUJAHIDUN, MUJAHIDIN). A fighter in a holy war (**jihad**). A fallen mujahid is a **martyr** who is assured paradise. In wars of liberation against the French in North Africa and the Soviet occupation in Afghanistan, popular forces proclaimed their guerrilla war a jihad and themselves mujahidin. *See* MUJAHIDIN-I KHALQ.

MUJAHIDIN-I ISLAM. Religio–political movement founded by Ayatollah Abu 'l-Qasem **Kashani** in 1945 in Iran. It called for the elimination of secular laws and the establishment of an Islamic state, with enforcement of the **shari'ah**. It also demanded the adoption of a clerical council (as provided for in the Iranian Constitution of 1906) to pass judgment on the compatibility of all legislation with Islamic law. Kashani was banished to Lebanon in 1949, and his movement was superseded by other, similar groups.

MUJAHIDIN-I KHALQ (MIK). Religio–political movement founded in 1965 by Sa'id Muhsin and Muhammad Hanif Nezhad that demanded the establishment of a classless society by combating imperialism, capitalism, dictatorship, and conservative clericalism in Iran. The movement turned increasingly Marxist, which led to a split in its ranks in 1975, but both factions engaged in armed attacks against Muhammad Reza Shah's government. In December 1978, the only surviving member of the original central committee, Mas'ud Rajavi, was freed.

The Mujahidin were one of the forces supporting the Iranian Revolution, but they refused to be disarmed and therefore turned against the regime of Ayatollah **Khomeyni**. In June 1981, they were responsible for planting a bomb that killed 74 leading members of the revolutionary government. In protracted fighting, some 1,200 religious and political leaders were said to have been killed and some 10,000 mujahidin massacred. Rajavi fled to Paris and eventually into exile in Iraq. He formed the National Liberation Army during the Iran–Iraq war, but his forces were badly mauled. After the conclusion of peace between Iran and Iraq, the mujahidin resumed sporadic attacks, but they were decimated to the extent that their activities were reduced to isolated bomb attacks. After 1995, the movement tried to moderate its policies.

In 1997, the United States declared the MIK a **terrorist** organization. A force of about 5,000 fighters remained in Camp Ashraf in Iraq, near the Iranian border. When the United States invaded Iraq, there was a question of whether to eliminate them or use them in activities against Iran. Apparently, this question has not yet been resolved. The MIK was largely disarmed, but continues to remain in their camp. Maryam Azodanlu, Rajavi's wife and coleader of MIK, was arrested in France in June 2003. *See also* ISLAMIC REPUBLIC OF IRAN.

MUJTAHID. "One who strives." One versed in canon law; in **Sunni** Islam it is the title of the founders of the four orthodox schools of jurisprudence. **Shi'i** mujtahids are jurists of the **Usuli school** who, by virtue of their **education**, are entitled to make an independent effort (**ijtihad**) to arrive at a decision regarding Islamic law and theology. The mujtahid formulates new rules based on reason (**'aql**) and the **Koran** and Traditions (**Sunnah**), including those of the **imams**. They differ from Sunni **muftis**, who can give only opinions (**fatwas**), in that their decisions are authoritative, because the mujtahids are the deputies of the **Hidden Imam**. The founders of the Sunni schools of jurisprudence decided in the 10th century to discontinue the use of ijtihad and called on the **believers** to emulate, or imitate (**taqlid**), the existing body of law.

MUKHTAR, AL- (ca. 622–687). A native of Ta'if and leader of a revolt against **Umayyad** rule in **Kufah** in the name of 'Ali's son, Muhammad ibn al-**Hanafiyyah**. He claimed to avenge the martyrdom of al-**Husayn** at **Karbala** and to establish an egalitarian Islamic state. He captured Kufah in 686 and defeated the Syrian army. He was the first to proclaim himself the Redeemer (**Mahdi**) and gained wide support among the Persian and Arab converts, whom the Umayyads treated as second-class citizens. Mukhtar tried to emancipate the mawalis and was reproached by a leading Arab, who said: "You have taken away our clients who are the booty which God bestowed upon us together with this country. We emancipated them, hoping to receive the Divine recompense and reward, but you would not rest until you made them sharers in our booty" (**Tabari**, quoted by Nicholson, 1962). Eventually Mukhtar was defeated in battle and killed at Harura by **Mus'ab ibn al-Zubayr**, brother of **'Abdallah ibn al-Zubayr**, who had himself proclaimed **caliph** in **Mecca**. Some scholars maintain that Mukhtar's movement contributed to transforming **Shi'ism** from a political movement into a religious **sect**.

MULLA. "Maula, master." In Iran and Afghanistan, a preacher and spiritual adviser as well as a teacher in elementary **mosque** schools. A mulla (from *mawla*, master—or *mala'*, meaning to fill, one full of learning) also performs such religious functions as recitation of the adhan (call to **prayer**) in the ear of the newborn, and he presides at **marriage** and burial ceremonies. He is paid for his services by donations from his parish and often needs to supplement his income by pursuing a trade or agricultural work. Mullas vary in educational background, from the barely literate to those with **madrasah education**.

MU'MINUN. *See* BELIEVERS.

MUNAFIQUN. *See* HYPOCRITES.

MUNKAR AND NAKIR. "The Unknown" and the "Repudiating." Two **angels** who interrogate the dead in their graves regarding their opinion about **Muhammad** and punish the unbelievers severely. If they say, "he is the Apostle of **God**," they are left unharmed until the **Day of Judgment**. The **Koran** says: "But how (will it be) when the angels take their souls at death, and smite their faces and their backs?"(47:27). They are described as black angels with blue eyes.

MUNTAZAR, MUHAMMAD AL-. The Twelfth **Imam**, who disappeared in 878 and is believed to have commenced a period of occultation to return at the end of time as the **Mahdi**. *See also* HIDDEN IMAM; OUUIION.

MUQADDIMAH. The first volume, *Prolegomena*, of the monumental history by **Ibn Khaldun**, the *Book of Examples* (*Kitab al-'ibar*), in which he argues that history is subject to universal laws. He presented a theory of cyclical change of humanity, from barbarism and primitive nomadism to rural and urban culture and to state and empire, and the growth of luxury, and finally to eventual decline, only to become prey to a new wave of barbarians. Ibn Khaldun established a critical methodology for the study of history. He stated that:

> The rule for distinguishing what is true from what is false in history is based on its possibility or impossibility: that is to say, we must examine human society (civilization) and discriminate between the characteristics

which are essential and inherent in its nature and those which are accidental and need not be taken into account, recognizing further those which cannot possibly belong to it. If we do this we have a rule for separating historical truth from error by means of a demonstrative method that admits of no doubt. . . . It is a genuine touchstone whereby historians may verify whatever they relate. (R. A. Nicholson, 438)

MUQAFFA, IBN AL- (720–750). The one with the "withered hand." A Zoroastrian Persian, born in Fars, who adopted Islam and served as secretary to the 'Abbasid Caliphs al-Saffah and al-Mansur. He introduced Persian themes into Arabic literature and translated from Persian into Arabic the famous collection of fables *Kalilah wa Dimnah*, *The Book of Kings* (*Khwoda-i-namah*), and a number of other works. He produced an abridgment of Aristotle's works on logic and wrote in a pure style of Arabic; his writings stimulated the development of Arabic prose. His hand was crippled from torture because he was suspected of embezzlement. He was burned at the stake, allegedly for imitating the style of the Koran and translating a book "which corrupted the faith of Muslims." According to another version, he was suspected of intriguing with Caliph Mansur's uncle, 'Abdallah ibn 'Ali.

MUQANNA, HASHIM IBN HAKIM AL- (d. 785/786). "The Veiled Prophet of Khurasan," who claimed to be an incarnation of God and started a revolt against the 'Abbasid caliph. He ruled for 14 years but was eventually defeated and committed suicide so as not to fall into the hands of his enemies. He was veiled to conceal his dazzling (or ugly) face and was said to have worn a mask of gold. Ibn Khallikan describes him as "low in stature, ill made, blind in an eye, and a stutterer; he never let his face be seen, but always veiled it with a mask of gold, and it was from this circumstance that he received his name" (II, 205). He made his followers believe that he could make the moon rise by placing quicksilver in a well.

MURABITUN. Fighters who garrisoned desert outposts (**ribat**) for the defense of the borders of the Islamic world. One force of Berber murabitun succeeded in founding an empire in North Africa and Spain. *See also* ALMORAVIDS.

MURID. A "novice," or devotee, of a spiritual master (**murshid**) of a **Sufi** order.

MURJI'ITES. "Postponers." The Murji'ites derive their name from the **Arabic** *arja'a*, meaning to defer. It is an early Islamic school that disagreed with the **Kharijites** on the question of **sin** and refused to declare one who had committed a grave sin an **apostate** (murtadd), subject to being killed. They held that judgment should be postponed to God's merciful decision. They were quiescent, accepting the **Umayyad caliphate** for the sake of unity and the well-being of the state, holding that it is better to obey even a sinful ruler than to revolt. The Murji'ites were moderates also in accepting the equality of the newly converted non-Arabs, who were treated as second-class citizens by the Umayyads. They emphasized faith over works. They introduced a quietism that continued to a certain extent even after the demise of the **Murji'ite sect** in the **Hanif**ite school of jurisprudence. Murji'ites see justification for their view in the **Koran**ic passage that says: "Others held in suspense (are deferred) for the command of **Allah**, whether He will punish them, or turn in mercy (relent) to them" (9:106).

MURSHID. A spiritual master and guide of a **Sufi** order.

MURUWWA. "Manliness." Arab virtue, as exemplified in pre-Islamic nomad poetry. Courage, loyalty, generosity, and hospitality characterized the virtuous man. Examples of this abound in the **Mu'allaqat**, where courage did not require one fighting a superior force, but fighting to the death for one's womenfolk. Loyalty meant devotion to one's tribe or clan, the Arab counterpart of "right or wrong, my country." Another example is Samuel, the Jew, who sacrificed the life of his son rather than surrender some coats of armor that were entrusted to him. **Hatim al-Ta'i'** slaughtered three camels to entertain three wayfarers who only asked for some milk. Not to protect someone who was in need of help would bring dishonor on the person, his clan, or his tribe. Vengeance must be exacted, and it is shameful to take blood money (**diyyah**) for injury. Muruwwa is still a living virtue in tribal societies and is practiced as Pashtunwali by the frontier Afghans and under other names elsewhere.

MUSA IBN NUSAYR (640–715). Muslim general who finished the conquest of North Africa and subjugated large areas of Spain. The son of a Christian prisoner, he was appointed governor of Ifriqiyah (698), present-day Libya and Tunis, from where he started his campaigns. He was "prudent, generous, and brave, and no army put under his command had ever suffered defeat." His lieutenant, the Berber Ziyad ibn **Tariq**, crossed into Spain and defeated the Visigothic King Roderic before Musa followed with a large army. Musa returned to **Damascus** with fabulous booty he had amassed in Spain, but he eventually fell into disfavor and died in poverty.

MUS'AB IBN AL-ZUBAYR (647–691). Brother of the anti-**Caliph** 'Abdallah ibn al-**Zubayr** and his governor in Iraq. He fought the **Kharijites** and defeated the uprising of al-**Mukhtar** in 687. He was defeated and killed in 691 by the army of **Umayyad** Caliph **'Abd al-Malik**.

MUSA AL-KAZIM (745–799). Son of **Ja'far al-Sadiq** and the seventh **imam** of the **Twelver Shi'ites**. His brother, **Isma'il**, is recognized as the seventh and last imam of the **Isma'ilis**. Musa was born in **Medina** and lived there until he was called to **Baghdad**. He was repeatedly imprisoned under **'Abbasid Caliphs** al-Mahdi and **Harun al-Rashid**. He was given the surname al-'Abd al-Salih (the holy servant) "because of his piety and his efforts to please God." Musa al-Kazim died in prison, probably of poisoning, and his tomb in al-Kazimayn, Baghdad, has become an important place of **pilgrimage** for Twelver (or Imami) Shi'ites. *See also* SHI'ISM.

MUSAWI, ZACARIAS (MOUSSAOUI). A French-born Moroccan accused by the United States of being the 20th hijacker, who took flying lessons in America in preparation for the 11 September attack on the World Trade Center. His instructor at the Pan Am International Flying Academy in Egan, Minnesota, became suspicious, and the school called the FBI. A burly figure, the 33-year-old Musawi was arrested on 17 August 2001 and held as a material witness. He originally denied having been a part of the suicide team, but during his trial in the United States, he claimed he was to have hijacked a fifth airliner to fly it into the White House. He named the would-be "shoe bomber" **Richard Reid** as his accomplice.

MUSAYLIMAH (MASLAMA). A contemporary of the Prophet **Muhammad** who claimed prophethood in imitation of Muhammad, for which he was given the name of contempt, "Little Muslim." He was of the Banu Hanifa of Yamama and had a considerable following among his tribe. After the death of Muhammad, **Caliph Abu Bakr** ordered his general, **Khalid ibn al-Walid**, to take action against Maslama, who was defeated in a bloody battle at Aqraba in 633. Khalid's army killed some 7,000 of Maslama's followers and suffered the loss of about 700 **Companions**. Musaylimah was the most powerful of a number of false prophets who appeared at the time of Muhammad. The *Sira* (Guillaume, 1924, 649), citing letters of correspondence between Musaylima and the Prophet, in which the former wanted to divide Arabia between them, states:

> From Musaylima [he would not have used this term] the apostle of **God** to Muhammad the apostle of God. Peace be upon you. I have been made partner with you in authority. To us belongs half the land and to **Quraysh** half, but Quraysh are hostile people.

Muhammad said to the messengers: "By God, were it not that heralds are not to be killed I would behead the pair of you!" Then he wrote:

> From Muhammad the apostle of God to Musaylima the liar. Peace be upon him who follows the guidance. The earth is God's. He lets whom He will of His creatures inherit it and the result is to the pious.

MUSIC. Music and musicians have an ambivalent status in much of the Islamic world. Music is frowned upon by theologians of most schools of jurisprudence and by members of the newly emergent **Islamist** movement. Although not expressly forbidden (**haram**) in the **Koran**, music is considered reprehensible (**makruh**). Some theologians refer to a passage in the Koran that says, "And be moderate in thy pace, and lower thy voice" (31:19) to justify its prohibition. One **hadith** calls musical instruments "the devil's **muezzin**, calling all men to his worship." But there are other traditions that condone music, and **Sufi**

rituals include music and dancing. Apart from the popularity of music, musicians have traditionally been persons of low status.

MUSLIM. An adherent of Islam who submits, *aslama*, to **Allah**'s commands. Muslims reject the term **Muhammad**an because Muhammad was a man and not a **prophet** with claims to divinity.

MUSLIM, ABU. *See* ABU MUSLIM.

MUSLIM BROTHERHOOD. The Society of Muslim Brethren (Al-Ikhwan Al-Muslimin) was founded in 1929 in Isma'iliyya, Egypt, by Hasan al-Banna (1906–1949). It was a religio-political organization that eventually spread to other parts of the Islamic world. Al-Banna, an ascetic and charismatic teacher, was the "Supreme Guide" (*murshid al-'amm*), who advocated social and economic reforms, expulsion of the British from Egypt, and establishment of an Islamic state. The movement is Pan-Islamic in outlook and aims at imposing Islamic law on all aspects of the social and political life of the Muslim nation (**ummah**). As a political party it was never very successful, but it was able to mobilize considerable support among the masses of the lower urban and rural classes. The Ikhwan was accused of political assassinations, and Hasan al-Banna was assassinated in 1949 (reputedly by government agents). The Ikhwan was banned in 1954 but renounced violence in the 1970s. Although outlawed, the Ikhwan was represented in the Egyptian Parliament, where its representatives run as independents. The party is said to have branches in 70 countries and has been called the "grandmother" of radical Islam because it has spawned such groups as **al-Qaeda** and the **jihadist** movement.

There has been a recent change in its fortunes. The Brotherhood has evolved from a popular underground organization into the largest opposition bloc in the parliament since the November/December 2005 elections, when it won 88 out of 454 seats. Muhammad Mahdi Akef, the seventh Supreme Guide, showed a willingness to adopt a de facto coexistence with the state. He had been sentenced to death in 1954 but was released from jail after serving for 20 years. There are said to be as many as 1,200 Brothers in Egyptian jails.

MUSLIM COUNCIL OF BRITAIN (MCB). The largest Muslim organization in Great Britain, acting as an umbrella for some 400 affiliated groups. It was founded in 1997 "to defend the rights of Muslims, improve relations between traditional Muslims and wider society and to promote cooperation, consensus and unity on Muslim affairs." Its secretary general, Iqbal Sacranie, was awarded a knighthood in the 2005 Queen's Birthday Honours List for his "long standing service to the community and interfaith dialogue." Politicians consult with the Council to formulate or review British government policy. The MCB has not, however, escaped criticism. Liberals have objected to its ostracism of gay organizations, such as the gay Muslim group Al-Fatiha; others have criticized its lack of cooperation in the Holocaust Remembrance, when Sacranie remarked that it neglected the "ongoing genocide and human rights abuses around the world and in the occupied territories of Palestine." The mayor of London condemned what he called a "witch-hunt" of the mainstream representative body of British Muslims, saying it would damage community relations and hinder the fight against terrorism.

MUSLIM IBN AL-HAJJAJ (820–875). Islamic scholar from Nishapur who compiled one of the six canonical **hadith** collections. It is similar to al-**Bukhari**'s *Sahih* and carries the same title. Muslim traveled widely, collecting **hadith** from all over the Islamic world, and died in his native Nishapur. he claimed that he collected his *Sahih* from 3,000 Traditions. During one of his sessions, Muhammad ibn Taliya challenged Muslim, saying: "Whoever holds the pronunciation (of the **Koran**) to be created, I forbid that person to attend my lessons;" thereupon Muslim "passed his cloak (*rida*) over his turban, and, standing up in the midst of the assembly, left the room" (Khallikan, trans. Slane, III, 349). He held that the Koran is not created, but that the pronunciation (its utterance) is created.

MUSLIM MODERNISTS. *See* SALAFIYYAH.

MUSLIMS, BLACK. *See* NATION OF ISLAM.

MUSTADH'AFUN (MOSTAZAFUN). A name given to the class of "downtrodden, meek, and poor" in the **Islamic Republic of Iran** to show the regime's sympathy for those who had suffered hardships during the Pahlavi regime. Ayatollah Ruhollah **Khomeyni** claimed that the revolution was made by them and should therefore serve their interests. He referred to a passage in the **Koran** that states: "And We wished to be gracious to those who were being depressed (*istadha'i-fun*) in the land, to make them leaders (in faith) and make them heirs" (28:5). Khomeyni renamed the well-endowed Pahlavi Foundation of the Shah the Mustadh'afun Foundation and gave it the task of providing social services for the poor. The war with Iraq and its effect on the economy have made the promise of a better life for the poor an aim rather than an accomplished fact.

'MUT'AH. "Enjoyment." Temporary **marriage** for a specified time in exchange for a commensurate payment. It can be as short as one day or be valid for years, and children of such marriages are considered legitimate. The partners do not have a right of **inheritance**. It existed in pre-Islamic times, but it is said to have been prohibited by **Caliph 'Umar** (632–634). Only in **Twelver Shi'ism** is the 'mut'ah marriage still practiced. It has been explained as a necessity in olden times, when merchants were away from home for many months or years and therefore deprived of the companionship of their wives. Shi'ites base it on the **Koran** (4:24), but there are certain conditions: a proper marriage (nikah) must be performed; the woman must be Muslim or of the **People of the Book** (such as a **Christian** or Jew); she must be chaste; some dowry must be specified or the contract is void; there must be a fixed period; and if there is a child, it must belong to the husband (*Baillie's Digest*, from Hughes). *See also* WOMEN.

MUTAKALLIM. Theologian.

MUTANABBI, ABU AL-TAYYIB AHMAD (915–965). Considered one of the greatest Arab poets, al-Mutanabbi was the son of a water carrier, born in **Kufah** and educated in his hometown and **Damascus**. He is said to have been a propagandist for the **Qarmatians**, called al-Mutannabi (pretender to prophesy) by the Bedouins, for which blasphemy he was imprisoned for two years. After his release, he went from one princely court to another, producing panegyrics for Sayf al-

Dawla at Aleppo and **Kafur**, the black ruler of Egypt. Nicholson (310) gives one of his erotic preludes:

> She uncovered: pallor veiled her at farewell:
> No veil 'twas, yet her cheeks it cast in shade.
> So seemed they, while tears trickled over them,
> Gold with a double row of pearls inlaid.
> She loosed three sable tresses of her hair,
> And thus of night four nights at once she made;
> But when she lifted to the moon in heaven
> Her face, two moons together I surveyed.

While traveling near **Baghdad**, he was attacked by bandits and fled, but his **slave** admonished Mutanabbi, author of the verse: "The horse, and the night, and the desert know me (well); the sword also, and the lance, and paper and the pen." Therefore Mutanabbi turned back and fought until he was slain (Khallikan, trans. Slane, I, 106).

MUTATAWI'AH. Individuals who enforce attendance at prayers and supervise popular morality, similar to the position of the **muhtasib**. In modern times, the urban police have taken over this function, except in Saudi Arabia and a few traditional states. In the newly established Islamic states of Iran and Afghanistan, the governments have reintroduced this institution.

MU'TAZILITE. Called the "rationalist" theological school, influenced by Greek philosophy, which sees no contradiction between reason and belief. It was founded by **Wasil ibn 'Ata'** in **Basra** in a dispute about whether committing a grave **sin** makes a Muslim an unbeliever. The **Kharijites** maintained that a sinner has become an **apostate** (*murtadd*) and should be killed. The **Murji'ites** (Postponers), on the other hand, held that a grave sinner remains a Muslim, and that his fate is to be left to God's merciful decision. In the circle of Hasan al-**Basri** (d. 728), someone raised this question. Wasil Ibn 'Ata' (d.748) answered that such a sinner is in an intermediate position, and he left. Hasan al-Basri said "he has separated himself from us" (*i'tazala*), which gave the new school its name.

The Mu'tazilites held five fundamental principles: (1) affirmation of God's unity (*tawhid*), which denied anthropomorphic divine attributes and the uncreatedness of the **Koran**; (2) affirmation of man's free will and God's justice; (3) affirmation of promise and threat (*al-wa'd wa'l-wa'id*), paradise or eternal punishment in **hell**; (4) acceptance of an intermediate state between belief and unbelief, that the sinner is neither an infidel nor a believer; and (5) the duty of the believer to command the right and forbid the sinful (*al-amr bi'l-ma'ruf wa-'l-nahy 'an al-munkar*).

The Mu'tazilites enjoyed the support of **Caliph** al-**Ma'mun** (r. 813–833), who enforced the dogma in an inquisition (**mihna**), but al-Mutawakkil (847–861) abandoned the doctrine of the **createdness of the Koran**. Orthodox dogma has since accepted that the Koran was not created. The Mu'tazilites call themselves the "People of Justice and God's Unity" (*ahl al-'adl wa 'l-tawhid*).

MUTUAL CURSING. *See* LI'AN.

MUWAHHID. "Unitarian." Believer in *tawhid*, divine unity. *See also* ALMOHADS; WAHHABIS.

MYSTICISM. *See* SUFI(ISM).

– N –

NABI. A **prophet** (pl. *nabiyun* or *anbiya*), "one to whom God has spoken." All **rasuls** (**messengers**) are nabis, but all nabis are not rasuls. A rasul brings a book; a nabi does not.

NADAWI, ABU AL-HASAN AL- (1914–). Indian **Islamist** philosopher and one of the most important theorists of the revivalist movement. He traveled widely in the Islamic world and met many of the founders of the Islamist movement, including **Sayyid Qutb** and Abul A'la al-**Maududi**. He became a member of the **Jama'at-i Islami** in 1941, but he resigned from it in 1978. His book *What the World Lost by Muslims' Deterioration* has been of considerable influence in the Islamic world.

NADHIR. "Warner." **Muhammad**'s task was to transmit God's message to the people. He was only a man, not an infallible authority (although **Shi'ites** would grant him and the **imams** this special quality). He was a "warner," calling on people to accept his message and prepare for the **Day of Judgment**. The **Koran** says: "Verily We have sent thee in truth as a bearer of glad tidings and a warner: But of thee no question shall be asked of the companions of the Blazing Fire" (2:119). Other **prophets** also were warners, especially **Noah**, who warned people of the impending flood.

NADIM, ABU AL-FARAJ AL- (936–995). A native of **Baghdad**, also called al-Warraq (Stationer), a librarian and bookdealer who gained fame for his *Fihirist* (*Catalogue*), which listed virtually all publications of the first four centuries of Islam. The book was annotated with information about the authors and included Egyptian papyri, Chinese paper, and leather scrolls. He was a tolerant person, a **Shi'ite** with **Mu'tazilite** sympathies.

NADIR, BANU. Jewish tribe residents in Yathrib (**Medina**); they cultivated the growing of palms and acted as money lenders and traders in weapons and jewelry. The tribe had come from Palestine to Medina in the first century and became clients of the Banu **Aws**. After the establishment of the Muslim community, they coexisted with **Muhammad**'s government, but they were accused of conspiring with the **Quraysh** and were expelled after the Battle of **Uhud** in 625.

NADIR SHAH. *See* AFSHARID DYNASTY.

NAFS. The "soul," an intellectual substance, incorporeal and immortal. Upon death, the soul leaves the body, and the pure soul returns to the intellectual substance created by God. The **Koran** says: "To the righteous soul will be said: 'O (thou) soul, in complete rest and satisfaction! Come back thou to the Lord, well pleased (thyself), and well-pleasing unto Him! . . . Yea, enter thou My heaven'" (89:27–30).

NAHRAWAN, BATTLE OF (659). Battle at a village and canal of the same name near **Baghdad**, in which **Caliph 'Ali** decisively defeated the **Kharijites** commanded by 'Abdullah ibn Wahb al-Rashidi. A survivor of the battle killed 'Ali in 661 in revenge. The Kharijites continued to be a force of rebellion long into the **'Abbasid** period.

NAJAF. A town in Iraq where **Caliph 'Ali** is believed to be buried. Caliph **Harun al-Rashid** built the tomb of 'Ali there in 791, making it an important **Shi'ite** place of **pilgrimage**. Afghans believe that Ali's body was brought to Afghanistan and buried at a site that is the present town of Mazar-i Sharif (The Noble Tomb). Al-Najaf is also an important center of Shi'ite **education**, where Ayatollah **Khomeyni** taught during his exile in Iraq. The city was a center of opposition to the **Sunni** government of Saddam Husayn.

NAKIR. *See* MUNKAR AND NAKIR.

NAMES AND NAMEGIVING. Names in **Arabic** generally consist of five elements: First is the personal name, *ism*, for example, **Muhammad**, **'Ali**, or Husayn—or two names, like Muhammad Ali or Ghulam Siddiq. 'Abd Allah (also spelled Abdullah) is a construct meaning the Servant of **Allah**. Second is the formal name, **kunyah**, which denotes a personal relationship, for example, Abu Muhammad, the father of Muhammad, or Umm Ahmad, the mother of Ahmad. Third, the patronymic, *nasab*, indicates the family origin, the name being preceded by *ibn*, the son of, or *bint*, the daughter of, as for example, **Ibn Khaldun** or Bint Khadijah. Fourth, the group name, **nisbah**, indicates origin or residence, tribe, or occupation, for example, al-Harawi, the Herati, or al-Misri, the Egyptian. Fifth, the honorific can be a nickname or title, for example, al-'Abbas al-Saffah, 'Abbas the "Shedder of Blood," or Muhammad al-Haddad, Muhammad the smith. The most common name in the Islamic world is Muhammad. **Shi'ites** prefer the names of their **imams**—'Ali, **Hasan**, **Husayn**. Upon **conversion** a person usually adopts a Muslim name.

NAMES OF ALLAH. *See* ALLAH, MOST BEAUTIFUL NAMES OF.

NAQSHBANDIS (NAQSHBANDIYYAH). A **Sufi** order originating in Central Asia that takes its name from its founder, Muhammad Baha al-Din Naqshband (1317–1389). It is most commonly found in Muslim Asia and areas formerly under **Ottoman** control. It advocates strict adherence to the **shari'ah**, shunning music and **dance**, and unlike other orders prefers silent **dhikrs**. The order was greatly invigorated as a result of the activities of the reformer Shaykh Ahmad Sirhindi (1564–1624), called the "Renewer of the Second Millennium" (Mujaddid Alf-i Thani).

NASA'I, AHMAD AL- (830–915). Compiler of the **Sunnah** (Traditions), one of the six canonic collection of **hadith**. He traveled in Egypt and Syria and seemed to be a supporter of the party of **'Ali** (*shi'atu 'ali*). **Ibn Khallikan** quotes a witness in **Damascus**, saying: "This doctor was an advocate for the rights of the **caliph** 'Ali; so the people began to strike him on the sides, nor did they discontinue till they thrust him out of the **mosque**. He was then borne to Ramla where he expired" (I, 58). He was buried in **Mecca**.

NASIR KHUSRAW (1004–1060). Persian poet, philosopher, scholar, and traveler. He was born in Qubadian and died in Yamagan in present-day northern Afghanistan. He traveled widely in the Islamic world and spent some time at the court of the **Fatimid** ruler Al-Mustansir when the dynasty was at the height of its power. Upon his return to **Khorasan**, he acted as an **Isma'ili** missionary and was eventually forced to flee to Yamagan, where he spent the last years of his life in seclusion. His most famous book, the *Safarnamah*, is an account of his travels and remains required reading in Iran even today.

NASKH. *See* ABROGATION.

NASRALLAH, SAYYID HASAN (1960–). Secretary general of the Islamist party **Hizbullah** in Lebanon. He succeeded Abbas al-Musawi after Abbas and his wife and child were killed in an Israeli attack in 1992. Nasrullah's campaign against Israeli occupying forces in Southern Lebanon was credited with resulting in the Israeli evacuation in 2000. The "Second" Lebanon War (12 July–8 September 2006) was precipitated when Hizbullah units crossed into Israel, killing three and capturing two soldiers. For 33 days, massive Israeli air strikes were met with Hizbullah missile attacks, resulting in the killing of more than a thousand, most of them Lebanese. Much of the infrastructure of Southern Lebanon was destroyed. Having been able to face Israeli military might made Nasrallah a hero in the "Arab street," although various Arab countries condemned the action as a reckless provocation. Nasrallah conceded that he intended to achieve a prisoner exchange and would not have started the action if he had known its consequences.

NATION OF ISLAM. Originally a black religio-nationalist movement, founded in the 1930s by W. Fard (or Farrad). After his mysterious disappearance in 1934, his deputy, who adopted the name Elijah Muhammad, founded the Temple of Islam in Chicago in 1936 and established his national headquarters there. Elijah Muhammad claimed prophethood and evolved an Islamic body of doctrines as well as a basis for economic self-sufficiency. During his 41-year period of leadership, he established more than 100 temples and numerous small businesses. He forbade the use of **alcohol** and drugs and the consumption of pork.

Malcolm X, a deputy of Muhammad, left the Nation of Islam in March 1964 and converted to orthodox Islam, founding his own organization. A gradual trend to Islamic orthodoxy began, which accelerated after the death of the founder in February 1975, when his son, **Imam** Warith Deen Muhammad, assumed the position of Supreme Minister. He adopted the name "American Muslim Mission" for his organization, but he eventually disbanded it to accept union with **Sunni** Islam. Muhammad Ali, the boxing champion, was a celebrated convert. Louis Farrakhan continued the "Nation of Islam" on a more black-nationalist line, but there seems to have been a rapprochement between the groups.

NAWAWI, YAHYA IBN SHARAF AL- (1233–1277). Shafi'ite jurist and **hadith** scholar who flourished in **Damascus**. He is the author of *Search of the Investigators* (*Minhaj al-talibin*), which, with its commentaries, is a text of Shafi'ite jurisprudence. Forty **hadith** and *Gardens of the Pious* (*Riyadh al-salihin*) are among his most important works. He emphasizes the devotional aspects of the **Koran**. Nawawi was born in Nawa, south of Damascus, and he died there. It was said of him that

> Imam al-Nawawi had three distinctive commendable qualities in his person. If anybody has only one out of these three, people turn to him in abundance for guidance. First, having knowledge and its dissemination. Second, to evade completely from the worldly inclina-

tions, and the third, inviting to all that is good (Islam) enjoining Ma'ruf (monotheism) and forbidding Munkar (polytheism). Imam had all three in him.

NIDHAM AL-MULK. *See* NIZAM AL-MULK, HASAN IBN ALI.

NIGHT JOURNEY. *See* NOCTURNAL JOURNEY.

NIGHT OF POWER. *See* LAYLAT AL-QADR.

NIHAVAND, BATTLE OF (640). Al-Nu'man ibn Muqarrin defeated a Sassanian army under Firuzan, which led to the collapse of the Sassanid dynasty. Both generals died in the battle, and Yastdijird III fled in 651, but he was killed by a miller with whom he had sought refuge. It was the last great battle of the Persians, and three years later the Muslim Arabs reached the Oxus (Amu Dariyah) River and the Indian border.

NIKAH. *See* MARRIAGE.

NISBAH. "Noun of relationship." Part of the name of a person, indicating a group, origin, tribe, or occupation, for example, Jamal al-Din al-Afghani—Jamal, the Afghan. *See* NAMES AND NAMEGIVING.

NIYYAH. "Intention." A formula expressed before **prayer** or commencement of a **pilgrimage** to validate a ritual act. The formula vows: "I intend to offer to God only, with a sincere heart, this morning (or, as the case may be) and with my face toward **Mecca**, two (or more) **rak'ah** prayers **fardh**" (**Sunnah**, nafl, etc.).

NIZAM AL-MULK, HASAN IBN ALI (1018–1092). Grand **vizier** of the Great **Saljuq** rulers Alp Arslan and Malik Shah (1063–1092). He contributed to the centralization of government and developed the system of military feudalism (*iqta*). He founded orthodox theological schools (**Nizamiyyah**) in **Baghdad**, **Damascus**, and other major cities to counter **Shi'ite** propaganda. He appointed al-**Juwayni** and al-**Ghazali** to teach in the Nizamiyyah. **Hasan al-Sabbah** studied there, before he founded his order of the Assassins. Nizam al-Mulk (his title, meaning "Order of the Realm") was the author of a book on governance, entitled *Siyasat-nama*. It provided instruction on state-craft but also contained attacks on Shi'ites, especially **Isma'ilis**. He was assassinated by an Isma'ili follower of Hasan al-Sabbah.

Nizam al-Mulk was born in Nawkan (Radkan? Sources list different towns), near Tus in Iran. He had memorized the **Koran** at age 11, and he continued studying with **Shafi'ite** teachers at Nishapur. He became secretary to the **Ghaznavid** ruler before he started his 20 years at the **Saljuq** court. Legend has it that when Nizam al-Mulk traveled near **Nihavand**, the site of a battle at the time of **Caliph 'Umar**, he said: "Happy is the man who is with them (the **martyrs**)." When a boy from Dailam in the dress of a **Sufi** called out to him and the vizier reached out his hand, the boy stabbed him in the heart with a dagger (Khallikan, trans. Slane, I, 414–415).

NIZAMIYYAH, AL-MADRASA AL-. The first real academy of Islam in **Baghdad**, built under the **Saljuq vizier Nizam al-Mulk** in 1065–1067, and therefore named after him. It represented the **Shafi'ite** school of **Sunni** Islam and offered the complete curriculum of the Islamic sciences. It promoted **Ash'arite** orthodoxy and counted among its scholars and students the most brilliant minds. Al-Ghazali lectured there for four years, and the school survived the ca-tastrophe of the **Mongol invasion** in 1258 to become the model for similar institutions elsewhere.

NIZARIS (NIZARIYYAH). A branch of **Isma'ilis** who gave alle-giance to Nizar, son of the **Fatimid Caliph** Mustansir (d. 1094) and his descendants. Headed at one time by the Shaykh of **Alamut**, **Hasan al-Sabbah**, the order lasted for 150 years until the **Mongol** conquest of Alamut. The **Agha Khan** claims descent from this **sect**.

NOAH (NUH). In the **Koran**, Noah is a warning **prophet** who was saved from the flood: "They rejected him (Noah), but We delivered him, and those with him in the ark, and We made them inherit (the earth), while We drowned in the flood those who rejected our signs. They see what was the end of those who were warned (but heeded not)" (10:73). He is said to have lived to be 950 years old (29:14). *See also* NADHIR.

NOBLES. *See* SHARIF.

NOCTURNAL JOURNEY (MI'RAJ). Journey of **Muhammad** from **Mecca** to **Jerusalem** and, in the company of the angel **Gabriel**, to the Seventh Heaven. He was riding a white animal, called **Buraq**, which was the size of a mule with a woman's head and a peacock's tail and two wings. Muhammad is said to have brought from **heaven** the instructions for the five ritual **prayers**. The **Koran** says: "Glory to (**Allah**) who did take his servant for a journey by night from the sacred **Mosque** whose precincts We did bless—in order that We might show him some of Our Signs" (17:1). A number of **hadith**, narrated by Abu Dhar, **Malik ibn Anas**, and **Ibn Hazm**, describe the Mi'raj as follows: "Gabriel descended, opened my chest and washed it with the water of **Zamzam** spring. He brought a golden tray full of wisdom and faith and poured it into my chest, and then closed it. He took hold of my hand and ascended to the sky. . . . Muhammad saw **Adam**, **Moses**, **Jesus**, and **Abraham** in heaven, and God prescribed 50 prayers, which He finally reduced to five. After entering several heavens, Muhammad was admitted to paradise "where there were strings of pearls and its soil was of musk" (Bukhari, VII, 345). This is how the daily five prayers were prescribed.

NORTH AMERICAN SHI'A ITHNA-ASHERI MUSLIM COMMUNITIES ORGANIZATION (NASIMCO). An umbrella organization of Shi'ites in North America and the Caribbean. Its mission is "to provide a common structure and framework to meet the religious, cultural and political needs of the Shia within its area of operation." It aims to "harness talents and resources available in member communities for the greater good of global humanity and our communities." It proposes to establish and run centers, encourage intrafaith and interfaith relationships, and develop and nurture relationships with the Marja'iat (Shi'i clergy) and world and regional Islamic Shia Ithna-asheri bodies. It cooperates with a number of organizations in Canadian and American cities and the Karbala Islamic Center in Dearborn, Michigan.

NU'MAN, ABU HANIFA ABI ABDULLAH AL- (d. 974). Arab jurist, generally known as al-Qadi al-Nu'man, who served at the **Fatimid**

court in Egypt as **judge** and as **Isma'ili** propagandist. He is credited as the founder of Isma'ili jurisprudence. His *Da'a'im al-Islam* is an exposition of Fatimid jurisprudence. Another major work is the *Beginning of the Mission and Establishment of the State* (*Kitab iftitah al-da'wa wa'inbtida' al daula*), which describes the rise of the Fatimids. He was described as a man of great talent, learning, and accomplishments; a prolific author; and an upright judge. He created the juridical and legal system of the Fatimid state and appeared to work toward reconciliation with **Sunni**sm. Of 44 works attributed to him, 18 are still extant.

NUR MUHAMMADI. The Light, or blessing (**barakah**), which inspired the Prophet Muhammad and became inherent in his descendants, according to **Shi'ite** Islam. From this derives the dogma of the infallibility of the Twelve **Imams**. The Nur Muhammadi is also an important **Sufi** concept.

NUSAYRIS. *See* 'ALAWIS.

NUWAS, ABU. *See* ABU NUWAS.

– O –

OATH. "Yamin." The **Koran** enjoins **believers** to be responsible for an oath, and if one breaks an oath, one must make atonement: "And make not **Allah**'s (name) an excuse in your oaths against doing good, or acting rightly, or making peace between persons; for Allah is one who heareth and knoweth all things" (2:224) and "Allah will not call you to account for what is void in your oaths, but He will call you to account for your deliberate oaths: for expiation feed ten indigent persons on a scale for the average for the food of your families; or clothe them; or give a slave his freedom. If that is beyond your means, fast for three days" (5:89).

OCCULTATION. "Ghaybah." *See* CONCEALMENT; SHI'ISM.

OMAR. *See* 'UMAR.

ORGANIZATION OF THE ISLAMIC CONFERENCE (OIC). Established in Jidda, Saudi Arabia, in 1971, to promote Islamic solidarity and foster political, economic, social, and cultural cooperation among Muslim states. The organization comprises 45 member countries, including some with only a minority Muslim population, for example, the African countries of Sierra Leone, Uganda, and Cameroon, with Muslim populations of 30 percent, 16 percent, and 22 percent, respectively. In addition to accomplishing the above tasks, the OIC sees its mission as fighting racial discrimination, eradicating colonialism, supporting international peace and security, safeguarding the Holy Places, and assisting the Palestinians in regaining their rights and liberating their land. It is a pan-Islamic organization that wants to unite the Islamic community (**ummah**), which is not only territorial but also includes all Muslims wherever they may be.

The foundation of the organization was shocked into action as a result of the arson attack on the Al-**Aqsa mosque** in **Jerusalem** by an Australian Zionist in August 1969. The OIC organizes conferences on matters of common interest and supports publications on religious and political subjects. Affiliated institutions include the Islamic Development Bank, the Al-Quds (Jerusalem) fund, the Islamic Commission of the International Crescent (equivalent of the Red Cross), and others. In spite of political and sectarian differences, the organization includes representatives from primarily **Shi'ite** Iran, as well as predominantly **Sunni** Saudi Arabia.

ORTHODOXY. The major **sect** in Islam, "The People of the Tradition and the Community" (*ahl al-sunnah wa'l-jama'a*), are called **Sunnites**. They comprise about 80 percent of Muslims and claim to represent orthodoxy, in distinction from the **Shi'ites** and other, smaller, groups.

OSAMA BIN LADEN. *See* LADEN, OSAMA BIN.

OSMAN. *See* 'UTHMAN, IBN 'AFFAN.

OTTOMAN EMPIRE (OSMANLI, 1342–1922). Named after Osman ('Uthman), the first of a Turkish dynasty that lasted until the end of the First World War and comprised at the height of its power an area from the borders of Iran westward across North Africa, south to Yemen, and north to the gates of Vienna. The empire emerged from a small principality in northwestern Anatolia and in less than a century included much of the Balkans and Anatolia. A setback that occurred when **Timur-i Lang** (Tamerlane) defeated Ottoman **Sultan** Bayezit in the Battle of Ankara in 1404 proved to be only temporary, and in 1453, Mehmet the Conqueror reunited the empire and captured the city of Constantinople. Renamed **Istanbul**, the city remained the capital of the Eurasian empire. The empire achieved its greatness under **Sulayman the Magnificent**, so called in the West, and known as "The Lawgiver" (al-Qanuni) to his people.

The spectacular military success of the Ottoman empire was due largely to its institutions and skill in military technology. It had an infantry army, drafted primarily from Christian subjects in the Balkans and equipped with firearms, at a time when its neighbors were still fighting a cavalry war. Ottoman rulers were able to stay in power by surrounding themselves with a bureaucracy and officers corps of their **slaves**, who held the highest offices in the state. The government was based on a system of military feudalism and tax farming, which worked well as long as the checks and balances were maintained. Members of the subject class were organized into autonomous nationalities (**millets**), which provided tranquility and left Muslims, **Christians**, and Jews subject to the jurisdiction of their traditional courts.

The Ottomans had a powerful navy, which for a time made them the masters of most of the Mediterranean, but a gradual decline set in when Ottoman expansion had reached its maximum extent. After an unsuccessful siege of Vienna in 1529, Hungary was annexed, but when the Ottomans again laid siege to Vienna in 1683, Hungary was lost and Ottoman weakness was clear to the world. Russia and Austria gained territory in the Balkans, and the Ottomans lost control of the seas. Decline was gradual, but by the 19th century, only the distrust and rivalry of European powers prevented the empire from being dismembered. The Young Turk revolution of 1908 ended the power of the **sultan/caliph**, and Ottoman participation in World War I on the side of the Central Powers led to the end of the empire and the emergence of the Republic of Turkey in 1923. *See also* DEVSHIRME; KEMALISM.

– P –

PACT OF UMAR. After the conquest of Syria and Palestine in 637, an agreement was concluded between the Christian population and Caliph Umar, which regulated the relationship of Muslims and ahl-al dhimma (peoples of the covenant, i.e., monotheists like **Christians** and Jews). Whereas the Charter of **Medina** was a pact between Muslims and Jews, the Pact of Umar was with the Christian community. These agreements arranged for the coexistence of Muslims and **Peoples of the Book**. Several versions of the Pact of Umar exist, one of which is given here:

In the name of God, the Merciful, the Compassionate!

This is a writing to Umar from the Christians of such and such a city. When You [Muslims] marched against us [Christians], we asked of you protection for ourselves, our posterity, our possessions, and our co-religionists; and we made this stipulation with you, that we will not erect in our city or the suburbs any new monastery, church, cell or hermitage; that we will not repair any of such buildings that may fall into ruins, or renew those that may be situated in the Muslim quarters of the town; that we will not refuse the Muslims entry into our churches either by night or by day; that we will open the gates wide to passengers and travellers; that we will receive any Muslim traveller into our houses and give him food and lodging for three nights; that we will not harbor any spy in our churches or houses, or conceal any enemy of the Muslims. [At least six of these laws were taken over from earlier Christian laws against infidels.]

That we will not teach our children the Qu'ran [some nationalist Arabs feared the infidels would ridicule the Qu'ran; others did not want infidels even to learn the language]; that we will not make a show of the Christian religion nor invite any one to embrace it; that we will not prevent any of our kinsmen from embracing Islam, if they so desire. That we will honor the Muslims and rise up in our assemblies when they wish to take their seats; that we will not imitate them in our dress, either in the cap, turban, sandals, or parting of the hair; that we will not make use of their expressions of speech, nor adopt their surnames [infidels must not use greetings and special phrases employed only by Muslims]; that we will not ride on saddles, or gird on swords, or take to ourselves arms or wear them, or engrave Arabic inscriptions on our rings; that we will not sell wine [forbidden to Muslims]; that we will shave the front of our heads; that we will keep to our own style of dress, wherever we may be; that we will wear girdles round our waists [infidels wore leather or cord girdles; Muslims wore cloth and silk.]

That we will not display the cross upon our churches or display our crosses or our sacred books in the streets of the Muslims, or in their market-places; that we will strike the clappers in our churches lightly [wooden rattles or bells summoned the people to church or synagogue]; that we will not recite our services in a loud voice when a Muslim is present; that we will not carry Palm branches [on Palm Sunday] or our images in procession in the streets; that at the burial of our dead we will not chant loudly or carry lighted candles in the streets of the Muslims or their market places; that we will not take any slaves that have already been in the possession of Muslims, nor spy into their houses; and that we will not strike any Muslim.

All this we promise to observe, on behalf of ourselves and our co-religionists, and receive protection from you in exchange; and if we violate any of the conditions of this agreement, then we forfeit your protection and you are at liberty to treat us as enemies and rebels. (From Jacob Marcus, *The Jews in the Medieval World: A Sourcebook*).

PAKISTAN. Pakistan was founded as an Islamic state when the British government gave up its control of India in 1947. Muslims in India feared that, even in a democratic state, their cultural and religious interests would be endangered by the Hindu majority. But partition could include only the contiguous Muslim populations of East and West Pakistan, separated by about 1,000 miles, and did not include millions of Muslims in what became India. The Hindu Maharajah of Kashmir opted for union with India, even though the population of the state was primarily Muslim. **Afghanistan** disputed control of the North-West Frontier Province that became part of Pakistan. Therefore, irredentist disputes with both India and Afghanistan prevented the establishment of harmonious neighborly relations.

Sayyid Abu'l A'la **Maududi**, founder of the **Jama'at-i Islami**, advocated the establishment of an "Islamic state," governed according to the dictates of the **Koran** and Traditions, but **Islamist** parties never had much appeal to the voters or the military rulers who established themselves periodically. It was left to General Zia-ul-Haq, who staged a coup against an elected government, to implement much of

Maududi's program. Pakistan became heavily involved in the war against the communist regime in Afghanistan and helped create a veritable Islamic "foreign legion," which eventually became the nucleus of the **Taliban**, al-**Qaeda**, and the **jihadi** movements. In this process, both the Afghan and Pakistan governments became destabilized and threatened by the new **Islamist** forces, long after the demise of the communist regime. *See also* AHMADIS.

PAN-ISLAMISM. The concept of political unification of the Islamic world to gain strength for defense against European imperialism. The idea was propounded by Sayyid Jamal al-Din **Afghani** and his disciple, **Muhammad 'Abduh**, in the late 19th century. They advocated reforming the Islamic world by selectively borrowing Western technology and administration. In exile in Paris, both collaborated on a journal called *The Firmest Bond* (*al-'Urwat al-wuthqa*) and a magazine, *The Minaret* (*al-Manar*). Afghani was a revolutionary. He enjoyed the support of **Sultan 'Abd al-Hamid** (1876–1908), whose claim to the **caliphate** would have made him the head of a pan-Islamic empire. Unity was not to be attained; rather, nationalism and, for a time, socialism became the ideologies of the 20th century and, only with the foundation of the **Organization of the Islamic Conference** in 1969 have new attempts been made at creation of a pan-Islamic organization.

PARADISE. *See* HEAVEN.

PARTY OF ALLAH. *See* HIZBULLAH.

PASDARAN. *See* REVOLUTIONARY GUARD.

PASSION PLAYS. *See* HUSAYN IBN 'ALI; HUSAYNIYYAH.

PENSIONS. For pensions paid to the early Muslim communities, *see* 'UMAR IBN AL-KHATTAB.

PEOPLES OF THE BOOK. *Ahl al-kitab*, also called *dhimmis*. Adherents of monotheistic religions with a revealed scripture, such as

Christians and Jews. As the Islamic empire grew, Zoroastrians in Iran, Buddhists in Transoxania, and Hindus in India were included in this category. They were invited to believe in **Muhammad** and the **Koran** (3:110) because the Christian and Jewish scriptures promised the prophesy of Muhammad. The Peoples of the Book were protected subjects—"peoples of the covenant" (*ahl al-dhimma*)—and under the jurisdiction of their own laws. They had to pay a special poll tax (**jizyah**) but were usually exempt from military service. Under the **Ottoman empire**, they were organized according to **sects** or nationalities (**millets**) under their respective bishops, patriarchs, and rabbis, who had civil and criminal jurisdiction over their communities. They often held high financial, clerical, and professional positions in the empire. The treatment of dhimmis varied with time and place; generally well treated, discriminating restrictions were, however, imposed on them at times, especially under the **caliphs 'Umar** II (717–720), **Harun al-Rashid** (786–809), Mutawakkil (847–861), and the **Fatimid** Caliph al **Hakim** (996–1021). Since the 19th century, and with the emergence of nation-states in the Middle East, most countries have given equal citizenship to non-Muslims, and the poll tax obligation has been abolished.

PILGRIMAGE. "Hajj." Pilgrimage to the **Ka'bah** in **Mecca** once in a lifetime is an obligation for Muslims who are in good health and can afford the cost. A pilgrim cannot borrow the cost and must have paid the alms tax (**zakat**) on the money he pays for the trip. It is the "right" of God upon men (3:97). According to tradition, it is a practice dating from **Abraham**, which was subsequently corrupted and then restored to its proper function by the Prophet **Muhammad**.

There are two types of pilgrimage: the *hajj* and the *'umrah*, the greater and lesser pilgrimage. The pilgrim begins the hajj in a state of consecration (**ihram**), in which one keeps away from things forbidden, performs **ablutions**, and puts on ihram clothing, consisting of two unsewn linen sheets. The hajj is performed in the last month of the lunar calendar, the Dhu 'l-Hijjah, and takes several days to complete. The pilgrim performs the circumambulation, walks seven times around the **Ka'bah**, approaches the **Black Stone** and touches it, if possible, and proceeds to the **Station of Abraham** and performs a

prayer. After performing the rites in the Grand **Mosque**, the pilgrims perform the rite of **sa'y**, walking or running between the hills of Safa and Marva. Then they set out for the plain of **'Arafat**, stopping on the way at **Mina** and upon return at Muzdalifah, where they spend the night. An animal is slaughtered as a sacrifice (this may be replaced by **fasting** for three days).

A person who has performed the pilgrimage obtains the honorific title "Hajji," pilgrim, and one who dies during the process has become a **martyr** and wins immediate entrance to paradise. In recent years, an increasing number of individuals have performed the hajj, and the presence of more than two million pilgrims has led to major accidents. Fires, crowds out of control, and political demonstrations have led to fatalities, and it is becoming increasingly difficult to channel the flow of pilgrims smoothly.

Shi'ites visit, in addition to Mecca and **Medina**, also the **Atabat**, the shrine cities of Iraq where six of the twelve Shi'ite **imams** are buried, and **Mashhad** and **Qom**, which contain numerous shrines.

PILGRIMAGE, FAREWELL. In 632, in the final days of **Muhammad**'s life, he set out on a **pilgrimage** to **Mecca**, accompanied by some 90,000 persons. On the first day of his pilgrimage, he preached to the pilgrims, and the following day he set out for **Mina**. He halted in the valley of **'Arafat** and delivered his farewell address. In it, he supported the sanctity of life and property, opposed usury, prohibited bloodshed, forbade changes in the **calendar**, appealed for the rights of wives, proclaimed the equality and brotherhood of all Muslims, and called for kind treatment of **slaves**. The Prophet then had a **revelation** that states: "This day have I perfected your religion for you, completed My favor upon you, and have chosen for you Islam as your religion" (5:3).

PILLARS OF ISLAM. *See* FIVE PILLARS OF ISLAM.

PIOUS FOUNDATION. *See* WAQF.

PIOUS SULTAN. *See* SULTAN.

PIR. The Persian word for a spiritual guide of a mystical (**Sufi**) order who initiates the novice (**murid**) in the Sufi practices. The **Arabic** equivalents for the term are **murshid** or **shaykh**.

PLUNDER. *See* GHANIMA.

POLL TAX. *See* JIZYAH.

POLYGAMY. Permitted in Islam, the **Koran** limited previously un-limited polygamy to a maximum of four wives. The Koran says: "Marry **women** of your choice, two, three, or four: but if ye fear that ye shall not be able to deal justly (with them), then only one, or that which your hand possesses [a slave]" (4:3).

Muslim modernists reason that it is impossible to treat several women equally and therefore discourage polygamy. They hold that during the time of the early conquests, men had to marry the wives of **martyrs**. Women had to be integrated into the clan and, when a man died, a brother or close relative had to marry the widow. But in modern society, those conditions no longer exist. *See also* MAR-RIAGE.

POLYTHEISM. Polytheism (**shirk**) is a **sin** that cannot be forgiven. *See* IDOLATRY; KAFIR.

PRAYER. "Salah." The **Koran** says God alone listens to prayer (3:38), and the best way to pray is with humility and in seclusion (7:55). There are several types of prayer, the ritual prayer, *salat*, which Muslims perform five times a day, and the **du'a'**, or personal prayer for special occasions.

The time for the ritual prayer is announced by the **muezzin** from a **minaret**, balcony, or the door of a **mosque**. The five prayers are performed a few minutes after sunset, at night when the sky is quite dark, at daybreak, a few minutes after noon, and in mid-afternoon. A person goes to the nearest mosque or prayer room, or performs his prayers at home or at work. A carpet, or mat, is usually spread out, on which the person prays, facing **Mecca**, the prayer direction (**qiblah**). In mosques, people line up in rows and follow the prayer leader (**imam**) to perform their bowings (rak'ah) in unison. **Women** pray at home, or in a mosque in a special area behind the men. Before prayer, a person performs the ritual washing (**ghusl** or **wudhu**) and recites his intention (**niyah**) to offer his prayer to God. **Friday** prayer should be performed in a major mosque where the preacher (**khatib**) gives his sermon (**khutbah**). According to a **hadith**, **'Umar ibn al-Khattab** used to say: "Do not intend to do your prayer at either sunrise or sunset, for the horns of Shaytan rise with the rising of the sun and set with its setting" (*Muwatta*, trans. Doi, 15.949). *See also* FIVE PILLARS OF ISLAM; PRAYER RUG.

PRAYER DIRECTION. *See* QIBLAH.

PRAYER NICHE. *See* MIHRAB.

PRAYER RUG. To perform the required ritual **prayers**, a Muslim must touch the floor with his forehead. To protect his face, a person may use a shawl, turban, or special prayer rug. Some rugs are provided with a compass to indicate the prayer direction (**qiblah**). Prayers can be performed anywhere, and **major mosques** are carpeted to eliminate the need for individual carpets. The Sultan Qabus Grand Mosque houses the world's largest hand-woven carpet, which contains 1,700 million knots and weighs 21 tons. The carpet was produced in Iran, measures in excess of 70 by 60 meters, and covers the 4,343-square-meter area of the praying hall.

PREDESTINATION. "Qadar." On the question of free will and predestination, the **Koran** says: "All bounties are in the hands of **Allah**: He granteth them to whom he pleaseth"(3:73) and "O Allah! Lord of Power (and Rule) Thou givest power to whom Thou pleasest, and Thou strippest off power from whom Thou pleasest: Thou endowest with honor whom Thou pleasest and Thou bringest low whom Thou pleasest: in Thy hand is all good. Verily, over all things Thou hast power" (3:26). These and similar passages in the Koran are taken by some schools, such as the **Jabrites** (from *jabr*, compulsion), to deny free will. The **Ash'arites** maintained that God wills "what is preserved on the table," seemingly denying man's free will, but they accept the idea of acquisition (**kasb**), which holds that God produces the act, but it is acquired by His creatures. There exists a measure of fatalism in popular Islam, manifest in such expressions as "it is written" (*maktub*), "it is decided" (*maqdur*), or "it is my lot (*kismat*)," that is, the "**kismet**" that is known in the West. *See also* FATALISM.

PRESERVED TABLET. "Al-Lauh al-Mahfudh." The belief that human actions were recorded before **creation** on a "preserved tablet" in **heaven** has led some schools to deny the capacity of free will. The **Koran** says: "Of all things have We taken account. In a clear Book (of evidence)" (36:12). *See also* PREDESTINATION.

PRIDE. The **Koran** considers pride a sin. It was out of pride that **Iblis** (a fallen **angel**) refused to bow before **Adam** (2:34, 7:13, 38:74–76). The causes of pride are affluence, a sense of superiority, and whims and desires.

PRIESTS. There is no priesthood in **Sunni** Islam, and all Muslims have equal rights and duties. There is no ordination of its functionaries, no teaching office that issues decrees of dogma, and no ritual that cannot be performed by any believer. Legislative power belongs to God, and the head of state is to follow the God-given law (**shari'ah**). The **'alim** (pl. **'ulama'**) is a learned man, qualified to interpret the law, acting in the name of the community (**ummah**).

The **Usuli school** of **Twelver Shi'ism** has permitted the creation of a hierarchy of clergy to act as intermediaries between the **Hidden Imam** and the **believers**. This led to the principle of "governance of the jurist" (**vilayat-i faqih**), which has led to the establishment of theocratic rule in the **Islamic Republic of Iran**.

PRIVACY OF DWELLINGS. It is unlawful to enter the house of a person without asking permission. The **Koran** says: "O ye who believe! Enter not houses other than your own, until ye have asked permission and saluted those in them" (24:27).

PROFESSION OF FAITH. *See* SHAHADA.

PROPHETS. "Nabi; Rasul." A prophet is a bringer of good tidings and a warner. The **Koran** says: "To every people (was sent) a **Messenger**: when their Messenger comes (before them), the matter will be judged between them with justice, and they will not be wronged" (10:47).

There are two classes of prophets: the rasul (Messenger) and the nabi. Rasuls bring a major new revelation; they include **Adam**, Seth, **Noah**, **Abraham**, Ihmael, **Moses**, Lot, Salih, Hud, Shuyaib, **Jesus**, and **Muhammad**, the last prophet. The nabi is a warner and a person who brings glad tidings. According to a **hadith**, there were 124,000 nabis.

PULPIT. *See* MINBAR.

PUNISHMENTS. There are three types of punishments in **Islamic law**: **hadd** punishments are defined in the **Koran** or Traditions (**Sunnah**) and include **adultery**, **fornication**, false accusation of adultery, **apostasy**, drinking **alcoholic** beverages, theft, and highway robbery. Qisas, **retaliation**, is exacted for bloodshed but is optional for the aggrieved. Ta'zib results from the **judge**'s discretional decision.

PURDAH. A **woman**'s garment, also called *burqa'* or *chatri*, that covers the entire body and is worn primarily in South Asia and Afghanistan. *See also* CHADOR; VEIL.

PURIFICATION. In preparation for **prayer**, a person must observe ritual purity (*tahara*), and **wudhu**, minor ablution, is obligatory. It requires one to wash the hands, wash the face and beard, wash the arms up to the elbows, rub the scalp, and wash the feet up to the ankles. Major ablution, **ghusl**, is obligatory on **Fridays** and on the '**Id al Fitr** and '**Id al-Adha** and after sexual intercourse, menstruation, and childbirth. It consists, in addition to wudhu, of washing the head by pouring water over it, washing the body—beginning with the right side— and washing the crevices of the body. If there is no water available, sand can be used for a symbolic purification. *See also* ABLUTION,

– Q –

QADARIYYAH. An early Islamic school of theology that upheld the Divine Decree (*al-Qadar*), God's omnipotence, but nevertheless accepted the idea of free will against the proponents of **predestination**. Qadar (power) seemed to denote the power of God to determine human actions, and the power of man to determine his own actions ("**Allah** will leave to stray those who do wrong: Allah doeth what He willeth," 14:27–32). Their opponents held that men act under compulsion (jabr), hence they were called the **Jabrites**. The contradiction has been resolved for orthodox Islam by al-**Ash'ari**'s postulation of **kasb**. *See also* ASH'ARITES.

QADHI (KAZI). *See* JUDGE.

QADIANIS. *See* AHMADIS.

QADIRIYYAH. A **Sufi** order named after Shaykh 'Abdul Qadir al-**Jilani** (1088–1166), an ascetic preacher, acclaimed one of the most popular **saints** in the Islamic world (*qutb al-qutb*—saint of saints). His tomb in **Baghdad** is a place of **pilgrimage**, maintained by the Naqib, custodian of the shrine, who is the descendant and hereditary head of the Qadiriyyah Sufi fraternity. From Iraq they spread in numerous branches across Asia and Africa.

QADISIYAH, BATTLE OF (637). A place near the present-day city of **Najaf** where Sa'd ibn abi **Waqqas** met the Persian general Rustam in a decisive battle, in which the Muslims captured Iraq. They sacked the capital Ctesiphon (Mada'in) and acquired an enormous amount of booty. Like Yarmuk, this battle became a turning point in the history of Muslim conquests in the east.

QAEDA, AL-. "The Base." A **terrorist** organization, founded by **Osama bin Laden**, Abu Ubayda al-Banshiri, and Muhammad Atif in 1988, for the purpose of "cleansing of the Muslim countries from corrupt and secular rulers, and fighting against the powers that threaten Muslim states and the holy places of Islam." Specifically, this meant achieving the withdrawal of U.S. troops from Saudi Arabia and winning independence for the Palestinian people (most American forces have since been withdrawn from Saudi Arabia). Al-Qaeda allied itself with **Islamist** forces in most parts of the Islamic world. It espouses a Hanbali interpretation of Islam, whose major protagonist is the 14th-century jurist **Ibn Taimiyyah**. The organization established its headquarters in Khartoum, Sudan, in 1992, and in response to American threats, moved to Afghanistan in May 1996. Al-Qaeda set up training camps in bases, established partly with American support during the war against the communist government, and subsequently provided considerable military assistance to the **Taliban** regime. Young Muslims from many parts of the Islamic world were trained in Afghanistan for military action in Kashmir, Chechnya, Bosnia, and other regions of conflict. The U.S. government holds al-Qaeda responsible for numerous attacks, including the 7 August 1998 bombings of its embassies in Kenya and Tanzania. In retaliation, President Bill Clinton ordered cruise missile attacks on Afghan terrorist training camps and the al-Shifa pharmaceutical plant in Sudan. Awards were offered for the capture or assassination of bin Laden and Muhammad Atif. The suicide attacks on the World Trade Center in New York and the Pentagon in Washington on 11 September 2001 resulted in war and the destruction of the al-Qaeda network in Afghanistan. At the time of this writing, American military actions continue. *See also* INTERNATIONAL COALITION AGAINST "TERROR"; JIHADIS DECLARATION OF WAR.

QAEDA, AL-, INTERNATIONAL. Once based in Sudan, then in Afghanistan, **al-Qaeda** is a worldwide organization whose aim is to establish a pan-Islamic caliphate under the banner of the "World Islamic Front for Jihad against the Jews and Crusaders." It is organized in cells, with members and sympathizers in the Islamic world and elsewhere. It is led by **Osama bin Laden**, who rose to prominence when he called for the withdrawal of American troops from the territory of Saudi Arabia. Because of his hostility to the Saudi government, he was deprived of his citizenship and began his search for a base elsewhere.

Al-Qaeda is only one of many **jihadi** groups, but, correctly or not, it has come to be blamed for **terrorist** actions in many countries, including Iraq, where insurgents fight Coalition forces and their collaborators. Abu Musab al-**Zarqawi** headed the al-Qaeda wing in Iraq. Al-Qaeda has lost its base in Afghanistan but seems to have moved some of its operations to Iraq. *See also* JIHADIS DECLARATION OF WAR.

QANUN (KANUN). Civil law in the **Ottoman empire**, issued by the **sultan** and collected into codes of law, the *Kanun-Name*. The name comes from the Greek, which designates religious (canon) law. A qanun had to be accompanied by a **fatwa**, indicating that it was not in conflict with any provision in **Islamic law** (**shari'ah**). Qanuns were easily changed to adapt to changing situations and enabled Ottoman rulers to borrow from their Persian and Byzantine neighbors and later from the West. In most countries of the Islamic world, a dual system of God's law and king's law (or local tradition) has coexisted to this day.

QARI'. "Reciter." A person who is versed in the science of reading the **Koran** correctly. A number of individuals have won fame as reciters of the Koran and have been in great demand for their skills.

QARMATIANS (CARMATIANS). A religio–political movement of **Isma'ilis**, named after Hamdan Qarmat, who led a revolt against the **'Abbasid caliphate** and created a state in 894. The **Qarmatians** were located primarily in **Kufah** and Bahrain, the coastal areas of eastern Arabia, and southern Iraq. The state was organized on the basis of an egalitarian, communist system with shared property. The people elected their **imam** and an advisory council and organized workers and artisans into guilds. The **sect** was messianic and revolutionary. Successors of Qarmat sacked Kufah, occupied Oman, and in 929 sacked **Mecca** and carried off the **Black Stone**, returning it only some 20 years later. Parts of the Qarmatian state survived until the end of the 11th century. Nasir-i Khusraw, the poet and world traveler, says of the Qarmatian state:

> It is ruled by the six sons of Abu Sa'id in common; in their palace there is a dais on which sit a council and from which they promulgate their orders and degrees after they have come to an agreement. They are asisted by six **viziers** who sit behind them on another platform. All matters are decided by them in consultation. . . . These princes possess 30,000 negro slaves . . . who are employed in agriculture and gardening. The people have to pay neither taxes nor tithes. To anyone who becomes poor or gets into debt, advances are made from public funds until his affairs are in good state again. Only the capital has to be paid back, no **interests** are claimed. (quoted by Steven and Randy Ronart, 433–34)

QASIDAH. An ode, composed for the purpose of gaining "a rich reward in return for praise and flattery," which consists of anywhere from 25 verses to more than 100. It follows a rigid pattern and depicts Bedouin life, then proceeds to the erotic prelude (*nasib*), which is followed by a eulogy or invective (*hija'*) for reward or to hurl invective at a person. Nicholson calls it "an illustrative criticism of Pre-Islamic life and thought" (78–79).

QAYNUQAH. One of three Jewish tribes in **Medina** who were merchants and jewelers and attained a measure of wealth. They were allied with the Muslim community until the Battle of **Badr** (624), when they were accused of collaborating with the **Meccans** and expelled from the Arabian Peninsula.

QAZWINI, ZAKARIA AL- (1203–1283). Author of a geographical dictionary titled *Monument of Places and History of God's Bondsmen* (*Athar al-bilad wa akhbar al-ibad*) and a cosmography, *Marvels of Creatures and Strange Things Existing* (*'Aja'eb al-makhluqat wa ghara'ib al-mawjudat*). He was an Iranian physician from Qazvin who served as legal expert and **judge** in various locations in Iran and Baghdad.

QIBLAH. "Direction of Prayer." This was toward **Jerusalem** until 623, and afterward it was directed toward the **Ka'bah** in **Mecca**. In **mosques** all over the world, the prayer niche (**mihrab**) indicates the direction of Mecca. Outdoors, a stone or landmark indicates the direction. The qiblah has a special sanctity: animal sacrifices are performed with the animal's head pointing in the direction of Mecca, and Muslims are buried with the head facing the qiblah. The change in the prayer direction was announced in the **Koran**: "We see the turning of thy face (for guidance) to the heavens: now shall We turn thee to a Qibla that shall please thee. Turn then thy face in the direction of the Sacred Mosque: Wherever ye are, turn your face in that direction" (2:144). Another **Surah** presents the change as a test from God: "And we appointed the Qibla to which thou wast used, only to test those who followed the **Messenger** from those who would turn on their heels" (2:143).

QISAS. *See* RETALIATION.

QIYAS. "Compare." Reasoning by analogy, an extension of personal judgment (**ra'y**) is one of the four pillars of Islamic law. By analogical reasoning, general principles found in the **Koran**, the Traditions (**Sunnah**), and the consensus of the doctors of law (**ijma**) are employed in judging a case. For example, the Koranic prohibition against wine applies to all intoxicating substances, including narcotic drugs, because they have a similar effect, even though they are not mentioned by name in the Koran.

QIZILBASH. *See* KIZILBASH.

QOM. One of the holy places of **Twelver Shi'ism** Islam in Iran, located south of Tehran. Some 400 imamzadeh (descendants of Shi'ite **imams**) are said to be buried there, including Fatima (d. 816), sister of the Eighth Imam, 'Ali al-**Ridha**. Her shrine is a celebrated sanctuary and an important object of **pilgrimage**, and it is visited prior to visiting the holy places of **Mashhad** and **Karbala**. Iran's largest theological college, the Fayziyyah, was opened there in 1920. Because most holy places of pilgrimage, Najaf and Karbala, are located in present-day Iraq, Qom and Mashhad are the only shrine cities readily available to Iranian pilgrims. Ayatollah **Khomeyni** taught in Qom, and the city became his headquarters after the Iranian revolution. It has continued to be the seat of the highest Shi'ite clergy.

QUDS. The Arabic name for **Jerusalem**.

QUR'AN. *See* KORAN.

QURAYSH. A tribe that ruled over the city-state of **Mecca** and conducted trade between the Arab Peninsula and Syria. It was divided into the subtribes of **Umayya**, Makhzum, Zuhra, Taim, and Hashim, among others. The Quraysh ruled Mecca and were the guardians of the **Ka'bah** when it was still a pre-Islamic shrine. The dialect of the Quraysh became the classical standard of **Arabic** because the **Koran** was revealed in it (but some claim that it was the language of the wider Arab community). The Prophet **Muhammad** was of the

Hashimite clan. Initially, leaders of the Quraysh opposed Muhammad and his invitation to **conversion**, so he was forced to flee to **Medina**. They waged a number of wars against the early Muslim community, but they eventually surrendered when Muhammad entered Mecca in 630. The Quraysh subsequently held leading positions, including the **caliphate**, in the **Umayyad** and **'Abbasid** dynasties, so that it came to be accepted by the Arabs that the caliphate is reserved for members of the Quraysh.

QURAYZAH. One of three Jewish tribes at **Medina** who were in a treaty relationship with the Prophet **Muhammad**. Accused of collaborating with the **Meccans** in the Battle of the **Trench** in 627, some 600 were killed and the rest expelled from the Arabian Peninsula.

QUTAYBAH IBN MUSLIM (669–715). Arab general and governor of Khurasan, who was responsible for **Umayyad** conquests in Central Asia. Various expeditions led him to Bukhara, Samarkand, Khiwa, and as far east as Farghana, establishing nominal Islamic rule. After the death of **Caliph al-Walid** (715), he refused to recognize his successor and was killed by rebellious soldiers.

QUTAYBAH, MUHAMMAD IBN MUSLIM AL-DINAWARI IBN-AL- (828–889). Historian, philologist, and literary critic of Persian origin, living in **Baghdad**. For a short time he acted as **judge** in Dinawar, before moving to Baghdad. He was a master of every known branch of science and a prolific author. His major works include *The Book of Knowledge* (*Kitab al-ma'arif*), a manual of history and genealogies; a *Guide for Secretaries* (*Adab al-katib*) on orthography, philology, synonyms, and grammar; and *Sources of Information* (*Uyun al-akhbar*), a work in 10 volumes, each of which covers a different subject. He died quite suddenly, after uttering a loud cry, and was buried in Baghdad.

QUTB. "Axis" or "pole." The highest stage of sanctity among **Sufi saints**. Qutb al-Din is a title given to eminent Muslim **pirs**.

QUTB, SAYYID (1906–1966). A leading member of the **Muslim Brotherhood** (*Ikhwan*) and one of the "Founding Fathers" of the modern **Islamist** movement. Born in a village near Asyut, he attended a village school and by the age of 10 had memorized the **Koran** and thus earned the title of **hafiz.** He then transferred to a teacher's training school and graduated in 1933 with a B.A. in **education.** He briefly taught at the Dar al-'Ulum in **Cairo** and then found employment in the ministry of education. Winning a fellowship, he went to the United States, where he earned a master's degree in education at the University of Northern Colorado's Teachers' College (1948–1950). His experience in the West caused an intellectual transformation—he was shocked by racism, seeming sexual permissiveness, and the pro-Zionist attitude of the American people.

Upon returning to Egypt, Qutb joined the Muslim Brotherhood and became editor of its paper, *al-Ikhwan.* Originally he supported the Free Officers who toppled the monarchy in Egypt in 1952, but then he opposed the Nasser regime when it became clear that the government was not going to Islamize the state. Arrested several times, Qutb was executed on 29 August 1966. In his writings, Qutb stated that "true Islam existed only in the time of the Prophet and his **Companions,**" and he called for the reestablishment of the state according to the early example. He advocated the use of violence to overthrow the existing Muslim rulers because they had strayed from the Islamic way. He rejected capitalism, communism, nationalism, liberalism, and secularism as ideologies that had failed and demanded the establishment of an Islamic state. He called for the public ownership of "fire, grass, and water," and demanded the redistribution of wealth not properly acquired. His teachings inspired the formation of such radical Islamic movements as Jama'at al-**Takfir wa al-Hijrah** (Excommunication and Exile), al-Jihad (Holy War), and **Jama'at-I Islami** (Islamic Society) in Egypt, as well as the al-**Qaeda** of **Osama bin Laden.**

– R –

RABB. One of the 99 **beautiful names of Allah** (*al-asma' al-husna'*). It means "nourisher, sustained provident being," and "master or lord" and also appears in such compounds as "The Lord of the Worlds" (*rabb al-'alamin*). Allah is the Lord and the **believers** are his servants, or slaves (**'Abd**). The **Koran** says: "It is Allah who is my Lord and your Lord; then worship Him. This is a way that is straight" (3:51).

RABI'AH AL-'ADAWIYYAH (714(?)–801). Famous female mystic of the tribe of 'Adi, who was born in **Basra** and died in **Jerusalem**. She led an ascetic life in the desert near Basra and attracted many disciples to her idea of Divine Love and union with God. Miracles were attributed to her. She wrote **Sufi** poetry, some of which is still extant. Kidnapped in youth and sold into **slavery**, she was manumitted because of her piety. Her grave was a much-visited object of **pilgrimage**. One verse of Rabi'ah quoted by Shaykh Al-Suhrawardi states:

> I reserve my heart for Thy converse, (o Lord!) And leave my body to keep company with those who desire my society. My body is thus the companion of the visitor, but my dearly beloved is the companion of my heart. (Khallikan, trans. Slane, I 156)

RAFSANJANI, AYATOLLAH AKBAR HASHEMI (1934–). President of the **Islamic Republic of Iran**, 1989–1997, losing to Mahmoud Ahmadinejad in the 2005 election. He was a major member of the Revolutionary Council and became the first speaker of the parliament, serving until 1989. In 2006, he was elected to the **Assembly of Constitutional Experts**, and in 2007 he became chairman of the Assembly of Experts. Rafsanjani was a founding member of the Islamic Republic Party. Considered a "pragmatic conservative," he favored a free-market economy, good relations with the Arab world, and accommodation with the West. He was born near the city of Rafsanjan in Kerman Province, hence his name, and educated in **Qom**, where he was taught also by Ruhollah **Khomeyni**. He is supposed to be quite wealthy.

RAHIM. One of the **beautiful names of Allah**, generally translated as "compassionate," and found in such phrases as *al-rahman al-rahim* "The Compassionate, The Merciful." It occurs in the **Basmalah**, the invocation of all **Surahs** except Surah 9, in which it says: "In the Name of the Merciful, the Compassionate" (*bism 'llah 'rahman 'l-rahim*).

RAHMAN. *See* RAHIM.

RAIDS. *See* GHAZWAH.

RAJ'AH. The return, referring to the return of the **Hidden Imam** in **Twelver Shi'ism**. *See also* SHI'ISM.

RAJM. Stoning, one of the **hadd** punishments commanded in the Traditions. *See also* HADD.

RAK'AH. A complete series of bowings (*ruku'*) performed during **prayer**.

RAMADHAN (RAMAZAN). The ninth month of the Islamic lunar **calendar**, during which daylight **fasting** is obligatory. Fast (sawm) begins with the sighting of the new moon (*laylat al-ruyah*) and continues until dawn, when a white thread can be distinguished from a black one. It ends with the **'Id al Fitr**. In addition to not eating any food, it is also prohibited to drink any liquids, including saliva—which can be ejected—or to engage in sexual relations. Children; the sick or elderly; travelers; and **women** menstruating, giving birth, or breast feeding are exempted. It is the sacred month in which the **Koran** was first revealed in the Night of Power (laylat al-qadr), when the Battle of **Badr** was fought, and when the Muslims captured **Mecca**

The Ramadhan War (Yom Kippur War, October 1973), started by Egyptian President Anwar Sadat to break the impasse in the Arab–Israeli conflict, was indicative of the religio–historical significance of the conflict. The Koran says: "The Night of Power is better than a thousand months. Therein come down the **angels** and the Spirit (**Gabriel**) by **Allah**'s permission." *See also* 'ID AL-ADHA.

RAMLA. *See* UMM HABIBAH BINT ABI SUFYAN.

RASHID RIDHA. *See* RIDHA, MUHAMMAD RASHID.

RASHIDUN. *See* RIGHTLY GUIDED CALIPHS.

RASUL. "**Messenger.**" **Muhammad** was the *Rasul Allah*, the Messenger of God. Other **prophets** accorded the title rasul, including **Abraham**, **Noah**, Lot, Isma'il, **Moses**, Shu'aib, Hud, Salih, and **Jesus** (Isa).

RATIONALISTS. *See* MU'TAZILITES.

RAWDHAH KHANI (RUZEH KHANI). Ritual mourning, commemorating the martyrdom of **Husayn**, the son of **Caliph 'Ali**, in which **Shi'ites** reenact the events of 680. On **'Ashura**, the 10th day of **Muharram** (but also at other times), meetings in **mosques** or homes are held for communal mourning and lamentation. Some mourners conduct processions through the streets, flagellating themselves and cutting the skin of their heads or bodies. Shi'ite communities stage passion plays, called **ta'ziyah**, in public squares, and coffee houses, dramatizing the events of their **imam**'s death.

RA'Y. "Informed opinion." Resort to the personal opinion of the jurist (**faqih**) in cases where the **Koran** and **Sunnah** do not give any clear decision regarding a point of law or theology. It was employed during the first two centuries of Islam as a "third source" of Islamic law. Ra'y is permitted primarily by the Hanafi **school** of **Sunni** Islam.

RAYHANA BINT ZAID. Wife of **Muhammad** who belonged to the Jewish tribe Nadhir and had married into the Banu Qurayzah of **Medina**. Taken as a captive, she converted and married the Prophet in the month of Muharram 628. She died before Muhammad, during the Farewell **Pilgrimage**. According to some sources, Rayhana decided to remain a concubine, so that she could keep her former religion.

RAZI, ABU BAKR AL- (865–925). Persian physician, philosopher, and universal thinker from Rayy in present-day Iran, known in the medieval West as Rhazes. He published works on various diseases and their symptoms, which were translated into Latin, Greek, and modern Western languages. His first medical book, dedicated to the Samanid Prince al-Mansur (*Kitab al-mansuri*), established him as a medical authority. In more than 100 medical treatises, he described the medical achievements up to his time. As a philosopher, he postulated, in addition to God, the world soul, time, space, and matter as eternal principles. As a youth, he sang and played the lute, but later he renounced this, saying that "**music** proceeding from between mustachoes and a beard had no charms to recommend it" (Khallikan, trans. Slane, III, 312). A failed alchemical experiment resulted in his being whipped by al-Mansur, which caused him to be blinded.

RAZI, FAKHR AL-DIN AL- (1149–1209). Persian philosopher, theologian, and commentator on the **Koran**, said to have been one of the last encyclopedic writers of Islam. He was an adherent of the **Ash'arite** school and violent opponent of **Mu'tazilism**. His most important works are *The Resumé* (*Kitab al-muhassal*), about philosophical and theological ideas, as well as commentary on the Koran, entitled *The Key to God's Secret* (*Mafatih al-ghayb*). **Ibn Khallikan** described Razi as "the pearl of the age, a man without a peer; he surpassed all his contemporaries in scholastic theology, metaphysics, and philosophy" (II,652). He was born in Rayy and died in Herat in present-day Afghanistan.

RAZZIA. *See* GHAZWAH.

RECITER. *See* QARI'.

RECOMPENSE. Mankind will be judged according to actions, good or evil, and will be recompensed by God in this world or in the world to come. The **Koran** says: "That Day will every soul be requited for what it earned; no injustice will there be that Day, for **Allah** is swift in taking account" (40:17). Nations rise and fall as recompensed by God: "And thou wilt see every nation bowing the knee: every nation will be called to its record: 'This day shall ye be recompensed for all ye did'" (45:28).

RECONQUISTA. The Spanish term for the reconquest in the 15th century of the last remnants of the Iberian Peninsula under Muslim control. *See also* CORDOVA.

REFAH. *See* WELFARE PARTY.

REFORM OR REVIVAL MOVEMENTS. *See* SALAFIYYAH.

REFORMER. See MUJADDID.

REID, RICHARD. The "shoe bomber" who attempted to light explosive devices in his shoes while traveling on American Airlines Flight 63 from Paris to Miami, carrying 197 people, on 22 December 2001. French customs became suspicious because Reid was traveling without luggage and prevented him from boarding the plane on 21 December, but he was permitted to take the flight on the following day. About 90 minutes after takeoff, he tried to use a match to light explosives hidden in his shoes and was subdued by passengers and members of the crew. The explosive was said to have been triaceton triperoxide, or TATP, also referred to as the "Mother of Satan" used in other **terrorist** acts. Was he not ready for "martyrdom" by acting within sight of other passengers, after already having attracted the suspicions of the French authorities? He initially denied any link with al-**Qaeda**, but at a court hearing he pleaded guilty to all charges and claimed to be a follower of **Osama bin Laden**.

Reid was born in London, the son of an English mother and a Jamaican father. He lived in the London suburb of Bromley and attended Thomas Tallis secondary school in Blackheath. He was repeatedly imprisoned for petty crimes until he converted to Islam. Taking the name Abdul Rahim, he was said to have associated with radical Islamists.

RELIGIOUS POLICE. *See* ENJOINING THE GOOD AND FORBIDDING EVIL.

REMEMBRANCE. In **Sufism**, *dhikr* is the remembrance of God. It is the glorification of God by repeating a fixed phrase in a ritual order, accompanied by bodily movements and rhythmic breathing, until a trance or unity with God is achieved. The **Koran** is also called dhikr, reminder.

RENEWER. *See* MUJADDID.

REPENTANCE. Return (*tawbah*) of an individual to God after falling into **sin** or error. Repentance wipes out sins, if it is made in a state of belief and is accompanied by the will to abstain from sin in the future. A nominal believer will not suffer perpetual damnation. The

Koran says: "But those who reject faith after they accepted it, and then go on adding to their defiance of faith—never will their repentance be accepted" (3:90).

RESURRECTION. *See* DAY OF JUDGMENT.

RETALIATION. "Qisas." The principle of "an eye for an eye, a tooth for a tooth" requires retaliation for killing or the shedding of blood. It is the system of pre-Islamic blood revenge, in which retaliation could be targeted against any male member of the offender's family, clan, or tribe. In a tribal conflict, peace could be restored when the party with a blood debt made material amends. **Women could be** given in **marriage** or blood money (**diyyah**), in the form of cash, camels, or other livestock. In Islam, a court has to decide the offense, and the aggrieved is permitted to kill a murderer or inflict an injury of equal nature. Blood money must be paid if the relatives of the aggrieved accept it, or they can pardon the culprit.

In most Islamic countries, the state has prohibited qisas, but in tribal and traditional societies in the Middle East, qisas is still practiced. The British, during their rule in India, codified tribal law to the extent that exact amounts of blood money were stipulated for an injury to the body, the face, the loss of a limb, or the loss of life. The **Koran** stipulates: "O ye who believe! The law of equality is prescribed to you in cases of murder: The free for the free, the slave for the slave, the woman for the woman. But if any remission is made by the brother of the slain, then grant any reasonable demand, and compensate him with handsome gratitude. This is a concession and a mercy from your Lord. After this whoever exceeds the limits shall be in grave chastisement" (2:178).

REVELATION. "Wahy." Guidance for mankind is given in the form of revelation by a **prophet**. Every prophet receives a message from God, which he conveys to his people to guide them on the Right Path. There are three types of revelation: inspiration, revelation "from behind a veil," and the message conveyed to the heart of the prophet by an **angel**. The **Koran** says: "It is not fitting for a man that **Allah** should speak to him except by inspiration, or from behind a veil, or by the sending of a **Messenger**" (42:51). Divine revelation is necessary to guide humanity to attain the ultimate truth.

REVENGE. *See* RETALIATION.

REVOLUTIONARY GUARDS (ARMY OF THE GUARDIANS OF THE ISLAMIC REVOLUTION). "Sepah-e Pasdaran-e Enqelab-e Eslami." Part of the **Islamic Republic of Iran** military, but separate from the Iranian army. It has its own ground forces, navy, air force, intelligence, and special forces. It also controls the **Basij**. Established in 1979, Sepah's main role is in national security, internal and border security, as well as law enforcement. It consists of about 90,000 regular soldiers and 300,000 reservists. It was the ideological force of the government, to counterbalance the power of the regular army. During the Iran–Iraq war, it fought alongside the army and suffered considerable casualties. Sepah, or **Pasdaran** as they are commonly called, were involved in support of **Hamas** and **Hizbullah**.

REWARD. "Ajr." God will reward the good by opening paradise to them, and good actions will be rewarded at least tenfold. The **Koran** says: "He that doeth good shall have ten times as much to his credit: he that doeth evil shall only be recompensed according to his evil" (6:160).

REZA. *See* RIDHA, 'ALI AL-.

RHYMED PROSE. "Saj'." Rhymed prose, one of the oldest forms of **Arabic** literary speech, also used in the **revelations** of **Muhammad**. It was the speech of the **Kahin**, the soothsayers, dealers in oracles whose form of expression was thought to possess magical powers. From saj' evolved another poetic form, the *rajaz*, which had a somewhat irregular iambic meter that is said to have been adopted from the rhythm of the gait of the camel. Because he used this medium of expression, Muhammad was accused by his enemies of being a Kahin. The **Koran** says: "This is verily the word of an honored **messenger**, it is not the word of a poet . . . nor is it the word of a soothsayer" (69:40–42).

RIBA'. *See* INTEREST.

RIBAT. Originally a fortified camp on the edges of the desert for the protection of Muslim communities. Ribats were manned by religious fighters, who often followed a purist, revivalist concept of Islam. The

Almoravids were such a community, which succeeded in founding an empire in North Africa and Spain.

RIDDAH. "**Apostasy**" is forbidden in Islam. If an apostate has become an infidel (**kafir**), he may lose his property and is considered **divorced** from his wife, because a Muslim **woman** may not be married to a non-Muslim. Some radical **sects**, like the seventh-century **Kharijites**, would even kill an apostate and his family. After the death of **Muhammad**, some of the Arab tribes considered their alliance with the Prophet terminated, and the **caliphate** of **Abu Bakr** (632–634) was devoted to forcing them to renew their loyalty and convert others in what came to be known as the "Riddah Wars." During European colonial occupation, **Islamic laws** of apostasy could not be enforced, and missionary activity, though with little success, was permitted. After independence, many Muslim states adopted Western legal institutions and, although apostasy was considered forbidden, they did not enforce punishments.

RIDHA, 'ALI AL- (**REZA, 765–818**). The eighth of the **Twelver Shi'ite imams**. He resided in **Medina** and was called to **Baghdad** by **'Abbasid Caliph** al-Ma'mun in 817 to be his successor. He gave him his daughter Umm Habib in **marriage** and had coins struck in his name. The 'Abbasid caliph wanted to end the schism in Islam, but al-Ridha died before him, reputedly of poisoning. 'Ali al-Ridha's death ended 'Abbasid attempts at unifying the Islamic community. Al-Ridha is buried beside **Harun al-Rashid** and his shrine has become one of the most venerated places of **Twelver Shi'ite pilgrimage**. The city of **Mashhad** has grown around the shrine. A **Companion** chided the poet **Abu Nuwas**, saying: "I never saw a more shameless fellow than you; there is not a sort of wine nor beast of chase but you have made some verses on it; and here is 'Ali Ibn Musa ar-Rida, living in your own time, and yet you have never noticed him." In a poem, Abu Nuwas excused himself, saying: I am unable to utter praises suited to the merits of an imam to whose father (the **angel**) Gabriel acted as a servant" (Khallikan, trans. Slane, II, 213).

RIDHA, MUHAMMAD RASHID (1865–1935). Islamic revivalist and reformer. Born near Tripoli, Syria, he left for Egypt in 1897 and cooperated with Muhammad **Abduh** in publishing the monthly journal *The Lighthouse* (*Al-Manar*) in **Cairo**. The journal demanded reform and the revitalization of Islam and Islamic society. Ridha advocated the reinterpretation of Islam on the basis of the **Koran** and the **Sunnah** through the exercise of **ijtihad** (informed reasoning in deciding matters of doctrine in **Islamic law**).

Like his mentors **Afghani** and Abduh, he wanted the Islamic community to progress by acquiring the positive aspects of European civilization. He opposed nationalism and secularism and demanded the restoration of the **caliphate**. But he wanted the Islamic world to gain strength to stem the tide of European colonialism and to fight tyranny and stagnation at home. He published a number of works, including *The Caliphate of the Supreme Imamate* as well as a biography of Muhammad Abduh and a commentary on the Koran. His teachings inspired both moderates and conservatives.

RIFA'I, AHMAD IBN ALI AL- (1106?–1183). Islamic mystic and founder of a religious fraternity, named after him the Rifa'iyyah. He was a native of Iraq and educated in **Basra**, and he attracted a large following with his teachings. He was an ascetic and inspiring teacher whose students believed that he could perform miracles. The order is centered primarily in Egypt, Syria, and Turkey; it stresses poverty, abstinence, and self-mortification.

RIGHTLY GUIDED CALIPHS (RASHIDUN). The first four caliphs in **Sunni** Islam are called the Rightly Guided successors to the Prophet (*al-khulafa al-rashidun*). **Abu Bakr** (r. 632–634), **'Umar ibn al-Khattab** (r. 634–644), **'Uthman ibn 'Affan** (r. 644–656), and **'Ali ibn Abi Talib** (r. 656–661) were contemporaries and closest to **Muhammad** and succeeded him after his death in the leadership of the Islamic community. Abu Bakr was elected by a council of **Companions** and contributed to the consolidation of the Islamic state in the **Riddah** wars. During 'Umar's **caliphate**, the Islamic domains extended into Persia and North Africa; he adopted the title **caliph** and "Prince of **Believers**" (*amir al-mu'minin*) and created some of the first institutions of the Islamic state. His assassination brought 'Uthman to the caliphate. He is said to have collected the text of the **Koran** as it exists today, but his rule was generally described as consisting of six good and six bad years.

Nepotism increased, and the Umayyads succeeded to leading positions in the empire. 'Uthman's assassination resulted in civil war and the gradual beginnings of schism, which eventually divided the Islamic world into the orthodox Sunnis and the **Shi'ites**, who denied the legitimacy of the first three caliphs and considered 'Ali the rightful successor to Muhammad. 'Ali's tenure was challenged by **Mu'awiyah**, a second cousin of 'Uthman, and neither force of arms nor arbitration had resolved the dispute when 'Ali was assassinated in 661. This ended the period of the patriarchal caliphs and ushered in the **Umayyad caliphate** (661–750), which many considered an Arab kingdom rather than a true Islamic theocracy.

RIGHT PATH, THE. Muslims are enjoined to follow the Right Path (*al-sirat al-mustaqim*), which leads directly to God and salvation (11:56).

RITUAL PRAYER. *See* PRAYER.

ROSARY. The Muslim rosary (*subhah* or *misbahah*) has 33 beads, divided into three sections, sometimes adding up to 99 or more beads. A person recites or thinks of the 99 **beautiful names of Allah** as he walks in public or sits in a coffee house. Probably originating in India, use of the rosary came into the Islamic world and was widespread after the 15th century. It is accepted by most schools, except for the Hanbalis, and even non-Muslims in the Mediterranean regions carry the rosary to keep their fingers busy.

ROWZEH. Persian name for **fasting** (sawm).

RUH. "Spirit or life." **Allah** gave life to **Adam** when he blew his ruh into him. "The faithful spirit" (*ruh al-amin*) and "the Holy Spirit" (*ruh al-quds*) seem to refer to the angel **Gabriel**, who was the means of communication in bringing the message of Allah to **Muhammad**. Ruh Allah, the Spirit of God, is the title of **Jesus** in the **Koran**.

RUKU' (RAK'AH). *See* PRAYER.

RULE BOOK OF TALIBAN. *See* TALIBAN.

RUM. "Rome," a term referring to the Eastern Roman (Byzantine) empire. After the conquest of Asia Minor by the **Saljuq** Turks, they were referred to as the Rum Seljuqs. During **Ottoman** times (13th to 20th centuries), their European possessions came to be called Rumelia, as compared to Anatolia, but Persians and Arabs continued to call Turks Rumis (those from Rome).

RUMI. *See* JALAL AL-DIN RUMI.

RUQAYYAH. Daughter of **Muhammad** by **Khadijah**. Ruqayyah married the son of **Abu Lahab**, an enemy of the Prophet, but she was **divorced** before consummation of the **marriage**. She accepted Islam at the same time as her mother and then married **'Uthman ibn 'Affan** and went into Abyssinian exile with him. She died at the time of the Battle of **Badr** (624).

RUSHDIE AFFAIR. When Salman Rushdie published his fourth novel, *The Satanic Verses*, in 1988, Muslims in a number of countries violently protested what they considered a blasphemous act. Ayatollah Ruhollah **Khomeyni** issued a **fatwa** in February 1989 calling for his assassination and offered a bounty for his death. Rushdie spent a number of years in hiding, but in June 2007 he was awarded a British knighthood "for services to literature." Rushtie was born a **Shi'ah** Muslim in Bombay, now Mumbai, and has been married four times.

RUZEH KHANI. *See* RAWDHAH KHANI.

– S –

SABBAH, HASAN AL-. *See* HASAN AL-SABBAH.

SACRED MONTHS, THE. From the time of **Abraham**, four months (Dhu 'l-Qa'dah, Dhu 'l-Hijjah, **Muharram**, and Rajab) were sacred months. During the first three it was forbidden to wage war, loot, or plunder, and general peace prevailed. Fairs were held in certain places, where Bedouin poets competed for prizes and honors. The **Mu'allaqat** was one of these collections of pre-Islamic poetry. The

10th of Rajab was celebrated in Islam as the day when **Noah** entered the ark. The **Koran** says: "It is no crime in you if ye seek of the bounty of your Lord (during **pilgrimage**)" (2:198), which has been interpreted to mean that commerce can continue even during the month of pilgrimage.

SACRIFICE. Islam took over the custom of ritual sacrifice from pre-Islamic times. It is in commemoration of the Prophet **Abraham**'s sacrifice, but Muslim modernists now see it as an act of social welfare and charity. On the 10th of Dhu 'l-Hijjah, pilgrims are required to make an animal sacrifice at **Mina**, usually of camels, cows, sheep, and goats. Those who cannot afford the cost may substitute a number of **fast** days. The pilgrims may eat some of the flesh and donate the rest to the poor. Formerly, the meat was buried because it could not be kept, but nowadays much of it is transported to feed poor people in countries of great need. An animal sacrifice is optional in celebration of the **'Id ul-Adha**, which marks the end of the month of **pilgrimage**, or the birth of a child, or in expiation of a **sin**. The **Koran** says: "The sacrificial camels We have made for you as among the signs from **Allah**: in them is (much) good for you: then pronounce the name of Allah over them as they line up (for sacrifice); when they are down on their sides (after slaughter), eat ye thereof, and feed such as (beg not but) live in contentment" (22:36).

SADAQA. Voluntary **almsgiving** to the needy. It can be done publicly or secretly and is one of the principal forms of making atonement. There is also the mandatory charity, **zakat**. If one has nothing to give, to refrain from evil is also considered a sadaqa.

SA'D IBN ABI WAQQAS. *See* WAQQAS, SA'D IBN ABI.

SA'DI, MUSLIH AL-DIN MUSHRIF IBN ABDULLAH (1184–1283/ 1292?). One of the great Iranian poets of the medieval period. A great panegyrist and lyricist, his major works include *The Rose Garden* (*Bostan*), *The Orchard*, and *Gulistan*, which have been translated into German, French, English, and other languages. Sa'di was born in Shiraz, in present-day Iran, and educated at the famous **Nizamiyyah**

of **Baghdad**. He traveled widely in the Islamic world and returned to Shiraz, where he enjoyed the sponsorship of the Seljuk Sultan Sa'd ibn Zengi.

SADR, MUSA AL- (1928–1978?). An Iranian-born **Shi'ite** cleric who became a dominant factor in Lebanese politics. Educated in **Qom** and at Tehran University, and subsequently in **Najaf**, Iraq, he came to Lebanon in 1959, where he became a religious leader in Tyre. He established a vocational institute in the vicinity of Tyre and wrote the covenant of the "Movement of the Deprived" (*al-mahrumin*) in 1974. He founded the Lebanese Resistance Detachments (AMAL). In August 1978, he visited Libya with two companions and disappeared. He is believed by his followers to have been killed by the Libyan leader Mu'ammar al-Qadhdhafi. **Amal** and **Hizbullah** are offshoots of the newly politicized Shi'ite movement in eastern and southern Lebanon.

SAFAVID DYNASTY (1501–1732). A dynasty named after Shaykh Safi al-Din (d. 1334), a **Sufi saint**, who established the Safavid order in Ardabil in northwestern Iran. A descendant of the **shaykh**, Shah Isma'il, founded the dynasty in 1501, unified the country, and established **Twelver Shi'ism** as the religion of the new state. He created a personal force, the **Kizilbash** (Red Heads), and a tribal force, the Shah Sevan (Friends of the Shah) as praetorian guards. His tribes venerated **Isma'il** and thought him invincible. It was only when the **Ottomans** defeated the Shah in the battle of Chalidran in 1514 that the ruler lost some of his charisma. But the Safavids retained some of the quasi-divine status. An Afghan army finally defeated the Safavids in the battle of Gulnabad in 1722.

SAFFARID DYNASTY. See YAQUB IBN LAYTH AL-SAFFAR.

SAFIYYAH BINT HUAYY. The 17-year-old widow of Kinanah, chief of the Jews of Khaybar, married **Muhammad**. She was captured in the Battle of Khaybar in 629 and enslaved, but she converted to Islam and was set free. She died long after the Prophet in 674 and left a third of her estate to her Jewish nephew.

SAINTS. "Awliyah, Friends of God." In popular Islam, there exists a cult of saints who are the source of a special blessing (**barakah**). They were often the founders of **Sufi** orders, and their tombs are objects of **pilgrimage**. Devotees fasten pieces of cloth from a garment to the enclosure or a tree nearby of a saint's tomb to find recovery from an affliction, or they may wear the cloth as a talisman. Some saints are believed to perform miracles (**karamah**) and dispense **amulets**, and are patrons of communities or tribes.

The terms for saints are **pir** (spiritual master), **wali** (friend), *murabit* (the North African *marabout*), *shafi* (intercessor), and **shaykh** (leader). They are believed to have the power of **intercession**, and the ability to give advice and bestow blessings. A person becomes a saint by acclamation and is often associated with a shrine. They receive offerings of money from their devotees. Although saint cults are frowned upon by orthodoxy, they are an expression of popular Islam, which could not be suppressed. **Twelver Shi'ism** accepts only a lesser type of sainthood, the imam-zadeh shrines, and the **Sunni Wahhabis** of Saudi Arabia and the Hanbali **school of law** reject the cult of saints as sinful innovations.

SAJ'. *See* RHYMED PROSE.

SAJDAH. Prostration, such as during prayer. A person stands, then lowers himself to the ground, and touches the ground with both hands and the forehead. *See* PRAYER.

SALADIN. *See* SALAH AL-DIN.

SALAF. "Ancestor." The virtuous forefathers, and a person who draws on the **Koran** and the **Sunnah** as the only valid sources of Islam. The Salaf included the Prophet's **Companions** and the early generations of Islam, ending with Ahmad **Ibn Hanbal** in the ninth century, although a number of later Islamic scholars are included. *See* SALAFIYYAH.

SALAFIYYAH. A reform movement in Islam that tried to respond to stagnation and weakness in the Islamic world and advocated a return to the basics of Islam on the basis of the **Koran**, the **Sunnah**, and the practices of the pious fathers (**Salaf**). It included such scholars as **Ibn Hanbal, Ibn Taimiyyah**, and, in the 19th century, **'Abd al-Wahhab**, whose ideas influenced later reformers. Most important, they influenced an Egyptian reform and revival movement at the turn of the century inspired by Jamal al-Din **Afghani** (18 39–1897) and Muhammad **'Abduh** (1849–1905). Impressed by the threat of European colonialism, they demanded a reinterpretation of Islam in the light of modernity and rejected the blind adherence to legal decisions of the past (**taqlid**). They felt that **revelation** and reason were fully compatible and favored **education** in the sciences and adoption of those technologies of the West that would strengthen the Islamic world.

A conservative trend, promoted by Rashid **Ridha**, inspired an **Islamist** movement that demanded the establishment of an Islamic state in which the **shari'iah** is the supreme law and all manifestations of Western culture are eliminated. Inspired by the Iranian revolution and the writings of Ayatollah **Khomeyni** (ca. 1900–1989), **Hasan al-Banna** (1906–1949), and Abu'l A'la **Maududi**, radical Islamic parties emerged that used Islam as a political doctrine of action. The **Taliban** of Afghanistan, the **Jihad** of Egypt, and the **Islamic Salvation Front** of Algeria sought to create a new Islamic society.

SALAH. *See* PRAYER.

SALAH AL-DIN, YUSUF IBN AYYUB (SALADIN) (1138–1193).

Military and diplomatic genius who founded the **Ayyubid dynasty** of Egypt. He replaced the **Fatimid** kingdom and restored orthodoxy to Egypt. He conducted a **jihad** against the crusaders, and in the battle of **Hittin** (1187) recaptured **Jerusalem**. He was respected as a tolerant ruler and became a hero in the Islamic world. He was born in Takrit, Iraq, the son of a Kurdish officer in the service of Nur al-Din, and he was educated in the **Shafi'ite** tradition. At the age of about 30 he joined forces with a Syrian army and gained control of Egypt. After the death of his suzerain Nur al-Din in 1174, he proclaimed himself independent under nominal **'Abbasid** suzerainty with the title of **sultan**. His mausoleum is located in Damascus.

According to **Ibn Khallikan**, "when Salah al-Din died 'he left' neither gold nor silver in his treasury, with the exception of forty-seven Nasirian dirhems and one gold piece coined at Tyre. He possessed neither estates, nor houses, nor lands, nor gardens, nor villages nor tillage grounds" (IV, 545).

SALAMAH BINT ABI UMAYYAH (UMM SALAMAH, d. 681). A widow of Abu Salamah with children, who became the wife of **Muhammad**, after she had rejected a proposal by **Abu Bakr** and **'Umar I**. She confessed to Muhammad that she was jealous, but he replied that "**Allah** will remove her jealousy." Her dowry is said to have consisted of a bed stuffed with palm leaves, a bowl, a dish, and a hand mill. She died at age 59, outliving most of Muhammad's wives.

SALAT. *See* PRAYER.

SALJUQ DYNASTY (1037–1307). Warriors of the Turkoman Oghuz clan who entered the Islamic world as mercenaries and protectors of the **'Abbasid caliphs** and, under Toghrul Bey (r. 1037–1063), became rulers of a new dynasty. They defeated the **Shi'ite Buyids** and established themselves in **Baghdad** in 1055. To get rid of their unruly nomadic fighters, they encouraged them to move west, leading to the conquest of Anatolia, where they defeated the Byzantine army in the Battle of Manzikert (1071). This led to the establishment of the Rum Saljuq empire in Anatolia and a period of great cultural revival. The period of **Nizam al-Mulk**, the grand vizier of Malik Shah (1072–1092), marked Saljuq power at its zenith. Its borders extended from Kashghar in the east to Jerusalem and from Constantinople to the Caspian Sea. Nizam al-Mulk published a treatise on government, the *Siyasatnamah*, and founded the **Nizamiyyah Madrasa** in 1065–1067, which became a model for higher education in the East and West. After a period of internal decline, the Mongols and Ottomans ended Saljuq control.

SALMAN THE PERSIAN. A **Companion** of the Prophet and the first Persian convert to Islam, who is credited with having suggested the construction of a trench (khandaq) that protected the Muslim community in **Medina** from a **Meccan** attack in the Battle of the Trench (627). Salman was born Zoroastrian, then was attracted to Christianity. He was sold to a Jew of the Banu **Qurayzah** but became a Muslim when he was ransomed by the Prophet. He became governor of Mada'in (Ctesiphon) near **Baghdad**, where he was also buried. Both **Sunnis** and **Shi'ites** claim him as one of their own, and the **'Alawis** put Salman on a par with **Muhammad** and 'Ali.

SALVATION. "Naja." **Believers** are promised "gardens with rivers flowing beneath, their eternal home [in paradise]" (5:119). A good Muslim will find salvation; a bad one will suffer in purgatory until his **sins** are atoned for. An unbeliever will suffer the pains of eternal hellfire.

SAMA'. A **Sufi** practice, "listening," is used in **musical** gatherings together with dhikr, "**remembrance**," to achieve ecstasy or union with God.

SAMANID DYNASTY (819–1005). A dynasty, named after its eponymous ancestor Saman, that reached its greatest extent under Nasr II ibn Ahmad (913–943) and included eastern Iran, Tranoxania, and present-day Afghanistan. Virtually independent of the **'Abbasid caliphs**, the Samanids defeated the Saffarids and captured 'Amr ibn Layth (d. 901). They established their capital at Bukhara, which was one of the great centers of Islamic civilization. Under the Samanids, there was a great revival of Persian culture. They patronized Persian language and literature, which assumed its modern form during this period. The first Persian poet of the Islamic period, Rudaki (d. 940), and the great physicians and philosophers **Ibn Sina** (Avicenna) and Abu Bakr al-Razi, flourished at the Samanid court. Eventually the Samanids succumbed to the **Ghaznavids** and Qarakhanids.

SAMARRA. Capital of the **'Abbasid caliphate** founded by al-Mu'tasim (r. 833–842) in 836, when his Turkish bodyguard became a menace to **Baghdad**. The name is a corruption of "pleased is he who sees it" (*surra man ra'a*). The city flourished in 847–861 under Caliph al-Mutawakkil, but after 688 it began its decline, and in the 10th century it was deserted. Remnants of the 'Abbasid architecture can still be seen, and the tombs of the **imams** 'Ali al-Hadi (d. 868) and Hasan al-'Askari (d. 874) make it an important place of **pilgrimage** for **Twelver Shi'ites**. The tomb of al-Askar was bombed by unknown persons in February 2006 and badly damaged.

SAMUEL, IBN ADIYA AL- (SAMAW'AL). Sixth-century Jewish poet who lived in a castle called al-Ablaq, north of **Medina**. His name has become proverbial as the epitome of unlimited loyalty because he sacrificed his son rather than surrender armor entrusted to him. The Bedouin poet **Imru 'l-Qays**, who had been entrusted with five suits of armor, was being pursued by men of the king of al-Hira. When the pursuers got to the gates of the castle, they demanded the armor—they had managed to capture his son while out on a hunting trip—and threatened to kill the son. Samaw'al sacrificed his son rather than betray a trust. Hence, the Arab saying, "more loyal than Samaw'al."

SANAD. *See* ISNAD.

SANCTUARY OF PEACE, THE. The city of **Mecca** is called the "sanctuary of peace" in the **Koran** (28:57, 29:67). The Koran says that **Abraham** prayed to God that the city of Mecca be designated a city of peace, because of the location of the **Ka'bah** in it (2:126).

SANUSIYYAH. A **Sufi** fraternity in North Africa, founded by Muhammad Ibn Abi al-Sanusi in 1833. The order won many followers in Libya, Egypt, and the Saharan desert region, where it established peace and security and introduced a puritanical practice of Islam. Under Sayyid Muhammad al-Mahdi (1859–1902) and Ahmad al-Sharif al-Sanusi (1905–1925), they fought the **Ottoman**, French, and subsequently Italian governments, and in 1951 their leader, Idris, became king of Libya. In 1969, the monarchy was overthrown in a military revolt under Colonel Mu'ammar al-Qadhdhafi.

SATAN. *See* IBLIS.

SA'UD, IBN. *See* IBN SA'UD.

SAWDAH BINT ZAM'AH. Wife of **Muhammad**. She and her first husband adopted Islam in Mecca and went into Abyssinian exile. When her husband died, she was the first woman after **Khadijah** whom **Muhammad** married. The **marriage** was in the month of **Ramadhan** in 620, and she received 400 **dirhams** as dowry. Described as a charitable woman, large and heavy, as she grew older, she deferred to **'A'ishah** to please Muhammad. She died in **Medina** in 676.

SAWM. *See* FASTING.

SA'Y. "Walking or running." One of the rituals of **pilgrimage** after circumambulation of the **Ka'bah**, sa'y consists of jogging between the hills al-Safa and al-Marwah within the area of the Grand **Mosque**. At each stop the pilgrim says certain **prayers**. The practice goes back to a tradition according to which **Hagar**, concubine of **Abraham** and mother of his son Isma'il, was running between the hills in search of water for her son.

SAYYID. "Lord, master." Title of a tribal chief in pre-Islamic times, it came to be a title of honor for the descendants of the Prophet through al-**Husayn**, son of **Fatimah** and **'Ali ibn Abi Talib**. Especially honored in **Shi'ism**, but also in **Sufism**, sayyids attained a measure of political influence. In some countries, sayyids live in their own communities and do not intermarry with the local population. Although not an aristocracy, sayyids enjoyed a number of privileges, including at times dispensation from physical punishment. In most Arab countries, the term is now equivalent to "Mister."

SAYYID AHMAD. *See* BARELVI, SAYYID AHMAD.

SCHOOLS OF LAW. Madhhab," meaning direction. By the middle of the ninth century, four **Sunni** schools had been established and gained general acceptance in the orthodox Islamic community. These schools, named after their teachers, evolved out of the legal practices in various areas of the Islamic world.

The Malikite school was named after **Malik ibn Anas**, who died in **Medina** in 795. Malik placed great importance on **Sunnah**, but he supplemented the Traditions with the practices of the community of Medina. He employed **ijma'**, consensus of the doctors of law, and permitted consideration of the welfare of the community (**istislah** and **istihsan**) and informed opinion (**ra'y**). At present the Malikite school is found primarily in North Africa and parts of Central and West Africa.

The Hanifite school, named after **Abu Hanifah** (d. 767), who taught at **Kufah**, Iraq, is considered the most liberal in the use of legal techniques. It gives preponderance to the use of informed opinion, ra'y, and also permits the use of preferential judgment (istihsan) and reasoning by analogy (**qiyas**). The school is the largest of the four and is found primarily in Iraq, Syria, Turkey, Central Asia, and India.

The Shafi'ite school was named after Idris al-**Shafi'i**, a member of the **Quraysh** who died in Egypt in 820. Shafi'i rejected the use of ra'y and istihsan, but permitted ijma', consensus of the community (rather than the scholars), and makes this, in addition to the **Koran** and the Sunnah of the Prophet, the basis for argument by reason of analogy (**qiyas**). The Shafi'ite school is prevalent in northern Egypt, the **Hijaz**, southern Arabia, East Africa, and Southeast Asia.

The Hanbali school, named after Ahmad **Ibn Hanbal**, an Arab who died at **Baghdad** in 855, wants to confine the sources of Islamic law solely to the Koran and the Sunnah. The school permits the use of reasoning by analogy (qiyas) only when the Koran, ijma', and even a weak **hadith** are not available. Everything else is sinful innovation (**bid'ah**). Hanbal favored a literalist interpretation of the Koran and Sunnah and rejected informed reasoning. This school is dominant in Saudi Arabia.

All four schools are considered orthodox, and individuals are under the jurisdiction of their particular school (**madhhab**). Because of interference by **caliphs** in matters of dogma, such as the question of the **createdness of the Koran**, the jurists decided in the 10th century that the "gate of **ijtihad**" was closed, and **believers** were henceforth bound to imitate or emulate the law (**taqlid**). The jurist **Ibn Taimiyyah** (d. 1328) and the founder of "Wahhabism," **'Abd al Wahhab** (d. 1792), became major exponents of this approach.

According to Muslim jurists, the fundamental human condition is liberty. But since it is in human nature to be weak, covetous, and ungrateful, it is in the interest of the individual and society that limits be set on human freedom of action. These limits, **hadd**, constitute the law. They were ordained for the soul of man to define his relationship to God. The principle of liberty of mankind limits man only in cases about which revealed information exists, or in which a need for limitations was felt. The majority of human actions do not come under the scope of law. The criteria for good and evil were therefore more than just two. There are five general classes of acts: actions obligatory on believers (**fardh**), for example, the **Pillars of Islam** and **prayers**; actions desirable or recommended, but not obligatory (**mandub**), such as the manumission of slaves; actions that are indifferent (**mubah**); actions that are objectionable but not forbidden (**makruh**), such as the eating of certain types of fish; and actions that are forbidden (**haram**), like the drinking of wine.

The **Kharijites**, **Twelver**, **Fiver Shi'ite**s, and the other **sects** differ from the orthodox interpretation. The Fivers are closest to the **Sunni**s, and the Twelvers recognize the Koran and the Sunnah of the Prophet as well as of the **imams**, whom they consider infallible. In the absence of the **Hidden Imam**, qualified scholars (**mujtahid**) continue the practice of ijtihad. *See also* ISLAMIC LAW; SHI'ISM.

SCRIPTURES. "Kitab." With the **Koran**, Muslims gained a scripture like that of the **Christians** and Jews. The Prophet announced that to him was revealed the Koran in the **Arabic** language, so that the Arabs too would have a scripture that they could understand: "We have sent it down as an Arabic Qur'an, in order that ye may learn wisdom" (12:2). The book provides verbal guidance, and the **prophets** provide practical instructions. The book is preserved on a tablet that is called the "Mother of the Book" (13:39, *Umm al-kitab*). The Koran says that **Moses** received the Torah (tawrat), David the Psalms (*zabur*), **Jesus** the Gospel (injil), and **Muhammad** the Koran—each successive book confirms the preceding ones, but the Koran is the last, free of any accretions or falsifications. *See also* KORAN.

SEAL OF THE PROPHETS, THE. Muhammad is called the "Seal of the Prophets," meaning that he is the final **prophet** and that the institution of prophesy is ended after him.

SECEDERS. *See* KHARIJITES.

SECLUSION OF WOMEN. *See* CHADOR; PURDAH; VEIL; WOMEN.

SECTS. "Mashab." According to a **hadith, Muhammad** said that there will be 73 sects in Islam, but only one will be saved. Some theologians deny that there are any sects in Islam, because all agree on the essentials. In addition to the majority of Muslims, the **Sunnis**, there are a number of sects and movements that disagree on specific details. They are the **Kharijites**, the **Shi'ites** (including the **Twelvers**, **Zaydis**, **Isma'ilis**, **Qarmatians**, Assassins, **Bohras**, and **Khojas**), and those derived from them (the **Druzes**, Nusairis, **Bahai'is**, and **Ahmadis**). There are also other small groups. The Twelvers (or **imamis**) are the largest of the Shi'ite sects.

SELJUQ DYNASTY (1038–1194). *See* SALJUQ DYNASTY.

SERMON. *See* KHUTBAH.

SEVENERS. *See* ISMA'ILIS.

SEVEN ODES. *See* MU'ALLAQAT.

SHADHILI, ABU 'L-HASAN 'ALI AL- (1196–1258). Islamic mystic born in Tunisia, who established himself in Egypt, where his devotees founded the Shadhiliyya **Sufi** fraternity. The order has many adherents in North Africa, Syria, Palestine, Iraq, and portions of southern Arabia. Shadhili died in the Egyptian desert on his way to the Holy Cities and his tomb in Humaithra is a much-venerated shrine.

SHAFI'I, MUHAMMAD IBN IDRIS AL- (767–820). Eponymous founder of the Shafi'ite school. He was born in Khurasan (Gaza?) and traveled widely in the Arab world and is buried in **Cairo**. He was the first to formulate the classical theory of the bases of **Islamic law**, the **Koran**, the Traditions (**Sunnah**), reasoning by analogy (**qiyas**), and consensus (**ijma'**), and restricted the use of informed opinion (**ra'y**). Famous members of his school include al-**Ash'ari** (d. 935), al-**Mawardi** (d. 1058), al-**Ghazali** (d. 1111), and al-**Nawawi** (d. 1277). Al-Shafi'i spent his childhood in **Mecca** and at the age of seven was able to recite the Koran by heart. He continued his **education** in **Medina** as a pupil of **Malik ibn Anas**, founder of the **Malikite** school, and reached the rank of **mufti** at the age of 15. Finally, he settled in al-Fustat (**Cairo**), where he won a large following. To-day, Shafi'ites are found predominantly in Syria, the southern part of the Arabian Peninsula, East Africa, and Southeast Asia. Shafi'i was described as

> unrivalled by his abundant merits and illustrious qualities; to the knowl-edge of all the sciences concerned with the book of **God** (the Koran), the Sunna (the Tradition), the sayings of the Companions, their history, the conflicting opinions of the learned (jurisconsults), etc., he united a deep acquaintance with the language of the Arabs of the Desert, philol-ogy, grammar, and poetry. (569) He lived without a rival, and, on his death, he left none to replace him." (Khallikan, trans. Slane, II, 570)

See also SCHOOLS OF LAW.

SHAFI'ITES. *See* SCHOOLS OF LAW; SHAFI'I, MUHAMMAD IBN IDRIS AL-.

SHAHADA. "Testimony." The profession of faith that contains the for-mula "There is no god but **Allah** and **Muhammad** is the **Messenger of Allah.**" It is the first of the **Five Pillars of Islam**. This formula (*kalima*) is part of the ritual prayer and an expression of piety. It makes a person a Muslim if he testifies to it before two witnesses. There are six conditions: it must be recited aloud; it must be perfectly understood; it must be believed in the heart; it must be professed un-til death; it must be recited correctly; and it must be professed and de-clared without hesitation. *See also* ISLAM.

SHAHID. "Witness." *See* MARTYR.

SHAHRASTANI, ABU 'L-FATH MUHAMMAD IBN 'ABD AL-KARIM (1076–1153). Muslim theologian from Shahrastan in Khurasan who specialized in the history of religion. He studied in **Baghdad** but returned to his hometown to spend the rest of his life there. A member of the **Ash'arite** school, he examined in his *Book of Religions and Sects* (*Kitab al-milal wa'l-nihal*) various Islamic and non-Islamic religions, **sects**, and philosophical currents. His work has been translated into German by T. Haarbrücker (Halle, 1850–1851). It was said of Shahrastani: "He knew by heart a great quantity of traditional information, his conversation was most agreeable, and he used to address pious exhortations to his auditors" (Khallikan, trans. Slane, II, 675).

SHAH WALI ALLAH. *See* WALI ALLAH, SHAH.

SHAJAR AL-DURR (d. 1257). "Tree of Pearls." Former **slave** and wife of the **Ayyubid** ruler Malik al-Salih (1240–1249), who adopted the title "**Sultana** of Egypt" after the death of her husband. As a sign of her authority, she had coins struck in her name. Subsequently, she married 'Izz al-Din Aybak, the commander of her Turkish bodyguard, and surrendered her title to Aybak. When Aybak took a second wife, she had him assassinated and was finally killed herself. This ended the unprecedented rule of a woman in the Islamic world.

SHA'RANI, ABD AL-WAHHAB AL- (1493–1565). Shafi'ite Islamic scholar and original thinker, who tried to find a synthesis of **Sufism** and the **shari'ah**. He studied and resided in **Cairo**, where he practiced the trade of a weaver. He was a tolerant person who pleaded for social justice and the equality of all and is said to have objected to the institution of **polygamy**. Nicholson (464) said of him he "could beat the scholastic theologians with their own weapons. Indeed, he regarded theology as the first step towards Sufism, and endeavored to show that in reality they are different aspects of the same science." He was a member of the Shadhiliyyah Sufi fraternity. *See* SHADHILI, ABU 'L-HASAN 'ALI AL-.

SHARI'AH. "The path to the water hole." *See also* ISLAMIC LAW.

SHARI'ATI, 'ALI (1933–1977). Iranian social and religious critic who provided the radical interpretation of Islam for the revolution. Born in Mazin, a village near **Mashhad**, and educated in Islamic studies in Mashhad, he worked as a teacher and in the 1950s became a political activist, supporting the Mussadeq government. Arrested and detained for a short time, he traveled to Paris and earned a doctorate in sociology from the Sorbonne in 1964. He was one of the founders of the National Front and edited its paper, *Iran Azad* (*Free Iran*). Upon his return to Iran, he was arrested. Jailed several times, he left Iran for

London, where he died under mysterious circumstances. He was a modernist **Shi'ite** reformer who criticized the **'ulama'** for "believing without thinking." He was attacked by the conservative 'ulama' as an agent of **Wahhabism**, communism, and **Christianity**. He emphasized independent reasoning and the principle of permanent revolution. He became famous as a fighter for progress and against the rule of the Iranian monarch and is credited by Iranians as the "Father of the Iranian Revolution" of 1979. He is buried in **Damascus**.

SHARIATMADARI, MUHAMMAD KAZIM (1903–1986). Senior religious leader in Iran and celebrated authority in his native Azerbaijan. Born in Tabriz of an Azari (Turkish) family, he was educated in **Najaf** and **Qom**. He was active as a religious teacher, before again moving to Qom, where he was elevated to the rank of **Ayatollah** in 1961. Although imprisoned for a short time, he remained loyal to the Pahlavi regime. After the ouster of the Shah in 1979, he joined the religio-political leadership. He differed with Ayatollah Ruhollah **Khomeyni** and the conservatives, demanding implementation of the Iranian constitution of 1906 and noninterference by the clerics in government affairs. Shariatmadari's son-in-law was accused of plotting a coup in April 1982 and of having been in contact with members of the American Central Intelligence Agency (CIA). Shariatmadari died in 1986 of natural causes.

SHARIF. "Noble." In pre-Islamic times the title of a Bedouin tribal chief. Subsequently a male descendant of the Prophet through **Fatimah** and her son, **Hasan**. The descendants of **Husayn** carry the title **Sayyid**. Sharifs (pl. *shurafa*) can be recognized by their green turbans. Since the 13th century, the position of the Grand Sharif of **Mecca** was hereditary in the **Hashimite** clan. Sharif Husayn was appointed as governor by the **Ottoman** ruler, but he led the Arab Revolt in the First World War against the Ottoman government.

SHAYKH (SHEIKH). "Old man." In pre-Islamic times the title of a Bedouin chief, who had to earn dignity through acts of bravery, generosity, and the ability to lead his tribe successfully in battle. In Islam, it was the designation for the heads of **Sufi** orders and leading Islamic scholars.

SHAYKH AL-ISLAM. Honorary title for Islamic scholars since the ninth century, and in the **Ottoman empire** the title of the Grand Mufti of **Istanbul**. He issued legal decisions (**fatwas**) testifying that the **sultan**'s laws were not in conflict with the **shari'ah** and appointed the **muftis** of the major Ottoman cities. The title was abolished in Turkey in 1924. In Iran, it was the title of a local paramount official.

SHAYKHIS (SHAYKHIYYAH). An Iranian **Shi'ite** movement founded by Ahmad al-**Ahsa'i** (1753–1826) that had syncretist features and therefore aroused the hostility of the **'ulama'**. He claimed to be the "**Bab**" (Gate) to the **Hidden Imam**. One of his successors, Sayyid Ali Muhammad, founded the **Babi sect**, an offshoot of which is the **Baha'i** religion.

SHAYTAN. *See* DEVIL; IBLIS.

SHEKH. *See* SHAYKH.

SHI'ISM (SHI'AH, SHI'ITES). "Party." The partisans of **'Ali Ibn Abi Talib**, the son-in-law and cousin of **Muhammad**, who maintain that 'Ali was the first legitimate **imam** (Khalifah), or successor, to the Prophet Muhammad. The "Party of Ali" (*shi'atu Ali*) began as an Arab political movement that was strongly supported by non-Arab converts and eventually developed into a **sect** combining many trends. They developed a doctrinal basis only gradually. The fundamental doctrine of Shi'ism is the exclusive right to the **caliphate** by members of 'Ali's family (**ahl al-bayt**), declaring the first three **Sunni caliphs** usurpers. Like the Sunnis, the Shi'ites accept the exoteric, literal interpretation of the **Koran**, but they also believe in an inner, esoteric, interpretation of a body of secret knowledge. This secret knowledge was believed to have been transmitted by Muhammad to 'Ali and his descendants. The imam has therefore also a spiritual function that exceeds that of the Sunni caliph. The imam became the only authoritative source of doctrine, which led to the eventual doctrine of the infallibility of the imam. The Divine Light, which came to the imams from **Adam** and a succession of prophets through

Muhammad, gave them a special **barakah** (blessing) and special authority. Some Shi'ites claim that the angel **Gabriel** had brought the
message wrongly to Muhammad instead of to 'Ali. The trends of le-
gitimism and esoterism merged with others and consolidated into
three major sects: the **Zaydis**, the **Isma'ilis**, and the Imamis (or
Twelvers).

The Zaydis are followers of Zayd, a grandson of **Husayn**. They are
also called the **Fivers** because Zayd was the fifth of the imams. Those
who did not accept Zayd continued to count imams until the seventh,
Isma'il, and are called Seveners, or Isma'ilis. Isma'il was appointed
by his father and later repudiated, but his followers rejected the repudiation. The Seveners eventually split into three major groups (also
called **Batinites**, because they believe in an inner, *batin*, interpretation of the Koran and the teachings of Islam): the **Fatimids** of Egypt,
the **Qarmatians** of **Basra** and Bahrain, and the Assassins of **Hasan
al-Sabbah**.

Finally there are the Imamis (also called Ja'fariyyah after the Sixth
Imam **Ja'far al-Sadiq**), who recognized **Musa al-Kazim** as the Sev-
enth Imam and continued to count 12 imams to Muhammad al-
Muntazar, who is believed not to have died when he disappeared as a
child but rather to have gone into occultation as the **Hidden Imam**.
They are the largest of all Shi'ite sects.

The Shi'ite concept of the state assigns the imam the functions of
interpreting and applying the Koranic laws. The imam is infallible
and sinless and is inspired by the Prophet or God. In the absence of
the imam, the shi'ite clergy are collectively responsible for the guidance of the community. The **mujtahid**, jurist, by virtue of his education, is entitled to make an independent effort (**itihad**) to arrive at a
decision regarding Islamic **law** and theology. The hierarchy of Islamic scholars, culminating in the **Ayatollah** al-'Uzma, permitted the
establishment of the theocratic regime in Iran founded by Ayatollah
Khomeyni.

The Shi'ite imams include the following:

1. 'Ali ibn Abi Talib (d. 661)   8. 'Ali al-Ridha (d. 818)
2. Hasan (d. 669)   7. Isma'il (d. 760)
3. Husayn (d. 680)   7. Musa al-Kazim (d. 799)

4. Ali Zayn al-Abidin (d. 712)	9. Muhammad al-Jawad (d. 835)
5. Muhammad al-Baqir (d. 731)	10. 'Ali al-Hadi (d. 868)
5. Zayd (d. 760) Imam of	11. Al-Hasan al-'Askari (d. 874)
the Zaydis	12. Muhammad al-Muntazar
6. Ja'far al-Sadiq (d. 765)	(878) Last imam of the "Twelvers."

The eponymic ancestor of the **Safavid dynasty** was Shaykh Safi al-Din, who established the Safaviyyah Sufi order at Ardabil in northwestern Iran. Shah Isma'il, the first of the Safavid rulers, imposed Shi'ism on most of Iran and started a theocracy that lasted until 1732. *See also* USULI SCHOOL; VILAYAT-I FAQIH.

SHI'ITE. *See* SHI'ISM.

SHIRK. "Association." It is a **sin** that cannot be forgiven. Islam espouses a strict monotheism that rejects "giving partners to God." The **Koran** says: "**Allah** forgiveth not (the sin of) joining other gods with Him; but he forgiveth whom He pleaseth other sins than this; one who joins other gods with Allah, hath strayed far, far away (from the right)" (4:116), and "Wonderful Originator of the heavens and the earth: How can He have a son when He hath no consort?"(6:101).

SHURAH. "Council, advice." Islamic rulers are enjoined to seek the advice of a council of experts; the Prophet himself did so, and the **Koran** says: "consult them in affairs (of moment), then, when thou hast taken a decision, put thy trust in **Allah**, for Allah loves those who put their trust (in Him)" (3:159). The shurah was started under **Caliph 'Umar** (634–644), who set up a council of six of the oldest and most respected **Companions** of the Prophet. The concept of shurah has been interpreted by Muslim modernists as a legitimization of parliamentary democracy. The term shurah is synonymous with **majlis** (tribal council), which is the term used in Iran for parliament.

SHU'UBIYYAH. A political and literary movement among the **mawla** from the 9th to 11th centuries that attacked the claimed superiority of the Arab Muslims over other races. It was especially connected with the Persian intelligentsia, who engaged in a literary feud contrasting their ancient culture with the Age of **Ignorance** of the Arabs.

SIBAWAYH, ABU BISHR AL- (d. 796). Arab philologist and grammarian, of Persian descent. For a long time, his *The Book* (*al-Kitab fi al-nahw*) was the most authoritative work on **Arabic** grammar. Sibawayh studied at **Basra** and became an outstanding member of the Basra school of grammarians. He abstracted grammatical rules from the **Koran** and Traditions, and from classical poetry and proverbs. His work left a lasting influence on Arabic linguistics. He was described as "a learned grammarian, and surpassed in this science every person of former and latter times: as for his Kitab, or Book, composed by him on that subject, it has never had its equal." Ibn Khallikan quotes Jahiz, saying "Never was the like of such a book written on grammar, and the books of other men have drawn their substance from it" (II, 396).

SIFAH (SIFAT). "Attributes." God has seven attributes, as distinct from His Essence, including: life—his existence has neither beginning nor end; knowledge—God is omniscient; power—God is almighty; will—God can do what He wants; hearing—**Allah** hears all without an ear; sight—Allah sees all things; and speech—Allah speaks to His servants like he spoke with **Moses**. This has encouraged the acceptance of a literalism and anthropomorphism in Islam. Some scholars also include **Allah**'s 99 **beautiful names** as additional attributes.

SIFFIN. A town on the right bank of the Euphrates River that became famous for the battle fought between **'Ali** and **Mu'awiyah** in July 657. After three days of fighting, Ali's forces seemed to gain the upper hand when Mu'awiyah appealed for arbitration of the dispute, culminating in the arbitration at **Adhruh**. The battle of Siffin and subsequent arbitration resulted in the creation of a new force of former supporters of 'Ali, the **Kharijites**, who now turned against him. **Caliph** 'Ali was subsequently assassinated by a Kharijite, and the schism in Islam began.

SIJISTANI, SULAYMAN ABU DAWUD AL- (817–888). Native of **Basra** and compiler of one of the six canonical collections of **Sunni**

hadith. His work, the *Book of Traditions* (*Kitab al-sunnan*), contains a collection of some 4,000 hadith, said to have been collected from a pool of 500,000. He used a measure of personal opinion (**ra'y**) in authenticating his choices. Abu Dawud said a man requires only four things for his religious conduct: deeds are to be judged by the intentions; proof of a man's sincerity in Islamism is his abstaining from what concerns him not; the **believer** is not truly a believer until he desireth for his brother that which he desireth for himself; and the lawful is clear and the unlawful is clear, but between them are things that are doubtful (Khallikan, trans. Slane, I, 590).

SILSILAH. "Chain." The line of succession in a **Sufi** order, traced to its founder or to the Prophet and his caliphs, or imams. It is the carrier of blessing (**barakah**), especially in the case of Sufi tradition. A silsilah is an unbroken tradition.

SINAN, MIMAR (1489–1588). Celebrated architect of the **Ottoman empire**, responsible for constructing or supervising 476 buildings. He has been called the greatest architect of the classical period. His greatest works are the Selimiye Mosque in Edirne, which rivaled the size of the dome of the **Aya Sofia**, and the Sulaimaniye Mosque in **Istanbul**. He was born of Christian , Greek, or Armenian background and drafted into Ottoman service through the **devshirme** process. He was recruited into the **Janissary** corps and served in a number of campaigns including the Battle of Mohacs, attaining the rank of commander. He assisted in the building of defenses and bridges and eventually became the "Architect of the Empire." He died in 1588 and is buried in a tomb just outside the walls of the Sulaimaniye Mosque.

SINF. "Guild." According to some authorities, the Muslim organization of crafts into guilds was started by the **Qarmatians**, which action then influenced the foundation of craft guilds in the rest of the Islamic world and medieval Europe.

SIN(NER). Sin is primarily disobedience to the law of God. There are two types of sin, major and minor. Disbelief and giving partners to God are great sins that cannot be forgiven and deserve eternal hellfire. The next category of great sins includes murder, **adultery**, and homosexuality. Next come theft, robbing of orphans, and receiving **interest**. A final category includes drinking wine, false accusation of unchastity, the practice of magic, and fleeing from the battlefield. A minor sin, committed intentionally, can become a major sin. Some theologians hold that a Muslim sinner will remain in hell for all eternity (**Kharijites**), but the orthodox view is that God will pardon all sins or the Prophet will intercede for the sinner. A **martyr** who dies for his faith is free of sin and goes directly to **heaven**. For **Sunnis**, only **Muhammad** is believed to be sinless, while the **Shi'ites** hold that their **imams** are impeccable.

SIQILLI, JAWHAR AL- (d. 992). "The Sicilian." **Fatimid** general who conquered Fez in 960, al-Fustat in 969, and the **Hijaz** in 976. He ruled as governor of Egypt and founded **Cairo**, where he remained until ousted by **Caliph** al-Mu'izz (952–975). He was a **Christian** slave, probably from Sicily; hence his name. Siqilli was presented to Caliph al-**Mansur** (946–952) and inherited by Caliph al-Mu'izz. The latter set him free and made him his personal secretary, then minister, and finally commander-in-chief of the army. His repeated attempts at conquering Syria failed, and he retired.

SIRHINDI, AHMAD AL-FARUQI AL- (1564–1624). A **Sufi** reformer claiming descent from **Caliph 'Umar** I, called the Renewer of the Second Millennium (Mujaddid Alf-i Thani). He was born and received his early education in Shrhind, Punjab, India. At age 28, he joined the **Naqshbandi** Sufi fraternity in Delhi. A collection of his letters details his teachings and activities. Some of his descendants carry the family name **Mujaddidi** and are active in Naqshbandi and political affaires.

SLAVERY. Slavery existed in pre-Islamic times, as elsewhere, and mainly resulted from war. Islam did not abolish it. Unlike the New World, where slaves were employed in a plantation economy to cultivate sugar, cotton, and tobacco, slaves in the Islamic world were largely employed as domestic servants and soldiers. As domestics, they became part of the family, and as soldiers they became the protectors of their masters, the **caliphs** and **sultans**. Eventually some slave forces made themselves independent and as sultans became the rulers of many parts of the Islamic world. They founded the **Mamluk** (slave) sultanates in Egypt and Syria (1250–1517) and slave dynasties in India, and they supported the **Ottoman** sultans, who were themselves the sons of slave **women**. The egalitarian **Kharijites** proclaimed that the position of caliph could be attained by anyone, even an Abyssinian slave. Islam encouraged the manumission of slaves, and **Abu Bakr**, the first caliph, is said to have spent his wealth on purchasing and freeing slaves.

Slavery in Islam was a condition from which recovery was possible. A contract (*kitaba*) enabled a slave to acquire his freedom in exchange for a future, or installment, payment. If a slave woman bore a child to a Muslim man, she could no longer be sold and was free when her master died (*Muwatta*, trans. Doi, 38.5.6). The **zakat**, the poor tax, is also to be used to purchase the freedom of slaves (9:60). Once freed, a slave enjoyed the same civil rights as a Muslim citizen. Slavery was officially abolished in the 19th and 20th centuries, and in 1962 also in Saudi Arabia. *See also* DEVSHIRME; ZANJ.

SOUL. *See* NAFS.

STATION OF ABRAHAM. "Maqam Ibrahim." A shrine near the **Ka'bah** where a stone with the footprint of Abraham is said to be kept. According to tradition, Abraham stood on this stone when he laid the foundations of the Ka'bah and left his footprint on it. The **Koran** says: "The Station of Abraham; whoever enters it attains security; **pilgrimage** thereto is a duty men owe to **Allah**" (3:97).

STONING TO DEATH. "Rajm." One of the punishments for **adultery**, not founded on the **Koran** but rather on the Traditions. The Koran says: "The woman and man guilty of adultery—flog each of them with a hundred stripes" (24:2). The severity of punishment is lessened by the condition of either a confession or four witnesses to the act. The Koran says: "And those who launch a charge against chaste women, and produce not four witnesses (to support their allegation), flog them with eighty stripes; and reject their evidence ever after: for such men are wicked transgressors" (24:4). Modern **Islamist** movements, such as the **Taliban** and al-**Qaeda**, have reintroduced stoning.

SUBHAH. *See* ROSARY.

SUBLIME PORTE. French term for the *Bab-i Ali* (High Gate), referring to the court of the Ottoman ruler. It may have denoted the gate at the tent of the ruler from which he conducted his court and subsequently have referred to the gate of the Top Kapu Serai, the Imperial palace in **Istanbul**. Later still, it referred to the executive offices of the grand vizier, and it finally became the name of the Turkish foreign ministry.

SUCCESSION TO MUHAMMAD. Schisms appeared in Islam over the question of succession to the Prophet to head the Islamic community. Muslims divided into three major groups: the **Sunnis**, **Shi'ites**, and **Kharijites**. The Sunnis held that the successor (khalifa—caliph) should be elected and, especially the Arabs, felt he must be of the **Quraysh** tribe. The Shi'ites held that he should be of the family of the Prophet, and three major subsects recognize either the Fifth (**Zayd**), the Seventh (**Isma'il**), or the Twelfth (al-Muntazar) as their **imam**. The egalitarian Kharijites would elect any pious man, "even an Abyssinian slave."

SUFI(ISM). "Tasawwuf." A member (*mutasawwif*) of one of the Sufi orders, a devotee of a mystical "path" (*tariqa*) or discipline that consists of graded esoteric teachings leading through a series of initiations to the status of an adept. The objective of the "path" is to achieve direct experiential knowledge (*ma'rifah*), which through illumination (kashf) leads to communion with God (*fana' fi llah*); it is achieved through personal devotion and a mastery of the techniques taught by the **shaykh**. The name probably comes from the **Arabic** "suf," meaning wool, the coarse wool garment worn by the early mystics. Sufism was systematically developed after the ninth century; al-Qushairy (d. 1072) was first to suggest stages of approach to the experience of God. The great Muslim philosopher al-**Ghazali** (d. 1111) succeeded in reconciling Sufism with orthodox Islam.

Sufi orders originated among the urban artisan classes that organized into brotherhoods, following a particular spiritual leader or saint (**pir**, shaykh, or **murshid**). Sufi lodges (**khanaqah**, tekke, zawiyya, ribat) were founded at the residence or tomb of a venerated pir and supported with contributions from the disciples (**murid**). Members meet regularly in homes or public places to perform remembrance (**dhikr**), pronounce ecstatic recitations of the names of **Allah**, or read passages of the **Koran**, accompanied by rhythmical breathing and physical movements; or engage in listening (**sama'**), participation in an ecstatic spiritual recital with music and dance.

Of about 200 orders, 70 are still active in the Islamic world. The line of famous mystics runs from the Persian al-**Hallaj**, executed in 922; to the pantheist Sufi Muhyi al-Din **Ibn al-Arabi** (1165 1240); to the Egyptian ibn al-Farid (1181–1235), who extolled Divine Love; to the great Persian poets of the 13th century, Sa'di, Hafiz, and **Rumi**. Famous founders of Sufi fraternities include 'Abdul Qadir al **Jilani** (1077–1166), the patron saint of the **Qadiriyyah**; Shihab al-Din al-**Suhrawardi**, of the Suhrawardiyyah; Ahmad al-**Rifa'i** (1106?–1182) of the Rifa'iyyah; Muhammad Naqshband (1317–1389) of the Naqshbaniyyah; and the eponymic ancestor of the **Safavid dynasty**, Shaykh Safi al-Din, who founded the Safaviyyah Sufi order in Ardabil in northwestern Iran. *See also* BASRI, HASAN AL-; RABI'AH AL-'ADAWIYYAH.

SUFI ORDERS

Ashraf	Nimatullahi
Azimiyya	Norbakshi
Ba'Alawiyya	Oveyssi-Shahmaghsudi
Badawlyyah	Owaisiyya
Bektashi	**Qadiriyyah**
Chishtiyya	Qadri Al-Muntahiyya
Darqawa	Qalandariyya
Galibiyya	Qarnaiyniyyah
Halvetiyya	Rifa'iyya
Hurufiyya	Safaviyeh
Idrisiyya	**Sanusiyyah**
Ismailiyya	Sarwari Qadiri
Jerrahiyya	Sarwariyya
Kibruyeh	Shadhiliyya
Mawlaviyya	**Tijaniyyah**
Nasiriyya	Zahediyehyya

SUFYAN. *See* ABU SUFYAN.

SUHRAWARDI, SHIHAB AL-DIN YAHYA (1154–1191). Muslim mystic and philosopher who traveled widely in the Middle East. His major work is *Wisdom of Illumination* (*Hikmat al-ishraq*), which combined **Shi'ite** views with the speculative philosophy of **Ibn Sina** and **Sufi** theosophy. **Ibn Khallikan** says of him:

> As-Suhrawardi was the first man of his time in the philosophical sciences, all of which he knew perfectly well. In the science of the fundamentals of jurisprudence, he stood pre-eminent; he was gifted with great acuteness of mind and the talent of expressing his thoughts with precision. His learning was greater than his judgment (IV, 154).

He was executed as a heretic in Aleppo and came to be known as "Suhrawardi the Martyr."

SUHRAWARDI, ABU HAFS UMAR (1144–1234). Eponymic founder of the Suhrawardi **Sufi** fraternity, which is represented mainly in the Indian subcontinent. He lived at the caliphal court in **Baghdad**, where he attracted a large following as Grand Master of the Sufi order. It was described as "not so much an Order as a school of mystic philosophy which has had a great influence on the teaching of many of the African Orders and fosters the growth of **fatalism** amongst them" Edward Sell, *The Religious Orders of Islam*. New York: Routledge, 2000, 46). His major work is the *awarif al-ma'arif* (divine gifts of knowledge), which is one of the most celebrated works on Sufism. **Ibn Khallikan** called him "a pious and holy **shaykh**, most assiduous in his spiritual exercises and the practice of devotion." He was born in Suhraward and died at Baghdad.

SUICIDE AND SUICIDE BOMBING. "Qatl nafsihi." Suicide is forbidden in Islam. **Allah** has bestowed upon human beings the gift of life, and humans are only his trustees of their own lives. Surah IV 29 says: "Do not kill (or destroy) yourself: for Allah hath been to you Most Merciful." Another verse says: "And make not your own hands contribute to (your) destruction" (II, 195). There are a number of

hadith that also prohibit suicide, "(indeed) whoever (intentionally) kills himself, then certainly he will be punished in the Fire of Hell, wherein he will dwell forever." (Bukhari, 5778, 1973).

However, suicide bombings have been justified with the doctrine of asymmetric warfare as a result of the imbalance of power. **Islamist** organizations see it as a form of **martyrdom** "committed out of despair against foreign occupation." The **Hamas Shaikh Ahmad Yassin** stated: "Once we have warplanes and missiles, then we can think of changing our means of legitimate self-defense. But now, we can only tackle the fire with our bare hands and sacrifice ourselves." (Quoted in Mia Bloom, *Dying to Kill: The Allure of Suicide Terror* [New York: Columbia University Press, 2005], 3–4.) *See also* REID, RICHARD; TERRORISM; ZARQAWI, ABU MUSAB AL-; ZAWAHIRI, AYMAN AL-.

SULAYMAN THE MAGNIFICENT (1494–1566). Ottoman sultan, called the "Magnificent" in Europe and "The Lawgiver" (*al-Qanuni*) by the Ottomans. During his reign, the empire reached its high point of power and success. His army captured Belgrade in 1521 and Rhodes in 1522, and defeated the Hungarians at Mohacs in 1526, taking direct control of the country in 1541. Vienna was able to withstand a siege in 1529. His navy successfully fought the Portuguese, British, and Dutch fleets in the Indian Ocean and the "Holy League" in the Mediterranean. He concluded a trade agreement with King Francis of France (r. 1515–1547), which granted the French considerable trade privileges. The "**capitulations,**" granted at a time of Ottoman power, were to weaken the state in subsequent centuries and permitted virtually unlimited European economic penetration. After Sulayman, the empire suffered a gradual decline, but it continued to exist until its defeat in the First World War.

SULTAN. "Power." Title, indicating de facto power, but eventually an independent king. The title was first assumed by Mahmud of Ghazna (r. 998–1030), but it was struck on coins for the first time by the **Saljuq** Toghrul Bey (d. 1063) at a time when the **caliphate** was in decline. The position of sultanate was legitimized as the "pious sultanate," in which the sultan was to perform all the functions the caliph no longer could. For a time, the fiction of caliphal supremacy was maintained, but eventually sultans became independent kings. The **Ottoman** sultanate was abolished in 1922.

SULTAN-GALIEV, MIRZA (d. 1939). A Tatar communist who cooperated with Joseph Stalin on the "nationalities question." He advocated the formation of a "Colonial International" to replace the Comintern. His call for a "dictatorship of the colonial nations over the metropolis," was not shared by Joseph Stalin, who had Sultan-Galiev killed in 1939.

SUNNAH (SUNNAN). "Path, way, custom." The customary way of life of the ancient Arabs. In Islam, the Sunnah comprises the Prophet's example: what he said, what he did, and what he approved or disapproved. In addition to the **Koran**, the Sunnah provides guidance in personal behavior as well as in matters of **Islamic law (shari'ah)** where it forms, together with the Koran, reasoning by analogy (**qiyas**) and the consensus of the scholars (**ijma'**), the bases **Islamic Law**. Matters not clearly stipulated in the Koran are supplemented by the "model behavior" of the Prophet, on the assumption that he led an exemplary life. The Koran says: "Ye have indeed in the **Messenger** of **Allah** an excellent exemplar" (33:21). **Hadith** is the story of a particular occurrence, and **Sunnah** is the rule of law deduced from it. Eventually, even the examples of the Prophet's **Companions** and their successors were taken as worthy of emulation. **Shi'ites** also follow the Sunnah of the infallible **imams**.

SUNNI (SUNNITES). The Sunnis are called the "people of custom and community" (*ahl al-sunnah wa 'l-jama'a*) or "orthodox" Muslims, who comprise about 80 percent of the Muslim population. They recognize the first four **caliphs** as rightful successors to the Prophet **Muhammad** and accept the legitimacy of the **Umayyad** and **'Abbasid caliphates**. They are divided into four **schools of law**: the Hanafi, **Maliki, Shafi'i**, and the Hanbali schools, the Hanafi being the largest and the Hanbali school the most restricted in its interpretation of the **Koran** and the **Sunnah**. Much of what has been described in this work is part of the Sunni tradition.

SURAH. A chapter in the **Koran**. There are 114 chapters, arranged roughly according to length, beginning with the longest, except for the **Fatiha**, "Opener," which is a short one. Each Surah has a special title and all, except the ninth, begin with the **Basmalah** formula.

SUYUTI, JALAL AL-DIN AL- (1445–1505). Scholar of Persian origin who flourished in **Cairo**. A prolific writer with some 500 publications (some only short pamphlets) to his name, including a history of Cairo, a history of the **caliphs**, and a commentary on the **Koran**. His major work is *The Flowering (al-Muzhir)*, in which he examines **Arabic** dialects and philology. He favored magical practices in medicine and rejected philosophy and logic. Suyuti knew the Koran by heart when he was eight years old. He traveled widely, but his vanity and arrogance frequently got him into trouble. He said about himself: "When I made the **pilgrimage**, I drank of the water of the well Zemzem with various intentions: among others that I should arrive in jurisprudence to the eminence of Shaykh Sirajuddin al-Bulqini, and in **Tradition** to the distinction of the Hafiz Ibn Hajr" and he left no doubt that he surpassed his teachers in erudition (*History of the Caliphs*, viii).

– T –

TABARI, MUHAMMAD IBN JARIR AL- (839–923). Islamic scholar from Tabaristan, in present-day Iran, whose *Annals of Prophets and Kings (Tarikh al-rusul wa'l-muluk)* is a history of the world from its creation to the 10th century. It is the first history of the world in **Arabic** and an important source for the early history of the **caliphate**. He also produced a 30-volume commentary (**tafsir**) on the **Koran**. The *Annals* have been translated into English, German, and French. Tabari is said to have memorized the Koran at age seven. He traveled widely and studied with famous scholars, including **Ibn Hanbal**, before he settled down in **Baghdad** as a teacher of Traditions (**Sunnah**) and jurisprudence (**fiqh**). Tabari refused to accept an appointment as **judge** to dedicate all his time to his research. **Ibn Khallikan** praised him as a jurisconsult of the **sect** of **al-Shafi'i**, . . . a high and sure authority as a doctor, veracious, learned, versed in dogmas and secondary points of the law, exact in his researches on the principles of Jurisprudence, conscientious, virtuous, and holy in his conduct.

However, he was not impressed by his poetry, saying that Tabari "composed poetry as good as might be expected from a jurisconsult" (II, 597). Tabari died at Baghdad in 923.

TABI'UN. "Successors." A class of people who had been in personal contact with **Companions** of the Prophet. They were important transmitters of Traditions, as were the *tabi'un al-tabi'in*, the next generation of "successors of the successors."

TAFSIR. "Explanation." Commentary on the **Koran**, a branch of Islamic theological science. *See also* EXEGESIS OF THE KORAN; TA'WIL.

TAGHRI BIRDI, ABU AL-MAHASIN AL- (1411–1469). Egyptian historian who wrote a history of Egypt from the Muslim conquest to his time, entitled *The Brilliant Stars Regarding the Kings of Egypt and Cairo (al-Nujum al-zahirah fi muluk misr wa 'l-qahirah)*. It is an important source on the history of the Bahri **Mamluk sultanate** (1250–1390).

TAHA HUSAIN. *See* HUSAIN, TAHA.

TAHAWI, AHMAD IBN MUHAMMAD (853–935). Hanafi scholar of **hadith** and most knowledgeable **fiqh** scholar in Egypt. He was described as "reliable, trustworthy, a faqih, intelligent, the likes of whom did not come afterward." His *Ma'ani al-athar* and *mushkel al-athar* clarified conflicting hadith. He was born in Taha and died in Egypt.

TAHIRID DYNASTY (822–873). First quasi-independent state, named after Tahir ibn Husayn (775–822), who helped al-**Ma'mun** win his struggle for the **caliphate** against his brother, al-**Amin**. For his help, Tahir was appointed governor of Khurasan and the Islamic east, and he made Nishapur his capital. Toward the end of his life,

Tahir made himself independent, having the **khutbah** read in his name, but his descendants continued to pay tribute to the **caliph** at **Baghdad**. Tahir was the descendant of a Persian slave, who made his fame as a military commander, nicknamed "The Ambidextrous" (*Dhu al-yaminayn*) because he could yield a sword effectively with either hand. During their short rule, the Tahirids provided a period of prosperity in Khurasan, until they were succeeded by the Saffarids.

TAHTAWI, RIFA'A RAFI' AL- (1801–1873). Egyptian modernist and reformer, born in Tahta, Upper Egypt, and educated at Al-**Azhar**. He was sent to accompany the first mission of Egyptian students to France and took advantage of the opportunity to study the French language, literature, and political philosophy. He was impressed by what he saw: the orderly life of the people, their social morality and seeming love of work, their intellectual curiosity and patriotism, and their democratic spirit. Upon his return he worked as a translator, and in 1836 he founded the School of Translation. In his writings, he advocated educational reforms, modern development, and parliamentary democracy. He wanted **education** for the people as well as the rulers and called for reform of the ornate and obfuscating style of **Arabic**. He was forced into exile for a number of years (1851–1854), but upon his return he resumed his cultural mission.

TAIMIYYAH. *See* IBN TAIMIYYAH, AHMAD.

TAKBIR. The *takbir* consists in saying "God is Most Great" (*Allahu Akbar*). It is part of the canonic prayers and a pious exclamation.

TAKFIR. *See* EXCOMMUNICATION.

TAKFIR WA AL-HIJRAH, JAMA'AT AL-. "Excommunication and exile." The name given to a radical **Islamist** group in Egypt led by Shukri Ahmad Mustafa (b. 1942), who was executed in 1978. He taught that only members of his movement, founded in 1972, were true Muslims, and that **Islamic law**, as compiled by the jurists of the traditional schools, was man-made and therefore to be rejected. He denied the legitimacy of Muslim rulers and wanted to establish an Islamic state ruled by a pious **amir**. The group was involved in the "bread riots" in 1977, attacking night clubs and bars in **Cairo**. They kidnaped Shaykh Muhammad Husayn al-Dhahabi of Al-**Azhar** University and killed him. The government reacted with mass arrests and tried some 465 members in military courts, executing five members, including Shukri. *See also* EXCOMMUNICATION.

TALAQ. "Repudiation, **divorce**." Originally it meant "unshackling" an animal, but the term came to mean the repudiation of a wife by a man. To divorce his wife, a man has to say "I divorce thee" three times in succession in front of witnesses. In many Muslim countries, this traditional process is no longer practiced and in some, such as Turkey, Western procedures have been adopted.

TALHAH IBN 'UBAYDULLAH (596–656). Member of the **Quraysh** and **Companion** of the Prophet, he fought in succession for all of the first four **caliphs**. He was a cousin and son-in-law of **Abu Bakr**. He joined the war against '**Ali** and was killed in the Battle of the **Camel** in 656. He was buried in **Basra**. Talha was one of 10 men promised paradise by the Prophet.

TALIBAN. A neofundamentalist movement recruited from students (*talib*, pl. *tullab*, or *taliban*) of **mosque** schools and **madrasahs**, who were organized into a military force and captured most of **Afghanistan**. The movement was headed by Maulawi **Muhammad 'Umar** (Omar), who was proclaimed Commander of the **Believers** (*amir al-mu'minin*) and set up a theocratic government with himself as the head. After the capture of Kabul, the capital of Afghanistan, the movement decreed that **women** be restricted to the home, men wear long **beards**, and both discard Western dress. The Taliban brought peace to about 85 percent of the country during their four-year rule. But they closed girls' schools and prohibited women, who had been active in the professions, the bureaucracy, business, etc., from pursuing their chosen careers. The Taliban started to enforce Islamic punishments, including the cutting off of a hand or a foot for theft and stoning for **adultery**. In the countryside, their policies caused little change. But in Kabul, a modern city with a population of a million and a half, these changes had a profound impact. The Taliban government was recognized only by **Pakistan**, the United Arab Emirates, and Saudi Arabia. Western recognition was not forthcoming in view of the discrimination against women, and the fact that Afghanistan had become a major producer of opium and its derivatives. Their collaboration with Osama bin **Laden** and the attack on the New York World Trade Center led to American retaliation and the destruction of the Taliban regime. *See also* DEOBAND; TORA BORA, BATTLE OF.

TAMERLANE. *See* TIMUR-I LANG.

TAQIYYAH. *See* CONCEALMENT

TAQLID. "Imitation." The obligation in **Sunni** Islam to imitate, or emulate, the law as frozen by the four orthodox **schools of law** that agreed to close the "gate of **ijtihad**" in the ninth century. Henceforth innovation (**bid'ah**) was forbidden. Various modernist and radical movements reject taqlid. **Shi'ites** accept the taqlid of their **mujtahids**.

TARAFA, IBN AL-ABD BIN SUFYA (d. 569). One of the seven **Mu'allaqat** poets of the tribe of the Bakr who spent his youth in Bahrain and, expelled from his home like "a mangy camel," went to the court of the king of Hira, Amr ibn Hind (d. 568). He was well received, but aroused the king's displeasure when he composed a satire on him and his brother. The king permitted him to return to Bahrain, but gave him a letter for the governor of the city. Despite his suspicions, he did not open the letter that carried his death sentence. Thus he "dug his grave with his tongue."

TARIQ, ZIYAD IBN (670–720). Berber commander of a force under **Musa ibn Nusayr** (640–715) that crossed from Ceuta into Spain in 711. Out on a mission of reconnaissance, he found little resistance and opened Spain to Muslim conquest, defeating the Visigothic King Roderic at the battle of Wadi Bakka. Tariq encouraged his troops, saying: "My men! Whither can you fly? [flee] The sea is behind you and the enemy before you; nothing can save you but the help of God, your bravery and your steadiness. Be it known to you that you are here as badly off as orphans at a miser's table. The foe is coming against you with his troops, his arms and all his forces; you have nothing to rely on but your swords, no food to eat except what you may snatch from the hands of the enemy" (Khalikan, III, 477). Gibraltar got its name from him, "Mountain of Tariq" (*Jabal al-Tariq*).

TARIQA. "Path." *See* SUFISM.

TASAWWUF. *See* SUFISM.

TAWBAH. "Repentance." First station of the **Sufi** path. *See also* REPENTANCE.

TAWHID (TAUHID). The doctrine of the unity of God, a strict monotheism; to give partners to God is an unforgivable sin. The **Koran** says: "Say: He is **Allah**, the One; Allah, the Eternal, the Absolute; he begetteth not, nor is He begotten; and there is none like unto Him" (112:1–4).

TA'WIL. "Interpretation." The science of interpreting the **Koran** and its complement, commentary (**tafsir**), begun by 'Abdallah ibn al-'Abbas in the late seventh century. Ta'wil is an allegorical interpretation practiced mainly by **Shi'ites**, especially **Isma'ilis** and mystics, whereas tafsir focuses on the exoteric, literal meaning of the Koran. Some Islamic scholars claim that everything, including the modern sciences, can be found in the Koran; they base this on a verse in the Koran that says: "Nothing have We omitted from the Book" (6:38).

TAXATION. There are three types of taxes in Islam: the poor tax (**zakat**), the poll tax (**jizyah**), and the land tax (**kharaj**). A kind of tithe (**'ushr**) eventually also became a land tax. Zakat is a transfer payment to help the poor and amounts in some countries to from 2.5 to 10 percent of liquid assets, or 5 to 10 percent on agricultural products. It is a wealth, rather than an income, tax. The jizyah, or poll tax, was levied on non-Muslim men, who did not pay the zakat and did not serve in the armed forces. **Women**, children, the elderly, beggars, monks, and **slaves** were exempt.

The kharaj was originally levied on non-Muslims, but after the eighth century also on Muslims. It was paid largely in kind. In many parts of the Islamic world, a military feudal system was set up in which land taxes were levied by officers or government officials to compensate them for their administrative or military duties, or by local notables contracted as tax farmers in exchange for a percentage of the income from land. In most countries, the jizyah has been abolished and the Islamic taxes replaced by an income tax, with the zakat levied independently by the **'ulama'**. In oil-rich countries, such as Saudi Arabia, the government levies only the zakat. **Shi'ites** reject the legitimacy of kharaj and 'ushr because they were introduced by **'Umar ibn al-Khattab** and are not mentioned in the **Koran**, but they accept a **khums**. They also consider zakat a charity rather than a religious tax. *See* KHUMS.

TAYAMMUM. Symbolic purification by sand or stone, where there is no water to perform the ritual **ablutions** of **wudhu** and **ghusl**. If water is available, but barely enough for drinking, or because of illness of a person or fear of contracting a disease, tayammum is permissible. The practice goes back to a **hadith**, which relates that the Prophet "struck his hand on earth once, then he shook off its dust and wiped with it the back of the (right) hand with the left or the back of the left with the (right) hand, then wiped his face with both hands" (Bukhari, 1951, 7:8).

TA'ZIR. Discretionary punishments for offenses that are not specified in the **Koran** or Traditions. Ta'zir permits the **judge** considerable discretion in a wide range of punishments, including admonition, reprimand, threat, boycott, public disclosure, fines, imprisonment, and flogging. It is usually imposed for less serious offenses and differs from the **hadd** offenses, for which punishment is prescribed in the Koran or Traditions. In exceptional cases, the death penalty has been allowed as a ta'zir punishment.

TA'ZIYAH. "Consolation." **Shi'ite** passion plays in remembrance of the martyrdom of Imam **Husayn** at **Karbala** in 680. They are performed on the 10th of **Muharram** in public places. The Ta'ziyah is perhaps the earliest serious drama developed in the Islamic world. *See also* 'ASHURA.

TEKKE. Turkish term for **Sufi** retreat. *See also* KHANAQAH.

TENTH OF MUHARRAM. *See* 'ASHURA; MUHARRAM.

TERRORISM. There seems to be no commonly agreed definition. President Ronald Reagan's "freedom fighters" in Afghanistan quickly became terrorists when they continued their **jihad** after the fall of the communist regime. One definition states:

> Criminal acts intended or calculated to provoke a state of terror in the general public, a group of persons or particular persons for political purposes are in any circumstances unjustifiable, whatever the considerations of a political, philosophical, ideological, racial, ethnic, religious or other nature that may be invoked to justify them. UN Resolution language. (1999)

A more concise definition calls terrorism a

> deliberate use of violence against noncombatants for political ends. Perpetrators can be states, agents of states, or individuals or groups acting independently or in cells. [It] does not apply to all acts of politically inspired violence. (*The Oxford Dictionary of Islam*, ed. John Esposito)

In other words, the criterion of a terrorist act is violence against the civilian population. In practice, much guerrilla activity also harmed noncombatants, as did counterinsurgency measures by the state and its allies. In the war against communism in **Afghanistan** and the subsequent civil war, combatants did not respect the laws of war as defined by the Geneva Conventions.

As a result of the attacks of 11 September 2001, President George W. Bush issued a declaration of war, stating that the United States would carry out strikes against al-**Qaeda** terrorist training camps and military installations of the Taliban regime in Afghanistan. Operation Enduring Freedom began with aerial bombardments on 7 October 2001, and by the end of December the Taliban regime had been destroyed. Far-reaching changes have been introduced in American society to forestall future terrorist attacks on the United States. *See* *also* INTERNATIONAL COALITION AGAINST "TERROR"; SUICIDE AND SUICIDE BOMBING.

TESTIMONY OF FAITH. *See* SHAHADA.

THABIT IBN QURRA (836–901). Mathematician, astronomer, philosopher, and member of the **Baghdad** school of scholars, who translated and revised important Greek works, which were thus preserved and later translated from **Arabic** into Latin. Thabit was born in Harran (in present-day Turkey) of a Sabian (non-Muslim) family. He was said to have been a money changer in his youth, but then came to Baghdad to study and later became the court astronomer of **Caliph** al-Mu'tadid.

THEOLOGY. *See* KALAM.

TIJANIYYAH. Sufi order founded in the 19th century by Ahmad ibn Muhammad al-Tijani (1737–1815) in Fez, in present-day Morocco. It gained considerable support in North Africa at the expense of the **Qadiriyyah** Sufi order. It was criticized for its political activities, especially its cooperation with the French. The members of the order believe that their chain of blessing (**silsilah**) led directly to Tijani from the Prophet **Muhammad.**

TIMUR-I LANG (TAMERLANE, 1336–1405). The "Lame Timur" was a military genius and the last of the great nomadic conquerors. He was born of humble origins in Kesh, a town near Samarkand in present-day Uzbekistan. He claimed descent from the family of Genghis Khan, but his real link to the family was his **marriage** to a **Mongol** noblewoman. He carried a number of titles, but only in 1388 did he call himself **sultan.** He was called the Lame Timur because he was disabled on the right hand and foot, an infirmity he suffered in war, or according to some sources, while stealing sheep. In 1941, Soviet scholars opened his tomb and found a skeleton, which they identified as his. Timur claimed to wage **jihad,** but in fact he fought primarily against Muslim states. His wars did not follow a general strategy of conquest. He moved from the Volga to the Ganges in India and from Mongolia to Syria. He defeated his opponents wherever he went, but he could not establish lasting rule over these areas. He was the most destructive of nomadic invaders, using terror as a tactical weapon. Timur sacked and destroyed Delhi, **Damascus**, **Baghdad**, Isfahan, Herat, and many other Islamic cities. He weakened the power of the Golden Horde in Russia, defeated the **Ottomans** at the battle of Ankara in 1404, and weakened the power of Muslim rulers in China and India. Timur built towers of skulls of the people he slaughtered and, while he destroyed many centers of Islamic civilization, he created his own cultural center in Samarkand. He seemed to be content with booty. Only in India did the house of Timur continue with the establishment of the Moghul (Mughal) dynasty in 1524.

TIRMIDHI, ABU JA'FAR (TIRMIZI, 816–907). A **Shafi'ite** jurist, "the ablest of them all in that age, the most devout and the most abstemious." When asked to comment on the Prophet's saying that "God descended to the heaven of the world" (i.e., the lowest of seven heavens) and that "what could be more exalting than the lowest heaven?" Tirmidhi replied: "The descent is intelligible; the manner how is unknown; the belief therein is obligatory, and the asking about it is a blamable innovation" (Khallikan, trans. Slane, II, 601).

TIRMIDHI, MUHAMMAD IBN 'ISA AL- (TIRMIZI, 825–892). Islamic **hadith** scholar who compiled the *Collection of Tirmidhi* (*Jami' al-tirmidhi*), one of the six canonical collections of Traditions in which he examined the differences among the **schools of law**. He was born and died in the village of Bugh near Tirmidh, Transcaspia. He was a pupil of al-**Bukhari** and, although blind, he was one of the great Traditionists.

TIRMIZI. *See* TIRMIDHI, MUHAMMAD IBN 'ISA AL-.

TOMBS. Monuments and tombs of saints and rulers exist in most parts of the Islamic world; they are forbidden by the Hanbali **school of law**. During their conquests in Arabia, the **Wahhabis** destroyed gravestones and monuments but spared the tomb of the Prophet. They also sacked the holy places of the **Shi'ites** at **Najaf** and **Karbala** in 1802.

TORA BORA, BATTLE OF. A campaign to destroy al-**Qaeda** and **Taliban** forces and capture Osama bin **Laden**, who controlled a complex of cave fortifications near the village of Tora, about 35 miles south of Jalalabad, near the **Pakistan** border. After the capture of Kandahar by U.S. and allied forces on 11 December 2001, U.S. Special Forces, supported by Hazrat Ali and Haji Zaman and their Pashai and Khugiani tribal contingents, moved east to trap the enemy, ensconced in the Tora Bora mountain range. Pakistani forces sealed the border. U.S. ground soldiers operated as spotters for B-52 sorties coming in at 20-minute intervals. Allied tribal forces did much of the fighting. The enemy, estimated at 1,500 Arab and Chechnyan fighters, proved to be fierce opponents, holding out until 16 December, when some 21 al-Qaeda fighters were taken prisoner, an unknown number were killed, and most managed to escape. Osama bin Laden was last seen in the final days of November 2001, when he made preparations to flee to the autonomous tribal area on the Pakistani side of the border. Although the American allies fought bravely, they may have permitted the enemy to escape. *See also* TORA BORA, CAVE FORTIFICATIONS; ZAWAHIRI, AYMAN AL-.

TORA BORA, CAVE FORTIFICATIONS. Caves in many parts of **Afghanistan** served to shelter the **mujahidin** in their war against the communist forces. They stored weapons, food, and the necessities of life in these caves, some of which, near the **Pakistan** border, were excavated to hold as many as 1,000 fighters. One such complex of caves at Tora Bora was carved 1,150 feet into a 13,000-foot mountain and was said to have served as Osama bin **Laden**'s headquarters. Mountain streams generated hydroelectric power, and a complex system of ventilation brought air into the caves. A main entrance led through a 50–foot tunnel, wide enough to permit vehicles to enter. Staircases connected to offices, dormitories, and communal rooms. Weapons were stored in armories. The complex was not visible from the air, and exits were closed with steel doors or hidden behind mud walls. Some exits were booby-trapped. According to one report, American bombing closed the main entrance, but another bomb opened it again. If it had not been for the American intervention, no Afghan rival could have defeated the **Taliban** and their **al-Qaeda** allies. *See also* TORA BORA, BATTLE OF.

TRADITIONS. *See* HADITH; SUNNAH.

TRENCH, BATTLE OF THE. "Khandaq." The battle between the forces of the Muslim community in **Medina** and the **Meccans** in 627. A Meccan army of some 10,000 men faced a Muslim force of about 3,000, and the Muslims were saved when, at the suggestion of a Persian convert, **Salman**, they built a defensive trench. After two weeks of desultory, long-distance fighting, a heavy storm blew away some of the Meccans' tents and disunity started, forcing the Meccans to lift the siege. This was the last encounter with the Meccans, and only 10 people were killed on both sides. The event caused a boost in the morale of the Muslim community and a loss of prestige for the Meccans. The last of the Jewish tribes of Medina, the Banu **Qurayzah**, was annihilated, having been accused of collaboration with the **Meccans**.

TULUNID DYNASTY (868–905). A dynasty founded by a deputy of the **'Abbasid caliphate** in Egypt, named Ahmad ibn Tulun (868–884), a Turkish slave from Bukhara. He had distinguished himself as a military commander while fighting the Byzantines, and became the **caliph**'s bodyguard. Once appointed deputy governor in Egypt, he remained in de facto control. His state's wealth was based on its agriculture and a flourishing textile industry. Ibn-Tulun established his capital at al-Qata'i (now **Cairo**), where he built the famed Tulunid **mosque**. When the 'Abbasid caliph tried to dislodge him, Ibn Tulun had the **khutbah** read in his name as a sign of his independence. When Ahmad died in 884, he was succeeded by his son Khumrawayh (884–895), who was able to add Syria to his possessions. Having been unable to oust him, the Caliph al-Mu'tadid (892–902) gave Khumrawayh his daughter in **marriage**. The latter displayed such prodigality on the occasion of his marriage that the state was seriously weakened, and it was finally recaptured by the forces of Caliph al-Muktafi in 905. The Tulunid example of the sudden rise of a **slave** to political power and the tendency of governors to make themselves independent was to become common in the Islamic world.

Ahmad ibn Tulun was described "a generous prince, just, brave, and pious; an able ruler, an unerring physiognomist; he directed in person all public affairs, repeopled the provinces, and inquired diligently into the condition of his subjects; he liked men of learning, and kept every day an open table for his friends and the public" (Khallikan, trans. Slane, I, 154).

TURABI, HASAN (b. 1932). Sudanese lawyer and politician who was instrumental in institutionalizing **shari'ah** law. Born in 1932 in Kassala, eastern Sudan, he studied law at the universities of Khartum (1951–1955), London (1955–1957), and the Sorbonne and obtained a Ph.D. in law from the Sorbonne in 1964. Upon his return to Sudan, he formed the Front for Islamic Constitution (FIC) and acted as its secretary general until 1969. Jailed for six years in 1969, and, after three years in exile, he joined the Numeiri government and was appointed attorney general (1977–1983). He demanded the introduction of Islamic law in 1983. Imprisoned briefly in 1985 and again in 1989, and after the overthrow of the Numeiri regime, Turabi founded the National Islamic Front, which came third in the national elections.

After the military coup of General Bashir in June 1989, the new military government implemented many of Turabi's ideas. He invited Osama bin **Laden** to Sudan in 1991 and supported his operations until 1996, when the al-**Qaeda** leader left for **Afghanistan**. In March 2004, the Bashir government accused Turabi of planning a coup and jailed him and some of his followers until June 2005. Turabi has inspired **Islamist** revivalists in other Muslim countries and was accused of assisting the group that attempted to assassinate Egyptian President Husni Mubarak in June 1995. His most important publication is *The Renewal of Islamic Thought* (*Tajdid al-fikr al-islami*).

TURBAN. A headdress consisting of a long piece of fabric, usually wound around a skullcap. It has existed since pre-Islamic times. The color, size, and shape of a turban usually indicated the ethnic, sectarian, or tribal identity of a person. Rulers would bestow turbans as an honor for distinguished service. In the 19th century, the Kufiyyah of the Arabs came into use, and the fez was worn by administrative and military officials. In some parts of the Middle East, fur caps came to be used. As a sign of Islamist revival, government officials in Afghanistan were ordered to wear a turban, rather than the previous choices of headgear.

TUSI, MUHAMMAD IBN AL-HASAN AL- (995–1067). Shi'ite theologian and compiler of one of the four canonical works on Traditions of the Prophet, the Istibsar. His works also include the 20-volume *The Catalogue* (*Fihrist*), which comprised all treatises on Shi'ite subjects published up to his time. He was born in Tus, Iran, but he spent most of his life in **Baghdad**. He finally left for **Najaf**, a center of Shi'ite learning, to escape from **Sunni** persecution.

TUSI, NASIR AL-DIN AL- (1201–1274). Shi'ite scholar, philosopher, astronomer, and mathematician born in Tus, Iran. He was probably an **Isma'ili**, who collaborated with the **Mongols** and entered the services of **Hulagu** Khan, founder of the Ilkhanid dynasty (1256–1353). Tusi made original contributions to the fields of mathematics and astronomy. Hulagu built an observatory and library for him at Maragha, where he compiled his astronomical tables (*al-Zij al-il-khani*) showing the planetary movements. Another of his many publications was a treatise on Shi'ite dogmatics.

TWELVER SHI'ITES. Also called Imamis, or Ja'faris, and in **Arabic** *Ithna 'Ashariyyah*; they recognize the twelfth as the last **imam** in descent from **'Ali**, the cousin and son-in-law of the Prophet **Muhammad**. *See also* SHI'ISM.

– U –

'UBAYDAH, IBN AL-JARRAH ABU (d. 639). **Companion** of the Prophet and important commander from **Mecca**. He participated in many battles and saved **Muhammad**'s life when the Prophet was wounded in the Battle of **Uhud** in 625. He participated in the election of the first **caliph**, **Abu Bakr** (r. 632–634), and was appointed commander-in-chief in Syria and governor of **Damascus** by Caliph **'Umar I** (r. 634–644). His tomb in Damascus is a much-venerated shrine.

'UBAYDAH, MA'MAR IBN AL-MUTHANNA ABU (728–825). Arab philologist and historian, who represented the **Basra** school of grammarians and was a proponent of the anti-Arab *Shu'ubiyyah* movement. Because of his extraordinary learning, he was summoned to the court of **Caliph Harun al-Rashid** (786–809), where he is said to have earned the animosity of many courtiers. Abu 'Ubaydah is said to have been of Judeo–Persian origin and is credited with some hundred publications, only a few of which are extant. Al-Jahiz said of him: "There was never on earth a **Kharijite** or an orthodox believer more learned in all the sciences than he." But **Ibn Khallikan** quotes Ibn Qutaybah as saying:

> The unusual expressions (of the **Arabic** language), the history of the (ancient) Arabs and their conflicts, were his dominant study; yet, with all his learning, he was not always able to recite a verse without mangling it; even in reading the **Koran**, with the book before his eyes, he made mistakes. (III, 388–389)

UBAYDULLAH IBN ZIYAD (648–686). Son of **Ziyad ibn Abihi**, appointed by the **Umayyad caliph** governor of Khurasan and subsequently of Iraq. He successfully fought **Kharijite** and **Shi'ite** revolts. His army, under Sa'd ibn abi **Waqqas**, was responsible for the massacre of **Husayn** and his forces at **Karbala** in 680.

UHUD, BATTLE OF. On 21 March 625, a year after their defeat at the Battle of **Badr**, the **Mecca**ns again manned an expedition against the Muslim community in **Medina**. This time they collected a force of some 3,000 men, headed by **Abu Sufyan**, with 3,000 camels and 200 horses. They engaged **Muhammad**'s force of some 700 men and defeated the Muslims. **Khalid ibn al-Walid**, then fighting on the side of the Meccans, was one of the decisive officers. Muhammad blamed the defeat of his men on their lack of devotion and called it God's trial of the sincerity of the faith of the Muslims. Although suffering great losses, and the Prophet himself being wounded, the Muslim community was able to recover from this defeat. Muhammad accused the Jewish tribe, Banu **Nadir**, of collaborating with the enemy, and expelled them from the **Hijaz**.

'UKAZ. A town in the **Hijaz** near **Mecca** that was the most important fair ground of pre-Islamic Arabia. It was a place of **pilgrimage** and a cultural center, where Bedouin poets would compete for prizes. The *Seven Odes* (**Mu'allaqat**) were suspended there and at the **Ka'bah** as prizewinning samples of Bedouin poetry. Annual fairs and periods of peace during three months made it possible for tribesmen to congregate. During this time, Meccan caravans could travel unmolested.

'ULAMA'. A collective term for the doctors of Islamic sciences. An 'alim (pl. 'ulama') is "one who possesses the quality of 'ilm, knowledge, or learning, of the Islamic traditions and the resultant canon law and theology." An 'alim is the product of a religious institution of higher **education** (**madrasah**). He is educated to be a religious functionary, for example, a **judge** (kadhi) who gives legal decisions in accordance with the **shari'ah**, a preacher (**khatib**) who reads the **Friday** sermon, a jurist (**faqih**), or a canon lawyer (**mufti**), who gives a formal opinion (**fatwa**) about the legality of a case. Often described as the Islamic "clergy," the 'ulama' is not tightly organized. It requires no ordination or hierarchy of authority, although in the **Ottoman empire** the **Shaykh al-Islam** was the grand mufti of **Istanbul** and appointed all muftis in the major cities. After independence, chief muftis were established in major cities, but the decision of one mufti is not necessarily binding on others. Only in **Twelver Shi'ism** has there been a development toward a centralized church, with the victory of the **Usuli** branch of jurisprudence. *See* SHI'ISM.

'UMAR, ABD AL-RAHMAN. *See* ABD AL-RAHMAN, 'UMAR.

'UMAR IBN 'ABD AL-AZIZ (OMAR II, 682–720). The eighth **Umayyad caliph** (r. 717–720), who solved the second-class status of the newly converted (**mawla**), giving them equality with Arab Muslims in matters of **taxation** and pensions if they had fought in the early conquests. He gave **Peoples of the Book**, the protected subjects (dhimmis), freedom of religion, but limited their religious observances to the privacy of their homes. Crosses could not be worn in public, and bells could not be sounded; they had to pay a poll tax (**jizyah**), but they did not have to serve in the military.

'Umar discontinued the practice of cursing **'Ali** at **Friday prayers**. The system introduced at this time was the model for subsequent Muslim states and extended throughout the **Ottoman empire** (1281–1924), where the **millets** (ethnic-sectarian) groups enjoyed cultural and juridical autonomy. With the emergence of nation-states, the poll tax and other limitations began to disappear. Although Abbasid historians did not give the Umayyads a good press, they did respect Umar II as a pious and just caliph.

UMAR BAKRI MUHAMMAD. London-based spiritual leader and founder of the radical al-Muhajirun (later disbanded), who caused considerable outrage by praising al-**Qaeda** and calling the **terrorist** acts "retaliation for British and American atrocities in Iraq." The Syrian-born cleric went to Great Britain in 1985 after being deported from Saudi Arabia. He founded Al-Muhajirun in 1996 and led a number of demonstrations, including one outside the U.S. embassy, protesting the desecration of the **Koran**. He left Britain for a visit to Lebanon and was told that he could not return. Arrested in Lebanon, he was freed because it appeared "that he had not committed any crime."

'UMAR IBN AL-KHATTAB (OMAR I, 585–644). One of the early **Companions** of the Prophet, who converted to Islam in 617 and became the second **caliph** in 634, after the death of **Abu Bakr**. He was a close adviser to the Prophet and gave him his daughter, **Hafsah**, in **marriage**. After the Prophet's death, 'Umar offered his allegiance to Abu Bakr and thus facilitated the election of the first **Sunni** caliph. 'Umar took the title "Prince of **Believers**" (*amir al-mu'minin*), and during his short period as caliph, the Muslim armies conquered Syria and Palestine (640), Egypt (639–642), and Tripolitania (643), and defeated the Persians at **Nihavand** (642). 'Umar made administrative reforms; he established a system of pensions, the **diwan**, which allocated funds to the Prophet's wives and to Muslims, ranked according to their dates of conversion. He ordered a cadastral survey for taxation of the newly conquered lands and founded the garrison towns of **Basra**, **Kufah**, and Fustat. He was assassinated in 644 by a slave who was a partisan of **'Ali**.

UMAR KHAYYAM. *See* KHAYYAM, OMAR.

UMAR, MULLA MUHAMMAD (OMAR, b. ca. 1960). Supreme leader and founder of the **Taliban** movement in 1994, who ruled over much of **Afghanistan** until the U.S. intervention in October 2001. Omar led his **madrasah** students in a spectacular campaign to capture Kandahar (1994), Herat (1995), Kabul (1996), and Mazar-i Sharif (1997), and finally to control most of the country (1998). Mulla **Umar**, a Pashtun, born in Oruzgan Province (or Nodeh village near Kandahar) was a **mujahid** in the Hizb-i Islami of Yunus Khalis and rose to the rank of deputy chief commander. Of heavy build, he is an expert marksman and is reputed to have destroyed several tanks in battle with Soviet and Marxist forces. He was wounded several times and lost one eye. Omar is said to be of Hotaki Ghilzai background. He taught in a village madrasah in Sangsag (Sang Hisar), some 24 miles west of Kandahar, but never finished his religious education; nevertheless, in April 1996 a **shurah** of about 1,000 members of the **'ulama'** recognized him as Amir al-Mu'minin (Commander of the Faithful). For this occasion, Omar wore what is believed to be the Cloak of the Prophet. He made Kandahar his center, from where he directed the organization.

Mulla Umar wanted to establish a "true" Islamic state in Afghanistan and issued a number of **fatwas** to this effect. Men were to wear beards and native dress. He ordered the closing of girls' schools and restricted **women** to their homes. He forbade photography of living creatures, music, television, videocassettes, cockfights, and kite flying, and made sportsmen wear pants from below the knee to the navel. Omar forbade women to walk in public without a male relative and initiated brutal punishment of enemies and "sinners," striking fear into those who did not accept his interpretation of Islam. He was also responsible for the destruction of the Buddha statues at Bamian. Mulla Umar had close relations with Osama bin **Laden**; some say he was dominated by the al-**Qaeda** leader. After the defeat of the Taliban regime, Omar fled and has not yet been captured. There is a bounty of $10 million on his head.

UMAYYA, BANU. A branch of the **Quraysh** to which **Caliph 'Uthman** and **Mu'awiyah** belonged. Mu'awiyah, founder of the **Umayyad** dynasty (661–750), challenged Caliph '**Ali** to demand vengeance for the murder of his clansman, 'Uthman, and eventually succeeded to the caliphate.

UMAYYAD CALIPHATE (661–750). The Umayyads gained power after **Mu'awiyah** successfully challenged the succession of **'Ali.** He demanded that the murder of **'Uthman** be avenged and implied that 'Ali was implicated in the deed. Mu'awiyah's first measure was to establish the Islamic capital at **Damascus,** where he had been governor and had the protection of his army. Mu'awiyah had himself proclaimed **caliph** in 660 and, after the assassination of 'Ali in 661 by a member of the **Kharijite sect,** there was no challenge to his claim. He gave **Hasan,** son of Caliph 'Ali, a handsome pension to renounce his claim, strengthened his army, and built the first Muslim navy. He paid the pensions of the soldiers and rendered justice according to the example of his predecessors. He issued coins fashioned after the Byzantine and Persian examples and appointed governors for the provinces. Mu'awiyah expanded the domains of the Islamic world from Central Asia across North Africa.

He broke precedence by appointing his son **Yazid** (r. 680–683) as his successor. **Husayn,** son of Caliph 'Ali, challenged the authority of Yazid and moved from his retirement in **Medina** to **Kufah** in response to an invitation from his supporters. He encountered an Umayyad army of some 4,000 men, and his group was wiped out almost to a man. The martyrdom of Husayn at **Karbala** sealed the schism in Islam. Yaszid's army defeated another challenger, 'Abdallah ibn **Zubayr,** near Medina in 683. **'Abd al-Malik** (r. 685–705), the fifth of the Umayyad rulers, began to reorganize the empire along **Arabic** Islamic lines. His general, al **Hajjaj,** pacified Iraq and suppressed a number of revolts. 'Abd al-Malik Arabized the administration of the empire, minted the first Islamic coins, and started construction of the great **Dome of the Rock** in **Jerusalem.** His was the greatest period of Umayyad power. **'Umar II** (r. 717–720) continued the reforms, but he also ended **Christian** participation in government and the army. He was later called the "Renovator of Islam."

But **'Abbasid** historians, perhaps to justify the 'Abbasid revolt, called the Umayyads Arab kings, rather than caliphs, who established secular rule based on dynastic succession. Historians have attributed the fall of the Umayyads to lack of an Islamic ideology, revival of Arab tribalism, and government of the Arabs for the Arabs. Only three caliphs—Mu'awiyah, Abdul Malik, and Umar II—were great rulers. The Umayyads, like subsequent Islamic rulers, did not have a clear rule of succession, and their governors and the generals who brought them great victories were eliminated as soon as they had accomplished their tasks. The pietist opposition, the **Kharijites**, the **Shi'ites**, and Iranian revivalism under the cover of international Islam all contributed to the 'Abbasid revolt, which ended the Umayyad empire in 750. Umayyad caliphs included the following:

660 Mu'awiyah ibn Abi Sufyan	717 'Umar ibn 'Abd al-Aziz
680 Yazid	720 Yazid II
683 Mu'awiyah II	724 Hisham
684 Marwan ibn al-Hakam	743 al-Walid
685 'Abd al Malik	744 Yazid III
705 al-Walid	744 Ibrahim
715 Sulayman	744–50 Marwan II

UMMAH. Originally a term for the **Medina** community, which included Muslims and Jews, but subsequently the term for the Islamic community, the Islamic "nation." It is not a territorial designation and includes Muslims wherever they may be. Arabs also use the term for the Arab nation.

UMM HABIBAH BINT ABI SUFYAN. Wife of **Muhammad** (also called Ramla), who was married to him in 629 when she was in Abyssinian exile. She was the daughter of **Abu Sufyan**, chief of the **Quraysh,** and half-sister of **Mu'awiyah,** the first **Umayyad caliph.** She was 35 years old when she married, and the Negus is said to have provided a dowry of 400 **dinars**. She died in about 646.

UMM AL-KITAB. A term used in the **Koran**, meaning "Mother of the Book." It refers to the **Preserved Tablet** in **heaven** as well as to verses in the Koran. The Koran says: "**Allah** doth blot out or confirm what He pleaseth: with Him is the Mother of the Book" (13:39).

UMM KULTHUM. Daughter of the Prophet **Muhammad** and **Khadijah**, who was to be married to her cousin 'Utaybah, son of **Abu Lahab.** Muhammad did not permit the **marriage**, because Abu Lahab was one of his worst enemies. She eventually married the future **Caliph 'Uthman** after the death of his wife **Ruqayyah**, another daughter of Muhammad. Umm Kulthum remained with 'Uthman until her death in 631. She had no children.

UMM AL-MU'MININ. "Mother of the **Believers**," a title given to **'A'ishah**, the wife of **Muhammad**.

UMM AL-QURRA. "Mother of Cities," a title given to **Mecca** in the **Koran** (6:92). The Koran says: "Thus We have sent by inspiration to thee an **Arabic** Qor'an: that thou mayest warn The Mother of Cities and all around her" (42:7).

UMM SALAMAH. Wife of **Muhammad**. *See also* SALAMAH BINT ABI UMAYYAH.

'UMRAH. The lesser **pilgrimage** that can be performed at any time of the year, unlike the hajj, which can be performed only during the month of pilgrimage (*Dhu 'l-Hijjah*). The Umrah consists of two ceremonies, the circumambulation (*tawaf*) of the **Ka'bah** and the **sa'y**, walking and running seven times between the hills of al-Safa and al-Marwa. Unlike the hajj, the 'umrah is not obligatory.

UNBELIEVER. *See* KAFIR.

'UQBAH IBN NAFI' (622–683). Arab general and governor of Ifriqiyyah (Tunis, 662–674) and the Maghrib (Northwest Africa) in 682. He founded the city of al-Qayrawan (Kerouan) in 670. With the support of Berber contingents, he fought Byzantine forces and advanced as far as Tangier (682), but he was eventually forced to retreat. Separated from his troops, with only a small force, 'Uqbah was killed. The village called Sidi 'Uqbah grew at the place of his tomb.

'URF. Local customs or laws, as distinguished from sacred law (**shari'ah**). In the Islamic world, a dualism has remained: the "king's law" and "God's law." Rulers could legislate and thus adapt the legal system to the changes of the times, but these laws ('urf, **qanun**, *siyasa*) were not to be in conflict with the sacred law. They had to be accompanied by a legal decision (**fatwa**) testifying to this fact (although this was at times ignored). The shari'ah is God's will; 'urf and qanun can be changed at the will of a ruler or government.

'URWA AL-WUTHQA, AL-. *The Firmest Bond* was a weekly magazine published in Paris in 1884 by Jamal al-Din **Afghani** and Muhammad **Abduh**. It advocated revivalist, **pan-Islamist** activism to save the Islamic world from Western imperialism and has had a considerable influence on revivalist movements to this day. The title comes from a verse in the **Koran** (2:256 and 31:22).

USAYBI'AH, IBN ABI (1230–1270). A native of **Damascus** who studied medicine, specialized in ophthalmology, and became head of the major hospital in **Cairo**. He won fame for his *Sources of Information on the Classes of Physicians* (*'Uyun al-anba' fi tabaqat al-atibbah*), which includes the biographies of some 600 **Arabic** and Greek physicians.

'USHR. "Tenth." A tithe levied by the state for public expenses that eventually became a land tax. **Shi'ites** dispute the legitimacy of the 'ushr because it was not mentioned in the **Koran** and was introduced by **'Umar II**, whose rule they did not recognize. .

'USMAN. *See* 'UTHMAN.

USUL AL-FIQH. The study of the origins, sources, and practice of Islamic jurisprudence. **Sunnis** accept four pillars: the **Koran**; the **Sunnah**, the Prophet's acts and statements; **qiyas**, judging by analogy; **ijma'**, consensus; and **ijtihad**, consensus. The Hanbali school accepts only the Koran and Traditions. The **Twelver Shi'ites** also accept the teachings of their imams and permit ijtihad of the clergy (**mujtahids**). *See also* FIQH.

USULI SCHOOL (USULIYYAH). One of two schools of jurisprudence in **Twelver Shi'ism**. The Usulis are the "followers of principles" and the **akhbaris** (akhbariyyah) are the "followers of tradition." First expounded by Aqa Muhammad Baqir Bihbihani

(1706–1790), the Usuli branch gained dominance in Iran in the 19th century and led to the centralization of the religious establishment as the representatives of the **Hidden Imam**. Whereas the Akhbari theologians based their legal argumentation on the Shi'ite Traditions, the Usulis used deductive reasoning based on the premises in the **Koran** and Traditions. This permitted the learned doctors (**mujtahids**) to claim a position of intellectual and moral leadership in the community. Eventually a hierarchy of mujtahids developed that culminated in a circle of the most prominent, requiring every believer to follow a living source for emulation (**marja' al-taqlid**). With the founding of the **Islamic Republic of Iran** in 1979, Ayatollah **Khomeyni** claimed supreme political powers with the establishment of the government of the highest jurist (**vilayat-i faqih**), whose **fatwa** is binding on the **believers**.

USURY. *See* INTEREST.

'UTHMAN, IBN 'AFFAN (r. 644–656). **Companion** of the Prophet, who married in succession **Ruqayyah** and **Umm Kulthum**, daughters of **Muhammad** by **Khadijah** (*see* WIVES OF THE PROPHET). He spent some time with refugees in Abyssinia. He was the third of the **Sunni caliphs**, whose tenure marked the beginning of division in the Arab world. 'Uthman was a member of the **Umayyad** clan of the **Quraysh** and was elected as a compromise candidate because he was a weak, old man. Opposition began over the division of revenues, which forced 'Uthman to reduce pensions. Muslim historians say that 'Uthman was a good ruler during his first six years. When he lost the Prophet's seal, six years of corruption and nepotism ensued. The partisans of **'Ali** (*shi'at 'ali*) disputed the legitimacy of the first three caliphs. Malcontents in the provinces, and the pious opposition, resented the supremacy of the Umayyads, most of whom were enemies of the Prophet and only recent converts. 'Uthman proclaimed the Arabian peninsula sacred territory, forbidden to non-Muslims. He conceived of the Arabs as a ruling elite and tried to prevent them from assimilation in the newly conquered lands by keeping them stationed in garrison towns. During his reign, the final version of the **Koran** is said to have been compiled to prevent the development of regional differences. Discontent increased, with **Zubayr ibn al-**

Awwam and **Talha ibn 'Ubaydullah,** two important Companions of the Prophet, among the opposition. A band of insurgents headed by Muhammad ibn Abi Bakr moved against **Medina** and assassinated 'Uthman in 656.

UZZA, AL-. With al-Lat and Manat, one of the three chief goddesses of pre-Islamic **Mecca.** They were known as the daughters of god.

– V –

VEIL. In the pre-Islamic Middle East, the veil was a status symbol, worn only by aristocratic ladies and subsequently by urban **women.** It became obligatory for Muslim women only in the ninth century. **Christian** and Jewish women also wore the veil, whereas Muslim peasant and nomad women only wore a kerchief because the veil would have interfered with agricultural labor and the mobility of the nomads. Increasing urbanization led to development of a variety of veils, from full body covers to those that revealed parts of the face. Modernization and the growth of Western influence in parts of the Islamic world have led to a demand for making the veil optional. Muslim modernists pointed out that there is no clear indication in the **Koran** that makes the veil obligatory.

Traditionists point to the example of the Prophet, who ordered a partition, **hijab,** put up in his room, separating the women from the daily conduct of affairs of state. They point to passages in the Koran, which say: "O Prophet! Tell thy wives and daughters, and the believing women, that they should cast their outer garments over their persons (when out of doors): That is most convenient, that they should be known (as such) and not molested" (33:59) and "Say to the believing women that they should lower their gaze and guard their modesty; that they should not display their beauty and ornaments except what (ordinarily) appear thereof; that they should draw their veils over their bosoms and not display their beauty except to their husbands, their fathers, their husbands' fathers, their sons, their husbands' sons, their brothers or their brothers' sons. Or their sisters' sons, or their women, or the slaves whom their right hands possess, or male attendants free of sexual desires [eunuchs], or small children who have no carnal knowledge of women" (24:31). The reference to women's breasts seems to forbid the pre-Islamic practice of Arab women baring their breasts to incite their men to bravery in battle. There is widespread disagreement on the obligation of seclusion and the wearing of the veil. Young women in many parts of the Middle East, and even Europe, have adopted "Islamic dress," consisting of a kerchief that covers the hair but leaves the face free. *See also* HIJAB.

VERSE. *See* AYAHS

VILAYAT-I FAQIH. A term used by Ayatollah Ruhollah **Khomeyni** in 1969 in a lecture in **Najaf**, which translates as the "guardianship of the Islamic jurist." It was implemented in 1979 when Khomeyni became the highest secular and religious authority in the **Islamic Republic of Iran**. The basis for Khomeyni's claim to temporal leadership is the **Usuli school** of **Twelver Shi'ism**, which became dominant in the 19th century and gave exclusive right to interpret Islamic law to the **mujtahids**. In his book on Islamic government (a compilation of lectures at **Najaf**), Khomeyni claimed for the highest jurist (**faqih**) the right to govern and the obligation of the people to obey him. Khamene'i, his successor, is not endowed with a special charisma, but he continues the line of spiritual leadership in Iran.

VIZIER (WAZIR). "One who carries a load." Title first given to ministers in the **'Abbasid** period and subsequently in other Islamic states. The grand vizier is a prime minister, ranking second only to the **sultan**. Some families held the vizierate for several generations, for example, the **Barmakids** under the 'Abbasids and the Chandarlis under the **Ottomans**. The **Koran** commanded the Prophet to "consult the intelligent and the learned" among his **Companions**, and it says that **Moses** asked God to "give me a vizier from my family . . . add to my strength through him, and make him share my task" (20:29–32). In al-**Ghazali**'s *Counsel for Kings*, the king is to observe three principles in his treatment of the vizier: not to punish him in haste when vexed with him, not to covet his wealth when he grows rich, and not to refuse him a (necessary) request when he makes one (Ghazali, 107). Abu Hamid al-. Cambridge: Islamic Texts, 2001.

– W –

WAFA', ABU AL- (BUZJANI, 940–997). Mathematician and astronomer from Buzjan, Khurasan, who went to **Baghdad** at age 19 and remained there until his death. He made his major contribution in the development of spherical trigonometry and geometrical constructions. His commentaries on Euclid, Diophanus, and al-**Khwarizmi**, as well as his astronomical tables, are lost. A moon crater was named in his honor.

WAHB IBN MUNABBIH (654–725). Arab chronicler of the **Umayyad** period. A native of Yemen, Wahb was a great transmitter of narrations and legends and "possessed information concerning the origin of things, the formation of the world, the history of the prophets and of (ancient) kings" (Khallikan, trans. Slane, III, 671).

WAHHAB, MUHAMMAD IBN 'ABD AL- (1703–1792). *See* 'ABD AL-WAHHAB, MUHAMMAD IBN.

WAHHABIS (AL-WAHHABIYYAH). A puritanical Islamic revivalist movement in the Arabian Peninsula that calls itself Unitarians (*muwahhidun*), founded by Muhammad Ibn **'Abd al-Wahhab** (1703–1792). 'Abd al-Wahhab allied himself with the tribal chief Muhammad ibn Sa'ud and conquered large areas of the Arabian Peninsula, including the Holy Cities of **Mecca** and **Medina**. They were defeated by Ibrahim, son of **Muhammad 'Ali**, the viceroy of Egypt, in 1818. During their raids, they destroyed some of the most holy shrines, including the tomb of **Husayn**, the son of **'Ali**. About 100 years later, **Ibn Sa'ud** ('Abd al-'Aziz ibn 'Abd al Rahman al-Sa'ud) was able to conquer much of the Arabian Peninsula and establish the Kingdom of Saudi Arabia.

Unitarianism (for the unity of God, **tawhid**) was established as the dominant school of Islamic jurisprudence in Saudi Arabia. It espouses a puritanical fundamentalism and opposes developments during the classical period of Islam as innovations (**bid'ah**). Wahhabism rejects **Sufism**, **intercession**, and **saint** cults, and considers the **Koran** and the early Traditions of the Prophet the only bases of **Islamic law**. Wahhabis enforce attendance at prayers and maintain a religious police force to promote virtue and forbid vice. In recent years, their practices have been somewhat mitigated, and great cathedral **mosques** were constructed in Mecca and Medina and elsewhere. The **Taliban** rulers, although of the liberal **Hanifi**te school, seem to have adopted the fundamentalist policies of Wahhabism in Afghanistan.

WAITING PERIOD, THE. "Iddah." The time a widow or **divorced** woman must wait before she can marry again. For widows the time is four months and 10 days; for divorced **women** it is three months. A child born during the waiting period is considered the offspring of the divorced or deceased man. For a pregnant woman, the period extends to the birth of the child. The husband is responsible for the support of the woman during the waiting period; he can also take her back and continue the **marriage**.

WAJIB. "Obligatory" or "necessary." Like **fardh** an essential duty, the fulfillment of which will be rewarded and neglect of which will be punished. *See also* FIVE PRINCIPAL ACTS IN ISLAM.

WALI. A "friend" or "patron," one who is "near" to God. Also the title of a governor of a province (*wilayat*). **Shi'ites** call **'Ali** the "Wali Allah," meaning "the Friend of God" and the "Vicegerent of God," thus the rightful successor to **Muhammad**'s leadership of the Muslim community. Wali also means guardian of a minor, benefactor, or helper, or a Muslim **saint** (pl. *awliya*).

WALI ALLAH, SHAH (1703–1762). One of the most important Muslim intellectuals of 18th-century India. Shah Wali Allah studied with his father, memorized the **Koran** at age 7, and at age 15 became a disciple of the **Naqshbandiyyah Sufi** order. He taught in Delhi and in 1731 left on a **pilgrimage** to **Mecca** and **Medina**, where he studied **hadith**, **fiqh**, and **Sufism**. On his return to Delhi, he published in **Arabic** and Persian. He attributed the decline of the Islamic world to the discontinuance of the spirit of **ijtihad** and the dominance of the dogma of imitation or emulation of the law (**taqlid**), as it was established by the four orthodox **schools of law**. He called for an intellectual revolution as a precondition to political change in India. He tried to create a united front for the purpose of establishing an Islamic state. His followers subsequently advocated a zealous puritanism, resembling the teachings of **Wahhabism**.

WALID, IBN 'ABDUL MALIK AL- (668–715). Sixth **Umayyad caliph**, during whose reign (705–715) the conquest of Spain began in 711 and the eastern part of the empire expanded to the Indus River. Walid was a great builder, who started the construction of the Al-**Aqsa mosque** and rebuilt the mosque of the Prophet in **Medina**. He continued the Arabization policy of his father and built the Umayyad mosque on the site of the Church of St. John in **Damascus**. The booty from territorial conquests permitted a period of unprecedented prosperity.

WALID. *See* KHALID IBN AL-WALID.

WAQF. "Detention." Pious foundation (pl. *awqaf*, also called *habs*), real estate, or property given to God in perpetuity in support of religious and charitable institutions. It provided for the construction of **mosques**, schools, hospitals, bridges, and the support of **education**, soup kitchens, and other social services. It was usually administered by a member of the **'ulama'**.

A **Hanif**ite definition of waqf is

the tying-up of the substance of a thing under the rule of the property of Almighty God, so that the proprietary right of the waqif [donor] becomes extinguished and is transferred to Almighty God for any purpose by which its profits may be applied to the benefit of His creatures. (Asaf A. A. Fyzee, 1967, 269)

There are certain conditions for establishing a waqf: the property must be real estate or a durable object; the property must be given in perpetuity; the donor must be of sound mind and legally fit; the purpose must be an act of charity; and the beneficiary must be alive. Eventually private awqaf were established to protect property from confiscation. Such provisions reserved for the donor and his descendants the use of a part of the property. It is said that in the later **Ottoman** period as much as a third of all lands comprised waqf property. Like church property in some Western countries, waqf property was exempt from **taxation** and could not be easily confiscated by the state. Nevertheless, governments took over control of awqaf when they had the power to defy popular opinion. In Turkey, three-fourths of arable lands consisted of waqf land; these lands were "nationalized" in 1925, and a minister (not a member of the 'ulama') took over their administration. In 1830, the French government took over the waqf (there called *habous*) in Algiers, where at the end of the 19th century almost one-half of arable land was dedicated to God (Fyzee, 266–267). It has been recognized that waqf property quickly deteriorated, as there was very little incentive for maintenance. Furthermore, the loss of taxation was a compelling reason for governments to take over the property.

WAQIDI, MUHAMMD IBN 'UMAR AL- (747–822). Arab historian from **Medina**, invited by **Caliph Harun al-Rashid** (r. 786–809) to **Baghdad**, where he won fame for his *Book of Wars* (*Kitab al-maghazi*), which describes the early wars and conquests of the Arabs. It served as an important source for biographies of the Prophet. His study of transmitters of **hadith** was important in evaluating the soundness of chains of transmitters.

WAQQAS, SA'D IBN ABI (603–675). Arab general, said to have been the seventh convert to Islam. He defeated the Sassanian forces at the Battle of **Qadisiyah** (637) and was appointed governor of **Kufah**. He retired from politics after the assassination of **Caliph 'Uthman** in 656.

WAR OF BASUS (ca. 494–534). A conflict between the rival clans of Taghlib and Bakr, which started over the killing of a she-camel belonging to a woman named Basus. It led to a 40-year cycle of vendettas, which was ended only through the intervention of the king of al-Hira, Amr Bin Hind. The Basus War has come to be a warning against the destructiveness of blood feuds among the Arabs. *See also* WAR, THE CLASSICAL ISLAMIC CONCEPT OF.

WAR, THE CLASSICAL ISLAMIC CONCEPT OF. Modernists claim that war is unavoidable, not desired or sought after. They stress that Muslims should "fight in the path of **Allah** against those who fight against you, but do not transgress" (II, 190). The **Koran** says: "But if the enemy incline towards peace, do thou (also) incline towards peace, and trust in Allah." Martial **jihad**, means "fighting in the path of Allah by means of life, property, tongue and other than these." It is a general duty that suffices, if accomplished by a sufficient number, and does not involve every Muslim.

Lawful wars include the continuation of war after a cease-fire or expiration of a peace treaty; a defensive measure if Muslim territory has been invaded, or if the enemy has behaved in an unbearable manner; a sympathetic measure to help Muslims suppressed by a non-Muslim government; and an idealistic measure to uproot godlessness and spread the faith. The latter is advocated by **Islamists** but repudiated by modernists, who claim that this was an injunction during the early period of Islam, when the small community was threatened.

A number of acts are forbidden, including unnecessarily cruel or tortuous ways of killing, killing of noncombatants, decapitation of prisoners, mutilations of men and beasts, treachery and perfidy, destruction of harvests, adultery with captive women, killing enemy hostages, killing of peasants when they do not fight, and so forth.

Muslim prisoners of war are to be ransomed (**zakat**, the arms tax, is to be used for this purpose), and enemy prisoners can arrange to be ransomed.

When a non-Muslim fortress was besieged, the enemy was given three choices: convert to Islam and become a Muslim citizen with all civil rights; surrender and become a protected resident (dhimmi) in Muslim lands, or have one year to decide to leave the Islamic domain; and fight to the end, letting Allah decide the outcome. In such case, the defeated enemy can be enslaved.

All these injunctions have been observed and violated at times. A jihad against Muslims was often justified by claiming the enemy was an **apostate**, infidel, and therefore subject to destruction. Non-Muslims were not involved in such disputes and generally were left in peace. Muslim modernists feel that the interpretation of Islam by 10th-century jurists was valid for the early period of Islamic history but must be reinterpreted to adapt to 21st-century conditions. They point out that jihad also means inwardly waging war against the carnal soul—a kind of moral imperative. The latter is called "The Great Effort" (*jihad al-akbar*) and is more important because it strives to achieve man's personal perfection. The "martial jihad," on the other hand, is the "Small Effort" (*jihad al-asghar*). *See also* DAR AL-HARB; TERRORISM.

WARNER. *See* NADHIR.

WASI. "Inheritor." The title **Shi'ites** give to **'Ali,** son-in-law and cousin of the Prophet, whom they consider the rightful successor to lead the Islamic community.

WASIL IBN 'ATA' (d. 748). Theologian and founder of the **Mu'-tazilite** school in **Basra.** Some claim that he was the first exponent of the five Mu'tazilite principles. A native of **Medina,** he went to **Baghdad** and became a student of Hasan al-**Basri** (d. 728). One day the question was raised whether a person who has committed a grave **sin** was a believer or not. According to one version, the **Murji'ites** held that the question should be postponed to the merciful decision of God, and the **Kharijites** declared a sinner a **kafir** destined for hell. Wasil held that the person was in between belief and unbelief, and then he withdrew and formed his own circle. Hasan said that "he separated from us" (*i'tazala 'anna*) and his followers came to be called the Mu'tazilites. Wasil had a long neck, for which he was ridiculed by his enemies, and he had a speech impediment that prevented him from pronouncing the letter "r"; therefore, "he never, in speaking, made use of words wherein it occurred. No one perceived the (difficulty he had to surmount), such was his mastery over the language and the fluency of his pronunciation."

WAZIER. *See* VIZIER.

WELFARE PARTY (REFAH PARTISI). A Turkish **Islamic** party, headed by Necmettin **Erbakan,** which rose from insignificant beginnings in 1983 to become the largest party in 1996. It succeeded previously banned Islamist parties, but was eventually forced out of power by the Turkish military in 1997. A year later the party was banned, but Islamic parties continued under different names, culminating in the election of 2003, which installed Recep Tayyip **Erdogan**, head of the Justice and Development Party, as prime minister. Because of the popularity of Islamic parties among the middle- and lower-class urban areas and the protest vote of Kurdish populations, the Islamic parties have been able to maintain themselves, in spite of secular opposition. In power, the Islamic parties have continued Turkey's policy of foreign affairs, including relations with Israel and demand for full membership in the European Union, but have also emphasized a return to "traditional values" and contributed to a gradual erosion of the secular policies of **Kemalism**.

WHIRLING DERVISHES. *See* MEVLEVIS.

WHITE STREAK, THE. The time when a **believer** can eat during **Ramadhan** "until the white thread of dawn appear to you distinct from its black thread" (2:187).

WIDOWS. According to **Tradition**, a widow must wait four months and 10 days after the death of her husband before she may take another husband, provided she is not pregnant at the time. The waiting period is called '**iddah**. *See also* WOMEN.

WINE. *See* ALCOHOL.

WITNESS. *See* MARTYR.

WIVES. "Zauj" (pl. *azwaj*). Muslims are permitted to marry up to four **women**, but they must treat them equally. A Tradition says: "When a man has two wives and does not treat them equally, he will come on the Day of Resurrection with half of his body fallen off." Surah 4:3 says: "Marry women of your choice, two, three, or four; but if ye shall not be able to deal justly (with them), then only one, or that which your right hand possesses." Muslim modernists maintain that it is not possible to treat several women equally; therefore, monogamy should be preferred. **Shi'ahs** also permit temporary marriages, **'mut'ah**, limited to a specific time. The children of such marriages are legal. Because of the existence of **slavery**, there was no limit on concubines (women whom your right hand possesses).

WIVES OF THE PROPHET. As long as he was married to **Khadijah, Muhammad** did not take any other **wives.** He married **'A'ishah** and **Hafsah** (a widow), the daughters of the subsequent **caliphs Abu Bakr** and **Umar**; then he took a number of widows, including **Umm Habibah**, the daughter of his erstwhile enemy **Abu Sufyan**, and **Sawdah, Zaynab bint Khuzaymah, Umm Salamah,** and **Safiyyah.** One wife, **Zaynab bint Jahsh,** was **divorced,** and one, **Juwayriyyah,** he married for political reasons. He also took a Jewish and a **Christian** concubine, **Rayhana** and **Mary the Copt,** for political reasons. The Tabaqat also lists **Maymuna,** and a number of **women** who proposed to Muhammad or whom he married and divorced. The wives who outlived Muhammad received a yearly pension of 10,000 **dirhams.** 'A'ishah was his favorite wife; she outlived him by 46 years and was subsequently called the "Mother of the **Believers.**" The descendants of Khadijah's daughter **Fatimah** and her husband **'Ali ibn Abi Talib** are the **Shi'ite imams.**

WOMEN. In the tribal society of pre-Islamic Arabia, women were part of the estate of their husbands, fathers, or close male relatives. The birth of a girl was considered a misfortune, and it was common for female infants to be buried alive. The **Koran** refers to this: "When news is brought to one of them of (the birth of) a female (child), his face darkens, and he is filled with inward grief! With shame does he hide himself from his people, because of the bad news he has had. Shall he retain it on (sufferance and) contempt, or bury it in the dust? Ah, what an evil (choice) they decide on" (16:58, 59). Islam brought change, giving women a right to **inheritance** and limiting the number of wives to four, although as a result of **slavery** there was no limit to the number of concubines. Women have a soul, like men, but the functions of the two differ: The woman is respected as a mother, and the man is responsible for her support. The Koran says: "Men are the protectors and maintainers of women, because **Allah** has given the one more (strength) than the other, and because they support them from their means" (4:34).

But even since the early period of Islam, women have played important roles in society. **Khadijah**, the wife of **Muhammad**, conducted business with Syria in which Muhammad was employed for a time. **Fatimah**, the **wife of the Prophet**, is an example of the virtuous woman, and **'A'ishah** is the transmitter of a great number of **hadith**. She participated in the Battle of the **Camel** in 656 during the civil war against **'Ali**. Shajar al-Durr (Tree of Pearls) was sultan of Egypt in the beginning of the **Mamluk** sultanate. **Rabi'ah al-'Adawiyyah** is a much-revered female mystic.

In **Islamic law**, the man possesses the right to punish a disloyal wife. **Adultery** requires four witnesses or a confession of the culprits to be punished, and an accusation of adultery by a husband can be voided, if the woman swears to her innocence (*see* LI'AN). It takes the testimony of two women to equal that of one man in a **shari'ah** court, but punishments and fines are half of those for a man. A woman does not have to fight in **war** and does not share in the booty, and she is not to be killed in war.

The position of Muslim women continues to be influenced by Tradition today. The number of women in public life is still limited, even in more Westernized states. Traditional occupations include the medical fields, education, business, and menial labor in the textile trades and agriculture. Although in urban areas a greater number of women attend public schools, illiteracy is much greater among women than men. As a result of the emergence of independent states in many parts of the Islamic world, women have gained leading positions in social and political life, including the position of prime minister in several states of South Asia. Many discriminatory practices against women have been outlawed. Women protest that, although limitations in public life were valid for a tribal society during the early period of Islam, present times call for a reinterpretation of old traditions.

On the other hand, the recent resurgence of **Islamist** movements in many parts of the Islamic world has led to demands to limit the spheres of female activity. An extreme example of this is the policy of the **Taliban** in **Afghanistan**, who, after their conquest of Kabul in

1994, closed schools for girls and restricted women to their homes. This caused incalculable hardship because many women were the sole support of their families. Even some of the most radical Islamist groups do not call for such measures. *See also* MARRIAGE; 'MUT'AH; WIVES.

WORSHIP. Laws concerning worship (**'ibadat**) refer to obedience and submissiveness to God and include such duties as ritual **prayers, fasting, almsgiving,** and the **pilgrimage.** *See also* FAITH.

WUDHU. The lesser **ablution.**

WUQUF. "Station, halt." The standing position during **prayer.** The obligation of "standing before the Lord" in the plain of 'Arafat on the ninth day of **pilgrimage.** The various schools differ about how long a pilgrim has to be there, but pilgrimage would be invalid without the wuquf.

– Y –

YAQUB IBN LAYTH AL-SAFFAR (867–879). Yaqub, the coppersmith (*saffar*), was the founder of a kingdom that came to be named after him, the Saffarid dynasty (867–1495). He began as a bandit, in which profession he showed great courage and generosity. He may have been a **Kharijite** before he turned orthodox. Appointed as commander of the army of Sistan, he captured Herat and Kerman, and raided into Fars. The **'Abbasid caliph** recognized his power and appointed him governor of Balkh and Tokharistan. From there, he expanded his realm farther east to Kabul, Afghanistan, and then turned to the west to conquer Nishapur from the Tahirids. Encouraged by his conquests, he demanded the province of Fars, but Caliph Mu'tamid (r. 870–892) sent an army against him and scored a decisive victory. Yaqub was succeeded by Amr (r. 879–901), but another defeat ended the Saffarids' control of Persian territory, although they continued to control parts of Sistan for several centuries.

YAQUBI, IBN WADIH AL- (d. 897). Arab historian and geographer, who won fame for his *World History* (*Tarikh ibn wadih*), which starts with the creation and continues to his time. His *Book of Countries* (*Kitab al-buldan*) provides statistical and topographical data on the Islamic world from Iran westward across North Africa. A **Twelver Shi'ite** and the son of a freed **slave**, he spent his childhood in **Baghdad** and subsequently lived in Armenia and Khurasan before moving to Egypt.

YAQUT AL-HAMAWI (1179–1229). Arab writer of Greek origin, who came to **Baghdad** as a **slave** and was manumitted there. He was a prolific writer, but only three of his works are extant: *Geographical Dictionary* (*Mu'ajam al-buldan*), *Dictionary of Men of Letters* (*Mu'ajam al-udaba'*), and *The Gazetteer* (*al-Mushtarik*). He traveled widely and eventually settled in Aleppo.

YARMUK, BATTLE OF AL-. A tributary of the Jordan River, where in 636 a Muslim force under the command of **Khalid ibn al-Walid** defeated a Byzantine army. Khalid's army of about 25,000 faced a superior Byzantine army of some 50,000 men, headed by Theodorus, brother of the Byzantine ruler Heraclius. Most of the Byzantine forces were killed, including Theodorus. This meant the loss of Syria (except for **Jerusalem**) for the Greeks.

YASIN, SHAIKH AHMAD ISMA'IL (1937–2004). Cofounder of **Hamas** with Abd al-Aziz al-Rantisi and its spiritual leader. Born in al-Jura, Palestine, a village destroyed during the 1948 Arab–Israeli war, he fled to Ghaza, where he spent most of his life. He was almost blind and a paraplegic, tied to a wheelchair after a sporting accident at age 12. He studied at Al-**Azhar** in **Cairo** and became a member of the **Muslim Brotherhood**. Arrested by the Israeli government, he was freed in 1997 in an arrangement between Jordan and Israel as a result of the Israeli assassination attempt on Khalid Mashal, a Hamas leader in Jordan. After an assassination attempt in September 2003, Yasin and two of his bodyguards were killed by a Hellfire missile from an Israeli helicopter gunship on 22 March 2004. Nine bystanders were also killed and more than a dozen injured during the operation. Al-Rantisi assumed leadership of Hamas. He was assassinated a month later.

YATHRIB. The pre-Islamic name of **Medina**.

YAWM AL-QIYAMAH. "Resurrection." *See* DAY OF JUDGMENT.

YAZID IBN MU'AWIYAH (r. 680–683). The second **Umayyad caliph**, appointed by his father, **Mu'awiyah**, as his successor, thus establishing the precedent of dynastic succession. The pious opposition in **Medina** and the followers of 'Ali ibn Abi Talib in Iraq contested the appointment. The Kufans invited **Husayn**, the son of 'Ali, from Medina but were unable to protect him from the army of Yazid, and on the 10th of **Muharram** 680, Husayn and his small group of followers were massacred. Yazid's forces defeated the opposition of Medina in the Harra. Once consolidated in power, Yazid sponsored the arts and introduced feasts with music and wine to his court.

YAZIDIS. Followers of a Kurdish enthno-sectarian community that probably derives its name from **Yazid**, the son of **Mu'awiyah**. Its modern creed was shaped by the **Sufi Shaykh** Adi ibn Musafir (d. 1160?) of Lalish near Mosul, Iraq. The **scriptures** of the Yazidis are the *Book of Revelation* and the *Black Book*. Their religion is said to have Sabaean, Muslim, Christian, and Zoroastrian elements and, because of the secrecy of their belief, they have been called devil worshipers and have been exposed to long periods of persecution. The tomb of Shaykh Adi is located near Mosul and is the location of an annual **pilgrimage**.

YEAR, ISLAMIC. *See* CALENDAR.

YUSUF IBN TASHFIN (d. 1106). Almoravid ruler (1061–1106) who founded Marrakesh in 1062 and eventually controlled virtually all of Muslim Spain, after he defeated King Alfonso VI of León and Castile in 1086. A Berber, Yusuf was described as, "of a middle size, a tawny complexion and a lean body; his cheeks were beardless and his voice feeble. . . . He was a man of resolution, skilled in the management of affairs, vigilant in maintaining the prosperity of his kingdom, favorable to the learned and religious men, whose advise also he had often recourse to."

– Z –

ZAB. Two tributaries of the Tigris. The Greater Zab, with its source near the Iraqi–Iranian border, was the site of a battle in January 750 between the last **Umayyad caliph**, Marwan II, and **'Abbasid** forces. The Umayyads were decisively defeated and replaced by the 'Abbasid **caliphate**.

ZABIH (DHABIH). The act of slaying an animal to make its meat lawful for consumption. According to **Sunni** tradition, the throat must be cut above the breast and the words "Allahu Akbar" must be recited. The person who kills the animal should be a Muslim, but a **Christian** or Jew is permissible. Surah 2:172 says: "O ye who believe! Eat of the good things that we have provided for you." Surah 2:173 says: "He hath forbidden you dead meat, and blood, and the flesh of swine, and that on which any other name hath been invoked besides that of **Allah**. But if one is forced by necessity, without wilful disobedience, nor transgressing due limits—then he is guiltless. For Allah is oft-forgiving most merciful."

ZABUR. "Psalms." Book given to David, mentioned in the **Koran**. It is one of a series of books, including the Torah, the Gospel, and the final **revelation**, the Koran. The Koran says: "Say: We believe in **Allah**, and in what has been revealed to us and what was revealed to **Abraham**, Isma'il, Isaac, Jacob, and the Tribes, and in (the Books) given to **Moses**, **Jesus**, and the Prophets from their Lord; we make no distinction between one or another among them, and to Allah do we bow our will (in Islam)" (4:163).

ZAHIR. "Outer." The literal meaning, especially of the **Koran**, the opposite of the esoteric (*batin*). *See also* BATINITES; ZAHIRITES.

ZAHIRITES (ZAHIRIYYAH). A school of jurisprudence, founded by Dawud al-Isfahani (d. 884), which demands an exoteric, **zahir**, interpretation of the **Koran** and the **Sunnah**. The Zahirites were "literalists," rejecting acceptance of authority (**taqlid**), the use of opinion (**ra'y**) by the jurist, and reasoning by analogy (**qiyas**), in interpreting the law. The Zahirites were established as an orthodox school in Iraq and then spread to other parts of the Islamic world. **Ibn Hazm** (d. 1064) was one of the school's most important proponents in Spain. It was also the school of jurisprudence of the **Almohad** ruler Yaqub al-Mansur (1184–1199), but it never found acceptance as a fifth orthodox **school of law**.

ZAKAT. "Purification." A tax incumbent on all Muslims. The **Koran** says: "Alms are for the poor and the needy, and those employed to administer the (funds); for those whose hearts have been reconciled (converted to truth); for those in bondage and in debt; in the cause of **Allah**; and for the wayfarer; thus it is ordained by Allah" (9:60). It is one of the obligations subsumed under the code of rituals called the **Five Pillars of Islam** and can be given in cash or in kind. Now largely voluntary, as much as 2.5 to 10 percent was customary.

According to the *Muwatta* of **Imam Malik ibn Anas**, zakat is paid on three things: the produce of cultivated land, gold and silver, and livestock. But there is no zakat obligation on fewer than five camels, on fewer than five awaq (200 **dirhams** of pure silver), or on less than five awaq of dates (1,500 double-handled scoops) (17.1.1–3.). Shi'ites look at zakat as charity rather than as a religious tax. *See also* SADAQA.

ZAMAKHSHARI, MAHMUD AL (1075–1144). Theologian and philologist of Persian origin, who was born at Zamakhshar and died at Korkanj in Transcaspia. **Ibn Khallikan** describes him as "The great master (**imam**) in the sciences of **Koran**ic interpretation, the Traditions, grammar, philology, and rhetoric, was incontrovertibly the first imam of the age in which he lived." He was a **Mu'tazilite**, supporting the **createdness of the Koran** and, in spite of his origin, an opponent of the anti-Arab **shu'ubiyyah** movement. His Koran commentary, *The Revealer* (*al-kashshaf*), was original, and his **Arabic** grammar (*al-mufassal*) is still used as a reference work today. Zamakhshari lost a foot as a result of an accident, and he carried a certificate with him to show that this was not the result of amputation for committing a crime.

ZAMZAM. "Abundant water." A sacred well at the southeast corner of the **Ka'bah**, which the angel **Gabriel** conjured to save **Hagar** and her son Isma'il from dying of thirst. Muslims drink from it during **pilgrimage** and treasure the water for its presumed healing qualities.

ZANJ. Arab name for the black inhabitants of the east African coast (Zanzibar), who were transported as **slaves** to work in the swampland of southern Iraq. As many as 5,000 slaves worked in the area, and they finally rose in rebellion, led by 'Ali Muhammad al-Zanji, under the banner of the **Qarmatian sect**. They captured **Basra** and cut off the trade route to the Gulf. The Zanj were defeated, and their capital, al-Mukhtara (The Chosen), was taken in 883, but their uprising accelerated the **'Abbasid** decline. Black slaves were usually employed as domestics or soldiers; the employment of large numbers of slaves in mines or plantations was an exception.

ZARQAWI, ABU MUSAB AL- (d. 2006). Osama bin **Laden**'s "amir" in Iraq, feared for directing guerrilla campaigns and **suicide** attacks against Coalition forces and **Shi'a** and Kurd communities. A former cell mate described the Jordanian terrorist as "a small man, with a small group, in a small cell," but he grew into a jihadist "more extreme than bin Laden." He had a bounty of $25 million on his head and was the most-wanted man in Iraq. On 9 November 2005 his group launched a triple suicide bombing on three American-owned hotels in Amman that caused the death of 59 civilians, most of them Jordanians, including 30 members of a wedding party. A message, purported to be from Zarqawi, stated: "We ask God to have mercy on the Muslims, who we did not intend to target. Even if they were in hotels which are centers of immorality." This caused a revulsion of feeling, and even his own family severed its links with Zarqawi "until doomsday." He was killed in a U.S. bombing raid on 7 June 2006.

ZAWAHIRI, AYMAN AL- (1951–). Head of the Egyptian Islamic Jihad who merged his movement in 1998, with Osama bin **Laden**'s al-**Qaeda** to create the "World Islamic Front for **Jihad** against Jews and

Crusaders." Accused of complicity in the 1995 **suicide** bombing of the Egyptian embassy in Islamabad, Zawahiri was sentenced to death in absentia by an Egyptian military court. In 1999, he and Osama bin Laden were indicted by a federal grand jury in New York for the U.S. embassy bombings in Nairobi and Dar es Salaam. Zawahiri moved to Sudan in 1991 and then to **Afghanistan** in 1996 and has been credited as the intellectual and ideological driving force behind the al-Qaeda organization. He was with bin Laden at the Battle of **Tora Bora** and is rumored to be based somewhere on the Afghan Pakistan border. There is a bounty on his head of $25 million.

Zawahiri was born of a prominent family on 19 June 1951 in al-Ma'adi, Cairo, the son of a pharmacology professor. Originally from Zawahir in Saudi Arabia, his great-grandfather came to Egypt and his grandfather had served as shaikh of Al-**Azhar**. Ayman graduated with a medical degree from Cairo University in 1974. He studied the writings of **Sayyid Qutb** and Abu A'la al-**Maududi** and at age 16 became a member of a jihad cell. In the early 1970s, at age 20, Zawahiri had attained the rank of "**amir**." He became increasingly radicalized, to the extent that he denounced the **Muslim Brotherhood** as infidel because of its participation in Egyptian elections.

ZAWIYAH. "Corner." A place of worship or **Sufi** lodge. *See also* KHANAQAH.

ZAYD IBN 'ALI (698–740). A grandson of **Husayn** and **imam** of the Zaydiyyah (or **Fiver**) Shi'ites. He fought the **Umayyads** but was defeated and killed in 740. *See also* ZAYDIS.

ZAYD IBN HARITH. A **slave** given to **Muhammad** by his wife **Khadijah** and later adopted as a son by Muhammad. Zayd **divorced** his wife **Zaynab** when the Prophet wanted to marry her. A **revelation** permitted the **marriage**, which would have been prohibited because adoption made Zayd a blood relative. He was the second male convert to Islam after '**Ali**.

ZAYD IBN THABIT (d. 666). Secretary of the Prophet and in charge of distributing the booty after the Battle of **Yarmuk** (636). In the wars of **apostasy**, a large number of reciters of the **Koran** were killed, and it was considered necessary to compile a definitive version from fragments, palm leaves, bones, and "the hearts of men." He was charged by **Caliph Abu Bakr** with the collection of texts of the Koran, a task he is believed to have later completed during the caliphate of **'Uthman**. When Ibn 'Abbas held the stirrup of Zayd, the latter exclaimed: "How, you, who are the uncle of the blessed Prophet, hold my stirrup?" Ibn Abbas replied: "Yes, it is thus we do with the learned." Caliphs **'Umar I** and 'Uthman considered him "without an equal as a judge, as a jurisconsult, a calculator in the division of **inheritance**, and a reader of the Koran" (Khallikan, trans. Slane, I, 372). Zayd is buried in **Damascus**.

ZAYDIS (ZAYDIYYAH). The followers of **Zayd ibn 'Ali** (d. 740), the fifth **Shi'ite imam**. They are closest to **Sunni** Islam and recognize the **Koran** and the **Sunnah** as the bases of their theology. They require that the imam be a descendant of either **Hasan** or **Husayn** and have de facto power as well as special doctrinal knowledge and political ability. Also an important qualification was that the imam excel in piety and valor, possess personal grace, and be free from physical defects. The Zaydis founded a state in Yemen in 897, and for a time they also existed in Iran. Their theology is a mixture of **Mu'tazilite** and **Murji'ite** doctrines, and they accept **Abu Bakr**, **'Umar I**, and part of **'Uthman**'s tenure as legitimate. Zaydis do not practice **taqiyah** and **'mut'ah marriage** and are opposed to **Sufism**. On the question of **sin** and the sinner, they believe the sinner is an unbeliever, but they do not demand that he be killed. They now constitute the majority of the population in southwestern Yemen. From the 10th century until 1962, their imam was also the head of state.

ZAYNAB BINT JAHSH. Wife of the Prophet who was married to his adopted son, **Zayd ibn Haritha**. When **Muhammad** came to visit Zayd, he refused to enter the house when he learned that Zayd was not at home. Sensing that Muhammad was interested in her, Zayd **divorced** Zaynab and became the Prophet's wife. A **revelation** said: "When Zayd no longer had any need of her, We married her to you" (33:37). She received a dowry of 400 **dirhams**.

ZAYNAB BINT KHADIJAH. Oldest daughter of **Muhammad** and **Khadijah**. She married Abu 'l-'As ibn al-Rabi' before the advent of Islam and had two children, **'Ali** and Umama. 'Ali died young, and Umama grew up and married 'Ali ibn Abi Talib after **Fatimah**'s death. Zaynab became Muslim and emigrated with her father to **Medina**. Her husband refused to convert; he was captured by the Medinans, and Zaynab won his release when she sent her necklace as ransom. When Abu 'l-'As converted, Muhammad gave Zaynab back to him. She died in about 630, before the death of the Prophet.

ZAYNAB BINT KHUZAYMAH, Wife of **Muhammad**, called "Mother of the Poor" because she spent much of her wealth on charity. Muhammad married her in the month of **Ramadhan** in 625 and gave her a dowry of 400 **dirhams**. She was **divorced** by her first husband and widowed by her second husband. Zaynab died at age 30 after only eight months of **marriage**.

ZAYN AL-'ABIDIN (658–712?). Son of **Husayn** ibn 'Ali and Sulafa, the daughter of Yazdegird III, the last Sassanian ruler. He is the fourth of the **Shi'ite imams**, and all the imams were his descendants. He was called Ibn al-Khiaratain (the son of two preferred ones), because a **hadith** quotes the Prophet as saying: "Of all the human race, Almighty **God** has preferred two (families); the tribe of Kuraish amongst the Arabs, and the Persians amongst the foreign nations." He had a reputation as a pious man and noted traditionalist and jurist.

ZIKR. See DHIKR.

ZINAH. See ADULTERY.

ZINDIQ. A heretic, atheist, or secularist. Also members of religions that had their origins in Islam, like **Baha'is**, and at times even **Druze** and **Ahmadis** who claim adherence to orthodox Islam.

ZIONISM. Jewish religio-nationalist movement founded in the late 19th century through the initiative of Theodor Herzl (1860–1904), a Paris correspondent of the *Neue Freie Presse* of Vienna. In his book

Der Judenstaat, Herzl asked the European governments to grant the Jewish people an area in which a Jewish homeland could be established. He suggested Argentina, Palestine, or some other area, but the First Zionist Congress in Basel, Switzerland (1897), demanded the establishment of a homeland in Palestine. The Zionist movement grew, and a Jewish National Fund was created, which specialized in land acquisitions in Palestine.

Attempts at winning **Ottoman Sultan Abd al-Hamid**'s approval for the settlement of Jews in Palestine in exchange for financing the Ottoman debt were unsuccessful. But during the First World War, the British foreign secretary, Arthur Balfour, trying to win the support of world Jewry, wrote a letter to Lord L. W. Rothschild in which he stated that his government favored "the establishment in Palestine of a national home for the Jewish people," with the proviso that "nothing shall be done which may prejudice the civil and religious rights of existing non-Jewish communities" (*Encyclopedia of Zionism and Israel*, 103).

The defeat of the **Ottoman empire** and the establishment of a British mandate for Palestine facilitated further Jewish immigration. The Arab population became increasingly hostile, fearing that unlimited Jewish immigration would lead to a loss of their political power. The result was armed clashes between the communities, which turned into war after the United Nations decreed to divide Palestine into Jewish and Arab states, with Jerusalem under a UN Trusteeship. Rather than helping to implement the Partition Plan, the British terminated the mandate in May 1948 and thus did not prevent the outbreak of war between the communities. Thus the Zionist objective was achieved.

ZIYAD IBN ABIHI (ca. 626–675). Proclaimed a half-brother by **Caliph Mu'awiyah** to tie him to the **Umayyad** regime, even though his name, the "Son of His Father" (*ibn abihi*), indicates that there was some doubt as to his descent (**Abu Sufyan** was rumored to be his father). He became governor of **Kufah**, later also of **Basra** and the eastern provinces, where he distinguished himself in fighting 'Alid and **Kharijite** forces and thus contributed to the consolidation of the **Umayyad caliphate**. He ruthlessly restored order in Iraq and Iran and maintained an elaborate spy system. Ziyad also wanted control of the Hijaz and wrote to the caliph: "Commander of the faithful! My left hand holds Iraq in submission unto you, and my right hand is unoccupied and waits to be employed in your service; appoint me therefore governor of **Hijaz**" (Khallikan, trans. Slane, 621). This was not granted, but Iraq prospered under his reign.

ZIYAD, TARIQ IBN. *See* TARIQ, ZIYAD IBN.

ZIYARAH. "Visitation." A visit to the graves of individuals for the purpose of praying for the dead. Also, a **pilgrimage** to a shrine that can be undertaken at any time.

ZUBAYR, 'ABDALLAH IBN AL- (624–692). Born in **Medina**, the son of Asmah, older sister of **'A'ishah**, the wife of **Muhammad**, and of **Zubayr ibn al-Awwam**, **Companion** of the Prophet. **Caliph 'Uthman** ordered Zubayr to make the first recension of the **Koran**. He was one of the leaders of the pious opposition who fought **'Ali ibn Abi Talib** in the Battle of the **Camel** in 656. He then lived in **Mecca** and subsequently refused to recognize **Yazid**, son of **Mu'awiyah**, as the new **Umayyad caliph**. Beaten in the battle of **Marj Rahit** in 684, he continued to rule as anti-caliph for 10 years at Mecca. He was defeated by **'Abd al-Malik**'s general al-**Hallaj** in the battle for Mecca and was killed in 692.

ZUBAYR, IBN AL-AWWAM (d. 656?). A cousin of the Prophet and the fifth convert to Islam, who fell in the Battle of the **Camel** fighting against **'Ali**. His wife, Asma', was the daughter of **Caliph Abu Bakr**, and his son, Abdallah ibn al-**Zubayr**, fought the **Umayyads** as counter-caliph in **Mecca**. He was one of 10 **Companions** whom the Prophet declared should enter paradise.

ZUHAYR, IBN ABI SULMA (ca. 520–609). One of the great pre-Islamic poets whose poems are part of the **Mu'allaqat**. He comes from a family of poets of the Muzaynah tribe and deals with raids and other aspects of nomadic life. He composed first a satire and later a eulogy on the Prophet. In his old age, he met the Prophet, who shouted on seeing him: "O God, preserve me from this demon!"

(Nicholson, 119). He was described as a man of wealth and the "gentleman-philosopher among Arab poets."

ZULM. "Tyranny." Acting tyrannically between man and God, between man and man, and between man and himself. It has come to mean oppression and tyranny by government, and for **Shi'ites** also oppression by the **Sunni** community.

Appendix: Estimates of the Muslim Population of the World

Country	Total Population	Percentage of Muslims	Muslim Population
Afghanistan	22,664,136	100.09%	22,664,136
Albania	3,249,136	75%	2,436,852
Algeria	29,183,032	99%	28,891,202
Angola	10,342,899	25%	2,585,725
Antigua and Barbuda	65,647	n/a	
Argentina	34,672,997	2	693,460
Aruba	67,794	5	3,390
Australia	18,260,863	2.09	382,000
Azerbaijan	7,676,953	93.4	7,170,274
Bahrain	590,042	100	590,042
Benin	5,709,529	15	856,429
Bangladesh	123,062,800	85	104,603,380
Bhutan	1,822,625	5	91,131
Bosnia and Herzegovina	2,656,240	40	1,062,496
Botswana	1,477,630	5	73,882
Brazil	162,661,214	0.6	1,000,000
Brunei	299,939	63	188,962
Bulgaria	8,612,757	14	1,205,786
Burkina Faso	10,623,323	50	5,311,662
Burma	45,975,625	10	4,597,563
Burundi	5,943,057	20	1,188,611
Cambodia	10,861,218	1	108,612
Cameroon	14,261,557	55	7,843,856
Canada	28,820,671	1.48	400,000
Central African Republic	3,274,426	55	1,800,934
Chad	6,976,845	85	5,930,318
China	1,210,004,956	11	133,100,545
Christmas Island	813	10	81
Cocos (Keeling) Island	609	57	347
Comoros	569,237	86	489,544
Congo	2,527,841	15	379,176

(continued)

345

Country	Total Population	Percentage of Muslims	Muslim Population
Cote d'Ivoire	14,762,445	60	8,857,467
Croatia	5,004,112	1.2	60,049
Cyprus	744,609	33	245,721
Djibouti	427,642	94	401,983
Egypt	63,575,107	94	59,760,601
Equatorial Guinea	431,282	25	107,821
Eritrea	3,427,883	80	2,742,306
Ethiopia	57,171,662	65	37,161,580
Fiji	782,381	11	86,062
France	58,317,450	7	4,082,222
Gabon	1,172,798	1	11,728
Gambia	1,204,984	90	1,084,486
Gaza Strip	923,940	98.7	911,929
Georgia	5,219,810	11	574,179
Germany	83,536,115	3.4	2,840,228
Ghana	17,698,271	30	5,309,481
Gibraltar	28,765	8	2,301
Greece	10,538,594	1.5	158,079
Guinea	7,411,981	95	7,041,382
Guinea-Bissau	1,151,330	70	805,931
Guyana	712,091	15	106,814
Hong Kong	6,305,413	1	63,054
India	952,107,694	14	133,295,077
Indonesia	206,611,600	95	196,281,020
Iran	66,094,264	99	65,433,321
Iraq	21,422,292	97	20,779,623
Israel	5,421,995	14	759,079
Italy	57,460,274	1	574,603
Japan	125,449,703	1	1,254,497
Jordan	4,212,152	95	4,001,544
Kazakstan	16,916,463	51.2	8,661,229
Kenya	28,176,686	29.5	8,312,122
Kuwait	1,950,047	89	1,735,542
Kyrgyzstan	4,529,648	76.1	3,447,062
Lebanon	3,776,317	70	2,643,422
Liberia	2,109,789	30	632,937
Libya	5,445,436	100	5,445,436
Lesotho	1,970,781	10	197,078
Macedonia	2,104,035	30	631,211
Madagascar	13,670,507	20	2,734,101
Malawi	9,452,844	35	3,308,495
Malaysia	19,962,893	52	10,380,704

Country	Total Population	Percentage of Muslims	Muslim Population
Maldives	270,758	100	270,758
Mali	9,653,261	90	8,687,935
Malta	375,576	14	52,581
Mauritania	2,336,048	100	2,336,048
Mauritius	1,140,256	19.5	222,350
Mayotte	100,838	99	99,830
Mongolia	2,496,617	4	99,865
Morocco	29,779,156	98.7	29,392,027
Mozambique	17,877,927	29	5,184,599
Namibia	1,677,243	5	83,862
Nepal	22,094,033	4	883,761
Netherlands	15,568,034	3	467,041
Niger	9,113,001	91	8,292,831
Nigeria	103,912,489	75	77,934,367
Norway	4,438,547	1.5	66,578
Oman	2,186,548	100	2,186,548
Pakistan	129,275,660	97	125,397,390
Panama	2,655,094	4	106,204
Philippines	74,480,848	14	10,427,319
Qatar	547,761	100	547,761
Reunion	679,198	20	135,840
Romania	21,657,162	20	4,331,432
Russia	148,178,487	18	26,672,127
Rwanda	6,853,359	1	68,534
Saudi Arabia	19,409,058	100	19,409,058
Senegal	9,092,749	95	8,638,112
Serbia and Montenegro	10,614,558	19	2,016,766
Sierra Leone	4,793,121	65	3,115,529
Singapore	3,396,924	17	577,477
Slovenia	1,951,443	1	19,514
Somalia	9,639,151	100	9,639,151
South Africa	41,743,459	2	834,869
Sri Lanka	18,553,074	9	1,669,777
Sudan	31,547,543	85	26,815,412
Suriname	436,418	25	109,105
Swaziland	998,730	10	99,873
Sweden	9,800,000	3.6	320,000
Syria	15,608,648	90	14,047,783
Tajikistan	5,916,373	85	5,028,917
Tanzania	29,058,470	65	18,888,006
Thailand	58,851,357	14	8,239,190

(continued)

Country	Total Population	Percentage of Muslims	Muslim Population
Togo	4,570,530	55	2,513,792
Trinidad and Tobago	1,272,385	12	152,686
Tunisia	9,019,687	98	8,839,293
Turkey	62,484,478	99.8	62,359,509
Turkmenistan	4,149,283	87	3,609,876
Uganda	20,158,176	36	7,256,943
United Arab Emirates	3,057,337	96	2,935,044
United Kingdom	58,489,975	2.7	1,579,229
United States	266,476,278	3.75	9,992,860
Uzbekistan	23,418,381	88	20,608,175
West Bank	1,427,741	75	1,070,806
Western Sahara	222,631	100	222,631
Yemen	13,483,178	99	13,348,346
Zaire	46,498,539	10	4,649,854
Zambia	9,159,072	15	1,373,861
Zimbabwe	11,271,314	15	1,690,697

Source: www.islamicwebcom/begin/population.htm

Bibliography

The sources listed in the following sections are a representative selection of books and articles in the field of Islamic studies. They are organized in four parts: "I. Reference," "II. History," "III. Islam," and "IV. Politics, Society, and the Arts."

Part I includes bibliographies, useful even at a time when one can access the Library of Congress catalog from a home computer. Most important are J. D. Pearson's *Index Islamicus*, which covers virtually all articles published on any aspect of Islamic studies in most European languages from 1905 to the present. The *Guide to Islam* (1983), by David Ede, is still useful. It lists a wide range of reference materials and historical works from pre-Islamic to modern times, as well as publications on religious thought, law, art, and other topics, with ample annotations. Specialized bibliographies include Samira R. Meghdessian's *The Status of the Arab Woman: A Select Bibliography*, and UNESCO's *Bibliographic Guide to Studies on the Status of Women*. K. A. C. Creswell covers the arts in his *Bibliography of the Architecture, Arts, and Crafts of Islam*. S. H. Amin, H. M . Steward, and Laila al-Zwaini list works on Islamic law in *Islamic Law in the Contemporary World: Introduction, Glossary, and Bibliography* and *A Bibliography of Islamic Law, 1980–1993*. Bibliographies on political Islam include Yvonne Haddad and John L. Esposito's *The Islamic Revival since 1988: A Critical Survey and Bibliography* and Yvonne Haddad's, John O. Voll's, and John L. Esposito's *The Contemporary Islamic Revival: A Critical Survey and Bibliography*. Ahmad S. Moussalli lists an excellent bibliography in his *Historical Dictionary of Islamic Fundamentalist Movements in the Arab World, Iran, and Turkey*.

Indispensable for the serious student of Islamic history for the period between 600 and 1500 CE is R. Stephen Humphreys *Islamic History: A Framework for Inquiry*, which combines a bibliographic study with an inquiry into method, surveying the principal reference tools available to historians of Islam. It is the most recent study of its type, replacing

J. Sauvaget's *Introduction to the History of the Middle East: A Bibliographical Guide*.

The most important reference works for the advanced student are the *Encyclopaedia of Islam*, a second edition (*EI2*), which was begun in 1954 and is still not completed (a CD-ROM edition exists up to the letter "S"), and the *Shorter Encyclopaedia of Islam*, which appeared in 1953 (reprinted in 1961) under the editorship of H. A. R. Gibb and J. H. Kramers. The emphasis is on the classical period rather than on modern Islam. The subjects are listed in Arabic terms, making it an academic work primarily for experts. These works are complemented by the *Encyclopaedia Iranica*, which includes greater coverage on Shi'ism and the eastern part of the Islamic world. It includes more contemporary materials, but the transliteration system may pose problems for the beginner. Furthermore, it is also still far from complete, and cross-listings of Persian terms in English are therefore not always available. A beginning student will prefer to consult Cyril Glassé's *The New Encyclopedia of Islam* and Stephan Ronart's and Nandy Ronart's *Concise Encyclopaedia of Arabic Civilization*, or the present work, which provides a historical outline of Islamic history as well as a study of classical Islam and modern revivalist movements subsumed under the general term of political Islam. *The Encyclopaedia Britannica*, now also available on the Internet, also has a wealth of information on all aspects of Islamic studies.

An important source for early "great men" is Guekin De Slane's *Ibn Khallikan's Biographical Dictionary*, which lists some 800 philosophers, theologians, scientists, and others and which the historian Reynold A. Nicholson has called the "best general biography ever written."

For reliable chronologies the reader may refer to C. E. Bosworth's *The New Islamic Dynasties: A Chronological and Genealogical Manual* and Robert Mantran's *Great Dates in Islamic History*.

Part II lists works on the history of individual countries, including the Arab world, Iran, the Ottoman empire, and Turkey, and a limited number of books and articles on Central Asia and Muslim Spain, an area that has been defined as the "Central Islamic Lands." One section includes general histories as well as the pioneering work of M. G. S. Hodgson, *The Venture of Islam: Conscience and History in a World Civilization*.

Part III contains books and articles on various aspects of Islamic studies, including sections on the Prophet Muhammad, Koran, hadith, mysticism, theology and philosophy, law, Shi'ism, and modernism. It presents a number of works that have been translated from Arabic, including classic authors such as Ibn Khaldun, Ibn Rushd (Averroës), and Ibn Sina (Avicenna).

Part IV covers politics, society, and the arts, with special emphasis on political Islam and women's studies, about which there exists an increasing amount of literature. The writings of the major ideologues of political Islam, for example Sayyid Abu'l A'la al-Maududi's *First Principles of the Islamic State*, Sayyid Qutb's *Milestones*, Hasan al-Banna's *Collections*, and Ayatollah Khomeyni's *Islam and Revolution*, have been presented in translations. An important work on political Islam is Ahmad S. Moussalli's *Historical Dictionary of Islamic Fundamentalist Movements in the Arab World, Iran, and Turkey.*

It must be stressed, however, that the following selection is necessarily only a representative sample of the considerable volume of material produced in the field of Islamic studies.

CONTENTS

III. Reference   352
  Bibliographies   352
  Encyclopedias and Handbooks   353
  Biographies   356
II. History   359
  General   359
  Arab World   360
    Pre-Islamic   360
    Islamic Period   361
  Iran   366
  Ottoman Empire and Turkey   369
  Turko–Mongols   373
  South and Central Asia   374
Islamic Spain   376
III. Islam   376
  General   376
Islamic Studies   381
  Muhammad   384
  Koran   385
  Hadith   388
  Mysticism   390

Medieval Theology and Philosophy 396
Law 406
Practices 412
Twelver Shi'ism 414
Other Sects 418
Modernism 422
IV Islamic Politics, Society, and the Arts 423
Political Islam 423
The Caliphate 440
Women 441
Art and Architecture 449
Education 452
Economics 453
Literature 456
Cities 457

I. REFERENCE

Bibliographies

Annes, M. A. "Study of Muslim Women and Family: A Bibliography." *Journal of Comparative Family Studies* 20 (1989): 263–274.

Creswell, K. A. C. *A Bibliography of the Architecture, Arts and Crafts of Islam to 1960.* Cairo: American University at Cairo Press, 1961.

Danishpazhouh, M., and A. Newman. "An Annotated Bibliography of Government and Statecraft." In *Authority and Political Culture in Shi'ism*, edited by S. A. Arjomand, 213–239. Albany: State University of New York Press, 1989.

Denffer, Ahmad von. *Literature on Hadith in European Languages: A Bibliography.* Leicester, UK: Islamic Foundation, 1981.

Ede, David. *Guide to Islam.* Boston: G. K. Hall, 1983.

Geddes, Charles L. *Guide to Reference Books for Islamic Studies.* Denver, CO: American Institute of Islamic Studies, 1985.

Haddad, Yvonne, and John L. Esposito. *The Islamic Revival since 1988: A Critical Survey and Bibliography.* Westport, CT: Greenwood Press, 1998.

Haddad, Yvonne, John O. Voll, and John L. Esposito. *The Contemporary Islamic Revival: A Critical Survey and Bibliography.* Westport, CT: Greenwood Press, 1991.

Hopwood, Derek, and Diana Grimwood-Jones, eds. *Middle East and Islam: A Bibliographic Introduction.* Zug, Switzerland: Inter-Documentation, 1972.

Howard, Harry N., et al. *The Middle East and North Africa: A Bibliography fore Undergraduate Libraries.* Williamsport, PA: Bro-Dart, 1971.

Humphreys, R. Stephen. *Islamic History: A Framework for Inquiry.* Princeton, NJ: Princeton University Press, 1991.

Makdisi, J. "Islamic Law Bibliography." *Law Liberty Journal* 78 (1986): 103–189.

Meghdessian, Samira R. *The Status of the Arab Woman: A Select Bibliography.* New York: Greenwood Press, 1980.

Modarressi, Hossein. *Tradition and Survival: A bibliographical Survey of Early Shi'ite Literature.* Oxford: Oneworld Publications, 2003.

Qazzaz, Ayad. *Women in the Arab World: An Annotated Bibliography.* Washington, DC: Association of Arab-American University Graduates, 1975.

Sauvaget, J. *Introduction to the History of the Muslim East: A Bibliographical Guide.* Berkeley: University of California Press, 1965.

Stewart, H. M. "Tribal Law in the Arab World: A Review of the Literature." *International Journal of Middle East Studies* 19 (1987): 473–490.

UNESCO. *Bibliographic Guide to Studies on the Status of Women.* London: Bowker, 1983.

Wickens, G. M., R. M. Savory, and W. J. Watson, eds. *Persia in Islamic Times: A Practical Bibliography of Its History.* Montreal: Institute of Islamic Studies, McGill University, 1964.

Wilson, Sir Arnold T. *A Bibliography of Persia.* Oxford: Clarendon Press, 1930.

Encyclopedias and Handbooks

Adamec, Ludwig. *Historical Dictionary of Afghanistan.* 3rd rev. ed. Lanham, MD: Scarecrow Press, 2003.

Amin, Hasan. *Islamic Shi'ite Encyclopaedia.* Beirut: n.p., 1968.

Bacharach, Jere L. *A Near East Studies Handbook.* Seattle: University of Washington Press, 1976.

Barthel, Günter, and Krisitina Stock, eds. *Lexikon Arabische Welt.* Wiesbaden, Germany: Dr. Ludwig Reichert Verlag, 1994.

Bidwell, Robin. *The Dictionary of Modern Arab History.* New York: Kegan Paul International, 1997.

Bosworth, Clifford Edmund. *The New Islamic Dynasties: A Chronological and Genealogical Manual.* Edinburgh: Edinburgh University Press, 1996.

Bowker, John, ed., *The Oxford Dictionary of World Religions.* New York: Oxford University Press, 1997.

Encyclopaedia of Islam, www.encislam.brill.nl.

Esposito, John. *Oxford Dictionary of Islam.* New York: Oxford University Press, 2003.

Ferguson, J. Ed. *Encyclopedia of Mysticism and Mystery Religions.* New York: Crossroads, 1982.

Freeman-Greenville, G. S. P. *Historical Atlas of Islam.* New York: Continuum International, 2002.

Fisher, W. B. *Cambridge History of Iran.* Cambridge: Cambridge at the University Press, 1968.

Freeman-Grenville, G. S. P. *Historical Atlas of Islam.* New York: Continuum International, 2002.

Gibb, Hamilton A. R., and J. H. Kramer. *Shorter Encyclopedia of Islam.* London: Luzac & Co. 1961.

Glassé, Cyril. *The New Encyclopedia of Islam.* Lanham, MD: Rowman & Littlefield, 2001.

Gresh, Alain, and Dominique Vidal. *The New A–Z of the Middle East.* London: I. B. Tauris, 2001.

Hazard, H. W. *Atlas of Islamic History.* 3rd ed. Princeton, NJ: Princeton University Press, 1954.

Hiro, Dilip. *Dictionary of the Middle East.* Houndmills, Basingstoke, Hampshire England: Macmillan, 1996.

Houtsma, M. T., et al., eds. *Encyclopedia of Islam: A Dictionary of the Geography, Ethnography, and Biography of Muhammadan Peoples, Prepared by a Number of Leading Orientalists.* 4 vols. Leiden, Netherlands: E. J. Brill, 1913–1936; Supplement, 1938.

Hughes, Thomas Patrick. *A Dictionary of Islam; Being a Cyclopaedia of the Doctrines, Rites, Ceremonies and Customs, together with the Technical and Theological Terms of the Muhammadan Religion.* Lahore, Pakistan: Premier Book House, 1964.

Ingrams, Doreen. "The Position of Women in Middle Eastern Arab Society." In *The Middle East: A Handbook,* edited by Michael Adams. New York: Praeger, 1971.

Juynboll, G. H. A. *Encyclopedia of Canonical Hadith.* Boston: Brill, 2007.

Khan, Muhammad Muhsin. *Summarized Sahih Al-Bukhari.* Riyadh, Saudi Arabia: Dar-us-Salam Publications, 1990.

Khoury, Adel Theodor, et al. *Islam Lexikon: Geschichte, Ideen, Gestalten.* Freiburg, Germany: Herder, 1991.

Leaman, Oliver. *The Biographical Encyclopedia of Islamic Philosophy.* 2 vols. New York: Maiden Lane, 2006.

Lewis, Bernard, and P. M. Hold, eds. *Historians of the Middle East.* London: Oxford, 1962.

Mantran, Robert, ed. *Great Dates in Islamic History.* New York: Facts on File, 1996. Translation of *Les grandes dates de l'Islam.* Paris: Librairie Larousse, 1990.

Margoliouth, D. S. *Lectures on Arabic Historians.* Calcutta, India: University of Calcutta, 1930.

McAuliffe, *Encyclopedia of the Qoran.* Leiden, Netherlands: E. J. Brill, 2001.

Meisami, Julie Scott, and Paul Starkey. *Encyclopedia of Arabic Literature.* London: Routledge, 1998.

Mir, Mustansir. *Dictionary of Quranic Terms and Concepts.* New York: Garland Publishing, 1987.

Mostyn, Trevor. *The Cambridge Encyclopedia of the Middle East and North Africa.* Cambridge: Cambridge University Press, 1988.

Moussalli, Ahmad S. *Historical Dictionary of Islamic Fundamentalist Movements in the Arab World, Iran, and Turkey.* Lanham, MD: Scarecrow Press, 1999.

Pearson, J. D. *Index Islamicus, 1906–1955: A Catalogue of Articles on Islamic Subjects in Periodicals and Other Collective Publications.* Cambridge: W. Heffer, 1958. Supplements continuing.

Penrice, J. A. *A Dictionary and Glossary of the Quran.* Delhi, India: Low Price Publications, 1873.

Philips, Cyril Henry, ed. *Handbook of Oriental History.* London: Office of the Royal Historical Society, 1951.

Reich, Bernard, ed. *Political Leaders of the Contemporary Middle East and North Africa: A Biographical Dictionary.* New York: Greenwood Press, 1991.

Reichert, Rolf. *A Historical and Regional Atlas of the Arabic World: Maps and Chronological Survey.* Translated by Phyllis Goetsch and Jose Luis Magalhaes. Salvador de Bahia, Brazil: Centro de Estudos Afro-Orientals, Universidade Federal, 1969.

Ronard, Stephan, and Nancy Ronard. *Concise Encyclopedia of Arabic Civilization.* Vol. 1, *The Arab East.* New York: Praeger, 1960.

Roolvink, R. *Historical Atlas of the Muslim Peoples.* London: G. Allen & Unwin, 1957.

Rosenthal, Franz. *A History of Muslim Historiography*. Leiden, Netherlands: E. J. Brill, 1968.

Shimoni, Yaacov, and Evyatar Levine. *Political Dictionary of the Middle East in the 20th Century*. Jerusalem: Jerusalem Publishing House, 1972.

Simon, Reeva S., et al. *Encyclopedia of the Modern Middle East*. New York: Macmillan Reference USA, 1996.

Wehr, Hans. *Arabic-English Dictionary*. Edited by J. M. Cowan. Ithaca, NY: Cornell University Press, 1960.

Wensinck, Arent J. *A Handbook of Early Muhammadan Tradition*. Leiden, Netherlands: E. J. Brill, 1927.

———, et al. *Handwörterbuch des Islam*. Leiden, Netherlands: E. J. Brill, 1941.

Zwaini, Laila al-, and Rudolph Peters. *A Bibliography of Islamic Law, 1980–1993*. Leiden, Netherlands: E. J. Brill, 1994.

Biographies

Abbott, Nabia. *Aishah, the Beloved of Mohammed*. Chicago: University of Chicago Press, 1942.

Aga Khan III, Sultan Muhammad. *The Memoirs of Aga Khan: World Enough and Time*. London: Simon & Schuster, 1954.

'Ali, Syed Ameer. "Memoirs." *Islamic Culture* 6 (1931): 509–42; 6 (1932):1–18.

Amin, 'Uthman. *Muhammad 'Abduh*. Translated by Charles Wendell. Washington, DC: Council of Learned Societies, 1953.

Amrouch, Fadhma. *My Life Story; The Autobiography of a Berber Woman*. New Brunswick, NJ: Rutgers University Press, 1989.

Aziz, K. K. *Ameer 'Ali: His Life and Work*. Lahore, Pakistan: Publishers United, 1968.

Baerlein, Henry. *Abu'l Ala, the Syrian*. Piscataway, NJ: Gorgias Press, 2004.

Baljon, J. M. S. *The Reforms and Religious Ideas of Sir Sayyid Ahmad Khan*. Leiden, Netherlands: E. J. Brill, 1949.

Bowen, Harold. *The Life and Times of 'Ali ibn 'Is'a, the "Good Vizier."* Cambridge: Cambridge University Press, 1928.

Dar, Bashir Ahmad. *A Study in Iqbal's Philosophy*. Lahore, Pakistan: Chulam Ali and Sons, 1971.

DeLong-Das, Natana. *Notable Muslims; Muslim Builders of World Civilization and Culture*. Oxford: Oneworld Publications, 2008.

Djemal Pasha, Ahmed. *Memories of a Turkish Statesman, 1913–1919.* New York: Doran, 1922.

Fischel, Walter J. *Ibn Khaldun in Egypt, His Public Functions and His Historical Research: A Study in Islamic Historiography.* Berkeley: University of California Press, 1967.

Gibb, H. A. R. *The Life of Saladin from the Words of 'Imad ad-Din and Baha' ad-Din.* Oxford: The Clarendon Press, 1973.

Graham, George F. Irving. *The Life and Work of Sir Sayyid Ahmad Khan.* Delhi, India: Idarah-i Adabiyat-i Delhi, 1974.

Haq, Mahmudul. *Muhammad Abduh: A Study of a Modern Thinker of Egypt.* Aligarh, India: Institute of Islamic Studies, Aligarh Muslim University, 1978.

Hart, Alan. *Arafat: Terrorist or Peacemaker?* London: Sidgwick and Jackson, 1984.

Haykal, Muhammad Husayn. *The Life of Muhammad.* Translated from the 8th edition by Ismail Ragi A. Faruqi. London: Shorouk International, 1983.

Jahiz, 'Amr ibn Bahr al-. *The Life and Works of Jahiz.* Translated by D. M. Hawke. London: Routledge and Kegan Paul, 1969.

Karsh, Efraim, and Inari Rautsi. *Saddam Hussein: A Political Biography.* New York: Free Press, 1991.

Keddie, Nikki R. *Sayyid Jamal ad-Din 'al-Afghani': A Political Biography.* Berkeley: University of California Press, 1972.

Kikhia, Masour O. El-. *Libya's Qaddafi: The Politics of Contradiction.* Gainesville: University Press of Florida, 1997.

Kinross, Lord. *Atatürk: A Biography of Mustafa Kemal, Father of Modern Turkey.* New York: Morrow, 1965.

Lane-Poole, Stanley. *Saladin and the Fall of the Kingdom of Jerusalem.* Beirut: Khayats, 1964.

Lees, Brian. *A Handbook of the Al Saud Ruling Family of Saudi Arabia.* London: n.p., 1980.

Malcolm X. *The Autobiography of Malcolm X* (1965). New York: Ballantine Books, 1992.

Malik, Hafeez, ed. *Iqbal: Poet-Philosopher of Pakistan.* New York: Columbia University Press, 1971.

———. *Sir Sayyid Ahmad Khan and Muslim Modernization in India and Pakistan.* New York: Columbia University Press, 1980.

Mansfield, Peter. *Nasser.* London: Methuen, 1969.

Matthews, C. D. "A Muslim Iconoclast (Ibn Taymiyyah) on the 'Merits' of Jerusalem and Palestine." *Journal of the American Oriental Society* 36 (1936): 1–21.

Mcdonald, D. B. "Life of al-Ghazzali." *Journal of the American Oriental Society* 20 (1899): 71–132.

McLoughlin, Leslie. *Ibn Saud: Founder of a Kingdom.* London: Macmillan, 1993.

Midhat, Ali Haidar. *The Life of Midhat Pasha.* London: Murray, 1903.

Monroe, Elizabeth. *Philby of Arabia.* London: Faber & Faber, 1973.

Nasr, Seyyed Hossein. *Three Muslim Sages.* Cambridge, MA: Harvard University Press, 1974.

Nizami, K. A. *Sayyid Ahmad Khan.* Delhi: Government of India, 1966.

O'Fahey, R. S. *Enigmatic Saint: Ahmad Ibn Idris and the Idrisi Tradition.* Evanston, IL: Northwestern University Press, 1990.

Pellat, Charles. *The Life and Works of Jahiz: Translations of Selected Texts.* Translated by D. M. Hawke. London: Routledge and Kegan Paul, 1969.

Philby, H. St. John. *Harun al-Rashid.* New York: Appleton-Century, 1934.

Rawlinson, H. G. "Sayyid Ahmad Khan." *Islam Culture* 4 (1930):386–396.

Sanyal, Usha. *Ahmad Riza Khan Barelwi: In the Path of the Prophet.* Oxford: Oneworld, 2005.

Shah, Mohammad, ed. *Writings and Speeches of Sir Syed Ahmad Khan.* Bombay, India: Nachiketa Publications, 1972.

Sharma, Arvind. "The Spiritual Biography of al-Ghaz_l." *Studies in Islam* 9 (1972): 65–85.

Slane, Mac Guckin de. *Ibn Khallikan's Biographical Dictionary.* Beirut: Khayat, 1970.

Topa, I. N. "Sir Sayyid Ahmad Khan: A Study in Social Thought." *Islamic Culture* 27 (1953): 225–241.

Tritton, A. S. "Ibn Hazm: The Man and the Thinker." *Islamic Studies* 3 (1964): 471–484.

Vahid, Syed Abdul. *Iqbal: His Art and Thought.* London: Murray, 1959.

Watt, W. Montgomery. *Muslim Intellectual: A Study of al-Ghazali.* Edinburgh: Edinburgh University Press, 1963.

Wessels, Antoine. *A Modern Arabic Biography of Muhammad: A Critical Study of Muhammad Husayn Haykal's Hayat, Muhammad.* Leiden, Netherlands: E. J. Brill, 1972.

Wolpert, Stanley A. *Jinnah of Pakistan.* New York: Oxford University Press, 1984.

II. HISTORY

General

Armanjani, Yahya. *Middle East, Past and Present*. Englewood Cliffs, NJ: Prentice Hall, 1970.

Brockelmann, Car. *History of the Islamic Peoples*. New York: Capricorn, 1944.

Choueiri, Youssef. *Arab Nationalism: A History*. New York: Blackwell, 2000.

Cleveland, William L. *A History of the Modern Middle East*. Boulder, CO: Westview Press, 1994.

Coll, Steve. *Ghost Wars: The Secret History of the CIA*. New York: Penguin, 2004.

El-Nawawy, Mohammed, and Adel Iskander. *Al-Jazeera: How the Free Arab News Network Scooped the World and Changes the Middle East*. Boulder, CO: Westwood Press, 2002.

El-Rewany, Hassan Ahmed. *The Ramadan War: End of Illusion*. Carlisle Barracks, PA: U.S. Army War College, 2001.

Fisher, Sydney Nettleton, and William Ochsenwald. *The Middle East: A History*. New York: McGraw-Hill, 1990.

Goldschmidt, Arthur, Jr. *A Concise History of the Middle East*. 4th ed. Boulder, CO: Westview Press, 1991.

Hitti, Philip. *The Near East in History: A 5,000 Year Story*. Princeton, NJ: Princeton University Press, 1961.

Hodgson, Marshall, G. S. *The Century of Islam: Conscience and History in a World Civilization*. 3 vols. Chicago: Chicago University Press, 1974.

Ibn Khaldun. *The Muqadimmah*. Princeton, NJ: Princeton University Press, 1958.

Lapidus, Ira. *A History of Islamic Societies*. Cambridge: Cambridge University Press, 1988.

Mansfield, Peter. *A History of the Middle East*. New York: Penguin Books, 1991.

Regan, Geoffrey. *First Crusader: Byzantium's Holy Wars*. New York: Palgrave Macmillan, 2001.

Said, Edward W. *Reflections on Exile and Other Essays*. Cambridge, MA: Harvard University Press, 2002.

Schaebler, Birgit, and Leif Stenberg. Eds. *Globalization and the Muslim World*. Syracuse, NY: Syracuse University Press, 2008.

Schroeder, Eric. *Muhammad's People*. Portland, ME: Bond Wheelwright, 1955.

Arab World

Pre-Islamic

Grunebaum, G. E. von. "The Nature of Arab Unity before Islam." *Arabica* 10 (1963): 5–23.

Hodgson, Marshall G. S. "The World before Islam." In *The Venture of Islam,* Vol. 1, 103–145. Chicago: Chicago University Press, 1974.

Kister, M. J. "Al-Hira: Some Notes on Its Relations with Arabia." *Arabica* 15 (1968): 143–169.

———. "Some Reports Concerning Mecca: From Jahiliyya to Islam." *Journal of the Economic and Social History of the Orient* 15 (1972): 63–93.

Levi della Vida, G. "Pre-Islamic Arabia." In *The Arab Heritage.* Princeton, NJ: Princeton University Press, 1946.

Moscati, S. "The Arabs." In *Ancient Semitic Civilizations.* London: Elek, (1957): 181–219.

Noldeke, Theodor. "Arabs (Ancient)." In *Encyclopaedia of Religion and Ethics*, 13 vols., edited by James Hastings, 1: 659–673. New York: Charles Scribner's Sons, 1962.

O'Leary, De Lacy. *Arabia before Muhammad.* London: K. Paul, Trench, and Trubner, 1927.

Ringgren, Helmer. *Islam: 'Aslama and Muslim.* Uppsala, Sweden: C. W. K. Gleerup, 1949.

Sergeant, R. B. "Haram and Hawtah: The Sacred Enclave in Arabia." In *Melanges Taha Husain*, edited by A. R. Badawi, 41–58. Cairo: Dar al-Maaref, 1962.

———. "Hud and Other Pre-Islamic Prophets of Hadramawt." *Le Museon* 67 (1959).

———. *The Sayyids of Hadramawt: An Inaugural Lecture.* London: School of Oriental and African Studies, University of London, 1957.

Shahid, Irfan. "Pre-Islamic Arabia." In *The Cambridge History of Islam,* Vol. 1, 3–29. Cambridge: Cambridge University Press, 1970.

Smith, W. Robertson. *Kinship and Marriage in Early Arabia.* Cambridge: Cambridge University Press, 1907.

Watt, W. M. "Belief in a 'High God' in Pre-Islamic Mecca." *Journal of Semitic Studies* 16 (1971): 35–40.

Wendell, Charles. "The Pre-Islamic Period of Sirat al-Nabi." *Muslim World* 62 (1972):12–41.

Islamic Period

Abdalla, Abdelgadir Mahmoud, et al., eds. *Sources for the History of Arabia*. Riyadh, Saudi Arabia: Riyadh University Press, 1979.

Abir, Mordechai. *Saudi Arabia in the Oil Era*. Boulder, CO: Westview Press, 1988.

Abun-Nasr, Jamil M. *A History of the Maghrib in the Islamic Period*. 3rd ed. Cambridge: Cambridge University Press, 1987.

Almana, Mohammed. *Arabia Unified: A Portrait of Ibn Saud*. Rev. ed. London: Hutchinson Benham, 1982.

Al-Rashid, Maddawi. *A History of Saudi Arabia*. Cambridge: Cambridge University Press, 2002.

Altorki, Soraya. *Women in Saudi Arabia: Ideology and Behavior among the Elite*. New York: Columbia University Press, 1986.

Anderson, Betty S. *Nationalist Voices in Jordan: The Street and the State*. Austin: University Texas Press, 2006.

Anderson, Irvine H. *Aramco, the United States, and Saudi Arabia: A Study of the Dynamics of Foreign Oil Policy, 1933–1950*. Princeton, NJ: Princeton University Press, 1981.

Antonius, George. *The Arab Awakening: The Story of the Arab National Movement*. London: Hamish Hamilton, 1945.

Armstrong, Harold C. *Lord of Arabia, Ibn Saud: An Intimate Study of a King*. London: Kegan Paul, 1934.

Belyaev, E. A. *Arabs, Islam and the Arab Caliphate in the Early Middle Ages*. Translated by A. Gourevitch. New York: Praeger, 1969.

Ben-Ami, Sholomo. *Scars of War, Wounds of Peace: The Israeli–Arab Tragedy*. Oxford: Oxford University Press, 2006.

Bligh, Alexander. *From Prince to King: Royal Succession in the House of Saud in the Twentieth Century*. New York: New York University Press, 1984.

Braude, Joseph. *The New Iraq: Rebuilding the Country for Its People, the Middle East, and the World*. New York: Basic Books, 2003.

Burckhardt, John Lewis. *Notes on the Bedouins and Wahabys Collected during His Travels in the East*. Vol. 2. London: Coulbourn and Bentley, 1931.

Burke, Edmund, III. *Prelude to Protectorate in Morocco: Precolonial Protest and Resistance, 1860–1912*. Chicago: University of Chicago Press, 1976.

Burkhardt, John L. *Travels in Arabia* (1829). London: F. Cass, 1968.

Carter, Jimmy. *Palestine Peace Not Apartheid*. Old Tappan, NJ: Simon & Schuster, 2006.

Crone, Patricia. *From Arabian Tribes to Islamic Empire: Army, State, and Society in the Near East, c. 600–850*. Burlington, VT: Ashgate, 2007.

———. *Meccan Trade and the Rise of Islam*. Piscataway, NJ: Georgias Press, 2004.

Davison, Christopher. *The United Arab Emirates: A Study of Survival*. Boulder, CO: Lynne Rienner, 2005.

De Gaury, Gerald. *Faisal, King of Saudi Arabia*. New York: Praeger, 1967.

———. *Rulers of Mecca*. London: Harrap, 1951.

Dickson, H. R. P. *The Arab of the Desert*. New York: Macmillan, 1949.

Donner, F. M. *The Early Islamic Conquests*. Princeton, NJ: Princeton University Press, 1981.

Doughty, Charles M. *Travels in Arabia Deserta*. New York: Random House, 1936.

Dunlop, D. *Arab Civilization to A.D. 1500*. London: Longmans, 1971.

Eppel, Michael. *Iraq from Monarchy to Tyranny: From the Hashemites to the Rise of Saddam*. Gainesville: University Press of Florida, 2004.

Fernea, Elizabeth. *Guests of the Sheikh*. New York: Doubleday, 1965.

———. *A View of the Nile*. Garden City, NJ: Doubleday, 1970.

Finnie, David H. *Desert Enterprise: The Middle East Oil Industry in Its Local Environment*. Cambridge, MA: Harvard University Press, 1958.

Fish, Robert. *Pity the Nation: The Abduction of Lebanon*. London: Deutsch, 1990.

Friedman, Lauri S. *The Iraq War*. Detroit: Greenhaven Press, 2008.

Gabrieli, Francesco. *The Arabs: A Compact History*. Translated by Salvator Attansio. New York: Hawthorn, 1963.

Golan, Galia. *Israel and Palestine: Peace Plans and Proposals from Oslo to Disengagement*. Princeton, NJ: Princeton University Press, 2006.

Goldberg, Jacob. *The Foreign Policy of Saudi Arabia: The Formative Years, 1902–1918*. Cambridge, MA: Harvard University Press, 1986.

Grunebaum, G. E. von. "The Nature of Arab Unity before Islam." *Arabica* 10 (1963): 5–23.

Habib, John S. *Ibn Saud's Warriors of Islam*. Leiden, Netherlands: E. J. Brill, 1978.

Helms, Christine Moss. *The Cohesion of Saudi Arabia: Evolution of Political Identity*. Baltimore, MD: Johns Hopkins University Press, 1981.

Herzl, Theodore. *The Jewish State*. Mineola, NY: Dover Publications, 1989.

Hinchcliffe, Peter, and Beverley Milton-Edwards. *Conflicts in the Middle East*. 3rd ed. New York: Routledge, 2007.

Hitti, Philip K. *The Arabs: A Short History*. Princeton, NJ: Princeton University Press, 1943.

———. *History of Syria Including Lebanon and Palestine*. 2nd ed. London: Macmillan, 1957.

———. *History of the Arabs from the Earliest Times to the Present*. 8th ed. New York: St. Martin's 1964.

———. *Lebanon in History from the Earliest Times to the Present*. London: Macmillan, 1957.

———. *Syria: A Short History*. London: Macmillan, 1959.

Hough, Roberts. *Embattled Algeria. 1988–2002. Studies in Broken Polity*. New York: Verso, 2003.

Hourani, Albert. *Arabic Thought in the Liberal Age, 1789–1939*. London: Oxford University Press, 1962, 1970.

———. *History of the Arab Peoples*. London: Faber and Faber, 1991.

Howarth, David. *The Desert King: Ibn Saud and His Arabia*. New York: McGraw-Hill, 1964.

Humphreys, R. Stephen. *Between Memory and Desire: The Middle East in a Troubled Age*. Berkeley: University of California Press, 2001.

Hurgronje, C. Snouck. *Mekka in the Latter Part of the Nineteenth Century*. Translated by J. H. Monahan. London: Luzac, 1931.

Jamal, Amal. *The Palestinian National Movement: Politics of Contention, 1967–2005*. Bloomington: Indiana University Press, 2005.

Joyce, Miriam. *Ruling Shaikhs and Her Majesty's Government: 1960–1969*. Portland, OR: Frank Cass, 2003.

Julien, Charles André. *History of North Africa: Tunisia, Algeria, and Morocco from the Arab Conquest to 1830*. Translated by John Petrie. Edited by C. C. Stewart. London: Routledge and Kegan Paul, 1970.

Kassem, Maye. *Egyptian Politics: The Dynamics of Authoritarian Rule*. Boulder, CO: Lynne Rienner Publishers, 2004.

Kennedy, Hugh. *The Prophet and the Age of the Caliphates: The Islamic Near East from the Sixth to the Eleventh Century*. London: Longman, 1986.

Khashan, Hilal. *Arabs at the Crossroads: Political Identity and Nationalism*. Gainesville: University Press of Florida, 2000.

Kimmerling, Baruch, and Joel S. Migdal. *The Palestinian People: A History*. Cambridge: Harvard University Press, 2003.

King, John. *Iraq Then and Now*. Chicago: Raintree, 2006.

Lane-Poole, Stanley. *A History of Egypt in the Middle Ages (600–1500)*. 2nd rev. ed. London: Methuen, 1914.

Laroui, Abdallah. *The History of the Maghrib: An Interpretive Essay*. Translated by Ralph Manheim. Princeton, NJ: Princeton University Press, 1977.

Le Strange, Guy. *Baghdad during the Abbasid Caliphate*. London: Oxford University Press, 1900.

———. *Palestine under the Moslems: A Description of Syria and the Holy Land (650–1500)*. London: A. P. Watt, 1890.

Lewis, Bernard. *The Arabs in History*. 4th ed. London: Hutchinson's, 1966.

Margoliouth, D. S. *Lectures on Arabic Historians*. Calcutta, India: University of Calcutta, 1930.

Massad, Joseph. *The Persistence of the Palestinian Question: Essays on Zionism and the Palestinian*. New York: Routledge, 2006.

McDougall, James. *History and Culture of Nationalism in Algeria*. Cambridge: Cambridge University Press, 2006.

Monroe, Elizabeth. *Philby of Arabia*. London: Faber and Faber, 1973.

Morony, Michael. *Iraq after the Muslim Conquest*. Princeton, NJ: Princeton University Press, 1984.

Morris, Benny. *The Birth of the Palestinian Refugee problem, 1947–1949*. New York: Cambridge University Press, 1987.

Moscati, S. "The Arabs." In *Ancient Semitic Civilizations*, 181–219. Princeton, NJ: Princeton University Press, n.d.

Muir, Sir William. *The Caliphate, Its Rise, Decline and Fall, from Original Sources*. Beirut: Khayats, 1963. Originally published in 1915.

Myers, Eugene A. *Arabic Thought and the Western World in the Golden Age of Islam*. New York: F. Unger, 1964.

Netton, Ian Richard, ed. *Arabia and the Gulf: From Traditional Society to Modern States*. Totowa, NJ: Barnes & Noble, 1986.

Niblock, Tim. *Saudi Arabia: Power, Legitimacy and Survival*. New York: Routledge, 2006.

———, ed. *State, Society and Economy in Saudi Arabia*. London: Croom Helm, 1982.

Nicholson, Reynold Alleyne. *A Literary History of the Arabs*. Cambridge: Cambridge University Press, 1969.

Ochsenwald, William. "Saudi Arabia." In *The Politics of Islamic Revivalism: Diversity and Unity*, edited by Shireen T. Hunter. Bloomington: Indiana University Press, 1988.

O'Leary, De Lacy. *A Short History of the Fatimid Khalifate*. New York: Dutton, 1925.

Oren, Michael. *Six Days of War: June 1967 and the Making of the Modern Middle East*. Oxford: Oxford University Press, 2002.

Philby, H. St. J. B. *Arabia*. New York: Scribner, 1930.

———. *Arabia of the Wabbabis*. London: Constable, 1928.

———. *Arabian Days*. London: Robert Hale, 1951.

———. *Arabian Jubilee*. London: R. Hale, 1952.

———. *A Pilgrim in Arabia*. London: R. Hale, 1946.

———. *Saudi Arabia*. London: Benn, 1955.

Rabinovitch, Itamar. *Waging Peace: Israel and the Arabs, 1948–2003*. Princeton, NJ: Princeton University Press, 2004.

Rubin, Barry. *The Modern Middle East*. Cambridge: Cambridge University Press, 2002.

———. *The Tragedy of the Middle East*. Cambridge: Cambridge University Press, 2002.

Said, Edward. *The Politics of Dispossession*. New York: Random House, 1994.

Salibi, Kemal. *A History of Arabia*. Delmar, Beirut: Caravan Books, 1980.

Scham, Paul, Walid Salem, and Benjamin Pogrund. *Shared Histories: A Palestinian–Israeli Dialogue*. Walnut Creek, CA: Left Coast Press, 2005.

Shaban, M. A. *The 'Abbasid Revolution*. Cambridge: Cambridge University Press, 1970.

Sheehi, Stephen. *Foundations of Modern Arab Identity*. Gainesville: University Press of Florida, 2004.

Sheikholislami, A. Reza S., and Rostam Kavoussi. *The Political Economy of Saudi Arabia*. Seattle: University of Washington Press, 1984.

Shoufani, Elias. *Al-Riddah and the Muslim Conquest of Arabia*. Toronto: University of Toronto Press, 1973.

Stansfield, Gareth R. V. *Iraqi Kurdestan: Political Development and Emergent Democracy*. London: Routledge, 2003.

Steele, Jonathan. *Defeat: Why They Lost Iraq*. London: I. B. Tauris, 2008.

Swisher, Clayton. *The Truth about Camp David: The Untold Story about the Collapse of the Middle East Peace Process*. New York: Thunder's Mouth Nation Books, 2004.

Synnott, Hilary. *Bad Days in Basra: My Turbulent Time as Britain's Man in Southern Iraq*. London: I. B. Tauris, 2008.

Telhami, Shibley. *The Stakes: America in the Middle East*. New York: Basic Books, 2002.

Troeller, Gary. *The Birth of Saudi Arabia: Britain and the Rise of the House of Saud.* London: Frank Cass, 1976.

Twitchell, Karl. *Saudi Arabia.* Princeton, NJ: Princeton University Press, 1953.

Van der Meulen, Daniel. *The Wells of Ibn Sa'ud.* New York: Praeger, 1957.

Vandewalle, Dirk. *A History of Modern Libya.* Cambridge: Cambridge University Press, 2006.

Watt, W. Montgomery. *Muhammad at Mecca.* Oxford: Clarendon, 1953.

———. *Muhammad, Prophet and Statesman.* London: Oxford University Press, 1961.

Wellhausen, Julius. *The Arab Kingdom and Its Fall.* Translated by N. G. Weir. Beirut: Khayats, 1963.

Winder, R. Bayly. *Saudi Arabia in the Nineteenth Century.* New York: St. Martin's Press, 1966.

Yassini, Ayman al-. *Religion and State in the Kingdom of Saudi Arabia.* Boulder, CO: Westview Press, 1985.

Iran

Abrahamian, Ervand. *Iran between Two Revolutions.* Princeton, NJ: Princeton University Press, 1982.

Akhavi, Shahrough. *Religion and Politics in Contemporary Iran: Clergy–State Relations in the Pablavi Period.* New York: Basic Books, 1986.

Algar, Hamid. *Mirza Malkum Khan: A Study in the History of Iranian Modernism.* Berkeley: University of California Press, 1973.

Arasteh, A. Reza. *Education and Social Awakening in Iran, 1850–1968.* 2nd ed. Leiden, Netherlands: E. J. Brill, 1969.

Arberry, J. J., ed. *The Legacy of Persia.* Oxford: Clarendon, 1968.

Armajani, Yaha. *Iran.* Englewood Cliffs, NJ: Prentice-Hall, 1972.

Axworthy, Michael. *Empire of the Mind: A History of Iran.* London: Hurst, 2008.

Bakhash, Shaul. *The Reign of the Ayatollahs: Iran and the Islamic Revolution.* New York: Basic Books, 1986.

Balyuzi, H. M. *The Bab: The Herald of the Day of Days.* Oxford: G. Ronald, 1973.

———. *Baha'u'llah: The King of Glory.* Oxford: G. Ronald, 1980.

Banani, Amin. *The Modernization of Iran, 1921–1941.* Stanford, CA: Stanford University Press, 1961.

Bernard, Cheryl, and Zalmay Khalilzad. *"The Government of God": Iran's Islamic Republic*. New York: Columbia University Press, 1984.

Bier, Carol, ed. *Woven from the Soul, Spun from the Heart: Textile Arts of Safavd and Qajar Iran, 16th–19th Centuries*. Washington, DC: The Textile Museum, 1987.

Binder, Leonard. *Iran: Political Development in a Changing Society*. Berkeley: University of California Press, 1962.

Bosworth, C. E. *The Ghaznavids: Their Empire in Afghanistan and Eastern Iran, 994–1040*. Edinburgh: Edinburgh University Press, 1963.

Bowden, Mark. *Guests of the Ayatollah: The First Battle in America's War with Militant Islam*. New York: Atlantic Monthly Press, 2006.

Brown, Edward G. "The Babis of Persia I: Sketch of Their History, and Personal Experiences amongst Them, Their Literature and Doctrines." *Journal of the Royal Asiatic Society* 21 (1889): 485–526, 881–1009. Reprinted with annotations in *Selections from the Writings of E. G. Browne on the Babi and Baha'i Religions*, edited by Moojan Momen, 145–315. Oxford: G. Ronald, 1987.

———. *The Persian Revolution of 1905–1909*. Cambridge: Cambridge University Press, 1910.

Dabashi, Hamid. *Theology of Discontent: The Ideological Foundations of the Islamic Revolution in Iran*. New Brunswick, NJ: Transaction Publishers, 2006.

Downes, Mark. *Iran's Unresolved Revolution*. Burlington, VT: Ashgate, 2002.

Fischer, Michael M. J. *Iran: From Religious Dispute to Revolution*. Cambridge, MA: Harvard University Press, 1980.

Fisher, W. B., ed. *The Cambridge History of Iran*. Vol. 1, *The Land of Iran*. Cambridge: Cambridge University Press, 1968.

Frye, Richard N. *The Cambridge History of Iran*. Vol. 4, *From the Arab Invasion to the Saljuqs*. Cambridge: Cambridge University Press, 1975.

———. *The Golden Age of Persia: The Arabs in the East*. London: Weidenfeld and Nicolson, 1975.

———. *The Heritage of Persia*. Cleveland, OH: World Publishing, 1963.

Ghamari-Tabrizi, Behrooz. *Islam and Dissent in Post-Revolutionary Iran: The Religious Politics of Abdolkarim Soroush*. London: I. B. Tauris, 2001.

Hiro, Dilip. *Iran Under the Ayatollahs*. London: Routledge and Kegan Paul, 1985.

Hooglund, Eric J. *Land and Revolution in Iran, 1960–1980*. Austin: University of Texas Press, 1982.

Katouzian, Homa. *Iranian History and Politics: The Dialectic State and Society.* London: Routledge Curzon, 2003.

———. *The Political Economy of Modern Iran: Despotism and Pseudo-Modernism, 1926–1979.* New York: New York University Press, 1981.

Katouzian, Homa, and Hossein Shahidi, eds. *Iran in the 21st Century: Politics, Economics, and Conflicts.* New York: Routledge, 2007.

Keddie, Nikki R. *Religion and Rebellion in Iran: The Iranian Tobacco Protect of 1891–1892.* New York: Humanities Press, 1966.

Keddie, Nikki, and Hooglund, Eric, eds. *The Iranian Revolution and the Islamic Republic.* Washington, DC: Middle East Institute, 1982.

Khomeini, Imam. *Islam and Revolution: Writings and Declarations of Imam Khomeini.* Translated by Hamid Algar. Berkeley, CA: Mizan Press, 1981.

Lambton, A. K. S. *Landlord and Peasant in Persia: A Study of Land Tenure and Land Revenue Administration.* London: Oxford University Press, 1953.

Levy, Reuben. *Persian Literature: An Introduction.* London: Oxford University Press, 1948.

Lockhart, Laurence. *Famous Cities of Iran.* Brentford, England: W. Pearce, 1939.

Loeffler, Reinhold. *Islam in Practice: Religious Beliefs in a Persian Village.* Albany: State University of New York Press, 1988.

Maleki, Abbas. *Iranian Foreign Policy: Past, Present, Future Scenarios.* New York: Routledge, 2008.

Nashat, Guity, ed. *Women and Revolution in Iran.* Boulder, CO: Westview Press, 1983.

Ramazani, Rouhollah K. *Revolutionary Iran: Challenge and Response in the Middle East.* Baltimore, MD: Johns Hopkins University Press, 1986.

Riza Shah Pahlavi, Mohammed. *Mission for My Country.* London: Hutchinson, 1961.

———. *Mohammed: The White Revolution.* Tehran: Imperial Pahlavi Library, 1967.

Rubin, Michael. *Into the Shadows: Radical Vigilantes in Khatami's Iran.* Washington, DC: The Washington Institute for Near Eastern Policy, 2001.

Rypka, Jan. *History of Iranian Literature.* Translated by Karl Jahn. New York: Humanities Press, 1968.

Sanasarian, Eliz. *The Women's Rights Movement in Iran: Mutiny, Appeasement, and Repression from 1900 to Khomeini.* New York: Praeger, 1982.

Savory, Roger. *Iran under the Safavids.* Cambridge: Cambridge University Press, 1980.

Schahgaldian, Nikola B. *The Iranian Military under the Islamic Republic.* Santa Monica, CA: Rand Corporation, 1987.

Vahdat, Farzin. *God and Juggernaut: Iran's Intellectual Encounter with Modernity.* Syracuse, NY: Syracuse University Press, 2002.

Varzi, Roxanne. *Warring Souls: Youth, Media, and Martyrdom in Post-Revolution Iran.* Durham, NC: Duke University Press, 2006.

Wickens, G. M., R. M. Savory, and W. J. Watson, eds. *Persia in Islamic Times: A Practical Bibliography of Its History.* Montreal: Institute of Islamic Studies, McGill University, 1964.

Wilber, Donald, N. *Iran, Past and Present.* Princeton, NJ: Princeton University Press, 1958.

Wilson, Sir Arnold T. *A Bibliography of Persia.* Oxford: Clarendon, 1930.

Zabih, Sepehr. *Iran since the Revolution.* Baltimore, MD: Johns Hopkins University Press, 1982.

Zuhur, Sherifa D. *Iran, Iraq, and the United States: The New Triangle's Impact on Sectarianism and the Nuclear Threat.* Carlisle Barracks, PA: Strategic Studies Institute, U.S. Army War College, 2006.

Ottoman Empire and Turkey

Abadan-Unat, Nermin, ed. *Women in Turkish Society.* Leiden, Netherlands: Brill, 1981.

Ahmad, Feroz. *Turkey: The Quest for Identity.* Oxford: Oneworld, 2003.

———. *The Turkish Experiment in Democracy, 1950–1975.* London: C. Hurst, 1977.

Alderson, A. D. *The Structure of the Ottoman Dynasty.* Oxford: Clarendon Press, 1956.

Allen, Henry Elisha. *The Turkish Transformation: A Study in Social and Religious Development.* Chicago: University of Chicago Press, 1935.

Armstrong, Harold C. *Grey Wolf, Mustafa Kamal: An Intimate Study of a Dictator.* London: Barker, 1932.

Atil, Esin. *The Age of Sultan Suleyman the Magnificent.* New York: Harry N. Abrams, 1987.

Berberoglu, Berch. *Turkey in Crisis: From State Capitalism to Neo-Colonialism.* London: Zed Press, 1982.

Berkes, Niyazi. *The Development of Secularism in Turkey.* Montreal: McGill University Press, 1964.

Birge, J. K. *The Bektashi Order of Dervishes.* Hartford, CT: Hartford Seminary Press, 1937.

——. *The Fall of Constantinople*. London: Cambridge University Press, 1955.

Bisbee, Eleanor. *The New Turks: Pioneers of the Republic, 1920–1950*. Philadelphia: University of Pennsylvania Press, 1951.

Çagaptay, Soner. *Islam, Secularism, and Nationalism in Turkey: Who Is a Turk?* New York: Routledge, 2006.

Çarkoglu, Ali, and Barry Rubin. *Religion and Politics in Turkey*. New York: Routledge, 2006.

Çinar, Alev. *Modernity, Islam, and Secularism in Turkey*. Minneapolis: University of Minnesota Press, 2005.

Creasy, Edward S. *History of the Ottoman Turks: From the Beginning of Their Empire to the Present Time*. Beirut: Khayats, 1961.

Davis, Fanny. *The Ottoman Lady: A Social History from 1718 to 1918*. New York: Greenwood, 1986.

Davison, Roderic H. *Reform in the Ottoman Empire, 1856–1876*. Princeton, NJ: Princeton University Press, 1963.

——. *Turkey*. Englewood Cliffs, NJ: Prentice-Hall, 1968.

Dawn, C. Ernest. *From Ottomanism to Arabism: Essays on the Origins of Arab Nationalism*. Urbana: University of Illinois Press, 1973.

Djemal Pasha, Ahmed. *Memories of a Turkish Statesman, 1913–1919*. New York: Doran, 1922.

Earle, Edward Mead. *Turkey, the Great Powers and the Baghdad Railway: A Study in Imperialism*. New York: Macmillan, 1923.

Eaton, William. *A Survey of the Turkish Empire*. London: Cadell and Davies, 1799.

Edib, Halide. *Memoirs of Halide Edib*. New York: Century, 1926.

——. *Turkey Faces West: A Turkish View of Recent Changes and Their Origins*. New Haven, CT: Yale University Press, 1930.

Emin, Ahmed. *Turkey in the World War*. New Haven, CT: Yale University Press, 1930.

Esposito, John L., and M. Hakan Yawuz. *Turkish Islam and the Secular State: the Gülen Movement*. Syracuse, NY: Syracuse University Press, 2003.

Evans, Laurence. *United States Policy and the Partition of Turkey, 1914–1924*. Baltimore, MD: Johns Hopkins University Press, 1965.

Faroqhi, Suraiya. *Peasants, Dervishes and Traders in the Ottoman Empire*. London: Variorum, 1986.

Fisher, Sydney Nettleton. *The Foreign Relations of Turkey, 1481–1512.* Urbana: University of Illinois Press, 1948.

Gerber, Haim. "Social and Economic Position of Women in an Ottoman City, Bursa, 1600–1700." *International Journal of Middle East Studies* 12 (1980): 231–244.

Gibbons, Herbert A. *The Foundation of the Ottoman Empire.* Oxford: Clarendon Press, 1916.

Göle, Nilüfer, and Ludwig Ammann. *Islam in Public: Turkey, Iran and Europe.* Istanbul: Istanbul Bilgi University Press, 2006

Hale, William. *The Political and Economic Development of Modern Turkey.* London: Croom Helm, 1981.

Heyd, Uriel. *The Foundations of Turkish Nationalism.* London: Harwell Press, 1950.

——. "The Ottoman Ulama and Westernization in the Time of Selim III and Mahmd II." In *Studies in Islamic History and Civilization.* Jerusalem: Hebrew University, 1961.

Holod, Renata, and Ahmet Evin, eds. *Modern Turkish Architecture.* Philadelphia: University of Pennsylvania Press, 1984.

Hurgronje, C. "Islam and Turkish Nationalism." In *Verspreide Geschriften van C. Snouck Hurgronje,* Vol. 6, 435–452. Leiden, Netherlands: E. J. Brill, 1927.

Inalcik, Halil. *The Ottoman Empire: Conquest, Organization and Economy.* London: Variorum, 1978.

——. *The Ottoman Empire: The Classical Age, 1300–1600.* Translated by Norman Itzowitz and Colin Imber. New York: Praeger, 1973.

——. *Studies in Ottoman Social and Economic History.* London: Variorum Reprints, 1985.

Issawi, Charles. *The Economic History of Turkey, 1800–1914.* Chicago: University of Chicago Press, 1980.

Karpat, Kemal H. *The Ottoman State and Its Place in World History.* Leiden, Netherlands: E. J. Brill, 1974.

Kasaba, Resat. *The Cambridge History of Turkey.* Oxford: Cambridge University Press, 2008.

Kazancigil, Ali, and Ergun Ozbudun, eds. *Ataturk: Founder of Modern State.* London: C. Hurst, 1981.

Kinross, Lord (Patrick Balfour). *Ataturk: A Biography of Mustafa Kemal, Father of Modern Turkey.* New York: Morrow, 1965.

———. *Ataturk: The Rebirth of a Nation.* London: Weidenfeld and Nicolson, 1964.

———. *The Ottoman Centuries: The Rise and Fall of the Turkish Empire.* New York: Morrow, 1977.

Koller, Markus, and Kemal H. Karpat. *Ottoman Bosnia: A History in Peril.* Madison: University of Wisconsin Press, 2004.

Kuneralp, Sinan, ed. *Studies on Ottoman Diplomatic History I.* Istanbul: Isis Press, 1987.

Kushner, David. *The Rise of Turkish Nationalism, 1876–1908.* London: Frank Cass, 1977.

Landau, Jacob M., ed. *Ataturk and the Modernization of Turkey.* Boulder, CO: Westview Press, 1984.

———. *Radical Politics in Modern Turkey.* Leiden, Netherlands: E. J. Brill, 1974.

Lewis, Bernard. *Istanbul and the Civilization of the Ottoman Empire.* Norman: University of Oklahoma Press, 1963.

Luke, Sir Harry. *The Old Turkey and the New: From Byzantium to Ankara.* London: G. Bles, 1955. New and rev. ed. of *The Making of Modern Turkey,* 1936.

Mardin, Serif. *The Genesis of Young Ottoman Thought: A Study in the Modernization of Turkish Political Ideas.* Princeton, NJ: Princeton University Press, 1962.

———. *Religion, Society, and Modernity in Turkey.* Syracuse, NY: Syracuse University Press, 2006.

Mears, Eliot Grinnell, ed. *Modern Turkey, A Politico-Economic Interpretation, 1908–1923, Inclusive, with Selected Chapters by Representative Authorities.* New York: Macmillan, 1924.

Merriman, R. B. *Suleiman the Magnificent, 1520–1566.* Cambridge, MA: Harvard University Press, 1944.

Midhat, Ali Haydar. *The Life of Midhat Pasha.* London: J. Murray, 1903.

Moorehead, Alan. *Gallipoli.* New York: Harper, 1956.

Petsopoulis, Yanni, ed. *Tulips, Arabesques and Turbans: Decorative Art from the Ottoman Empire.* New York: Abbeville Press, 1982.

Pitcher, D. *An Historical Geography of the Ottoman Empire from Earliest Times to the End of the Sixteenth Century.* Leiden, Netherlands: E. J. Brill, 1974.

Pope, Hugh. *Sons of the Conquerors: The Rise of the Turkic World.* New York: Overlook Press, 2005.

Ramsaur, Ernest E., Jr. *The Young Turks*: Princeton, NJ: Princeton University Press, 1957.

Renda, Gunsel, and C. Max Kortepeter, eds. *The Transformation of Turkish Culture: The Ataturk Legacy*. Princeton, NJ: Kingston Press, 1986.

Rice, Tamara Talbot. *The Seljuks in Asia Minor*. London: Thames and Hudson, 1961.

Robins, Philip. *Suits and Uniforms: Turkish Foreign Policy Since the Cold War*. Seattle: University of Washington Press, 2003.

Rustow, Dankwart A. *Turkey: America's Forgotten Ally*. New York: Council on Foreign Relations, 1987.

Shankland, David. *Structure and Function in Turkish Society: Essays on Religion, Politics and Social Change*. Istanbul: Isis Press, 2006.

Shaw, Stanford J. *History of the Ottoman Empire and Modern Turkey*. 2 vols. Cambridge: Cambridge University Press, 1976.

Stoye, John. *The Siege of Vienna*. New York: Holt, Rinehart & Winston, 1965.

Sugar, Peter F. *Southeastern Europe under Ottoman Rule, 1354–1804*. Seattle: University of Washington Press, 1977.

Tachau, Frank. *Turkey: The Politics of Authority, Democracy, and Development*. New York: Praeger, 1984.

Trumpener, Ulrich. *Germany and the Ottoman Empire, 1914–1918*. Princeton, NJ: Princeton University Press, 1968.

Tursun Beg. *The History of Mehmed the Conqueror*. Translated by Halil Inalcik and Rhoads Murphy. Minneapolis, MN: Bibliotheca Islamica, 1978.

Webster, Donald Everett. *The Turkey of Ataturk: Social Process in the Turkish Reformation*. Philadelphia: American Academy of Political and Social Science, 1939.

White, Jenny B. *Islamist Mobilization in Turkey: A Study in Vernacular Politics*. Seattle: University of Washington Press, 2002.

Wittek, Paul. *The Rise of the Ottoman Empire*. London: Royal Asiatic Society, 1958.

Yalman, Ahmed Emin. *Turkey in My Time*. Norman: University of Oklahoma Press, 1956.

Turko–Mongols

Ayalon, David. *Gunpower and Firearms in the Mamluk Kingdom*. London: Valentine, Mitchell, 1956.

Boyle, J. A., ed. *The Cambridge History of Iran*. Vol. 5, *The Saljuq and Mongol Periods*. Cambridge: Cambridge University Press, 1968.

Clavijo, Ruy Gonzalez de. *Narrative of the Embassy to the Court of Tamerlane at Samarcand A.D. 1403–1406*. Translated by Clemenes R. Markham. New York: B. Franklin, n.d.

Howorth, Henry. *History of the Mongols from the Ninth to the Nineteenth Century*. 5 vols. London: Longmans, Green, 1876–1927.

Ibn 'Arabshah. *Tamurlane, or Timur the Great Amir*. Translated by J. H. Saunders. London: Luzac, 1936.

Juvaini, 'Ata-Jalik. *The History of the World-Conqueror*. 2 vols. Translated by J. A. Boyle. Manchester, England: University of Manchester Press, 1958.

Prawdin, Michael. *The Mongol Empire, Its Rise and Legacy*. London: G. Allen & Unwin, 1961.

Saunders, J. J. *The History of the Mongol Conquests*. London: Routledge and Kegan Paul, 1971.

Spuler, Bertold. *History of the Mongols, Based on Eastern and Western Accounts of the Thirteenth and Fourteenth Centuries*. Translated by H. Drummond and S. Drummond. London: Routledge and Kegan Paul, 1972.

South and Central Asia

Adamec, Ludwig W. *Afghanistan's Foreign Affairs to the Mid-Twentieth Century: Relations with the USSR, Germany, and Britain*. Tucson: University of Arizona Press, 1974.

———. *Historical Dictionary of Afghanistan*. 3rd rev. ed. Lanham, MD: Scarecrow Press, 2003.

Ahmad, Aziz. "Cultural and Intellectual Trends in Pakistan." *Middle East Journal* 19 (1965).

———. *Islamic Modernism in India and Pakistan 1857–1964*. London: Oxford University Press, 1967.

Azad, (Mawlana) Abul-Kalam. *India Wins Freedom: An Autobiographical Narrative*. New York: Longmans, Green, 1960.

Barthold, V. V. *Four Studies on the History of Central Asia*. 3 vols. Translated by V. Minorsky and T. Minorsky. Leiden, Netherlands: E. J. Brill, 1956–1962.

Butler, A. J. *The Arab Conquest of Egypt and the Last Thirty Years of the Roman Domination*. Oxford: Clarendon, 1902.

Chayes, Sarah. *The Punishment of Virtue: Inside Afghanistan after the Taliban*. New York: Penguin Group, 2007.

Crews, Robert, and Amin Tarzi. *The Taliban and the Crisis of Afghanistan.* Cambridge, MA: Harvard University Press, 2008.

Dorronsoro, Gilles. *Revolution Unending: Afghanistan, 1979 to the Present.* New York: Columbia University Press, 2005.

Dupree, Louis. "Militant Islam and Traditional Warfare in Islamic South Asia." *American Universities Field Staff Reports, Asia* 21 (1980): 12.

Faris, Nabih Amin, ed. *The Arab Heritage.* Princeton, NJ: Princeton University Press, 1946.

Gibb, H. A. R. *The Arab Conquests in Central Asia.* New York: AMS Press, 1970.

Glubb, John B. *The Great Arab Conquests.* London: Hodder and Stoughton, 1964.

Gregorian, Vartan. *The Emergence of Modern Afghanistan.* Stanford, CA: Stanford University Press, 1969.

Hollister, J. N. *The Shi'a of India.* London: Luzac, 1953.

Hussain, Zahid. *Frontline Pakistan: The Path to Catastrophe and the Killing of Benazir Bhutto.* London: I. B. Tauris, 2008.

Ikram, S. M., and A. T. Embree, eds. *Muslim Civilization in India.* New York: Columbia University Press, 1964.

Johnson, Chris, and Jolyon Leslie. *Afghanistan: The Mirage of Peace.* London: Zed Books, 2004.

Lane-Poole, Stanley. *Medieval India under Mohammedan Rule (A.D. 712–1764).* London: T. Fisher Unwin, 1906.

Mujeeb, M. *Islamic Influence on Indian Society.* Delhi, India: Meenakshi Prakashan, 1972.

Muztar, A. D. *Shah Waliullah: A Saint Scholar of Muslim India.* Islamabad, Pakistan: National Commission on Historical and Cultural Research, 1979.

Rasanayagam, Angelo. *Afghanistan: A Modern History.* London: I. B. Tauris, 2003.

Rogers, Paul. *A War on Terror: Afghanistan and After.* New York: Pluto Press, 2004.

Schimmel, Annemarie. *Islam in the Indian Subcontinent.* Leiden, Netherlands: E.J. Brill, 1980.

Schofield, Victoria. *Afghan Frontier: Feuding and Fighting in Central Asian.* New York: I. B. Tauris, 2003.

Sharif, Ja'far. *Islam in India, or the Qanun-i-Islam: The Customs of the Musalmans in India.* New Delhi, India: Oriental Books Reprint Corporation, 1974.

Smith, Vincent. *The Oxford History of India.* Pt. 2, *Indian in the Muhammadan Period.* Oxford: Clarendon, 1920.

Utas, B. "Notes on Afghanistan: Sufi Orders and Khanaqahs." *Afghanistan Journal* 7, no. 2 (1980): 60–67.

Wilber, D. N. "The Structure and Position of Islam in Afghanistan." *Middle East Journal* 6, no. 1 (1952): 41–48.

Zahab, Mariam Abou, and Olivier Roy. *Islamist Networks: The Afghan–Pakistan Connection.* New York: Columbia University Press, 2004.

Ziring, Lawrence. *Pakistan: At the Crosscurrent of History.* Oxford: Oneworld, 2003.

Islamic Spain

Chejne, Anwar G. *Muslim Spain: Its History and Culture.* Minneapolis: University of Minnesota Press, 1974.

Coppee, Henry. *History of the Conquest of Spain by the Arab Moors.* Piscataway, NJ: Gorgias Press, 2002.

Dozy, Reinhart. *Spanish Islam: A History of the Moslems in Spain.* Translated by Francis Griffin Stokes. London: Chatto and Windus, 1913.

Glick, F. Thomas. *Islamic and Christian Spain in the Early Middle Ages.* Boston: Brill, 2005.

Imamuddin, S. M. *A Political History of Muslim Spain.* Dacca, Bangladesh: Najman, 1969.

Glick, F. Thomas. *Islamic and Christian Spain in the Early Middle Ages.* Boston: Brill, 2005.

Rodriguez, Jarbel. *Captives and their Saviors in the Medieval Town of Aragon.* Washington, DC: Catholic University of America Press, 2007.

Suhrawardy, Shahid. *The Art of Mussulmans in Spain.* New York: Oxford University Press, 2005.

Watt, W. Montgomery. *A History of Muslim Spain.* Edinburgh: University of Edinburgh Press, 1965.

III. ISLAM

General

Abdo, Geneive. *No God but God: Egypt and the Triumph of Islam.* New York: Cambridge University Press, 2002.

Abdullah, Saeed. *Islamic Thought: An Introduction.* New York: Routledge, 2006.

Adams, Charles J. "The Islamic Religious Tradition." In *Religion and Man,* edited by W. Richard Comstock, 553–617. New York: Harper & Row, 1971.

Ahmed, Akbar. *Islam: A Short Introduction to the Muslim World.* New York: I. B. Tauris, 1999.

'Ali, Muhammad. *The Religion of Islam.* Cairo: National Publication and Printing House, 1967.

'Ali, Syed Ameer. *The Spirit of Islam: A History of the Evolution and Ideals of Islam.* London: Chatto and Windus, 1964.

Arberry, A. J., and Rom Landau, eds. *Islam Today.* London: Faber and Faber, 1942.

Armstrong, Karen. Islam: *A Short History.* New York: Modern Library, 2002.

'Azzam,'Abd al-Rahman. *The Eternal Message of Muhammad.* Translated by C. E. Farah. New York: Devin-Adavi, 1964.

Bayat, Asef. *Making Islam Democratic.* Stanford, CA: Stanford University Press, 2007.

Bishai, Wilson B. *Humanities in the Arabic–Islamic World.* Dubuque, IA: Brown, 1973.

———. *Islamic History of the Middle East.* Boston: Allyn and Bacon, 1968.

Bulliet, Richard, W. *The Case for Islamo–Christian Civilization.* New York: Columbia University Press, 2004.

Butterworth, Charles E., and William Zartman, eds. *Between the State and Islam.* Washington, DC: Woodrow Wilson Center Press, 2001.

Chapman, Colin Gilbert. *Cross and Crescent: Responding to the Challenges of Islam.* Downers Grove, IL: Inter Varsity Press, 2008.

Christopher, John B. *The Islamic Tradition.* New York and London: Harper & Row, 1972.

Cragg, Kenneth. *The House of Islam.* 2nd rev. ed. Encino, CA: Dickenson Publishing, 1975.

Dawn, C. Ernest. "Islam in the Modern Age." *Middle East Journal* 19, no. 4 (1965).

Delong-Bas, Natana J. *Wahhabi Islam: From Revival and Reform to Global Jihad.* New York: I. B. Tauris, 2004.

Dermenghem, Emile. *Muhammad and the Islamic Tradition.* Translated by J. M. Watt. New York: Harper & Brothers, 1958.

Doi, A. Rahman I. "The Muwatta' of Imam Malik on the Genesis of the Shari'a Law: A Western Scholar's Confusion." *Hamdard Islamicus* 4, no. 3, 1981, pp. 27–41.

Endress, Gerard. *An Introduction to Islam*. Translated by Carole Hillenbrand. New York: Columbia University Press, 1988.

Esposito, John. *Islam the Straight Path*. New York: University of Oxford Press, 2005.

———. *The Islamic Threat: Myth or Reality?* New York: Oxford University Press, 1999.

———. *Unholy War: Terror in the Name of Islam*. New York: Oxford University Press, 2002.

———. *What Everyone Needs to Know About Islam*. New York: Oxford University Press, 2002.

Esposito, John, and Dalia Mogahed. *Who Speaks for Islam?: What a Billion Muslims Really Think*. New York: Gallup Press, 2008.

Farah, Caesar E. *Islam: Beliefs and Observances*. Woodbury, NY: Barron's Educational Series, 1968.

Fayzee, A. A. A. *A Modern Approach to Islam*. Bombay, India: Times of India, 1963.

Friedman, Lauri. *Islam*. San Diego: Greenhaven Press, 2006.

Freeman-Greenville, G. S. P., and Stuart C. Munro-Hay. *Islam: An Illustrated History*. London: Continuum, 2006.

Gardet, L. *Mohammedanism*. Translated by William Bunidge. London: Burns and Oates, 1961.

Gibb, H. A. R. "The Heritage of Islam in the Modern World." *International Journal of Middle East Studies* 1 (1970): 221–237; 2 (1972): 129–147.

———. *Mohammedanism*. 2nd ed. London: Oxford University Press, 1962. Reprinted with revisions, 1970.

Goldziher, Ignaz. *Introduction to Islamic Theology and Law*. Translated by Andras and Ruth Hamori. Princeton, NJ: Princeton University Press, 1981.

Gottschalk, Peter, and Gabriel Greenberg. *Islamophobia: Making Muslims the Enemy*. Lanham, MD: Rowman & Littlefield, 2007.

Gregorian, Vartan. *Islam: A Mosaic, Not A Monolith*. Washington, DC: Brookings Institution Press, 2003.

Grieve, Paul. *A Brief Guide to Islam: History, Faith, and Politics, the Complete Introduction*. New York: Carroll and Graf Publishers, 2006.

Haddad, Yvonne Yazeck. *Contemporary Islam and the Challenge of History*. Albany: State University of New York Press, 1982.

Hitti, Philip K. *Islam: A Way of Life*. New York: Humanities, 1971.

Hodgson, Marshall G.S. *The Venture of Islam*. Chicago: University of Chicago Press, 1974.

Hunter, Shireen T., ed. *Islam, Europe's Second Religion: The New Social, Cultural, and Political Landscape*. Washington, DC: Praeger Center for Strategic and International Studies, 2002.

———. "Islam, Modernization and Democracy: Are They Compatible?" *CSIS Insights* (March–April 2002).

Jeffery, Arthur, ed. *Islam: Muhammad and His Religion*. New York: Liberal Arts, 1958.

———. *A Reader on Islam: Passages from Standard Arabic Writings Illustrative of the Beliefs and Practices of Muslims*. The Hague: Mouton, 1962.

Kamrawa, Mehran, ed. *The New Voices of Islam: Rethinking Politics and Modernity—A Reader*. Berkeley: University of California Press, 2007.

Klein, F. A. *The Religion of Islam*. New York: Humanities Press, 1971. Reprint of 1906 edition.

Lahoud, Nelly, and Anthony H. Johns. *Islam in World Politics*. New York: Routledge, 2005.

Lawrence, Bruce B. *Shattering the Myth: Islam Beyond Violence*. Princeton, NJ: Princeton University Press, 1998.

Lewis Bernard, ed. *Islam and the Arab World: Faith, People, Culture*. New York: Knopf, 1976.

Lombard, Maurice. *The Golden Age of Islam*. Translated by Joan Spencer. New York: American Elsevier Publishing, 1975.

Mahajan, Rahul. *The New Crusade*. New York: Monthly Review Press, 2002.

Mamiya, Lawrence H. "Islam in the Americas." In *The Muslim Almanac*, edited by Azim A. Nanji. Detroit: Gale Research, 1996.

McNeill, William H., and Marilyn R. Waldman, eds. *The Islamic World*. Chicago: University of Chicago Press, 1973.

Moaddel, Mansoor, and Kamran Talattof. *Contemporary Debates in Islam: An Anthology of Modernist and Fundamentalist Thought*. New York: St. Martin's Press, 2000.

Morgan, Kenneth, ed. *Islam: The Straight Path   Islam Interpreted by Muslims*. New York: Ronald Press, 1958.

Nasr, Seyyed Hossein. *The Heart of Islam: Enduring Values for Humanity*. San Francisco: Harper Collins, 2002.

———. *Ideals and Realities of Islam*. London: Allen & Unwin, 1966.

Noss, John B. *Man's Religions*. 5th ed. New York: Macmillan, 1974.

Piscatori, James P. *Islam in a World of Nation-States*. New York: Cambridge University Press, 1986.

Rajaee, Farhang. *Islamism and Modernism: The Changing Discourse in Iran*. Austin: University of Texas Press, 2007.

Rejwan, Nissim, ed. *The Many Faces of Islam: Perspectives on a Resurgent Civilization*. Gainesville: University Press of Florida, 2000.

Renard, John, ed. *Windows on the House of Islam: Muslim Sources on Spirituality and Religious Life*. Berkeley: University of California Press, 1998.

Roberts, D. S. *Islam: A Concise Introduction*. San Francisco: Harper & Row, 1981.

Roy, Olivier. *Globalized Islam: The Search for a New Ummah*. New York: Columbia University Press, 2004.

Saeed, Abdullah, and Hassan Saeed. *Freedom of Religion, Apostasy and Islam*. Burlington, VT: Ashgate, 2004.

Saikal, Amin. *Islam and the West: Conflict or Cooperation?* New York: Palgrave Macmillan, 2003.

Saliba, George. *Islamic Science and the Making of the European Renaissance*. Boston: MIT Press, 2007.

Savory, R. M., ed. *Introduction to Islamic Civilization*. Cambridge: Cambridge University Press, 1976.

Schaebler, Birgit, and Leif Stenberg. *Globalization in the Muslim World: Culture, Religion and Modernity*. Syracuse, NY: Syracuse University Press, 2004.

Schimmel, Annemarie. "Islam." In *Historia Religionum: Handbook for the History of Religion*, Vol. 2, edited by C. J. Bleeker and George Widengren. Leiden, Netherlands: E. J. Brill, 1971.

Schroeder, Eric. *Muhammad's People: A Tale by Anthology*. Portland, OR: Band Wheelwright, 1955.

Schwedler, Jillian, "Islamic Identity: Myth, Menace, or Mobilizer?" *SAIS Review* 21, no. 2 (Summer–Fall 2001): 7.

Sha'ban, Muhammad 'Abd al-Hayy. *Islamic History: A New Interpretation*. Vol. 2. Cambridge: Cambridge University Press, 1976.

Smart, Ninian. "The Muslim Experience." In *The Religious Experience of Mankind*, 372–423. New York: Scribner, 1969.

Tritton, A. S. *Islam: Belief and Practices*. 2nd ed. London: Hutchinson's University Library, 1954.

Turam, Berna. *Between Islam and the State*. Stanford, CA: Stanford University Press, 2007.

Watt, W. Montgomery. *What Is Islam?* New York: Praeger, 1968.

Wickham, Carrie Rosefsky. *Mobilizing Islam*. New York: Columbia University Press, 2002.

Williams, John A. *Islam*. New York: George Braziller, 1961.

———, ed. *Themes of Islamic Civilization*. Berkeley: University of California Press, 1971.

Islamic Studies

Adams, Charles J. "The Islamic Religious Tradition." In *Religion and Man*, edited by W. Richard Comstock, 553–617. New York: Harper & Row, 1971.

Arberry, A. J. *Aspects of Islamic Civilization as Depicted in the Original Texts*. London: Allen & Unwin, 1964.

Arnold, Thomas, and A. Guillaume. *The Legacy of Islam*. Oxford: Clarendon, 1931.

Bell, Richard. "Muhammad's Pilgrimage Proclamation." *Journal of the Royal Asiatic Society* (1937): 233–244.

———. *The Origin of Islam in Its Christian Environment*. London: Macmillan, 1926.

Benningsen, Alexande, and Chantal Lemercier-Quelquejay. *Islam in the Soviet Union*. Translated by Geoffrey E. Wheeler and Hubert Evans. New York: Praeger, 1967.

Berger, Morroe. *Islam in Egypt Today: Social and Political Aspects of Popular Religion*. Cambridge: Cambridge University Press, 1970.

Boulares, Habib. *Islam: The Fear and the Hope*. Atlantic Highlands, NJ: Zed Books,1990.

Brown, Leon Carl. "The Role of Islam in Modern North Africa." In *State and Society in Independent North Africa*, edited by Leon Carl Brown. Washington, DC: The Middle East Institute, 1966.

Calverley, Edwin. *Worship in Islam: Al-Ghazzali's Book of the Ihya*. Piscataway, NJ: Gorgias Press, 2004.

Daniel, Norman. *Islam and the West: The Making of an Image*. Edinburgh: University Press, 1960.

Eickelman, Dale F. *Moroccan Islam: Tradition and Society in a Pilgrimage Center*. Modern Middle East Series, no. 1. Austin: University of Texas Press, 1976.

———. "Musaylima: An Approach to the Social Anthropology of Seventh Century Arabia." *Journal of the Economic and Social History of the Orient* 10 (1967): 17–52.

Fekrat, M. Ali. "Stress in the Islamic World," *Journal of South Asian and Middle Eastern Studies*. 4, no. 3 (Spring 1981).

Fitzgerald, Judith, and Michael Oren Fitzgerald. *The Universal Spirit of Islam: From the Koran and Hadith*. Bloomington, IN: World Wisdom, 2006.

Ghulam Ahmad, Hazrat Mirza. *Triumph of Islam*. Translated by Mirza Ma'-sum Bey. Lahore, Pakistan: Raheel Art, 1968.

Gibb, H. A. R. "The Community in Islamic History." *Proceedings of the American Philosophical Society* 107, no. 2 (1963): 173–176.

———. "Interpretation of Islamic History." *Journal of World History* 1 (1953): 39–62. Reprinted in *Studies on the Civilization of Islam,* edited by S. J. Shaw and W. R. Polk, 3–33. Boston: Beacon Press, 1962.

———. *Modern Trends in Islam*. New York: Octagon Books, 1972.

———. "Structure of Religious Thought in Islam." *The Muslim World*. 38 (1948). Reprinted in *Studies on the Civilization of Islam,* edited by S. J. Shaw and W. R. Polk. Boston: Beacon Press, 1962.

Goldziher, Ignaz. "The Appearance of the Prophet in Dreams." *Journal of the Royal Asiatic Society* (1912): 503–506.

Grunebaum, G. E. von. *Islam: Essays in the Nature and Growth of a Cultural Tradition*. 2nd ed. London: Routledge and Kegan Paul, 1961.

———. "The Sources of Islamic Civilisation." In *The Cambridge History of Islam,* Vol. 2. Cambridge: Cambridge University Press, 1970.

———. *Unity and Variety in Muslim Civilization*. Chicago: University of Chicago Press, 1955.

Hassan, Ahmad Y. al-, and Donald R. Hill. *Islamic Technology: An Illustrated History*. London: Cambridge University Press, 1992.

Jeffery, Arthur. "The Family in Islam." In *The Family: Its Function and Destiny,* edited by Ruth N. Ashen, 201–238. New York: Harper & Brothers, 1959.

Levy, Reuben. *The Social Structure of Islam: Being the Second Edition of the Sociology of Islam*. Cambridge: Cambridge University Press, 1957.

Lewis, Bernard. *Islam in History: Ideas, Men and Events in the Middle East*. New York: Library Press, 1973.

Makari, Victor E., *Ibn Taymiyyah's Ethics: The Social Factor*. Chico, CA: Scholar's Press, 1983.

Mez, Adam. *The Renaissance of Islam*. London: Luzac, 1937.

Nasr, Seyyid Hossein. *Science and Civilization in Islam*. Cambridge, MA: Harvard University Press, 1968.

Obermann, Julian. "Early Islam." In *The Idea of History in the Ancient Near East*, edited by Robert C. Dentan, 239–310. New Haven, CT: Yale University Press, 1955.

———. "Islamic Origins: A Study in Background and Foundation." In *The Arab Heritage*, 58–120. Princeton, NJ: Princeton University Press, 1946.

Padwick, Constance E. *Muslim Devotions: A Study of Prayer Manuals in Common Use*. London: Society for Promoting Christian Knowledge, 1961.

Peters, F. E. *Allah's Commonwealth: A History of Islam in the Near East 6900–1100 A.D.* New York: Simon & Schuster, 1973.

Rahman, Fazlur. *Islam and Modernity: Transformation of an Intellectual Tradition*. Chicago: University of Chicago Press, 1982.

———. *Islamic Methodology in History*. Karachi, Pakistan: Central Institute of Islamic Research, 1965.

Ringgren, Helmer. *Islam: Aslama and Muslim*. Uppsala, Sweden: C.W.K. Gleerup, 1949.

Sanyal, Usha. *Ahmad Riza Khan Barelwi: In the Path of the Prophet*. Oxford: Oneworld, 2005.

Saunders, J. J. *A History of Medieval Islam*. London: Routledge and Kegan Paul, 1965.

Schacht, Joseph, and C. E. Bosworth. *The Legacy of Islam*. 2nd ed. Oxford: Clarendon Press, 1974.

Schroeder, Eric. *Muhammad's People: A Tale by Anthology*. Portland, OR: Band Wheelwright, 1955.

Schuon, Frithjof. *Dimensions of Islam*. Translated by P. N. Townsend. London: Allen & Unwin, 1970.

———. *Understanding Islam*. Translated by D. M. Matheson. Baltimore, MD: Penguin, 1974.

Smith, Wilfred Cantwell. *Modern Islam in India*. Lahore, Pakistan: Minerva Book Shop, 1943.

Taylor, Alan R. *Islamic Question in Middle Eastern Politics*. Boulder, CO: Westview Press, 1988.

Toprak, Binnaz. *Islam and Political Development in Turkey*. Leiden, Netherlands: E. J. Brill, 1981.

Trimingham, J. S. *A History of Islam in West Africa*. London: Oxford University Press, 1962.

Turner, Bryan S. *Weber and Islam: A Critical Study*. London: Routledge and Kegan Paul, 1974.

Volpi, Frederic. *Islam and Democracy: The Failure of Dialogue in Algeria.* London: Pluto Press, 2003.

Waardenburg, Jacques. *Islam: Historical, Social, and Political Perspectives.* Berlin: Walter de Gruyter, 2002.

———. *Muslims and Others: Relations in Context.* Berlin: Walter de Gruyter, 2003.

Watt, W. Montgomery. *The Influence of Islam on Medieval Europe.* Edinburgh: University of Edinburgh Press, 1972.

Williams, John Alden, ed. *Themes of Islamic Civilization.* Berkeley: University of California Press, 1971.

Wingate, F. R. *Mahdism and the Egyptian Sudan.* 2nd ed. London: Frank Cass, 1968.

Wolf, Eric. R. "The Social Organization of Mecca and the Origins of Islam." *Southwestern Journal of Anthropology* 7 (1951): 329–356.

Muhammad

Abbott, Nabia. *Aishah, the Beloved of Mohammed.* Chicago: University of Chicago Press, 1942.

Andrae, Tor. *Mohammed: The Man and His Faith.* New York: Harper & Row, 1960.

Birkeland, Harris. *The Legend of the Opening of Muhammad's Breast.* Oslo, Norway: I Kommisjon Hos Jacob Dybwad, 1955.

Bodley, R. V. C. *The Messenger: The Life of Muhammad.* London: Robert Hale, 1946.

Brott, Bernard. *Muhammad.* New York: Collins, 1973.

Cook, Michael. *Muhammad.* Oxford: Oxford University Press, 1985.

Elahi, Maulana Muhammad Ashiq. *The Wives of the Prophet.* Translated by Muhammad Akram. Islamic Book Service, 2002.

Gabrieli, Francesco. *Muhammad and the Conquests of Islam.* New York: McGraw-Hill, 1968.

Glubb, John Bagot. *The Life and Times of Muhammad.* London: Hodder & Stoughton, 1970.

Goldziher, I. *Mohammad and Islam.* Translated by K. C. Seeyle. New Haven, CT: Yale University Press, 1917.

Haykal, Muhammad Husayn. *The Life of Muhammad.* Translated from the 8th edition by Isma'il Ragi A. Faruqi. London: Shorouk International, 1983.

Ibn Hisham, 'Abd al-Malik. *The Life of Muhammad.* Translated by Alfred Guillaume. Oxford: Oxford University Press, 1935.

Ibn Ishaq. *The Life of Muhammad: A Translation of (Ibn) Ishaq Rasul Allah.* Translated by A. Guillaume. London: Oxford: Oxford University Press, 1955.

Jeffery, Arthur, ed. *Islam: Muhammad and His Religion.* New York: Liberal Arts, 1958.

Margoliouth, D. S. *Mohammed and the Rise of Islam.* Piscataway, NJ: Gorgias Press, 2003

———. "Relics of the Prophet Mohammed." *Moslem World* 27 (1937): 20–27.

Muir, Sir William. *The Life of Mahomet from Original Sources.* London: Smith, Elder, 1894.

Newby, Gordon D. *The Making of the Last Prophet.* Columbia: University of South Carolina Press, 1989.

Rodinson, Maxime. "The Life of Muhammad and the Sociological Problem of the Beginnings of Islam." *Diogenes* 20 (1975): 28–51.

———. *Mohammed.* Translated by A. Carter. London: A. Lane, Penguin Press, 1971.

Rogerson, Barnaby. *The Prophet Muhammad: A Biography.* New York: Little, Brown, 2003.

Rubin, Uri. *The Life of Muhammad.* Burlington, VT: Ashgate, 1998.

Shati, Bint Al-. *The Wives of the Prophet Muhammad.* Translated by Matti Moosa and D. Nicholas Ranson. Lahore, Pakistan: Ashraf, 1971.

Sugana, Gabriele Mandel. *The Life and Times of Mohammed.* Translated by Francis Koval. London: Hamlyn Publishing, 1968.

Viorst, Milron. *In the Shadow of the Prophet.* Boulder, CO: Westview Press, 2001.

Wendell, Charles. "The Pre-Islamic Period of Sirat al-Nabi." *Muslim World* 62 (1972): 12–41.

Wessels, Antoine. *A Modern Arabic Biography of Muhammad: A Critical Study of Muhammad Husayn Haykal's Hayat Muhammad.* Leiden, Netherlands: E. J. Brill, 1972.

Zakaria, Rafiq. *Muhammad and the Quran.* New York: Penguin Books, 1991.

Koran

Abbott, Freeland. "Mawlana Maududi on Quranic Interpretation." *Muslim World* 48 (1958): 6–19.

Akhtar, Shabbir. *The Quran and the Secular Mind: A Philosophi of Islam.* New York: Routledge, 2007.

'Ali 'Abdallah Yusuf, trans. *The Holy Qur'an*. Lahore, Pakistan: Ashraf, 1983.
———, trans. *The Holy Qur'an: Text, Translation and Commentary*. 2 vols. Washington, DC: American International, 1946.
Arberry, A. J. Trans. *The Holy Koran: An Introduction with Selections*. London: Allen & Unwin, 1953.
———. *The Koran Interpreted*. 2 vols. London: Allen & Unwin, 1955.
Ayoub, Mahmoud M. *The Qur'an and Its Interpreters*. 2 vols. to date. New York: State University of New York Press, 1984.
Bakker, Dirk. *Man in the Qur'an*. Amsterdam: Drubberij Holland, 1965.
Baljon, J. M. S. *Modern Muslim Koran Interpretation (1800–1960)*. Leiden, Netherlands: E. J. Brill, 1961.
Bell, Richard. *Bell's Introduction to the Qur'an*. New edition revised and enlarged by W. M. Watt. Edinburgh: Edinburgh University Press, 1970.
———, trans. *The Qur'an: Translated with a Critical Re-arrangement of the Surahs*. 2 vols. Edinburgh: Clark, 1937.
Birkeland, Harris. *Muslim Interpretation of Surah 107*. Oslo, Norway: I Kommisjon Hos H. Aschehoug, 1958.
———. *Old Muslim Opposition against Interpretation of the Koran*. Oslo, Norway: I Kommisjon Hos Jacob Dybwad, 1955.
Burton, John. *The Collection of the Qur'an*. Cambridge: Cambridge University Press, 1977.
Cook, Michael. *The Koran: A Very Short Introduction*. Oxford, 2000.
Cragg, Kenneth. *The Mind of the Qur'an*. London: Allen & Unwin, 1973.
Dawood, N. A., trans. *The Koran*. Baltimore, MD: Penguin Books, 1961.
Denny, Frederick Mathewson. "Qur'an Recitation: A Tradition of Oral Performance and Transmission." *Oral Tradition* 4, nos. 1–2 (January–May 1989): 83–95.
Donaldson, Bess Allen. "The Koran as Magic." *Moslem World* 27 (1937): 254–266.
Esack, Farid. *The Qur'an: A Short Introduction*. Oxford: Oneworld, 2002.
Gathe, Helmut. *The Qur'an and Its Exegesis: Selected Texts with Classical and Modern Muslim Interpretations*. Translated and edited by Alford T. Welch. Berkeley: University of California Press, 1976.
Goldziher, Ignaz. *Die Richtungen der Islamischen Koranauslegung*. 2nd ed. Leiden, Netherlands: E. J. Brill, 1970. Reprint of 1920 edition.
———. *Schools of Koranic Commentators*. Edited by Wolfgang H. Behn. Wiesbaden, Germany: Harrassowitz, 2006.
Hawting, G. R., and Abdul-Kader, A. Shareet, eds. *Approaches to the Qur'an*. London: Routledge, 1993.

Izutsu, Toshihiko. *Ethico-Religious Concepts in the Qur'an.* Rev. ed. Montreal: McGill University, 1966. Originally published as *The Structure of Ethical Terms in the Koran.* Tokyo: Keio University, 1959.

Jansen, J. J. G. *The Interpretation of the Koran in Modern Egypt.* Leiden, Netherlands: E. J. Brill, 1974.

Jeffery, A. *Materials for the History of the Text of the Qur'an.* Leiden, Netherlands: E. J. Brill, 1937.

———. *The Qur'an as Scripture.* New York: Russell Moore, 1952.

Khaleel, Mohammed, and Andrew Rippin. *Coming to Terms with the Qur'an: A Volume in Honor of Professor Issa Boullata.* North Halden, NJ: Islamic Publications International, 2008.

Mahmud, Y. Zahid *The Meaning of the Quran.* 3th ed. Beirut: Dar al-Choura. 1980.

Mawdudi, Sayyid Abu al-A'la. *Towards Understanding the Qur'an.* Vol. I. Translated and edited by K. Ahmedition Lahore. Pakistan: Islamic Publications, 1963.

Nelson, Kristina. *The Art of Reciting the Qur'an.* Austin: Texas University Press, 1985.

Nieuwenhuijze, C. A. O. van. "The Qur'an as a Factor in the Islamic Way of Life." *Der Islam* 38 (1962): 215–257.

Noldeke, Theodor. "The Koran." In *Sketches from Eastern History*, 21–59. London: A. and C. Black, 1892.

O'Shaughnessy, Thomas. *The Development of the Meaning of Spirit in the Kur'an.* Rome: Pontifical Institute, 1953.

———. *The Koranic Concept of the Word of God.* Rome: Pontificio Instituto Biblico, 1948.

Palmer, E. H., trans. *The Qur'an.* 2 vols. *Sacred Books of the East.* Edited by Max Müller, vols. 6 and 9. Delhi, India: Motilal Banarsidass, 1965.

Paret, Rudi. *Der Koran: Kommentar und Konkordanz.* Stuttgart, Germany: V. M. Kohlhammer, 1971.

Parrinder, Geoffrey. *Jesus in the Qur'an.* New York: Barnes & Noble, 1965.

Pickthall, Muhammad N. *The Glorious Koran: A Bilingual Edition with English Translations, Introduction and Notes.* Albany: State University of New York Press, 1976. Reprint of 1938 edition.

Rahbar, Daud. *God of Justice: A Study in the Ethical Doctrine of the Qur'an.* Leiden, Netherlands: E. J. Brill, 1960.

Rahman, Fazlur. *Major Themes of the Qur'an.* Chicago: Bibliotheca Islamica, 1980.

Raisanen, Heibbi. *The Idea of Divine Hardening: A Comparative Study of the Notion of Divine Hardening, Leading Astray and Inciting to Evil in the Bible and the Qur'an.* Helsinki: Finnish Exegetical Society, 1972.

Rippin, Andrew. *The Qur'an: Formative Interpretation.* Burlington, VT: Ashgate, 1999.

———. *The Qur'an: Style and Contents.* Burlington, VT: Ashgate, 2001.

Roberts, Robert. *The Social Laws of the Qur'an.* London: Williams and Norgate, 1925.

Rodwell, J. M., trans. *The Koran.* London: Dent, 1989.

Sa'id, Labib al-. *The Recited Koran.* Translated by Bernard G. Weiss et al. Princeton, NJ: Darwin Press, 1975.

Stanton, H. A. Weitbrecht. *The Teachings of the Qur'an: With an Account of Its Growth and a Subject Index.* New York: Biblo and Tannen, 1969. Reprint of 1919 edition

Surty, Muhammad Ibrahim. *A Course in the Science of Reciting the Qur'an.* Leicester, England, 1988.

Wagtendonk, K. *Fasting in the Koran.* Leiden, Netherlands: E. J. Brill, 1968.

Wansbrough, John. *Quranic Studies.* Oxford: Oxford University Press, 1977.

Watt, W. Montgomery. *Companion to the Qur'an.* London: Allen & Unwin, 1967.

———. "God's Caliph: Qur'anic Interpretations and Umayyad Claims." In *Iran and Islam: In Memory of V. Minorsky,* edited by C. E. Bosworth, 565–574. Edinburgh: University Press, 1971.

Hadith

Adams, Charles J. "The Authority of Hadith in the Eyes of Some Modern Muslims." In *Essays on Islamics Civilization Presented to Niyazi Berkes,* edited by D. P. Little, 27–49. Leiden: E. J. Brill, 1976.

———. "The Islamic Religious Tradition." In *Religion and Man,* edited by W. Richard Comstock, 553–617. New York: Harper & Row, 1971.

Azmi, M. M. *Studies in Early Hadith Literature.* Beirut: Khayats, 1968.

Bravmann, M. M. "Sunnah and Related Concepts." In *The Spiritual Background of Early Islam,* 122–198. Leiden, Netherlands: E. J. Brill, 1972.

Bukhari, Muhammad ibn Ismail al-. "Appendix." In *The Concept of Believe in Islamic Theology.* Tokyo: Keio Institute of Cultural and Linguistic Studies, 1965.

———. *A Manual of Hadith.* 2nd ed. Translated by Muhammad Ali. Lahore, Pakistan: Ahmadiyyah Anjuman Isha'at Islam, 1951.

————. *The Translation of the Meanings of Sahih al-Bukhari.* 9 vols. Translated by Muhammad M. Khan. Medina: Islamic University, 1973.

Christopher, John B. *The Islamic Tradition.* London: Harper & Row, 1972.

Dermenghem, Emile. *Muhammad and the Islamic Tradition.* Translated by J. M. Watt. New York: Harper & Bros., 1958.

Graham, Willaim A. *A Divine Word and Prophetic Word in Early Islam: A Reconsideration of the Sources, with Special Reference to the Divine Saying or Hadith Qudsi.* The Hague: Mouton, 1976.

Guillaume, Alfred. *The Traditions of Islam.* Oxford: Oxford University Press, 1924.

Hamidullah, Muhammad. *The Earliest Extant Work on the Hadith: Sahifah Hammam Ibn Munabbih.* Translated by M. Rahimuddin. Paris: Publications du Centre Cultural Islamique, 1961.

Hosain, H. Hadayat. "The Development of the Hadath Concordance in Arabic Literature (Ilm al-Atraf)." *Journal of the Asiatic Society of Bengal* 20 (1924): 99–110.

————. "Islamic Apogrypha (Tadlis)." *Journal of the Royal Asiatic Society of Bengal* 2 (1936); 1–7.

Juynboll, G. H. A. "Ahmad Muhammad Shakir (1892–1958) and His Edition of Ibn Hanbal's Musnad." *Der Islam* 49 (1972): 221–247.

————. *The Authenticity of the Tradition Literature: Discussion in Modern Egypt.* Leiden, Netherlands: E. J. Brill, 1969.

Kister, M. J. "Al-Tahannuth: An Inquiry into the Meaning of a Term." *Bulletin of the School of Oriental and African Studies* 31 (1968): 223–236.

————. "You Shall Only Set Out for Three Mosques: A Study of Early Tradition." *Le Museon* 82 (1969): 173–196.

Motzki, Harald. *Hadith: Origins and Development.* Burlington, VT: Ashgate, 2004.

Nawawi, Muhyi al-Din. "The Forty (Two) Traditions of al-Nawawi." Translated by E. F. F. Bishop. *Moslem World* 29 (1939): 153–177.

————. *Gardens of the Righteous: Riyadh as Salihin of Imam Nawawi.* Translated by Muhammad Zafrullah Khan. London: Curzon Press, 1975.

Rahman, Fazlur. "The Origins and Development of Tradition." In *Islam,* 43–74. New York: Anchor Books, 1966.

Robson, James. "Hadith." In *EI2,* Vol. 3, 23–28. New ed. Leiden, Netherlands: E. J. Brill, 1960.

————. "The Material of Tradition." *Muslim World* 41 (1959): 166–180, 257–270.

———. "Standards Applied by Muslim Traditionists." *Bulletin of the John Rylands Library* 43 (1961): 459–479.

———. "Tradition: Investigation and Classification." *Muslim World* 41 (1951): 98–112.

———. "Tradition: The Second Foundation of Islam." *Muslim World* 41 (1951): 22–33.

———. "Traditions from Individuals." *Journal of Semitic Studies* 9 (1964): 327–340.

Samarqandi, Abu Layth al-. "The Angel of Death in Late Islamic Tradition." *Islamic Studies* 3 (1964): 285–519.

———. "The Creation of Man and Angels in the Eschatological Literature (Translated Excerpts from an Unpublished Collection of Traditions)." Translated by J. Macdonald. *Islamic Studies* 3 (1964): 285–308.

———. "The Day of Resurrection." *Islamic Studies* 5 (1966): 129–197.

———. "Paradise." *Islamic Studies* 5 (1966): 331–383.

———. "The Preliminaries to the Resurrection and Judgment." *Islamic Studies* 4 (1965): 137–179.

———. "The Twilight of the Dead." *Islamic Studies* 4 (1965): 55–102.

Schacht, Joseph. "Ahl al-Hadith." In *EI2*, Vol. 1, 258–259. New ed. Leiden, Netherlands: E. J. Brill, 1960.

———. "A Revaluation of Islamic Traditions." *Journal of the Royal Asiatic Society* (1949): 143–154.

Siddiqi, M. Zubayr. *Hadith Literature*. Calcutta, India: Calcutta University Press, 1961.

Smith, Jane I., and Y. Haddad. "Women in the Afterlife: The Islamic View as Seen from Quran and Tradition," In *The Islamic Understanding of Death and Resurrection*, 39–50. Albany: State University of New York Press, 1981.

Wensinck, A. J. *A Handbook of Early Muhammadan Tradition*. Leiden, Netherlands: E. J. Brill, 1927.

Yusuf, S. M. "The Sunnah—Its Transmission, Development and Revision." *Islamic Culture* 37 (1963): 271–282; 38 (1964): 15–25.

Mysticism

Abbas, Shemeem Burney. *The Female Voice in Sufi Ritual: Devotional Practices in Pakistan and India.* Austin: University of Texas Press, 2002.

Abun-Nasr, Jamil M. "The Salafiyya Movement in Morocco: The Religious Bases of the Moroccan Nationalist Movement." In *Social Change: The Colonial Situation*, edited by I. Wallerstein. New York: Wiley, 1966.

———. *The Tijaniyya: A Sufi Order in the Modern World*. M. E. Monographs, 7. Oxford: Oxford University Press, 1965.

Algar, Hamid. "A Brief History of the Naqshbandi Order" and "Political Aspects of Naqshbandi History." In *Naqshbandis: Cheminements et situation actuelle d'un ordre mystique musulman*, edited by Marc Gaborieau et al, 3–44, 123–152. Istanbul: Edition Isis, 1990.

———. "The Naqshbandi Order: A Preliminary Survey of Its History and Significance." *Studia Islamica* 44 (1976): 123–152.

Amedroz, H. F. "Notes on Some Sufi Lives." *Journal of the Royal Asiatic Society* (1912): 551–586, 1087–1089.

Anawati, G., and L. Gardet. *La mystique musulmane*. Paris: Vrin, 1961.

Ansari, 'Abdullah-i. "Ansari's Prayers and Counsels." Translated by A. J. Arberry. *Islamic Culture* 10 (1936): 369–389.

Ansari, Sarah D. F. *Sufi Saints and State Power: The Pirs of Sind, 1843–1947*. Cambridge: Cambridge University Press, 1992.

Anwarul Haq, M. *The Faith Movement of Mawlana Muhammad Llyas*. London: Allen & Unwin, 1972.

Arberry, A. J. "Mysticism." In *The Cambridge History of Islam*, 604–632. 2 vols. Cambridge: Cambridge University Press, 1970.

———. *Sufism: An Account of the Mystics of Islam*. London: Allen & Unwin, 1950; New York: Harper Torch, 1970.

Arnold, Sir Thomas. "Saints and Martyrs Muhammadan in India." In *Encyclopaedia of Religion and Ethics*, Vol. 11, 63–73. New York: Charles Scribner's Sons, 1962.

Bakhtiar, Laleh. *Sufi Women of America: Angels in the Making*. Chicago: Institute of Traditional Psychoethics and Guidance, 1996.

Biegmann, Nicolass. *Egypt: Moulids, Saints, Sufis*. London: Kegan Paul, 1990.

Birge, John Kingsly. *The Bektashi Order of Dervishes*. Hartford, CT: Hartford Seminary Press, 1937.

Bövering, Gerhard. *The Mystical Vision of Existence in Classical Islam*. Berlin: Walter de Gruyter, 1980.

Brown, J. P., and H. A. Rose. *The Dervishes or Oriental Spiritualism*. London: Cass, 1968. Reprint of 1868 edition.

Burckhardt, T. *An Introduction to Sufi Doctrine*. Lahore, Pakistan: Sharaf, 1959.

Canaan, Taufik. *Mohammedan Saints and Sanctuaries in Palestine*. Luzac's Oriental Religions Series, Vol. 5. London: Luzac, 1927.

Chittick, William. Trans. *Sufi Path of Love*. Albany: State University of New York Press, 1983.

———. *Sufism: A Short Introduction*. Oxford: Oneworld Publications, 2000.

Corbin, Henry. *Creative Imagination in the Sufism of Ibn 'Arabi*. Translated by R. Manheim. Bollingen Series, no. 91. Princeton, NJ: Princeton University Press, 1969.

Darqawi, al-. *Letters of a Sufi Master*. Translated by T. Burckhardt. London: Perennial Books, 1973.

DeJong, F. "Cairene Ziyara-Days: A Contribution to the Study of Saint Veneration in Islam." *Die Welt des Islam* new series 17 (1976–1977): 26–43.

Eaton, R. M. "Sufi Folk Literature and the Expansion of Indian Islam." *History of Religions* 14 (1974): 117–127.

Fakhry, Majid. "Three Varieties of Mysticism in Islam." *International Journal of Philosophy of Religion* 2 (1971): 193–207.

Faroqhi, Suraiya. "The Tekke of Haci Bektash: Social Position and Economic Activities." *International Journal of Middle Eastern Studies* 7 (1976):183–208.

Friedmann, Y. *Shaykh Ahmad Sirhindi: An Outline of His Thought and a Study of His Image in the Eyes of Posterity*. Montreal: McGill Queen's University Press, 1971.

Gardet, L. "Dhikr." In *EI2*, Vol. 2, 223–227. Leiden, Netherlands: E. J. Brill, 1960.

Gellner, Ernest. *Saints of the Atlas*. London: Weidenfeld and Nicolson, 1969.

Gilsenan, Michael. *Saint and Sufi in Modern Egypt: An Essay in the Sociology of Religion*. Oxford: Clarendon, 1973.

———. "Some Factors in the Decline of the Sufi Orders in Modern Egypt." *Muslim World* 57 (1967): 11–18.

Goldziher, Ignaz. "Veneration of Saints in Islam." In *Muslim Studies*, Vol. 1. London: Allen & Unwin, 1967.

Hawi, Sami S. *Islamic Naturalism and Mysticism: A Philosophic Study of Ibn Tufal's Hayy ibn Yaqzan*. Leiden, Netherlands: E. J. Brill, 1974.

Horten, Max. "Mystics in Islam." Translated by V. June Hager. *Islamic Studies* 13 (1974): 67–93.

Hosain, H. Haydatay. "Islamic Apocrypha (Tadlis)." *Journal of the Royal Asiatic Society of Bengal* 2 (1936): 1–7.

Hourani, A. "Shaikh Khalid and the Naqshbandi Order." In *Islamic Philosophy and the Classical Tradition: Essays Presented to R. Walzer on His Seventieth Birthday*, edited by S. M. Stern, 89–103. Columbia: University of South Carolina Press, 1972.

Huda, Qamar ul-. *Striving for Divine Union: Spiritual Exercises for Suhrawardi Sufis*. London: Routledge Curzon, 2003.

Ibn al-'Arabi. *The 'Tarjuman al-Ashwaq': A Collection of Mystical Odes by Muhiu'ddin Ibn al-'Arabi*. Edited and translated by R. A. Nicholson. London: Royal Asiatic Society, 1911.

Ibn 'Ata'Allah. "Counsels of a Sufi Master." *Studies in Comparative Religion* 5 (1971): 207–215.

———. *Ibn 'Ata' Allah's Sufi Aphorisms (Kitab al Hikam)*. Translated by V. Danner. Leiden, Netherlands: E. J. Brill, 1973.

Izutsu, Toshihiko. "Mysticism and the Linguistic Problem of Equivocation in the Thought of 'Ayn al-Qadat al-Hamadhani." *Studia Islamica* 31 (1970): 153–170.

Keddie, Nikki R., ed. *Scholars, Saints, and Sufis: Muslim Religious Institutions since 1500*. Berkeley: University of California Press, 1972.

Knysh, Alexander. *Islamic Mysticism: A Short History*. Leiden, Netherlands: E. J. Brill, 2000.

Krymsky, A. E. "A Sketch of the Development of Sufism to the End of the Third Century of the Hijra." Translated by N. S. Doniach. *Islamic Quarterly* 5 (1959–60): 109–126; 6 (1961): 79–106.

Landolt, Hermann. "Suhrawardi's 'Tales of Initiation.'" *Journal of the American Oriental Society* 107 (1987): 475–486.

Le Gall, Dina. *A Culture of Sufism: Naqshbandis in the Ottoman World*. Albany: State University of New York Press, 2005.

Lewis, I. M. "Sufism in Somaliland: A Study in Tribal Islam." *Bulletin of the School of Oriental and African Studies* 17 (1955): 581–602; 18 (1956): 145–160.

Lings, Martin. *A Sufi Saint of the Twentieth Century: Shaykh Ahmad al-'Alawi, His Spiritual Heritage and Legacy*. 3rd ed. Boston: Unwin Press, 1993.

———. *What Is Sufism?* Berkeley: University of California Press, 1975.

Macdonald, D. B. "The Development of the Idea of Spirit in Islam." *Muslim World* 22 (1932): 25–42, 153–168.

Mackeen, A. M. Mohamed. "The Rise of al-Shadhili (d. 656/1258)." *Journal of the American Oriental Society* 91 (1971): 477–486.

Makdisi, George. "Ibn Taymiyya: A Sufi of the Qadariya Order." *American Journal of Arabic Studies* 1 (1973): 118–129.

Martin, B. G. "A Short History of the Khalwati Order." In *Scholars, Saints, and Sufis*, edited by Nikki R. Keddie, 275–307. Berkeley: University of California Press, 1972.

McCown, Chester C. "Muslim Shrines in Palestine." *American School of Oriental Research in Jerusalem*, Annual 2 and 3 (1921–1922): 47–49.

Meier, Fritz. "The Mystery of the Ka'ba: Symbol and Reality in Islamic Mysticism." In *The Mysteries: Papers from the Eranos Yearbooks*, edited by R. Manheim. New York: Pantheon Books, 1955.

Nasr, S. H. "Shihab al-Din Suhrawardi Maqtul." In *A History of Muslim Philosophy*, Vol. 2, 372–398. Wiesbaden: Harrassowitz, 1963–1966.

———. *Sufi Essays*. London: Allen & Unwin, 1972.

Nicholson, R. A. "The Goal of Muhammadan Mysticism." *Journal of the Royal Asiatic Society* (1913): 55–69.

———. "A Historical Enquiry concerning the Origin and Development of Sufism." *Journal of the Royal Asiatic Society* (1906): 303–348.

———. *The Idea of Personality in Sufism*. Lahore, Pakistan: Ashraf, 1970. Originally published in 1923.

———. *The Mystics of Islam*. New York: Shocken Books, 1975.

Nizami, K. A. "Early Indo–Muslim Mystics and Their Attitudes toward the State." *Islamic Quarterly* 22 (1948): 387–398; 23 (1929): 13–21, 162–170, 312–321; 24 (1950): 60–71.

———. "Naqshbandi Influence on Mughal Rulers and Politics." *Islamic Culture* 39 (1965): 41–52.

———. "Some Aspects of Khanqah Life in Medieval India." *Studia Islamica* 8 (1957): 51–69.

Norton, J. D. "Bektashis in Turkey." In *Islam in the Modern World*, edited by D. MacEoin and A. al-Shah. London: Croom Helm, 1983.

Rahman, Fazlur. *Selected Letters of Shaikh Ahmad Sirhindi*. Karachi, Pakistan: Iqbal Academy, 1968.

Renard, John., ed. and trans. *Knowledge of God in Classical Sufism: Foundations of Islamic Mystical Theology*. Mahwah, NJ: Paulist, 2004.

Rizvi, Syed Athar Abbas. *Muslim Revivalist Movements in Northern India*. Agra, India: Agra University, 1965.

Rumi. *Discourse of Rumi.* Translated by A. J. Arberry. London: Murray, 1961.

———. *More Tales from the Mathnawi.* Translated by A. J. Arberry. London: Allen & Unwin, 1963.

———. *Mystical Poems of Rumi.* Translated by A. J. Arberry. Chicago: University of Chicago Press, 1968.

———. *Rumi: Poet and Mystic.* Translated by R. A. Nicholson. London: Allen & Unwin, 1950.

———. *Selected Poem from the Divan-i Shams-i Tabriz.* Translated and edited by R. A. Nicholson. Cambridge: Cambridge University Press, 1952. Reprint of 1898 edition.

———. *Tales from the Mathnawi.* Translated by A. J. Arberry. London: Allen & Unwin, 1961.

———. *The Teachings of Rumi: The Masnawi of Maulana Jalalu-'ddin Muhammad Rumi.* Translated by E. H. Whinfield. New York: Dutton, 1975.

Salik, S. A. *The Saint of Jilan.* Lahore, Pakistan: Ashraf, 1961.

Schimmel, Annemarie. "The Martyr-Mystic Hallaj in Sindhi Folk Poetry." *Numen* 9 (1962): 161–200.

———. "The Origin and Early Development of Sufism." *Journal of the Pakistan Historical Society* 8 (1959): 55–67.

———. "Some Aspects of Mystical Prayer in Islam." *Die Welt des Islam-*snew series 2 (1952): 112–125.

Schlegell, Barbara von, trans. *Principles of Sufism.* Berkeley, CA: Mizan, 1992.

Sells, Michael, ed. and trans. *Early Islamic Mysticism.* Mahwah, NJ: Paulist, 1996.

Shadhili, al-. *Illumination in Islamic Mysticism.* Translated by E. Jurhi. Princeton, NJ: Princeton University Press, 1938.

———. "Prayers of al-Shadhili." Translated by E. H. Douglas. In *Middle Eastern Studies in Honor of Aziz Suryal Atiya,* edited by Sami A. Hanna, 106–122. Leiden, Netherlands: E. J. Brill, 1972.

Sharib, Z. H. *Khawaja Gharib Nawaz.* Lahore, Pakistan: Ashraf, 1961.

Sharma, Arvind. "The Spiritual Biography of al-Ghazali." *Studies in Islam* 9 (1972): 65–85.

Smith, Margaret. *Al-Ghazali, the Mystic.* London: Luzac, 1944.

———. *An Early Mystic of Baghdad.* London: Sheldon, 1935.

———. *Rabi'a the Mystic and Her Fellow Saints in Islam.* Cambridge: Cambridge University Press, 1928.

Subhan, J. A. *Sufism, Its Saints and Shrines: An Introduction to the Study of Sufism with Special Reference to India and Pakistan.* 2d rev. ed. Lucknow, India: Lucknow Publishing, 1960. Reprint of 1938 edition.

Sviri, Sara. *Perspectives on Early Islamic Mysticism.* New York: Routledge, 2006.

Triaud, Jean-Louis. "Khalwa and the Career of Sainthood: An Interpretative Essay." In *Charisma and Brotherhood in African Islam,* edited by Christian Coulon and Connor Cruise O'Brien, 53–66. Oxford: Clarendon, 1988.

Trimingham, J. Spencer. *The Sufi Orders in Islam* Oxford: Oxford University Press, 1971.

Valiuddin, Mir. *Love of God: The Sufi Approach.* New Delhi, India: Asia House, 1968.

———. *The Qur'anic Sufism.* New Delhi, India: Asia House, 1959.

Van Ess, Josef. "Umar II and His Epistle against the Qadariya." *Abr-Nahrain* 12 (1971–1972): 19–26.

Vikor, Knut S. *Sufi and Scholar on the Desert Edge: Muhammad b. 'Ali al-Sanusi, 1787–1859.* London: Hurst & Co., 1995.

Wali Allah, Shah. *A Mystical Interpretation of Prophetic Tales by an Indian Muslim: Shah Wali Allah's 'Ta'wil al-hadith'.* Translated by J. M. S. Baljon. Leiden, Netherlands: E. J. Brill, 1973.

Zaehner, R. C. *Hindu and Muslim Mysticism.* London: Athlone, 1960.

Zarrinkoob, A. H. "Persian Sufism in Its Historical Perspective." *Iranian Studies* 3 (1970): 139–208.

Ziadeh, Nicola A. *Sanusiyah: A Study of a Revivalist Movement in Islam* (1958). Reprint. Leiden, Netherlands: E. J. Brill, 1983.

Medieval Theology and Philosophy

'Abduh, Mahammad. *The Theory of Unity.* Translated by Ishaq Musa al-Husaini and Kenneth Cragg. London: Allen & Unwin, 1966.

Affifi, A. E. "Ibn 'Arabi." In *A History of Muslim Philosophy,* Vol. 1, 398–421. Wiesbaden, Germany: Harrassowitz, 1963–1966.

Ahmad, Aziz, and G. E. von Grunebaum, eds. *Muslim Self-Statement in India and Pakistan, 1857–1968.* Wiesbaden, Germany: Harrassowitz, 1970.

Al-Alwani, Taha J. "Taqlid and the Stagnation of the Muslim Mind." *The American Journal of Islamic Social Sciences* 8, no. 3 (1991).

Arberry, A. J. *Aspects of Islamic Civilization as Depicted in the Original Texts.* London: Allen & Unwin, 1964.

———. *Revelation and Reason in Islam.* London: Allen & Unwin, 1957.

Arnold, Sir Thomas. *The Preaching of Islam.* London: Constable, 1913.

Ashari, al-. *The Theology of al-Ash'ari: The Arabic Texts of al-Ash'ari's Kitab al-Luma' and Risalat Istihsan al-Khaw fi 'Ilm al-Kalam.* Translated by R. J. McCarthy. Beirut: Imprimerie Catholique, 1953.

'Attar. *The Conference of the Birds.* Translated by C. S. Noth. London: Janus, 1954; Berkeley, CA: Shambala, 1971.

———. *The Ilahi-Nama or Book of God of Farid al-Din 'Attar.* Translated by John A. Boyle. Manchester, England: Manchester University Press, 1976.

———. *Muslim Saints and Mystics: Episodes from the Tadhkirat al-auliya' (Memorial of the Saints) by Farid al-Din 'Attar.* Translated by A. J. Arberry. Chicago. University of Chicago Press, 1966.

Baali, Fuad, and Ali Wardi. *Ibn Khaldun and Islamic Thought-Styles.* Boston: G. K. Hall, 1981.

Baghdadi, al-. "The Logical Basis of Early Kalam." Translated by W. M. Watt. *Islamic Quarterly* 6 (1961): 3–10; 7 (1963): 13–39.

Berg, Herbert. *The Development of Exegesis in Early Islam.* London: Curzon, 2000.

Bukhari, Muhammad ibn Isma'il al-. "Appendix." In *The Concept of Belief in Islamic Theology,* 235–50. Tokyo: Keio Institute, 1965.

Bulliet, Richard W. "The Shaikh al-Islam and the Evolution of Islamic Society." *Studia Islamica* 35 (1972): 53–67.

Cagatay, Nes'et. "Riba and Interest Concept and Banking in the Ottoman Empire." *Studia Islamica* 32 (1979): 53–68.

Calverley, Edwin. *Worship in Islam: Al-Ghazzali's Book of the Ihya.* Piscataway, NJ: Georgias Press, 2004.

Cherif-Chergui, Abderraham. "Justice and Equality in Islam." *The Month* 13, no. 2 (February 1980).

Corbin, Henry. *Avicenna and the Visionary Recital.* Translated by W. R. Trask. Bollingen Series, no. 46. New York: Bollingen, 1960.

Cragg, Kenneth. *Counsels in Contemporary Islam.* Edinburgh: University of Edinburgh Press, 1965.

———. *The House of Islam.* 2nd rev. ed. Encino, CA: Dickenson Publishing Co., 1975.

Cragg, Kenneth, and R. Marston Speight. *Islam from Within.* Belmont, CA: Wadstone Publishers, 1980.

Crone, Patricia. *From Kavad to al-Ghazali: Religion, Law, and Political Thought in the Near East, c. 600–c. 1100.* Burlington, VT: Ashgate, 2005.

Cureton, William, ed. *The Book of Religious and Philosophical Sects*. By Muhammad Shahrastani. Piscataway, NJ: Gorgias Press, 2002.

Denny, Frederick Mathewson. *An Introduction to Islam*. 2nd ed. New York: Macmillan, 1994.

Donaldson, D. M. *Studies in Muslim Ethics*. London: S.P.C.K., 1963.

Fakhry, Majid. "The Classical Islamic Arguments for the Existence of God." *Muslim World* 47 (1957): 133–145.

———. *A History of Islamic Philosophy*. New York: Columbia University Press, 1970.

———. *Islamic Occasionalism and Its Critique by Averoës and Aquinas*. London: Allen & Unwin, 1958.

———. "Philosophy and Scripture in the Theology of Averroes." *Medieval Studies* 30 (1968): 78–89.

Faris, Nabih A. "Al-Ghazzali." In *The Arab Heritage*, 142–158. Princeton, NJ: Princeton University Press, 1946.

Frank, R. M. "The Divine Attributes according to the Teaching of Abu'l-Hudhayl al-'Allaf." *Le Museon* 82 (1969): 451–506.

———. "The Structure of Created Causality according to al-Ash'ari." *Studia Islamica* 25 (1966): 13–75.

Fyzee, A. A. A. *A Modern Approach to Islam*. Bombay: Times of India, 1963.

Ghazali, Abu Hamid al-. *Al-Ghazali on Divine Predicates and Their Properties: A Critical and Annotated Translation of These Chapters in al-Iqtisad fi'l-i'tiqad*. Translated by 'Abd-r-Rahman Abu Zayd. Lahore, Pakistan: S. M. Ashraf, 1970.

———. "Al-Ghazali's Tract on Dogmatic Theology." Edited and translated by A. L. Tibawi. *Islamic Quarterly* 9 (1965): 65–122.

———. "Al-Risalat al-Laduniyya, by Abu Hamid Muhammad al-Ghazali." Translated by Margaret Smith. *Journal of the Royal Asiatic Society* 19 (1938): 177–200, 353–374.

———. *Book XX of al-Ghazali's Ihya' 'Ulum al-Din*. Translated by L. Zolondek. Leiden, Netherlands: E. J. Brill, 1963.

———. *The Book of Knowledge, Being a Translation with Notes of the Kitab al-'Ilm of al-Ghazzali's Ihya' 'Ulum al-Din*. Translated by N. A. Faris. Lahore, Pakistan: Ashraf, 1962.

———. "Emotional Religion in Islam as Affected by Music and Singing, Being a Translation of a Book of the *Ihya' Ulum ad-Din* of al-Ghazzali with Analysis, Annotation, and Appendices." Translated by D. B. Macdonald. *Journal of the Royal Asiatic Society* (1901): 195–253; (1902): 1–28.

———. *The Faith and Practice of al-Ghazali.* Translated by W. M. Watt. London: Allen & Unwin, 1952.

———. *The Foundations of the Articles of Faith, Being a Translation with Notes of the Kitab Qawa'id al-'Aqa'id of al-Ghazzali's Ihya' Ulum al-Din.* Translated by N. A. Faris. Lahore, Pakistan: S. M. Ashraf, 1963.

———. "Ghazali on Ethical Premises." Translated by Michael Marmura. *Philosophical Forum* 1 (1968): 393–403.

———. *Ghazali on Prayer.* Translated by Kojiro Nakamura. Tokyo: Tokyo University Press, 1983.

———. "Ghazzali's 'Epistle of the Birds': A Translation of the *Risalat at-Tayr.*" Translated by N. A. Faris. *Muslim World* 34 (1944): 46–53.

———. *The Mysteries of Almsgiving: A Translation from the Arabic, with Notes, of the Kitab Asrar al-Zakah of al-Ghazzali's Ihya' 'Ulum al-Din.* Translated by N. A. Faris. Beirut: American University of Beirut, 1966.

———. *The Mysteries of Purity, Being a Translation with Notes of the Kitab Asrar al-Taharah of Al-Ghazzali's Ihya' 'Ulum al-Din.* Translated by N. A. Faris. Lahore, Pakistan: S. M. Ashraf, 1966.

———. *Ninety-Nine Names of God in Islam: A Translation of the Major Portion of al-Ghazali's al-Maqsad Al-Asna.* Translated by R. C. Stade. Ibadan, Nigeria: Daystar, 1970.

———. *On the Duties of Brotherhood.* Translated by Muhtar Holland. Woodstock, NY: Overlook Press, 1976.

———. *Tahafut al-Falasifah, or Incoherence of the Philosophers.* Translated by S. A. Kamali. Lahore, Pakistan: Pakistan Philosophical Congress, 1958.

———. *Worship in Islam, Being a Translation, with Commentary and Introduction, of al-Ghazali's Book of the Ihya' on the Worship.* Translated by E. E. Calverley. 2nd ed. London: Luzac, 1957.

Goitein, S. D. "The Sanctity of Jerusalem and Palestine in Early Islam." In *Studies in Islamic History and Institutions.* Leiden: E. J. Brill, 1996, 135–49.

Goldziher, I. *Mohammad and Islam.* Translated by K. C. Seeyle. New Haven, CT: Yale University Press, 1917.

Goodman, L. E. "Ghazali's Argument from Creation." *International Journal of Middle East Studies* 2 (1971): 67–85, 168–188.

Grunebaum, G. E. von. *Classical Islam: A History, 600–1258.* London: Allen & Unwin, 1970.

———. "Islam: Experience of the Holy and Concept of Man." In *Islam and Medieval Hellenism: Social and Cultural Perspectives*, 1–39. London: Variorum, 1976.

———. *Modern Islam: The Search for Cultural Identity*. Berkeley: California University Press, 1962.

Hitti, Philip K. *Islam: A Way of Life*. New York: Humanities, 1971.

Hodgson, Marshall G.S. *The Venture of Islam*. Chicago: Chicago University Press, 1974.

Hoodbhoy, Pervez. *Islam and Science: Religious Orthodoxy and the Battle for Rationality*. London: Zed Books, 1991.

Hosain, M. Hadayat. "The Development of the Hadath Concordance in Arabic Literature (Ilm al-Atraf)." *Journal of the Asiatic Society of Bengal* new series 20 (1924): 99–110.

Hourani, Albert. "Islam and the Philosophers of History." *Middle Eastern Studies* 3 (1967): 206–268.

Hourani, G. F. "Averroes on Good and Evil." *Studia Islamica* 16 (1962): 14–40.

———. "The Basis of Authority of Consensus in Sunnite Islam." *Studia Islamica* 21 (1964): 13–60.

———. "The Dialogue between al-Ghazali and the Philosophers on the Origin of the World." *Muslim World* 48 (1958): 183–191, 308–314.

———. *Islamic Rationalism: The Ethics of 'Abd al-Jabbar*. Oxford: Clarendon, 1971.

———. "Juwayni's Criticism of Mu'tazilite Ethics." *Muslim World* 65 (1975): 161–173.

———. "Two Theories of Value in Medieval Islam." *Muslim World* 50 (1960): 269–278.

Ibn al-Kalbi, Hisham. *The Book of Idols: Being a Translation from the Arabic of the Kitab al Am*. Translated with introduction and notes by N. A. Faris. Princeton, NJ: Princeton University Press, 1952.

Ibn Khaldun, 'Abd al-Rahman b. Muhammad. *The Muqaddimah: An Introduction to History* 3 vols. Translated by F. Rosenthal. London: Routledge and Kegan Paul, 1985.

Ibn Rushd. *Averroes: On the Harmony of Religion and Philosophy. A Translation, with Introduction and Notes, of Ibn Rushd's Kitab Fasl al-Maqal, with Its Appendix and an Extract from Kitab al-Kashi 'an Manahij al-Adilla*. Translated by G. Hourani. Gibb Memorial Series, new series, no. 21. London: Luzac, 1967.

———. *Averroes' Tahafut al-Tahafut*. 2 vols. Translated by Simon van der Bergh. London: Luzac, 1954.

Ibn Sina. *Avicenna on Theology*. Translated by A. J. Arberry. London: Murray, 1951.

Ibn Tufayl. *Ibn Tufayl's Hayy ibn Yaqzan*. Translated by Lenn E. Goodman. New York: Twayne Publishers, 1972.

Iqbal, Muhammad. *The Mysteries of Selflessness*. Translated by A. J. Arberry. London: Murray, 1953.

———. *The Reconstruction of Religious Thought in Islam*. Lahore, Pakistan: Ashraf, 1934.

———. *The Secrets of the Self*. Rev. ed. Translated by R. A. Nicholson. Lahore, Pakistan: Ashraf, 1940.

Ivanow, W. *True Meaning of Religion*. Bombay, India: Ismaili Society, 1947.

Izutsu, Toshihiko. *A Comparative Study of the Key Philosophical Concepts in Sufism and Taoism*. Vol. 1. Tokyo: Keio Institute of Cultural and Linguistic Studies, 1966.

———. *The Concept and Reality of Existence*. Tokyo: Keio Institute of Cultural and Linguistic Studies, 1971.

Jalbani, G. N. *Teachings of Shah Waliyullah of Delhi*. Lahore, Pakistan: S. M. Ashraf, 1967.

Jeffery, Arthur, trans. *Materials for the History of the Text of the Qur'an*. Leiden, Netherlands: E. J. Brill, 1937.

———. *A Reader on Islam: Passages from Standard Arabic Writings Illustrative of the Beliefs and Practices of Muslims*. The Hague: Mouton, 1962.

Juynboll, G. H. A. "Ahmad Muhammad Shakir (1892–1958) and His Edition of Ibn Hanabal's Musnad." *Der Islam* 49 (1972): 221–247.

Kassem, Hammond. "The Idea of Justice in Islamic Philosophy." *Diogenes* 79 (1972): 81–103.

Katsh, A. I. *Judaism in Islam: Biblical and Talmudic Backgrounds of the Koran and Its Commentaries*. New York: Bloch, 1954.

Kister, M. J. "Al-Tahannuth: An Inquiry into the Meaning of a Term." *Bulletin of the School of Oriental and African Studies* 31 (1968): 223–236.

Landau, Rom. *The Philosophy of Ibn Arabi*. New York: Macmillan, 1959.

Lewis, James R. "Some Aspects of Sacred Space and Time in Islam." *Studies in Islam* 19 (1982): 167–178.

Macdonald, D. B. "The Development of the Idea of Spirit in Islam." *Muslim World* 22 (1932): 25–42, 153–168.

Mahdi, Muhsin. *Ibn Khaldun's Philosophy of History: A Study in the Philosophic Foundation of the Science of Culture.* Chicago: University of Chicago Press, 1957. Reprint. Chicago: Phoenix, 1964.

Makdisi, G. "Ash'ari and the Ash'arites in Islamic Religious History." *Studia Islamica* 17 (1962): 37–80; 18 (1963): 19–39.

Marmura, Michael. "Ghazali and Demonstrative Science." *Journal of the History of Philosophy* 3 (1965): 183–204.

Maryam Jameelah. *Islam in Theory and Practice.* Lahore, Pakistan: Kuhammad Yusuf Khan, 1973.

Mawardi, Abu al-Hasan 'Ali ibn Muhammad al-. *Al-Ahkam al-Sultaniyah.* Edited by M. Engri. London: Garnet Publishing, 1969.

McDonald, D. B. "Life of al-Ghazzali." *Journal of the American Oriental Society* 20 (1899): 71–132.

McDonough, Sheila. *The Authority of the Past: A Study of Three Muslim Modernists.* Chambersburg, PA: American Academy of Religion, 1970.

Memon, Muhammad Umar. *Ibn Taymiya's Struggle against Popular Religion.* The Hague: Mouton, 1976.

Modarressi, Hossein. "The Just Ruler." *Journal of the American Oriental Society* no. 3 (1991): 549–562.

Morgan, Kenneth, ed. *Islam: The Straight Path—Islam Interpreted by Muslims.* New York: Ronald Press, 1958.

Mufid, Muhammad ibn Muhammad al-. *Kitab al-Irshad: The Book of Guidance.* Translated by K. A. Howard. Elmhurst, NY: Tahrike Tarsile Quran, 1981.

Mutahhari, Murtaza. *Fundamentals of Islamic Thought: God, Man, and the Universe.* Translated by R. Campbell. Berkeley: Mizan Press, 1985.

Nadvi, Abulhasan 'Ali. *Four Pillars of Islam.* Translated by Mohammad A. Kidwai. Lucknow: Academy of Islamic Research and Publications, 1978.

Nakamura, Kojiro. *Ghazali on Prayer.* Tokyo: University of Tokyo Press, 1973.

Nasr, Seyyed Hossein. *Ideals and Realities of Islam.* Boston: Beacon Press, 1975.

———. *An Introduction to Islamic Cosmological Doctrine.* Cambridge, MA: Harvard University, 1964.

———. *Traditional Islam in the Modern World.* London: Routledge and Kegan Paul, 1987.

Netton, Ian Richard. *Al-Farabi and His School*. London: Routledge, 1992.

Noss, John B. *Man's Religions*. 5th ed. New York: Macmillan, 1974.

O'Shea, Stephen. *Sea of Faith: Islam and Christianity in the Medieval Mediterranean World*. New York: Walker, 2006.

Parens, Joshua. *An Islamic Philosophy of Virtuous Religious: Introducing Alfarabi*. Albany: State University of New York Press, 2006.

Parwez, Ghulam Chaudhri. *Islam: A Challenge to Religion*. Lahore, Pakistan: Zarreen Art, 1968.

Patton, W. M. *Ahmad B. Hanbal and the Mihna*. Leiden, Netherlands: E. J. Brill, 1897.

Qadir, C. A. *Philosophy and Science in the Islamic World*. London: Croom Helm, 1988.

Qaradawi, Yusuf al-. *The Lawful and the Prohibited in Islam*. Indianapolis, IN: American Trust Publication, 1980.

Rahman, Fazlur. *The Philosophy of Mulla Sadra*. Albany: State University of New York Press, 1975.

———. *Prophecy in Islam: Philosophy and Orthodoxy*. London: Allen & Unwin, 1958.

———. "Revival and Reform in Islam." In *The Cambridge History of Islam*, edited by P. M. Holt et al., Vol. 2, 632–656. Cambridge: Cambridge University Press, 1978.

Raisanen, Heibbi. *The Idea of Divine Hardening: A Comparative Study of the Notion of Divine Hardening, Leading Astray and Inciting to Evil in the Bible and the Qur'an*. Helsinki: Finnish Exegetical Society, 1972.

Razi, al-. *A Study of Fakhr al-Din al-Razi and His Controversies in Transoxiana*. Translated by Fahallah Khaleif. Beirut: Dar el-Machreq, 1966.

Ringgren, Helmer. *Studies in Arabia Fatalism*. Wiesbaden, Germany: Otto Harrassowitz, 1955.

Rodison, Maxime. *Islam and Capitalism*. Translated by Brian Perace. New York: Pantheon, 1973.

Rosenthal, Franz. *Knowledge Triumphant: The Concept of Knowledge in Medieval Islam*. Leiden, Netherlands: E. J. Brill, 1970.

Sachedina, A. A. *Islamic Messianism: The Idea of the Mahdi in Twelver Shi'ism*. Albany: State University of New York Press, 1981.

Samarqandi, Abu Layth al-. "The Angel of Death in Late Islamic Tradition." *Islamic Studies* 3 (1964): 285–519.

———. "The Creation of Man and Angels in the Eschatological Literature (Translated Excerpts from an Unpublished Collection of Traditions)." Translated by J. Macdonald. *Islamic Studies* 3 (1964): 285–308.

———. "The Day of Resurrection." *Islamic Studies* 5 (1966): 129–197.

———. "Paradise." *Islamic Studies* 5 (1966): 331–383.

———. "The Preliminaries to the Resurrection and Judgment." *Islamic Studies* 4 (1965): 137–179.

———. "The Twilight of the Dead." *Islamic Studies* 4 (1965): 55–102.

Schacht, J. "New Sources for the History of Mohammadan Theology." *Studia Islamica* 1 (1953): 23–42.

Schimmel, Annemarie. *Gabriel's Wing: A Study in the Religious Ideas of Sir Muhammad Iqbal.* Leiden, Netherlands: E. J. Brill, 1963.

———. "Islam." In *Historia Religionum: Handbook for the History of Religion,* edited by C. J. Bleeker and George Widengren, Vol. 2, 125–210. Leiden, Netherlands: E. J. Brill, 1971.

Schuon, Frithjof. *Dimensions of Islam.* London: Allen & Unwin, 1970.

Schwarz, Michael. "The Letter of al-Hasan al-Basri." *Oriens* 20 (1967): 15–30.

Seale, Morris S. *Muslim Theology: A Study of Origins with Reference to the Church Fathers.* London: Luzac, 1964.

Shari'ati, 'Ali. *On the Sociology of Islam.* Berkeley, CA: Mizan Press, 1979.

Sharif, M. M. *A History of Muslim Philosophy: With Short Accounts of Other Disciplines and the Modern Renaissance in Muslim Lands.* 2 vols. Wiesbaden, Germany: Harrassowitz, 1963–1966.

Sherif, Mohamed Ahmed. *Ghazali's Theory of Virtue.* Albany: State University of New York Press, 1975.

Smart, Ninian. "The Muslim Experience." In *The Religious Experience of Mankind,* 372–423. New York: Scribner, 1969.

Smith, Jane I., and Yvonne Yazbeck Haddad. *The Islamic Understanding of Death and Resurrection.* Albany: State University of New York Press, 1981.

Smith, W. Robertson. *Lectures on the Religion of the Semites: The Fundamental Institutions.* New York: Schroder, 1972.

Suhrawardi, al-. *A Sufi Rule for Novices: Kitab Adab al-Muridin of Abu al-Najib al-Suhrawardi.* Translated by M. Milson. Cambridge, MA: Harvard University Press, 1975.

Swartz, Merlin. "Acquisition (Kasb) in Early Kalam." In *Islamic Philosophy and the Classical Tradition: Essays Presented to R. Walzer on His Seventieth Birthday,* 355–389. Columbia: University of South Carolina Press, 1972.

Tabawi, A. L. "Philosophy of Muslim Education." *Islamic Quarterly* 4 (1957): 78–89.

Taleqani, Mahmud et al. *Jihad and Shahadat: Struggle and Martyrdom in Islam.* Houston: n.p., 1986.

Tritton, A. S. *Islam: Belief and Practices.* 2nd ed. London: Hutchinson's University Library, 1954.

———. *Muslim Theology.* London: Royal Asiatic Society, 1947.

———. "The Speech of God." *Studia Islamica* 36 (1972): 5–23.

Troll, Christian W. *Sayyid Ahmad Khan: A Reinterpretation of Muslim Theology.* Delhi, India: Vikas Publishing House, 1978.

Urvoy, Dominique. *Ibn Rushd.* London: Routledge, 1991.

Vesey-Fitzgerald, S. G. "Nature and Sources of the Shari'a." In *Law in the Middle East*, 85–112. Washington, DC: Middle East Institute, 1955.

Voll, John Obert. *Islam, Continuity, and Change in the Modern World.* Boulder, CO: Westview Press, 1982. 2nd ed. Syracuse, NY: Syracuse University Press, 1994.

Watt, W. Montgomery. "The Conception of Iman in Islamic Theology." *Islam* 43 (1967):1–10.

———. *The Formative Period of Islamic Thought.* Edinburgh: Edinburgh University Press, 1973.

———. *Free Will and Predestination in Early Islam.* London: Luzac, 1948.

———. *Islamic Philosophy and Theology.* Edinburgh: Edinburgh University Press, 1962.

———. *Islamic Revelation in the Modern World.* Edinburgh: Edinburgh University Press, 1969.

———. *Muslim Intellectual: A Study of Al-Ghazali.* Edinburgh: Edinburgh University Press, 1963.

———. "The Origin of the Islamic Doctrine of Acquisition." *Journal of the Royal Asiatic Society* (1943): 234–247.

———. "Some Muslim Discussions of Anthropomorphism." *Transactions of the Glasgow University of Oriental Society* 13 (1947–1949): 1–10.

———. *What Is Islam?* New York: Praeger, 1968.

Wensinck, A. J. *The Muslim Creed: Its Genesis and Historical Development.* Cambridge: Cambridge University Press, 1932; London: Cass, 1962.

Williams, John A. "The Expected Deliverer." In *Themes of Islamic Civilization.* Berkeley: University of California Press, 1971.

———. *Islam.* New York: George Braziller, 1961.

Wolfson, H. A. *The Philosophy of the Kalam.* Cambridge, MA: Harvard University Press, 1976.

Zwemer, Samual M. "The Palladium of Islam." *Moslem World* 23 (1933): 109–116.

———. *Studies in Popular Islam.* London: Sheldon Press, 1939.

Law

Ahmad, Aziz. *Islamic Law in Theory and Practice.* Lahore, Pakistan: All-Pakistan Legal Decision, 1956.

———. "An Eighteenth-Century Theory of Caliphate." *Studia Islamica* 28 (1968): 127–33.

Ahmad, Khwaja Harris. "The Concept and Principals of Quranic Justice." *The Law Journal* (Pakistan) 40, no. 1 (1978).

Ajijola, A. D. *Introduction to Islamic Law.* Karachi, Pakistan: International Islamic Publishers, 2002.

Akbarabadi, S. A. "Islamic Law in Modern Times." *Islamic and Comparative Law Quarterly* 1 (1981): 191–203.

Alami, Dawoud S. *The Marriage Contract in Islamic Law.* London: Graham and Trotman, 1992.

Ali, S. A. *Mahommedan Law.* 5th ed. 2 vols. New Delhi, India: Himalayan Books, 1985. Originally published in 1929.

Amin, S. H. *Islamic Law in the Contemporary World: Introduction, Glossary and Bibliography.* Glasgow, Scotland: Royston House, 1985.

———. *Middle East Legal Systems.* Glasgow, Scotland: Royston House, 1985.

Anderson, J. N. D. *Islamic Law in the Modern World.* New York: New York University Press, n.d.

———. "Islamic Law Today: The Background to Islamic Fundamentalism." *Arab Law Quarterly* 2 (1987): 339–351.

———. "Law as a Social Force in Islamic Culture and History." *Bulletin of the School of Oriental and African Studies* 20 (1957): 13–40.

———. "The Law of Islam." In *The World's Religions,* edited by R. P. Beaver. Tring, Sutherland, Australia: Lion, Albatross, 1982.

———. *Law Reform in the Muslim World.* London: Athlone Press, 1976.

Annes, M. A. "Study of Muslim Women and Family: A Bibliography." *Journal of Comparative Family Studies* 20 (1989): 263–274.

Azmeh, A. A. , ed. *Islamic Law: Social and Historical Contexts.* New York: Routledge, 1988.

Bassiouni, M. Cherif, ed. *The Islamic Criminal Justice System.* New York: Oceana Publications, 1988.

Bassiouni, M. C. et al."Islamic Law." *American Society of International Law, Proceedings* 76 (1982): 55–77.

Bhatia, H. S. *Studies in Islamic Law, Religion and Society.* New Delhi, India: Deep and Deep Publications, 1989.

Brohi, A. K. "Islam: Its Political and Legal Principle." In *Islam and Contemporary Society,* edited by M. Qutb, S. Nasr, et al. New York: Longman, 1982.

Brunschvig, R. "Logic and Law in Classical Islam." In *Logic in Classical Islamic Culture,* 113–30. Wiesbaden, Germany: Harrassowitz, 1970.

Calder, N. *Studies in Early Muslim Jurisprudence.* Oxford: Oxford University Press, 1993.

Coulson, Noel J. *Conflicts and Tensions in Islamic Jurisprudence.* Chicago: University of Chicago Press, 1969.

———. "Doctrine and Practice in Islamic Law: One Aspect of the Problem." *Bulletin of the School of Oriental and African Studies* 18 (1956): 211–226.

———. *A History of Islamic Law.* Edinburgh: Edinburgh University Press, 1964.

———. "Muslim Custom and Case-Law." *Die Welt des Islam* 6 (1959): 13–24.

———. "The State and the Individual in Islamic Law." *International and Comparative Law Quarterly* 6 (1957): 49–60.

Crone, Patricia. *From Kavad to al-Ghazali: Religion, Law, and Political Thought in the Near East, c. 600–c. 1100.* Burlington, VT: Ashgate, 2005.

Doi, A. R. I. "The Muwatta' of Imam Malik on the Genesis of the Shari's Law: A Western Scholar's Confusion." *Hamdard Islamicus* 4, no. 3 (Autumn 1981): 27–41.

———. "Shari'ah: A Misunderstood and Maligned System of Law." *Journal of Arabic and Religious Studies* 2 (1985): 33–45.

Dwyer, D. H. , ed. *Law and Islam in the Middle East.* New York: Bergin and Garvey, 1990.

———. "Law and Islam in the Middle East: An Introduction." In *Law and Islam in the Middle East,* edited by D. H. Dwyer. New York: Bergin and Garvey, 1990.

Esposito, John. "Law in Islam." In *The Islamic Impact,* edited by Y. Y. Haddad, B. Haines, and E. Findly, 69–88. Syracuse, NY: Syracuse University Press, 1984.

———. "Muslim Family Law Reform: Towards an Islamic Methodology." *Islamic Studies* 15 (1976):19–51.

———. *Women in Muslim Family Law.* Syracuse, NY: Syracuse University Press, 1982.

Faruki, I. "Humanism and the Law: The Case of the Shari'ah." *Journal of Islamic and Comparative Law (Shari'ah)* 10 (1981): 1–15.

———. *Islamic Jurisprudence.* New Delhi, India: Vanity Books, 1988.

Faruqi, I. R. "Humanism and the Law: The Case of the Shari'ah." *Journal of Islamic and Comparative Law (Sharia)* 10 (1981): 1–15.

Forte, D. F. "Islamic Law and the Crime of Theft: An Introduction." *Cleveland State Law Review* 34 (1985–1986): 47–67.

Fyzee, A. A. A. "Isma'ili Law and Its Founder." *Islamic Culture* 9 (1935): 107–112.

———. "Shi'i Legal Theories." In *Law in the Middle East*, edited by Majid Khadduri and H. J. Libesney. Washington, DC: Middle East Institute, 1995.

Ghazali, Al-, M. "Introduction to a Draft Islamic Constitution." *Islamic Studies* 2 (1981): 153–168.

Gibb, H. A. R. "Some Considerations on the Sunni Theory of the Caliphate." In *Studies on the Civilization of Islam*, 141–150. Boston: Beacon Press, 1962.

Gibb, H. A. R., and H. Bowen. "The Ulama." In *Islamic Society and the West*, Vol. 1, pt. 1, 81–114. London: Oxford University Press, 1951.

Goldziher, I. "The Principles of Law in Islam." In *The Historians' History of the World*, edited by H. S. Williams. New York: Hooper and Jackson, 1908.

Grunebaum, Gustav E. von. "The Body Politic: Law and the State." In *Medieval Islam*, 142–169. Chicago: Chicago University Press, 1956.

———. *Theology and Law in Islam.* Wiesbaden, Germany: Harrassowitz, 1971.

Hallaq, Wael. *The Formation of Islamic Law.* Burlington, VT: Ashgate, 2004.

———. *The Origins and Evolution of Islamic Law.* Cambridge: Cambridge University Press, 2005.

Hamidullah, M. "Sources of Islamic Law: A New Approach." *Islamic Quarterly* 1 (1954): 205–211.

Heer, N., ed. *Islamic Law and Jurisprudence: Studies in Honor of Farhat J. Ziadeh.* Seattle: University of Washington Press, 1990.

Heyd, Uriel. *Studies in Old Ottoman Criminal Law*. London: Clarendon Press, 1973.

Ibn Abi Zayd. *First Steps in Muslim Jurisprudence*. Translated by A. D. Russell and A. M. Suhrawardy. London: Luzac, 1906.

Ishaq, K. "Islam and Law in the Twenty-First Century." *Islamic and Comparative Law Quarterly* 5 (1985): 173–225.

Kamali, Muhammad Hashim. *Shari'ah Law: An Introduction*. Oxford: One World Publication, 2008.

———. "Source, Nature, and Objectives of Shari'a." *Islamic Quarterly* 33 (1989): 215–236.

Khadduri, Majid. "From Religious to National Law." In *Modernization of the Arab World*, 37–51. Princeton, NJ: Van Nostrand, 1966.

———. *The Islamic Conception of Justice*. Baltimore, MD: Johns Hopkins University Press, 1984.

———. *Islamic Jurisprudence: Shafi'i's Risala*. Baltimore, MD: Johns Hopkins University Press, 1961.

———. *War and Peace in the Law of Islam*. Baltimore, MD: Johns Hopkins University Press, 1955.

Khan, K. M. "Juristic Classification of Islamic Law." *Houston Journal of International Law* 6 (1983): 23–35.

Kielstra, N. "Law and Reality in Modern Islam." In *Islamic Dilemmas: Reformers, Nationalists and Industrialization: The Southern Shore of the Mediterranean*, edited by M. Geller. Berlin: Mouton, 1985.

Kohlberg. E. *Belief and Law in Imami Shi'ism*. Aldershot, England: Variorum, 1991.

Levy, Reuben. "Islamic Jurisprudence." In *The Social Structure of Islam*, 150–191. Cambridge: Cambridge University Press, 1957.

———. "Usage, Custom and Secular Law under Islam." In *The Social Structure of Islam*, 242–270. Cambridge: Cambridge University Press, 1957.

Liebesny, H. J. "Judicial Systems in the Near and Middle East: Evolutionary Development and Islamic Revival [Egypt, Saudi Arabia, Afghanistan, and Pakistan]." *Middle East Journal* 37 (Spring 1983): 202–217.

———. "Religious Law and Westernization in the Moslem Near East." *American Journal of Comparative Law* 2 (1953): 492–504.

———. "Stability and Change in Islamic Law." *Middle East Journal* 21 (1967):16–31.

Lippman, Matthew, Sean McConville, and Mordechai Yerushalmi. *Islamic Criminal Law and Procedure*. New York: Praeger, 1988.

Lombardi, Clark Benner. *State Law as Islamic Law in Modern Egypt: The Incorporation of the Shari'a into Egyptian Constitutional Law*. Studies in Islamic Law and Society. Leiden, Netherlands: E. J. Brill, 2006.

Macdonald, D. B. "Development of Jurisprudence." In *The Development of Muslim Theology, Jurisprudence, and Constitutional Theory*, 65–118. New York: Scribner, 1903.

———. *The Development of Muslim Theology, Jurisprudence, and Constitutional Theory*. Khayat's Oriental Reprint Series, no. 10. New York: Scribner, 1903.

Mahmood, Tahir. *Personal Law in Islamic Countries*. New Delhi: N. M. Tripathi, 1987.

Makdisi, J. "Islamic Law Bibliography." *Law Liberty Journal* 78 (1986): 103–189.

———. "Legal Logic and Equity in Islamic Law." *American Journal of Comparative Law* 33 (1985): 63–92

Mallat, Chibli. *The Renewal of Islamic Law: Muhammad Baqer As-Sadr, Najaf, and the Shi'i International*. Cambridge: Cambridge University Press, 1993.

Massignon, L. "The Juridical Consequences of the Doctrines of Al-Hallah." In *Studies on Islam*, edited by M. Swartz. New York: Oxford University Press, 1981.

Mawdudi, Sayyid Abu'l-A'la. *The Islamic Law and Constitution*. 2nd ed. Translated and edited by Khurshid Ahmad. Lahore, Pakistan: Islamic Publications, 1960.

———. *Purdah and the Status of Woman in Islam*. Lahore, Pakistan: Islamic Publications, 1978.

Mayer, A. E. "Islamic Law." In *Islam: The Religious and Political Life*, edited by M. Kelly. New York: Praeger, 1984.

———. "Law and Religion in the Muslim Middle East." *American Journal of Comparative Law* 35 (1987): 127–184.

———. "The Shari'a: A Methodology or a Body of Substantive Rules?" In *Islamic Law and Jurisprudence: Studies in Honor of Farhat J. Ziadeh*, edited by N. Heer. Seattle: University of Washington Press, 1990.

Misri, Ahmad ibn al-Naqib al-. *The Reliance of the Traveller: A Classical Manual of Islamic Sacred Law*. Translated by Noah H. M. Keller. Dubayy, UAE: Matbah al-Asiriya, 1991.

Muhammad Baqir as-Sadr. *Lessons in Islamic Jurisprudence.* Translated by Royn Mottahedeh. Oxford: Oneworld Publications, 2003.

Nasir, Jamal J. *The Islamic Law of Personal Status.* London: Graham and Trotman, 1986.

Othman, M. Z. B. "Origin of the Institution of Waqf." *Hamdard Islamicus* 6, no. 2 (Summer 1983): 3–23.

Peters, Rudolph. *Islam and Colonialism: The Doctrine of Jihad in Modern History.* The Hague: Mouton, 1979.

———, trans. *Jihad in Mediaeval and Modern Islam.* Leiden, Netherlands: E. J. Brill, 1977.

Powers, D. S. "The Islamic Inheritance System: A Socio-Historical Approach." In *Islamic Family Law*, edited by C. Mallat and J. Connors. London: Graham and Trotman, 1990.

Qureshi, T. A. "Justice in Islam." *Islamic Studies* 21, no. 2 (1982): 35–51.

Rahman, Fazlur. "The Controversy over the Muslim Family Laws." In *South Asian Religion and Politics*, edited by Donald E. Smith. Princeton, NJ: Princeton University Press, 1966.

———. "Law and Ethics in Islam." In *Ethics in Islam*, edited by R. H. Hovannisian. Malibu, CA: Undena Publications, 1985.

Rahman, M. H. "The Role of Pre-Islamic Customs in the Islamic Law of Succession." *Islamic and Comparative Law Quarterly* 8 (1988): 48–64.

Rahman, T. "Application of Shari'ah in the Muslim World." *Al-Ilm (Durban)* 3 (1983): 48–58.

Ramadan, Hisham M. *Understanding Islamic Law: From Classical to Contemporary.* Lanham, MD: Rowman & Littlefield, 2006.

Reinhart, A. K. "Islamic Law as Islamic Ethics." *Journal of Religious Ethics* 11 (1983): 186–203.

Safwat, Safiyah. "Islamic Laws in the Sudan." In *Islamic Law*, edited by Aziz al-Azmeh, 231–250. London: Routledge, 1988.

Schacht, Joseph. "Foreign Elements in Ancient Islamic Law." *Journal of Comparative Legislation* 32 (1950): 9–16.

———. *An Introduction to Islamic Law.* Oxford: Clarendon, 1964, 1979.

———. "Islamic Law in Contemporary States." *American Journal of Comparative Law* 8 (1959): 133–147.

———. "The Law." In *Unity and Variety in Muslim Civilization*, 65–86. Chicago: Chicago University Press, 1955.

———. "Law and Justice." In *The Cambridge History of Islam*, Vol. 2, 539–568. Cambridge: Cambridge University Press, 1970.

——. *The Origins of Muhammadan Jurisprudence.* Oxford: Clarendon, 1950.

——. "Pre-Islamic Background and Early Development of Jurisprudence." In *Law in the Middle East*, 28–56. Washington, DC: Middle East Institute, 1955.

——. "Problems of Modern Islamic Legislation." In *The Modern Middle East*, edited by R. H. Nolte, 172–200. New York: Atherton, 1963.

——. "The Schools of Law and Later Developments of Jurisprudence." In *Law in the Middle East*, 57–84. Washington, DC: Middle East Institute, 1955.

Shafi'i al-. *Islamic Jurisprudence: Shafi'i's Risala.* Translated by M. Khadduri. Baltimore, MD: Johns Hopkins University Press, 1961.

Siddiqi, Mohammad Suleman. "The Concept of Hudud and Its Significance." In *Islam and Contemporary Muslim World*, edited by Anwar Moazzam. New Delhi: Light and Life Publishers, 1981.

Siddiqi, M. Zubayr. "The Importance of Hadith as a Source of Islamic Law." *Studies in Islam* 1 (1964): 19–25.

Stewart, F. H. "Tribal Law in the Arab World: A Review of the Literature." *International Journal of Middle East Studies* 19 (1987): 473–490.

Tabatabai, H. M. *An Introduction to Shi'i Law: A Bibliographical Study.* St. Antony's Middle East Monographs, London: Ithaca Press, 1984.

——. "Rationalism and Traditionalism in Shi'i Jurisprudence." *Alserat* 10, no. 2 (1984): 30–42.

Tyan, Emile. "Judicial Organization." In *Law in the Middle East*, edited by Majid Khadduri and Herbert J. Liebesny, 236–278. Washington, DC: Middle East Institute, 1955.

Williams, John A. "The Law: Fiqh, Shari'a." In *Islam*, 78–121. New York: George Braziller, 1961.

Ziadeh, F. "Urf and Law in Islam." In *The World of Islam: Studies in Honour of P.K. Hitti*, edited by J. Kritzeck and R. B. Winder, 60–67. London: Macmillan, 1959.

Zubaida, Sami. *Law and Power in the Islamic World.* New York: I. B. Tauris, 2005.

Practices

Abdullah 'Ankawi. "The Pilgrimage to Mecca in Mamluk Times." *Arabian Studies* 1 (1974): 146–170.

Abu Zahra, Nadia. "The Comparative Study of Muslim Societies and Islamic Rituals." *Arab Historical Review for Ottoman Studies* 3–4 (December 1991): 7–38.

Bell, Richard. "The Origin of the 'id al-Adha." *Muslim World* 23 (1933): 117–120.

Burton, Richard F. *A Personal Narrative of a Pilgrimage to al-Madina and Meccah* (1855). 3rd ed. Reprint. New York: Dover, 1964.

Calverley, Edwin. *Worship in Islam: Al-Ghazzali's Book of the Ihya.* Piscataway, NJ: Georgias Press, 2004.

Cragg, Kenneth. "Pilgrimage Prayers." *Muslim World* 45 (1955): 269–280.

———. "Ramadan Prayers." *Muslim World* 47 (1957): 210–223.

Dennett, Daniel C., Jr. *Conversion and the Poll Tax in Early Islam.* Cambridge, MA: Harvard University Press, 1950.

Fischer, H. J. "Prayer and Military Activity in the History of Muslim Africa South of the Sahara." *Journal of African History* 12 (1971): 391–406.

Ghafuri, 'Ali. *The Ritual Prayer of Islam.* Translated by Laleh Bakhtiar and Mohammed Nematzadeh. Houston: Free Islamic Literature, 1982.

Goitein, S. D. " The Origin and Nature of Friday Worship." *Moslem World* 44 (1959): 183–195.

———. "Prayer in Islam." In *Studies in Islamic History and Institutions.* Leiden, Netherlands: E. J. Brill, 1966.

Haddad, Yvonne Yazbeck. "The Qur'anic Justification for an Islamic Revolution: The View of Sayyid Qutb." *Middle East Journal* 37, no. 1 (Winter 1983): 14–29.

Hawting, Gerald. *The Development of Islamic Ritual.* Burlington, VT: Ashgate, 2006.

Ibn Taymiyah. *Al-hisbah fi al-Islam.* Translated by Muhtar Holland as *Public Duties in Islam: The Institution of the Hisbah.* Leicester, England: Islamic Foundation, 1982.

Kamal, Ahmad. *The Sacred Journey.* New York: Duell, Sloan and Pierce, 1961.

Keddie, Nikki R. "The Roots of the Ulama's Power in Modern Iran." In *Scholars, Saints, and Sufis,* 211–229. Berkeley: University of California Press, 1972.

Othman, M. Z. B. "Origin of the Institution of Waqf." *Hamdard Islamicus* 6, no. 2 (Summer 1983): 3–23.

Padwick, Constance E. *Muslin Devotions: A Study of Prayer Manuals in Common Use.* London: Society for Promoting Christian Knowledge, 1961.

Rumi. *The Mathnawi-i Ma'nawi.* 8 vols. Edited and translated by R. A. Nicholson. Gibb Memorial Series, new series, no. 4. London: Luzac, 1925–1940.

Shari'ati, 'Ali. *Ali Shariati's Hajj: Reflections on Its Rituals.* Translated by Laleh Bakhtiar. Bedford, England: Free Islamic Literature, 1988.

Smith, Wilfred Cantwell. *The Faith of Other Men.* New York: New American, 1965.

Troll, Christian W., ed. *Muslim Shrines in India.* New York: Oxford University Press, 1989.

Twelver Shi'ism

Ahmad, Fazl. *Husain: The Great Martyr.* Lahore, Pakistan: n.p., 1969.

Ajami, Fouad. *The Vanished Imam: Musa al-Sadr and the Shia of Lebanon.* Ithaca, NY: Cornell University Press, 1986.

Alsarat. *The Imam Husayn.* Vol. 12. Edited by the Muhammadi Trust of Great Britain and Northern Ireland. London: n.p., 1986.

Amin, Hassan al-. *The Islamic Shi'ite Encyclopaedia.* Beirut: n.p., 1968.

Arjomand, Said Air. *The Shadow of God and the Hidden Imam: Religion, Political Order, and Societal Change in Shi-ite Iran from the Beginning to 1890.* Chicago: University of Chicago Press, 1984.

Ayoub, Mahmoud M. *Redemptive Suffering in Islam: A Study of the Devotional Aspects of 'Ashura in Twelver Shi'ism.* The Hague: Mouton Publishers, 1978.

Busse, M. "The Revival of Persian Kingship under the Buyids." In *Islamic Civilizations 950–1150,* 17–70. Oxford: R. Cassierer, 1973.

Calder, Norman. "Doubt and Prerogative: The Emergence of an Imami Shi'i Theory of Ijtihad." *Studia Islamica* 70 (1989): 57–78.

———. "The Structures of Authority in Imami Shi'i Jurisprudence." Ph.D. dissertation, School of Oriental and African Studies, University of London, 1980.

Canetti, Elias. "The Muharram Festival of the Shi'ites." In *Crowds and Power.* New York: Viking Press, 1978.

Chelkowski, Peter, ed. *Ta'ziyeh: Ritual and Drama in Iran.* New York: New York University Press, 1979.

Cole, Juan R. J. *Sacred Space and Holy War: The Politics, Culture, and History of Shi'ite Islam.* London: I. B. Tauris, 2002.

———. "Shi'i Clerics in Iraq and Iran, 1722–1780: The Akhbari-Usuli Conflict Reconsidered." *Iranian Studies* 18, no. I (Winter 1985): 3–34.

Cole, Juan R. J., and Nikki R. Keddie, eds. *Shi'ism and Social Protest*. New Haven, CT: Yale University Press, 1986.

Corbin, Henry. "Cyclical Time in Mazdaism and Ismailism." In *Man and Time: Papers from the Eranos Yearbooks*. Translated by R. Manheim. Bollingen Series 3, no. 30. New York: Bollingen Foundation, 1957.

———. *Spiritual Body and Celestial Earth: From Mazdean Iran to Shi'ite Iran*. Translated by Nancy Pearson. Princeton, NJ: Princeton University Press, 1977.

Dabashi, Hamid. *Theology of Discontent: The Ideological Foundation of the Islamic Republic of Iran*. New York: State University of New York Press, 1993.

Donaldson, Dwight M. *The Shiite Religion: A History of Islam in Persia and Iraq*. London: Luzac, 1933.

Eliash, J. "The Ithna 'Ashari-Shi'i Juristic Theory of Political and Legal Authority." *Studia Islamica* 29 (1969): 17–30.

———. "On the Genesis and Development of the Twelver Shi'i Three-Tenet Shahadah." *Der Islam* 47 (1971): 265–272.

Ende, Werner. "The Flagellations of Muharram and the Shi'ite Ulama." *Der Islam* 55 (1978): 19–36.

Gardet, L. "Dhikr." In *EI2*, Vol. 2, 223–227. Leiden, Netherlands: E. J. Brill, 1960.

Geoffrey, S. *Origins and Early Development of Shia Islam*. London: Longman, 1979.

Ha'iri, 'Abd al-Hadi. *Shi'ism and Constitutionalism in Iran*. Leiden: E. J. Brill, 1977.

Hasnain, Nadeem, and Abrar Husain. *Shias and Shia Islam in India*. Delhi, India: Harnam Publications, 1988.

Hegland, Mary. "Two Images of Husain: Accommodation and Revolution in an Iranian Village." In *Religion and Politics in Iran: Shi'ism from Quietism to Revolution*, edited by Nikki R. Keddie, 218–235. New Haven, CT: Yale University Press, 1983.

Hilli, Hasan Ibn Yusuf al-. *Al Bab al-Hadi 'Ashar*. Translated by W. M. Miller. Oriental Trust Fund, new series, no. 29. London: Luzac, 1958.

Hoffman, Valerie J. "An Islamic Activist: Zaynab al-Ghazali." In *Women and the Family in the Middle East: New Voices of Change*, edited by Elizabeth W. Fernea, 233–254. Austin: University of Texas Press, 1985.

Hollister, J. N. *The Shi'a of India*. London: Luzac, 1953.

Husain, A. F. Badshah. *The Holy Quran: A Translation with Commentary according to Shia Traditions and Principles* 2 vols. Lucknow: Matricidal Watson, 1936.

———. "How Did the Early Shi'ah Become Sectarian?" *Journal of the American Oriental Society* 75 (1955): 1–13.

Ibn Babawayh. *A Shi'ite Creed.* Translated by A. A. A. Fyzee. Bombay, India: Islamic Research Association, 1942.

Ibn Hazm. "The Heterodoxies of the Shiites in the Presentation of Ibn Hazm." Translated by I. Friedlander. *Journal of the American Oriental Society* 28 (1907): 1–80; 29 (1908): 1–183.

Ibn Sina. "A Treatise on Love." Translated by E. L. Fackenheim. *Medieval Studies* 7 (1945): 208–228.

Ivanow, W. *Ismaili Tradition concerning the Rise of the Fatimids.* London: Oxford University Press, 1992.

———, trans. *Kalami Pir: A Treatise on Ismaili Doctrine.* Bombay, India: Islamic Society, 1955.

Kabir, Mafizullah. *The Buwayhid Dynasty of Baghdad (334/946–447/1055).* Calcutta, India: Iran Society, 1964.

Khan, M. S. "The Early History of Zaydi Shi'ism in Daylaman and Gilan." *Zeitschrift der Deutschen Morgenlandischen Gesellschaft* 125 (1975): 301–315.

Khomeini, Ruhollah Mousavi. *A Clarification of Questions (Resaleh Towzih al-Masael).* Translated by J. Borujerdi. Boulder, CO: Westview Press, 1984.

Kohlberg, Etan. "Akhbariya." In *Encyclopaedia Iranica*, 716–718. London: Routledge and Kegan Paul, 1987.

———. "Aspects of Akhbari Thought in the Seventeenth and Eighteenth Centuries." In *Eighteenth-Century Renewal and Reform in Islam*, edited by Nehemia Levtzion and John Obert, Vol. 1, 133–160. Syracuse, NY: Syracuse University Press, 1987.

———. "The Development of the Imami Shi'i Doctrine of Jihad." *Zeitschrift der Deutschen Morgenlandischen Gesellschaft* 126 (1976): 64–86.

———. "Some Imami-Shi'i Views on Taqiyyah." *Journal of the American Oriental Society* 95 (1975): 395–403.

Kramer, Martin, "Sacrifice and Fratricide in Shiite Lebanon." In *Violence and the Sacred in the Modern World*, edited by Mark Juergens-meyer, 30–47. London: Frank Cass, 1992.

Lane-Poole, Stanley. "The Persian Miracle Plays." In *Studies in a Mosque*, 208–251. London: William H. Allen, 1883.

Mallat, Chibli. *Shi'i Thought from the South of Lebanon*. Oxford: Oxford University Press, 1988.

Massignon, Louis. *The Passion of al-Hallaj*. Vol. 1. *The Life of al-Hallaj*. Princeton, NJ: Princeton University Press, 1982.

Momen, Moojan. *An Introduction to Shi'i Islam: The History and Doctrines of Twelver Shi'ism*. New Haven, CT: Yale University Press, 1985.

Nakash, Yitzhak. *Reaching for Power: The Shi'a in the Modern Arab World*. Princeton, NJ: Princeton Univdrsity Press, 2006.

Naqvi, 'Ali Naqi. *The Martyrdom of Karbala*. Translated by S. Ali Akhtar. Karachi, Pakistan: n.p., 1984.

Naqvi, Sadiq. "The Socio-Cultural Impact of Karbala." In *Red Sand*, edited by Mehdi Nazmi, 211–220. Delhi, India: Abu Talib Academy, 1984.

Nasr, Seyyed Hossein. "Ithna 'Ashari Shi'ism and Iranian Islam." In *Religion in the Middle East*, Vol. 2, 96–118. Cambridge: Cambridge University Press, 1969.

Pelly, Sir Lewis. *The Miracle Play of Hassan and Husain Collected from Oral Tradition*. 2 vols. London: William H. Allen, 1879.

Pinault, David. *The Shiites: Ritual and Popular Piety in a Muslim Community*. New York: St. Martin's Press, 1992.

Piscatori, J. P. "The Shia of Lebanon and Hizbullah: The Party of God." In *Politics of the Future: The Role of Social Movements*, edited by Christine Jennett and Randal G. Stewart, 292–317. Melbourne: Macmillan, 1989.

Rizvi, Saiyid Athar Abbas. *A Socio-Intellectual History of the Isna 'Ashari Shi'is in India*. 2 vols. Canberra: Ma'rifat Publishing, 1986.

Robson, J. "The Muharrem Ceremonies." *Hibbert Journal* 54 (1955–1956): 267–274.

Sachedina, Abdulaziz A. *The Just Ruler (al-Sultan al-'Adil) in Shi'ite Islam: The Comprehensive Authority of the Jurist in Imamite Jurisprudence*. New York: Oxford University Press, 1988.

Shams al-Din, Muhammad Mahdi. *The Ring of Husayn: Its Impact on the Consciousness of Muslim Society*. Translated by I. K. A. Howard. London: Muhammadi Trust of Great Britain and Northern Ireland, 1985.

Shariati, Ali. *Red Shi'ism*. Translated by Habib Shirazi. Houston: Free Islamic Literatures, 1980.

Sheriff, Ahmed H. *The Leader of Martyrs*. Elmhurst, NY: Tahrike Tarsile Qur'an, 1986.

Tabataba'i, Muhammad Husayn. *An Introduction to Shi'i Law: A Bibliographic Study.* London: Ithaca Press, 1984.

———. *Shi'ite Islam.* Albany: State University of New York Press, 1977.

Thaiss, Gustav. "Religious Symbolism and Social Change: The Drama of Husain." In *Scholars, Saints, and Sufis,* 349–366. Berkeley: University of California Press, 1972.

Tritton, A. S. "Popular Shi'ism." *Bulletin of the School of Oriental and African Studies* 13 (1951): 829–839.

Watt, W. Montgomery. "The Muslim Yearning for a Savior: Aspects of Early 'Abbasid Shi'ism." In *The Savior God: Comparative Studies in the Concept of Salvation Presented to E.O. James,* edited by S. G. F. Brandon, 191–204. New York: Barnes and Noble, 1963.

———. "The Reappraisal of Abbasid Shi'ism." In *Arabic and Islamic Studies in Honor of H. A. R. Gibb,* edited by G. Makdisi. Leiden, Netherlands: E. J. Brill, 1965.

———. "Shi'ism under the Umayyads." *Journal of the Royal Asiatic Society* (1960): 158–172.

Other Sects

Abu Izzeddin, Nejla M. *The Druzes: A New Study of Their History, Faith, and Society.* Leiden, Netherlands: E. J. Brill, 1984.

Addison, J. T. "The Ahmadiyyah Movement and Its Western Propaganda." *Harvard Theological Review* 22 (1929):1–32.

Assaad, S. A. *The Reign of al-Hakim bi Amr Allah.* Beirut: Arab Institute for Research and Publishing, 1974

Baghdadi, al-. *Moslem Schisms and Sects.* Translated by R. C. Seeyle. Columbia University Oriental Studies, Vol. 15. New York: Ams, 1966.

Bar-Asher, Meir m., et al. *The Nusayri-Alawi Religion: An Enquiry into its Theology and Liturgy.* New York: E. J. Brill, 2002.

Betts, Robert B. *The Druze.* New Haven, CT: Yale University Press, 1988.

Borthwick, Bruce. "The Ismailis and Islamization in Pakistan." *American Council for the Study of Islamic Societies Newsletter* 1 (August 1990): 4–6.

Brush, Stanley E. "Ahmadiyyat in Pakistan: Rabwa and the Ahmadis." *Muslim World* 45 (1955): 145–171.

Bryer, D. "The Origins of the Druze Religion." *Der Islam* 52 (1975): 47–84, 239–262; 53 (1976): 5–27.

Cole, Juan. "Modernity in the Millennium: The Genesis of the Baha'i Faith in the Nineteenth-Century Middle East." In *Studies in the Babi and Baha'i Religions,* Vol. 9. New York: Columbia University Press, 1998.

Cureton, William, ed. *The Book of Religious and Philosophical Sects.* By Muhammad al-Shahrastani. Piscataway, NJ: Gorgias Press, 2002.

Daftary, Farhad. *The Asassin Legends: Myths of the Islam'ilis.* New York: I. B. Tauris, 1995.

——. *The Isma'ilis: Their History and Doctrines.* Cambridge: Cambridge University Press, 2007.

——. *Medieval Ismaili History and Thought.* Cambridge: Cambridge University Press, 1996.

Dana, Nissim. *The Druze in the Middle East: Their Faith, Leadership, Identity and Status.* Brighton, England: Sussex Academic Press, 2003.

Dodge, Bayard. "Al-Isma'iliyyah and the Origin of the Fatimids." *Muslim World* 49 (1959): 296–305.

——. "Aspects of the Fatimid Philosophy." *Muslim World* 50 (1960): 182–192.

——. "The Fatimid Hierarchy and Exegesis." *Muslim World* 50 (1960): 130–141.

——. "The Fatimid Legal Code." *Muslim World* 50 (1960): 30–38.

Firro, Kais. *A History of the Druzes.* Leiden, Netherlands: E. J. Brill, 1992.

Frank, R. M. *The Metaphysics of Created Being according to Abu l-Hudhayl al-'Allaf.* Leiden: Nederlands Historisch-Archaeologisch Instituut in het Nabije Oosten, 1966.

Friedmann, Yohanan. *Prophecy Continuous: Aspects of Ahmadi Religious Thought and Its Medieval Background.* Berkeley: University of California Press, 1989.

Hazrat Mirza, Bashiruddin Mahmud Ahmad. *Ahmadiyyat or True Islam.* 2nd ed. Washington, DC: American Fazl Mosque, 1951.

Hirschberg, J. W. "The Druzes." In *Religion in the Middle East*, Vol. 2, 330–349. Cambridge: Cambridge University Press. 1969.

Hitti, Philip K. *The Origins of the Druze People and Religion with Extracts from Their Sacred Writings.* New York: Columbia University Press, 1928.

Hodgson, M. G. S. "Al-Darazi and Hamza in the Origin of the Druze Religion." *Journal of the American Oriental Society* 82 (1962): 5–20.

——. "The Isma'ili State." In *The Cambridge History of Iran.* Vol. 5, *The Saljuq and Mongol Periods*, 422–482. Cambridge: Cambridge University Press, 1975.

———. *The Order of the Assassins.* New York: AMS Press, 1980.

Hourani, George F. "Islamic and Non-Islamic Origins of Mu'tazilite Ethical Rationalism." *International Journal of Middle Eastern Studies* 7 (1976): 59–87.

Husain, A. F. Badshah. "The Isma'ili State." In *The Cambridge History of Iran.* Vol. 5, *The Saljuq and Mongol Periods,* 422–482. Cambridge: Cambridge University Press, 1968.

Jurji, Edward J. "The 'Alids of North Syria." *Moslem World* 29 (October 1939): 329–341.

Jwaideh, Wadie. *The Kurdish National Movement: Its Origins and Development.* Syracuse, NY: Syracuse University Press, 2006.

Khan, Muhammad Zafrullah. *Ahmadiyyat: The Renaissance of Islam.* London: Kemp, 1978.

Khuri, Fuad I. *Being a Druze.* London: Druze Heritage Foundation, 2004.

Kohlberg, Eton. "Some Zaydi Views on the Companions of the Prophet." *Bulletin of the School of Oriental and African Studies* 39 (1976): 91–98.

Lewicki, T. "The Ibadites in Arabia and Africa." *Journal of World History* 13 (1971): 51–130.

Lewis, B. *The Assassins: A Radical Sect in Islam.* Oxford: Oxford University Press, 1967.

———. "An Isma'ili Interpretation of the Fall of Adam." *Bulletin of the School of Oriental and African Studies* 9 (1937–1939): 691–704.

———. *The Origins of Isma'ilism.* Cambridge: Heffer, 1990.

Lincoln, C. Eric. *The Black Muslims in America.* Boston: Beacon Press, 1961.

Makarem, Sami Nassib, trans. *Ash-Shafiya (The Healer); An Isma'ili Poem Attributed to Shihab ad-din Abu Firas.* Beirut: American University of Beirut, 1966.

———. *The Doctrine of the Ismailis.* Beirut: Arab Institute for Research and Publishing, 1972.

———. *The Druze Faith.* Delmar, NY: Caravan, 1974.

———. "The Philosophical Significance of the Imam in Isma'ilism." *Studia Islamica* 27 (1967): 41–53.

Moosa, Matti. *Extremist Shiites: The Ghulat Sects.* Syracuse, NY: Syracuse University Press, 1988.

Nasr, Seyyed Hossein, ed. *Isma'ili Contributions to Islamic Culture.* Tehran: Imperial Iranian Academy of Philosophy, 1977.

Natali, Denise. *The Kurds and the State: Evolving National Identity in Iraq, Turkey, and Iran.* Syracuse, NY: Syracuse University Press, 2005.

Pessagno, J. M. "The Murji's Iman and Abu 'Ubayd." *Journal of the American Oriental Society* 95 (1975): 382–394.

Phoenix. "A Brief Outline of the Wahabi Movement." *Journal of the Central Asian Society* 27 (1930): 401–416.

Rentz, George. "The Wahhabis." In *Religion in the Middle East,* Vol. 2, 270–285. Cambridge: Cambridge University Press, 1969.

Rubinacci, Roberto. "The Ibadis." In *Religion in the Middle East,* Vol. 2, 302–318. Cambridge: Cambridge University Press, 1969.

Sahas, D. J. *John of Damascus on Islam: The 'Heresy of the Ishmaelites.* Leiden, Netherlands: E. J. Brill, 1972.

Salisbury, E. E. "Translation of Two Unpublished Arabic Documents Relating to the Doctrines of the Isma'ilis and Other Batinian Sects." *Journal of the American Oriental Society* 2 (1851): 257–324.

Serjeant, R. B. "The Zaydis." In *Religion in the Middle East,* edited by A. J. Arberry, Vol. 2, 285–301. Cambridge: Cambridge University Press, 1969.

Shahrastani, al-. "The Kharijites and the Murhi'ites from Shahrastani's *Kitab al-Milal we'l-Nihal:* The Shi'tes." Translated by A. Kazi and J. C. Flynn. *Abr-Nahrain* 15 (1974–1975): 50–98.

———. "The Mu'tazilites." Translated by A. K. Kazi and J. C. Flynn. *Abr-Nahrain* 8 (1968–1969): 36–68.

Smith, Peter. *The Babi and Baha'i Religions: From Messianic Shi'ism to a World Religion.* Cambridge: Cambridge University Press, 1987.

Stansfield, Gareth. *The Kurds and Iraq.* New York: Routledge, 2008.

Stern, S. M. "The Early Isma'ili Missionaries in North-West Persia and in Khurasan and Transoxania." *Bulletin of the School of Oriental and African Studies* 23 (1960): 56–90.

———. *Studies in Early Isma'ilism.* Jerusalem: Magnus Press, 1983.

Toftbek, E. "A Shorter Druze Catechism." *Muslim World* 44 (1954): 38–42.

Tritton. A. S. "Theology and Philosophy of the Isma'ilis." *Journal of the Royal Asiatic Society* (1958): 178–188.

Trowbridge, Stephen, V. R. "The Alevis, or Deifiers of Ali." *Harvard Theological Review* 2 (1909): 340–352. Republished as "The 'Alevis.'" *Muslim World* 2 (July 1921): 253–266.

Walker, Paul E. "Cosmic Hierarchies in Early Isma'ili Thought: The View of Abu Ya'qub al-Sijistani." *Muslim World* 66 (1976): 14–28.

———. "An Ismaili Answer to the Problems of Worshipping the Unknowable, Neoplatonic God." *American Journal of Arabic Studies* 2 (1974): 7–21.

Watt, W. Montgomery. "Kharijite Thought in the Umayyad Period." *Der Islam* 36 (1961): 215–231.

———. "The Kharijites." In *The Formative Period of Islamic Thought*. Edinburgh: Edinburgh University Press, 1973.

———. "The Political Attitudes of the Mu'tazilah." *Journal of the Royal Asiatic Society* (1963): 38–57.

Modernism

Adams, Charles C. *Islam and Modernism in Egypt: A Study of the Modern Reform Movement Inaugurated by Muhammad 'Abduh*. New York: Russell and Russell, 1968.

Ahmad, Aziz. *Islamic Modernism in India and Pakistan, 1857–1964*. London: Oxford University Press, 1967.

Badawi, M. A. Zaki. *The Reformers of Egypt*. London: Croom Helm, 1978.

Chehabi, H. E. *Iranian Politics and Religious Modernism: The Liberation Movement of Iran under the Shah and Khomeini*. Ithaca, NY: Cornell University Press, 1990.

Faghfoory, Mohammad H. "Modernization and Professionalism of the 'Ulama' in Iran, 1925–1941." *Journal of Iranian Studies* 26, nos. 3–4 (Summer–Fall 1993).

Ikram, S. M. *Modern Muslim India and the Birth of Pakistan*. Lahore, Pakistan: Shaikh Muhd Aswal, 1965

Johnson, Nels. *Islam and the Politics of Meaning in Palestinian Nationalism*. London: Kegan Paul, 1982.

Kazamias, Andreas M. *Education and the Quest for Modernity in Turkey*. London: Allen & Unwin, 1966.

Keddie, Nikki R. *Sayyid Jamal ad-Din al-Afghani: A Political Biography*. Berkeley: University of California Press, 1972.

Kurzman, Charles. *Modernist Islam, 1840–1940: A Source Book*. New York: Oxford University Press, 1998.

Leiden, Carl, ed. *The Conflict of Traditionalism and Modernism in the Middle East*. Austin: University of Texas Press, 1966.

Martin, Vanessa. *Islam and Modernism: The Iranian Revolution of 1906*. London: Tauris, 1989.

Millward, G. W. "Aspects of Modernism in Shi'a Islam." *Studia Islamica* 37 (1973): 111–128.

Moaddel, Masoor. *Islamic Modernism, Nationalism, and Fundamentalism: Episode and Discourse*. Chicago: University of Chicago Press, 2005.

Rahman, Fazlur. "Islamic Modernism: Its Scope, Method, and Alternatives." *International Journal of Middle East Studies* 1 (1970): 317–333.

———. "Muslim Modernism in the Indo-Pakistan Sub-Continent." *Bulletin of the School of Oriental and African Studies* 21 (1958): 82–99.

Vahdat, Farzin. *God and Juggernaut: Iran's Intellectual Encounter with Modernity.* Syracuse, NY: Syracuse University Press, 2002.

IV. ISLAMIC POLITICS, SOCIETY, AND THE ARTS

Political Islam

Abbott, Freeland. "The Jama'at-i-Islami of Pakistan." *Middle East Journal* 11 (1957): 37–51.

Abrahamian, Ervand. *Radical Islam: The Iranian Mojahedin.* London: Tauris, 1989.

Abu Amr, Ziad. *Islamic Fundamentalism in the West Bank and Gaza: Muslim Brotherhood and Islamic Jihad.* Bloomington: Indiana University Press, 1994.

Abu Rabi. *Intellectual Origins of Islamic Resurgence in the Modern Arab World.* Albany: State University of New York Press, 1996.

Adams, Charles J. "The Ideology of Mawlana Maududi." In *Religions and Politics in South Asia,* edited by Donald Smith, 371–397. Princeton, NJ: Princeton University Press, 1966.

Affendi, Abdelwahab. *Turabi's Revolution: Islam and Power in Sudan.* London: Grey Seal, 1991.

Ahmad, Akbar S. *Islam under Siege.* London: Polity Press, 2003.

———. *Postmodernism and Islam: Predicament and Promise.* New York: Routledge, 1992.

Ahmad, Aziz. "Afghani's Indian Contacts." *Journal of the American Oriental Society* 89 (1969): 476–491.

———. "Delhi Sultanate and the University Caliphate." In *Studies in Islamic Culture in the Indian Environment,* 3–11. Oxford: Clarendon Press, 1964.

———. "Maududi and Orthodox Fundamentalists in Pakistan." *Middle East Journal* 21 (1967).

———. "Political and Religious Ideas of Shah Wali-Ullah of Delhi." *Muslim World* 52 (1962): 22–30.

———. "Sayyid Ahmad Khan, Jamal al-Din Al-Afghani, and Muslim India," *Studia Islamica* 13 (1960).

Ahmad, Mumtaz. "Islam and the State: The Case of Pakistan." In *The Religious Challenge to the State*, edited by Metthew Moen and Lowell Gustafson. Philadelphia: Temple University Press, 1992.

———. "Islamic Fundamentalism in South Asia: The Jamatt-i Islami and the Tablighi Jamaat." In *Fundamentalisms Observed*, edited by Martin E. Marty and R. Scott Appleby. Chicago: University of Chicago Press, 1991.

———. "Islamic Revival in Pakistan," In *Islam in the Contemporary World*, edited by Cyriac Pullapilly. Notre Dame, IN: Cross Roads Books, 1980.

Ahsan, Abdullah. *OIC: The Organization of the Islamic Conference*. Islamization of Knowledge Series. Herndon, VA: International Institute of Islamic Thought, 1988.

Ahsan, Manazir. "Mawlana Mawdudi't Defense of Sunnah," *Arabia*, no. 26 (October 1983).

Ajami, Fouad. *The Arab Predicament: Arab Political Thought and Practice since 1967*. Cambridge: Cambridge University Press, 1981.

Akhavi, Shahrough. "Elite Factionalism in the Islamic Republic of Iran." *Middle East Journal* 4, no.12 (Spring 1987): 181–202.

———. "The Politics of War: Islamic Fundamentalisms in Pakistan." In *Islamic Fundamentalisms and the Gulf Crisis*, edited by James Piscatori. Chicago: American Academy of Arts and Sciences, 1991.

———. "Sayyid Qutb: The Poverty of Philosophy and the Vindication of Islamic Tradition." In *Cultural Transitions in the Middle East*, edited by Sharif Mardin, 130–152. Leiden, Netherlands: E. J. Brill, 1994.

———. "Shariati's Social Thought," In *Roots of Revolution: An Interpretive History of Modern Iran*, edited by Nikki R. Keddie, New Haven, CT: Yale University Press, 1981.

Akhtar, Karm B., and Ahmad H. Sakr. *Islamic Fundamentalism*. Cedar Rapids, IA: Ingram Press, 1982.

Algar, Hamid. "The Oppositional Role of the Ulama in Twentieth Century Iran." In *Scholars, Saints, and Sufis*, edited by Nikkie R. Keddie. Berkeley: University of California Press, 1972.

———. *Religion and State in Iran, 1785–1906*. Berkeley: University of California Press, 1969.

———. *The Roots of the Islamic Revolution*. Markham, Ontario: Open Press. 1983.

Ali, Tariq. *The Clash of Fundamentalisms: Crusades, Jihads and Modernity*. London: Verso, 2002.

Altman, I. "Islamic Movements in Egypt." *Jerusalem Quarterly* 10 (1979).

Aly, Abd al-Moneir Said, and Manfred W. Wenner. "Modern Islamic Reform Movements: The Muslim Brotherhood in Contemporary Egypt," *Middle East Journal* 36, no. 3 (Summer 1982).

Amad, Queyamuddin. *The Wahabi Movement in India*. Calcutta, India: K. L. Mukhopadhyay, 1966.

Amin, Osman. "Some Aspects of Religious Reform in the Muslim Middle East." In *The Conflict of Traditionalism and Modernism in the Muslim Middle East*, edited by Carl Leiden. Austin: University of Texas Press, 1966.

Anderson, J. N. D. "Islamic Law Today: The Background to Islamic Fundamentalism." *Arab Law Quarterly* 2 (1987): 339–351.

Anderson, Raymond H. "Ayatollah Ruhollah Khomeini, Relentless Founder of the Islamic Republic." *New York Times*, June 5, 1989.

Aneer, Gudmar. *Imam Ruhullah Khumaini, Shah Muhammad Riza Pahlavi, and the Religious Traditions of Iran*. Uppsala, Sweden: Academia Upsalensis, 1985.

Ansari, Hamied N. "The Islamic Militants in Egyptian Politics." *International Journal of Middle East Studies* 16 (1984): 123–144.

Ansari, Javed. "Themes in Islamic Revivalism." Arabia, no. 24 (August 1983).

Antoun, Richard T. *Understanding Fundamentalism: Christian, Islamic, and Jewish*. Lanham, MD: Rowman & Littlefield, 2001.

Arjomand, Said Amir. *From Nationalism to Revolutionary Islam*. London: Macmillan. 1984.

———. "Ideological Revolution in Shi'ism." In *Authority and Political Culture in Shi'ism*, edited by Said Amir Arjomand, 178–209. New York: State University of New York Press, 1988.

———. *The Turban for the Crown*. New York: Oxford University Press, 1988.

Auda, Gehad. "Islamic Movement and Resource Mobilization: A Political Culture Perspective." In *Political Culture and Democracy in Developing Countries*, edited by Larry Diamond, 379–407. Boulder, CO: Rienner, 1993.

———. "The Normalization of the Islamic Movement in Egypt." In *Accounting for Fundamentalisms*, edited by Martin E. Marty and R. Scott Appleby, 374–412. Chicago: University of Chicago Press, 1994.

Ayubi, Nazih N. *Political Islam: Religion and Politics in the Arab World*. London: Routledge, 1991.

———. "The Politics of Militant Islamic Movements in the Middle East." *Journal of International Affairs* 36, no. 2 (Fall/Winter, 1982/1983).

Azm, Sadik al-. "Islamic Fundamentalism Reconsidered: A Critical Outline of Problems, Ideas and Approaches." *South Asia Bulletin* Part I and II (1993 and 1994), 93–131, 73–98.

Azmeh, Aziz al-. *Islam and Modernity*. London: Verso, 1993.

Bahadur, Kalim. "The Jamaat-i-Islami of Pakistan: Ideology and Political Action." *International Studies* (India) 14 (January 1995).

Bailey, Clinton. "Lebanon's Shi'is after the 1982 War." In *Shi'ism, Resistance, and Revolution*, edited by Martin Kramer. Boulder, CO: Westview Press, 1987.

Baker, Raymond William. *Islam without Fear: Egypt and the New Islamists*. Cambridge, MA: Harward University Press, 2003.

Banna, Hasan al-. *Five Tracts of Hasan al-Banna (1906–1949)*. Translated by Charles Wendell. Berkeley: University of California Press, 1975.

Banuazizi, Ali. "Faltering Legitimacy: The Ruling Clerics and Civil Society in Contemporary Iran." *International Journal of Politics, Culture and Society* 4 (1995): 563–577.

Banuazizi, Ali, and Myron Weiner, eds.. *The State, Religion, and Ethnic Politics: Afghanistan, Iran, and Pakistan*. Syracuse, NY: Syracuse University Press, 1986.

Bari, M. A. "A Nineteenth-Century Muslim Reform Movement in India." In *Arabic and Islamic Studies in Honor of H.A.R. Gibb*, 84–102. Leiden, Netherlands: E. J. Brill, 1965.

———. "The Politics of Sayyid Ahmad Barelwi." *Islamic Culture* 31 (1957): 156–164.

Batatu, Hama. "Iran's Underground Shi'ah Movements: Characteristics, Causes and Prospects." *Middle East Journal* 35, no. 4 (Autumn 1981).

Bayat, Mangol. *Iran's First Revolution: Shi'ism and the Constitutional Revolution of 1905–1909*. New York: Oxford University Press, 1991.

Bayat-Philipp, Mangol. "Shi'ism in Contemporary Iranian Politics: The Case of Ali Shariati." In *Towards a Modern Iran: Studies in Thought, Politics, and Society*, edited by Elie Kedourie and Sylvia G. Haim. London: F. Cass, 1980.

Beeman, William. "Khomeini's Call to the Faithful Strikes Fear in the Arab World." *Philadelphia Inquirer*, May 29, 1992.

Bergen, Peter. *Holy War, Inc: Inside the Secret World of Osama bin Laden*. New York: Free Press, 2001.

Bergesen, Albert. *The Sayyid Qutb Reader: Selected Wrtings on Politics, Religion, and Society*. New York: Routledge, 2008.

Bill, James A. "Resurgent Islam in the Persian Gulf." *Foreign Affairs* 63 (Fall 1984): 108–127.

———. *The Shah, The Ayatollah, and the U.S.* Headline Series, No. 285. New York: Foreign Policy Association, June 1988.

Bill, James A., and Robert Springborg. *Politics in the Middle East.* 3rd ed. Glenview, IL: Scott, Foresman & Company, 1990.

Binder, Leonard. "Al-Ghazali's Theory of Government." *Muslim World* 45 (1955): 229–241.

———. "Pakistan and Modern Islamic Nationalist Theory." *Middle East Journal* 12 (1958).

———. "The Proofs of Islam: Religion and Politics in Iran." In *Arabic and Islamic Studies,* edited by George Makdisi. Leiden, Netherlands: E. J. Brill, 1965.

———. *Religion and Politics in Pakistan.* Berkeley: University of California Press, 1961.

———. "The Religious Aesthetic of Sayyid Qutb." In *Islamic Liberalism,* 170–205. Chicago: University of Chicago Press (1988).

Black, Antony. *The History of Islamic Political Thought: From the Prophet to the Present.* Edinburgh: Edinburgh University Press, 2001.

Blum, Patrick. "Islamic Revival Fuels Maghreb Discontent." *Middle East Economic Digest* 24, no. 9 (February 29, 1980).

Bonney, Richard. *Jihad from the Qur'an to Bin Laden.* London: Palgrave Macmillan, 2004.

Bowden, Mark. *Guests of the Ayatollah: The First Battle in America's War with Militant Islam.* New York: Atlantic Monthly Press, 2006.

Brachman, Jarret. *Global Jihadism: Theory and Practice.* New York: Routledge, 2008.

Brisard, Jean-Charles, and Damien Martinez. *Zarqawi: The New Face of Al-Qaeda.* New York: Other Press, 2005.

Burgat, François. *Face to Face with Political Islam.* London: I. B. Tauris, 2003.

Butterworth, Charles E. *Political Islam.* The Annals of the American Academy of Political and Social Sciences, 524 (November 1992).

———. "State and Authority in Arab Political Thought." In *The Foundations of the Arab State,* edited by Ghassan Salame, 91–111. London: Croom Helm, 1987.

Carre, O. "The Impact of the Muslim Brotherhood's Political Islam since the 1950's." In *Islam, Nationalism, and Radicalism in Egypt and the*

Sudan, edited by G. R. Warburg and U. M. Kupferschmidt, 262–280. New York: Praeger, 1983.

Chayes, Sarah. *The Punishment of Virtue: Inside Afghanistan after the Taliban*. New York: Penguin Group, 2007.

Chehabi, H. E. "The Impossible Republic: Contradictions of Iran's Islamic State." *Contention* 3 (Spring 1996): 135–154.

Choueiri, Youssef M. *Islamic Fundamentalism*. London: Pinter, 1990.

Chowdhury, Anwar. "State and Politics in Islam. *The Muslim*, September 28, 1983.

Cook, David. *Understanding Jihad*. Berkeley: University of California Press, 2005.

Cudsi, Alexander S., and Ai Hillal Dessouki, eds. *Islam and Power*. London: Croom Helm, 1981.

Dabashi, Hamid. *Islamic Liberation Theory: Resisting the Empire*. New York: Routledge, 2008.

Dallal, Ahmad. "The Origins and Objectives of Islamic Revivalist Thought, 1750–1860." *Journal of the American Oriental Society* 113, no. 3 (July–September 1993): 341–359.

Dar, Bashir Ahmad. *Religious Thought of Sayyid Ahmad Khan*. Lahore, Pakistan: Shaikh Muhammad Ashraf, 1957.

Davis, Elizabeth V. W., and Rouben Azizian. *Islam, Oil, and Geopolitics: Central Asia After September 11*. Lanham, MD: Rowman & Littlefield, 2006.

Dekmejian, Richard H. "The Anatomy of Islamic Revival: Legitimacy Crisis, Ethnic Conflict and the Search for Islamic Alternatives." *Middle East Journal* 34, no. 1 (Winter 1980)

Dekmejian, Richard H., and Margaret J. Wyszomirski. "Charismatic Leadership in Islam: The Mahdi of the Sudan." *Comparative Studies in Society and History*. 14 (1972).

Dessouki, Ali E. Hillal, ed. *Islamic Resurgence in the Arab World*. New York: Praeger, 1982.

Devji, Faisal. *Landscapes of the Jihad*. Ithaca, NY: Cornell University Press, 2005.

Dil, Shaheen F. "The Myth of Islamic Resurgence in South Asia." *Current History* no. 456 (April 1980).

Dorronsoro, Gilles. *Revolution Unending: Afghanistan, 1979 to the Present*. New York: Columbia University Press, 2005.

Duran, Khalid. *Islam und Politischer Extremismus*. Hamburg, Germany: Deutsches Orient-Institut, 1985.

Eccel, A. Chris. *Egypt, Islam and Social Change: Al-Azhar in Conflict and Accommodation.* Berlin: Klaus Schwarz Verlag, 1984.

Edwards, David B. "Summoning Muslims: Print, Politics, and Religious Ideology in Afghanistan." *Journal of Asian Studies* 53, no. 3 (August 1993): 609–628.

Eickelman, Dale. "Changing Interpretations of Islamic Movements." In *Islam and the Political Economy of Meaning*, edited by William R. Roff, 13–30. London: Croom Helm, 1987.

El-Affendi, Abdelwahab. "Martyrdom, Godhead and Heresy." *Arabia* 4, no. 43 (March 1985).

———. *Turabi's Revolution: Islam and Power in Sudan.* London: Grey Seal, 1991.

El-Guindi, Fadwa. "Veiling Infitah with Muslim Ethic: Egypt's Contemporary Islamic Movement." *Social Problems* 28, no. 4 (1981): 465–485.

Enayat, Hamid. "The Resurgence of Islam: The Background." *History Today* 30 (1980).

Eqbal, Ahmad. *Terrorism: Theirs and Ours.* New York: Seven Stories Press, 2001.

Esposito, John L. *The Iranian Revolution: Its Global Impact.* Gainesville: University of Florida Press, 1990.

———. *Islam and Politics.* 3rd ed. Syracuse, NY: Syracuse University Press, 1991.

———. *The Islamic Threat: Myth or Reality?* Rev. ed. New York: Oxford University Press, 1995.

———. *Unholy War: Terror in the Name of Islam.* New York: Oxford University Press, 2002.

Esposito, John L., and James P. Piscatori. "Democratization and Islam." *Middle East Journal* 45, no. 3 (Summer 1991): 427–440.

Esposito, John L., and John O. Voll. *Islam and Democracy.* New York: Oxford University Press, 1996.

Faruqi, Ziya-ul-Hasan. *The Deoband School and the Demand for Pakistan.* Bombay, India: Asia Publishing House, 1963.

Ferdows, Amir K. "Khomeini and Fadayan's Society and Politics." *International Journal of Middle East Studies* 15 (May 1983): 241–257.

Fluehr-Lobban, Carolyn. *Islamic Law and Society in Sudan.* London: Frank Cass, 1987.

Franzius, Enno. *History of the Order of Assassins.* New York: Funk and Wagnalls, 1969.

Fuller, Graham E. *The Future of Political Islam*. New York: Palgrave Macmillan, 2003.

———. *Islamic Fundamentalism in the Northern Tier Countries: An Integrative View*. Santa Monica, CA: Rand Corporation, 1991.

Fuller, Graham E., and Iran Lesser. *A Sense of Siege: The Geopolitics of Islam and the West*. Boulder, CO: Westview Press, 1995.

Gellner, E. *Muslim Society*. Cambridge: Cambridge University Press, 1983.

Gerges, Fawaz. *The Far Enemy: Why Jihad Went Global*. Cambridge: Cambridge University Press, 2005.

Germanus, Julius. *Modern Movements in the World of Islam*. Lahore, Pakistan: al-Biruni, reprinted 1978.

Ghazali, Al-, M. "Introduction to a Draft Islamic Constitution." *Islamic Studies* 2 (1981): 153–168.

Gibb, H. A. R. "Al-Mawardi's Theory of the Khilafah." *Islamic Culture* 11 (1937): 291–302. Reprinted in *Studies on the Civilization of Islam*, edited by S. J. Shaw and W. R. Polk, 151–165. Boston: Beacon Press, 1966.

Giustozzi, Anthony. *Koran, Kalshnikov and Laptop: The Neo-Taliban Insurgency in Afghanistan, 2000–2007*. London: Hurst, 2008.

Gorenberg, Gershom. *The End of Days: Fundamentalism and the Struggle for the Temple Mount*. New York: Oxford University Press, 2000.

Gunaratna, Rohan. *Inside Al-Qaeda: Global Network of Terror*. New York: Columbia University Press, 2002.

Gunning, Jeroen. *Hamas in Politics: Democracy, Religion, Violence*. London: Hurst, 2008.

Habeck, Mary. *Knowing the Enemy: Jihadist Ideology and the War on Terror*. New Haven, CT: Yale University Press, 2006

Haddad, Yvonne Y., and John L. Esposito, eds. *Islam, Gender, and Social Change*. New York: Oxford University Press, 1997.

Halliday, Fred. *Two Hours that Shook the World: September 11, 2001: Causes and Consequences*. Basingstoke, UK: Palgrave, 2002.

Hamzeh. Ahmad Nizar. *In the Path of Hizbullah: Modern Intellectual and Political History of the Middle East*. Syracuse, NY: Syracuse University Press, 2004.

Hardy, Peter. *Partners in Freedom and True Muslims: The Political Thought of Some Muslim Scholars in British India, 1912–1947*. Scandinavian Institute of Asian Studies, no. 5. Lund, Sweden: Student Litteratur, 1972.

Harik, Judith Palmer. *Hezbullah: The Changing Face of Terrorism*. London: I. B. Tauris, 2004.

Hasan, Masudul. *Sayyid Abul Aala Maududi and His Thought*. Vol. 1. Lahore, Pakistan: Islamic Publications, 1984.

Hegland, Mary Elaine. "Ritual and Revolution in Iran." In *Culture and Political Change*, edited by Myron J. Aronoff, 75–100. New Brunswick, NJ: Transaction, 1983.

———. "Sayyid Qutb: The 'Poverty of Philosophy' and the Vindication of Islamic Tradition." In *Cultural Transitions in the Middle East*, edited by Serif Mardin, 130–152. Leiden, Netherlands: E. J. Brill, 1994.

Hiro. Dilip. *Iran under the Ayatollahs*. London: Routledge and Kegan Paul, 1985.

———. "Islamist Strengths and Weaknesses in Central Asia." *Middle East International*, no. 443 (February 5, 1993).

Hitti, Philip K. *Makers of Arab History*. New York: St. Martin's Press, 1968.

Hodgson, Marshall G. S. "Muhammad Abduh: The Pre-Eminent Muslim Modernist of Egypt." *Hamdard Islamicus* 9, no. 3 (Autumn 1986).

———. "Muslim Modernists: The Torch-Bearers of Progressive Islam." *The Islamic Quarterly* 31, no. 3 (1987).

———. "The Prototypical Muslim Pragmatist and Unconventional Islamic Revivalist: Muhammad Ali Jinnah (1875–1949). *Journal of the Pakistan Historical Society* 36, no. 4 (October 1988).

———. "The Role of Islam in World History." *International Journal of Middle Eastern Studies* 1, no. 2 (April 1970).

Holt, P. M. *The Mahdist State in the Sudan 1881–1898: A Study of its Origins, Development and Overthrow*. 2nd rev. ed. Oxford: Clarendon Press, 1970.

Hopwood, Derek. "A Pattern of Revival Movements in Islam?" *The Islamic Quarterly* 15, no. 4 (October–December 1971).

Hunter, W. W. *The Indian Musulmans*. Lahore: Premier Book House, 1964. Originally published in 1871.

Husain, Mir Zohair. "Ayatollah Ruhollah al-Musavi al-Khomeini." *The Search: Journal for Arab and Islamic Studies* 7 (Winter 1986).

———. "Hassan al-Banna: Founder of the Ikhwan al-Muslimin." *Islam and the Modern Age* 17, no. 4 (November 1986).

———. "Iqbal on the Islamic Agenda." *Journal of the Institute of Muslim Minority Affairs* 7, no. 2 (July 1986).

———. "Maulana Abd al-Bari Farangi Mahalli: Scholar and Political Activist." *Pakistan Journal of History and Culture* 7, no. 1 (January–June 1986).

———. "Maulana Sayyid Abul A'la Maududi: Founder of the Fundamentalist Jammat-e-Islami." *South Asia: Journal of South Asian Studies* 9, no. 1 (June 1986).

———. "Shah Waliullah Al-Dihlawi: The Indian Subcontinent's Most Revered Scholar." *Journal of Religious Studies* 14, no. 2 (Autumn 1986).

———. "A Typology of Islamic Revivalists." In *The Third World at the Crossroads*, edited by Sheikh R. Ali. New York: Praeger Publishers, 1989.

Ibn Khaldun. *Muqaddimah.* Translated by Franz Rosenthal. New York: Pantheon, 1958.

Ibrahim, Saad Eddin. "Anatomy of Egypt's Militant Islamic Groups." *International Journal of Middle East Studies* 12, no. 4 (December 1980): 423–453.

Ismael, Tareq Y. *Government and Politics of the Contemporary Middle East.* Homewood, IL: Dorsey Press, 1970.

Ismail, Salma. *Rethinking Islamist Politics: Culture, the State and Islamism.* London: I. B. Tauris, 2003.

Jacquard, Roland. *In the Name of Osama bin Laden: Global Terrorism and the Bin Laden Brotherhood.* Durham, NC: Duke University Press, 2002.

Jansen, G. H. *Militant Islam.* New York: Harper & Row, 1979.

Karpat, Kemal, ed. *Political and Social Thought in the Contemporary Middle East.* New York: Praeger, 1968.

Kazemi, Farhad. "The Fada'iyan-e Islam: Fanaticism, Politics, and Terror." In *From Nationalism to Revolutionary Islam*, edited by Said Amir Arjomand, 158–176. Albany: State University of New York Press, 1984.

———. "State and Society in the Ideology of the Devotees of Islam." *State, Culture, and Society* I (Spring 1985): 118–135.

Keddie, Nikki R, ed. "The Role of the Ulama in the Politics of an Islamic State." *International Journal of Middle East Studies* 18 (February 1986): 53–71.

Keddie, Nikki R, ed. "Iran: Change in Islam; Islam and Change." *International Journal of Middle East Studies* 11 (1980).

———. "The Origins of the Religious-Radical Alliance in Iran." *Past and Present* 34 (1966): 70–80.

———. *Religion and Politics in Iran: Shi'ism from Quietism to Revolution.* New Haven, CT: Yale University Press, 1983.

———. "The Revolt of Islam and Its Roots." In *Comparative Political Dynamics,* edited by Dankwart A. Rustow and Kenneth Paul Erickson. New York. HarperCollins, 1991.

———. *Roots of Revolution: An Interpretive History of Modern Iran.* New Haven, CT: Yale University Press, 1981.

Keddie, Nikki, and Beth Baron, eds. *Women in Middle Eastern History.* New Haven, CT: Yale University Press, 1991.

Keddie, Nikki, and Eric Hooglund, eds. *The Iranian Revolution and the Islamic Republic.* Syracuse, NY: Syracuse University Press, 1986.

Kepel, Gilles. *Jihad: The Trail of Political Islam.* Cambridge, MA: Harvard University Press, 2002.

———. *Muslim Extremism in Egypt: The Prophet and Pharaoh.* Berkeley: University of California Press, 1986.

———. *The Prophet and Pharaoh.* London: Al-Saqi Books, 1985.

Kerr, Malcolm. *Islamic Reform: The Political Theories of Muhammad Abduh and Rashid Rida.* Berkeley: University of California Press, 1966.

Khomeini, Ruhollah al-Musavi. *Islam and Revolution: Writings and Declarations of Imam Khomeini.* Translated and edited by Hamid Algar. Berkeley: Mizan Press, 1981.

Khuri, Fuad. *Imams and Emirs: State, Religion, and Sect in Islam.* London: Al-Saqi Press, 1990.

Kohlmann, Evan F. *Al-Qaida's Jihad in Europe: The Afghan-Bosnia Network.* New York: Berg, 2004.

Kramer, Martin, ed. "Hizbullah: The Calculus of Jihad." In *Fundamentalisms and the State: Remaking Polities, Economies, and Militance,* edited by Martin E. Marty and R. Scott Appleby, 539–556. Chicago: University of Chicago Press, 1992.

———. "The Ideals of an Islamic Order." *The Washington Quarterly* 3, no. 1 (Winter 1980).

———. "Islam vs. Democracy." *Commentary* 95, no. 1 (January 1993): 35–42.

———. "The Moral Logic of Hizballah." In *Origins of Terrorism: Psychologies, Ideologies, Theologies, States of Mind.* Edited by Walter Reich. Cambridge: Cambridge University Press, 1990: 131–157.

———. "Muhammad Husayn Fadlallah." *Orient,* no. 2 (1985): 147–149.

———. "Political Islam." *The Washington Papers* 8, no. 73 (1990).

———. "Redeeming Jerusalem: The Pan-Islamic Premise of Hizballah." In *The Iranian Revolution and the Muslim World,* edited by David Menashri, 105–130. Boulder, CO: Westview Press, 1990.

———. *Shi'ism, Resistance and Revolution.* Boulder, CO: Westview Press, 1987.

Kudsi-Zadeh, A. A. "Islamic Reform in Egypt: Some Observations on the Role of Afghani." *Muslim World* 61 (1971): 1–12.

Ladd, Valerie J. Hoffman. "Women's Religious Observances." In *Oxford Encyclopedia of the Modern Islamic World*, edited by John L. Esposito, Vol. 4, 327. New York: Oxford University Press, 1995.

Lambton, Ann K. S. "Islamic Political Thought." In *The Legacy of Islam*, 404–424. Oxford: Clarendon Press, 1974.

———. "A Nineteenth Century View of Jihad." *Studia Islamica* 32 (1970): 181–192.

———. "Secret Societies and the Persian Revolution of 1905–1906." *St. Anthony's Papers*, no. 11 (1956): 43–60.

———. *State and Government in Medieval Islam*. New York: Oxford University Press, 1981.

Landau, Jacob M. *The Politics of Pan-Islam: Ideology and Organization*. Oxford: Oxford University Press, 1990.

Lapidus, Ira M. "The Separation of State and Religion in the Development of Early Islamic Society." *International Journal of Middle East Studies* 6, no. 4 (October 1975): 363–385.

Lawrence, Bruce B. *Defenders of God: The Fundamentalist Revolt against the Modern Age*. San Francisco: Harper & Row, 1989.

———. *Religious Fundamentalism*. Durham, NC: Duke University Press, 1993.

Lee, D. A. "The Origins of Pan-Islamism." *American Historical Review* 47, no. 2 (January 1942): 278–287.

Lelyveld, David. *Aligarh's First Generation: Muslim Solidarity in British India*. Princeton, NJ: Princeton Universty Press, 1978.

LeVine, Mark. *Why They Don't Hate Us: Lifting the Veil on the Axis of Evil*, Oxford: One World Publication, 2005

Lewis, Bernard. "Islamic Revival in Turkey." *International Affairs* 18 (1952): 38–48.

———. "The Roots of Muslim Rage." *The Atlantic* 266, no. 3 (September 1990).

Lia, Brynjar, *Architect of Global Jihad: The Life of Al-Qaeda Strategist Abu Mus'ab al-Suri*. London: Hurst, 2008.

Magnarella, Paul J. "The Republican Brothers: A Reformist Movement in the Sudan." *Muslim World* 72 (January 1982): 14–24.

Makdisi, George. "The Sunni Revival." In *Islamic Civilization: 950–1150*. Oxford: B. Cassierer, 1973.

Malik, Hafeez. "Islamic Political Parties and Mass Politicization." *Islam and the Modern Age* 3, no. 2 (May 1972).

———. "Islamic Theory of International Relations. *Journal of South Asia and Middle Eastern Studies* 2, no. 3 (Spring 1979).

Mallat, Chibli. *Shi'i 'Ulama' (including Fadlallah) Which Informed Hizbullah's Doctrine*. London: Graham and Trotman, 1988.

Marty, Martin E., and R. Scott Appleby, eds. *Accounting for Fundamentalisms: The Dynamic Character of Movements*. Chicago: American Academy of Arts and Sciences, 1994.

———. *Fundamentalisms Observed*. Chicago: University of Chicago Press, 1991.

———. *The Glory and the Power: The Fundamentalist Challenge to the Modern World*. Boston: n.p., 1992.

Maryam Jameelah. *Islam versus the West*. Lahore, Pakistan: Muhammad Yusuf Khan, 1988. Reprint.

———. *A Manifesto of the Islamic Movement*. Lahore, Pakistan: Muhammad Yusuf Khan, 1969.

Mawdudi, Sayyid Abu'l-A'la. *Islam aur Jahiliyat*. Translated into English as *Islam and Ignorance*. Lahore, Pakistan: Islamic Publications, 1976.

———. *Let Us Be Muslims*. Translated and edited by Khurram Murad. Leicester, England: n.p., 1981.

——— *A Short History of the Revivalist Movement in Islam*. 3rd ed. Translated by Al-Ashari. Lahore, Pakistan: Islamic Publications, 1976.

Menashri, David, ed. *The Iranian Revolution and the Muslim World*. Boulder, CO: Westview Press, 1990.

Metcalf, Barbara D. *Islamic Revival in British India: Deoband, 1860–1900*. Princeton, NJ: Princeton University Press, 1982.

Milani, Mohsen. "The Evolution of the Iranian Theocracy." *Iranian Studies* 26, nos. 3–4 (Summer/Fall 1994): 359–374.

———. *The Making of Iran's Islamic Revolution*. Boulder, CO: Westview Press, 1994.

Miller, Judith. "The Challenge of Radical Islam." *Foreign Affairs* 72, no. 2 (Spring 1993): 43–56.

Mohaddessin, Mohammad. *Islamic Fundamentalism: The New Global Threat*. Washington, DC: Seven Locks Press, 1993.

Mottahedeh, Roy P. *The Mantle of the Prophet: Religion and Politics in Iran*. New York: Simon & Schuster, 1985.

Moussalli, Ahmad S. "Hasan al-Banna's Islamist Discourse on Constitutional Rule." *Journal of Islamic Studies* 4, no. ii (1993): 161–174.

———. "Hasan al-Turabi's Discourse on Democracy and Shura." *Middle East Studies* 30 (January 1994): 52–61.

———. *Historical Dictionary of Islamic Fundamentalist Movements in the Arab World, Iran, and Turkey*. Lanham, MD: Scarecrow Press, 1999.

———. *Islamic Fundamentalism: Myths and Realities.* Ithaca, NY: Ithaca Press, 1998.

———. *Moderate and Radical Fundamentalism: The Quest for Modernity, Legitimacy and the Islamic State.* Gainesville: University Press of Florida, 1999.

———. "A New Interpretation of the Theory of Velayat-e Faqih." *Middle Eastern Studies* 28, no. 1 (1992): 101–107.

———. *Radical Islamic Fundamentalism: The Ideological and Political Discourse of Sayyid Qutb.* Beirut: American University of Beirut, 1992.

Munson, Henry, Jr. *Islam and Revolution in the Middle East.* New Haven, CT: Yale University Press, 1988.

———. "Islamic Revivalism in Morocco and Tunisia. *Muslim World* 76, nos. 3–4 (July-October 1986): 203–218.

———. *Religion and Power in Morocco.* New Haven, CT: Yale University Press, 1993.

Muztar, A. D. *Shah Waliullah: A Saint Scholar of Muslim India.* Islamabad, Pakistan: National Commission on Historical and Cultural Research, 1979.

Naby, Eden. "The Changing Role of Islam as a Unifying Force in Afghanistan." In *The State, Religion, and Ethnic Politics: Afghanistan, Iran and Pakistan,* edited by Ali Banuazizi and Nyron Weiner, 124–154. Syracuse, NY: Syracuse University Press, 1986.

Naim, 'Abd Alla Ahmad. *Toward an Islamic Reformation: Civil Liberties, Human Rights, and International Law.* Syracuse, NY: Syracuse University Press,1990.

Nait Belkacem, Mouloud Kassim. "The Concept of Social Justice in Islam." In *The Challenge of Islam,* edited by Altaf Gauhar. London: Islamic Council of Europe, 1978.

Nasr, S. H. "Sadar al-Din Shirazi (Mulla Sadra)." In *A History of Muslim Philosophy,* vol. 2, 932–961. Wiesbaden, Germany: Harrassowitz, 1963–1966.

Nasr, Seyyed Vali Reza. *The Vanguard of the Islamic Revolution: The Jamaat-i Islami of Pakistan.* Berkeley: University of California Press, 1994.

Naumkin, Vitaly. "Islam in the States of the Former USSR." *Annals of the American Academy of Political and Social Science,* no. 524 (November 1992).

Nizam al-Mulk. *The Book of Government.* London: Routledge and Kegan Paul, 1960.

Nizami, Khaliq Ahmad. "Shah Wali-Ullah Dehlavi and Indian Politics in the 18th Century." *Islamic Culture* 25 (January, April, July, and October 1951).

———. *Some Aspects of Religion and Politics in India during the Thirteenth Century.* Aligarh, India: Department of History, Aligarh Muslim University, 1961.

———. "The Ulama." In *Some Aspects of Religion and Politics in India during the Thirteenth Century,* 150–173. Aligarh, India: Department of History, Aligarh Muslim University, 1961.

Noorani, A. G. *Islam and Jihad: Prejudice Versus Reality.* Global Issues Series. London: Zed Books, 2002.

Norton, Augustus Richard. *Amal and the Shi'a: Struggle for the Soul of Lebanon.* Austin: Texas University Press, 1987.

Obermann, J. "Political Theology in Early Islam: Hasan al-Basri's Treatise on Qadar." *Journal of the American Oriental Society* 55 (1935): 138–162.

Ochsenwald, William. "Saudi Arabia and the Islamic Revival." *International Journal of Middle East Studies* 13 (1981): 271–286.

Osman, Fathi. "The Life and Works of Abu al-A'la al-Mawdudi." *Arabia* 4, no. 40 (December 1984).

Pedahzur, Ami. *Suicide Terrorism.* Cambridge: Polity Press, 2005.

Piscatori, James P., ed. "Ideological Politics in Saudi Arabia." In *Islam in the Political Process,* edited by James P. Piscatori. Cambridge: Cambridge University Press, 1983.

———. *Islamic Fundamentalism and the Gulf Crisis.* Chicago: American Academy of Arts and Sciences, 1991.

Qureshi, Ishtiaq Husain. *Ulema in Politics.* Karachi, Pakistan: Ma'aref, 1972.

Qutb, Sayyid. *Milestones.* Cedar Rapids, IA: Unity, 1981.

———. *Social Justice in Islam.* Translated by J. B. Hardie. Washington, DC: American Council of Learned Societies, 1953.

Rahbar, Muhammad Daud. "Shah Wali Ullah and Ijithad." *The Muslim World* 45 no. 4 (October 1955).

Rahman, Fazlur. *Islam and Modernity: The Transformation of an Intellectual Tradition.* Chicago: University of Chicago Press, 1982.

———. "Islam and the New Constitution of Pakistan." *Journal of African and Asian Studies* 8 (1973).

———. "The Principle of Shura and the Role of the Umma in Islam." *American Journal of Islamic Studies* 1, no. 1 (1984): 1–9.

————. "The Thinker of Crisis: Shah Waliy-Ullah." *Pakistan Quarterly* 6, no. 2 (Summer 1956).

Rana, Mohammed. "The Concept of State in Islam." *Law Journal* (Pakistan) 40, no. 1 (1978).

Rizvi, S. A. A. *Shah Wali-Allah and His Times*. Canberra, Australia: Marifat Publishing, 1980.

Rogers, Paul. *A War on Terror: Afghanistan and After*. New York: Pluto Press, 2004.

Rosenthal, E. I. J. *Political Thought in Medieval Islam: An Introductory Outline*. Cambridge: Cambridge University Press, 1962.

Roy, Olivier. *Islam and Resistance in Afghanistan*. Cambridge: Cambridge University Press, 1986.

————. *The Politics of Chaos in the Middle East*. London: Hurst, 2008.

Rubin, Barry. *Political Islam: Critical Concepts in Islamic Studies*. New York: Routledge, 2007.

Rubin, Uri. "The 'Constitution of Medina': Some Notes." *Studia Islamica* 62 (1985): 5–23.

Saad-Ghorayeb, Amal. *Hizbullah: Politics of Religion*. Pluto, 2002.

Sachedina, Abdulaziz. "Ali Shariati: Ideologue of the Iranian Revolution." In *Voices of Resurgent Islam*, edited by John Esposito. Oxford: Oxford University Press, 1983.

Sageman, Marc. *Understanding Terror Networks*. Philadelphia: Pennsylvania Press, 2004.

Said, Edward W. "Islam Rising." *Columbia Journalism Review* (March/April 1980).

————. "Islam through Western Eyes," *The Nation*, April 26, 1980.

Salem, Elie Adib. *Political Theory and Institutions of the Khawarij*. Baltimore, MD: Johns Hopkins University Press, 1956.

Sayeed, Khalid Bin. "The Jama'at-i-Islami Movement in Pakistan." *Pacific Affairs* 30, no. 1 (March 1957).

Sayid, A. L. "The Role of the Ulama in Egypt in the Early Nineteenth Century." In *Political and Social Change in Modern Egypt*, 264–280. London: Oxford University Press, 1992.

Scott, Joan Wallach. *The Politics of the Veil*. Princeton, NJ: Princeton University Press, 2007.

Serjeant, R. B. "The Constitution of Madinah." *Islamic Quarterly* 8 (June 1964): 3–16.

Shadid, Anthony. *Legacy of the prophet: Despots, Democrats, and the New Politics of Islam*. Boulder, CO: Westview Press, 2002.

Shahi, Agha. "Roots of Islamic Reassertion." *The Muslim* (Karachi) (July 1984).

Shapira, Shimon. "The Origins of Hizballah." *Jerusalem Quarterly* 46 (Spring 1988): 115–130.

Shari'ati, A. *Marxism and Other Western Fallacies.* Translated by R. Campbell. Edited by H. Algar. Berkeley, CA: Mizan Press, 1980.

Sheikh, Naveed S. *The New Politics of Islam: Pan Islamic Foreign Policy in a World of States.* London: RoutledgeCurzon, 2003.

Siba'i Mustafa as-. "Islam as a State Religion: A Muslim Brotherhood View in Syria." Translated by R. B. Winder. *Muslim World* 44 (1954): 215–226.

Siddiqi, A. H. "Caliphate and Sultanate." *Journal of the Pakistan Historical Society* 2 (1954): 35–50.

Sivan, Emmanuel. *Radical Islam.* New Haven, CT: Yale University Press, 1985.

———. "Sunni Radicalism in the Middle East and the Iranian Revolution." *International Journal of Middle East Studies* 21 (1989): 1–30.

Soares, Benjamin F. And René Otayck. *Islam and Muslim Politics in Africa.* New York: Palgrave Macmillan, 2007.

Stevens, Richard P. "Sudan's Republican Brothers and Islamic Reform." *Journal of Arab Affairs* 1 (October 1981): 135–146.

Stowasser, Barbara. *The Islamic Impulse.* Washington, DC: Georgetown University Center for Contemporary Arab Studies, 1987.

Tadesse, Medhane. *Al-Ittihad: Political Islam and Black Economy in Somalia.* Addis Ababa, Ethiopia: Meag, 2002.

Theroux, Peter. *The Strange Disappearance of Imam Moussa Sadr.* London: Weidenfeld and Nicolson, 1988.

Tibi, Basam. *The Challenge of Fundamentalism: Political Islam and the New World Disorder.* Berkeley: California University Press, 2002.

———. *Political Islam, World Politics and Europe: Democratic Peace and Euro-Islam versus Global Jihad.* New York: Routledge, 2008.

Tritton, A. S. *The Caliphs and Their Non-Muslim Subjects: A Critical Study of the Covenant of 'Umar.* London: F. Cass, 1970.

Turabi, Hasan al-. "The Islamic State." In *Voices of Resurgent Islam*, edited by John L. Esposito, 241–251. New York: Oxford University Press, 1983.

Usher, Graham. *What Kind of a Nation?* London: Pluto Press, 1999.

Vatikiotis, P. J. *The Fatimid Theory of State.* Lahore, Pakistan: Orientalia, 1957.

———. "Religion and the State." In *Islam, Nationalism and Radicalism in Egypt and the Sudan*, edited by G. R. Warburg and U. M. Kupferschmidt. New York: Praeger, 1983.

Vertigans, Donncha Marron, and Philip Sutton. *Militant Islam: A Sociology of Characteristics, Causes and Consequences*. New York: Routledge, 2008.

Voll, John O. "The Islamic Past and the Present Resurgence." *Current History* 456 (April 1980).

———. "The Sudanese Mahdi: Frontier Fundamentalist." *International Journal of Middle East Studies* 10, no. 2 (May 1979).

Warburg, G. R., and U. M. Kupferschmidt, eds. *Islam, Nationalism and Radicalism in Egypt and the Sudan*. New York. Praeger, 1983.

Watt, W. Montgomery. *Islamic Fundamentalism and Modernity*. London: Routledge, 1988.

———. *Islamic Political Thought*. Edinburgh: Edinburgh University Press, 1968.

Wendell, Charles. *Five Tracts of Hasan al-Banna (1906–1949)*. Berkeley: University of California Press, 1975.

Wiktorowicz, Quintan. *Radical Islam Rising: Muslim Extremism in the West*. Lanham, MD: Rowman & Littlefield, 2005.

Williams, John Alden. "Struggle: Jihad." In *Themes of Islamic Civilization*, 253–303. Berkeley: University of California Press, 1971.

Woollacott, Martin. "Coming to Power. Theocracy Envelopes New Urban Masses." *World Press Review* (February 1980).

Wyatt, W. M. *Islamic Political Thought*. Islamic Surveys, no. 6. Edinburgh: University of Edinburgh Press, 1968.

Zahab, Mariam Abou, and Olivier Roy. *Islamist Networks: The Afghan-Pakistan Connection*. New York: Columbia University Press, 2004.

Zeidan, David. *The Resurgence of Religion: A Comparative Study of Selected Themes in Christian and Islamic Fundamentalist Discourses*. Leiden, Netherlands: E. J. Brill, 2003.

Zinn, Howard. *Terrorism and War*. New York: Seven Stories Press, 2002.

The Caliphate

Ahmad, Manzooruddin. "The Classical Muslim State." *Islamic Studies* (Karachi) 1, no. 3 (September 1962).

Arnold, Sir T. W. *The Caliphate*. Rev. edition New York: Barnes & Noble, 1966.

Bowen, J., and H. A. R. Gibb. "Caliphate and Sultanate." In *Islamic Society and the West* vol. 1, pt. 1, 26–38. Oxford: Oxford University Press, 1963.

Crone, Patricia, and Martin Hinds. *God's Caliph: Religious Authority in the First Centuries of Islam*. Cambridge: Cambridge University Press, 1986.

Farsakh, A. M. "A Comparison of the Sunni Caliphate and the Shi'i Imamate." *Muslim World* 59 (1969): 50–63, 127–141.

Hitti, Philip. *The Origins of the Islamic State*. Translation of Ahmad Al-Baladhuri of Kitab futuh al-buldan. Piscattaway, NJ: Gorgias Press, 2002.

Macdonald, D. B. "The Caliphate." *Muslim World* 7 (1917): 349–357.

Margoliouth, David S. "The Caliphate Historically Considered." *Muslim World* 11 (1921): 332–343.

Muir, Sir William. *The Caliphate, Its Rise, Decline and Fall, from Original Sources*. Beirut: Khayats, 1963. Originally published in 1915.

Omar, Farouk. *The Abbasid Caliphate 132/750–170/786*. Baghdad: National, 1969.

Women

Abadan, Nermin. "Turkey." In *Women in the Modern World*, edited by Raphael Patai. New York: The Free Press, 1967.

Abadan-Unat, Nermin, ed. *Women in Turkish Society*. Leiden, Netherlands: E. J. Brill, 1981.

Abbas, Shemeem Burney. *The Female Voice in Sufi Ritual: Devotional Practices in Pakistan and India*. Austin: University of Texas Press, 2002.

Abbott, Nadia. *Aisha: The Beloved of Mohammad*. London: Saqi Books, 1986.

———. *Two Queens of Baghdad*. London: Saqi Books, 1986.

Abdalati ('Abd al'Ati), Hammudah. *The Family Structure in Islam*. Indianapolis, IN: American Trust Publication, 1977.

Abu-Lughud, Janet, and Lucy Amin. "Egyptian Marriage Advertisements: Microcosm of a Changing Society." *Marriage and Family Living* 23, no. 2 (1961): 127–136.

Abu Nassr, Julinda, ed. *Women, Employment and Development in the Arab World*. New York: Mouton, 1985.

Abu-Zahra. Nadia M. "On the Modesty of Women in Arab Muslim Villages: A Reply." *American Anthropologist* 72, no. 5 (1970): 1079–1088.

Afetinan, A. *The Emancipation of the Turkish Woman*. Paris: UNESCO, 1962.

Afkhami, Mahnaz. *"Introduction."* In *Faith and Freedom: Women's Human Rights in the Muslim World,* edited by Mahnaz Afkhami, 1–15. London: I. B. Tauris, 1995.

Afkhami, Mahnaz, and Helen Vaziri. *Claiming Our Rights: A Manual for Women's Human Rights Education in Muslim Societies.* Bethesda, MD: Sisterhood Is Global Institute, 1996.

Afza, N. "Woman in Islam," *Islamic Literature* 13, no. 10 (1967): 5–24.

Ahmed, Feroz. "Age at Marriage in Pakistan." *Journal of Marriage and the Family* 31, no. 4 (1969): 799–807.

Ahmed, Kazi Nasir-un-Din. *The Muslim Law of Divorce.* Islamabad, Pakistan: Islamic Research Institute, 1972.

Ahmed, Shereen Azia. "Pakistan." In *Women in the Modern World,* edited by Raphael Patai. New York: The Free Press, 1967.

Ali, A. "Social Dynamics and Status of Women in Islam." In *Status of Women in Islam,* edited by A. Ali. Delhi, India: Agenda, 1987.

Ali, Zahida Amjad. "The Status of Women in Pakistan." *Pakistan Quarterly* 6, no. 4 (1956): 46–55.

Al-Mughni, Haya. *Women in Kuwait: The Politics of Gender.* New York: St. Martin's Press, 2001.

Altorki, Soraya. *Women in Saudi Arabia: Ideology and Behavior among the Elite.* New York: Columbia University Pres, 1988.

Altorki, Soraya, and Camilla F. el-Sohl. *Arab Women in the Field: Studying Your Own Society.* Syracuse, NY: Syracuse University Press, 1988.

Amar, Hamed. *Growing Up in an Egyptian Village.* London: Kegan Paul, 1954.

Amin, Cameron Michael. *The Making of the Modern Iranian Woman.* Gainesville: University Press of Florida, 2002.

Annes, M. A. "Study of Muslim Women and Family: A Bibliography." *Journal of Comparative Family Studies,* 20 (1989): 263–274.

Antoun, Richard T. "On the Modesty of Women in Arab Muslim Villages: A Study in the Accommodation of Traditions." *American Anthropologist* 70, no. 4 (1968): 671–697.

Arasteh, Reza. "The Struggle for Equality in Iran." *Middle East Journal* 18, no. 2 (1964): 189–205.

Astin, Helen S., and Carol Leland. *Women of Influence, Women of Vision: A Cross Generational Study of Leaders and Social Change.* San Francisco: Jossey Bass Publishers, 1991.

Atiya, Nayra. *Khul Khaal: Five Egyptian Women Tell Their Stories.* Syracuse, NY: Syracuse University Press, 1982.

Augustin, Ebba, ed. *Palestinian Women: Identity and Experience*. London: Zed Books, 1993.

Badran, Margo, ed. "Competing Agenda: Feminism, Islam and the State in Nineteenth and Twentieth Century Egypt." In *Women, Islam and the State*, edited by Deniz Kandiyoti, 201–236. London: Macmillan, 1991.

———. "Gender Activism: Feminists and Islamists in Egypt." In *Identity Politics and Women: Cultural Reassertions and Feminisms in International Perspective*, edited by Valentine M. Moghadam. Boulder, CO: Westview Press, 1994.

———. *Huda Sharawi's Harem Years: Memoirs of an Egyptian Feminist*. London: Virago Press, 1986.

Badran, Margo, and Miriam Cooke, eds. *Opening the Gates: A Century of Arab Feminist Writing*. Bloomington: Indiana University Press, 1990.

Bakhtiar, Laleh. *Sufi Women of America: Angels in the Making*. Chicago: Institute of Traditional Psychoethics and Guidance, 1996.

Basu, Amrita, ed. *The Challenge of Local Feminisms: Women's Movements in Global Perspective*. Boulder, CO: Westview Press, 1995.

Beck, Lois, and Guitty Nashat. *Women in Iran from 1800 to the Islamic Republic*. Urbana: University of Illinois Press, 2004.

Berkey, Jonathan P. "Circumcision Circumscribed: Female Excisions and Cultural Accommodation in the Medieval Near East." *International Journal of Middle East Studies* 28 (1996): 19–38.

Bewley, Aisha. *The Women of Medina*. London: Ta-Ha, 1997.

Caspi, Mishael Maswari, trans. *Daughters of Yemen*. Berkeley: University of California Press, 1985.

Celarte, Henriette. *Behind Moroccan Walls*. Translated by Constance Lily Morris. Freeport, NY: Books for Libraries Press, 1931.

Cooke, Miriam. *Women Write War: The Centering of the Beirut Decentrists*. Oxford: Centre for Lebanese Studies, 1987.

Doolittle, M. "The Education of Women." *Muslim World* 18 (1928): 395–403.

Esposito, John. *Women in Muslim Family Law*. Syracuse, NY: Syracuse University Press, 1982.

Fakhiro, Munira A. *Women at Work in the Gulf: A Case Study of Bahrain*. New York: Routledge, 1990.

Ferdows, Adele. "Shariati and Khomeini on Women." In *The Iranian Revolution and the Islamic Republic: Proceedings of a Conference*, edited by Nikki R. Keddie and Eric Hoogland. Washington, DC: Middle East Institute in cooperation with Woodrow Wilson International Center for Scholars, 1982.

Fernea, Elizabeth Warnock. *Guests of the Sheik: An Ethnography of an Iraqi Village*. New York: Anchor Books/Doubleday, 1965.

Fernea, Elizabeth Warnock, and Basima Bezirgan, eds. *Middle Eastern Muslim Women Speak*. Austin: University of Texas Press, 1985.

Gauch, Suzanne. *Liberating Sharazad Feminism, Postcolonialism, and Islam*. Ann Arbor: University of Michigan Press, 2006.

Gerber, Haim. "Social and Economic Position of Women in an Ottoman City, Bursa, 1600–1700." *International Journal of Middle East Studies* 12 (1980): 231–244.

Golley, Nawar al-Hassan. *Arab Women's Lives Retold*. Syracuse, NY: Syracuse University Press, 2008.

Gray, Doris H. *Muslim Women on the Move*. Lanham, MD: Rowman & Littlefield, 2007.

Hawley, John S., ed. *Fundamentalism and Gender*. New York: Oxford University Press, 1994.

Heggoy, Alf Andrew. "Cultural Disrespect: European and Algerian Views on Women in Colonial and Independent Algeria." *Muslim World* 62, no. 4 (October 1972): 323–334.

Helie-Lucas, M. A. *Poverty and Development: Women and Islam in Muslim Societies*. The Hague: Ministry of Foreign Affairs, 1994.

Hijab, Nadia. *Womanpower: The Arab Debate on Women at Work*. New York: Cambridge University Press, 1988.

Hilal, J. "The Management of Male Dominance in 'Traditional' Arab Culture: A Tentative Model." *Civilisations* 21, no. 2 (1971): 85–95.

Huber, Joan. *Changing Women in Changing Societies*. Chicago: University of Chicago Press, 1973.

Hussain, Igbalunnisa. *Changing India: A Muslim Woman Speaks*. Bangalore, India: Hosali Press, 1940.

——. *Purdah and Polygamy: Life in an Indian Muslim Household*. Bangalore, India: Hosali Press, 1944.

Hussaini, Amal. "The Come-Back of the Hijab in Syria." *Al Nahj Center for Socialist Research and Studies in the Arab World*, no. 5 (1995): 162–166.

Ingrams, Doreen. "The Position of Women in Middle Eastern Arab Society." *The Middle East: A Handbook*. Editor Michael Adams. New York: Praeger, 1971.

Jacobs, Sue-Ellen. *Women in Perspective: A Guide for Cross-Cultural Studies*. Urbana: University of Illinois Press, 1974.

Jayawardena, Kumari. *Feminism and Nationalism in the Third World*. London: Zed Books, 1986.

Joekes, Susan. *Women in the World Economy.* New York: Oxford University Press, 1990.

Jones, V. R. et al. *Women in Islam.* Lucknow: Lucknow Publishing House, 1961.

Joseph, Saud. "Gender and Citizenship in Middle Eastern States." *Middle East Report* 198 (1996): 4–10.

Kandiyoti, Deniz. "Identity and Its Discontents: Women and the Nation." In *Colonial Discourse and Post-Colonial Theory,* edited by Patrick Williams and Laura Chrisman. Harvester: Wheatsheaf, 1993.

———. *Women, Islam and the State.* Philadelphia: Temple University Press, 1991.

Keddie, N. and Baron, B., eds. *Women In Middle East History: Shifting Boundaries of Sex and Gender.* New Haven, CT: Yale University Press, 1992.

Khalaf, S. *Prostitution in a Changing Society: A Sociological Survey of Legal Prostitution in Beirut.* Beirut: Khayats, 1965.

Khayyat, Sana, *Honour and Shame: Women in Modern Iraq.* London: Saqi Books, 1990.

Kudat, Ayse, and Helen Abadzi. *Participation of Women in Higher Education in Arab States.* Washington, DC: World Bank, 1989.

Kuttab, Eileen. "Palestinian Women and the Intifada: Fighting on Two Fronts." *Journal of Arab Studies Quarterly* 14 no. 2 (1993): 69–85.

Ladd, Valerie J. Hoffman. "Women's Religious Observances." *Oxford Encyclopedia of the Modern Islamic World,* edited by John L. Esposito, vol. 4, 327. New York: Oxford University Press, 1995.

Lattouf, Mirna. *Women, Education and Socialization in Modern Lebanon: 19th and 20th Centuries Social Histories.* Boulder, CO: University Press of America, 2004.

Lazreg, Marnia. *The Eloquence of Silence: Algerian Women in Question.* New York: Routledge, 1994.

Lichtenstadter, I. "The Muslim Woman in Transition, Based on Observations in Egypt and Pakistan." *Sociologus* 7, no. 1 (1957): 23–28.

Lorfing, I., and M. Khalaf. *Economic Contribution of Women and Its Effect on the Dynamics of the Family in Two Lebanese Villages.* Geneva: International Labour Organisation, 1985.

Mahmood, Saba. *Politics of Piety: The Islamic Revival and the Feminine Subject.* Princeton, NJ: Princeton University Press, 2005.

Malik, F. H. "Women in Islam." *The Muslim Digest* 21, no. 10 (1971): 20–23.

Malti-Douglas, Fedwa. *Women's Body, Women's World: Gender and Discourse in Arabo-Islamic Writing.* Princeton, NJ: Princeton University Press, 1992.

Meghdessian, Samira R. *The Status of the Arab Woman: A Select Bibliography.* New York: Greenwood Press, 1980.

Mernissi, Fatima. *Doing Daily Battle.* New Brunswick, NJ: Rutgers University Press, 1989.

———. "Femininity as Subversion: Reflections on the Muslim Concept of Nushuz." In *Speaking of Faith: Crosscultural Perspectives on Women, Religion and Social Change,* edited by Diana Eck and Devaka Jain, 95–108. New Delhi, India: Kali for Women, 1986.

———. *The Forgotten Queens of Islam.* Translated by Mary Jo Lakeland, Ann Arbor: University of Michigan Press, 1992.

———. *Islam and Democracy: Fear of the Modern World.* London: Virago, 1993.

———. "The Moslem World: Women Excluded from Development." In *Women and World Development,* edited by Irene Tinker and M. B. Brauman. Washington, DC: AAAS, 1976.

———. *The Veil and the Male Elite: A Feminist Interpretation of Women's Rights in Islam.* New York: Addison-Wesley, 1991.

———. "Women, Saints, and Sanctuaries." *Signs* 3, no. 1 (1977): 101–112.

Mies, Maria. *Fighting on Two Fronts: Women's Struggles and Research.* The Hague: Institute of Social Studies, 1982.

Mikhail, Mona. *Images of Arab Women: Fact and Fiction.* Washington, DC. Three Continents Press 1978.

Moghadam, Valentine M. Ed. *From Patriarchy to Empowerment.* Syracuse, NY: Syracuse University Press, 2008.

———. *Modernizing Women: Gender and Social Change in the Middle East.* Boulder, CO: Lynne Rienner, 1993.

Muhyi, I. A. "Women in the Arab Middle East." *Journal of Social Issues,* no. 5 (1959).

Mumtaz, Khawar, and Farida Shaheed. *Women of Pakistan: Two Steps Forward, One Step Back.* London: Zed Books, 1987.

Nagavi, Sayyid Ali. "Modern Reforms in Muslim Family Laws: A General Study." *Islamic Studies* 13 (1974): 235–252.

Naghibi, Nima. *Rethinking Global Sisterhood: Western Feminism and Iran.* Minneapolis: University of Minnesota Press, 2006.

Nagnarella, Paul J. "Conjugal Role Relationships in a Modernizing Turkish Town." *International Journal of Sociology of the Family* 2, no. 2 (1972): 179–192.

Najjar, Orayb Aref. *Portraits of Palestinian Women.* Salt Lake City: Utah University Press, 1992.

Nashat, Guity (ed.). *Women and Revolution in Iran.* Boulder, CO: Westview Press, 1983.

Papanek, Hanna. "The Woman Field Worker in a *Purdah* Society." *Human Organization* 23, 2 (1964): 160–163.

Perlmann, M. "Women and Feminism in Egypt." *Palestine Affairs* 4, no. 3 (1949): 36–39.

Peteet, Julie. *Gender in Crisis: Women and the Palestinian Resistance Movement.* New York: Columbia University Press, 1982.

Qazzaz, Ayad. *Women in the Arab World: An Annotated Bibliography.* Washington, DC: Association of Arab-American University Graduates, 1975.

Rutenberg, Taly. "Learning Women Studies," In *Theories of Women Studies*, edited by Gloria Bowles and Renate Klein, 72–78. London: Routledge, 1983.

Sa'adawi, Nawal. *Memoirs from the Women's Prison.* London: The Women's Press, 1983.

Sabbagh, Suha, and Ghada Talhami, eds. *Images and Reality: Palestinian Women under Occupation and in the Diaspora.* Washington, DC: Institute for Arab Women's Studies, 1989.

Sabbah, Fatna A. *Woman in the Muslim Unconscious.* Oxford: Pergamon Press, 1984.

Sabri, M. A. *The Hidden Face of Eve: Women in the Arab World.* London: Zed Books, 1980.

———. *Memories of a Woman Doctor.* Berkeley, CA: City Lights Books, 1989.

———. *Pioneering Profiles: Beirut College for Women.* Beirut: Khayats, 1967.

Saleh, Saneya. "Women in Islam: Their Status in Religious and Traditional Culture." *International Journal of Sociology of the Family* (March 1972): 35–42.

Sanabary, Nagat. *Women in Muslim Family Law.* Syracuse, NY: Syracuse University Press, 1992.

Sanasarian, Eliz. *The Women's Rights Movement in Iran: Mutiny, Appeasement, and Repression from 1900 to Khomeini.* New York: Praeger, 1982.

Sayegh, R. "The Changing Life of Arab Women." *Middle East Journal* 8, no. 6 (1968): 19–23.

Schneider, Jane. "Of Vigilance and Virgins: Honor, Shame and Access to Resources in Mediterranean Societies." *Ethnology* 10 (1971): 1–24.

Scott, Joan Wallach. *The Politics of the Veil*. Princeton, NJ: Princeton University Press, 2007.

Sha'aban, Bouthaina. *Both Right and Left Handed*. Bloomington: Indiana University Press, 1988.

———. "The Muslim Women in Syria." *Al Nahj, Center for Socialist Research and Studies in the Arab World*, no. 5 (1995): 87–99.

Shafik, Doria. "Egyptian Feminism." *Middle Eastern Affairs* (August–September 1952): 233–238.

Shakir, Evelyn. *Remember Me to Lebanon: Stories of Lebanese Women in America*. Syracuse, NY: Syracuse University Press, 2008.

Sharawi, Huda. *Harem Years*. New York: Feminist Press, 1987.

Sims, Holly. "Western Models, Indian Women: The Legacy of Foreign Aid." In *Bridging Worlds: Studies on Women in South Asia*, edited by Sally J. M. Sutherland, 225–239. Berkeley: University of California Press, 1991.

Smith, Jane I., and Yvonne Y. Haddad. " Eve: Islamic Image of Women." In *Women and Islam*, edited by Al-Hibri. Special issue of *Women's Studies International Forum* 5, no 2 (1982): 135–144.

Strum, Philippa. *The Women Are Marching: The Second Sex and the Palestinian Revolution*. New York: Lawrence Hill Books, 1992.

Sultana, Farrukh. "Status of Women in Iqbal's Thought." *Islamic Literature* 17, no. 1 (1971): 49–54.

Tabatabao. Shanin. "Women in Islam." *Islamic Revolution*, no. 1 (1979).

Talib, N. al-. "Status of Women in Islam." *Islamic Literature* 15, no. 6 (1969): 57–64.

Tawil, Raymonda. *My Home, My Prison*. London: Zed Books, 1986.

Tillion, Germaine. *The Republic of Cousins: Women's Oppression in Mediterranean Society*. London: Saqi Books, 1986.

Toubia, Nahid. *Women of the Arab World*. London: Zed Books, 1988.

Tucker, Judith E. *Women in Nineteenth-Century Egypt*. New York: Cambridge University Press, 1984.

Tuqan, Fadwa. *A Mountainous Journey: An Autobiography*. London: The Women's Press, 1990.

UNESCO. *Bibliographic Guide to Studies on the Status of Women*. London: Bowker, 1983.

Ungor, B. "Women in the Middle East and North Africa, and Universal Suffrage." *Annals of the American Academy of Political and Social Science*, no. 375 (1968): 71–81.

Van Ess, D. *Fatima and Her Sisters*. New York: John Day, 1961.

Warnock, Kitty. *Land Before Honor: Palestinian Women in the Occupied Territories*. New York: Monthly Review Press, 1990.

Wikan, Unni. *Behind the Veil in Arabia*. Chicago: University of Chicago Press, 1982.

Young, Elise. *Keepers of Our History: Women and the Israeli-Palestinian Conflict*. New York: Teachers College Press, 1992.

Yuval-Davis, Nira, and Foya Anthias, eds. *Woman, Nation, State*. London: Macmillan, 1989.

Art and Architecture

Arnold, Thomas. *Printing in Islam, A Study of the Place of Pictorial Art in Muslim Culture*. Piscataway, NJ: Gorgias Press, 2002.

Arnold, Sir T. W., and A. Grohmann. *The Islamic Book: A Contribution to Its Art and History from the VII-XVIII Century*. New York: Harcourt, Brace, 1929.

Aslanapa, Oktay. *Turkish Art and Architecture*. New York: Praeger, 1971.

Atil, Esin. *Turkish Art*. Washington, DC: Smithsonian Institution Press, 1980.

Atil, Esin et al. *Islamic Metalwork in the Freer Gallery of Art*. Washington, DC: The Gallery, Smithsonian Institution, 1985.

Behrens-Abouseif, D. *Islamic Architecture in Cairo*. Leiden, Netherlands: E. J. Brill, 1989.

Binyon, L. J., V. S. Wilkinson, and B. Gray. *Persian Miniature Painting*. New York: Dover Publications, 1933.

Blair, Sheila S., and Jonathan M. Bloom. *The Art and Architecture of Islam, 1250–1800*. New Haven, CT: Yale Pelican History of Art, 1994.

Blanc, J.-C. *Afghan Trucks*. New York: Stonehill Punlishing Co., 1976.

Briggs, M. S. *Muhammadan Architecture in Egypt and Palestine*. Oxford: Clarendon, 1924.

Creswell, K. A. C. *Early Muslim Architecture I: Umayyads, A.D. 622–750*. Oxford: Clarendon, 1932.

———. *Early Muslim Architecture, II: Abbasids, Umayyads of Cordova, Aghlabids, Tulunids, and Samanids, A.D. 751–905*. Oxford: Oxford University Press, 1940.

———. *Muslim Architecture of Egypt and Palestine*. New York: Hacker Arts Books, 1979.

———. *A Short Account of Early Muslim Architecture*. Baltimore, MD: Penguin Books, 1960.

Dimand, M. S. *A Handbook of Muhammadan Art*. New York: n.p., 1958.

Elgood, R., ed. *Islamic Arms and Armour*. London: Scolar Press, 1979.

Erdmann, K. *Oriental Carpets: An Essay on Their History*. London: Universe Books, 1961.

Ettinghausen, R. *Arab Painting*. New York: Rizzoli, 1977.

———. *Islamic Art and Archeology: Collected Papers*. Berlin: G. Mann Verlag, 1984.

Ferrier, R., ed. *The Arts of Persia*. New Haven, CT: Yale University Press, 1989.

Goodwin, Godfred. *A History of Ottoman Architecture, with 4 Colour Plates and 521 Illustrations, Including 81 Plans*. Baltimore, MD: Johns Hopkins University Press, 1971.

Grabar, Oleg. *The Alhambra*. Cambridge, MA: Harvard University Press, 1987.

———. *The Formation of Islamic Art*. New Haven, CT: Yale University Press, 1973.

———. "The Umayyad Dome of the Rock in Jerusalem." *Ars Orientalia* 3 (1959).

Grabar, Oleg, and R. Ettinghausen. *The Art and Architecture of Islam, 650–1250*. Harmondsworth, England: Penguin Books, 1987.

Gray, B. *The Arts of India*. Oxford: Phaidon, 1981.

The Arts of the Book in Central Asia. Boulder, CO: Shambala Publication/UNESCO, London, 1979.

———. *Persian Painting*. Cleveland, OH: World Publishing, 1961.

Grube, Ernst J. *The World of Islam: Landmarks of the World's Art*. New York: McGraw-Hill, 1966.

Holod, Renata, and Ahmet Evin, eds. *Modern Turkish Architecture*. Philadelphia: University of Pennsylvania Press, 1984.

Hubel, R. J. *The Book of Carpets*. New York: Praeger, 1970.

Hutt, A. *Islamic Architecture: Iran*. London: Scorpion Publications, 1985.

Irwin, Robert. *Islamic Art*. London: L. King, 1997.

Kühnel, E. *Islamic Art and Architecture*. London: Bell, 1966.

Kuran, Aptullah. *The Mosque in Early Ottoman Architecture*. Chicago: University of Chicago Press, 1968.

Lane, A. *Early Islamic Pottery: Mesopotamia, Egypt, and Persia.* New York: Van Nostrand Co., 1958.

———. *Later Islamic Pottery: Persia, Syria, Egypt, Turkey.* London: Faber and Faber, 1971.

Mayer, L. A. *Islamic Architects and Their Works.* Geneva: A. Kundig, 1956.

———. *Islamic Armourers and Their Works.* Geneva: A. Kundig, 1962.

———. *Islamic Metalworkers and Their Works.* Geneva: A. Kundig, 1959.

———. *Islamic Woodcarvers and Their Works.* Geneva: A. Kundig, 1958.

McChesney, Robert D. "Economic and Social Aspects of the Public Architecture in Bukhara in the 1560s and 1570s." *Islamic Art* 2 (1987): 217–242.

Michell, G. *Architecture of the Islamic World.* New York: Morrow, 1978.

Nasr, Seyyed. *Islamic Art and Spirituality.* New York: Oxford University Press, 1990.

Otto-Dorn, K. *Art of Islam.* Paris: A. Michel, 1967.

Petsopoulis, Yanni, ed. *Tulips, Arabesques and Turbans: Decorative Art from the Ottoman Empire.* New York: Abbeville Press, 1982.

Pinder-Wilson, R. *Studies in Islamic Art.* London: Pindar Press, 1985.

Pope, A. U., with P. Ackerman. *A Survey of Persian Art.* Costa Mesa, CA: Mazda Publishers, 1981.

Rogers, J. M. *Islamic Art and Design, 1500–1700.* London: British Museum Publication, 1983.

Safadi, Y. H. *Islamic Calligraphy.* London: Thames and Hudson, 1978.

Sarre, F. *Islamic Bookbindings.* London: K. Paul, Trench, Trubner and Co., 1923.

Sarre, F., and H. Trenkwald. *Old Oriental Carpets Issued by the Austrian Museum for Art and Industry.* 2 vols. New York: Dover Publications, 1926–1929.

Schimmel, A. *Calligraphy and Islamic Culture.* New York: New York University Press, 1990.

Slyomovics, Susan. *The Walled City in Literature, Architecture and History: The Living Medina in the Maghrib.* London: Frank Cass, 2001.

Talbot Rice, D. *Islamic Art.* New York: Praeger, 1965.

Unsal, Behcet. *Turkish Islamic Architecture in Seljuk and Ottoman Times, 1071–1923.* London: Tiranti, 1959.

Wilson, R. P. *Islamic Art.* London: Benn, 1957.

Wulff, H. E. *The Traditional Crafts of Persia.* Cambridge, MA: MIT Press, 1966.

Education

Ahmed, Munir-ud-Din. *Muslim Education and the Scholars' Social Status up to the Fifth Century Muslim Era in the Light of Ta'rikh-i Baghdad.* Zurich: Verlag Der Islam, 1968.

Arab Information Center. *Education in the Arab States.* New York: Arab Information Center, 1966.

Arasteh, A. R. *Education and Social Awakening in Iran, 1850–1968.* Leiden, Netherlands. E. J. Brill, 1969.

Benor, J. L. "Arab Education in Israel." *Middle Eastern Affairs* 1 (1950): 224–229.

Buchanan, J. R. "Muslim Education in Syria (before the War)." *Muslim World* 12 (1922): 394–406.

Dodge, Bayard. *Al-Azhar: A Millennium of Muslim Learning.* Washington, DC: Middle East Institute, 1961.

———. *Muslim Education in Medieval Times.* Washington, DC: Melustit, 1962.

Doolittle, M. "The Education of Women." *Muslim World* 18 (1928): 395–403.

———. "Moslem Religious Education in Syria." *Muslim World* 18 (1928): 374–380.

Gilliot, Claude. *Education and Learning in the Early Islamic World.* Burlington, VT: Ashgate, 2007.

Goldziher, Ignaz. "Education." In *Encyclopaedia of Religion and Ethics,* vol. 5, 198–207. New York: Charles Scribner's Sons, 1962.

Hamiuddin Khan, M. *History of Muslim Education.* Vol. 1, *712 to 1750 A.D.* Karachi: Academy of Education Research, 1967.

Heyworth-Dunne, J. *An Introduction to the History of Education in Modern Egypt.* London: Luzac, 1938.

Khan, Mu'id. "The Muslim Theories of Education during the Middle Ages." *Islamic Culture* 18 (1944): 418–423.

Kraemer, J. "Tradition and Reform at al-Azhar University." *Middle Eastern Affairs* 7 (1956): 89–94.

Lattouf, Mirna. *Women, Education and Socialization in Modern Lebanon: 19th and 20th Centuries Social Histories.* Boulder, CO: University Press of America, 2004.

Makdisi, G. "Muslim Institutions of Learning in Eleventh Century Baghdad." *Bulletin of the School of Oriental and African Studies* 24 (1961): 1–56.

Nakosteen, M. *History of Islamic Origins of Western Education, 800–1350.* Boulder: University of Colorado Press, 1964.

Pederson, J. "Some Aspects of the History of the Madrasa." *Islamic Culture* 3 (1929): 525–537.

Pinto, O. "The Libraries of the Arabs during the Time of the Abbasides." *Islamic Culture* 3 (1929): 210–243.

Rahman, Fazlur. "Education." In *Islam*, 221–237. New York: Doubleday, 1968.

Sadiq, Issa Khan. *Modern Persia and Her Educational System*. New York: Bureau of Publications, Teachers' College, Columbia University, 1931.

Shalaby, Ahmad. *History of Muslim Education*. Beirut: Dar al-Kashahaf, 1954.

Snider, N. "Mosque Education in Afghanistan." *Muslim World* 58 (1968): 24–35.

Tibawi, A. L. "Arab Education under the Caliphate." *Islamic Review* 42 (June 1954): 13–18.

———. *Islamic Education: Its Traditions and Modernization into the Arab National Systems*. London: Luzac, 1972.

———. "Muslim Education in the Golden Age of the Caliphate." *Islamic Culture* 28 (1954): 418–438.

———. "Origin and Charter of al-Madrasah." *Bulletin of the School of Oriental and African Studies* 25 (1962): 225–38.

Tota, Khalil A. *The Contribution of the Arabs to Education*. New York: Bureau of Publications, Teachers' College, Columbia University, 1926.

Tritton, A. S. *Materials on Muslim Education in the Middle Ages*. London: Luzac, 1957.

———. "Muslim Education in the Middle Ages (c. 600–800 A.D.)." *Muslim World* 43 (1953): 82–94.

Williams, James. *Education in Egypt before British Control*. Birmingham, AL: F. Juckes, 1939.

Economics

Abdul Mannan, Muhammad. *Islamic Economics: Theory and Practice*. Sevenoakes, England: Hodder and Stoughton, 1986.

Ahmad, Feroz. "The Political Economy of Kemalism." In *Atatürk: Founder of the Modern State*. Hamden, CT: Archon Books, 1980.

Ashtor, E. *A Social and Economic History of the Near East in the Middle Ages*. Berkeley: University of California Press, 1976.

Chapra, Mohammad Umer. *Islam and the Economic Challenge*. Leicester, England: Islamic Foundation, 1992.

Charnay, Jean-Paul, *Islamic Culture and Socio-Economic Change*. Social, Economic and Political Studies of the Middle East, vol. 4. Leiden, Netherlands: E. J. Brill, 1971.

Choudhury, Masudul Alam. *An Advanced Exposition of Islamic Economics and Finance*. Lewiston, NY: Edwin Mellen Press, 2004.

———. *The Islamic World System: A Study in Polity-Market Interaction*. New York: Routhledge Curzon, 2004.

Cook, M. A., ed. *Studies in the Economic History of the Middle East: From the Rise of Islam to the Present Day*. London: Oxford, 1970.

Crone, Patricia. *Meccan Trade and the Rise of Islam*. Piscataway, NJ. Gorgias Press, 2004.

El-Gamal, Mahmoud A. *Islamic Finance: Law, Economics, and Practice*. London: Cambridge University Press, 2006.

Gaspard, Toufic K. *A Political Economy of Lebanon, 1948–2002: The Limits of Laissez-Faire*. Leiden, Netherlands: Brill, 2004.

Gerber, Haim. "Social and Economic Position of Women in an Ottoman City, Bursa, 1600–1700." *International Journal of Middle East Studies* 12 (1980): 231–244.

Hanna, Nelly. *Money, Land and Trade: An Economic History of the Muslim Mediterranean*. London: I. B. Tauris, 2001.

Ikram, Khalid. *The Egyptian Economy, 1952–2000: Performance, Policies, and Issues*. New York: Routledge, 2006.

Inalcik, Halil. *The Ottoman Empire: Conquest, Organization and Economy*. London: Variorum, 1978

Iqbal, Munawar. *Distributive Justice and Need Fulfillment in an Islamic Economy*. Islamabad, Pakistan: International Institute of Islamic Economics, 1988.

———. *Islamic Banking and Finance: Current Developments in Theory and Practice*. Leicester, England: Islamic Foundation, 2001.

———. *Islamic Economic Institutions and the Elimination of Poverty*. Leicester, England: Islamic Foundation, 2002.

Issawi, Charles. "Economic Change and Urbanization in the Middle East." *Middle Eastern Cities*, edited by Ira M. Lapidus. Berkeley: University of California Press, 1969.

Johnson, F. E. *The Seven Poems Suspended from the Temple at Mecca*. Piscataway, NJ: Gorgias Press, 2002.

Kapil, Arun. "Islamic Economics: The Surest Path?" *MESA Bulletin* 29:1 (July 1995): 22–24.

Katouzian, Homa. *The Political Economy of Modern Iran: Despotism and Pseudo-Modernism, 1926–1979*. New York: New York University Press, 1981.

Khan, Muhammad Akram. *Islamic Economics and Finance: A Glossary*. New York: Routledge, 2003.

Kuran, Timur. *Islam and Mammon: The Economic Predicaments of Islamism*. Princeton, NJ: Princeton University Press, 2004.

Kuran, Timur. "The Economic System in Contemporary Islamic Thought." In *Islamic Economic Alternatives*, edited by K. S. Jomo. Kuala Lumpur: Iqraq, 1992.

Lewis, Bernard. "Sources for the Economic History of the Middle East." In *Studies in the Economic History of the Middle East*, 78–92. London: Oxford University Press, 1970.

Mannan, Mohammed. *Institutional Settings of an Islamic Economic Order: A Comparative Study of Economic Practices*. Jeddah, Saudi Arabia: International Center for Research in Economics, King Abdul Aziz University, 1981.

Mawdudi, Sayyid Abu'l-A'la. "Economic and Political Teachings of the Quran." In *A History of Muslim Philosophy*, Vol. 1. Lahore, Pakistan: Islamic Publications, n.d.

Morad, Munir. "Current Thought on Islamic Taxation: A Critical Synthesis" In *Islamic Law and Finance*, edited by Chibli Mallat, 117–127. London: Graham and Trotman, 1988.

Morony, Michael. *Islamic Theories of Finance*. Piscataway, NJ: Gorgias Press, 2005.

Niblock, Tim. *The Political Economy of Saudi Arabia*. New York: Routledge, 2008.

Nomani, Farhad, and Ali Rahnema. *Islamic Economic Systems*. London: Zed Books, 1994.

Pramanik, Ataul Huq. *Poverty, Inequality, and the Role of Some Islamic Economic Institutions*. Islamabad, Pakistan: n.p., 1981.

Rabie, Hassanein. *The Financial System of Egypt—A.H. 564–741/A.D. 1169–1341*. London: Oxford University Press, 1972.

Rahman, Fazlur. "Islam and the Problem of Economic Justice." *Pakistan Economist* 14 (August 24, 1974): 14–36.

Rahnema, Ali, and Farhad Nomani. *The Secular Miracle: Religion, Politics, and Economic Policy in Iran*. London: Zed Books, 1990.

Richards, D. S., ed. *Islam and the Trade of Asia: A Colloquium*. Oxford: Cassirer, 1970.

Rodinson, Maxime. *Islam and Capitalism*. New York: Pantheon Books, 1974.

Saleh, Nabil. *Unlawful Gain and Legitimate Profit in Islamic Law.* Cambridge: Cambridge University Press, 1986.

Sheikholislami, A. Reza, and Rostam Kavoussi. *The Political Economy of Saudi Arabia.* Seattle: University of Washington Press, 1984.

Siddiqi, Muhammed Nejaullah. *Insurance in an Islamic Economy.* Leicester, England: n.p., 1985.

Siddiqi, S. A. *Public Finance in Islam.* Lahore, Pakistan: Saikh Muhammad Ashraf, 1952.

Szyliowicz, Joseph. *Education and Modernization in the Middle East.* Ithaca, NY: Cornell University Press, 1973.

Tabataba'i, Husayn Mudarrisi. *Khardj in Islamic Law.* Ithaca, NY: Ithaca Press, 1983.

Taleqani, Seyyed Mahmood (Taleqani, Mahmud). *Islam and Ownership.* Translated by Ahmad Jabari and Farhang Rajaee. Lexington, KY: n.p., 1983.

Wilson, Rodney. *Islamic Business Theory and Practice.* London: Routledge, 1985.

Literature

Al-Musawi, Muhsin J. *Arabic Poetry: Trajectories of Modernity and Tradition.* New York: Routledge, 2006.

Aminrazawi, Mehdi. *The Wine of Wisdom: The Life, Poetry, and Philosophy of Omar Khayyam.* Oxford: Oneworld, 2005.

Arberry, A. J. *The Seven Odes: The First Chapter in Arabic Literature.* London. Allen & Unwin, 1961.

Baerlein, Henry. *The Divan of Abu 'l-Ala.* Piscataway, NJ: Gorgias Press, 2003.

Browne, Edward G. *A Literary History of Persia.* 4 vols. Cambridge: Cambridge University Press, 1951–1953. Originally published in 1928.

Burckhardt, John Lewis. *Arabic Proverbs and the Manners and Customs of Modern Egyptian.* Piscataway, NJ: Gorgias Press, 2002.

Gibb, E. J. W. *A History of Ottoman Poetry.* 6 vols. London: Luzac, 1900–1909.

Gibb, H. A. R. *Arabic Literature: An Introduction.* 2nd rev. ed. Oxford: Clarendon, 1963.

Green, Dunton. *Philosophy, Literature, and Fine Arts.* Dunton Gree, Kent, England: Hodder and Stoughton, 1982.

Johnson, F. E. *The Seven Poems Suspended From the Temple at Mecca*. Piscataway, NJ: Gorgias Press, 2002.

Levy, Reuben. *Persian Literature: An Introduction*. London: Oxford University Press, 1948.

Nicholson, Reynold A. *A Literary History of the Arabs*. Cambridge: Cambridge University Press, 1962.

Rypka, Jan. *History of Iranian Literature*. Translated by Karl Jahn. New York: Humanities Press, 1968.

Cities

Al-Fahim, Mohammed. *From Rags to Riches: A Story of Abu Dhabi*. London: I. B. Tauris, 2001.

Brown, Leon Carl, ed. *From Madina to Metropolis: Heritage and Change in the Near Eastern City*. Princeton, NJ: Darwin, 1973.

Davidson, Christopher D. *Dubai: The Vulnerability of Success*. London: Hurst, 2008.

Duncan, Alistair. *The Noble Sanctuary: Portrait of a Holy Place in Arab Jerusalem*. London: Longmans Group, 1972.

Esin, Emel, and Haluk Doganbey. *Mecca the Blessed, Madinah the Radiant*. London: Elek Books, 1963.

Ford, Nick. *Jerusalem under Muslim Rule in the Eleventh Century*. New York: Rosen Publication Group, 2004.

Ismail, Salwa. *Political Life in Cairo's New Quarters*. Minneapolis: University of Minnesota Press, 2006.

Lammens, Henri, and A. J. Wensinck. "Mecca." In *EI1* Vol. 3, 437–438. Leiden, Netherlands: E. J. Brill, 1960.

Lapidus, Ira, ed. *Middle Eastern Cities: A Symposium on Ancient, Islamic, and Contemporary Middle Eastern Urbanism*. Berkeley: University of California Press, 1969.

———. *Muslim Cities in the Later Middle Ages*. Cambridge, MA: Harvard University Press, 1967.

Levy, Reuben. *A Baghdad Chronicle*. Cambridge: Cambridge University Press, 1929.

Mayer, Tamar, and Suleiman A. Mourad. *Jerusalem*. New York: Routledge, 2008.

Philipp, Thomas. *Acre: Rise and Fall of a Palestinian City, 1730–1831*. New York: Columbian University Press, 2002.

Slyomovics, Susan. *The Walled City in Literature, Architecture and History: The Living Medina in the Maghrib.* London: Frank Cass, 2001.

Watenbaugh, Hegnar Zeitlian. *The Image of an Ottoman City: Imperial Architecture and Urban Experience in Aleppo in the 16th and 17th Centuries.* Leiden, Netherlands: E. J. Brill, 2004.

Wolf, Eric R. "The Social Organization of Mecca and the Origins of Islam." *Southwestern Journal of Anthropology* 7 (1951): 329–356.

Zwemer, S. M. "Al-Haramain." *Moslem World* 37 (1947): 7–15.

About the Author

Ludwig W. Adamec (B.A., political science; M.A., journalism; Ph.D., Islamic and Middle East Studies, UCLA), is a professor of Middle East Studies at the University of Arizona and was director of its Near Eastern Center for 10 years. Widely known as a leading authority on Afghanistan, he is the author of a number of reference works on Afghanistan and books on Afghan history, foreign policy, and international relations, including *Afghanistan 1900–1923: A Diplomatic History*; *Afghanistan's Foreign Affairs to the Mid-Twentieth Century*; the six-volume *Political Gazetteer of Afghanistan*; *Historical Dictionary of Afghanistan*; and *Historical Dictionary of Afghan Wars, Revolutions, and Insurgencies*. His publications have been translated into Persian, Pashtu, Urdu, Arabic, French, and German. Adamec has traveled widely throughout the Middle East, most recently visiting Kabul, Afghanistan, in August 2008 to attend a conference in the ministry of foreign affairs. He has received numerous awards and was elected an Honorary Member of the Central Eurasian Studies Society, hosted by Harvard University.